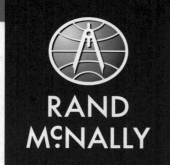

RAND McNALLY

Road Atlas

P9-AFO-547

2016 LARGE SCALE

CONTENTS

2

3

10

Photo credits:
Table of contents: (t to b) ©Rand McNally, ©Juli Scalzi Photography/ istockphoto, ©Rand McNally; p. 3 (t to b), ©Juli Scalzi Photography/istockphoto, ©2G1R / istockphoto, p. 4 (t to b) ©Cathy Melloan / Alamy, ©Brent Waltermire / Alamy, ©Danita Delimont / Alamy; p. 5 (t to b) ©Daniela Duncan / Getty, ©jctdesign / istockphoto, ©visionsofmaine / istockphoto; p. 6 (t to b) ©laddio1234 / istockphoto, ©Natalia Bratslovsky / istockphoto, ©Daniel Dempster Photography / Alamy; p. 7 (t to b) ©Thye Gn / Alamy, ©KingWu / istockphoto, ©Design Pics Inc. / Alamy.

©2015-2016 RM Acquisition, LLC d/b/a Rand McNally. Rand McNally, the globe logo, and Best of the Road are registered trademarks of RM Acquisition, LLC. All other trademarks appearing in this publication are trademarks of third parties and are the responsibility of their respective owners.

For licensing information and copyright permissions, contact us at permissions@randmcnally.com.

If you have a comment, suggestion, or even a compliment, please visit us at randmcnally.com/contact or write to:
Rand McNally Consumer Affairs
P.O. Box 7600
Chicago, Illinois 60680-9915

Published in U.S.A.
Printed in China

1-2-3-LE-16-15

Quick Map References

Mileage Chart

This handy chart offers more than 2,400 mileages covering 77 North American cities and U.S. national parks. Want more mileages? Visit **randmcnally.com/MC** and type in any two cities or addresses.

	Albuquerque, NM	Atlanta, GA	Billings, MT	Boston, MA	Charlotte, NC	Chicago, IL	Cincinnati, OH	Dallas, TX	Denver, CO	Detroit, MI	Houston, TX	Indianapolis, IN	Kansas City, MO	Los Angeles, CA	Memphis, TN	Miami, FL	Milwaukee, WI	Minneapolis, MN	New Orleans, LA	New York, NY	Omaha, NE	Orlando, FL	Philadelphia, PA	Phoenix, AZ	Pittsburgh, PA	Portland, OR	Saint Louis, MO	Salt Lake City, UT	San Francisco, CA	Seattle, WA	Washington, DC	Wichita, KS
Albuquerque, NM		1386	998	2219	1626	1333	1387	647	446	1570	884	1279	784	786	1008	1952	1354	1225	1165	2001	863	1730	1924	462	1641	1363	1037	599	1086	1438	1885	591
Amarillo, TX	284	1102	965	1935	1342	1049	1103	363	424	1286	589	995	570	1072	720	1668	1132	1009	881	1716	647	1446	1640	746	1357	1669	752	883	1370	1743	1600	382
Atlanta, GA	1386		1831	1095	244	715	461	780	1404	722	794	533	800	2174	379	661	809	1127	468	882	992	440	780	1844	684	2603	555	1878	2472	2649	637	955
Atlantic City, NJ	1985	831	2072	338	590	818	632	1518	1792	644	1598	703	1187	2774	1063	1248	910	1232	1273	126	1272	1038	60	2447	365	2922	948	2201	2934	2889	188	1379
Austin, TX	705	920	1495	1959	1164	1121	1128	193	950	1358	157	1067	702	1381	643	1341	1204	1136	503	1737	839	1124	1658	1010	1411	2068	825	1304	1760	2143	1524	542
Baltimore, MD	1887	683	1953	400	442	699	513	1368	1673	524	1448	584	1068	2670	914	1082	792	1112	1124	192	1153	889	98	2349	246	2804	829	2081	2816	2771	39	1260
Billings, MT	998	1831		2236	1990	1246	1546	1425	551	1535	1652	1435	1026	1240	1477	2497	1173	838	1868	2041	845	2275	2011	1210	1713	891	1278	552	1173	818	1951	1064
Birmingham, AL	1241	146	1780	1177	390	660	466	636	1329	724	668	478	749	2030	235	746	754	1072	343	960	939	534	880	1700	748	2551	502	1826	2327	2598	745	810
Boise, ID	938	2177	621	2660	2336	1693	1943	1702	830	1960	1930	1835	1372	842	1825	2844	1732	1461	2216	2465	1225	2622	2435	914	2137	428	1622	339	639	503	2375	1338
Boston, MA	2219	1095	2236		841	983	870	1764	1970	724	1844	937	1421	2983	1312	1482	1074	1396	1520	207	1436	1288	306	2681	570	3086	1182	2365	3098	3054	439	1613
Branson, MO	864	652	1241	1433	868	545	601	435	806	784	602	493	209	1651	274	1284	630	643	597	1201	402	1062	1138	1326	851	2013	249	1288	1950	2060	1081	292
Calgary, AB	1542	2357	541	2615	2400	1627	1925	1967	1096	1916	2209	1814	1567	1557	2028	3018	1555	1221	2419	2439	1387	2797	2391	1524	2093	787	1820	869	1500	678	2334	1606
Charleston, SC	1703	317	2133	970	207	908	620	1099	1706	826	1105	726	1103	2491	696	583	1002	1324	742	768	1294	380	668	2165	654	2904	857	2180	2789	2951	532	1272
Charlotte, NC	1626	244	1990	841		769	477	1023	1566	616	1038	583	961	2414	619	728	867	1180	712	641	1151	526	539	2088	446	2761	714	2037	2712	2808	398	1092
Chicago, IL	1333	715	1246	983	769		289	926	1002	280	1085	181	526	2015	531	1381	90	408	923	787	470	1153	757	1795	459	2118	296	1398	2130	2063	697	724
Cincinnati, OH	1387	461	1546	870	477	289		934	1187	259	1055	108	584	2172	482	1127	381	703	804	637	722	905	571	1849	288	2369	348	1647	2380	2363	512	779
Cleveland, OH	1598	714	1597	638	514	342	248	1194	1330	168	1315	315	799	2342	729	1240	434	756	1057	460	797	1043	428	2060	131	2446	560	1725	2458	2414	370	992
Columbus, OH	1457	567	1606	763	426	354	106	1039	1261	191	1174	176	657	2244	587	1164	445	766	910	533	792	954	468	1920	184	2439	421	1718	2451	2425	411	851
Corpus Christi, TX	855	1001	1622	2051	1244	1338	1262	410	1077	1542	207	1228	919	1494	782	1394	1421	1353	554	1844	1056	1172	1754	1122	1561	2218	1042	1454	1873	2292	1619	758
Dallas, TX	647	780	1425	1764	1023	926	934		880	1163	228	873	489	1437	453	1307	1010	928	519	1548	656	1086	1467	1066	1221	2128	630	1403	1734	2193	1332	361
Denver, CO	446	1404	551	1970	1566	1002	1187	880		1270	1035	1083	603	1015	1097	2069	1042	913	1398	1775	534	1851	1732	908	1447	1256	854	533	1268	1320	1671	519
Des Moines, IA	983	902	946	1299	1057	332	580	683	670	599	938	474	193	1682	617	1567	371	242	1008	1105	137	1339	1074	1445	777	1786	354	1065	1798	1764	1015	391
Detroit, MI	1570	722	1535	724	616	280	259	1163	1270		1319	288	764	2281	742	1354	374	696	1066	613	736	1144	583	2032	285	2385	533	1664	2397	2353	522	964
Duluth, MN	1375	1187	860	1370	1239	466	760	1092	1063	754	1331	651	586	2076	963	1852	394	152	1354	1264	530	1632	1230	1838	932	1749	679	1458	2033	1677	1171	785
Edmonton, AB	1724	2391	722	2549	2443	1670	1968	2149	1278	1958	2391	1857	1626	1755	2147	3058	1598	1264	2538	2482	1445	2836	2434	1721	2136	966	1878	1069	1695	793	2377	1787
El Paso, TX	260	1418	1257	2373	1662	1455	1569	635	707	1702	744	1398	929	796	1089	1934	1497	1377	1095	2202	1004	1712	2102	424	1774	1630	1157	866	1175	1705	1967	730
Fargo, ND	1318	1361	607	1629	1414	641	937	1079	873	930	1321	825	600	1848	1054	2025	569	235	1445	1438	420	1807	1405	1780	1107	1497	841	1160	1781	1424	1348	685
Gatlinburg, TN	1439	196	1803	922	202	578	290	884	1376	552	964	396	773	2226	431	865	672	994	640	707	964	640	625	1901	493	2574	527	1850	2525	2621	490	905
Guadalajara, JA	1194	1739	2194	2789	1982	1954	1962	1028	1639	2191	948	1901	1535	1501	1482	2131	2037	1969	1292	2592	1672	1910	2492	1212	2261	2545	1658	1792	1963	2631	2356	1377
Gulfport, MS	1221	399	1912	1482	643	896	767	562	1386	1025	403	780	883	1949	365	792	988	1196	78	1266	1073	572	1180	1577	1052	2633	647	1909	2307	2730	1036	867
Houston, TX	884	794	1652	1844	1038	1085	1055	228	1035	1319		1021	732	1550	575	1186	1163	1171	347	1632	898	965	1547	1178	1354	2356	784	1634	1929	2431	1411	595
Indianapolis, IN	1279	533	1435	937	583	181	108	873	1083	288	1021		482	2068	464	1198	272	591	818	707	613	968	643	1742	359	2260	243	1541	2273	2253	582	674
Jacksonville, FL	1636	346	2183	1146	379	1068	796	992	1756	1002	871	874	1152	2421	677	349	1163	1474	547	939	1344	141	844	2050	825	2954	907	2230	2723	3001	706	1272
Kansas City, MO	784	800	1026	1421	961	526	584	489	603	764	732	482		1616	451	1466	565	436	844	1196	187	1246	1127	1246	840	1797	250	1073	1808	1844	1066	193
Key West, FL	2099	809	2646	1659	886	1534	1275	1455	2222	1515	1334	1348	1617	2884	1159	162	1632	1944	1010	1446	1807	387	1357	2514	1332	3417	1370	2693	3186	3464	1213	1735
Las Vegas, NV	572	1959	973	2714	2199	1746	1932	1220	747	2013	1457	1828	1349	270	1581	2525	1786	1656	1739	2518	1278	2303	2480	286	2190	1023	1600	419	569	1128	2428	1164
Lexington, KY	1371	369	1610	917	400	370	83	876	1186	344	996	184	581	2158	423	1030	464	782	745	701	771	817	638	1833	370	2381	334	1657	2392	2428	533	773
Little Rock, AR	877	515	1407	1447	754	650	617	319	965	885	439	583	381	1666	137	1147	724	815	425	1230	574	925	1150	1340	905	2211	345	1488	1963	2275	1015	446
Los Angeles, CA	786	2174	1240	2983	2414	2015	2172	1437	1015	2281	1550	2068	1616		1794	2735	2055	1925	1894	2787	1546	2515	2713	370	2428	963	1821	688	380	1134	2670	1377
Memphis, TN	1008	379	1477	1312	619	531	482	453	1097	742	575	464	451	1794		1012	622	831	394	1094	641	778	1014	1471	768	2245	283	1524	2095	2299	879	577
Mexico City, DF	1404	1718	2301	2768	1962	2017	1979	1090	1756	2254	924	1963	1598	1839	1500	2111	2100	2032	1272	2571	1735	1889	2471	1469	2279	2768	1721	2003	2218	2842	2336	1440
Miami, FL	1952	661	2497	1482	728	1381	1127	1307	2069	1354	1186	1198	1466	2735	1012		1475	1791	861	1288	1658	229	1180	2362	1173	3260	1221	2544	3038	3315	1044	1587
Milwaukee, WI	1354	809	1173	1074	867	90	381	1010	1042	374	1163	272	565	2055	622	1475		336	1015	879	509	1258	849	1817	551	2062	379	1437	2170	1990	788	763
Minneapolis, MN	1225	1127	838	1396	1180	408	703	928	913	696	1171	591	436	1925	831	1791	336		1223	1204	372	1573	1171	1687	874	1727	563	1308	2040	1655	1110	634
Mobile, AL	1234	328	1874	1427	571	917	721	589	1414	978	468	733	850	2014	382	719	1011	1224	144	1202	1038	497	1101	1643	1000	2661	645	1936	2320	2727	965	894
Montréal, QC	2129	1218	2099	310	980	847	824	1722	1832	560	1884	847	1330	2845	1314	1647	938	1262	1640	382	1302	1437	454	2591	603	2948	1092	2228	2960	2916	587	1529
Nashville, TN	1219	248	1586	1099	407	469	273	664	1158	534	786	287	555	2006	212	913	564	881	532	884	747	692	802	1682	560	2357	310	1633	2306	2404	667	688
New Orleans, LA	1165	468	1868	1520	712	923	804	519	1398	1066	347	818	844	1894	394	861	1015	1223		1304	1032	641	1222	1523	1090	2642	675	1920	2252	2716	1087	880
New York, NY	2001	882	2041	207	641	787	637	1548	1775	613	1632	707	1196	2787	1094	1288	879	1204	1304		1245	1089	97	2463	369	2891	954	2170	2902	2858	228	1391
Norfolk, VA	1910	558	2132	569	328	878	605	1350	1758	704	1362	720	1155	2707	898	950	969	1295	1026	370	1335	755	271	2373	425	2962	911	2238	2973	2949	189	1349
Oklahoma City, OK	542	844	1203	1678	1084	792	846	204	631	1029	437	739	348	1326	466	1476	876	788	722	1460	452	1254	1384	1005	1101	1922	496	1200	1627	1948	1344	158
Omaha, NE	863	992	845	1436	1151	470	722	656	534	736	898	613	187	1546	641	1658	509	372	1032	1245		1436	1212	1325	914	1650	439	930	1662	1663	1151	298
Orlando, FL	1730	440	2275	1288	526	1153	905	1086	1851	1144	965	968	1246	2515	778	229	1258	1573	641	1089	1436		986	2145	975	3048	999	2323	2816	3093	849	1365
Ottawa, ON	2039	1158	1768	428	920	760	732	1632	1748	471	1804	757	1240	2763	1230	1618	859	1032	1582	440	1213	1408	447	2501	546	2660	1002	2142	2877	2586	566	1439
Philadelphia, PA	1924	780	2011	306	539	757	571	1467	1732	583	1547	643	1127	2713	1014	1180	849	1171	1222	97	1212	986		2387	304	2861	888	2140	2873	2828	137	1319
Phoenix, AZ	462	1844	1210	2681	2088	1795	1849	1066	908	2032	1178	1742	1246	370	1471	2362	1817	1687	1523	2463	1325	2145	2387		2104	1332	1499	653	749	1414	2348	1053
Pittsburgh, PA	1641	684	1713	570	446	459	288	1221	1447	285	1354	359	840	2428	768	1173	551	874	1090	369	914	975	304	2104		2563	604	1842	2574	2530	244	1035
Portland, ME	2315	1192	2333	110	938	1079	967	1861	2067	825	1940	1034	1518	3082	1408	1585	1176	1492	1616	304	1533	1385	402	2778	666	3186	1279	2461	3196	3151	535	1710
Portland, OR	1363	2603	891	3086	2761	2118	2369	2128	1256	2385	2356	2260	1797	963	2245	3260	2062	1727	2642	2891	1650	3048	2861	1332	2563		2050	765	635	172	2800	1764
Rapid City, SD	843	1508	323	1900	1670	912	1208	1061	397	1200	1291	1100	704	1312	1160	2173	840	575	1551	1708	525	1956	1675	1305	1378	1215	959	649	1384	1142	1618	699
Reno, NV	1019	2396	958	2881	2555	1913	2163	1668	1051	2180	1904	2056	1591	470	2029	3063	1953	1818	2186	2685	1445	2841	2656	733	2357	578	1844	518	217	720	2595	1558
Richmond, VA	1832	532	2051	547	293	797	512	1278	1671	622	1329	627	1069	2620	824	944	888	1210	1002	334	1259	742	245	2294	344	2869	822	2145	2880	2868	108	1261
Saint Louis, MO	1037	555	1278	1182	714	296	348	630	854	533	784	243	250	1821	283	1221	379	563	675	954	439	999	888	1499	604	2050		1326	2061	2096	827	442
Salt Lake City, UT	599	1878	552	2365	2037	1398	1647	1403	533	1664	1634	1541	1073	688	1524	2544	1437	1308	1920	2170	930	2323	2140	653	1842	765	1326		735	839	2079	1042
San Antonio, TX	712	986	1480	2039	1230	1202	1210	276	935	1439	197	1149	766	1357	727	1379	1285	1205	541	1822	920	1160	1742	985	1495	2076	906	1311	1736	2150	1607	625
San Diego, CA	810	2138	1302	3046	2381	2080	2196	1359	1077	2346	1472	2089	1597	120	1819	2656	2118	1986	1816	2809	1613	2436	2738	352	2452	1083	1845	750	501	1256	2693	1401
San Francisco, CA	1086	2472	1173	3098	2712	2130	2380	1734	1268	2397	1929	2273	1808	380	2095	3038	2170	2040	2252	2902	1662	2816	2873	749	2574	635	2061	735		807	2812	1775
Santa Fe, NM	58	1379	943	2212	1618	1313	1379	640	391	1562	877	1272	766	846	998	1944	1336	1207	1158	1994	891	1723	1917	520	1634	1388	1029	625	1144	1463	1879	572
Sault Ste. Marie, ON	1777	1040	1273	923	947	471	577	1370	1428	347	1527	540	951	2465	972	1685	398	538	1355	921	850	1475	911	2240	614	2166	740	1848	2581	2090	854	1150
Seattle, WA	1438	2649	818	3054	2808	2063	2363	2193	1320	2353	2431	2253	1844	1134	2299	3315	1990	1655	2716	2858	1663	3093	2828	1414	2530	172	2096	839	807		2768	1828
Spokane, WA	1320	2369	541	2774	2528	1785	2084	1964	1091	2075	2192	1973	1564	1216	2018	3035	1712	1377	2409	2580	1383	2814	2550	1381	2252	351	1817	720	874	278	2490	1600
Tampa, FL	1746	451	2293	1342	578	1166	916	1102	1860	1178	980	984	1252	2525	779	255	1260	1578	651	1138	1445	84	1040	2153	1023	3064	1008	2340	2832	3111	904	1381
Toronto, ON	1800	963	1771	548	756	519	493	1393	1504	232	1551	518	1001	2517	983	1483	609	933	1306	489	974	1284	497	2262	316	2620	763	1899	2632	2588	486	1188
Tulsa, OK	645	782	1234	1576	1022	687	738	258	692	927	487	635	243	1433	402	1414	773	704	671	1350	380	1192	1282	1107	994	1938	392	1215	1731	2012	1234	173
Vancouver, BC	1575	2785	953	3188	2944	2198	2499	2338	1465	2487	2565	2389	1980	1275	2437	3451	2125	1790	2851	2993	1799	3229	2963	1550	2665	313	2232	973	947	141	2903	1973
Washington, DC	1885	637	1951	439	398	697	512	1332	1671	522	1411	582	1066	2670	879	1044	788	1110	1087	228	1151	849	137	2348	244	2800	827	2079	2812	2768		1258
Wichita, KS	591	955	1064	1613	1092	724	779	361	519	964	595	674	193	1377	577	1587	763	634	880	1391	298	1365	1319	1053	1035	1764	442	1042	1775	1828	1258	

Mileages in this chart are based upon the routes usually followed by motorists. Highway systems include interstate, U.S., and state highways.

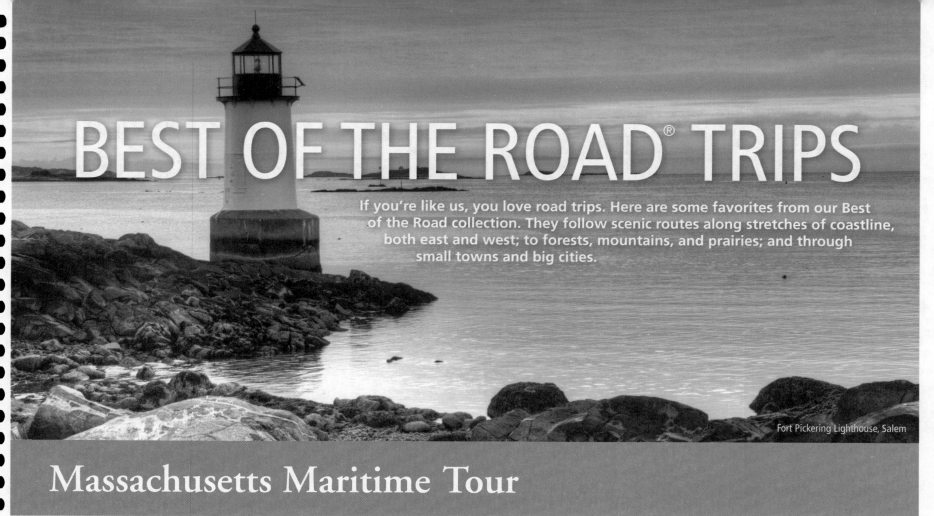

BEST OF THE ROAD® TRIPS

If you're like us, you love road trips. Here are some favorites from our Best of the Road collection. They follow scenic routes along stretches of coastline, both east and west; to forests, mountains, and prairies; and through small towns and big cities.

Fort Pickering Lighthouse, Salem

Massachusetts Maritime Tour

The close proximity to the Atlantic has long fostered a co-dependence between Massachusetts's coastal towns and the sea. To immerse yourself in the (aptly nicknamed) Bay State's rich maritime traditions, start at Newburyport's Custom House Maritime Museum on Boston's North Shore. Move from water to witches in Salem, home of the infamous trials.

A bit farther south, you'll hit the vibrant city of Boston, where history meets sports meets culture at every turn. Beyond, on the South Shore, you'll find Plymouth, famous landing place of the Pilgrims, and the Plimoth Plantation Living History Museum, where you can experience 17th-century life. Sights in the one-time whaling center of New Bedford highlight still more maritime history.

Plimoth Plantation

Newburyport

Custom House Maritime Museum. Settled in 1653 at the intersection of the Merrimack River and the Atlantic Ocean, Newburyport almost immediately solidified its importance as a commercial port. The museum, housed in a handsome Greek-revival building, contains objects that represent the town's maritime history. There are stunning models and paintings of the clipper ships that once plied their trade in this area as well as artifacts from actual ships that made it back to port and those salvaged from ships lost at sea. The museum's Coast Guard Room tells its history through art and photos and helps to explain exactly what the Coast Guard does. *25 Water St., (978) 462-8681, www.customhousemaritimemuseum.org.*

Salem

The Salem Witch Museum. Salem is most known for, of course, the 1692 Witch Trials, one of the strangest episodes in Anglo-American colonial history. Fourteen women and five men were hanged after being convicted of sorcery, and one man died after being pressed to death over the course of two days. The museum has stage-sets that use figures and narration to bring this frightening era to life. The gift shop sells all sorts of one-of-a-kind witchy paraphernalia including Salem witch bottles (small glass vessels filled with sand, salt, a nail, and a charm that colonists used to use to ward off evil). *Washington Sq., (978) 744-1692, www.salemwitchmuseum.com.*

Boston

Faneuil Hall. Wealthy merchant Peter Faneuil built his namesake hall in 1741 to handle imported and exported goods (including, sadly, slaves). The building was used by Samuel Adams and other Sons of Liberty in the 1760s and '70s to denounce British Colonial rule. Still a popular venue for political speeches and public meetings, it now encompasses the original hall, as well as the North, South, and Quincy Market buildings. True to its commercial past, the whole complex is home to retail outlets, restaurants and bars, and small spaces that sell take-away food and souvenirs. *1 Faneuil Hall Sq., (617) 635-3105, www.cityofboston.gov/freedomtrail.*

New England Aquarium. Penguins, though not native to Boston, take pride of place here, but they're only a fraction of the aquarium's thousands of examples of marine life. Many different environments are recreated such as an Amazon rainforest, a coral reef, coastal Maine, and a harbor seal habitat. If you want to see whales—right whales, humpbacks, pilot whales—and dolphins, take the **Boston Harbor Cruises' New England Aquarium Whale Watch** (617/227-4321, www.bostonharborcruises.com/whale-watch), a three-hour tour offered in conjunction with the Aquarium. *1 Central Wharf, (617) 973-5200, www.neaq.org.*

Boston Tea Party Ships and Museum. On the evening of December 16, 1773, members of the underground group, Sons of Liberty, boarded three British trade ships anchored at Griffin's Wharf, and dumped their payload of tea chests into Boston Harbor. At this museum, you can board a replica of the *Beaver*, one of the ships at the wharf that night, and throw simulated bales of tea into the harbor. Abigail's Tea Room has tea (ahem), soft drinks, beer and wine, and assorted pastries and sandwiches. *Congress St. Bridge, (617) 338-1773, www.bostonteapartyship.com.*

Plymouth

Plimoth Plantation. This living-history museum recreates the daily life of Pilgrims and the native Wampanoags in 1627 through recreated homesteads, costumed re-enactors, and cooking demonstrations, lectures, and games. There's a crafts center, where

MASSACHUSETTS

Atlas map B-15, p. 100

Distance: 135 miles point to point.

workers use traditional tools and techniques to produce most of the items used on the grounds; a working grist mill; and the Nye Barn, where many of the animals are direct descendants of the cattle, sheep, goats, pigs, and birds the Pilgrims would have encountered or brought with them from England. The visitor center has a gift shop and a café. *137 Warren Ave., (508) 746-1622, www.plimoth.org.*

New Bedford

New Bedford Whaling National Historical Park. Whale-oil lamps were ubiquitous in the mid-19th century, and New Bedford was the world's premier whaling port and thus, the richest city. With a collection of museums, historic homes and buildings, and a working waterfront, the park invites you to explore the town in context of its golden past and its importance to the nation and the world. The visitors center has self-guided brochures and maps and a brief movie. Guided tours of New Bedford leave from the center daily and last about an hour. *33 William St., (508) 996-4095, www.nps.gov/nebe.*

Eiteljorg Museum of American Indians and Western Art, Indianapolis

Heart of Indiana Tour

This tour samples the cultural vitality, scenic beauty, and increasingly sophisticated food scene in central Indiana. It begins in Indianapolis, the state capital, and then heads south to Columbus, one of the nation's top destinations for architecture lovers.

From Columbus, the road winds west into Brown County, a landscape of rolling ridges, mysterious hollows, and mist rising from forested valley floors. The American Impressionists of the Hoosier School migrated here to capture the countryside in watercolors and oils. Visit the T.C. Steele State Historic Site to hear their stories, or explore the wooded glens in Brown County State Park. A little farther west is Bloomington, a lively college town.

Indianapolis

Conner Prairie Interactive History Park. One of the nation's premier living-history museums brings 19th-century Indiana to life through costumed interpreters who go about their daily activities in five historic areas. Here you can be part of a Civil War raid, dance to a water drum and a gourd rattle in the Lenape Indian Camp, dip a candle at the William Conner Homestead, or learn about early aviation history at the 1859 Balloon Village. Note that the park is in the suburb of Fishers, about 25 miles northeast of downtown. *13400 Allisonville Rd., (317) 776-6006, www.connerprairie.org.*

Eiteljorg Museum of American Indians and Western Art. This museum celebrates the art, history, and cultures of North America's indigenous peoples and the American West. It has one of the nation's finest collections of contemporary Native American art as well as classic works by the likes of N.C. Wyeth, Frederic Remington, Charles Russell, and Kay WalkingStick. Its café serves Southwestern fare, and its store has many items produced by Native American artists. *500 W. Washington St., (317) 636-9378, www.eiteljorg.org.*

Brown County State Park

Edinburgh

Exit 76 Antique Mall. There's nothing fancy about this establishment, but treasures abound from more than 340 dealers displaying their wares in 600 booths and cases. Its 72,000 square feet make it one of the Midwest's largest antique malls. Those tired of shopping can relax in a lounge area with TV and vending machines. *12595 N. Executive Dr., (812) 526-7676, www.exit76antiques.com.*

Columbus

Columbus Architectural Tours. The Columbus Visitor Center offers a variety of tours of the city's internationally acclaimed architecture. Its signature two-hour guided bus excursion will introduce you to many of the nearly 70 eye-popping churches, commercial buildings, schools, and art installations. Along the way you'll learn about architects and artists that include I.M. Pei, Eliel Saarinen, Richard Meier, Harry Weese, Dale Chihuly, and Henry Moore. *506 5th St., (812) 378-2622, columbus.in.us.*

Columbus architecture

Gnaw Bone

Bear Wallow Distillery. This woman-owned business is continuing the long tradition of Hoosier moonshine, only with an upscale twist. Its copper stills create artisanal spirits from locally grown grains. Tours include samples of its signature liquors: Hidden Holler Corn Whisky Moonshine, Bear Trap Barrel Strength White Whiskey, and Liar's Bench Rye Whiskey. No need to worry about revenue agents—this moonshine is legal. *4484 E. Old State Rd. 46, (812) 657-4923, www.bearwallowdistillery.com.*

Nashville

Brown County State Park. Founded in 1929, this 16,000-acre oasis is nicknamed the Little Smokies because of its resemblance to the Great Smoky Mountains. Densely forested hills and valleys, rugged ridges, and deep ravines entice hikers and fall-foliage enthusiasts. *1450 State Rd. 46 E (812) 988-6406, www.in.gov/dnr.*

T.C. Steele State Historic Site. Landscape painter Theodore C. Steele (1847–1926), the most highly respected of Indiana's painters, moved to Brown County in 1907 and helped introduce the area's beauty to an international audience. This state historic site preserves Steele's studio and home, which you can tour, as well as the gardens planted and tended by Selma Steele, the artist's wife. Five scenic hiking trails, from

INDIANA

Atlas map J-9, p. 75

Distance: 97 miles point to point.

easy to steep, wind through the property, which also has a gift shop. *4220 T.C. Steele Rd., (812) 988-2785, www.tcsteele.org.*

Beanblossom

Bill Monroe Music Park & Campground. Known as the father of bluegrass music, Bill Monroe spent much of his life in tiny Beanblossom. His former home is now the site of the Bill Monroe Bluegrass Hall of Fame & Museum, featuring instruments, clothing, and memorabilia from the greats of bluegrass and country music collected during Monroe's 60 years as a performer. This is also where the world's oldest, continuous-running bluegrass festival is held: June's eight-day Bill Monroe Memorial Bluegrass Festival, which began in 1967 (make reservations well in advance). *5163 State Rd. 135 N, (812) 988-6422, www.billmonroemusicpark.com.*

Bloomington

Indiana University Art Museum. With a dramatically angled building designed by famed architect I.M. Pei and 40,000 objects dating from ancient Mesopotamia to the present, this is considered one of the country's top university art museums. There are paintings by Claude Monet, Jackson Pollack, and Pablo Picasso, and highly regarded collections of ancient jewelry and African masks and art. Angles Café—named after the building's unusual design—refreshes you with beverages and pastries. *1133 E. 7th St., (812) 855-5445, www.indiana.edu.*

Marsh near Charleston

South Carolina: Highlights of Lowcountry

A road trip along coastal South Carolina means a relatively straight shot through seaside towns, many of which seem frozen in the elegance of a different era. From the 60-mile stretch of golden Grand Strand beaches to the mansions of historic Charleston to the plantations and seaside towns in between, Lowcountry charms you with its historical and natural beauty, great food, and Southern hospitality.

And, when you're not learning to dance the shag in North Myrtle Beach, you'll be touring centuries-old plantations and some of the country's oldest public gardens or following in the footsteps of movie stars in Beaufort, which served as the backdrop for classics like *Forrest Gump*.

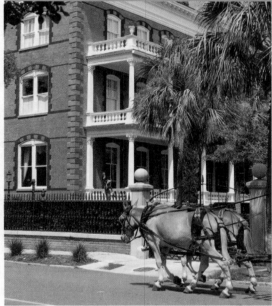
Charleston

North Myrtle Beach

Fat Harold's Beach Club. You can't blend in with the locals until you can dance like them, and in Lowcountry that means learning the shag. This is one of the best places to get in step. The king of shag and founder of this club, Harold Bessent, wouldn't have it any other way. The Society of Stranders (SOS), a group devoted to the dance, holds events here, and the calendar is chockablock with lessons—some of them free. *212 Main St., (843) 249-5779, www.fatharolds.com.*

Myrtle Beach

Myrtle Beach Boardwalk and Promenade. The heart of Myrtle Beach is its boardwalk, which runs from a pier at 14th Avenue North to another at 2nd Avenue North. Take a spin on the SkyWheel, or fly above things on a Myrtle Beach Zipline Adventures experience. **Broadway at the Beach** (www.broadwayatthebeach.com) has over two dozen

restaurants; several theaters; myriad specialty shops; and attractions like WonderWorks, Ripley's Aquarium, and the Hollywood Wax Museum. The Pavilion Nostalgia and Carousel Park has tamer vintage offerings. *14th Ave. N to 2nd Ave. N., myrtlebeachdowntown.com.*

Murrells Inlet

Brookgreen Gardens. In 1931, four rice fields were transformed into public gardens that, today, often make top-10 lists of the nation's best. Themed landscape areas include Live Oak Allee, with trees planted as far back as the 18th century; a medieval-style labyrinth; and the Palmetto Garden, which features the Sabal palmetto, South Carolina's state tree. Kids love the zoo filled with Lowcountry creatures, the Enchanted Storybook Forest, and the Children's Discovery Room and Sensory and Nature Trail. *1931 Brookgreen Dr., (843) 235-6000, www.brookgreen.org.*

Charleston

Fort Sumter National Monument. There's an eerie calmness at Fort Sumter, the same place that was shaken by explosions that set the American Civil War in motion. In the early hours of April 12, 1861, the fort came under Confederate attack and surrendered 34 hours later. It was left a smoldering heap of ruins in Charleston Harbor. Over time, it was rebuilt and is now listed on the National Register of Historic Places, a testament to the resiliency of the American South. Vessels operated by **Fort Sumter Tours** (843/722-2628, fortsumtertours.com) depart several times daily from Liberty Square, near the Fort Sumter Visitor Education Center. Trips last just over two hours. *Liberty Square, 340 Concord St., (843) 883-3123, www.nps.gov/fosu.*

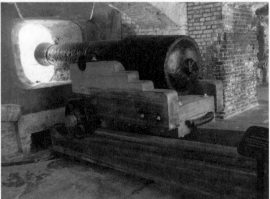
Cannon at Fort Sumter

Middleton Place. The estate of Henry Middleton, President of the First Continental Congress, has decorative and fine arts from the mid-18th to the mid-19th centuries that document the history of this affluent South Carolina family. In addition to taking a 45-minute guided house tour, you can explore America's oldest formally designed garden, a vast landscape

where there's something blooming just about year round: camellias in the winter; azaleas in the spring; magnolias, crepe myrtles, and roses in the summer. This National Historic Landmark site also has a restaurant serving plantation cuisine for lunch and dinner and an inn offering modern accommodations. *4300 Ashley River Rd., (843) 556-6020, www.middletonplace.org.*

Kiawah Island

Beachwalker Park. Just 15 miles south of Charleston, the barrier island's only public park consistently makes the Forbes list of America's best beaches. There are dressing areas and bathrooms, picnic areas with grills, and seasonal beach chair and umbrella rentals as well as showers. The beach is just one reason to visit the island. Golf is another. The island, much of which is a gated resort community, has five championship courses. *8 Beachwalker Dr., (843) 768-2395, www.ccprc.com.*

Beaufort

Beaufort Tours. Voted America's Happiest Seaside Town, Beaufort Tours aims to show you why. See locations used in films like *Forrest Gump* and *Something to Talk About*. Explore a haunted graveyard on a ghost tour, or visit a cotton plantation on the Plantation and Gullah Tour. A two-hour walking tour of Beaufort's historic district is also available. *1006 Bay St., (843) 838-2746, www.beauforttoursllc.com.*

St. Helena Island

Hunting Island State Park. Along with miles of sandy beaches and a working lighthouse, this island has more than 5,000 acres waiting to be explored. White egrets, great blue herons, osprey, bald eagles, pelicans, loggerhead turtles, and alligators are some of the creatures that make their homes here. The park also has nature trails and a nature center, a fishing pier, a boat ramp, and a store. *2555 Sea Island Pkwy., (843) 838-2011, www.huntingisland.com.*

Atlas map E-13, p. 187

Distance: 230 miles point to point.

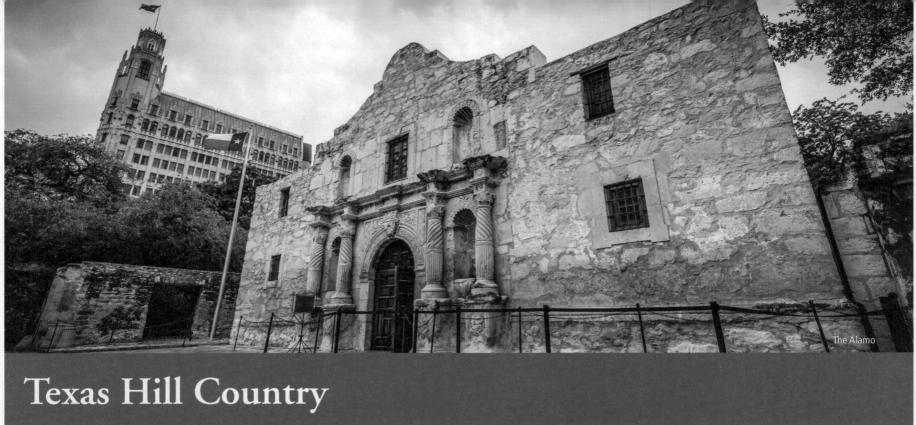

The Alamo

Texas Hill Country

In this state, as the miles keep passing, you come to understand why Texans boast that everything is bigger here.
A trip through Hill Country, though, is manageable, packing a lot of history and culture into a compact area that includes two great cities.

San Antonio seems to embody the full history of Texas, from its days under Spanish and Mexican rule to its struggle for independence ("Remember the Alamo," as the saying goes) and eventual statehood. Cutting-edge Austin, on the other hand, is the repository of all that history. Between them, you'll discover Wild West towns (some on the region's Wine Trail) that seem in no hurry to leave the 19th century.

San Antonio

The Alamo. In 1836, nearly 200 farmers, lawyers, surveyors, frontiersmen (including Jim Bowie and Davy Crockett), and others barricaded themselves inside the Alamo, determined to protect what they hoped would be the provisional capital of the Republic of Texas. Despite desperate requests for reinforcements, fewer than 100 men answered the call. Outside the walls, Mexico's Santa Anna marshaled his 1,800 men and waited. On March 6, the 13th day of the siege, Mexican soldiers breached the walls and killed all but a few women, children, and slaves, who were told to share what they had seen.

Hearing what happened on fact-filled ranger-led or self-guided-audio tours of the Alamo provides insight into one of the most unforgettable stories in American history. So does touring the museum within the Long Barrack, where the defenders made their final stand, and exploring the surrounding grounds, built as part of a WPA project. *300 Alamo Plaza, (210) 225-1391, www.thealamo.org.*

Field of Indian Paintbrush and Bluebonnets

River Walk. Designer Robert Hugman's vision of a lovely "scenescape" called Paseo del Rio, or River Walk, caught the imagination of San Antonio's citizens. It was completed as a WPA project, and to this day, its sinuous canals are enchanting, whether you walk along the promenade with its restaurants, cafés, bars, hotels, and boutiques, or embark with **San Antonio Cruises** (210/244-5700, www.riosanantonio.com) on a sail past scenes of old San Antonio. *110 Broadway, (210) 227-4262, www.thesanantonioriverwalk.com.*

Fredericksburg

National Museum of the Pacific War. Chester Nimitz grew up in land-locked Fredericksburg, but he went on to become one of the most respected of the U.S. Navy's admirals during WW II. This complex includes not only the Admiral Nimitz Museum but also the Center for Pacific War Studies, Plaza of Presidents, Memorial Courtyard, and Japanese Garden of Peace. Displays are packed with singular items like a PT boat, a Quonset hut, a mock field hospital, a midget Japanese sub that tried to reach Pearl Harbor, and the casing for a spare Fat Man atomic bomb. *340 E. Main St., (830) 997-8600, www.pacificwarmuseum.org.*

Dooley's 5-10-25. This place is a blast from the past, selling everything from broomstick toy ponies to Mexican jumping beans. What else can you stock up on? Things like Radio Flyer wagons, cast-iron cookware, kitchen gadgets, wind-up alarm clocks, plastic flowers, coonskin caps, Beemans gum, Blue Waltz perfume. . . the list goes on. *131 E. Main St., (830) 997-3458.*

Auslander. Combine a Bavarian biergarten with a Texas sports bar, and you get the Auslander. Drop into its bar or its German restaurant and select from roughly 70 beers, including those from Texas, Colorado, California, and Pennsylvania as well as those from Mexico, Holland, Belgium, Germany, and England. *323 E. Main St., (830) 997-7714, theauslander.com.*

Austin

Bullock Texas State History Museum. You can't miss this museum: Just look for the giant, bronze Lone Star sculpture. The first floor has Native American and Western artifacts, including an original wooden gate from the Alamo. Second-floor exhibits focus on the people and events that made Texas what it is—information you'll glean from diaries and letters dating from the days of early Mexican settlers, the Republic of Texas, the Civil War, and the Great Depression. The third level covers state geography, climate, infrastructure, and resources. *1800 N. Congress Ave., (512) 936-8746, www.thestoryoftexas.com.*

Waterloo Records. Music is the motor that moves Austin, and that motor is fueled by places like Waterloo Records. One of the city's finest record shops is packed with new and used CDs and LPs, including alternative/indie, rock/pop, folk/country, or blues/jazz. Texas artists are well represented, and the music-loving staffers will

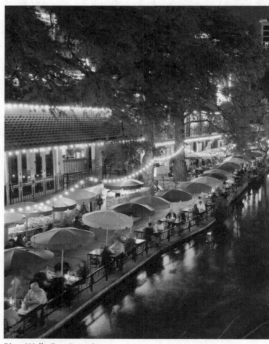

River Walk, San Antonio

Atlas map EM-4, p. 204

Distance: 185 miles point to point.

help you find new sounds. *600 N. Lamar Blvd., (512) 474-2500, www.waterloorecords.com.*

Congress Avenue Bridge Bat Colony. More than a million Mexican free-tail bats, comprising North America's largest urban colony, hang out beneath the Ann W. Richards Congress Avenue Bridge. Just after sunset, you can stand on its span, and watch the entire colony emerge for its nightly food foray. The viewing "season" runs March through November; late July or early August sees lots of young pups starting to fly. Want viewing-time information? Call the Bat Hotline, which is really just the main number for a local branch of Bat Conservation International. *(512) 327-9721.*

Cannon Beach

A Pacific Northwest Passage

Woods, water, and historic wonders await on this trip between two great metropolises of the Pacific Northwest. Few cities balance culture and commerce, nature and architecture, the past and the future as well as Seattle. The Emerald City makes a great jumping off point for a visit to the Olympic National Park and Forest.

The coastal route south from forested Washington to Oregon is as fun to drive as it is breathtaking. It also promises unique maritime experiences in towns like Astoria and Cannon Beach. Inland, you'll travel through one of Oregon's wine regions before reaching Portland, the so-called City of Roses, known for its gardens and its greenery. Here, as elsewhere along the route, expect great food, great views, and great stories—old and new.

Seattle, WA

Pike Place Market. Founded in 1907, "the Market" is a multilevel complex overlooking Elliott Bay and part of a 9-acre historic district. At street level on its western side are produce, fish, meat, flower, and craft stands. Across the narrow, cobblestoned Pike Place are more shops and restaurants. Watch fishmongers toss salmon, visit the first Starbucks outpost, and enjoy the antics of talented street performers. *85 Pike St., (206) 682-7453, www.pikeplacemarket.org.*

Space Needle and Seattle Center. The 1962 Seattle World's Fair left a legacy of icons, including the 605-foot Space Needle and its 360-degree views. Glass elevators travel up to 10 mph to the observation deck, with its displays, shops, lounge, and revolving SkyCity restaurant.

Below the Space Needle are the Experience Music Project, with rock-and-roll memorabilia; the Pacific Science Center; and the Seattle Children's Museum. Arrive via the Monorail, which zips (in about 2 minutes!) between downtown's Westlake Center Station and Seattle Center Station. *400 Broad St., (206) 905-2100, www.spaceneedle.com.*

Bill Speidel's Underground Tour. This 90-minute guided tour travels beneath historic Pioneer Square to 1890s walkways, where many storefronts and some interiors remain intact. You'll learn about Seattle's early timber days and famous Skid Row and get the back story of this three-block area, where the street level was raised from 8 to 35 feet after the 1889 Seattle Fire. *608 1st Ave., (206) 682-4646, www.undergroundtour.com.*

Port Angeles

Olympic National Park. Three ecosystems make up this 1,427-square-mile peninsular park: Pacific shoreline, subalpine forest and meadowland, and coastal-Northwest rain forest. You can readily combine a visit here with explorations of Olympic National Forest—which rings the park—and the coast.

The drive along U.S. 101 has many overlooks and short trails down to the beach. Near shore, in the park's southwestern reaches, is the Hoh Rain Forest. Learn about the mild climate and lush vegetation at its visitors center before exploring the mile-long Hall of Mosses or one of eight other trails. *3002 Mount Angeles Rd., (360) 565-3130, www.nps.gov/olym.*

Hoh Rain Forest, Olympic National Park

Astoria, OR

Columbia River Maritime Museum. A massive window overlooks the Columbia River, and displays tell the stories of its vessels and the dangers they face on "the bar" at the river's mouth. Indeed, the collection of 30,000 maritime artifacts has many items salvaged from wrecks in the so-called Graveyard of the Pacific. Step into a simulator to see what it's like to pilot a tugboat before visiting the lightship *Columbia*. *1792 Marine Dr., (503) 325-2323, www.crmm.org.*

Cannon Beach

Ecola State Park. Kayakers and swimmers like the waters off this park's beautiful, half-mile Crescent and Indian beaches. You can also hike to a spot overlooking the 19th-century Tillamook Rock Lighthouse (in spring and fall, watch for gray whales). It's just off the 2.5-mile Clatsop Loop Trail, which travels through forests of giant Sitka spruce in the footsteps of Lewis and Clark. *Off Hwy. 101, (503) 436-2844, www.oregonstateparks.org.*

Pittock Mansion, Portland

Atlas map F-7, p. 218

Distance: 442 miles point to point.

Forest Grove

David Hill Vineyards and Winery. Established by a German pioneer family in the late 1800s, David Hill has some of Willamette Valley's oldest Pinot Noir vines and also produces Gewürztraminer, Riesling, and other varieties. Stop by the tasting room any day of the week. *46350 N.W. David Hill Rd., (503) 992-8545, www.davidhillwinery.com.*

Portland

Pittock Mansion and Washington Park. Mansion is an understatement. It's more like a castle, or rather, a French Renaissance–style chateau. In the 1850s, Henry and Georgiana Pittock each traveled west along the Oregon Trail before meeting and marrying in Portland. Henry took over the *Daily Oregonian* newspaper and made a fortune in several endeavors.

Their 22-room sandstone residence was completed in 1914, and tours of it and the 46-acre estate highlight architecture, decorative arts, and the family. In nearby Washington Park, check out the Rose Test Garden, Japanese Garden, Discovery Museum, Portland Children's Museum, and Oregon Zoo. *3229 N.W. Pittock Dr., (508) 823-3623, pittockmansion.org.*

Powell's City of Books. It's been around for a while, is open 365 days a year, stocks new and used tomes, and has staffers and customers who truly love to read. Shop for books on local history or lore, scan the national best sellers, grab a cheap paperback, and have a cuppa at World Cup Coffee & Tea. *1005 W. Burnside, (503) 228-4651, www.powells.com.*

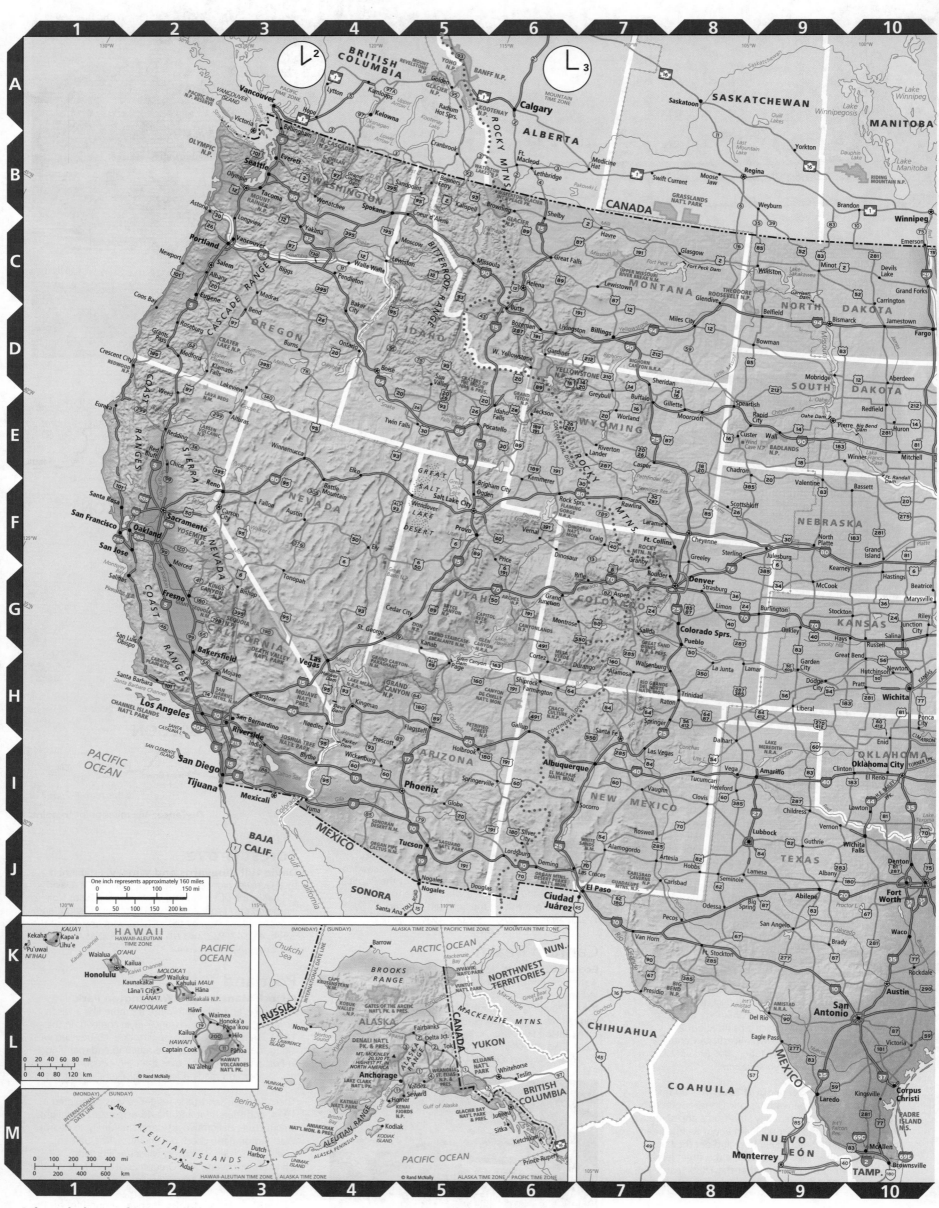

Selected places of interest

- Acadia National Park, C-20
- Arches National Park, G-6
- Badlands National Park, E-9
- Big Bend National Park, L-8
- Biscayne National Park, M-18
- Bryce Canyon National Park, G-5
- Canyonlands National Park, G-6
- Capitol Reef National Park, G-5
- Carlsbad Caverns National Park, J-7
- Channel Islands National Park, H-1
- Congaree National Park, I-17
- Crater Lake National Park, D-2
- Cuyahoga Valley National Park, F-16
- Death Valley National Park, G-3
- Denali National Park, L-4
- Dry Tortugas National Park, M-17
- Everglades National Park, M-17
- Glacier Bay National Park, M-5
- Glen Canyon National Recreation Area, G-5
- Grand Canyon National Park, H-4
- Grand Teton National Park, E-6
- Great Sand Dunes Nat'l Park & Pres., H-7
- Great Smoky Mountains Nat'l Park, H-15
- Guadalupe Mountains National Park, J-7

Land area: 3,537,438 sq. mi. | Population: 308,745,538 | Largest city: New York, 8,175,133

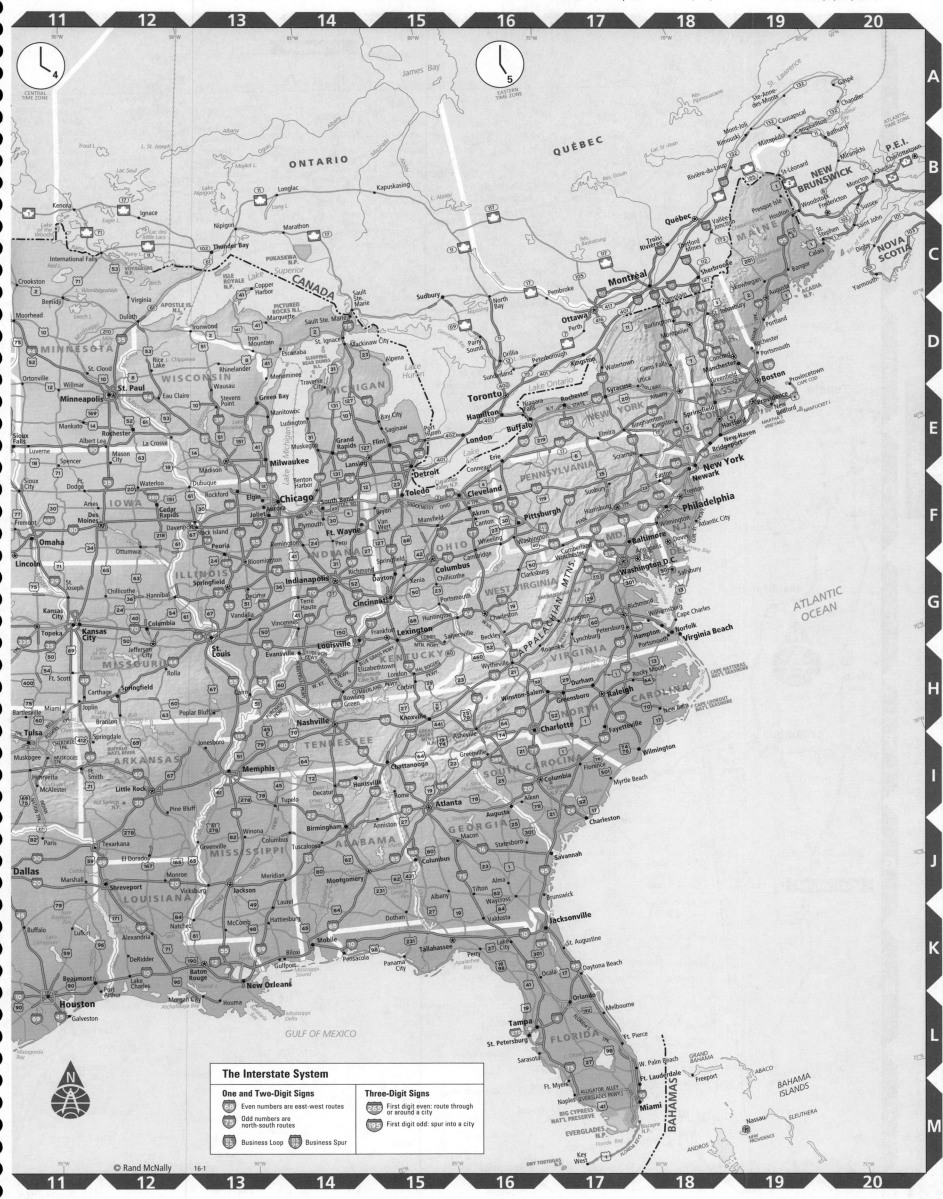

The Interstate System

One and Two-Digit Signs
- **66** Even numbers are east-west routes
- **75** Odd numbers are north-south routes
- **81** Business Loop · **82** Business Spur

Three-Digit Signs
- **265** First digit even: route through or around a city
- **195** First digit odd: spur into a city

© Rand McNally   16-1

Index of cities Pg. 236

Mileages between cities

	Andalusia	Anniston	Auburn	Birmingham	Chattanooga, TN	Columbus, GA	Dothan	Florence	Gadsden	Grove Hill	Huntsville	Meridian, MS	Mobile	Montgomery	Selma	Tuscaloosa
Atlanta, GA	252	90	108	146	117	106	206	263	119	294	181	289	328	160	210	201
Birmingham	181	64	109		146	141	196	118	61	155	102	146	258	90	87	58

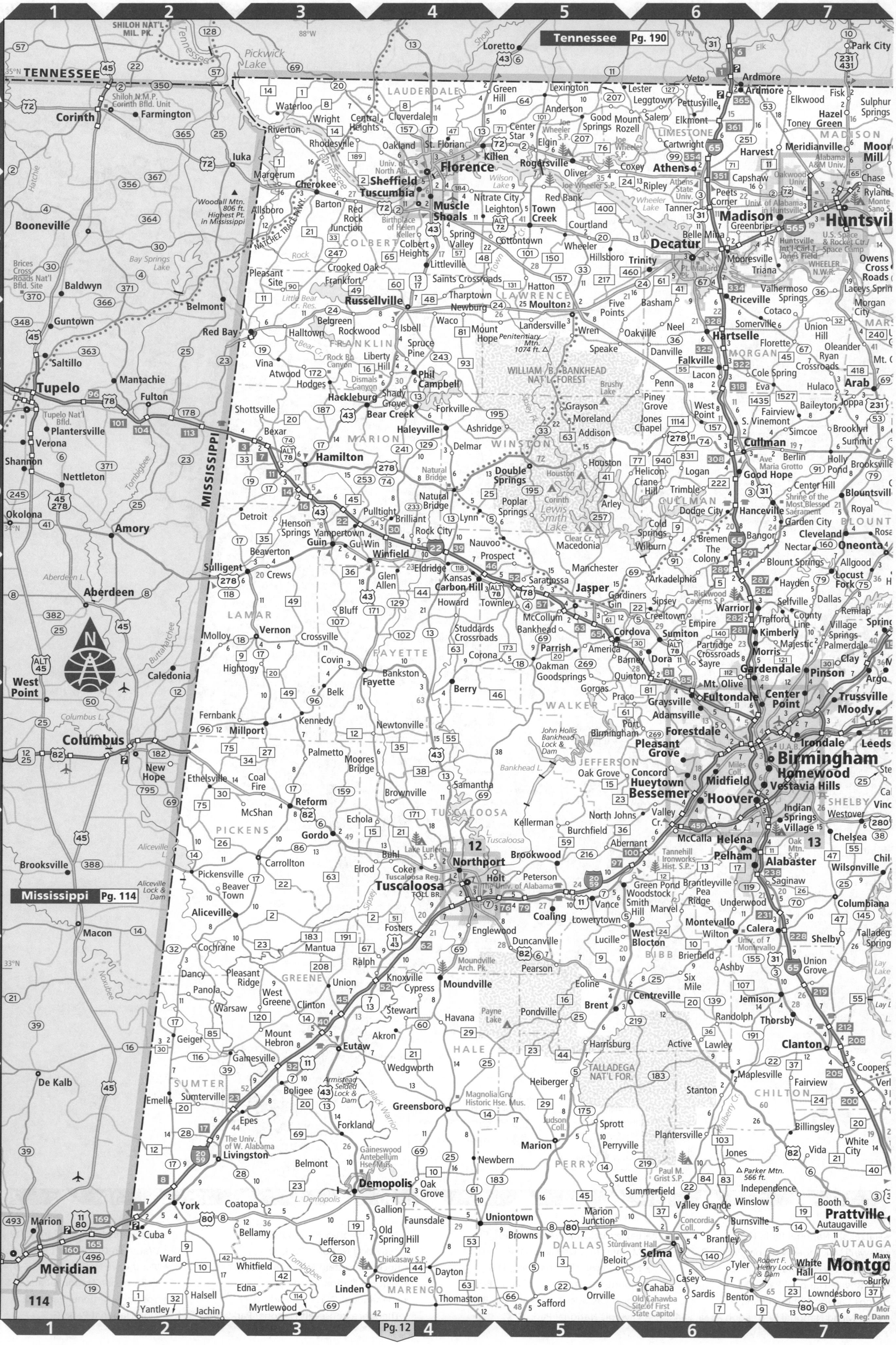

Alabama state facts

Nickname: The Heart of Dixie
Capital: Montgomery, J-8

Population: 4,779,736 (rank: 23rd)
Largest city: Birmingham, 212,237, F-7

Land area: 50,744 sq. mi. (rank: 28th)
Highest point: Cheaha Mountain, 2,407 ft., F-9

Determining distances along roads

Highway distances (segments of one mile or less not shown):
Cumulative miles (red): the distance between red arrows
Intermediate miles (black): the distance between intersections & places

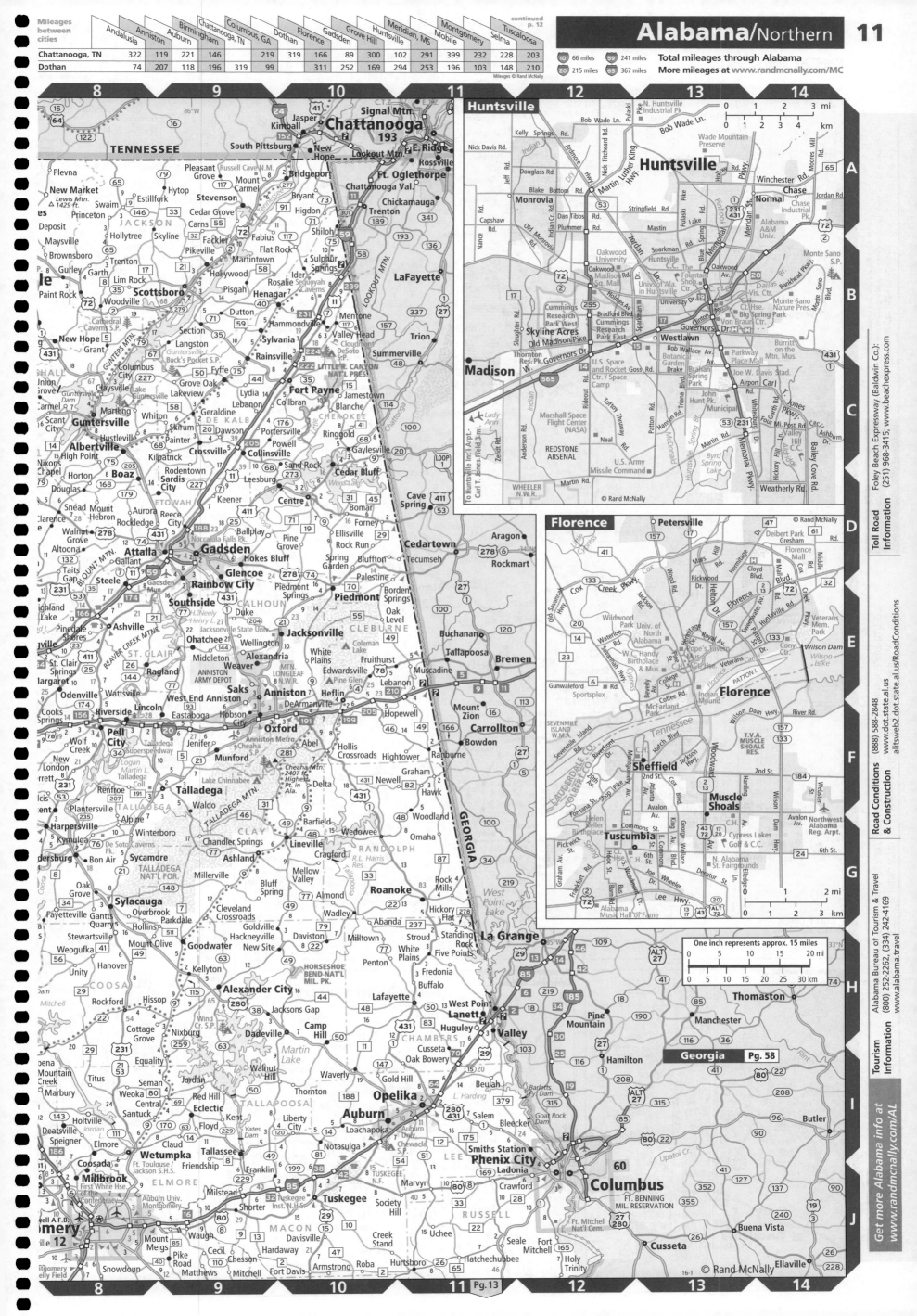

10 66 miles **59** 241 miles **Total mileages through Alabama**
20 215 miles **65** 367 miles **More mileages at www.randmcnally.com/MC**

Huntsville

Florence

One inch represents approx. 15 miles

Georgia Pg. 58

Pg. 13

© Rand McNally

Mileages between cities	Andalusia	Anniston	Auburn	Birmingham	Chattanooga, TN	Columbus, GA	Dothan	Florence	Gadsden	Grove Hill	Huntsville	Meridian, MS	Mobile	Montgomery	Selma	Tuscaloosa
Huntsville	279	104	210	102	102	243	294	64	72	254		244	356	189	188	155
Mobile	123	280	222	258	399	256	196	376	313	82	356	133		168	159	203

Mileages © Rand McNally

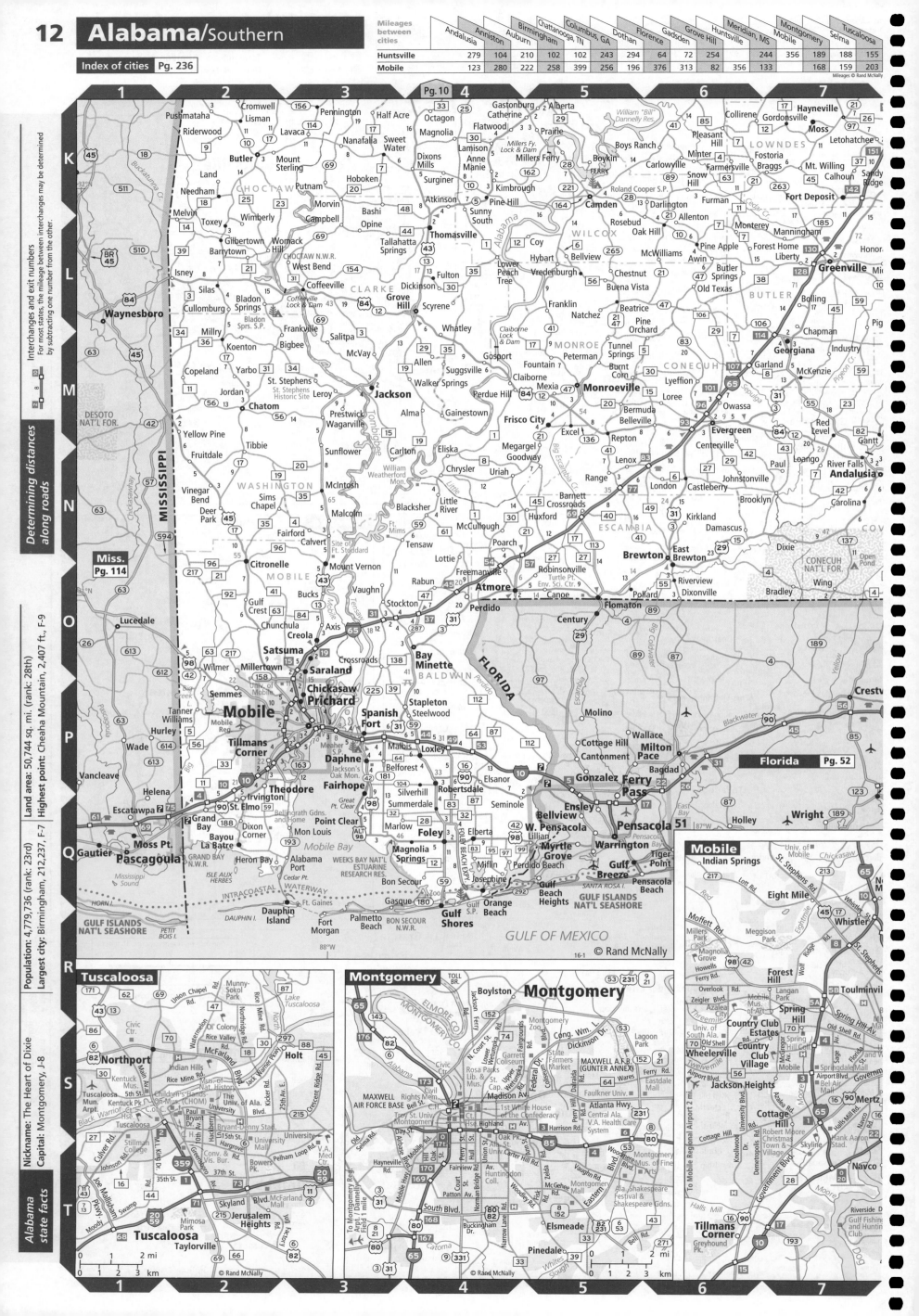

© Rand McNally

Mileages between cities

	Andalusia	Anniston	Auburn	Birmingham	Chattanooga, TN	Columbus, GA	Dothan	Florence	Gadsden	Grove Hill	Huntsville	Meridian, MS	Mobile	Montgomery	Selma	Tuscaloosa
Montgomery	91	110	54	90	232	87	103	205	148	134	189	153	168		50	104
Tuscaloosa	194	118	159	58	203	192	210	123	118	121	155	93	203	104	75	

10 66 miles · 59 241 miles · 20 215 miles · 65 367 miles

Total mileages through Alabama
More mileages at www.randmcnally.com/MC

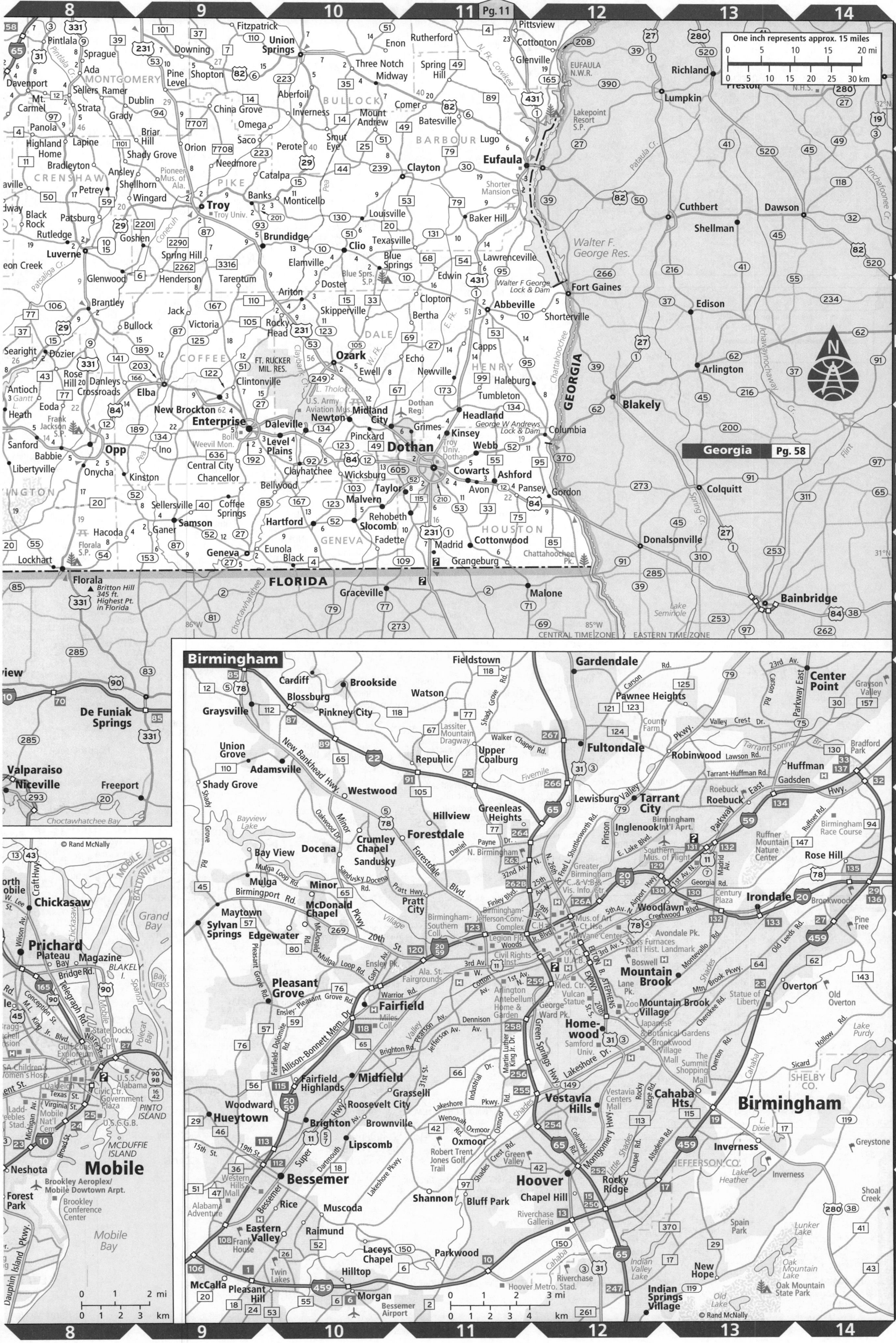

Toll Road Information
Foley Beach Expressway (Baldwin Co.): (251) 968-3415; www.beachexpress.com

Road Conditions & Construction
(888) 588-2848
www.dot.state.al.us
alitsweb2.dot.state.al.us/RoadConditions

Tourism Information
Alabama Bureau of Tourism & Travel
(800) 252-2262, (334) 242-4169
www.alabama.travel

Get more Alabama info at www.randmcnally.com/AL

Index of cities Pg. 236

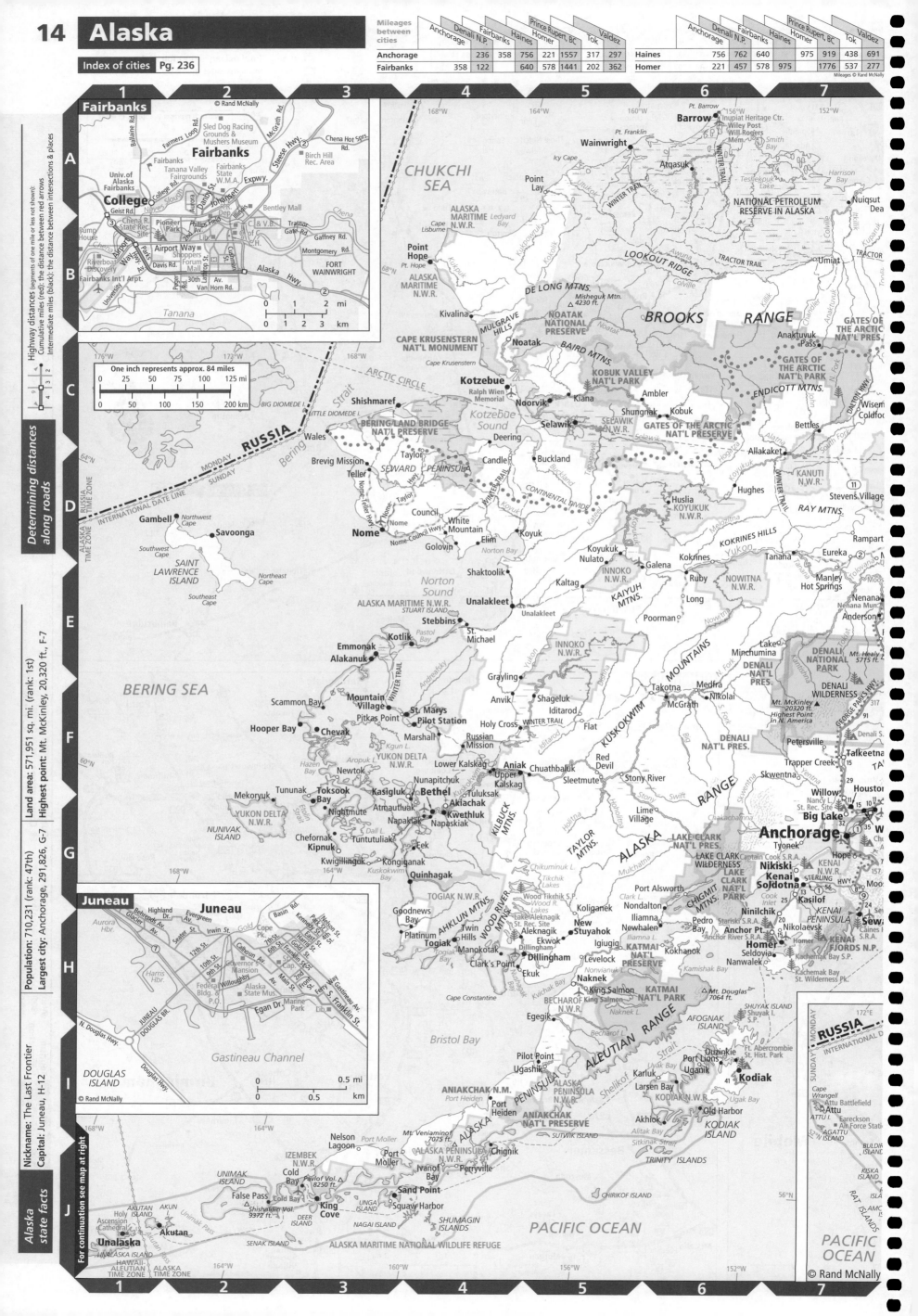

Mileages between cities	Anchorage	Denali N.P.	Fairbanks	Haines	Prince Rupert, BC / Homer	Tok	Valdez
Anchorage		236	358	756	221 / 1557	317	297
Fairbanks	358		122	640	578 / 1441	202	362
Haines	756	762	640		975 / 919	438	691
Homer	221	457	578	975	1776	537	277

Mileages © Rand McNally

Alaska state facts

Nickname: The Last Frontier
Capital: Juneau, H-12

Population: 710,231 (rank: 47th)
Largest city: Anchorage, 291,826, G-7

Land area: 571,951 sq. mi. (rank: 1st)
Highest point: Mt. McKinley, 20,320 ft., F-7

Determining distances along roads

Highway distances (segments of one mile or less not shown):
Cumulative miles (red): the distance between red arrows
Intermediate miles (black): the distance between intersections & places

For continuation see map at right

© Rand McNally

Mileages between cities

	Anchorage	Denali N.P.	Fairbanks	Haines	Homer	Prince Rupert, BC	Tok	Valdez
Kenai	157	393	514	911	83	1713	473	213
Seward	126	362	483	880	168	1682	442	182

	Anchorage	Denali N.P.	Fairbanks	Haines	Homer	Prince Rupert, BC	Tok	Valdez
Tok	317	324	202	438	537	1240		252
Valdez	297	346	362	691	277	1493	252	

① 408 miles ② 202 miles ③ 325 miles

Total mileages through Alaska

More mileages at www.randmcnally.com/MC

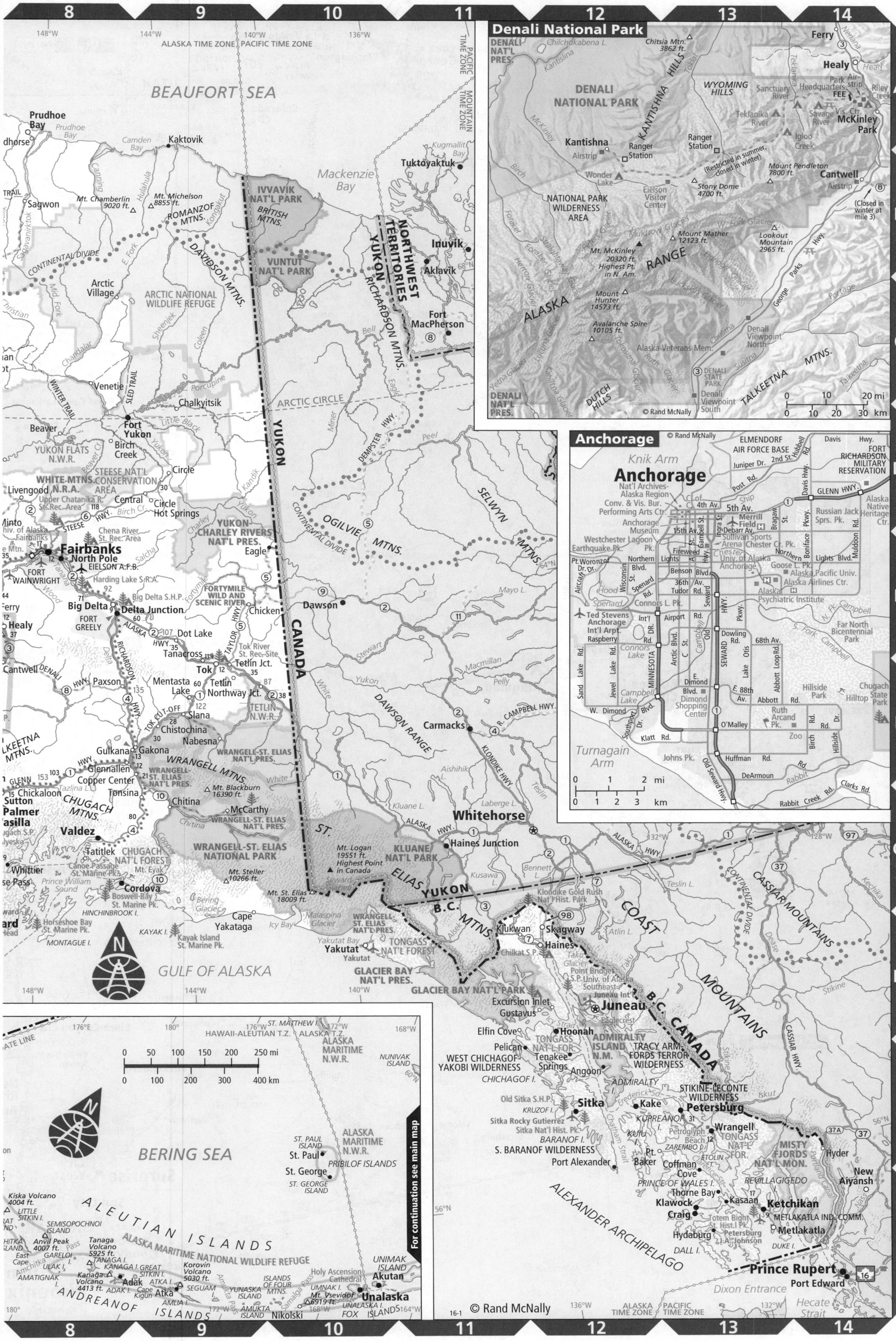

Road Conditions & Construction
511
511.alaska.gov
www.dot.state.ak.us

Tourism Information
State of Alaska Tourism Office
(800) 862-5275
www.travelalaska.com

Toll Road Information
No toll roads

Explore Alaska at www.randmcnally.com/AK

Index of cities Pg. 236

Mileages between cities	Casa Grande	Chinle	Eagar	Flagstaff	Gallup, NM	Grand Canyon	Holbrook	Kingman	Lake Havasu City	Las Vegas, NV	Lordsburg, NM	Nogales	Page	Phoenix	Tucson	Yuma
Flagstaff	191	213	176		185	79	90	146	204	250	374	321	133	139	255	318
Holbrook	220	123	86	90	94	167		237	295	340	264	304	214	230	278	409

Mileages © Rand Nally

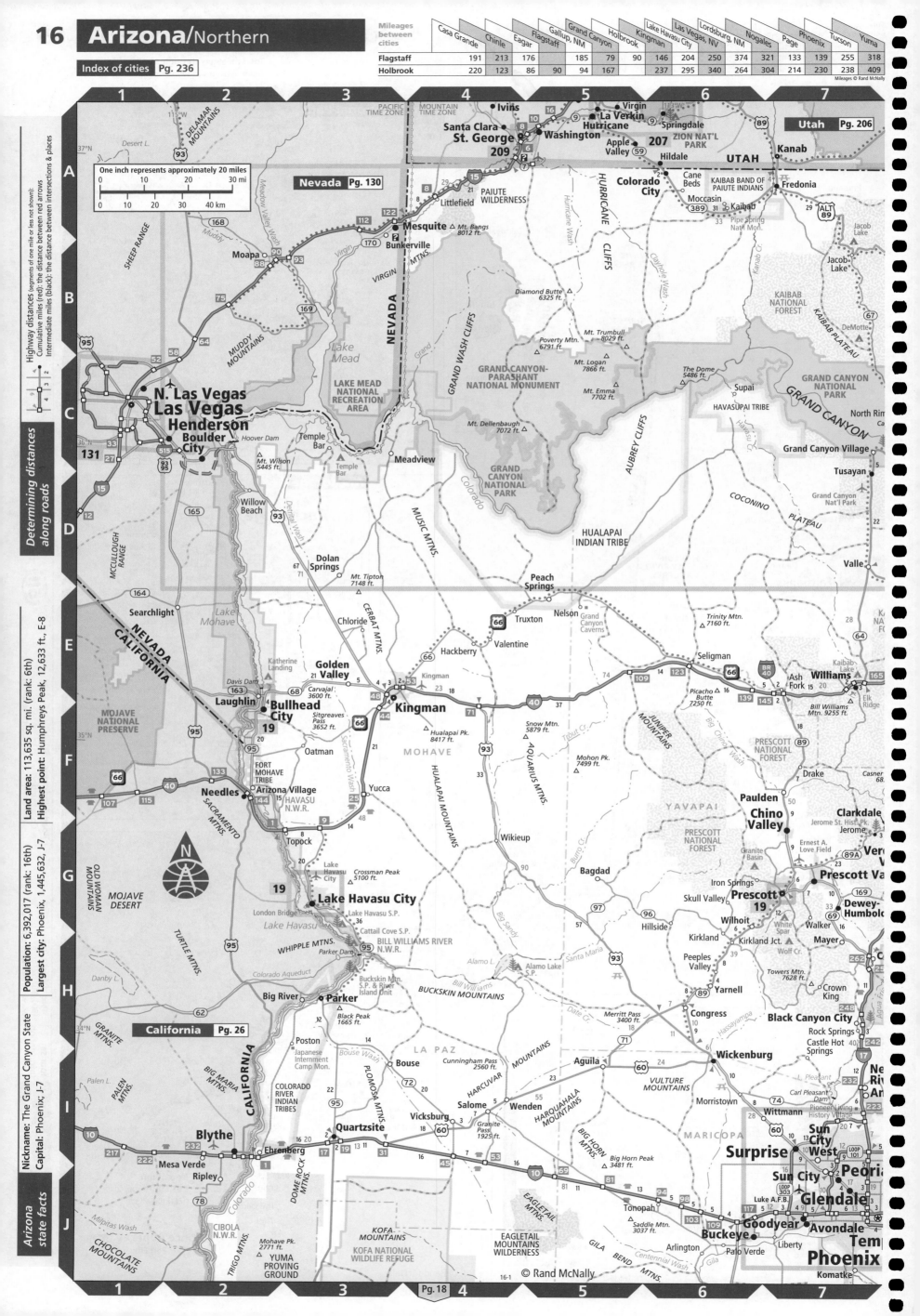

Mileages between cities	Casa Grande	Chinle	Eagar	Flagstaff	Gallup, NM	Grand Canyon	Holbrook	Kingman	Lake Havasu City	Las Vegas, NV	Lordsburg, NM	Nogales	Page	Phoenix	Tucson	Yuma
Las Vegas, NV	336	463	427	250	435	275	340	104	152		558	467	271	285	401	292
Page	324	204	301	133	255	137	214	281	340	271	499	455		275	390	453

Mileages © Rand McNally

continued p. 18

Total mileages through Arizona
8 — 178 miles   17 — 146 miles
10 — 392 miles   40 — 359 miles
More mileages at www.randmcnally.com/MC

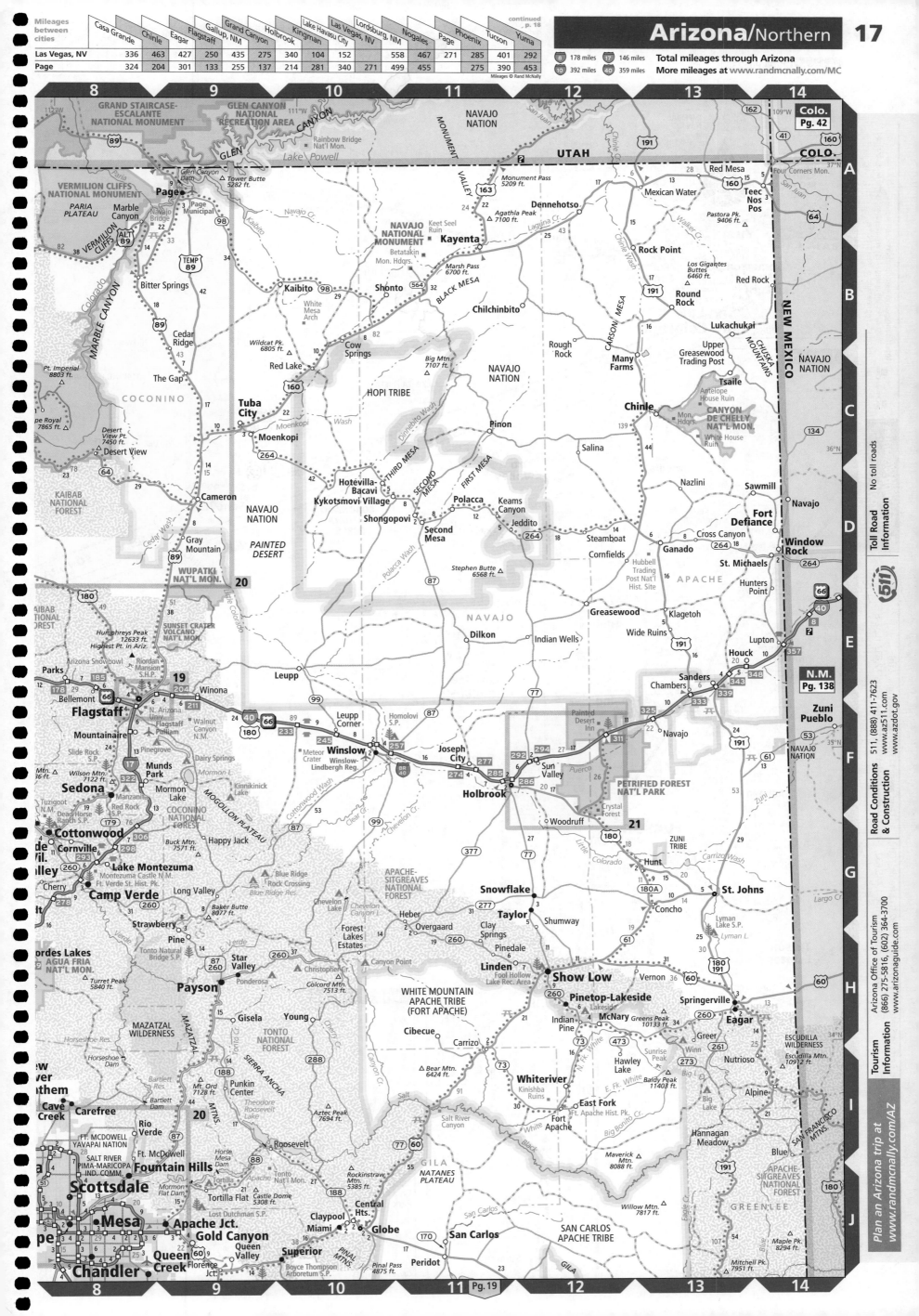

Index of cities Pg. 236

Mileages between cities	Casa Grande	Chinle	Eagar	Flagstaff	Gallup, NM	Grand Canyon	Holbrook	Kingman	Lake Havasu City	Las Vegas, NV	Lordsburg, NM	Nogales	Page	Phoenix	Tucson	Yuma
Phoenix	48	353	226	139	324	218	230	182	198	285	268	179	275		116	181
Prescott	148	306	270	93	278	126	184	148	206	251	368	278	227	97	213	214

Mileages © Rand McNally

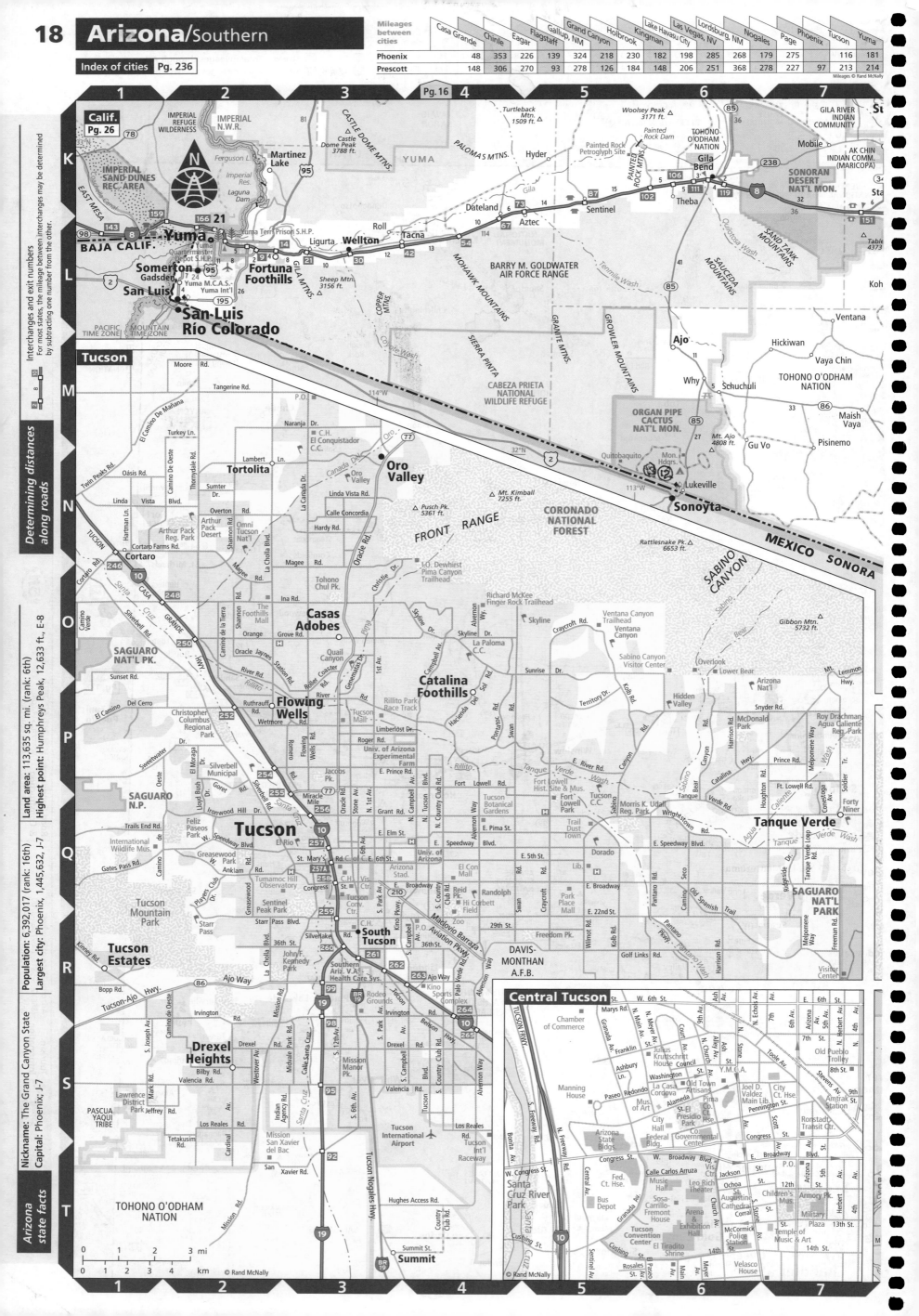

Nickname: The Grand Canyon State
Capital: Phoenix; J-7

Population: 6,392,017 (rank: 16th)
Largest city: Phoenix, 1,445,632, J-7

Land area: 113,635 sq. mi. (rank: 6th)
Highest point: Humphreys Peak, 12,633 ft., E-8

Determining distances along roads

Interchanges and exit numbers
For most states, the mileage between interchanges may be determined by subtracting one number from the other.

Mileages between cities	Casa Grande	Chinle	Eagar	Flagstaff	Gallup, NM	Grand Canyon	Holbrook	Kingman	Lake Havasu City	Las Vegas, NV	Lordsburg, NM	Nogales	Page	Phoenix	Tucson	Yuma
Tucson	66	361	238	255	333	334	238	297	314	401	156	66	390	116		236
Yuma	172	532	399	318	502	397	409	213	155	292	392	301	453	181	236	

Mileages © Rand McNally

Total mileages through Arizona
8 — 178 miles 17 — 146 miles 10 — 392 miles 40 — 359 miles
More mileages at www.randmcnally.com/MC

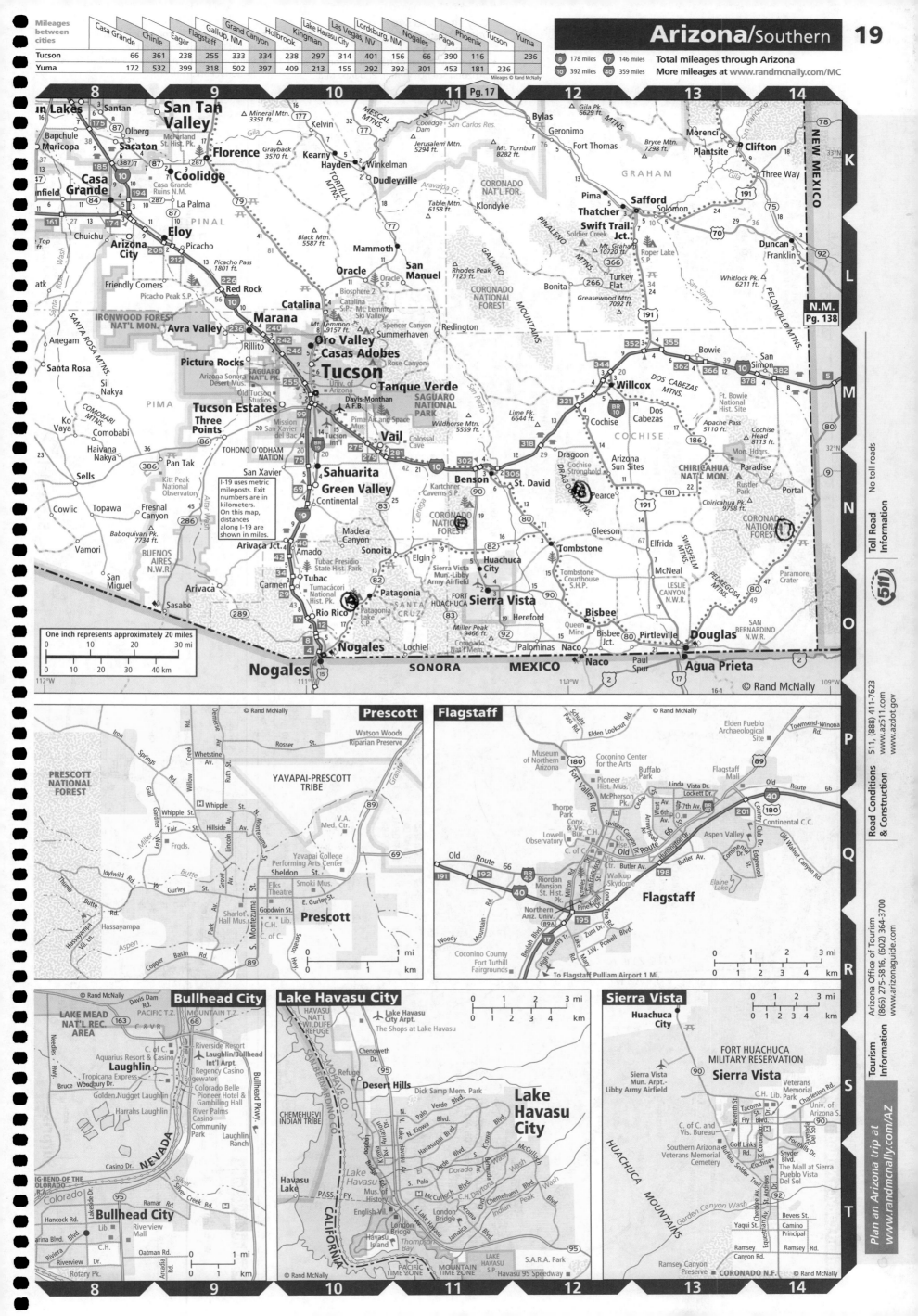

One inch represents approximately 20 miles

I-19 uses metric mileposts. Exit numbers are in kilometers. On this map, distances along I-19 are shown in miles.

© Rand McNally

City sights to see

- Arizona Historical Society Sanguinetti House Museum, Yuma, L-6
- Arizona Museum of Natural History, Mesa, J-7
- Arizona Science Center, Phoenix, M-3
- Arizona State Capitol, Phoenix, M-1
- Heard Museum, Phoenix, L-2
- Painted Desert Inn Museum, Petrified Forest National Park, L-10

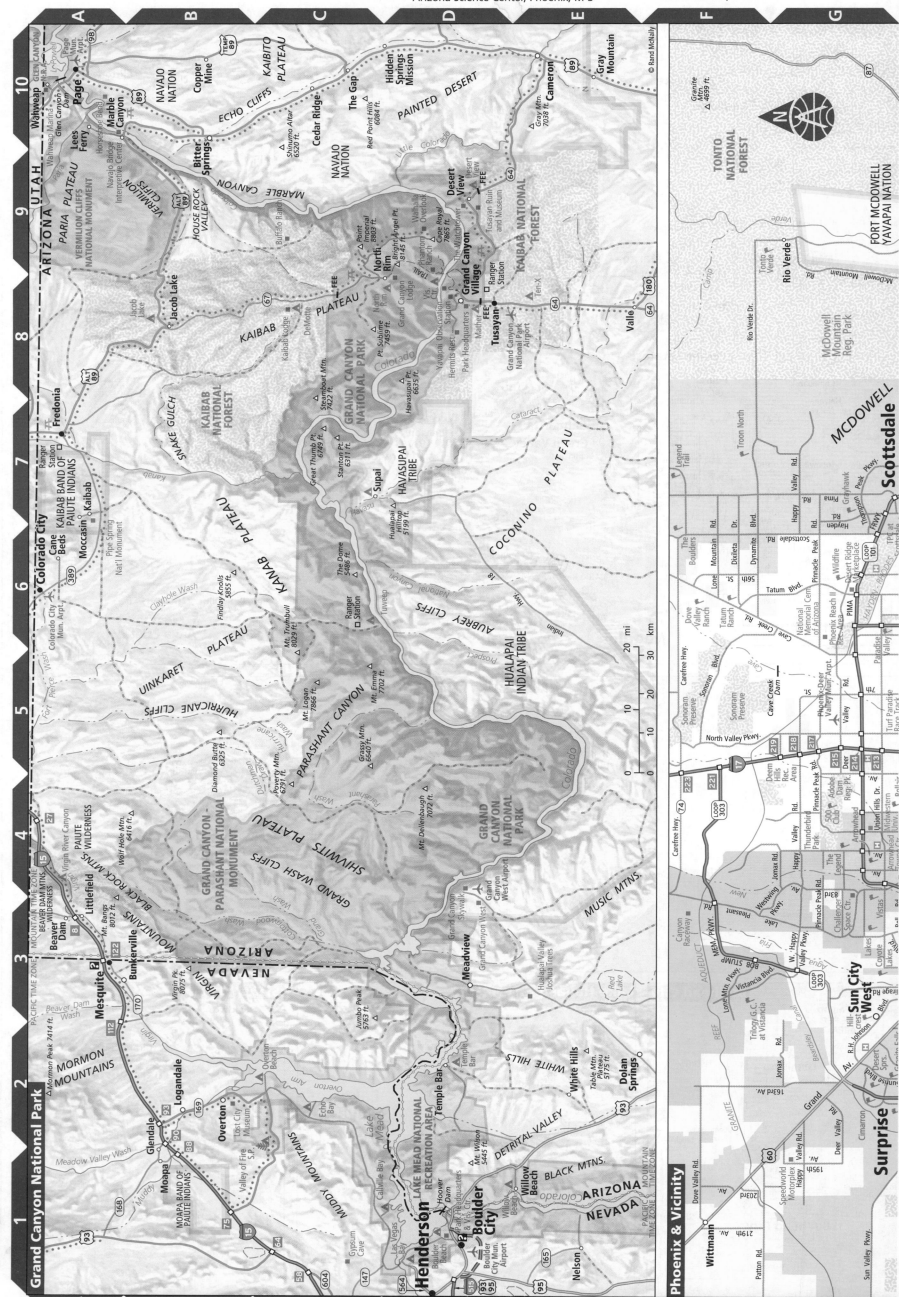

- Phoenix Art Museum, Phoenix, L-2
- Taliesin West, Scottsdale, H-7
- Tusayan Ruin and Museum, Grand Canyon National Park, D-9
- Yavapai Observation Station, Grand Canyon National Park, D-8
- Yuma Territorial Prison State Historic Park, Yuma, L-6

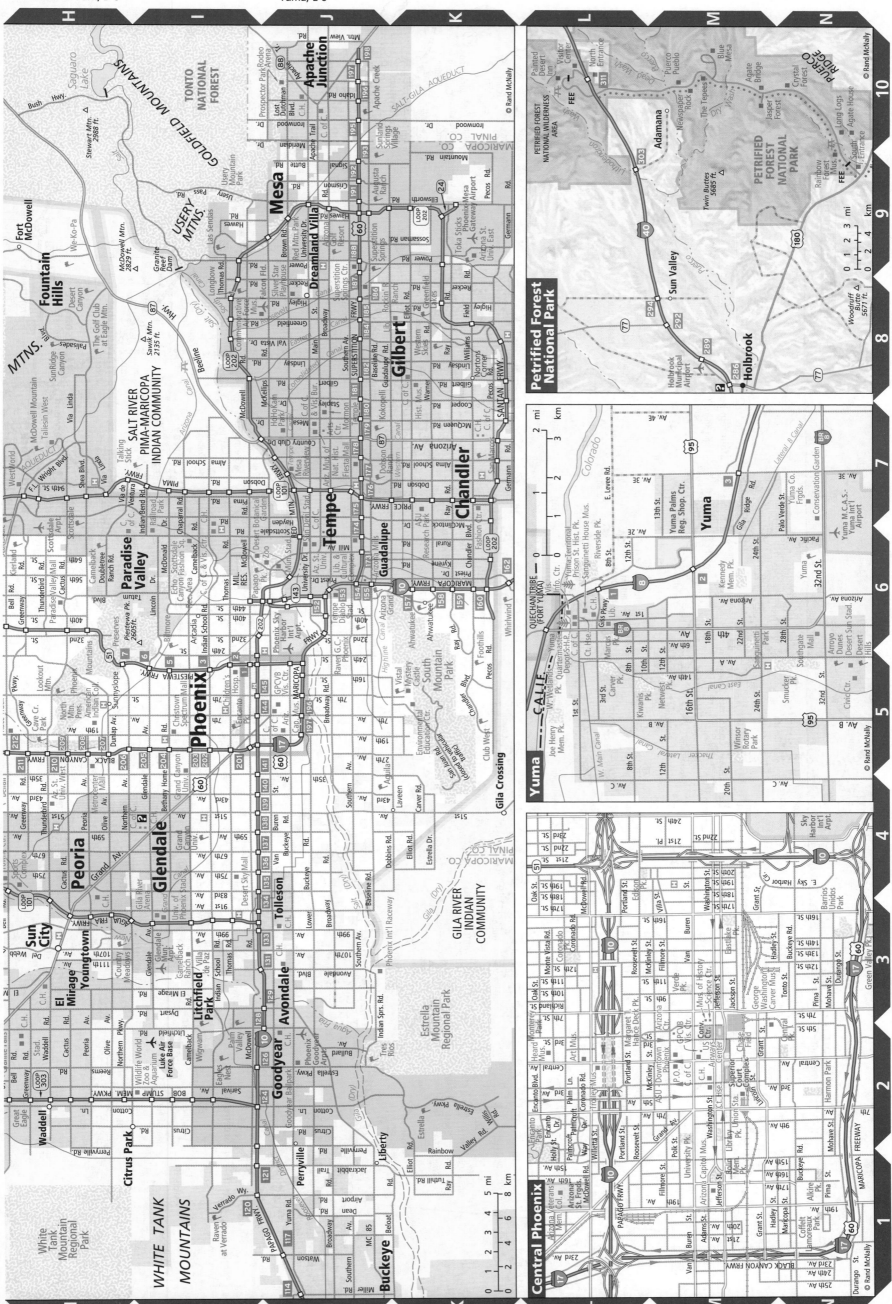

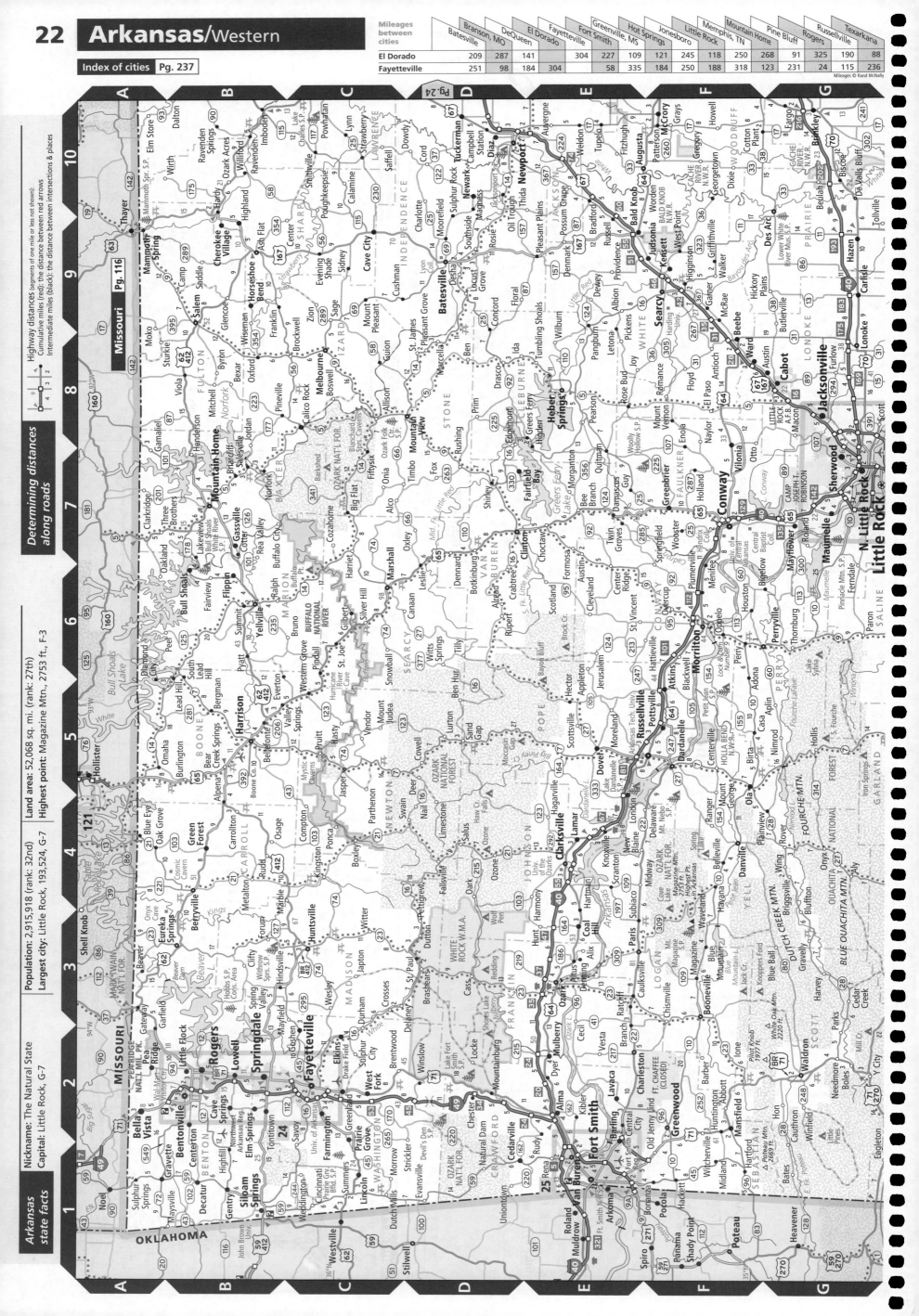

Mileages © Rand McNally

Mileages between cities	Batesville	Branson, MO	DeQueen	El Dorado	Fayetteville	Fort Smith	Greenville, MS	Hot Springs	Jonesboro	Little Rock	Memphis, TN	Mountain Home	Pine Bluff	Rogers	Russellville	Texarkana
El Dorado	209	287	141		304	227	109	121	245	118	250	268	91	325	190	88
Fayetteville	251	98	184	304		58	335	184	250	188	318	123	231	24	115	236

Arkansas state facts

Nickname: The Natural State
Capital: Little Rock, G-7

Population: 2,915,918 (rank: 32nd)
Largest city: Little Rock, 193,524, G-7

Land area: 52,068 sq. mi. (rank: 27th)
Highest point: Magazine Mtn., 2753 ft, F-3

Determining distances along roads

Highway distances (segments of one mile or less not shown):
Cumulative miles (red): the distance between red arrows
Intermediate miles (black): the distance between intersections & places

Mileages between cities	Batesville	Branson, MO	DeQueen	El Dorado	Fayetteville	Fort Smith	Greenville, MS	Hot Springs	Jonesboro	Little Rock	Memphis, TN	Mountain Home	Pine Bluff	Rogers	Russellville	Texarkana
Fort Smith	219	158	130	227	58		304	130	261	158	286	187	199	81	84	182
Jonesboro	68	203	272	245	250	261	219	182		130	70	126	171	253	173	270

Mileages © Rand McNally

Total mileages through Arkansas

30	143 miles	55	72 miles
40	284 miles	65	309 miles

More mileages at www.randmcnally.com/MC

continued p. 24

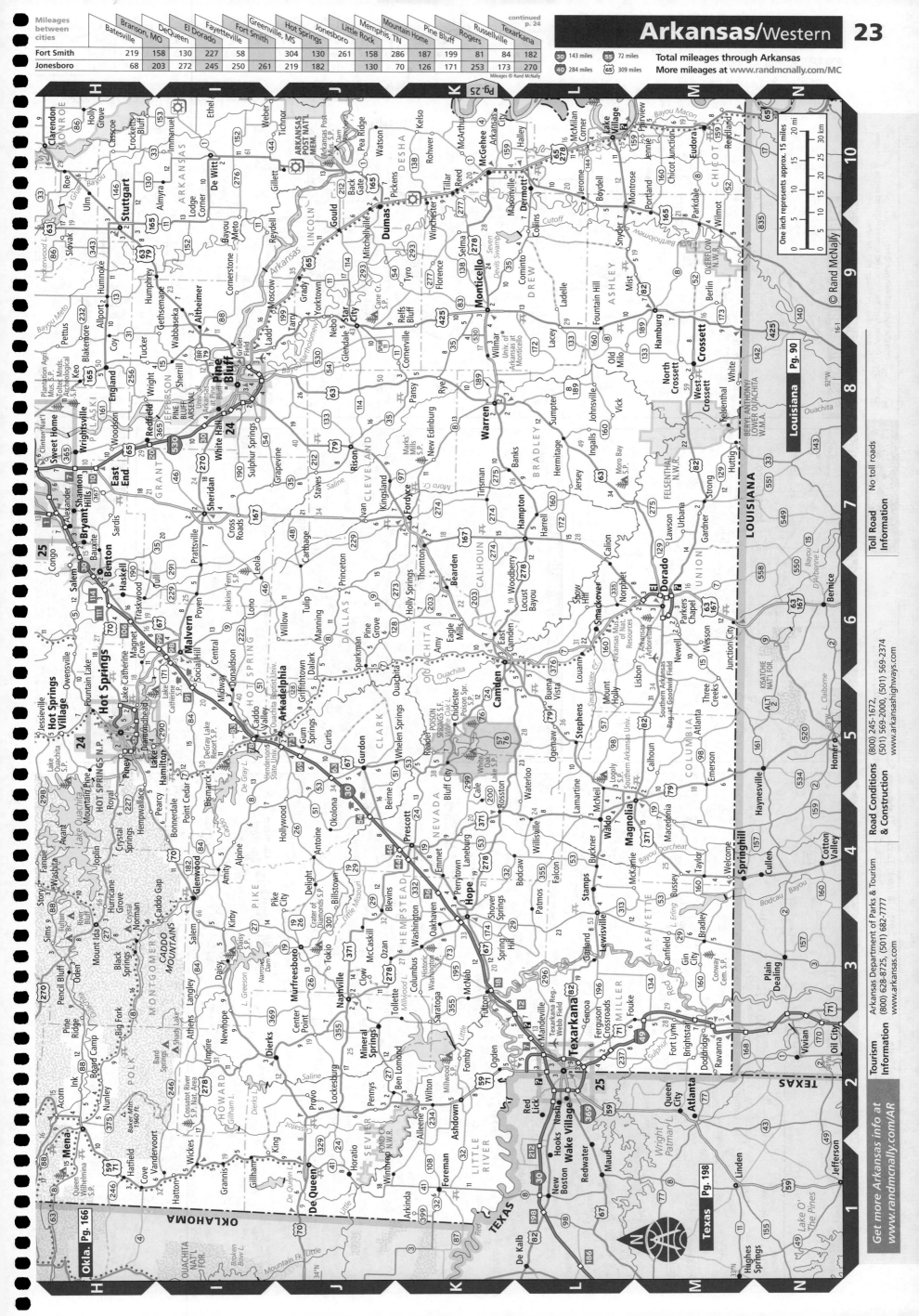

One inch represents approx. 15 miles

© Rand McNally

Tourism Information — Arkansas Department of Parks & Tourism (800) 628-8725, (501) 682-7777 www.arkansas.com

Road Conditions & Construction — (800) 245-1672, (501) 569-2000, (501) 569-2374 www.arkansashighways.com

Toll Road Information — No toll roads

Louisiana Pg. 90

Okla. Pg. 166

Texas Pg. 198

Get more Arkansas info at www.randmcnally.com/AR

Mileages between cities	Batesville	Branson, MO	DeQueen	El Dorado	Fayetteville	Fort Smith	Greenville, MS	Hot Springs	Jonesboro	Little Rock	Memphis, TN	Mountain Home	Pine Bluff	Rogers	Russellville	Texarkana
Little Rock	94	172	143	118	188	158	147	54	130		137	151	43	208	74	142
Memphis, TN	119	274	278	250	318	286	152	188	70	137		195	152	339	204	276

Mileages © Rand McNally

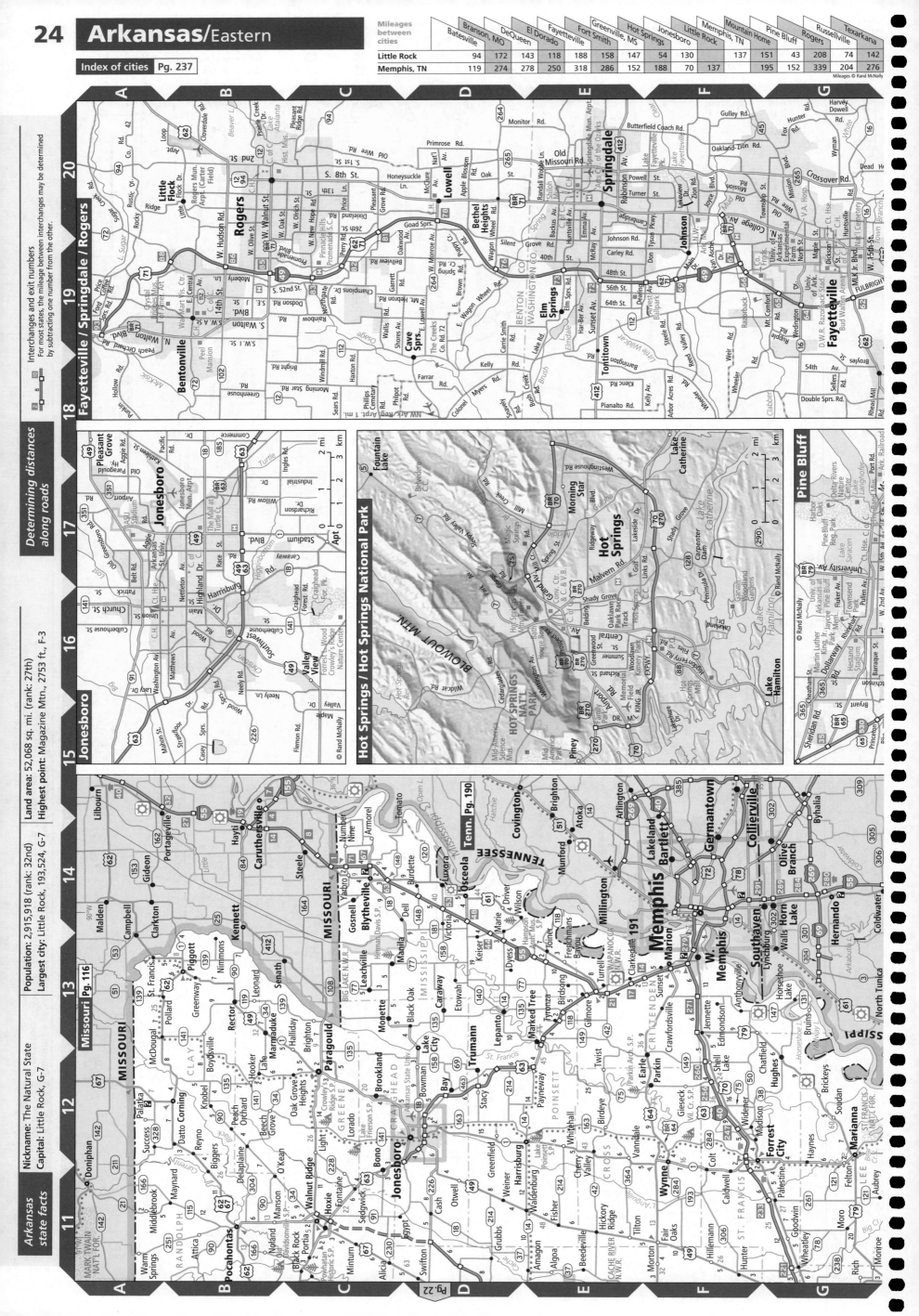

Arkansas state facts

Nickname: The Natural State
Capital: Little Rock, G-7

Land area: 52,068 sq. mi. (rank: 27th)
Highest point: Magazine Mtn., 2753 ft., F-3

Population: 2,915,918 (rank: 32nd)
Largest city: Little Rock, 193,524, G-7

Determining distances along roads

Interchanges and exit numbers
For most states, the mileage between interchanges may be determined by subtracting one number from the other.

Fayetteville / Springdale / Rogers

Jonesboro

Hot Springs / Hot Springs National Park

Pine Bluff

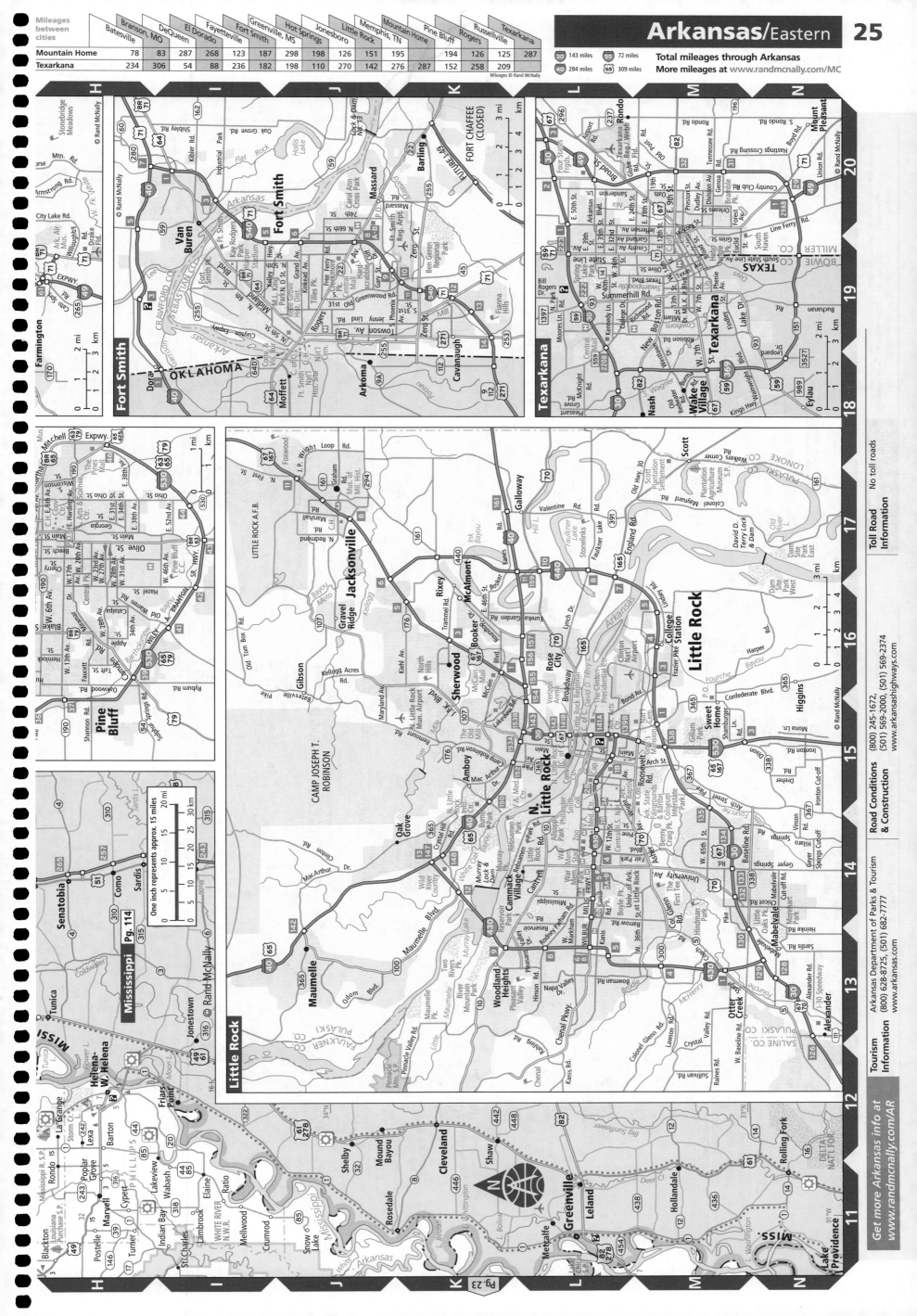

	Batesville	Branson, MO	DeQueen	El Dorado	Fayetteville	Fort Smith	Greenville, MS	Hot Springs	Jonesboro	Little Rock	Memphis, TN	Mountain Home	Pine Bluff	Rogers	Russellville	Texarkana
Mountain Home	78	83	287	268	123	187	298	198	126	151	195		194	126	125	287
Texarkana	234	306	54	88	236	182	198	110	270	152	276	287	152	258	209	

Mileages © Rand McNally

Total mileages through Arkansas

30	143 miles	55	72 miles
40	284 miles	65	309 miles

More mileages at www.randmcnally.com/MC

Toll Road Information No toll roads

Road Conditions & Construction (800) 245-1672, (501) 569-2000, (501) 569-2374 www.arkansashighways.com

Tourism Information Arkansas Department of Parks & Tourism (800) 628-8725, (501) 682-7777 www.arkansas.com

Get more Arkansas info at www.randmcnally.com/AR

Mileages between cities	Bishop	Crescent City	Los Angeles	Oroville	Redding	Sacramento	San Francisco	San Jose	Santa Rosa	S. Lake Tahoe	Stockton	Susanville	Ukiah	Vallejo	Yosemite N.P.	Yreka
Alturas	371	280	648	225	144	302	357	385	365	228	349	103	330	329	392	176
Bishop		614	265	326	400	269	295	290	364	176	224	286	418	328	138	454

Mileages © Rand McNally

California state facts

Nickname: The Golden State
Capital: Sacramento, NK-7

Population: 37,253,956 (rank: 3rd)
Largest city: Los Angeles, 3,792,621, SJ-11

Land area: 155,959 sq. mi. (rank: 1st)
Highest point: Mt. Whitney, 14,494 ft., SC-11

Determining distances along roads

Highway distances (segments of one mile or less not shown):
Cumulative miles (red): the distance between red arrows
Intermediate miles (black): the distance between intersections & places

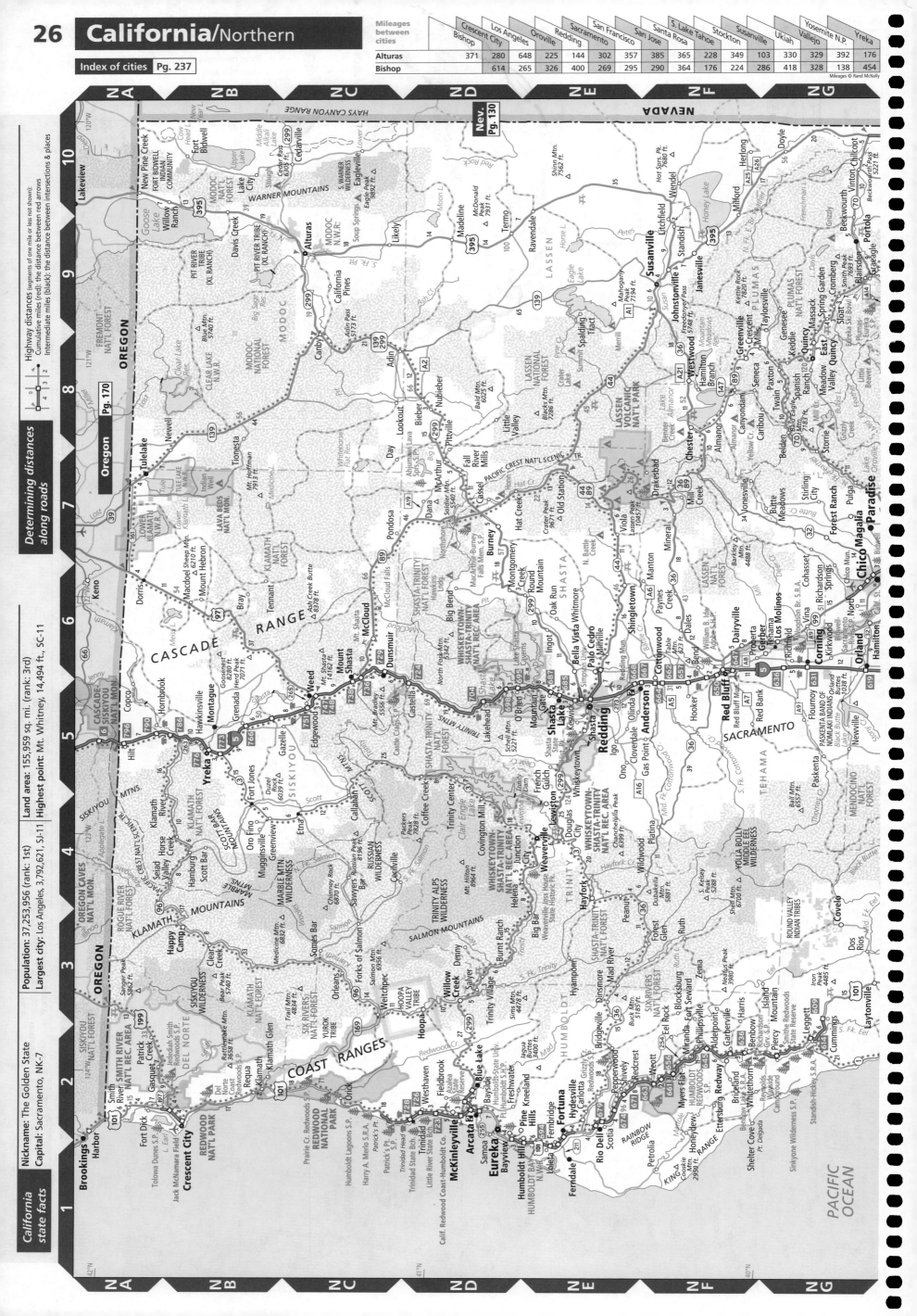

Mileages between cities	Bishop	Crescent City	Los Angeles	Oroville	Redding	Sacramento	San Francisco	San Jose	Santa Rosa	S. Lake Tahoe	Stockton	Susanville	Ukiah	Vallejo	Yosemite N.P.	Yreka
Eureka	546	81	644	222	146	289	272	315	217	392	325	259	158	262	454	198
Redding	400	208	544	94		161	216	244	198	264	209	112	188	187	332	98

continued p. 28

Mileages © Rand McNally

Total mileages through California

5: 797 miles   101: 791 miles   80: 199 miles

More mileages at www.randmcnally.com/MC

Yosemite National Park

One inch represents approximately 18 miles

Explore California at www.randmcnally.com/CA

Tourism Information — California Tourism (877) 225-4367, (916) 444-4429; www.visitcalifornia.com

Road Conditions & Construction — (800) 427-7623; www.dot.ca.gov; Sacramento region: 511; www.sacregion511.org; San Francisco Bay area: 511; www.511.org

Toll Bridge Information — Golden Gate Bridge (San Francisco Bay area) (FasTrak): (415) 921-5858; www.goldengatebridge.org; Bay Area Toll Authority (all other San Francisco Bay area bridges) (FasTrak): (510) 817-5700; bata.mtc.ca.gov

Mileages between cities	Bishop	Crescent City	Los Angeles	Oroville	Redding	Sacramento	San Francisco	San Jose	Santa Rosa	S. Lake Tahoe	Stockton	Susanville	Ukiah	Vallejo	Yosemite N.P.	Yreka
Sacramento	269	372	383	68	161		87	115	95	100	47	217	145	58	160	257
San Francisco	295	355	380	150	216	87		45	55	187	82	303	115	30	189	312

Mileages by Rand McNally

San Francisco Bay Area:
San Francisco / Oakland / San Jose

Nev. Pg. 130

Mileages between cities	Bishop	Crescent City	Los Angeles	Oroville	Redding	Sacramento	San Francisco	San Jose	Santa Rosa	S. Lake Tahoe	Stockton	Susanville	Ukiah	Vallejo	Yosemite N.P.	Yreka
San Jose	290	396	340	178	244	115	45		96	215	74	330	156	64	182	340
S. Lake Tahoe	176	472	445	157	264	100	187	215	195		147	143	248	159	189	311

Mileages © Rand McNally

Total mileages through California
5 797 miles 101 791 miles
80 199 miles
More mileages at www.randmcnally.com/MC

Tourism Information
California Tourism (877) 225-4367, (916) 444-4429; www.visitcalifornia.com
Explore California at www.randmcnally.com/CA

Road Conditions & Construction
(800) 427-7623; www.dot.ca.gov; Sacramento region: 511; www.sacregion511.org San Francisco Bay area: 511; www.511.org

Toll Road Information
Golden Gate Bridge (San Francisco Bay area) (FasTrak): (415) 921-5858; www.goldengatebridge.org Bay Area Toll Authority (all other San Francisco Bay area bridges) (FasTrak): (510) 817-5700; bata.mtc.ca.gov

City sights to see

- AT&T Park, San Francisco, E-10
- California State Capitol, Sacramento, I-6
- California State Railroad Museum, Sacramento, H-6
- Chinatown, San Francisco, C-8
- Coit Memorial Tower, San Francisco, B-8
- Crocker Art Museum, Sacramento, I-5
- Fisherman's Wharf, San Francisco, A-7

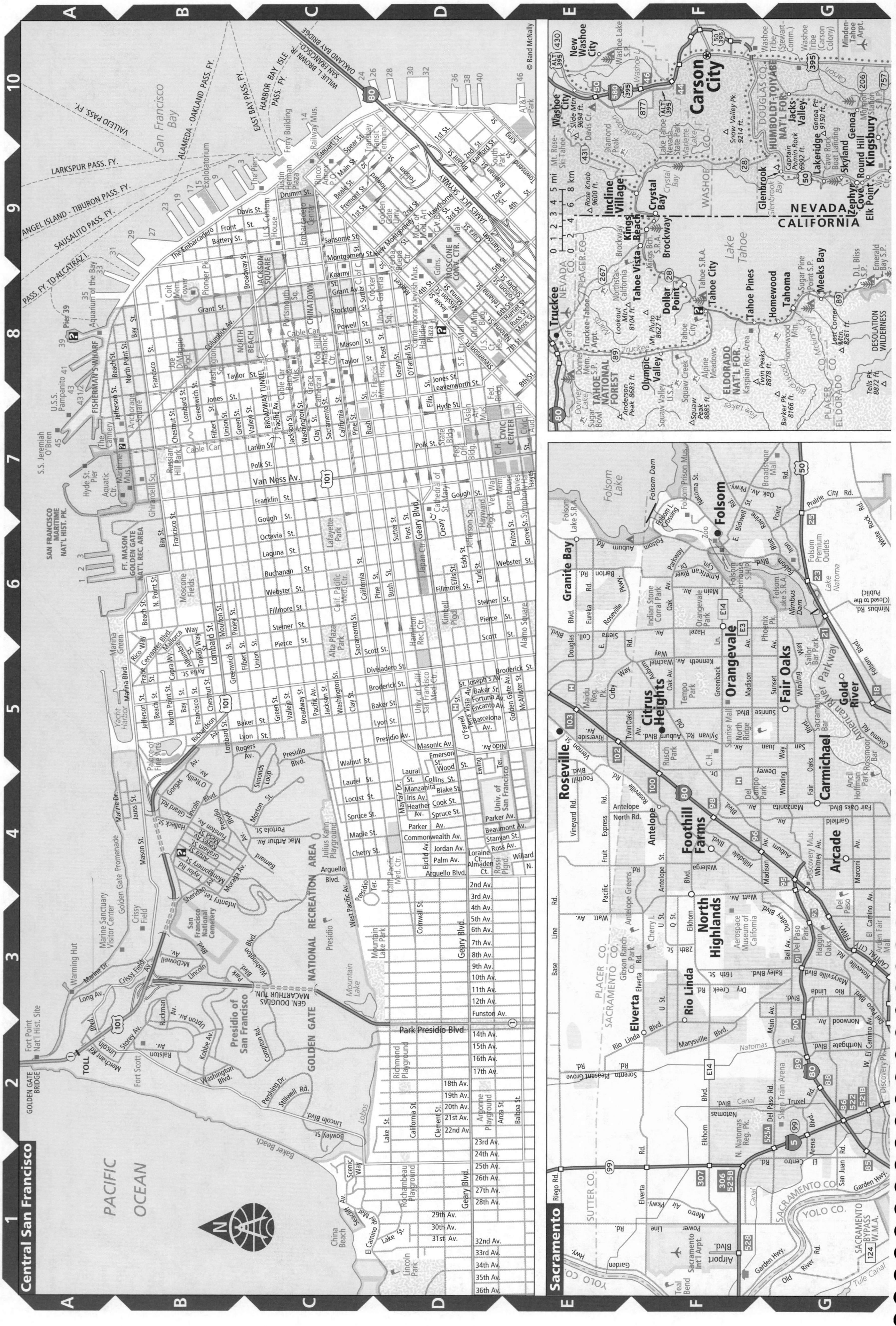

© Rand McNally

Central San Francisco

Sacramento

NEVADA
CALIFORNIA

- Ghirardelli Square, San Francisco, B-7
- Golden Gate Bridge, San Francisco, A-2
- Monterey Bay Aquarium, Monterey, M-1
- National Steinbeck Center, Salinas, K-5
- Pier 39, San Francisco, A-8
- San Francisco Cable Car Museum, San Francisco, C-8
- Squaw Valley U.S.A., Olympic Valley, F-8

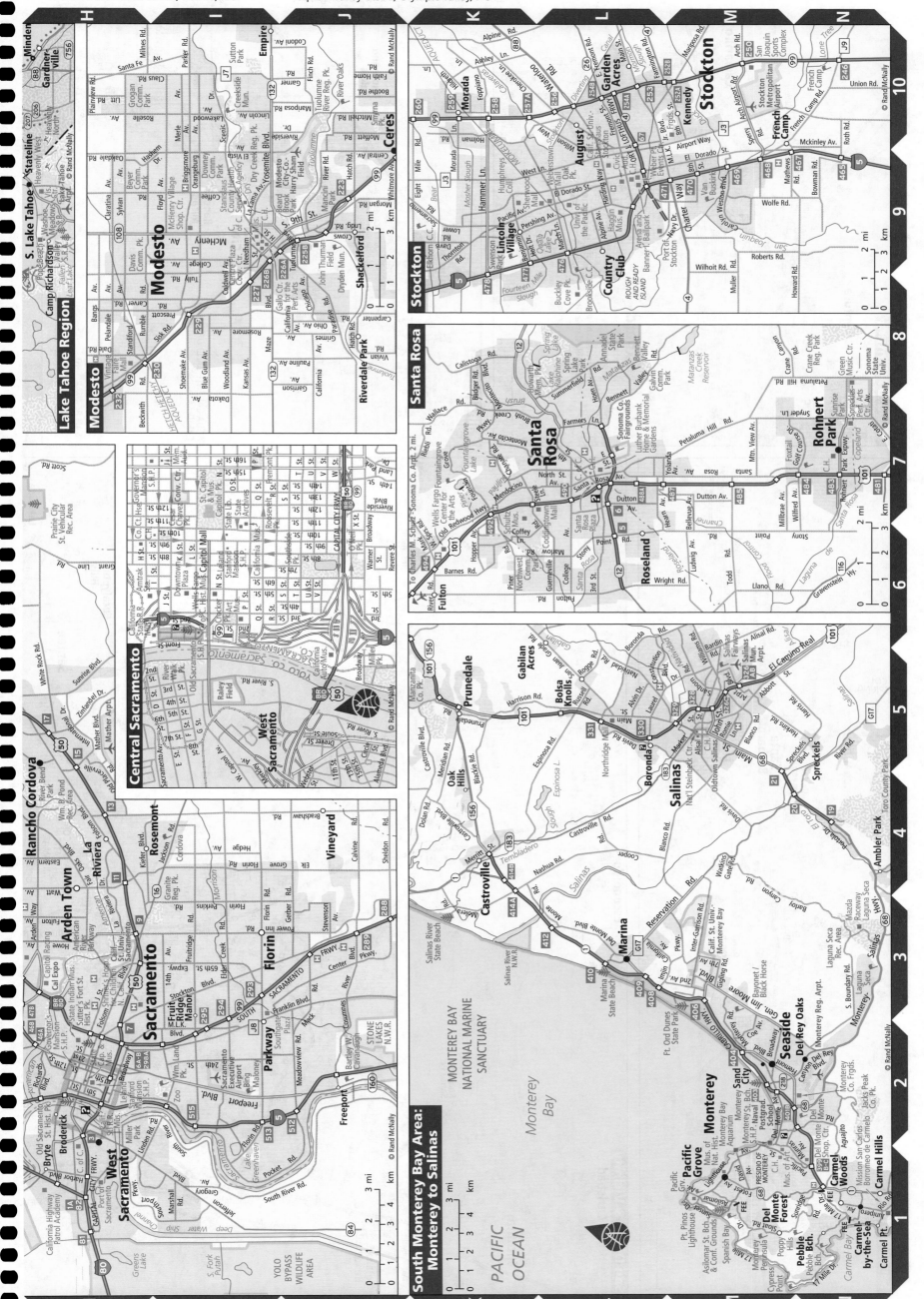

City sights to see
• Balboa Park, San Diego, K-10
• Birch Aquarium at Scripps Institute, San Diego, G-1
• Cabrillo National Monument, San Diego, K-1
• Channel Islands National Park Visitor Center & Headquarters, Ventura, B-8
• Gaslamp Quarter Historic District, San Diego, M-9

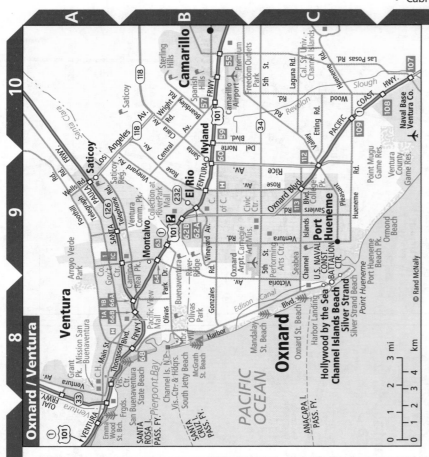

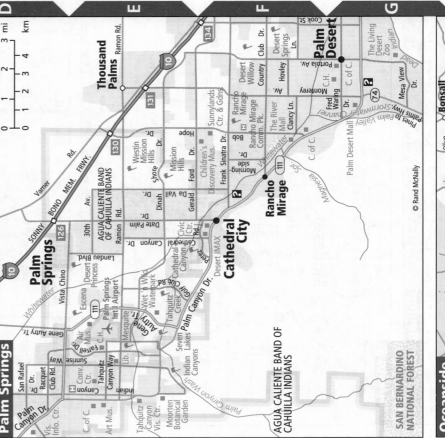

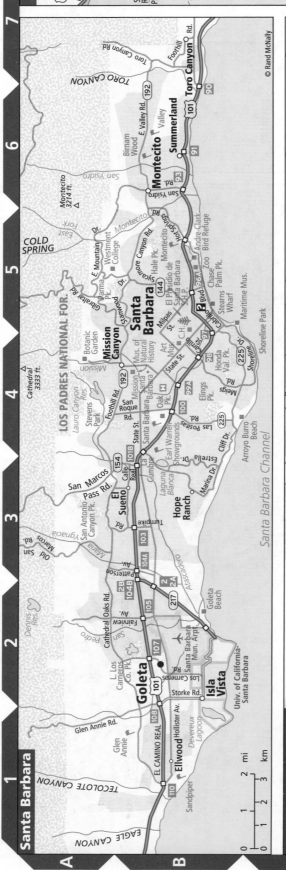

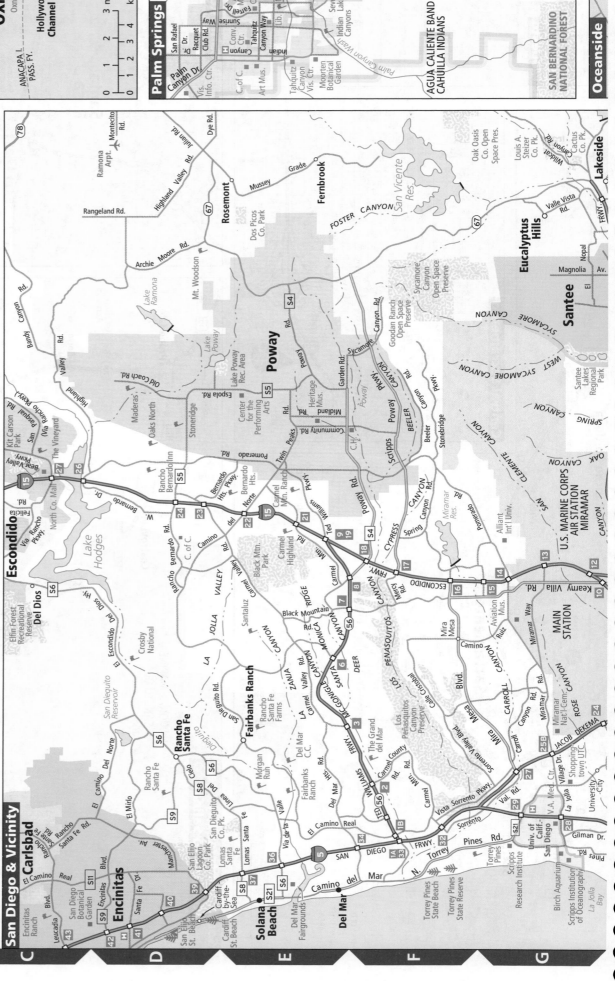

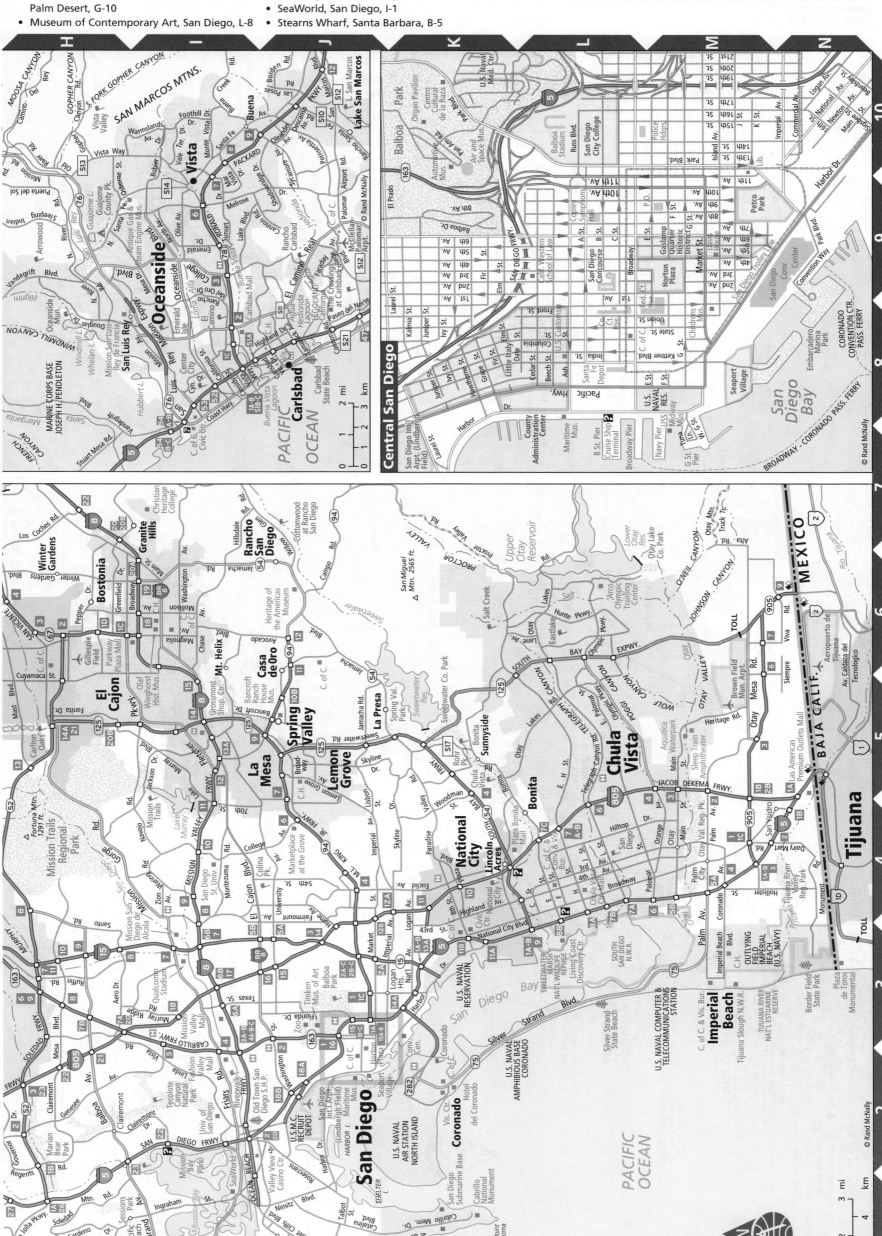

Index of cities Pg. 237

Pg. 36
Pg. 27

Mileages between cities	Bakersfield	Barstow	El Centro	Fresno	Las Vegas, NV	Los Angeles	Monterey	Needles	Palm Springs	Riverside	San Bernardino	San Diego	San Francisco	San Luis Obispo	Santa Barbara	Sequoia N.P.
Bakersfield		129	322	109	286	112	222	272	216	166	166	232	284	130	147	122
Fresno	109	239	429		395	218	150	381	323	271	273	339	183	130	254	77

Mileages © Rand McNally

California state facts

Nickname: The Golden State
Capital: Sacramento, NK-7
Population: 37,253,956 (rank: 1st)
Land area: 155,959 sq. mi. (rank: 3rd)
Largest city: Los Angeles, 3,792,621, SJ-11
Highest point: Mt. Whitney, 14,494 ft., SC-11

Determining distances along roads

Highway distances (segments of one mile or less not shown):
Cumulative miles (red): the distance between red arrows
Intermediate miles (black): the distance between intersections & places

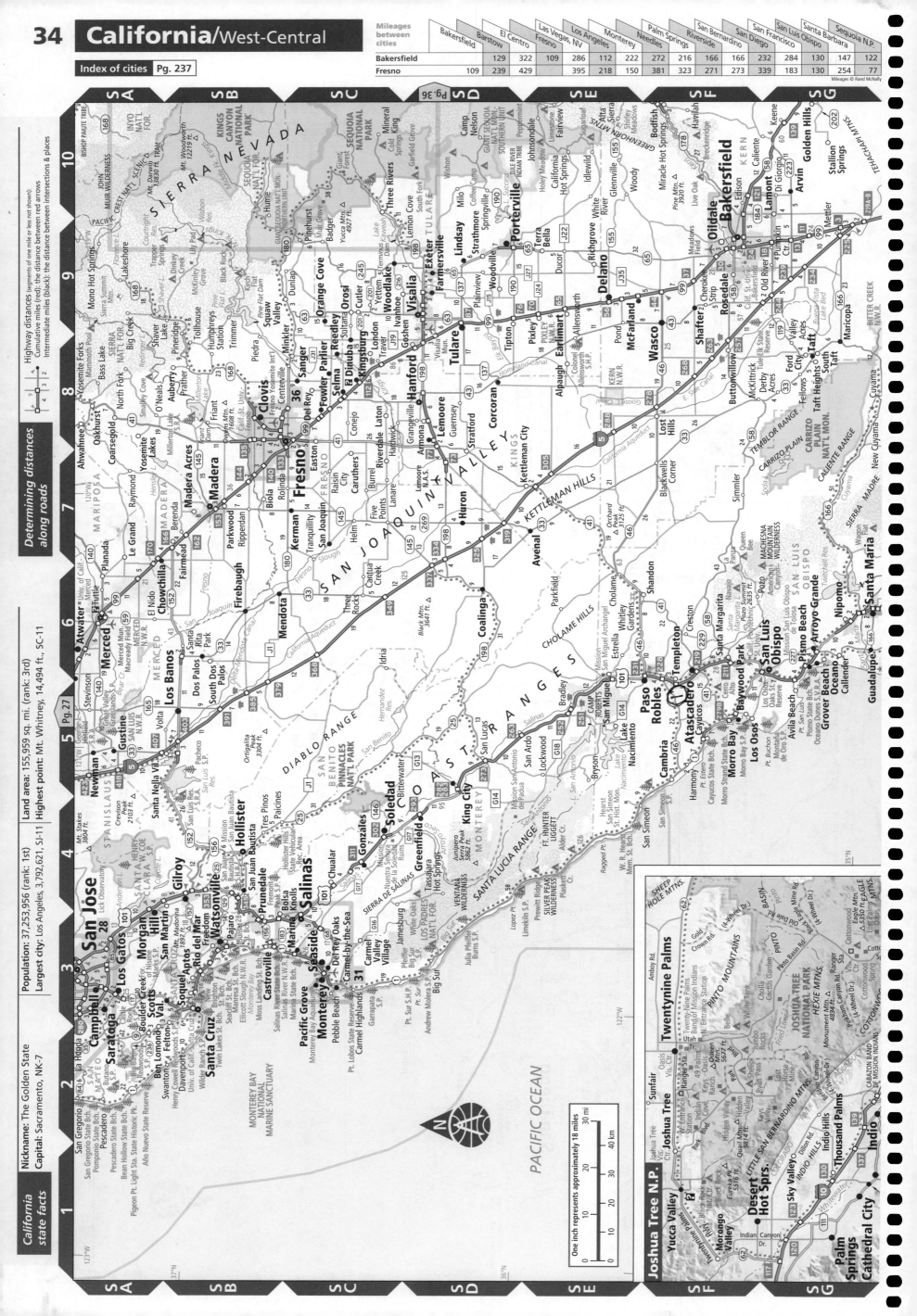

Joshua Tree N.P.

One inch represents approximately 18 miles

0 10 20 30 mi
0 20 40 km

One inch represents approximately 18 miles
30 mi
40 km

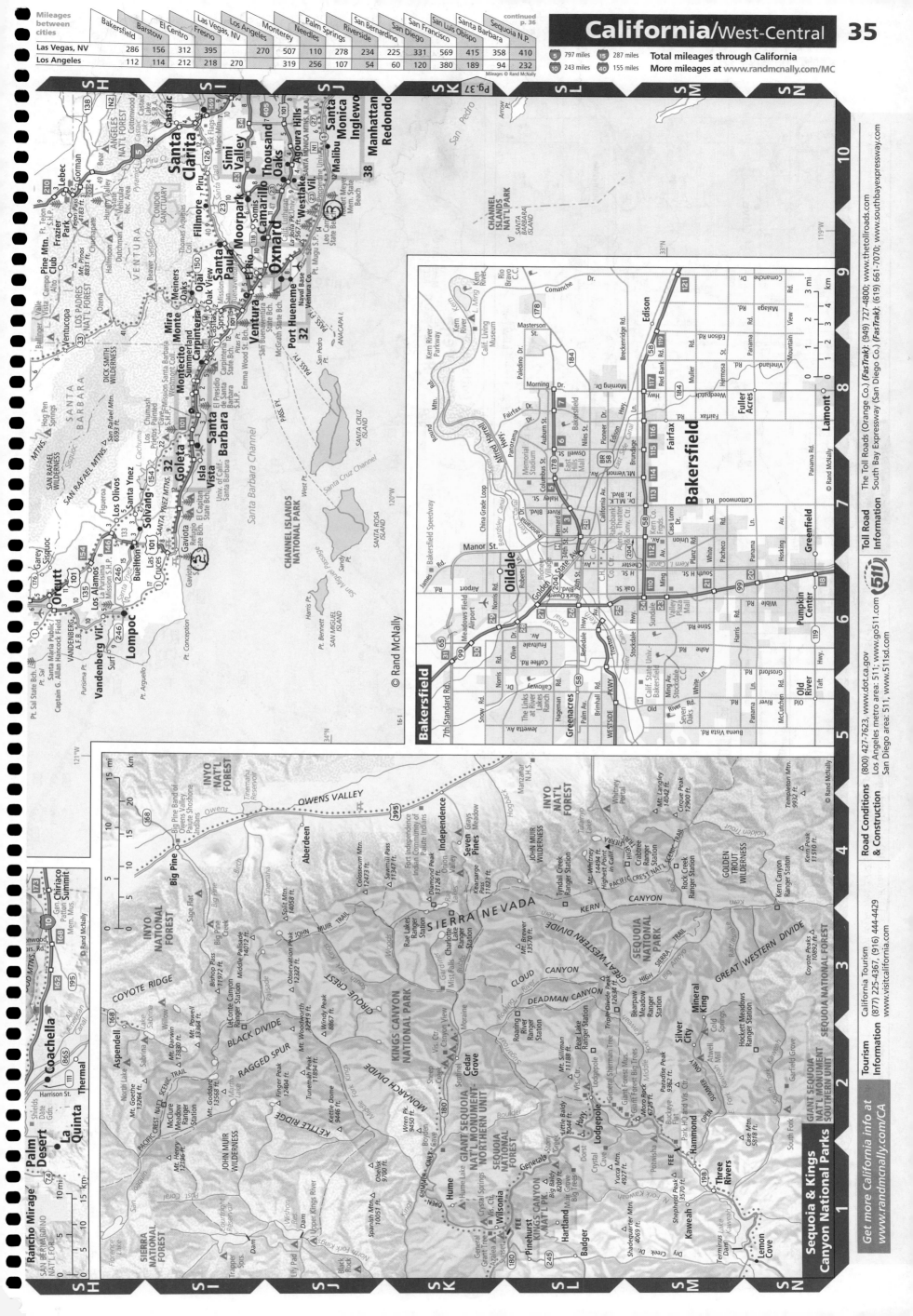

Mileages between cities

	Bakersfield	Barstow	El Centro	Fresno	Las Vegas, NV	Los Angeles	Monterey	Needles	Palm Springs	Riverside	San Bernardino	San Diego	San Francisco	San Luis Obispo	Santa Barbara	Sequoia N.P.
Las Vegas, NV	286	156	312	395		270	507	110	278	234	225	331	569	415	358	410
Los Angeles	112	114	212	218	270		319	256	107	54	60	120	380	189	94	232

Mileages © Rand McNally

continued p. 36

Total mileages through California
5 = 797 miles 15 = 287 miles
10 = 243 miles 40 = 155 miles
More mileages at www.randmcnally.com/MC

Index of cities Pg. 237

Mileages between cities	Bakersfield	Barstow	El Centro	Las Vegas, NV	Los Angeles	Monterey	Needles	Palm Springs	Riverside	San Bernardino	San Diego	San Francisco	San Luis Obispo	Santa Barbara	Sequoia N.P.
Monterey	222	350	530	150	507	319	494	424	372	373	439	112	142	237	226
Palm Springs	216	123	108	323	278	107	424	188	52	54	139	486	296	201	338

Mileages by Rand McNally

California state facts

Nickname: The Golden State
Capital: Sacramento, NK-7
Population: 37,253,956 (rank: 1st)
Largest city: Los Angeles, 3,792,621, SJ-11
Land area: 155,959 sq. mi. (rank: 3rd)
Highest point: Mt. Whitney, 14,494 ft., SC-11

Determining distances along roads

Interchanges and exit numbers
For most states, the mileage between interchanges may be determined by subtracting one number from the other.

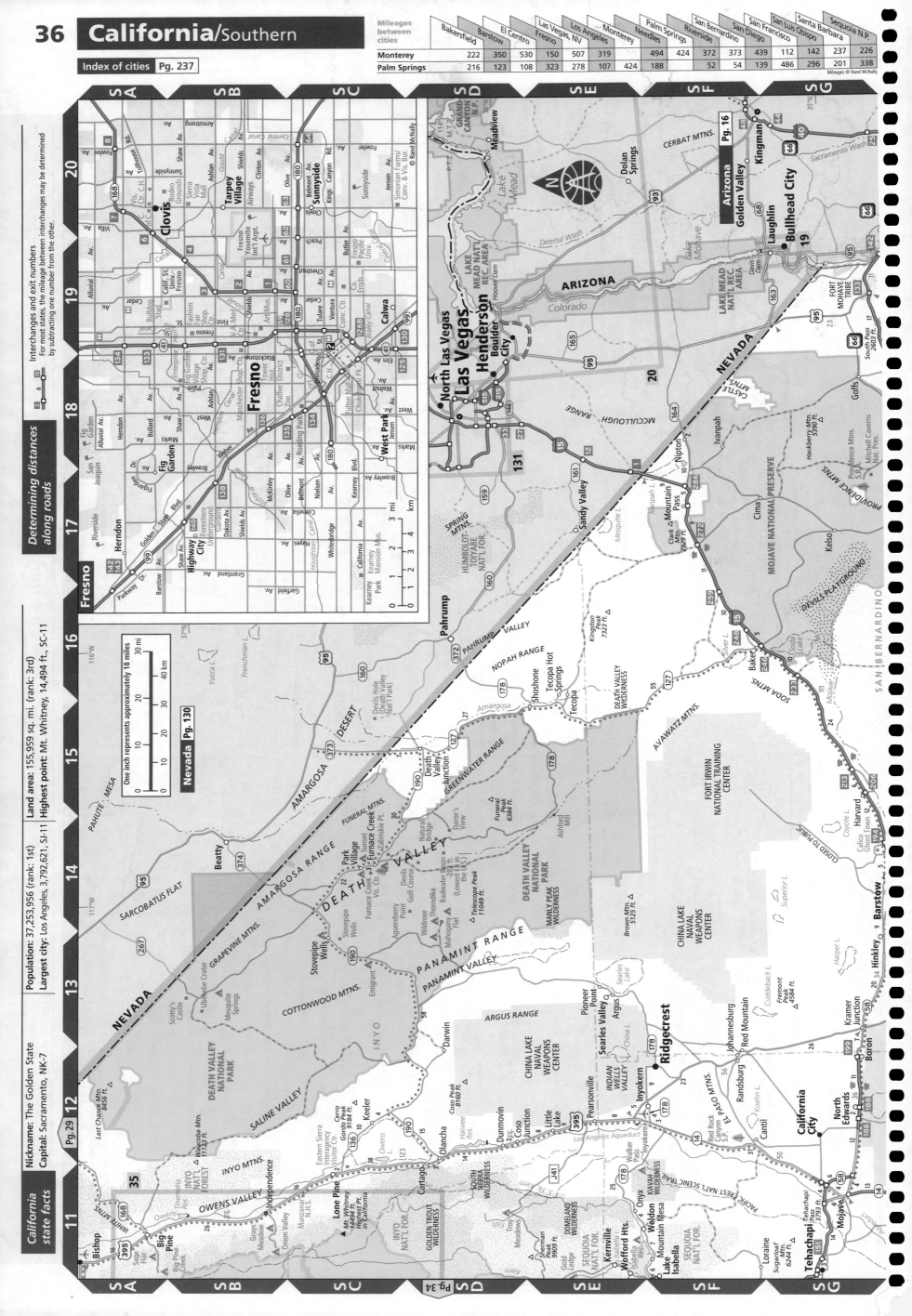

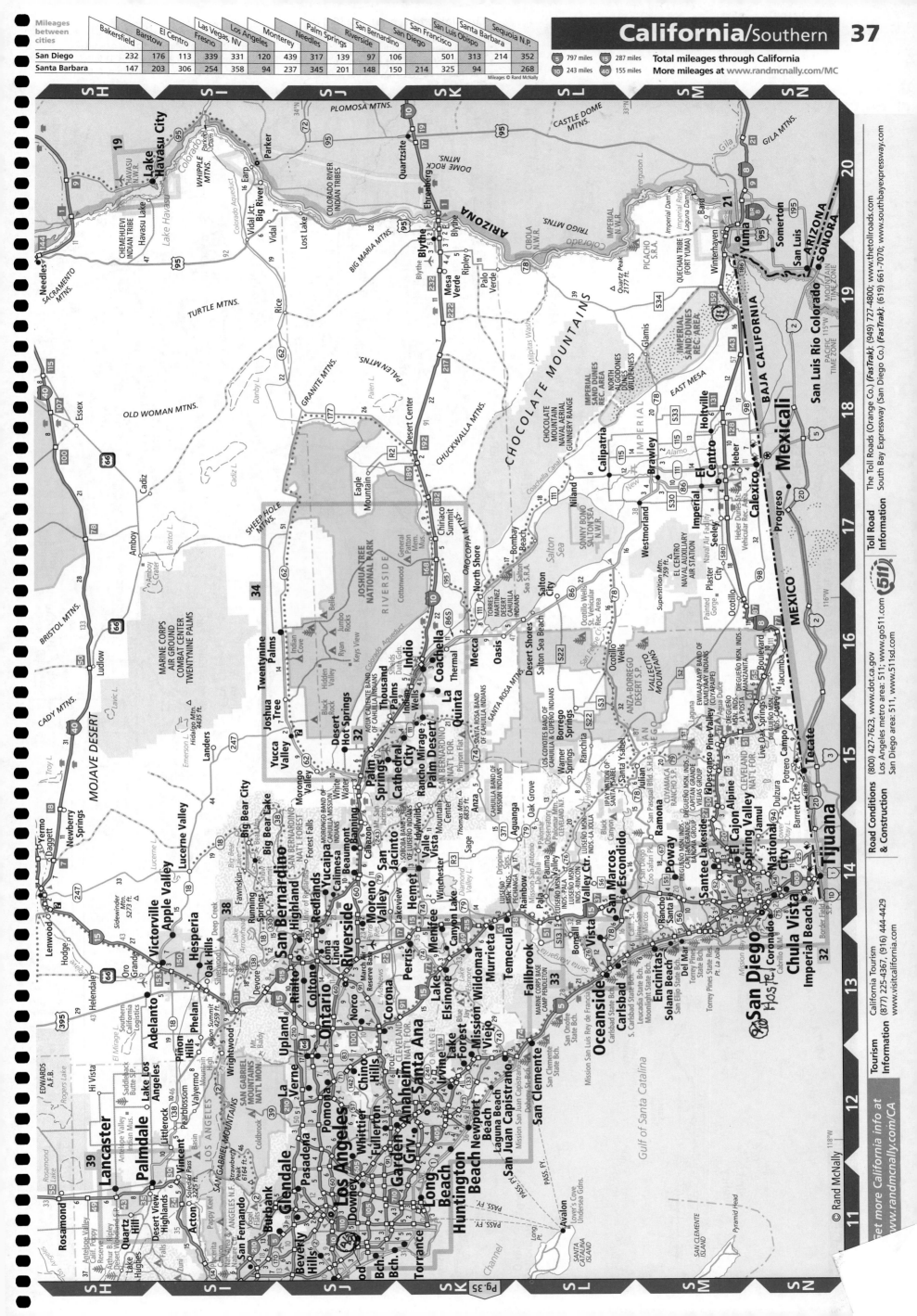

Mileages between cities	Bakersfield	Barstow	El Centro	Fresno	Las Vegas, NV	Los Angeles	Monterey	Needles	Palm Springs	Riverside	San Bernardino	San Diego	San Francisco	San Luis Obispo	Santa Barbara	Sequoia N.P.
San Diego	232	176	113	339	331	120	439	317	139	97	106		501	313	214	352
Santa Barbara	147	203	306	254	358	94	237	345	201	148	150	214	325	94		268

Mileages © Rand McNally

Total mileages through California
More mileages at www.randmcnally.com/MC

5 797 miles   15 287 miles
10 243 miles   40 155 miles

City sights to see (pages 38-41)

- Aquarium of the Pacific, Long Beach, J-8
- Disneyland, Anaheim, I-11
- Dodger Stadium, Los Angeles, E-7
- El Pueblo de Los Angeles, Los Angeles, K-2
- Getty Center, Los Angeles, E-4
- Grand Central Market, Los Angeles, L-2
- Hollywood Bowl, Los Angeles, D-6
- Huntington Library, San Marino, D-9

Los Angeles & Vicinity

Central Los Angeles

- Japanese American National Museum, Los Angeles, K-3
- Knott's Berry Farm, Buena Park, H-10
- Los Angeles Co. Art Mus., Los Angeles, E-6
- Los Angeles Maritime Museum, Los Angeles, J-7
- Los Angeles Zoo and Botanical Gardens, Los Angeles, D-7

list continued p.40

City sights to see (pages 38-41)
- Mission San Juan Capistrano, San Juan Capistrano, M-14
- Mount Wilson Observatory, Mt. Wilson, C-9
- Old Pasadena, Pasadena, D-8
- Oldest Winery in Calif., Rancho Cucamonga, D-15
- The Queen Mary, Long Beach, J-8
- Richard M. Nixon Library & Birthplace, Yorba Linda, H-12

SAN BERNARDINO NATIONAL FOREST

SAN GABRIEL MOUNTAINS

SAN GABRIEL MOUNTAINS NAT'L MONUMENT

SAN BERNARDINO MTNS.

PACIFIC CREST NATIONAL SCENIC TRAIL

LOS ANGELES CO. / SAN BERNARDINO CO.

SAN BERNARDINO CO. / RIVERSIDE CO.

LOS ANGELES CO. / ORANGE CO.

Cedar Glen, Lake Arrowhead, Skyforest, Blue Jay, Twin Peaks, Crestline, Cedarpines Park, Devore, Hesperia, Cajon Junction, Scotland, Lytle Creek, Applewhite, Mount Baldy, Crystal Lake

San Bernardino, Highland, Redlands, Loma Linda, Grand Terrace, Colton, Muscoy, Verdemont, Rialto, Bloomington, Fontana, Highgrove, Riverside, Moreno Valley

Jurupa Valley, Norco, Eastvale, Rancho Cucamonga, Ontario, Upland, Montclair, San Antonio Heights, Chino, Chino Hills

Claremont, La Verne, San Dimas, Glendora, Charter Oak, Covina, West Covina, Walnut, Pomona, Diamond Bar, Brea

Azusa, Duarte, Bradbury, Baldwin Park, Irwindale, Citrus, Valinda, La Puente, S. San Jose Hills, Rowland Heights, La Habra Heights, La Habra

DAY CANYON, WATERMAN CANYON, RECHE CANYON, CUCAMONGA WILDERNESS, BIG DALTON CANYON, LITTLE DALTON CANYON, COLD WATER CANYON

MARCH AIR RESERVE BASE

Pg. 38

- Rose Bowl, Pasadena, D-8
- Santa Monica Pier, Santa Monica, F-4
- Universal City, Los Angeles, D-6
- Venice Boardwalk, Los Angeles, F-4
- Walt Disney Concert Hall, Los Angeles, K-2
- Warner Bros. Studio, Burbank, D-6
- Will Rogers State Historic Park, Pacific Palisades, E-4

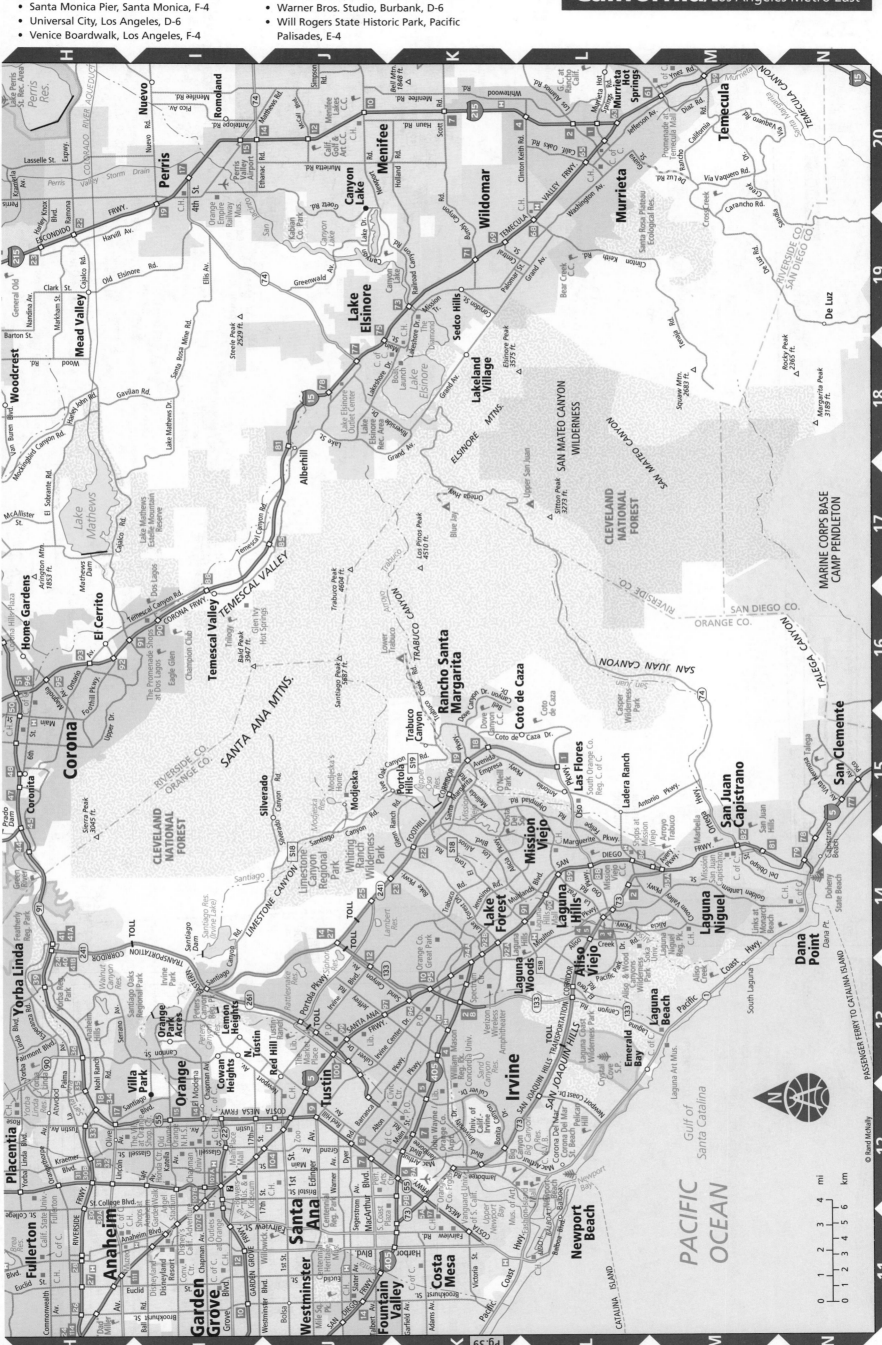

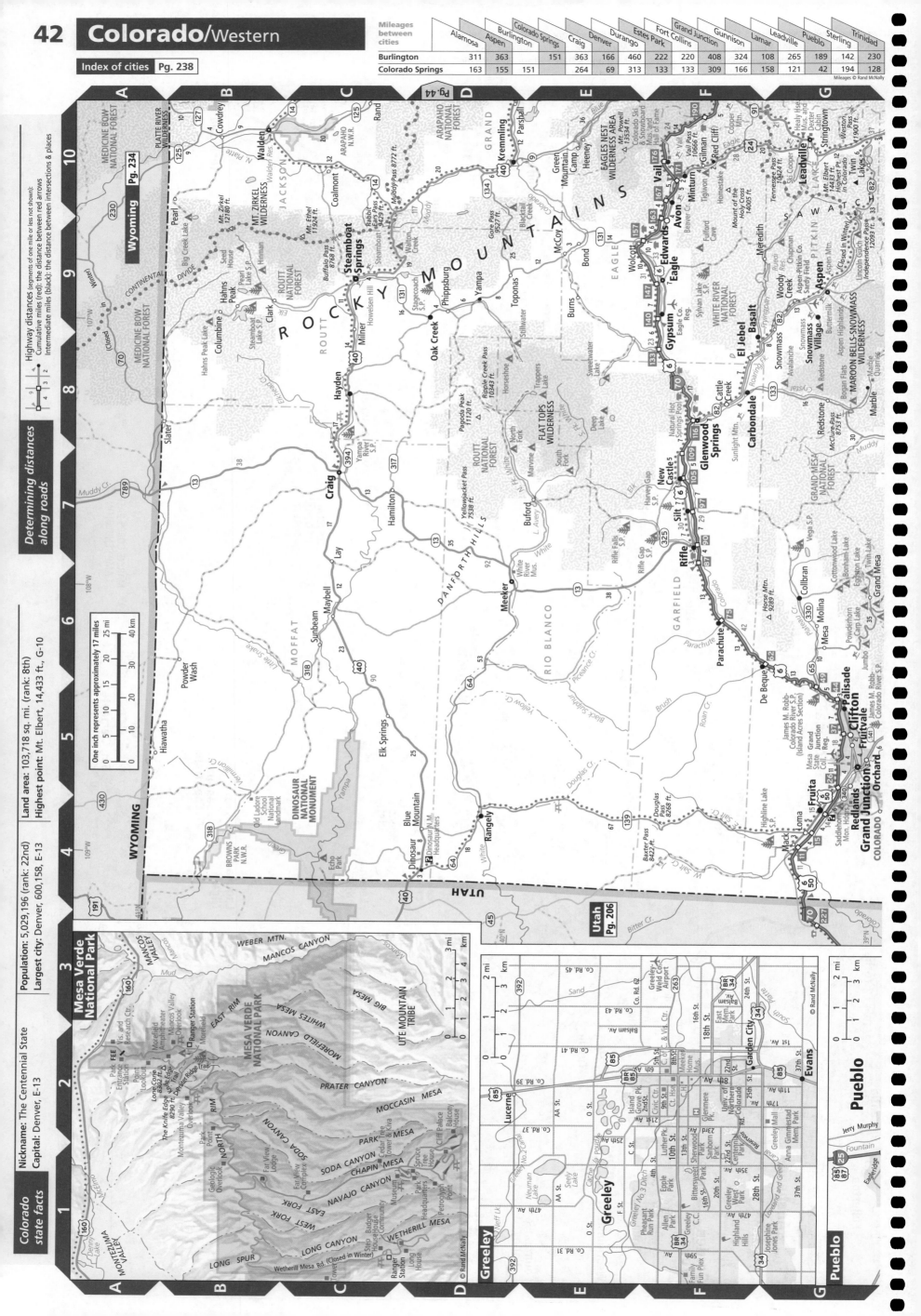

Mileages between cities	Alamosa	Aspen	Burlington	Colorado Springs	Craig	Denver	Durango	Estes Park	Fort Collins	Grand Junction	Gunnison	Lamar	Leadville	Pueblo	Sterling	Trinidad
Burlington	311	363		151	363	166	460	222	220	408	324	108	265	189	142	230
Colorado Springs	163	155	151		264	69	313	133	133	309	166	158	121	42	158	121

Mileages © Rand McNally

Colorado state facts

Nickname: The Centennial State
Capital: Denver, E-13

Population: 5,029,196 (rank: 22nd)
Largest city: Denver, 600,158, E-13

Land area: 103,718 sq. mi. (rank: 8th)
Highest point: Mt. Elbert, 14,433 ft., G-10

Determining distances along roads

Highway distances (segments of one mile or less not shown):
Cumulative miles (red): the distance between red arrows
Intermediate miles (black): the distance between intersections & places

One inch represents approximately 17 miles

Mesa Verde National Park

Greeley

Pueblo

Mileages between cities	Alamosa	Aspen	Burlington	Colorado Springs	Craig	Denver	Durango	Estes Park	Fort Collins	Grand Junction	Gunnison	Lamar	Leadville	Pueblo	Sterling	Trinidad
Denver	234	197	166	69	197		336	64	63	243	200	208	99	112	125	198
Durango	149	246	460	313	312	336		402	396	168	142	351	253	269	458	258

continued p. 44

Mileages © Rand McNally

Total mileages through Colorado
More mileages at www.randmcnally.com/MC

| 25 | 300 miles | 76 | 185 miles |
| 70 | 451 miles | 50 | 467 miles |

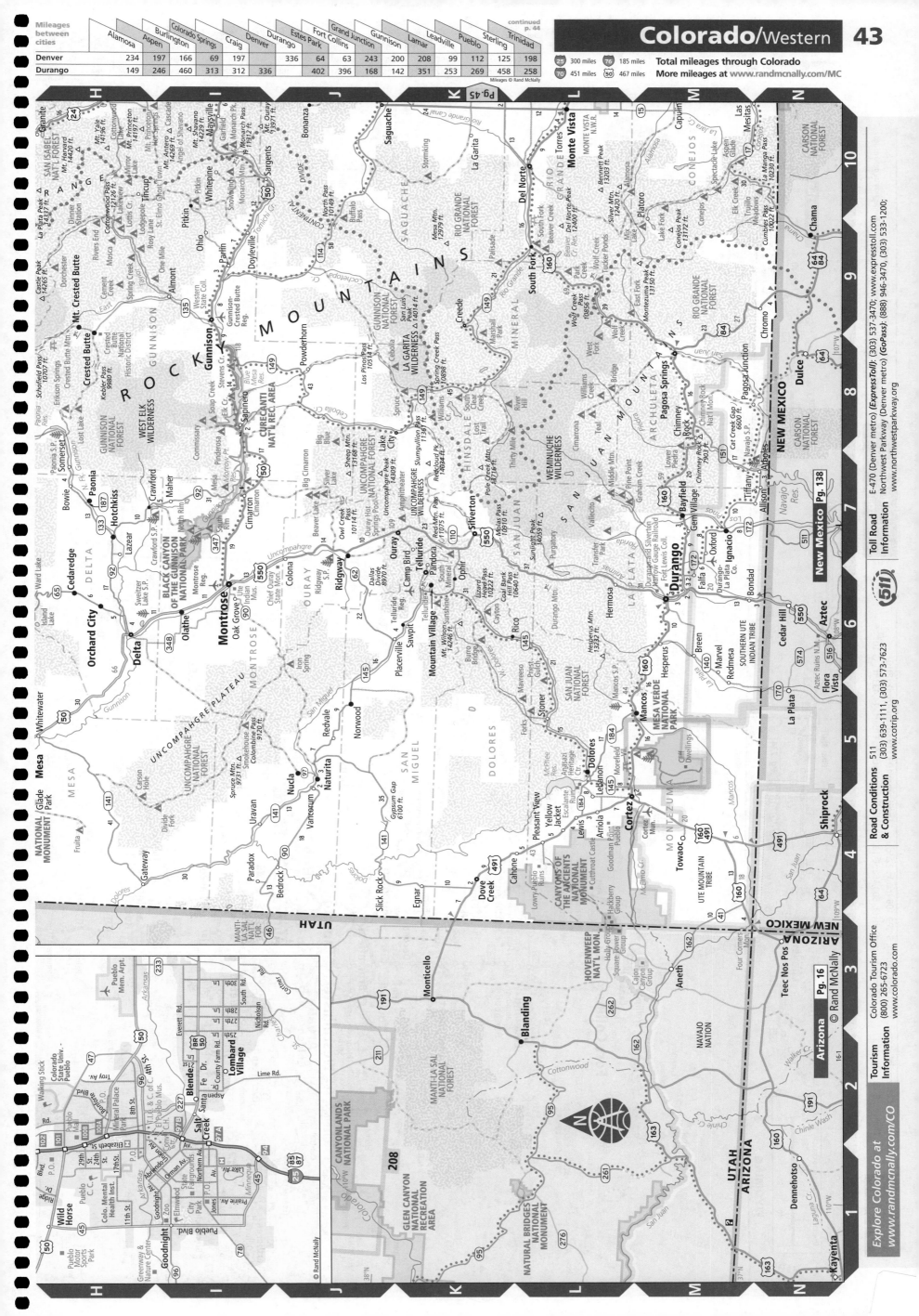

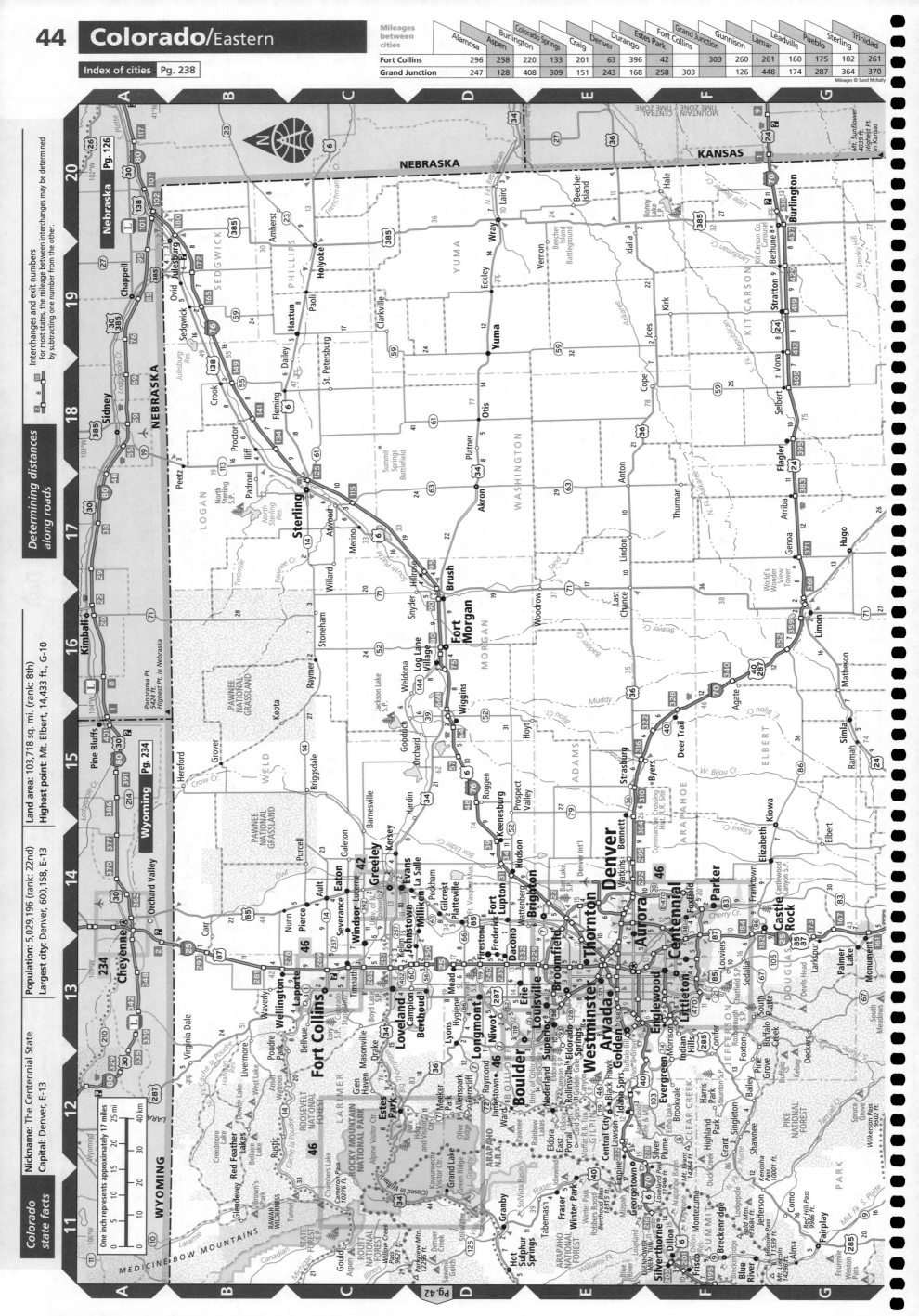

Mileages between cities	Alamosa	Aspen	Burlington	Colorado Springs	Craig	Denver	Durango	Estes Park	Fort Collins	Grand Junction	Gunnison	Lamar	Leadville	Pueblo	Sterling	Trinidad
Fort Collins	296	258	220	133	201	63	396	42		303	260	261	160	175	102	261
Grand Junction	247	128	408	309	151	243	168	258	303		126	448	174	287	364	370

Mileages © Rand McNally

Colorado state facts

Nickname: The Centennial State

Capital: Denver, E-13

Population: 5,029,196 (rank: 22nd)

Largest city: Denver, E-13

Land area: 103,718 sq. mi. (rank: 8th)

Highest point: Mt. Elbert, 14,433 ft., G-10

Determining distances along roads

For most states, the mileage between interchanges may be determined by subtracting one number from the other.

Interchanges and exit numbers

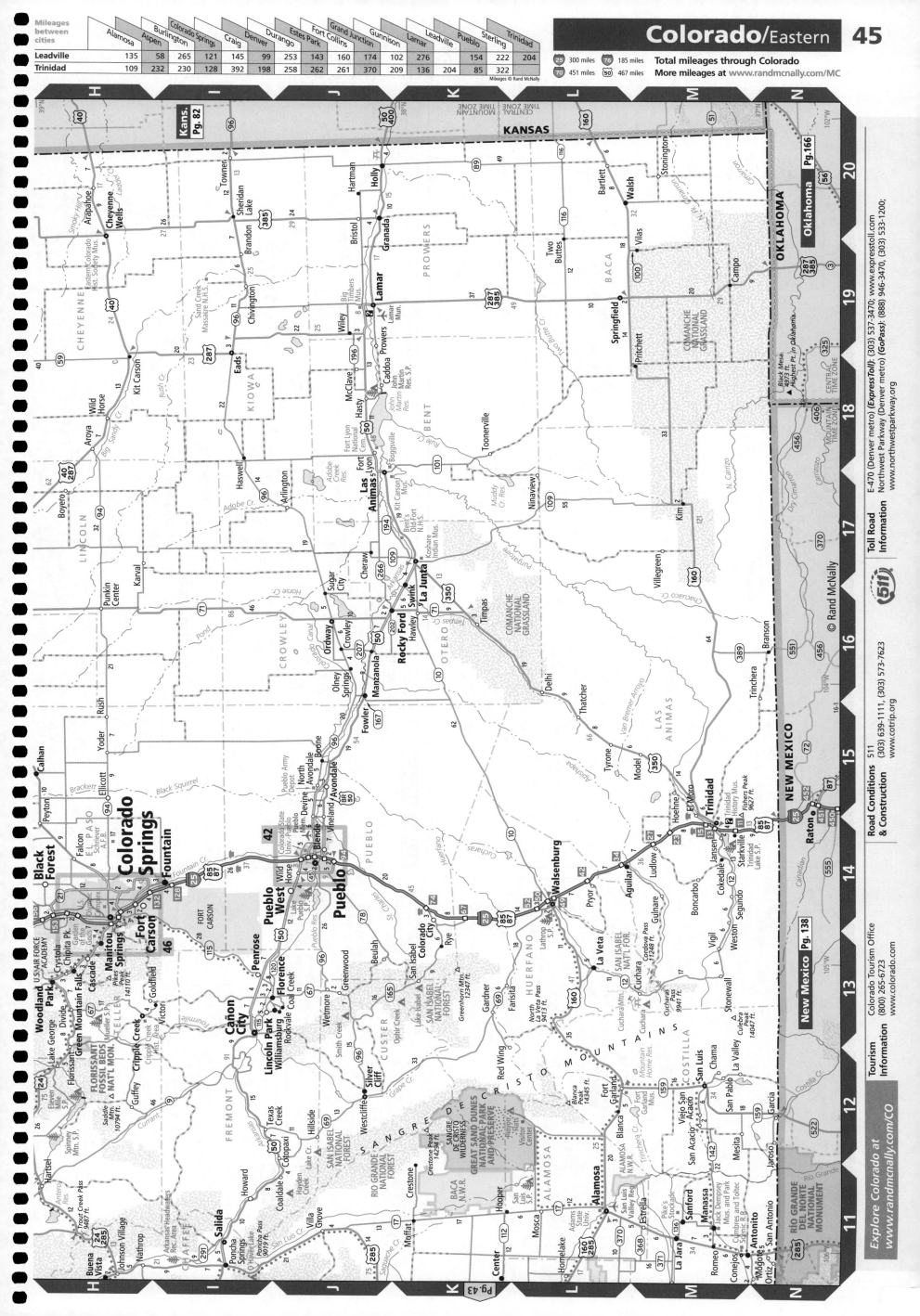

Mileages © Rand McNally

Total mileages through Colorado
More mileages at www.randmcnally.com/MC

| 25 | 300 miles | 76 | 185 miles |
| 70 | 451 miles | 50 | 467 miles |

City sights to see

- Black American West Museum & Heritage Center, Denver, L-3
- Cave of the Winds, Colorado Springs, G-1
- Colorado History Museum, Denver, M-2
- Colorado State Capitol, Denver, M-2
- Denver Art Museum, Denver, M-2
- Denver Museum of Nature & Science, Denver, L-4
- Garden of the Gods, Colorado Springs, G-1

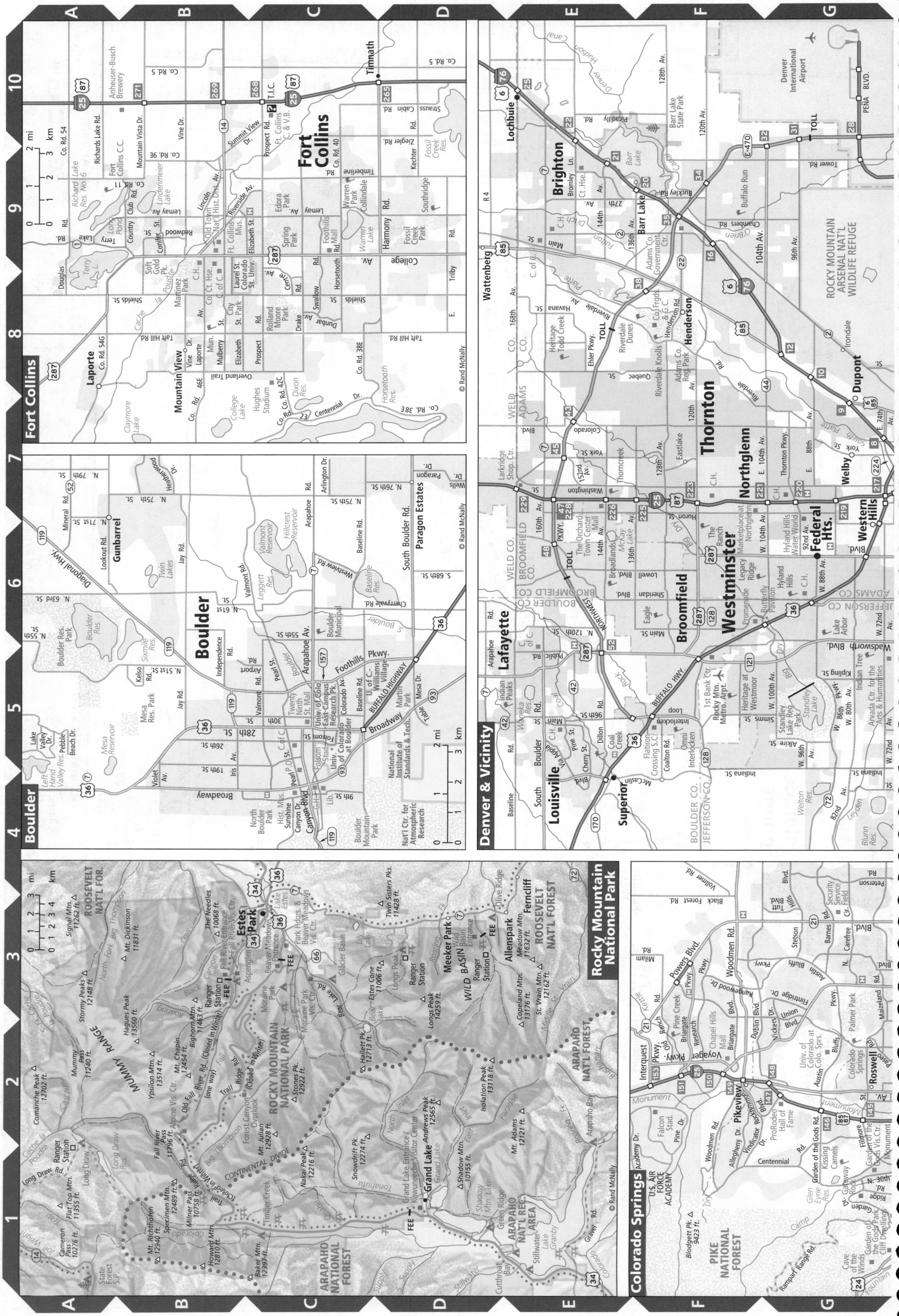

Fort Collins

Boulder

Denver & Vicinity

Rocky Mountain National Park

Colorado Springs

© Rand McNally

- National Center for Atmospheric Research, Boulder, D-4
- Old Town National Historic District, Fort Collins, B-9
- ProRodeo Hall of Fame, Colorado Springs, G-2
- Red Rocks Amphitheatre, Morrison, J-4
- U.S. Airforce Academy, Colorado Springs, F-1
- United States Mint, Denver, M-2
- World Figure Skating Hall of Fame, Colorado Springs, I-2

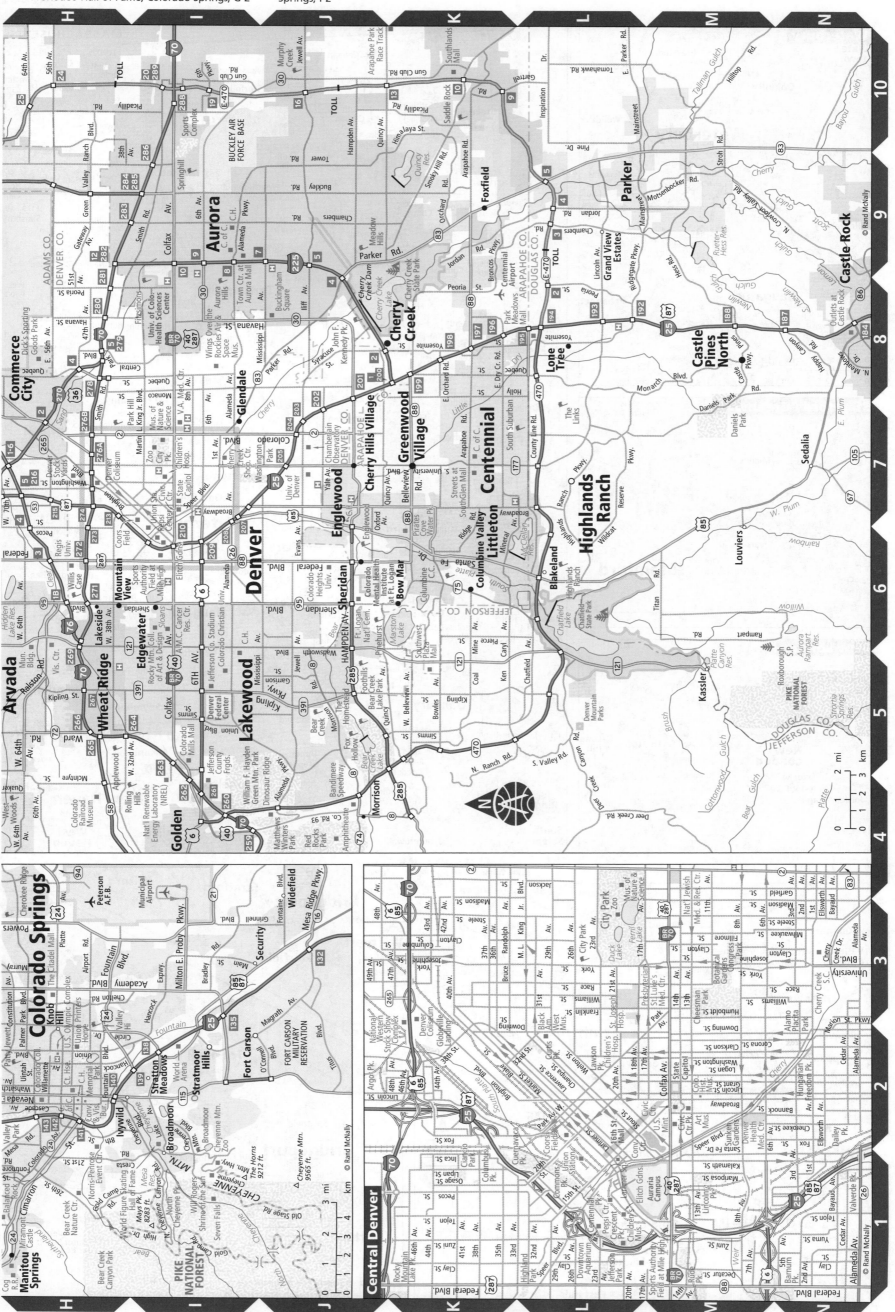

© Rand McNally

Index of cities Pg. 239

Mileages between cities

	Bridgeport	Hartford	New Haven	New London	New York, NY	Putnam	Torrington	Waterbury
Bridgeport		55	18	64	54	107	50	30
Danbury	29	57	35	81	62	104	47	27
Hartford	55		38	45	108	47	26	30
New Haven	18	38		46	72	89	43	22

Mileages © Rand McNally

Connecticut state facts

Nickname: The Constitution State
Capital: Hartford, C-9

Population: 3,574,097 (rank: 29th)
Largest city: Bridgeport, 144,229, H-5

Land area: 4,845 sq. mi. (rank: 48th)
Highest point: Mt. Frissell, 2,380 ft., A-4

Determining distances along roads

Interchanges and exit numbers
For most states, the mileage between interchanges may be determined by subtracting one number from the other.

Mileages between cities

	Bridgeport	Hartford	New Haven	New London	New York, NY	Putnam	Torrington	Waterbury
New London	64	45	46		118	47	79	63
Putnam	107	47	89	47	162		73	78

	Bridgeport	Hartford	New Haven	New London	New York, NY	Putnam	Torrington	Waterbury
Torrington	50	26	43	79	109	73		20
Waterbury	30	30	22	63	89	78	20	

Mileages © Rand McNally

84 98 miles | 95 112 miles | 91 58 miles | 395 55 miles

Total mileages through Connecticut
More mileages at www.randmcnally.com/MC

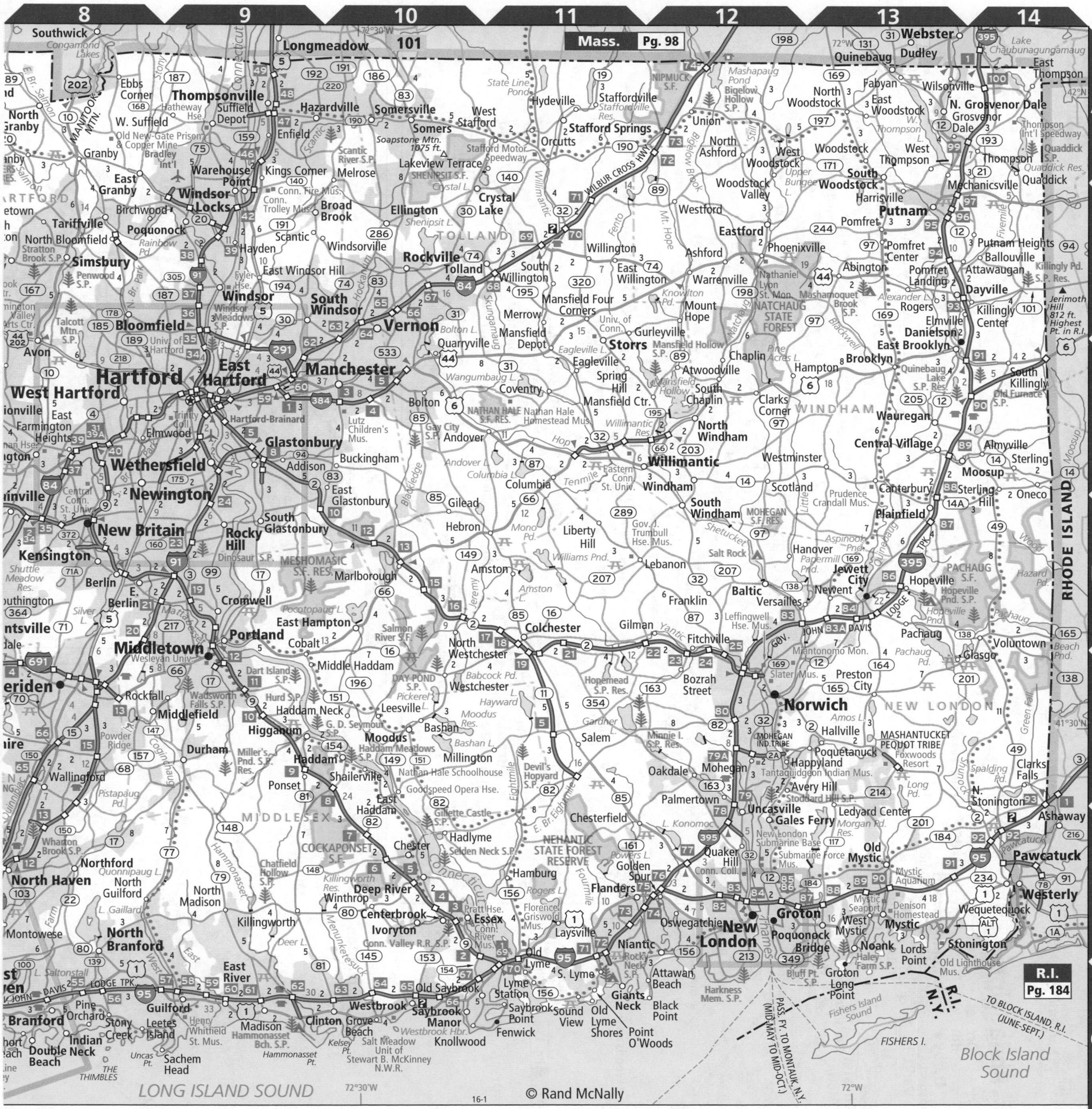

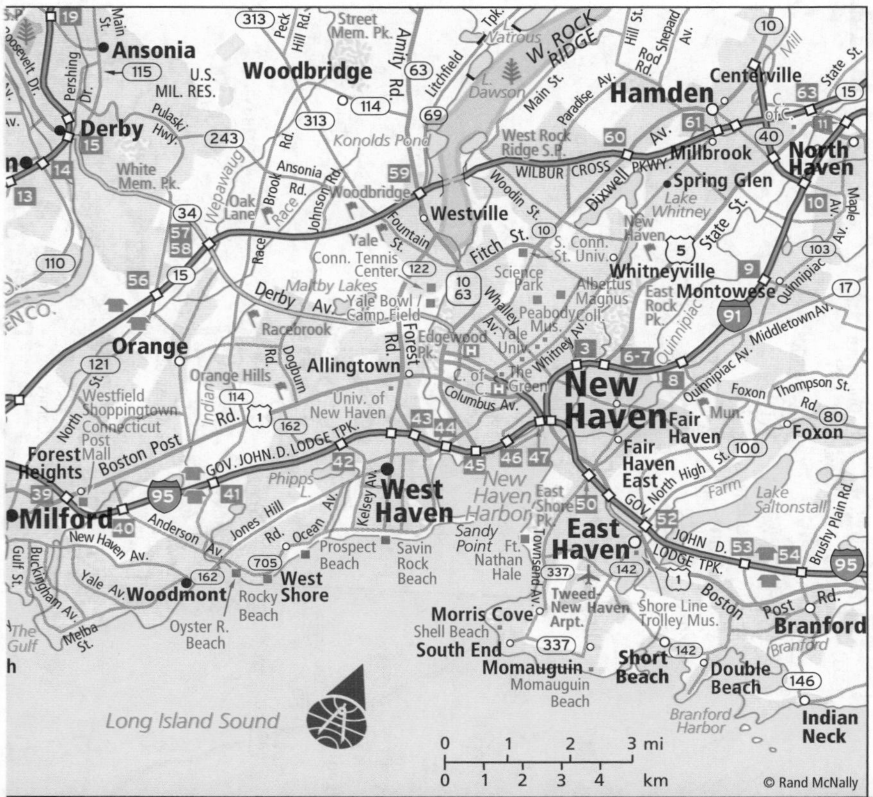

Toll Road Information: No toll roads

Road Conditions & Construction: (860) 594-2000, (860) 594-2650, www.ct.gov/dot

Tourism Information: Connecticut Office of Tourism (860) 256-2800, www.ctvisit.com

Plan a Connecticut trip at www.randmcnally.com/CT

Delaware state facts

Nickname: The First State

Capital: Dover, G-2

Population: 897,934 (rank: 45th)

Largest city: Wilmington, 70,851, C-2

Land area: 1,954 sq. mi. (rank: 49th)

Highest point: Ebright Azimuth, 448 ft., B-3

Determining distances along roads

Highway distances (segments of one mile or less are not shown):
Cumulative miles (red): the distance between red arrows
Intermediate miles (black): the distance between intersections & places

© Rand McNally

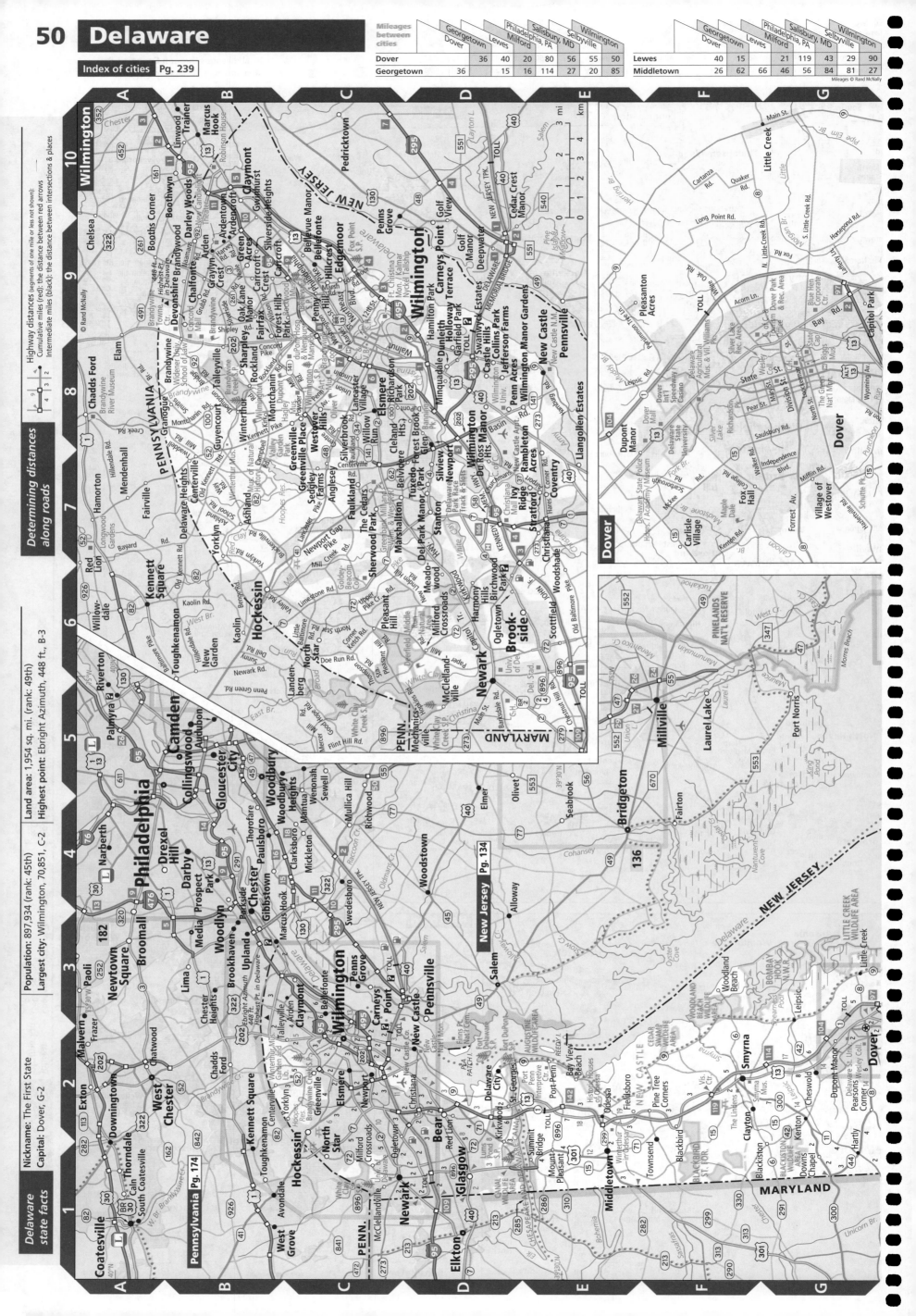

Pennsylvania Pg. 174

New Jersey Pg. 134

Dover

MARYLAND

Mileages between cities	Georgetown	Lewes	Philadelphia, PA	Salisbury, MD	Selbyville	Wilmington
		Dover		Milford		
Millville, NJ	94	124	128	108	45	147	143	53
Newark	46	80	85	64	43	102	99	14

	Georgetown	Lewes	Philadelphia, PA	Salisbury, MD	Selbyville	Wilmington
		Dover		Milford		
Selbyville	55	20	29	36	133	24		104
Wilmington	50	85	90	70	29	107	104	

Mileages © Rand McNally

Total mileages through Delaware
More mileages at www.randmcnally.com/MC

95	23 miles	1	104 miles
13	108 miles		

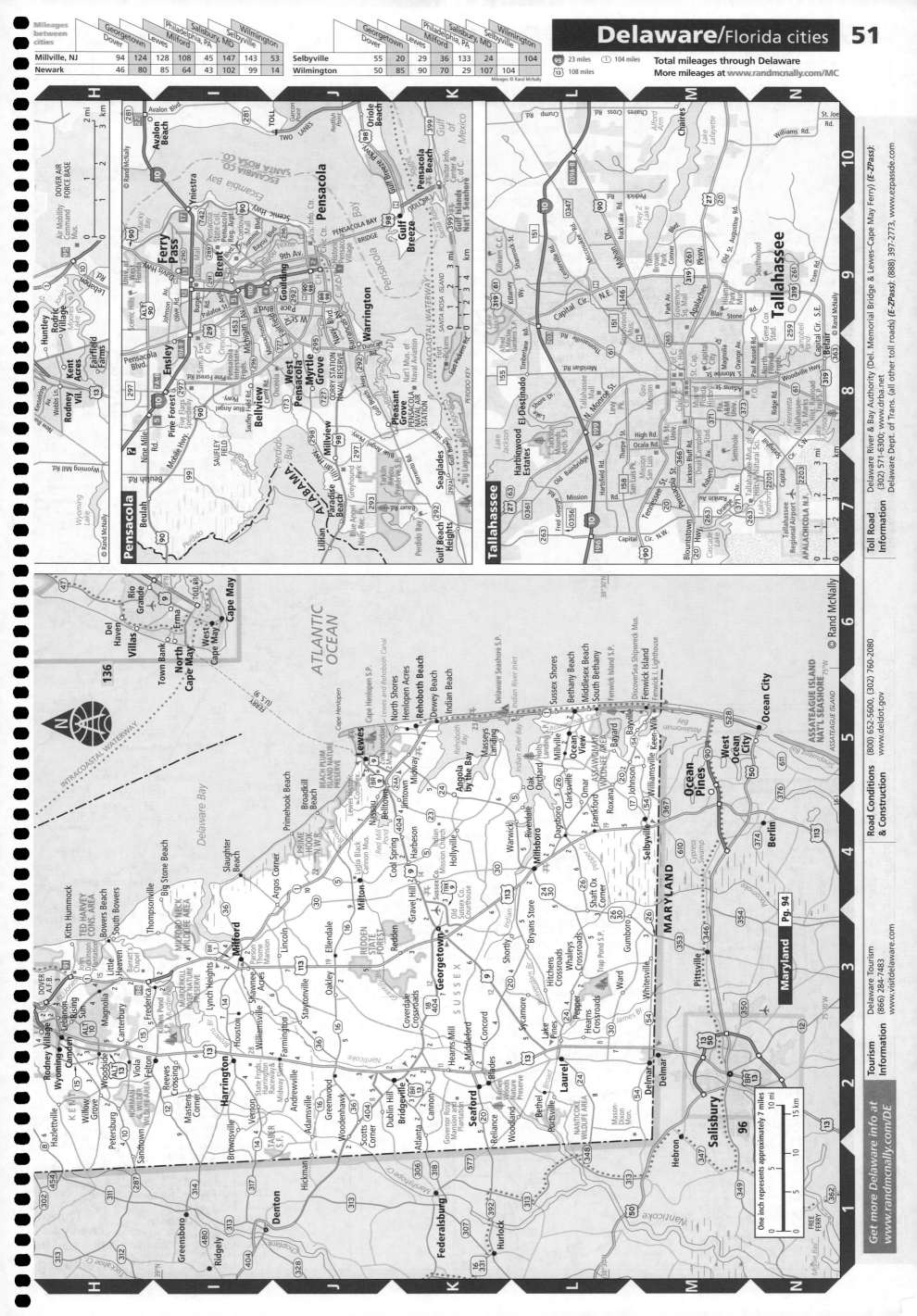

Tourism Information — Delaware Tourism (866) 284-7483 www.visitdelaware.com

Road Conditions & Construction — (800) 652-5600, (302) 760-2080 www.deldot.gov

Toll Road Information — Delaware River & Bay Authority (Del. Memorial Bridge & Lewes–Cape May Ferry) (302) 571-6300; www.drba.net — Delaware Dept. of Trans. (all other toll roads) (E-ZPass): (888) 397-2773, www.ezpassde.com

Get more Delaware info at www.randmcnally.com/DE

continued p. 54

Mileages between cities

	Daytona Beach	Fort Myers	Fort Pierce	Gainesville	Jacksonville	Key West	Miami	Orlando	Panama City	Pensacola	St. Petersburg	Sarasota	Tallahassee	Tampa	Titusville	W. Palm Beach
Key West	414	279	284	483	507		162	387	727	821	390	352	627	402	371	231
Miami	256	152	123	336	349	162		229	579	663	262	225	479	255	213	68

Mileages © Rand McNally

Total mileages through Florida — More mileages at www.randmcnally.com/MC

4	132 miles	75	471 miles
10	362 miles	95	382 miles

Inset maps: **Daytona Beach**, **Melbourne / Titusville**

Toll Road Information — Florida's Turnpike (SunPass): (800) 749-7453 — floridasturnpike.com

511 — Road Conditions & Construction — 511 (866) 374-3368 www.fl511.com, www.dot.state.fl.us

Tourism Information — Visit Florida (888) 735-2872, (850) 488-5607 www.visitflorida.com

Plan a Florida trip at www.randmcnally.com/FL

© Rand McNally

Pg. 55

Mileages between cities	Daytona Beach	Fort Myers	Fort Pierce	Gainesville	Jacksonville	Key West	Miami	Orlando	Panama City	Pensacola	St. Petersburg	Sarasota	Tallahassee	Tampa	Titusville	W. Palm Beach
Orlando	54	171	110	114	141	387	229		357	451	106	132	257	84	39	159
Pensacola	442	589	549	338	355	821	663	451	102		458	511	193	459	487	594

Mileages © Rand McNally

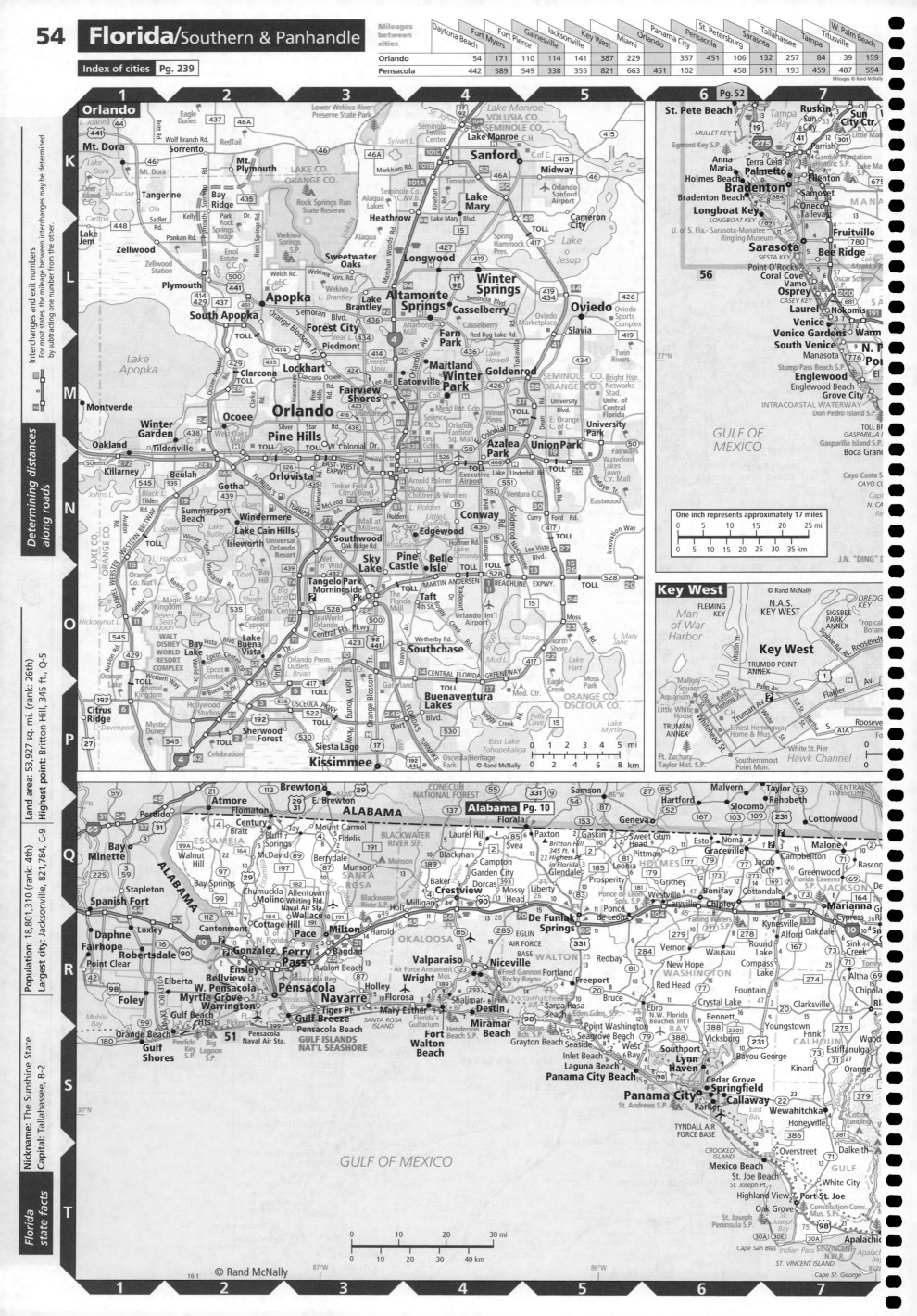

Florida state facts

Nickname: The Sunshine State
Capital: Tallahassee, B-2

Population: 18,801,310 (rank: 4th)
Largest city: Jacksonville, 821,784, C-9

Land area: 53,927 sq. mi. (rank: 26th)
Highest point: Britton Hill, 345 ft., Q-5

© Rand McNally

Mileages between cities	Daytona Beach	Fort Myers	Fort Pierce	Gainesville	Jacksonville	Key West	Miami	Orlando	Panama City	Pensacola	St. Petersburg	Sarasota	Tallahassee	Tampa	Titusville	W. Palm Beach
Tallahassee	253	397	364	148	164	627	479	257	96	193	257	328		273	295	413
Tampa	137	130	151	127	198	402	255	84	373	459	23	60	273		124	202

Mileages © Rand McNally

Total mileages through Florida
4 132 miles   75 471 miles
10 362 miles   95 382 miles
More mileages at www.randmcnally.com/MC

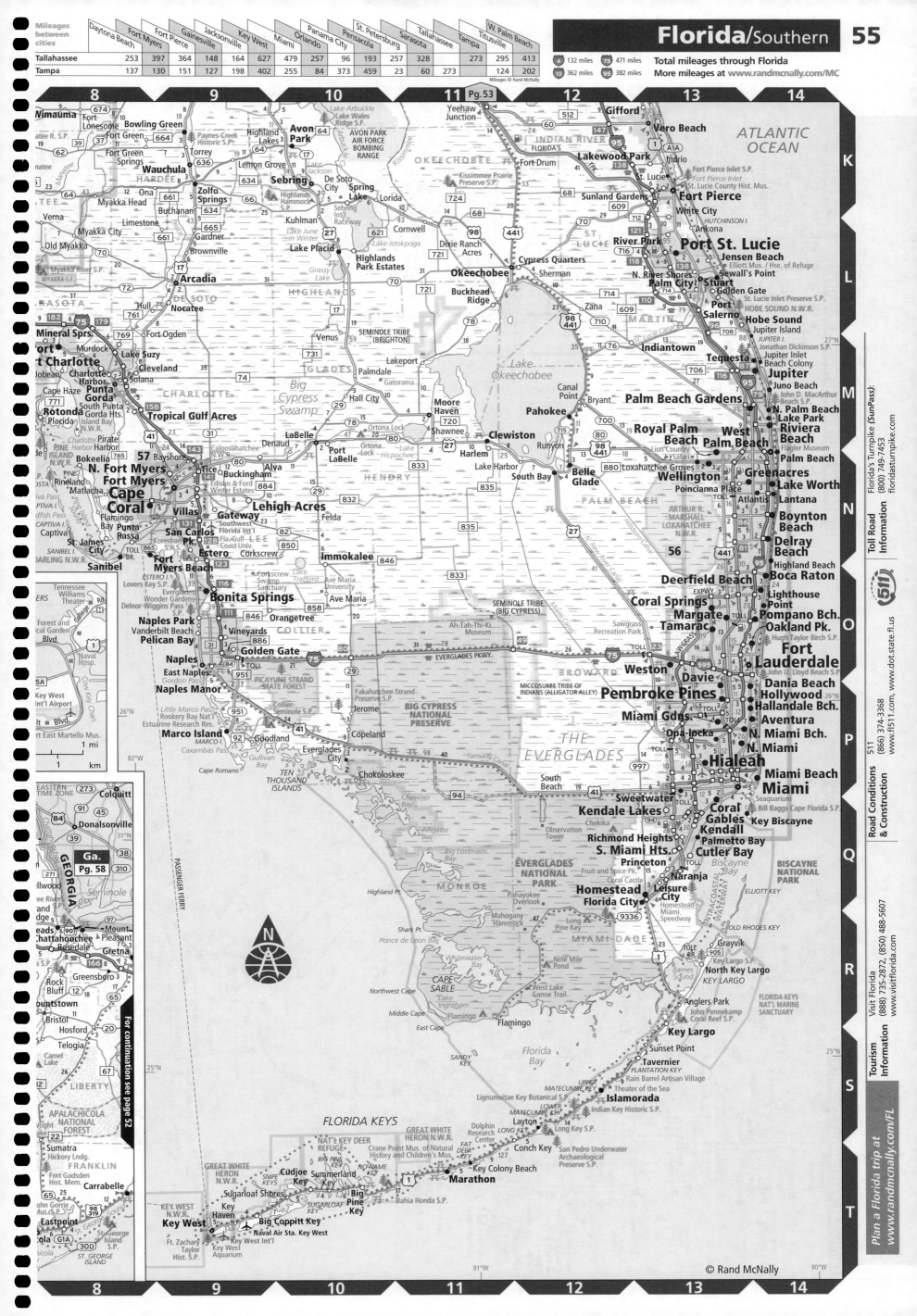

Florida's Turnpike (*SunPass*): (800) 749-7453 floridasturnpike.com — **Toll Road Information**

511 (866) 374-3368 www.fl511.com, www.dot.state.fl.us — **Road Conditions & Construction**

Visit Florida (888) 735-2872, (850) 488-5607 www.visitflorida.com/FL — **Tourism Information**

Plan a Florida trip at www.randmcnally.com/FL

For continuation see page 52

Ga. Pg. 58

City sights to see
- Art Deco National Historic District, Miami Beach, L-9
- Busch Gardens, Tampa, B-4
- Goodyear Blimp Base, Pompano Beach, G-9
- Hugh Taylor Birch State Park, Fort Lauderdale, H-9
- Marie Selby Botanical Gardens, Sarasota, H-3
- Miami Seaquarium, Miami, M-9

Tampa / St. Petersburg / Sarasota

Miami / Fort Lauderdale & Vicinity

- Norton Mus. of Art, West Palm Beach, B-10
- Ringling Museum of Art / Ringling Center for the Cultural Arts, Sarasota, G-3
- Salvador Dali Museum, St. Petersburg, D-2
- St. Petersburg Mus. of Hist., St. Petersburg, D-2
- Thomas A. Edison & Henry Ford Winter Estates, Fort Myers, M-1
- Vizcaya Museum and Gardens, Miami, M-8

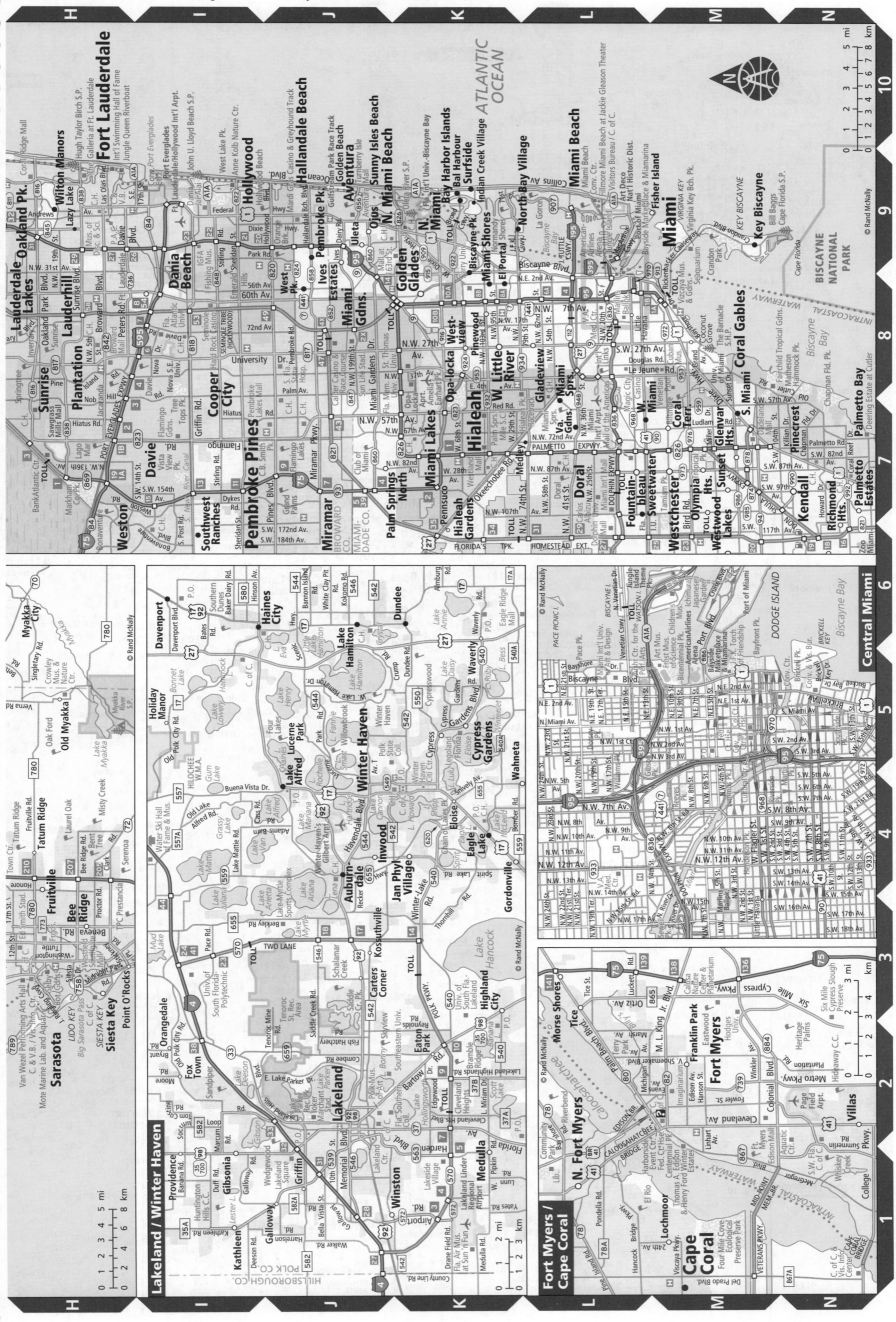

© Rand McNally

Index of cities Pg. 240

Mileages between cities

	Albany	Athens	Atlanta	Augusta	Bainbridge	Brunswick	Chattanooga, TN	Columbus	Gainesville	Jacksonville, FL	Macon	Rome	Savannah	Toccoa	Valdosta	Vidalia
Atlanta	182	69		148	240	275	117	106	54	346	82	70	247	94	228	172
Augusta	211	98	148		268	193	265	249	140	254	123	217	134	132	217	99

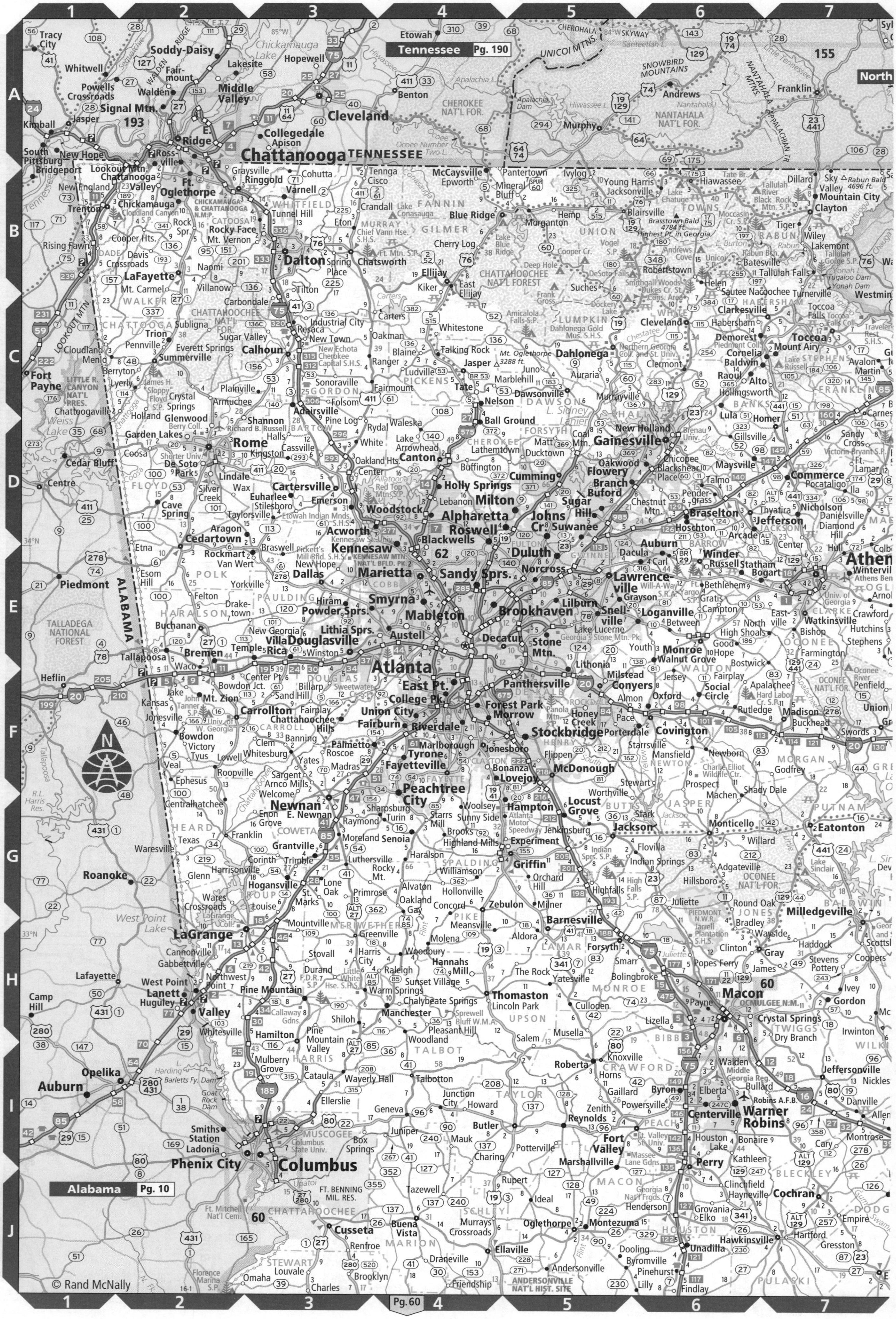

Georgia state facts

Nickname: The Peach State
Capital: Atlanta, E-4

Population: 9,687,653 (rank: 9th)
Largest city: Atlanta, 420,003, E-4

Land area: 57,906 sq. mi. (rank: 21st)
Highest point: Brasstown Bald, 4,784 ft., B-6

Determining distances along roads

Highway distances (segments of one mile or less not shown):
Cumulative miles (red): the distance between red arrows
Intermediate miles (black): the distance between intersections & places

Mileages between cities	Albany	Athens	Atlanta	Augusta	Bainbridge	Brunswick	Chattanooga, TN	Columbus	Gainesville	Jacksonville, FL	Macon	Rome	Savannah	Toccoa	Valdosta	Vidalia
Chattanooga, TN	300	172	117	265	348	397		219	121	465	201	71	364	155	346	289
Columbus	85	171	106	249	128	258	219		161	292	98	144	249	201	173	175

continued p. 60

Mileages © Rand McNally

Total mileages through Georgia

| 20 | 203 miles | 85 | 180 miles |
| 75 | 355 miles | 95 | 112 miles |

More mileages at www.randmcnally.com/MC

continued p. 60
Carolina Pg. 150
South Carolina Pg. 186
Pg. 61
Pg. 61

Georgia/Northern map, including insets for Augusta and Albany.

One inch represents approximately 16 miles

Toll Road Information — No toll roads

511 — **Road Conditions & Construction** — 511, (888) 635-8287, (877) 694-2511, (404) 635-8000, www.511ga.org

Tourism Information — Georgia Dept. of Economic Development, (800) 847-4842, www.exploregeorgia.org

Explore Georgia at www.randmcnally.com/GA

Index of cities Pg. 240

Mileages between cities	Albany	Athens	Atlanta	Augusta	Bainbridge	Brunswick	Chattanooga, TN	Columbus	Gainesville	Jacksonville, FL	Macon	Rome	Savannah	Toccoa	Valdosta	Vidalia
Jacksonville, FL	198	310	346	254	204	66	465	292	396		270	416	135	375	121	164
Macon	106	91	82	123	163	193	201	98	132	270		152	165	143	152	90

Mileages © Rand McNally

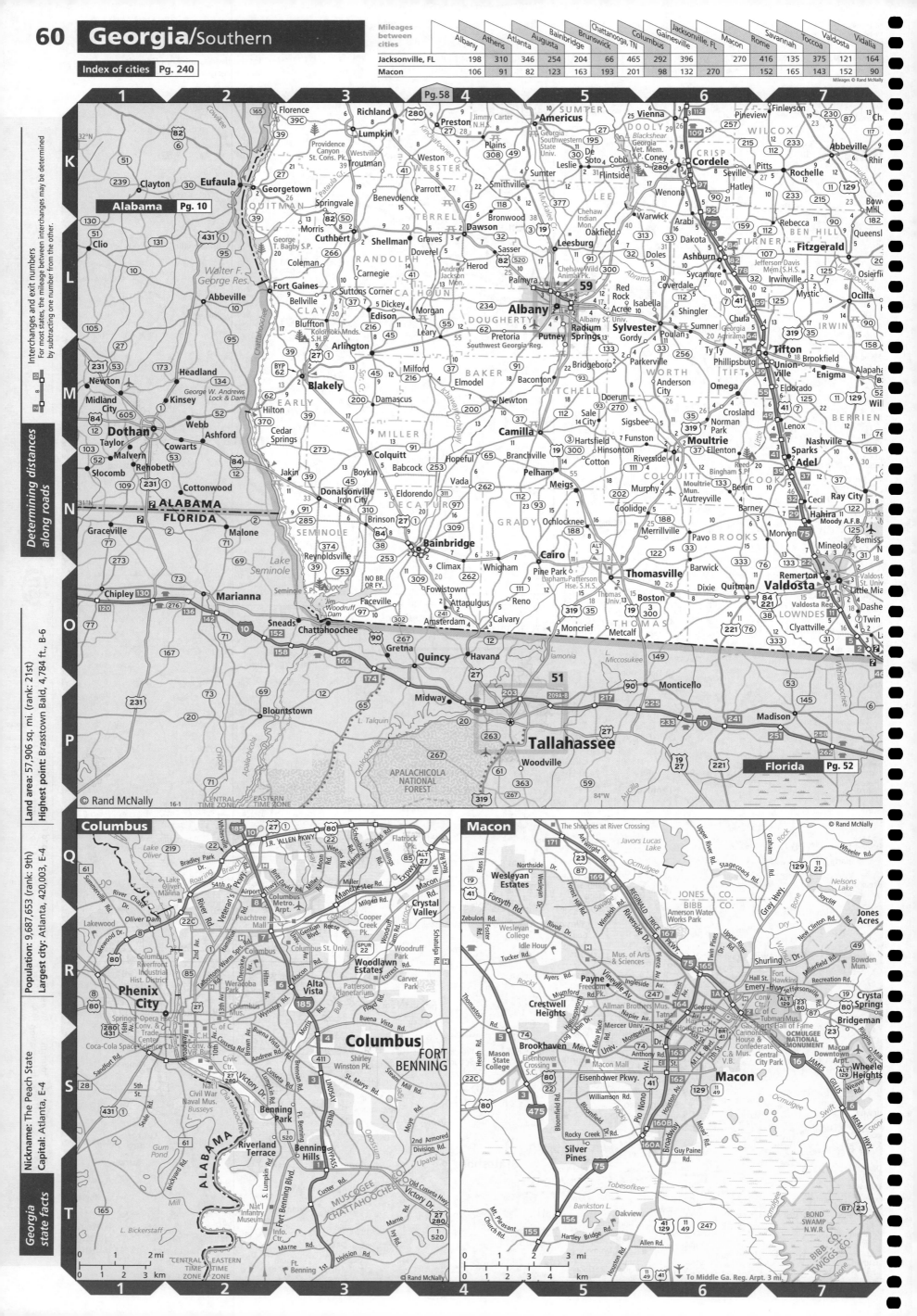

© Rand McNally

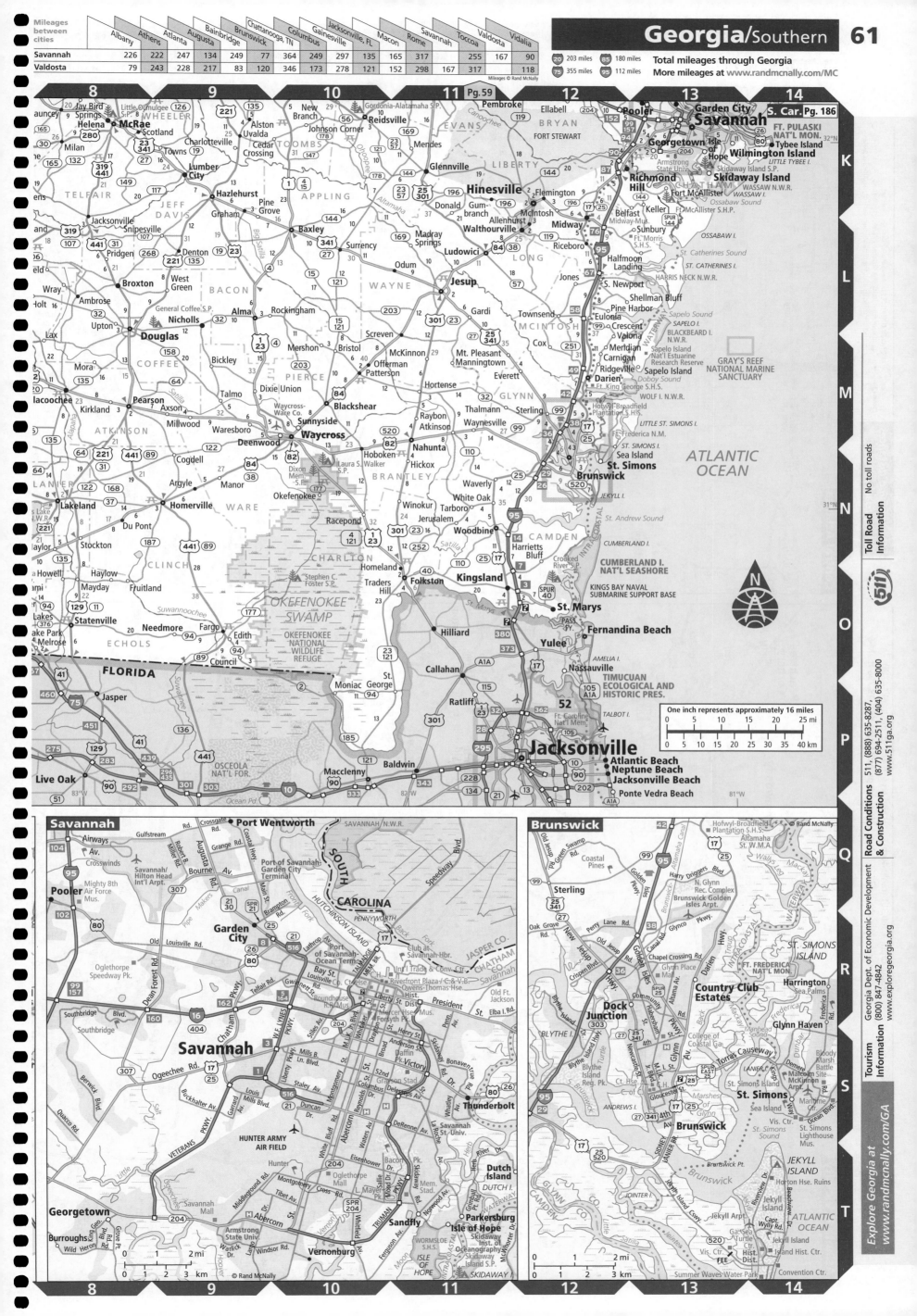

Mileages between cities	Albany	Athens	Atlanta	Augusta	Bainbridge	Brunswick	Chattanooga, TN	Columbus	Gainesville	Jacksonville, FL	Macon	Rome	Savannah	Toccoa	Valdosta	Vidalia
Savannah	226	222	247	134	249	77	364	249	297	135	165	317		255	167	90
Valdosta	79	243	228	217	83	120	346	173	278	121	152	298	167	317		118

Mileages © Rand McNally

Total mileages through Georgia

| 20 | 203 miles | 85 | 180 miles |
| 75 | 355 miles | 95 | 112 miles |

More mileages at www.randmcnally.com/MC

Index of cities Pg. 240

Mileages between cities	Hilo	Honolulu	Kahului	Kailua	Kailua Kona	Kapa'a	Lahaina	Wahiawa
Hilo		225*	127*	237*	74	337*	149*	236*
Honolulu	225*		108*	11	177*	116*	130*	20

	Hilo	Honolulu	Kahului	Kailua	Kailua Kona	Kapa'a	Lahaina	Wahiawa
Kahului	127*	108*		22*	93*	214*	22	119*
Kailua Kona	74	177*	93*		188*	283*	116*	188*

*via plane

Mileages © Rand McNally

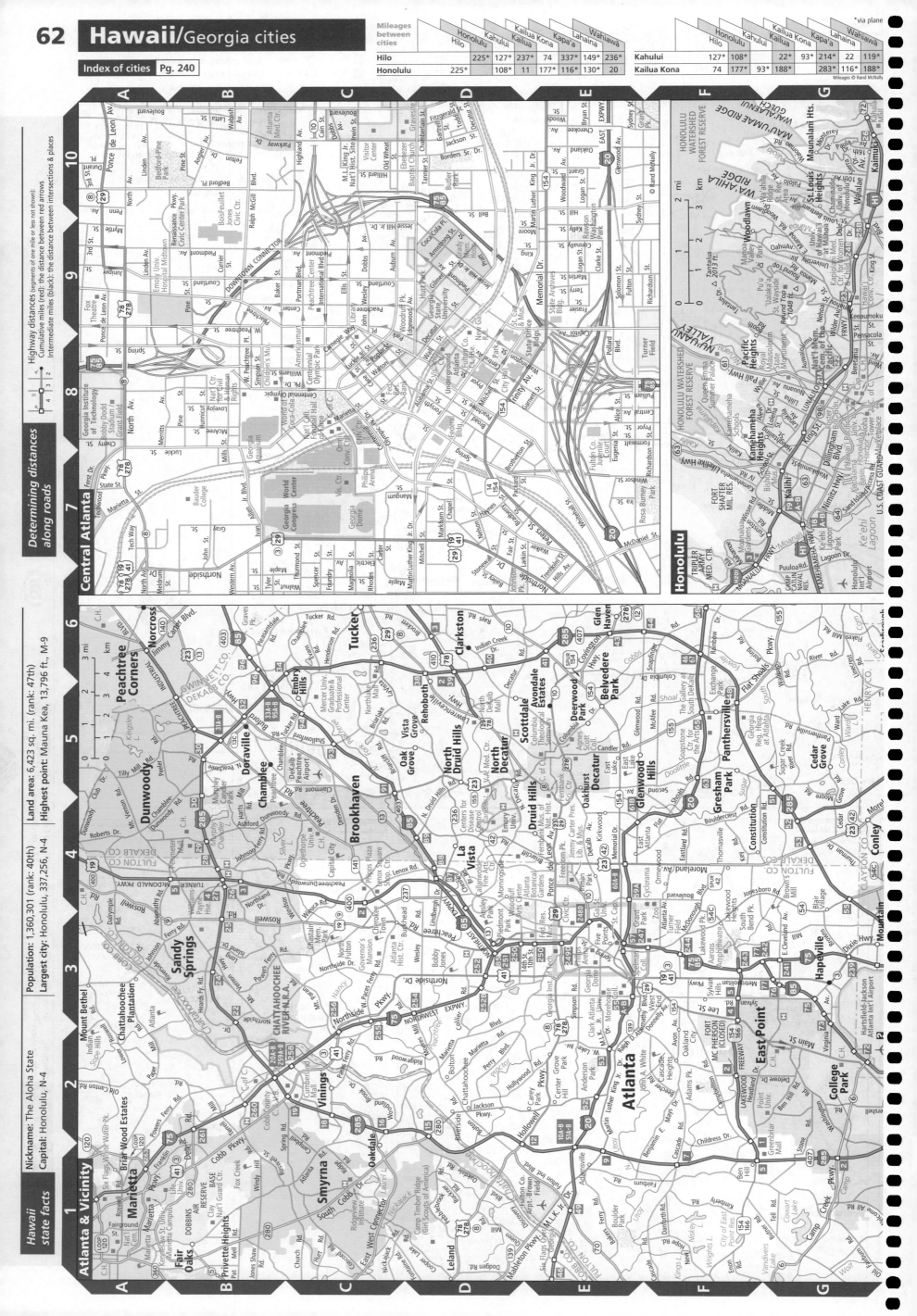

Mileages between cities	Honolulu Hilo	Kahului	Kailua Kona Kailua	Kapa'a	Wahiawā Lahaina	
Kapa'a	337*	116*	214*	128*	283*	236*	128*
Kaunakakai	177*	68*	55*	79*	144*	174*	77*	79*

	Honolulu Hilo	Kahului	Kailua Kona Kailua	Kapa'a	Wahiawā Lahaina	
Lahaina	149*	130*	22	43*	116*	236*	141*
Wahiawā	236*	20	119*	26	188*	128*	141*

*via plane

Mileages © Rand McNally

Total mileages through Hawaii
More mileages at www.randmcnally.com/MC

H1 27 miles   H3 15 miles
H2 8 miles

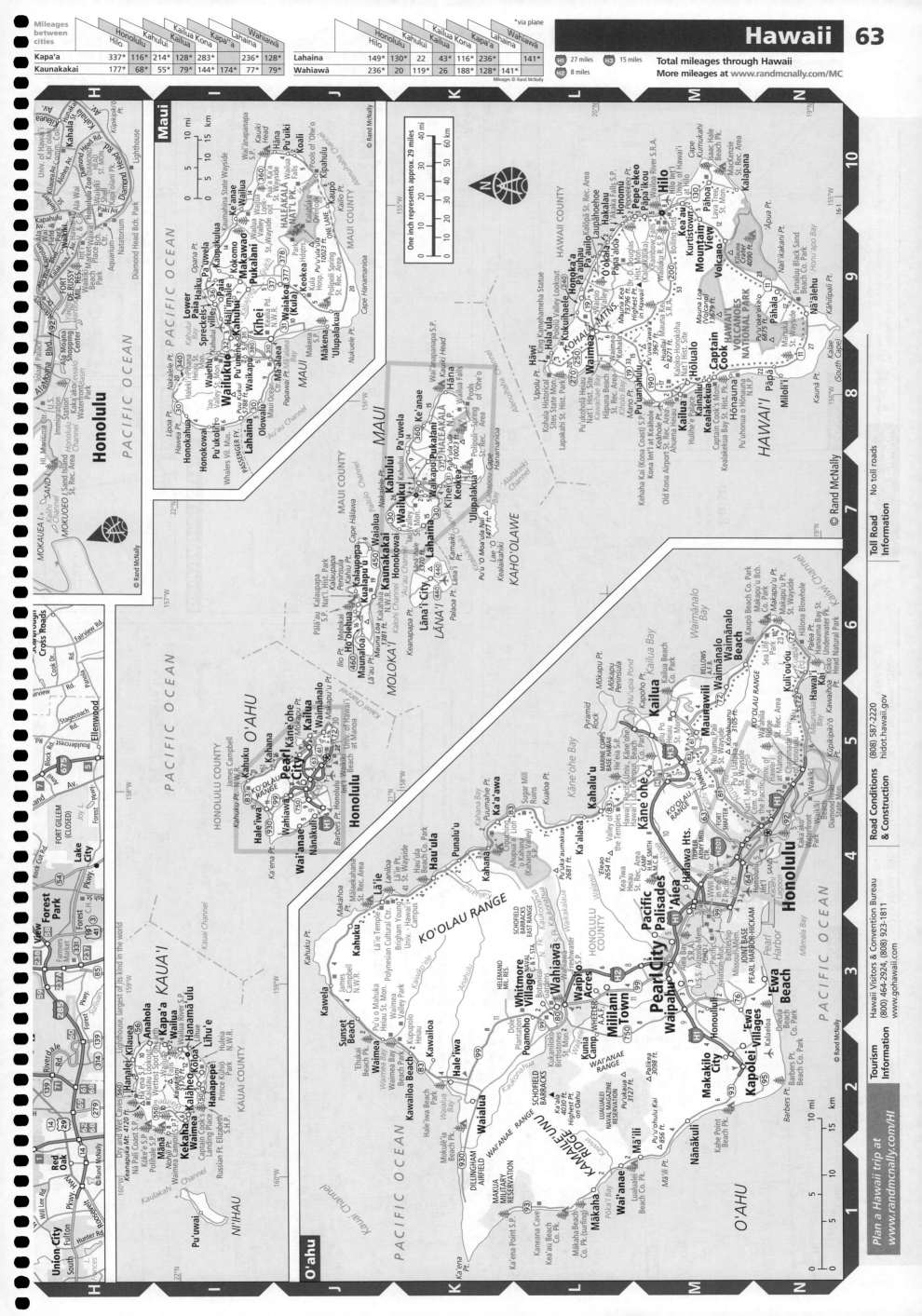

Tourism Information: Hawaii Visitors & Convention Bureau (800) 464-2924, (808) 923-1811 www.gohawaii.com

Road Conditions & Construction: (808) 587-2220 hidot.hawaii.gov

Plan a Hawaii trip at www.randmcnally.com/HI

Index of cities Pg. 241

Idaho state facts

Nickname: The Gem State
Capital: Boise, K-2
Population: 1,567,582 (rank: 39th)
Largest city: Boise, 205,671, K-2
Land area: 82,747 sq. mi. (rank: 11th)
Highest point: Borah Peak, 12,662 ft., J-5

Mileages between cities	Boise	Coeur d'Alene	Lewiston	Missoula, MT	Mountain Home	Pocatello	Salmon	Twin Falls
Boise		383	268	367	44	234	247	128
Bonners Ferry	459	76	191	212	504	573	351	589

	Boise	Coeur d'Alene	Lewiston	Missoula, MT	Mountain Home	Pocatello	Salmon	Twin Falls
Coeur d'Alene	383		115	166	428	525	303	513
Idaho Falls	279	478	526	312	237	49	160	159

Mileages © Rand McNally

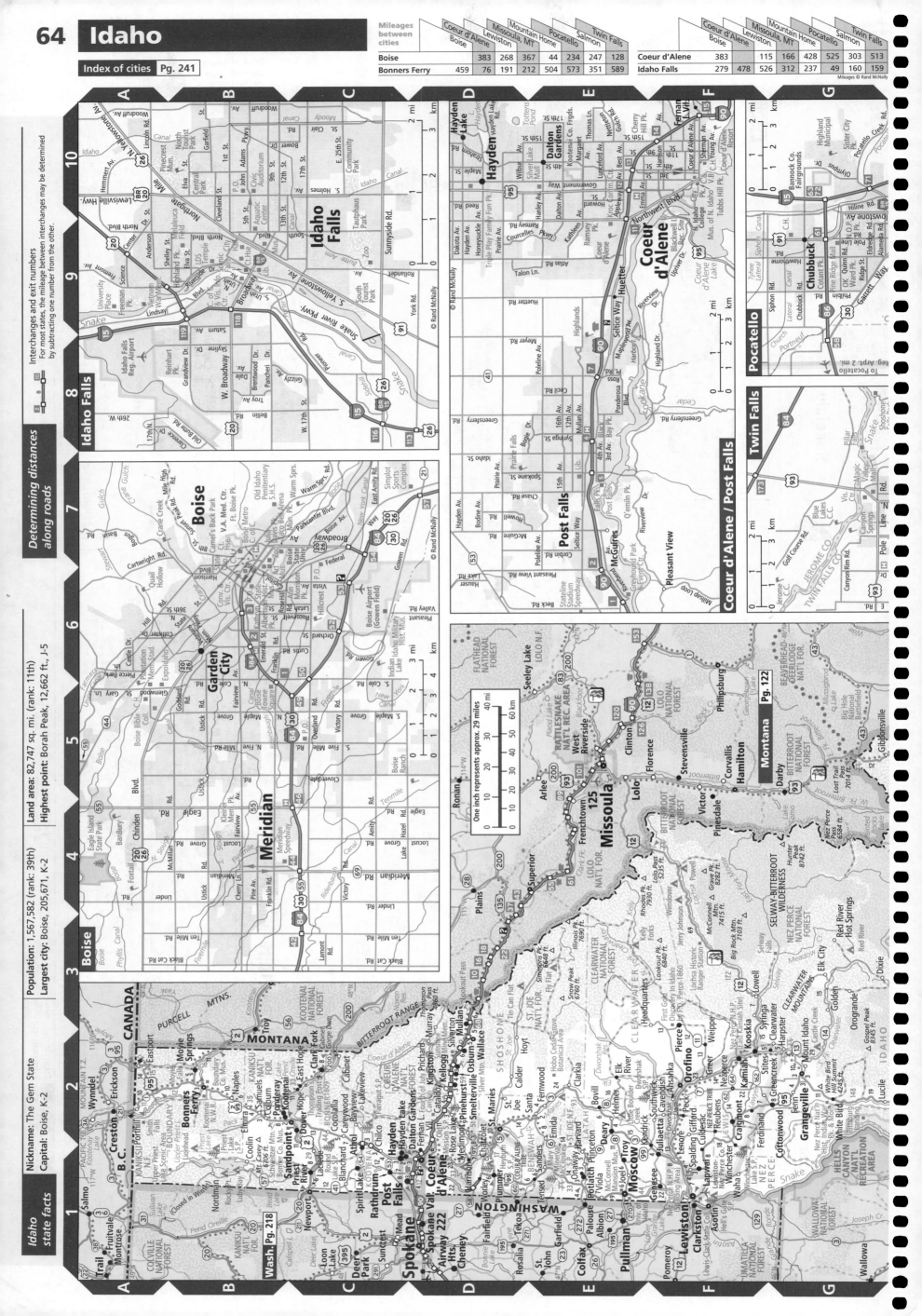

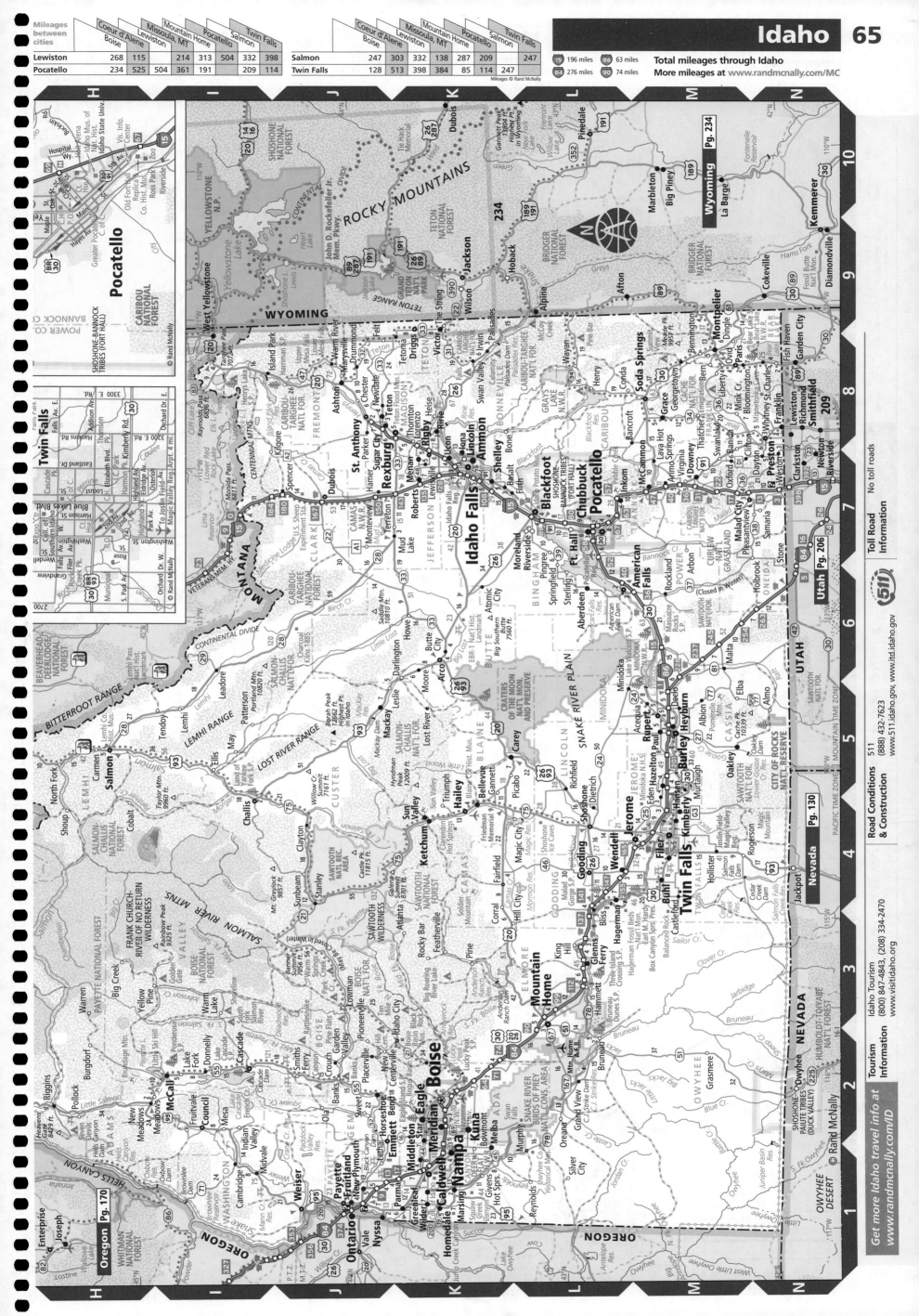

Mileages between cities

	Coeur d'Alene / Boise	Lewiston	Missoula, MT	Mountain Home	Pocatello	Salmon	Twin Falls
Lewiston	268	115	214	313	504	332	398
Pocatello	234	525	504	361	191	209	114

	Coeur d'Alene / Boise	Lewiston	Missoula, MT	Mountain Home	Pocatello	Salmon	Twin Falls
Salmon	247	303	332	138	287	209	247
Twin Falls	128	513	398	384	85	114	247

Mileages © Rand McNally

Total mileages through Idaho
15 196 miles   86 63 miles
84 276 miles   90 74 miles
More mileages at www.randmcnally.com/MC

Mileages © Rand McNally

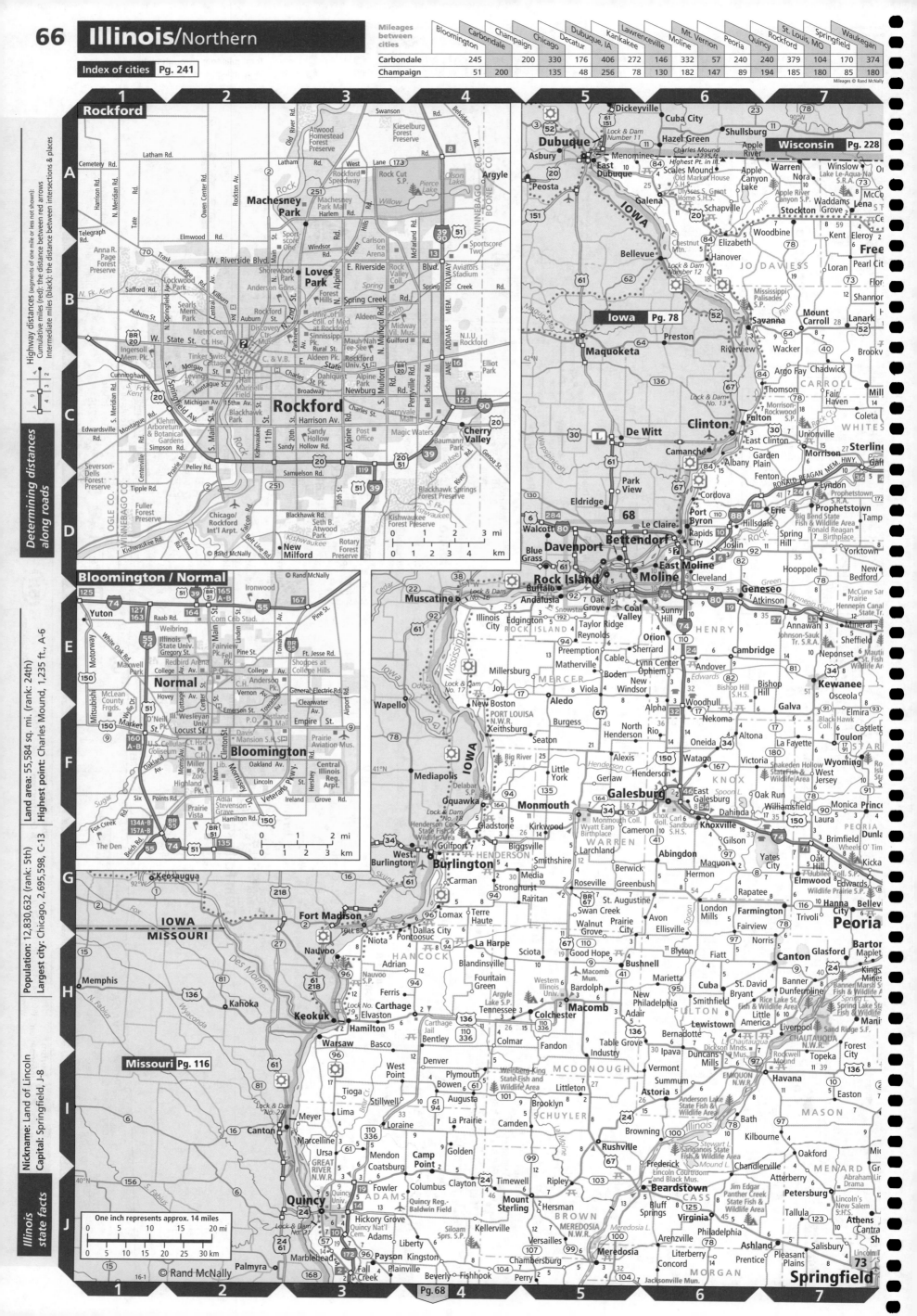

Rockford

Bloomington / Normal

One inch represents approx. 14 miles

© Rand McNally

Mileages between cities	Bloomington	Carbondale	Champaign	Chicago	Dubuque, IA	Decatur	Kankakee	Lawrenceville	Mt. Vernon Moline	Peoria	Quincy	Rockford	St. Louis, MO	Springfield	Waukegan
Chicago	132	330	135		179	177	58	247	166 277	154	309	84	296	198	38
Moline	131	332	182	166	171	75	158	307	308	93	148	120	261	164	190

continued p. 68

Mileages © Rand McNally

Total mileages through Illinois

55	313 miles	80	164 miles
70	156 miles	90	124 miles

More mileages at www.randmcnally.com/MC

Toll Road Information
Chicago Skyway (I-Pass): (312) 552-7100; www.chicagoskyway.org
Illinois Tollway (all other toll roads) (I-Pass): (800) 824-7277; I-Pass: www.illinoistollway.com

Road Conditions & Construction
(800) 452-4368, (312) 368-4636
www.gettingaroundillinois.com
www.dot.il.gov

Tourism Information
Illinois Office of Tourism
(800) 226-6632
www.enjoyillinois.com

Plan an Illinois trip at www.randmcnally.com/IL

Index of cities Pg. 241

Mileages between cities

	Bloomington	Carbondale	Champaign	Chicago	Decatur	Dubuque, IA	Kankakee	Lawrenceville	Moline	Mt. Vernon	Peoria	Quincy	Rockford	St. Louis, MO	Springfield	Waukegan
Peoria	38	240	89	154	78	167	108	214	93	215		130	138	168	71	184
Rockford	132	379	185	84	180	93	139	309	120	326	138	268		294	197	73

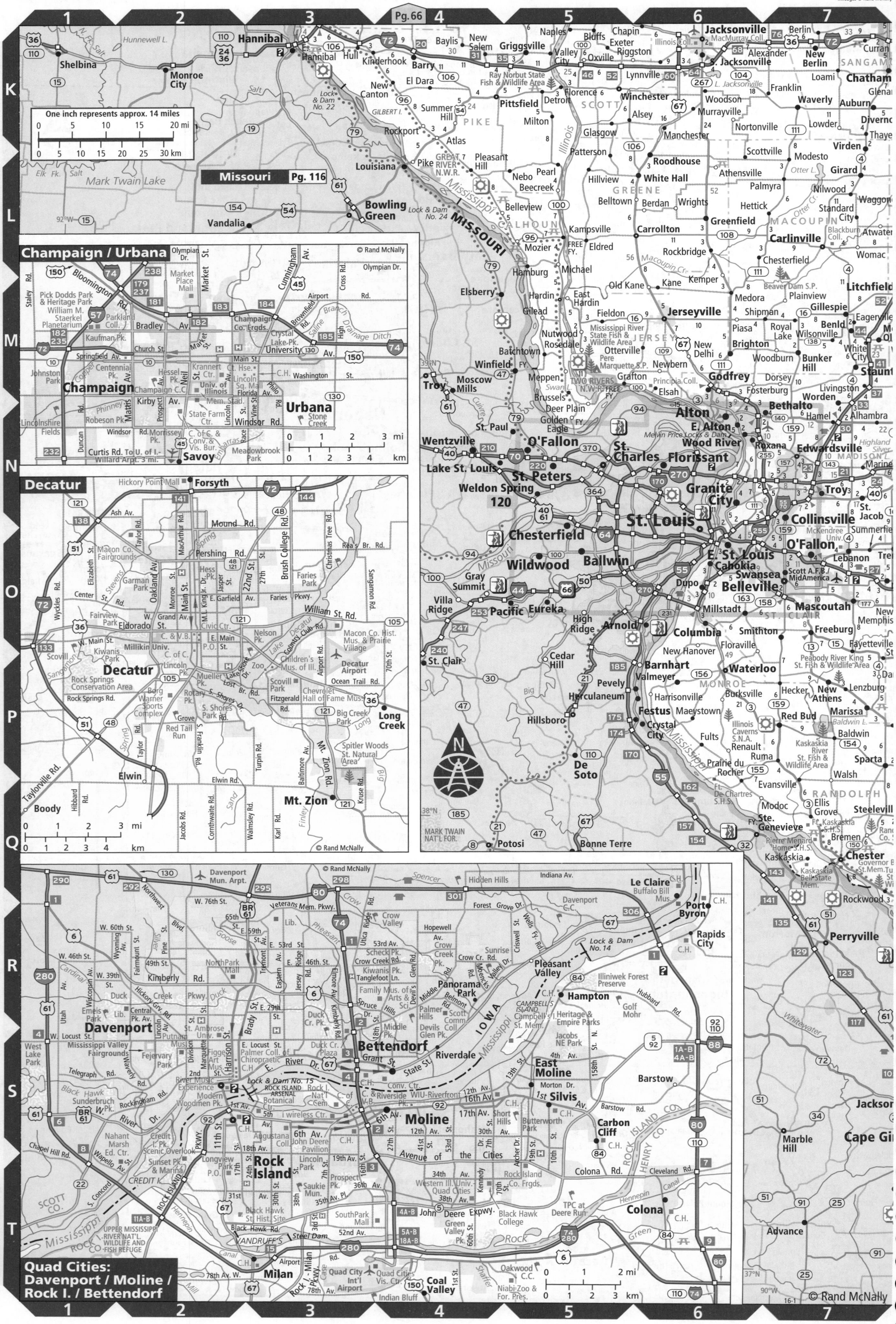

Interchanges and exit numbers
For most states, the mileage between interchanges may be determined by subtracting one number from the other.

Determining distances along roads

Land area: 55,584 sq. mi. (rank: 24th)
Highest point: Charles Mound, 1,235 ft., A-6

Population: 12,830,632 (rank: 5th)
Largest city: Chicago, 2,695,598, C-13

Nickname: Land of Lincoln
Capital: Springfield, J-8

Illinois state facts

Mileages between cities	Bloomington	Carbondale	Champaign	Chicago	Decatur	Dubuque, IA	Kankakee	Lawrenceville	Mt. Vernon	Moline	Peoria	Quincy	Rockford	St. Louis, MO	Springfield	Waukegan
St. Louis, MO	162	104	180	296	135	335	252	144	261	79	168	139	294		98	326
Springfield	66	170	85	198	38	238	157	153	164	138	71	112	197	98		229

Mileages © Rand McNally

Total mileages through Illinois

55	313 miles	80	164 miles
70	156 miles	90	124 miles

More mileages at www.randmcnally.com/MC

Toll Road Information

Chicago Skyway (I-Pass): (312) 552-7100; www.chicagoskyway.org
Illinois Tollway (all other toll roads) (I-Pass): (800) 824-7277; www.illinoistollway.com

Road Conditions & Construction

(800) 452-4368, (312) 368-4636
www.gettingaroundillinois.com
www.dot.il.gov

Tourism Information

Illinois Office of Tourism
(800) 226-6632
www.enjoyillinois.com

Plan an Illinois trip at
www.randmcnally.com/IL

Indiana Pg. 74

Kentucky Pg. 86

City sights to see
- Adler Planetarium, Chicago, G-15
- Art Institute of Chicago, Chicago, E-13
- Baha'i Temple, Wilmette, E-8
- Chicago Botanic Garden, Glencoe, D-8
- Field Museum, Chicago, G-14
- Frank Lloyd Wright Home & Studio, Oak Park, H-8
- Illinois Holocaust Museum, Skokie, F-8

- John G. Shedd Aquarium, Chicago, G-14
- John Hancock Center, Chicago, C-13
- Lincoln Park Zoo, Chicago, H-9
- Millennium Park, Chicago, E-13
- Museum of Science & Industry, Chicago, J-10
- Navy Pier, Chicago, D-14
- Willis Tower, Chicago, E-12
- Wrigley Field, Chicago, G-9

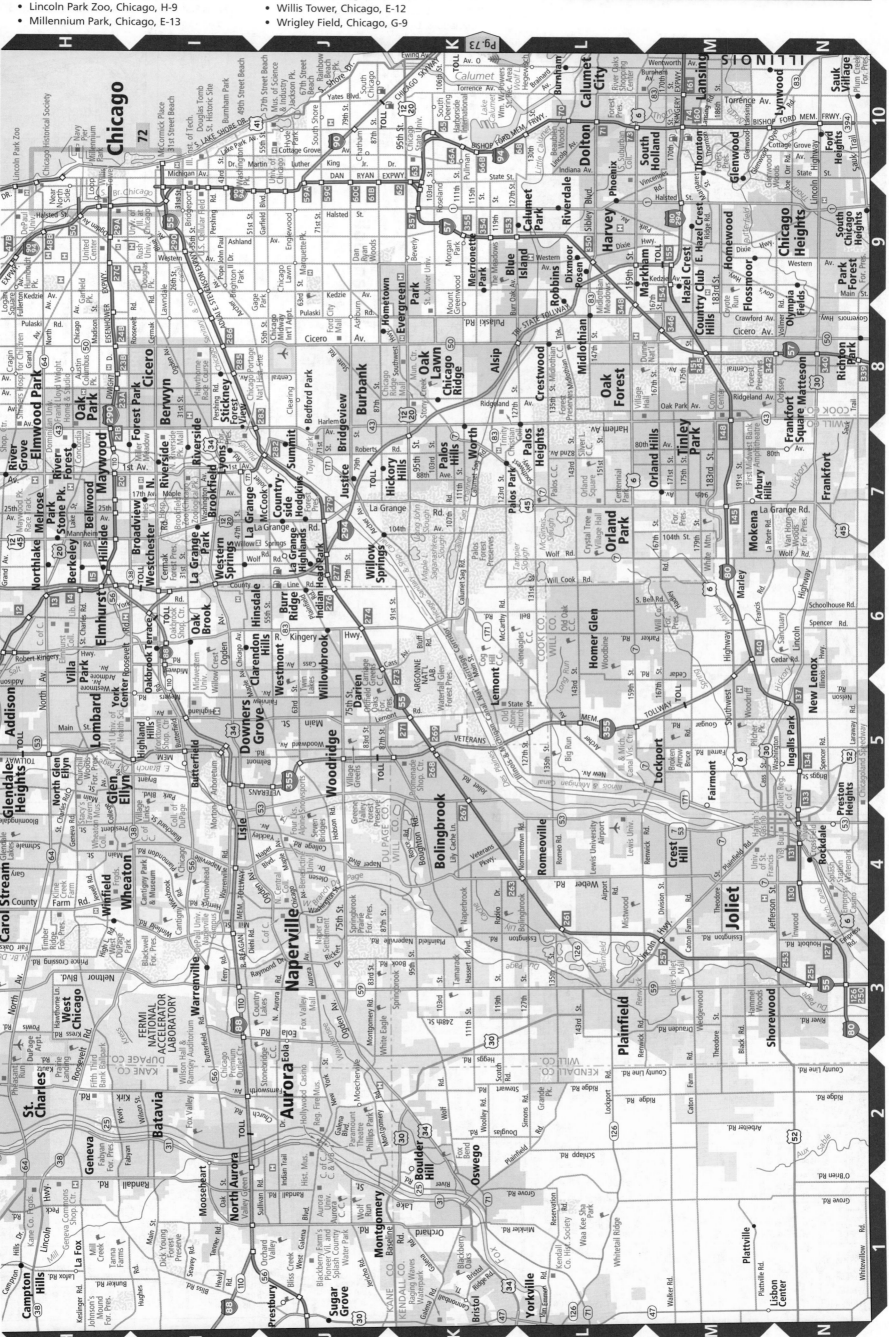

City sights to see

- Abraham Lincoln Presidential Library & Museum, Springfield, M-16
- Children's Museum of Indianapolis, Indianapolis, D-18
- Eiteljorg Museum, Indianapolis, E-17
- Fort Wayne Children's Zoo, Fort Wayne, L-19
- Illinois State Capitol Complex, Springfield, M-16
- Indiana State Capitol, Indianapolis, E-18

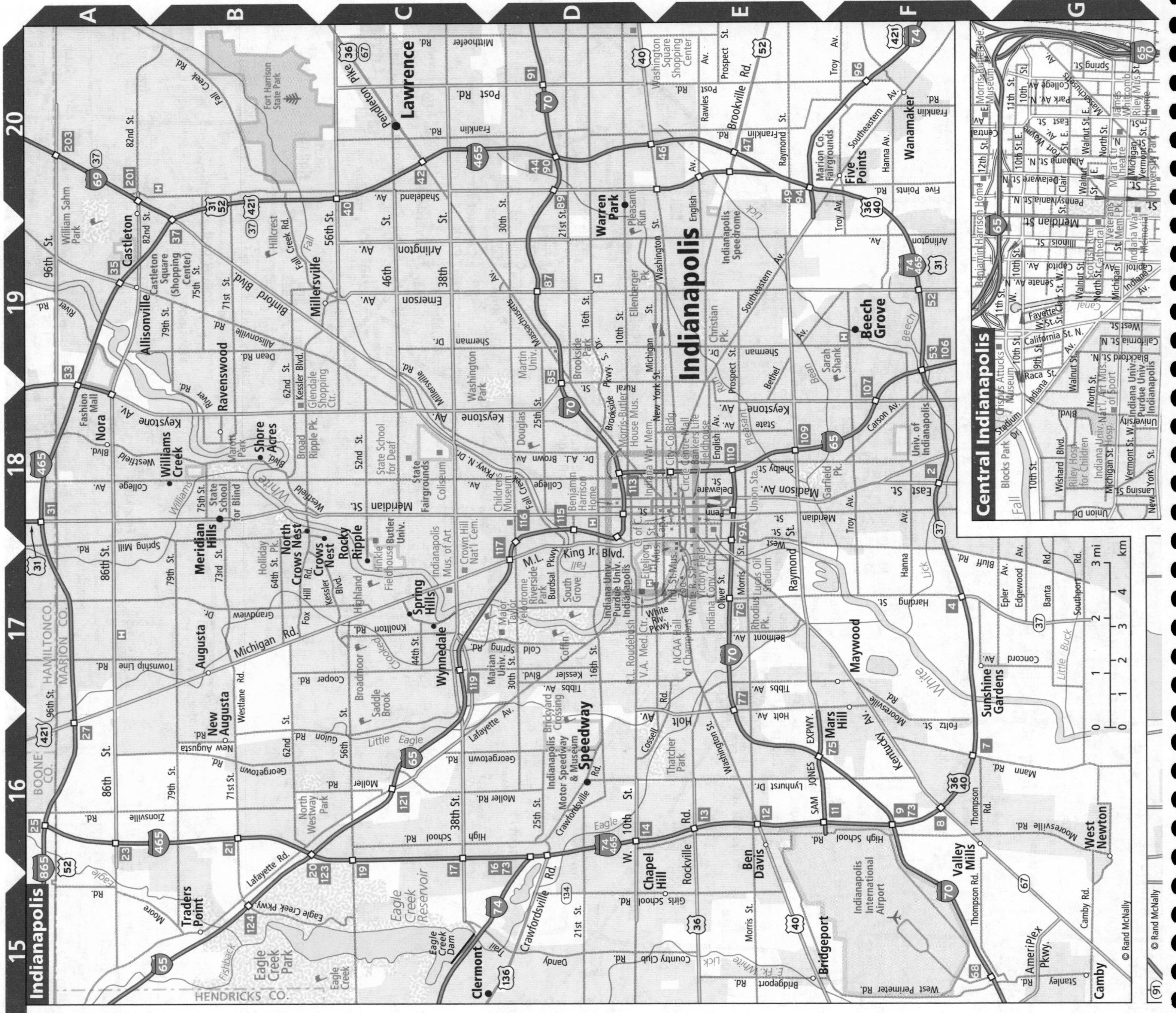

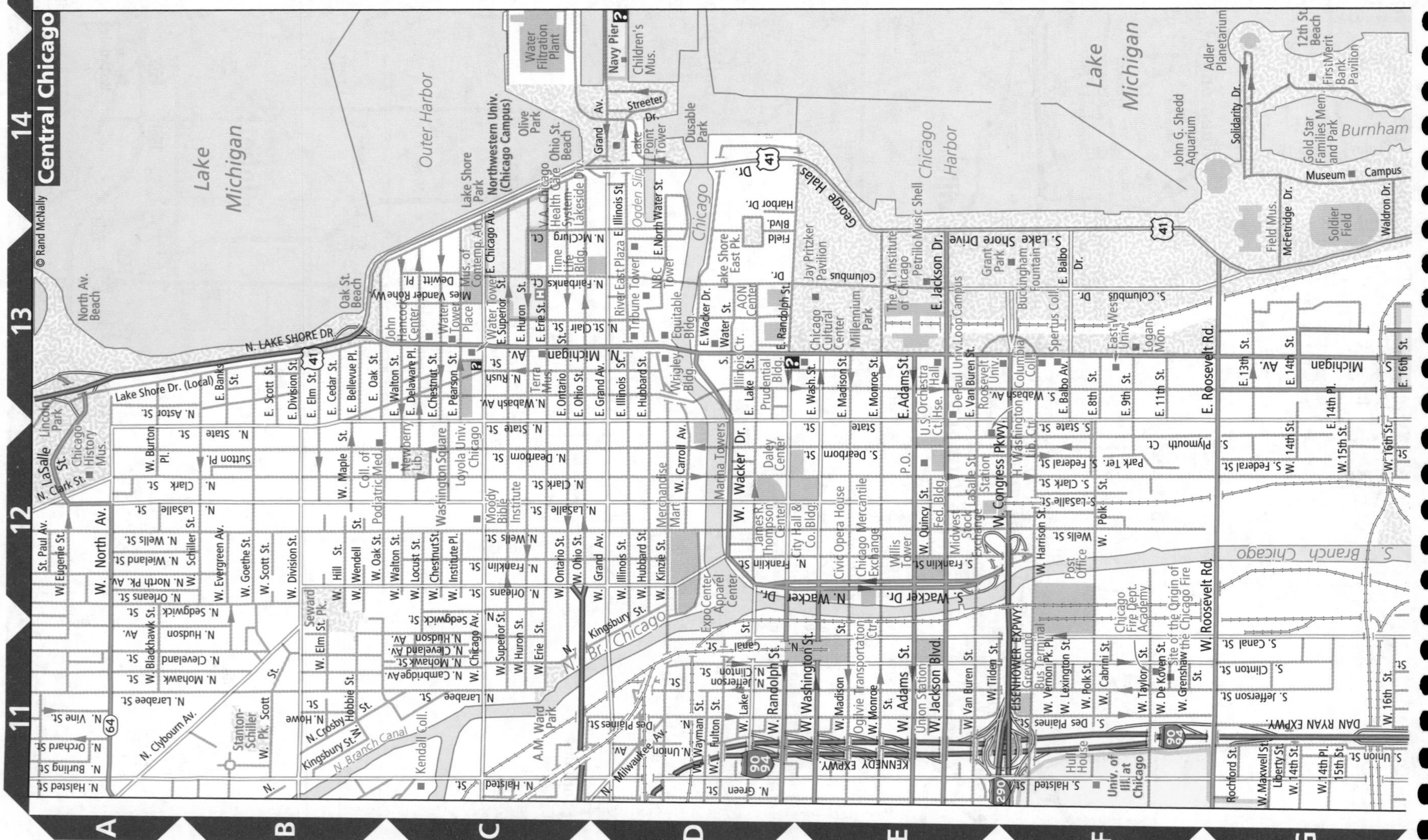

Indianapolis

Central Indianapolis

Central Chicago

© Rand McNally

- Indiana State Museum, Indianapolis, E-17
- Indianapolis Motor Speedway and Hall of Fame Museum, Indianapolis, D-16
- NCAA Hall of Champions, Indianapolis, H-18
- President Benjamin Harrison Home, Indianapolis, D-18

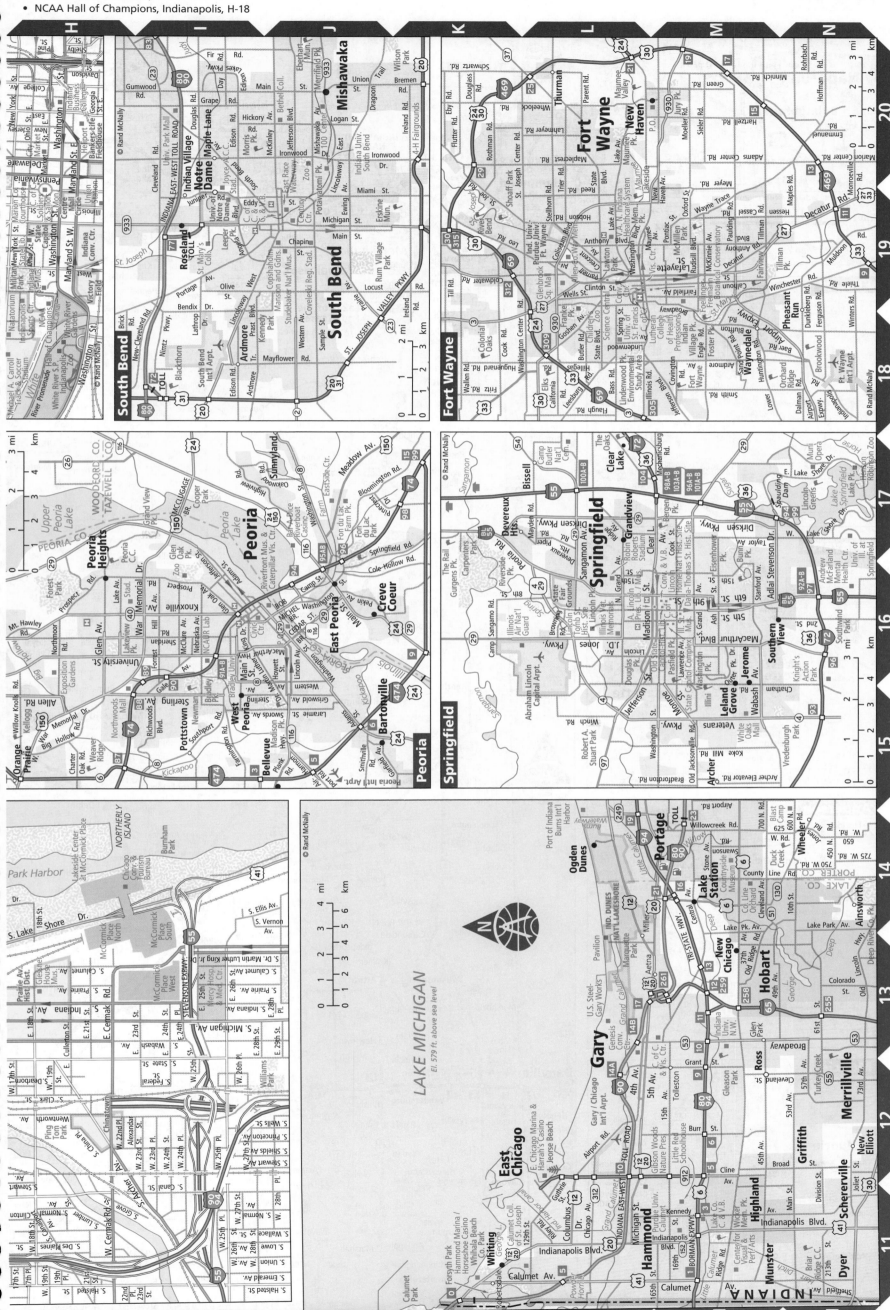

© Rand McNally

LAKE MICHIGAN
El. 579 ft. above sea level

Pg.71

Index of cities Pg. 242

Mileages between cities

	Angola	Bloomington	Chicago, IL	Crawfordsville	Evansville	Fort Wayne	Gary	Greensburg	Indianapolis	Kokomo	Lafayette	Muncie	New Albany	Richmond	South Bend	Terre Haute
Evansville	347	120	289	178		309	273	202	180	234	198	244	112	255	320	109
Fort Wayne	39	178	160	162	309		132	147	129	86	117	72	238	92	89	205

Mileages © Rand McNally

Determining distances along roads

Highway distances (segments of one mile or less not shown): Cumulative miles (red): the distance between red arrows. Intermediate miles (black): the distance between intersections & places

Indiana state facts

Nickname: The Hoosier State
Capital: Indianapolis, J-9

Population: 6,483,802 (rank: 15th)
Largest city: Indianapolis, 820,445, J-9

Land area: 35,867 sq. mi. (rank: 38th)
Highest point: Hoosier Hill, 1,257 ft., I-14

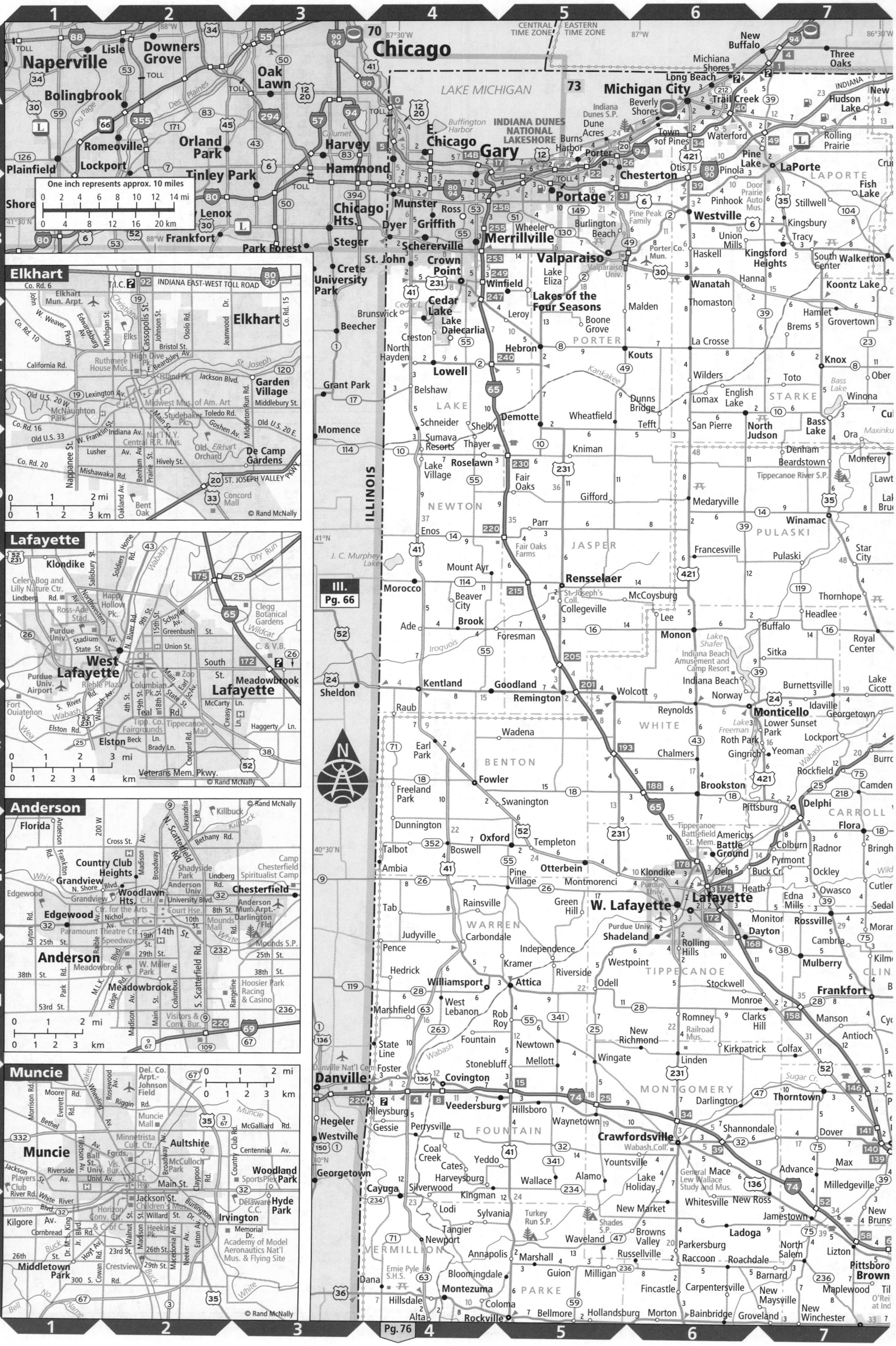

Mileages between cities	Bloomington	Chicago, IL	Crawfordsville	Evansville	Fort Wayne	Gary	Greensburg	Indianapolis	Kokomo	Lafayette	Muncie	New Albany	Richmond	South Bend	Terre Haute
Gary	135	200	30	118	273		132		203	151	127	91	196	266	222	64	164
Indianapolis	166	52	181	49	180	129	151		50		51	63	61	114	73	145	76

Mileages © Rand McNally

continued p. 76

Total mileages through Indiana
More mileages at www.randmcnally.com/MC

65 261 miles 74 172 miles
70 157 miles 90 156 miles

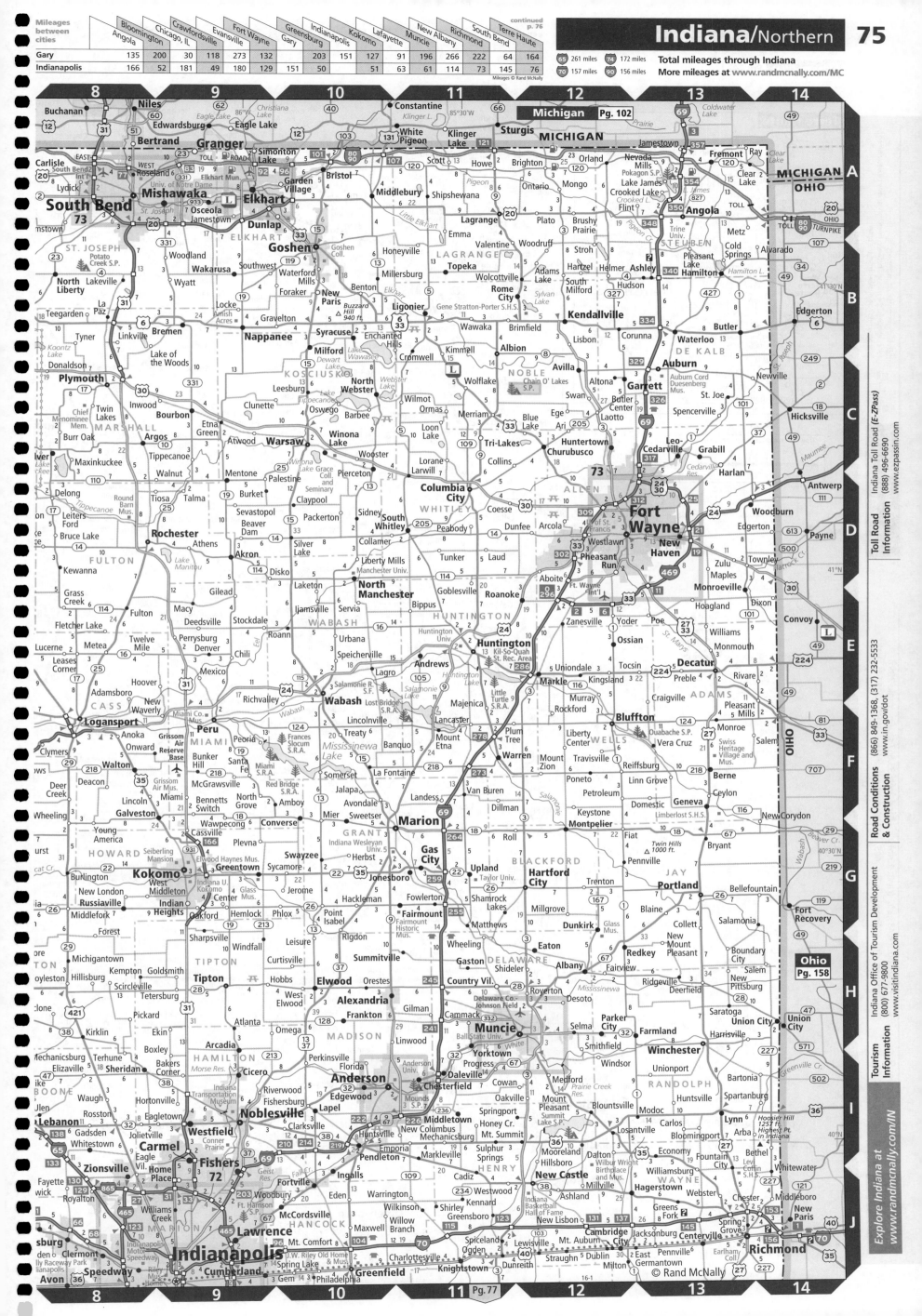

© Rand McNally

Index of cities Pg. 242

Mileages between cities

	Angola	Bloomington	Chicago, IL	Crawfordsville	Evansville	Fort Wayne	Gary	Greensburg	Indianapolis	Kokomo	Lafayette	Muncie	New Albany	Richmond	South Bend	Terre Haute
New Albany	276	88	296	163	112	238	266	94	114	168	178	172		184	256	146
Richmond	139	123	252	119	255	92	222	62	73	115	134	43	184		202	150

Determining distances along roads

Interchanges and exit numbers
For most states, the mileage between interchanges may be determined by subtracting one number from the other.

Indiana state facts

Nickname: The Hoosier State
Capital: Indianapolis, J-9
Population: 6,483,802 (rank: 15th)
Largest city: Indianapolis, 820,445, J-9
Land area: 35,867 sq. mi. (rank: 38th)
Highest point: Hoosier Hill, 1,257 ft., I-14

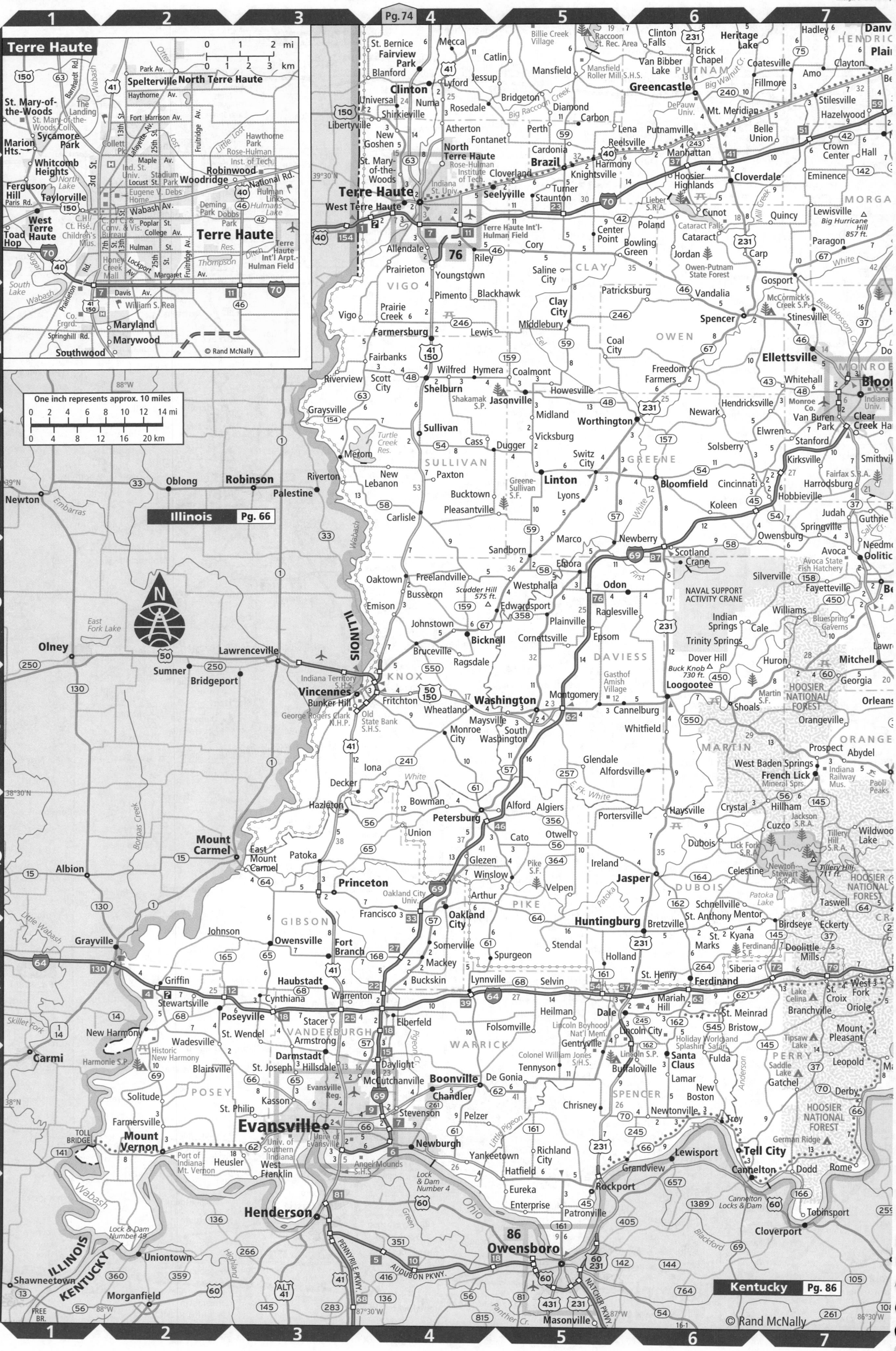

Mileages between cities	Angola	Bloomington	Chicago, IL	Crawfordsville	Evansville	Fort Wayne	Gary	Greensburg	Indianapolis	Kokomo	Lafayette	Muncie	New Albany	Richmond	South Bend	Terre Haute
South Bend	77	195	93	135	320	89	64	183	145	87	106	143	256	202		216
Terre Haute	242	58	180	58	109	205	164	123	76	129	89	139	146	150	216	

Mileages © Rand McNally

Total mileages through Indiana
More mileages at www.randmcnally.com/MC

65 261 miles 74 172 miles
70 157 miles 90 156 miles

Toll Road Information — Indiana Toll Road (E-ZPass) (888) 496-6690 www.ezpassin.com

Road Conditions & Construction — (866) 849-1368, (317) 232-5533 www.in.gov/dot

Tourism Information — Indiana Office of Tourism Development (800) 677-9800 www.visitindiana.com

Explore Indiana at www.randmcnally.com/IN

Mileages between cities	Ames	Burlington	Cedar Rapids	Council Bluffs	Davenport	Decorah	Des Moines	Dubuque	Iowa City	Mason City	Ottumwa	Sioux City	Sioux Falls, SD	Spirit Lake	Storm Lake	Waterloo
Burlington	209		100	294	77	206	167	150	77	238	78	366	451	355	312	155
Cedar Rapids	108	100		253	82	105	126	70	28	136	110	268	357	252	212	53

Mileages © Rand McNally

Iowa state facts

Nickname: The Hawkeye State
Capital: Des Moines

Population: 3,046,355 (rank: 30th)
Largest city: Des Moines, 203,433, I-10

Land area: 55,869 sq. mi. (rank: 23rd)
Highest point: Hawkeye Point, 1,670 ft., B-4

Determining distances along roads

Highway distances (segments of one mile or less not shown):
Cumulative miles (red): the distance between red arrows
Intermediate miles (black): the distance between intersections & places

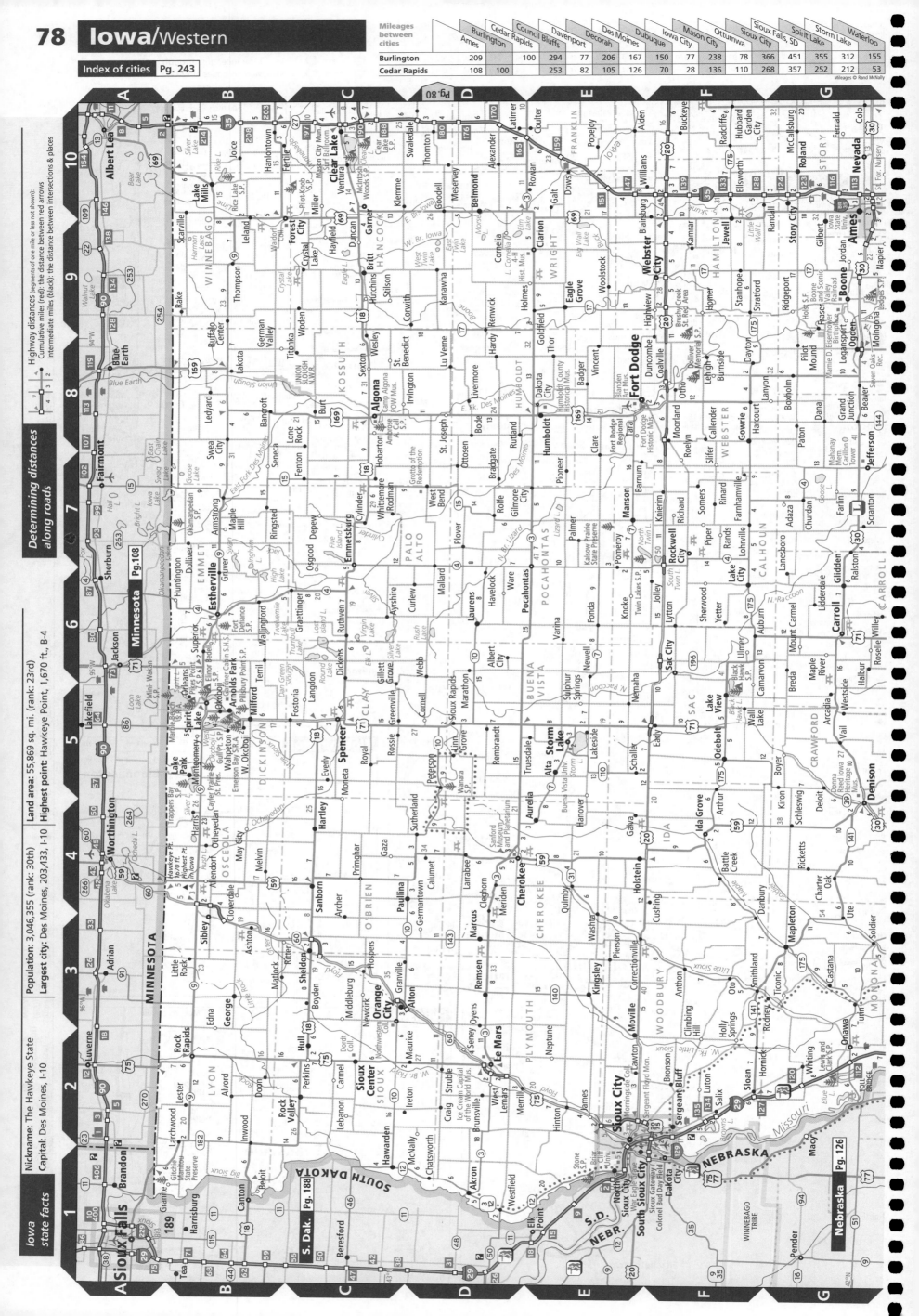

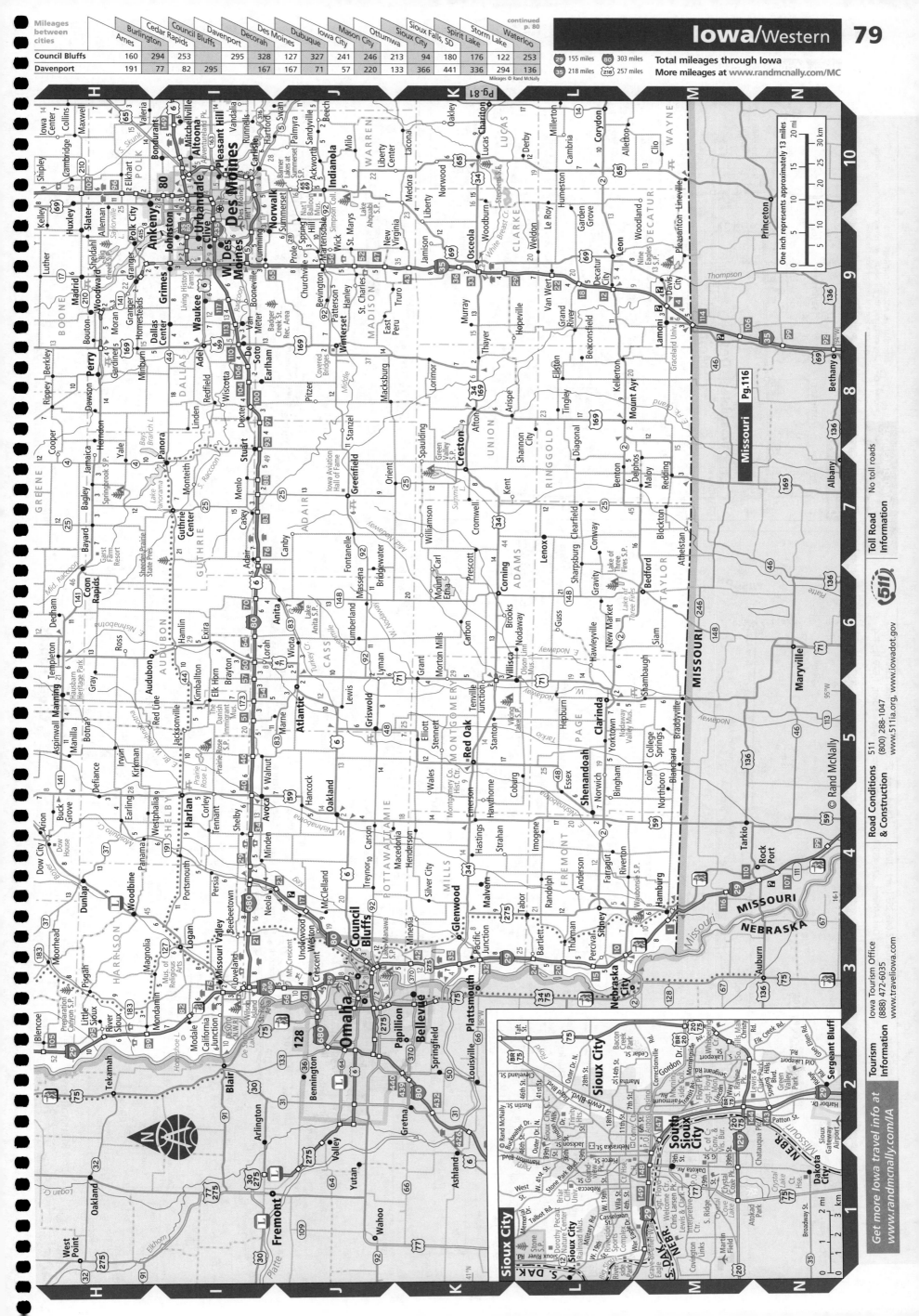

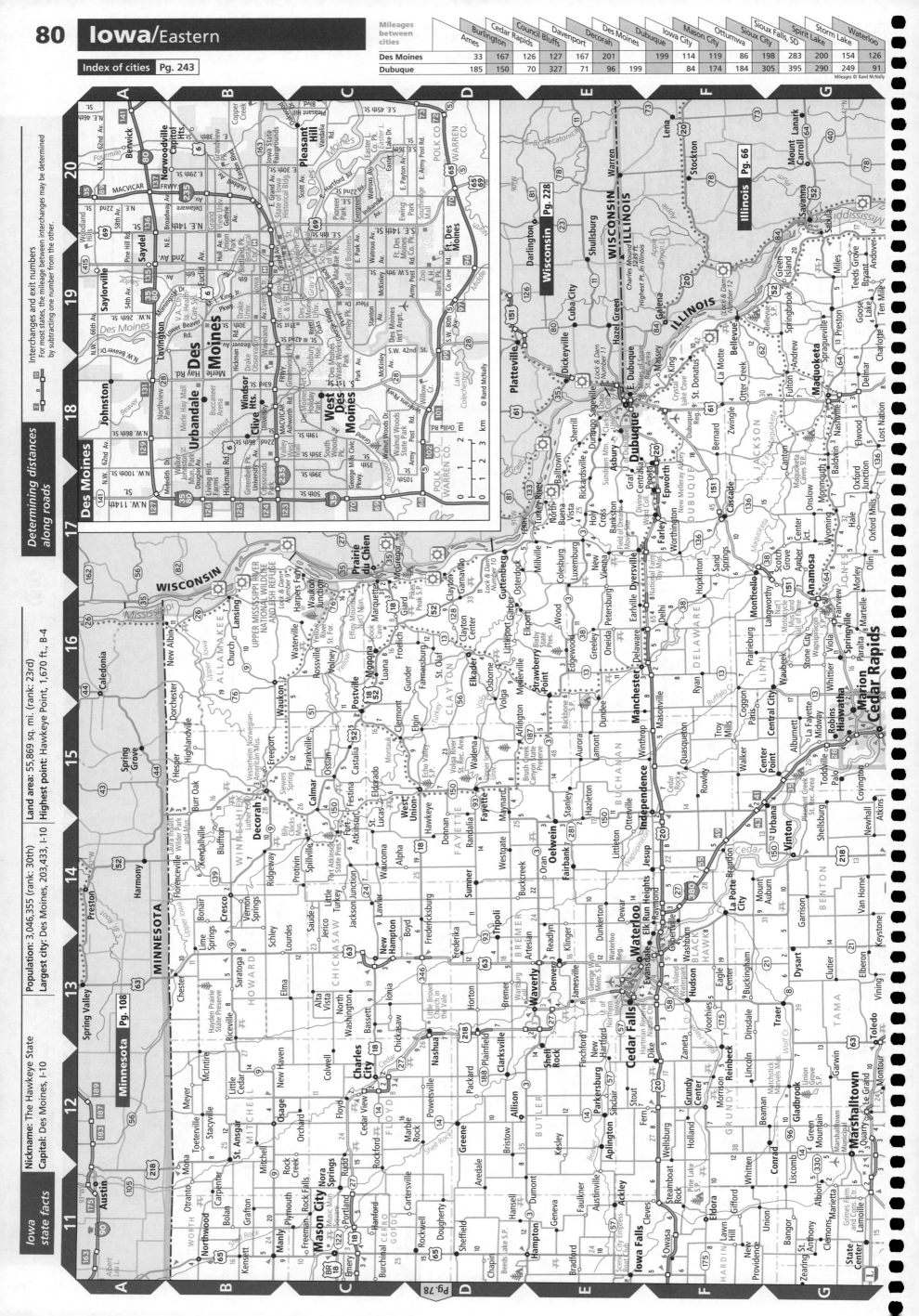

Illinois Pg. 66
Wisconsin Pg. 228
Minnesota Pg. 108
Pg. 78

Mileages between cities

	Ames	Burlington	Cedar Rapids	Council Bluffs	Davenport	Decorah	Des Moines	Dubuque	Iowa City	Mason City	Ottumwa	Sioux City	Sioux Falls, SD	Spirit Lake	Storm Lake	Waterloo
Des Moines	33	167	126	127	167	201		199	114	119	86	198	283	200	154	126
Dubuque	185	150	70	327	71	96	199		84	174	184	305	395	290	249	91

Mileages © Rand McNally

Iowa state facts

Nickname: The Hawkeye State
Capital: Des Moines

Population: 3,046,355 (rank: 30th)
Largest city: Des Moines, 203,433, I-10

Land area: 55,869 sq. mi. (rank: 23rd)
Highest point: Hawkeye Point, 1,670 ft., B-4

Determining distances along roads

For most states, the mileage between interchanges may be determined by subtracting one number from the other.

Interchanges and exit numbers

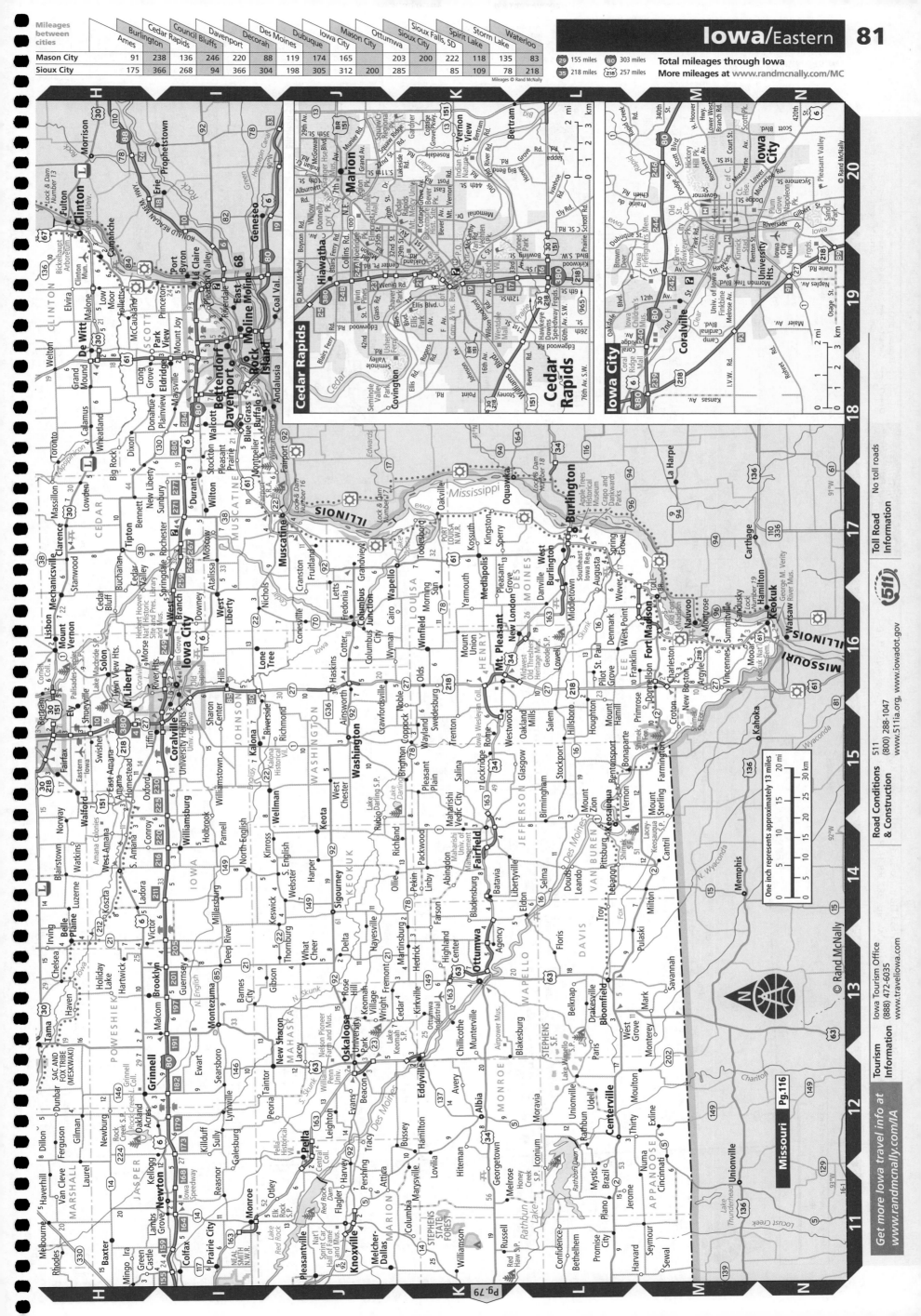

Mileages between cities

	Ames	Burlington	Cedar Rapids	Council Bluffs	Davenport	Decorah	Des Moines	Dubuque	Iowa City	Mason City	Ottumwa	Sioux City	Sioux Falls, SD	Spirit Lake	Storm Lake	Waterloo
Mason City	91	238	136	246	220	88	119	174	165		203	200	222	118	135	83
Sioux City	175	366	268	94	366	304	198	305	312	200	285		85	109	78	218

Mileages © Rand McNally

29 155 miles	80 303 miles
35 218 miles	218 257 miles

Total mileages through Iowa
More mileages at www.randmcnally.com/MC

Tourism Information — Iowa Tourism Office (888) 472-6035 www.traveliowa.com

Road Conditions & Construction — 511 (800) 288-1047 www.511ia.org, www.iowadot.gov

Get more Iowa travel info at www.randmcnally.com/IA

Toll Road Information — No toll roads

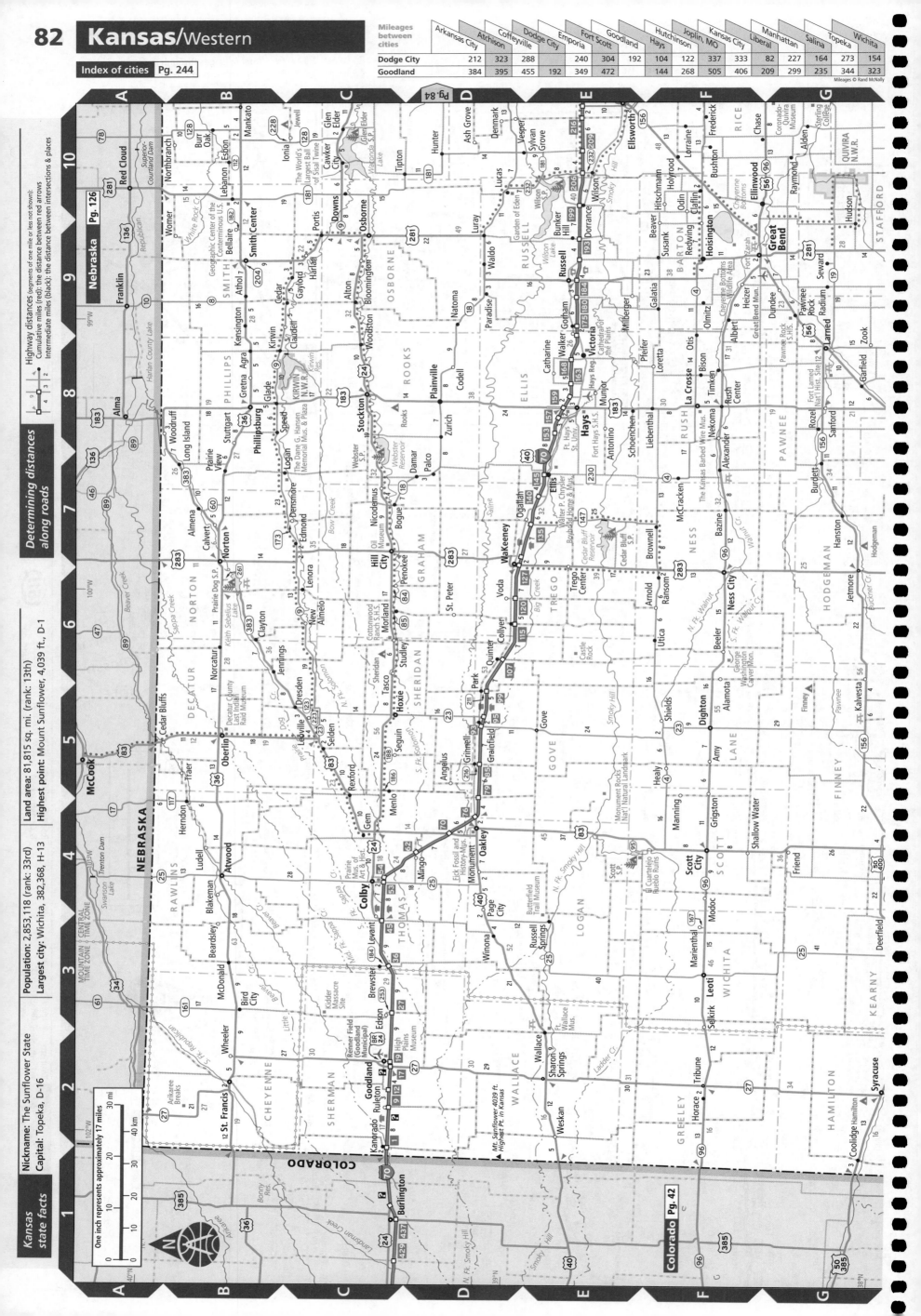

Mileages between cities	Arkansas City	Atchison	Coffeyville	Dodge City	Emporia	Fort Scott	Goodland	Hays	Hutchinson	Joplin, MO	Kansas City	Liberal	Manhattan	Salina	Topeka	Wichita
Dodge City	212	323	288		240	304	192	104	122	337	333	82	227	164	273	154
Goodland	384	395	455	192	349	472		144	268	505	406	209	299	235	344	323

Mileages © Rand McNally

Pg. 84

Pg. 126

Colorado Pg. 42

Determining distances along roads

Highway distances (segments of one mile or less not shown); the distance between red arrows
Cumulative miles (red); the distance between intersections & places
Intermediate miles (black); the distance between intersections & places

Kansas state facts

Nickname: The Sunflower State
Capital: Topeka, D-16

Population: 2,853,118 (rank: 33rd)
Largest city: Wichita, 382,368, H-13

Land area: 81,815 sq. mi. (rank: 13th)
Highest point: Mount Sunflower, 4,039 ft., D-1

One inch represents approximately 17 miles
0   30 mi
0   40 km

Mileages between cities	Arkansas City	Atchison	Coffeyville	Dodge City	Emporia	Fort Scott	Goodland	Hays	Hutchinson	Joplin, MO	Kansas City	Liberal	Manhattan	Salina	Topeka	Wichita
Joplin, MO	150	196	65	337	177	60	505	366	233		154	395	252	274	196	183
Kansas City	228	58	172	333	109	94	406	266	220	154		406	117	173	62	196

Mileages © Rand McNally

Total mileages through Kansas
More mileages at www.randmcnally.com/MC

| 35 | 235 miles | 56 | 464 miles |
| 70 | 424 miles | 81 | 220 miles |

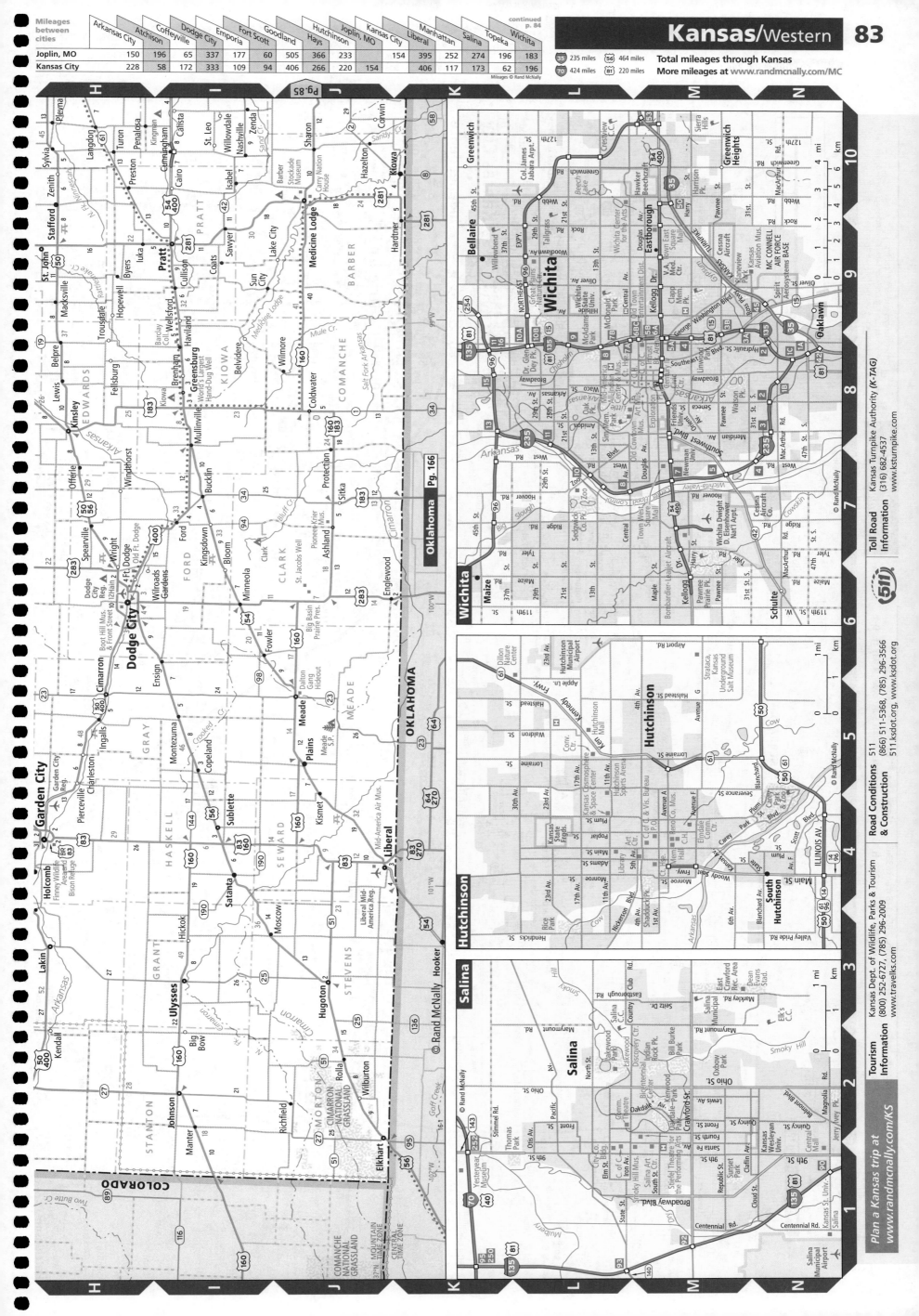

Tourism Information — Kansas Dept. of Wildlife, Parks & Tourism (800) 252-6727, (785) 296-2009 www.travelks.com

Road Conditions & Construction — 511 (866) 511-5368, (785) 296-3566 511.ksdot.org, www.ksdot.org

Toll Road Information — Kansas Turnpike Authority (K-TAG) (316) 682-4537 www.ksturnpike.org

Plan a Kansas trip at www.randmcnally.com/KS

Mileages between cities	Arkansas City	Atchison	Coffeyville	Dodge City	Emporia	Fort Scott	Goodland	Hutchinson	Joplin, MO	Kansas City	Liberal	Manhattan	Salina	Topeka	Wichita
Salina	151	160	224	164	117	238	235	96	65	274	173	246	65	109	90
Smith Center	266	213	338	195	231	342	175	91	155	387	263	277	150	117	206	205

Mileages © Rand McNally

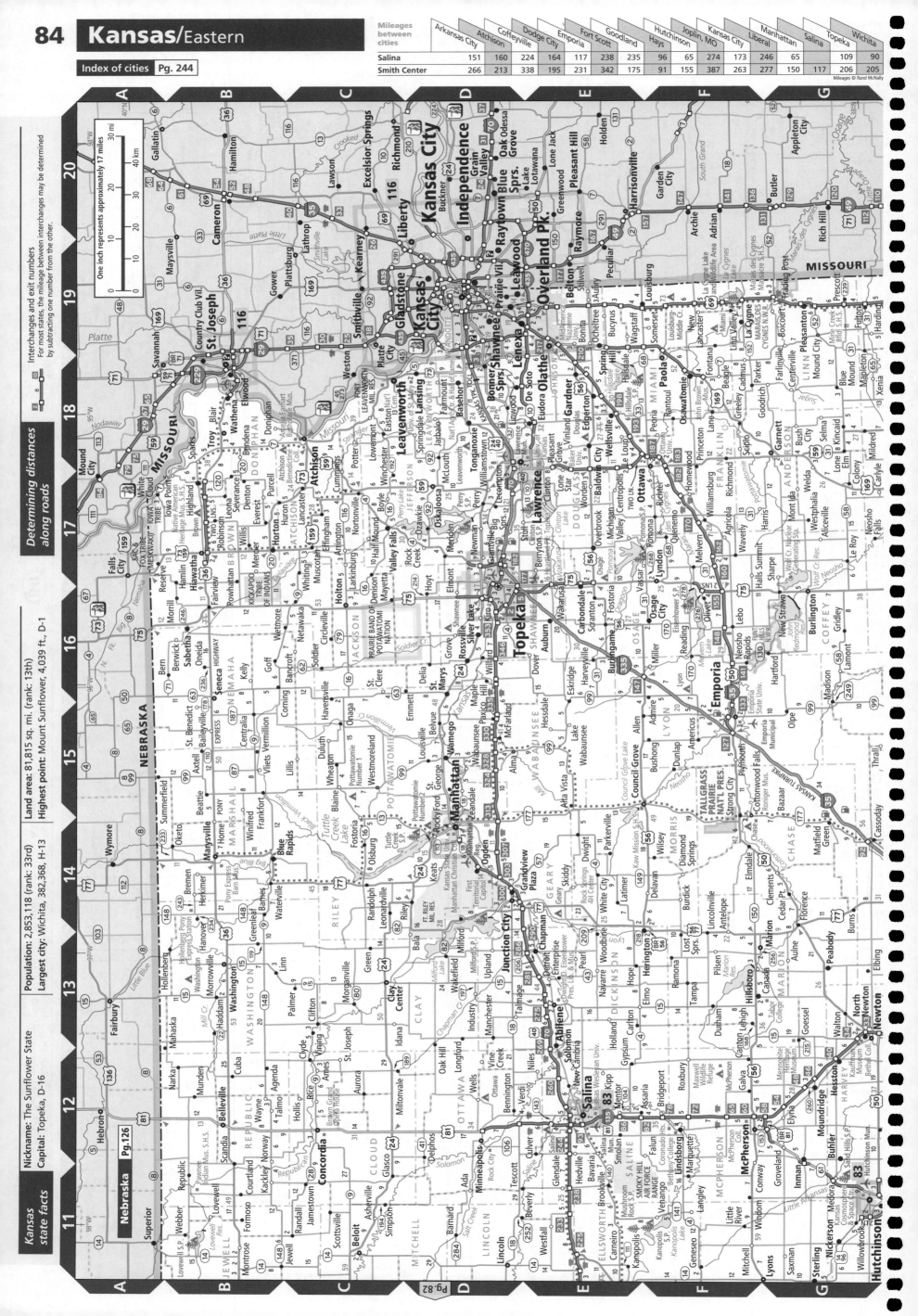

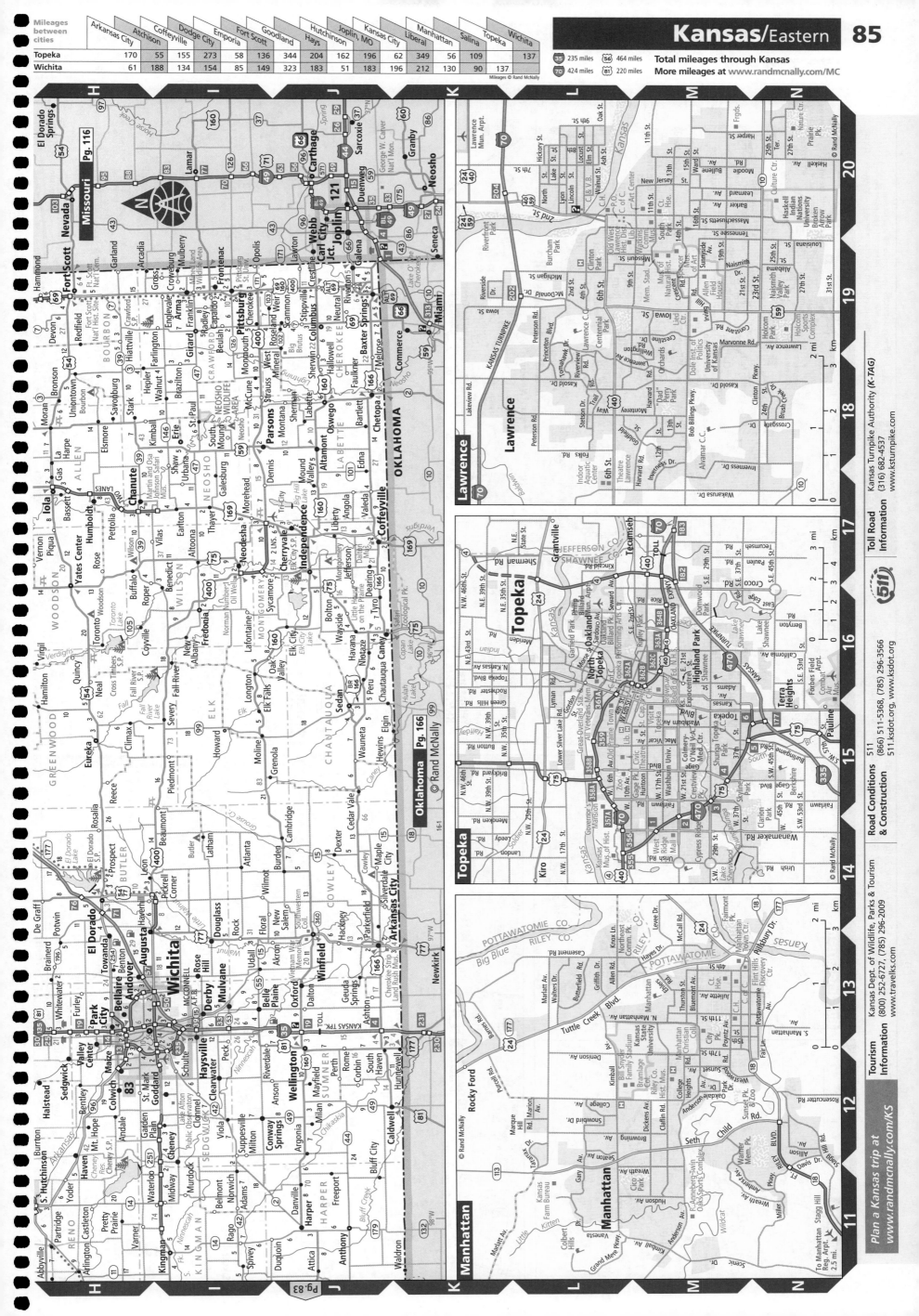

Total mileages through Kansas

More mileages at www.randmcnally.com/MC

Mileages between cities	Arkansas City	Atchison	Coffeyville	Dodge City	Emporia	Fort Scott	Goodland	Hays	Hutchinson	Joplin, MO	Kansas City	Liberal	Manhattan	Salina	Topeka	Wichita
Topeka	170	55	155	273	58	136	344	204	162	196	62	349	56	109		137
Wichita	61	188	134	154	85	149	323	183	51	183	196	212	130	90	137	

Mileages © Rand McNally

Total mileages through Kansas

35 235 miles 56 464 miles
70 424 miles 81 220 miles

Mileages between cities	Ashland	Bowling Green	Cave City	Covington	Elizabethtown	Frankfort	Hopkinsville	Lexington	Louisville	Mayfield	Maysville	Middlesboro	Owensboro	Paducah	Pikeville	Somerset
Ashland		269	242	138	202	140	325	117	187	383	76	227	294	372	96	175
Bowling Green	269		31	209	70	147	64	151	113	160	216	198	71	151	265	109

Mileages © Rand McNally

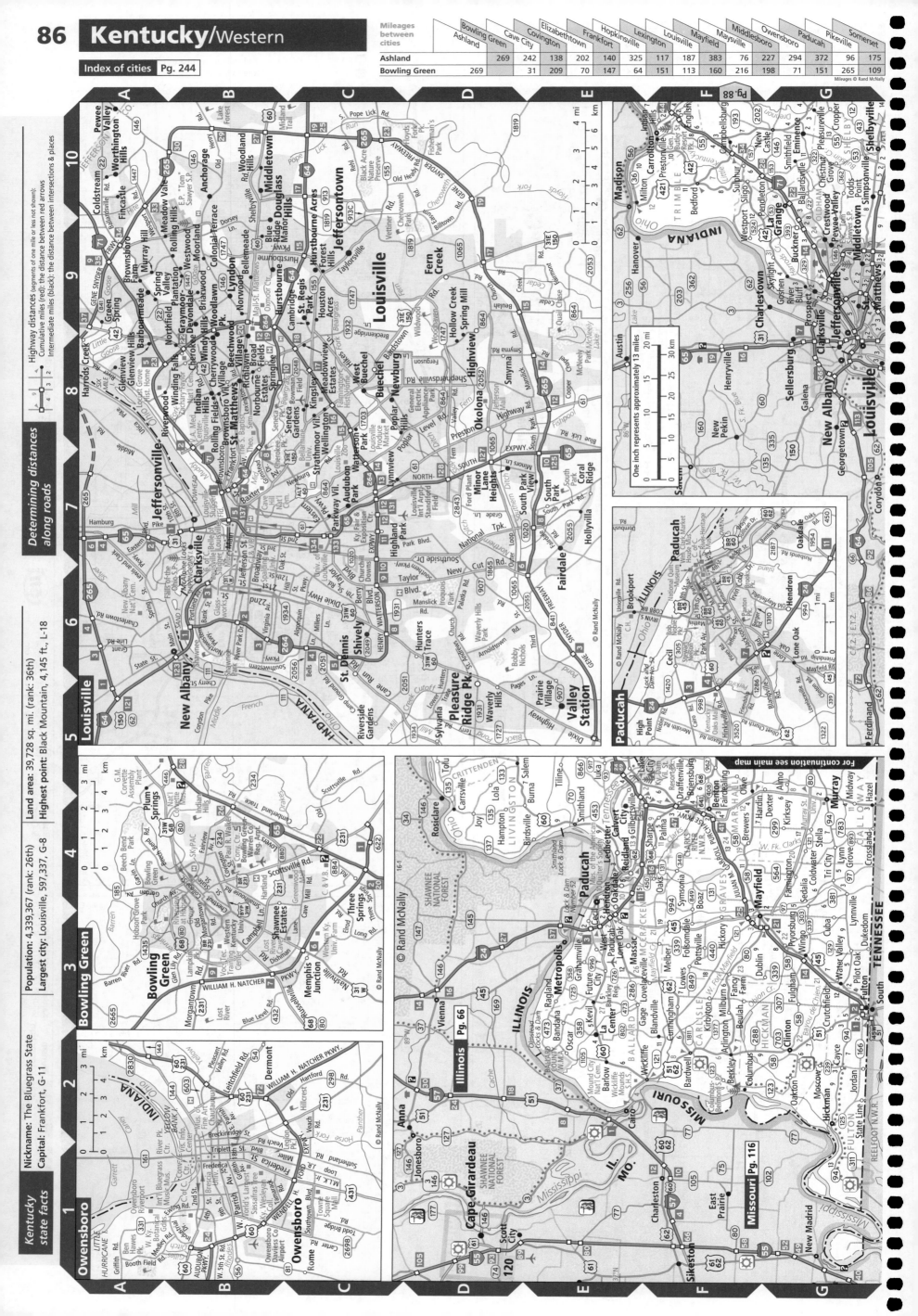

Mileages between cities	Ashland	Bowling Green	Cave City	Covington	Elizabethtown	Frankfort	Hopkinsville	Lexington	Louisville	Mayfield	Maysville	Middlesboro	Owensboro	Paducah	Pikeville	Somerset
Covington	138	209	181		140	78	265	81	97	322	59	208	203	312	216	157
Lexington	117	151	124	81	84	29	207		76	266	63	130	177	256	140	78

continued p. 88

64 185 miles	71 97 miles
65 137 miles	75 192 miles

Total mileages through Kentucky
More mileages at www.randmcnally.com/MC

Mileages © Rand McNally

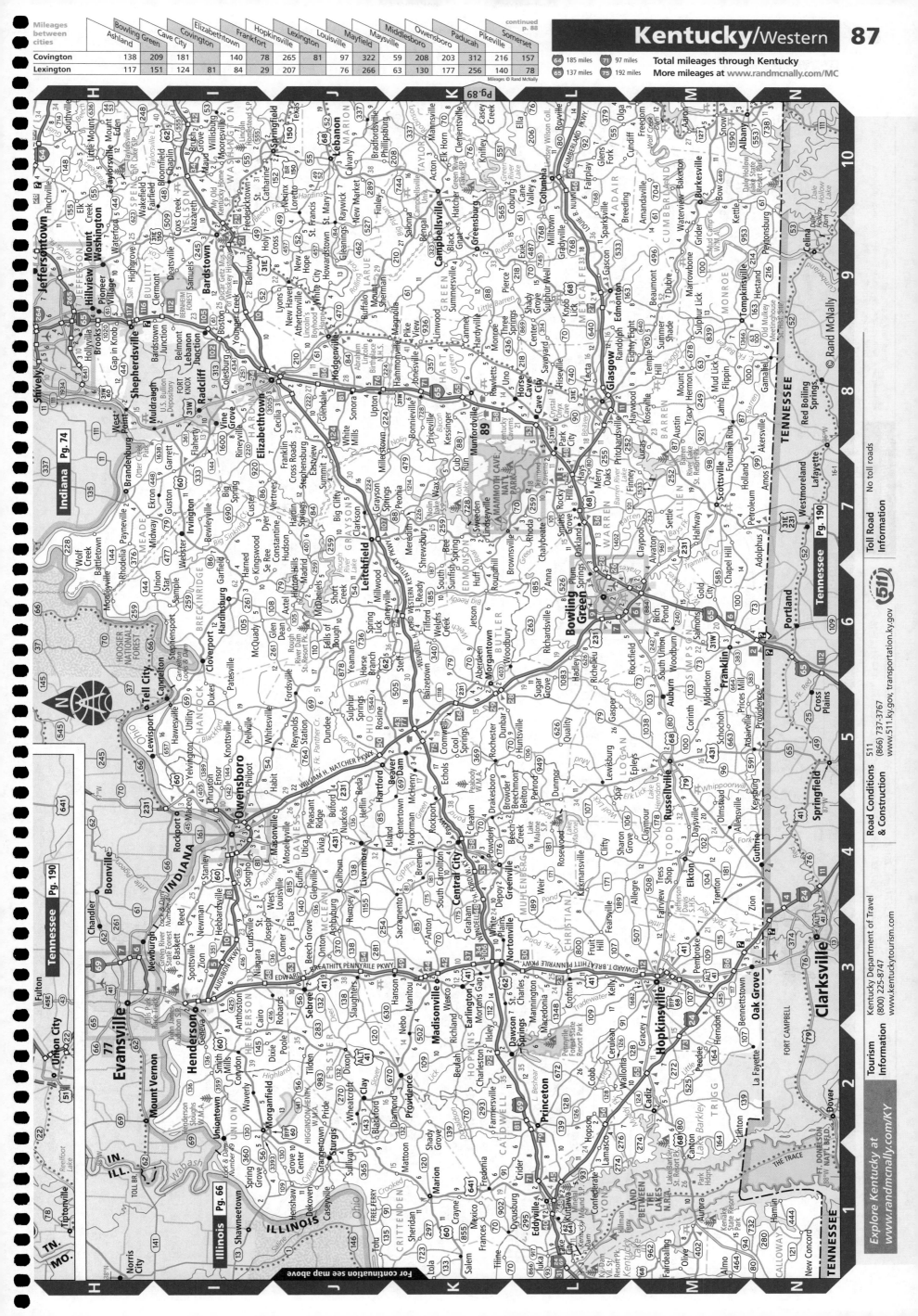

Mileages between cities	Ashland	Bowling Green	Cave City	Covington	Elizabethtown	Frankfort	Hopkinsville	Lexington	Louisville	Mayfield	Maysville	Middlesboro	Owensboro	Paducah	Pikeville	Somerset
Louisville	187	113	85	97	44	50	170	76		227	133	203	106	216	211	124
Middlesboro	227	198	176	208	182	157	265	130	203	363	191		275	353	125	88

Mileages © Rand McNally

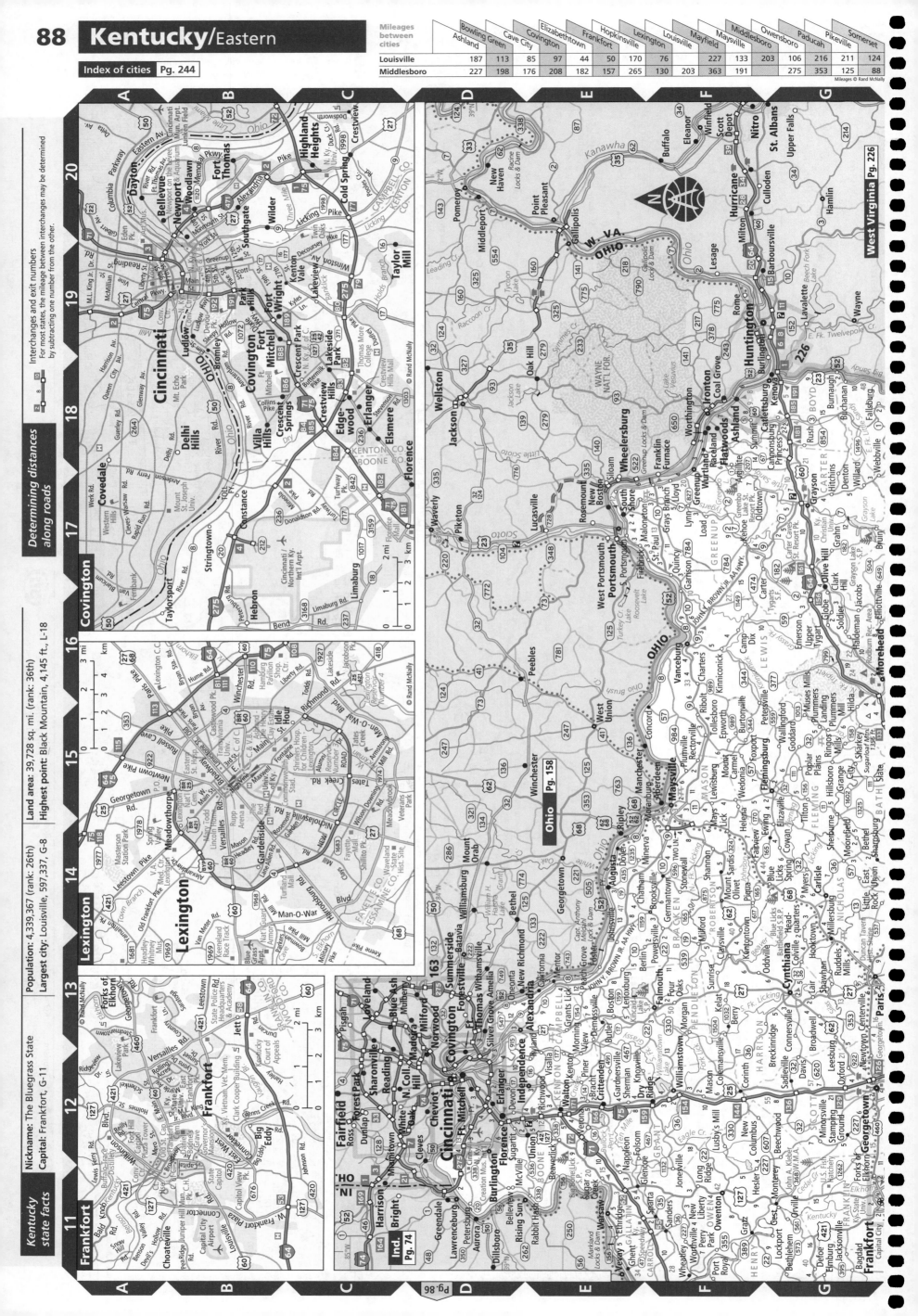

Mileages between cities	Ashland	Bowling Green	Cave City	Covington	Elizabethtown	Frankfort	Hopkinsville	Lexington	Louisville	Mayfield	Maysville	Middlesboro	Owensboro	Paducah	Pikeville	Somerset
Owensboro	294	71	108	203	94	159	96	177	106	154	242	275		143	318	187
Paducah	372	151	186	312	172	250	72	256	216	24	319	353	143		396	265

Mileages © Rand McNally

64	185 miles
65	137 miles
71	97 miles
75	192 miles

Total mileages through Kentucky
More mileages at www.randmcnally.com/MC

Virginia Pg. 212

One inch represents approximately 13 miles

Mammoth Cave National Park

Tourism Information — Kentucky Department of Travel — (800) 225-8747 — www.kentuckytourism.com

Road Conditions & Construction — 511 — (866) 737-3767 — www.511.ky.gov, transportation.ky.gov

Explore Kentucky at www.randmcnally.com/KY

Mileages between cities	Beaumont, TX	Houma	Lake Charles	Monroe	New Orleans	Shreveport	Vicksburg, MS			Beaumont, TX	Houma	Lake Charles	Monroe	New Orleans	Shreveport	Vicksburg, MS
Alexandria	125	155	190	97	95	218	123	147	Gulfport, MS	134	318	131	258	276	78	375	201
Baton Rouge		183	85	124	186	79	250	157	Lafayette	55	133	102	73	182	134	211	212

Mileages © Rand McNally

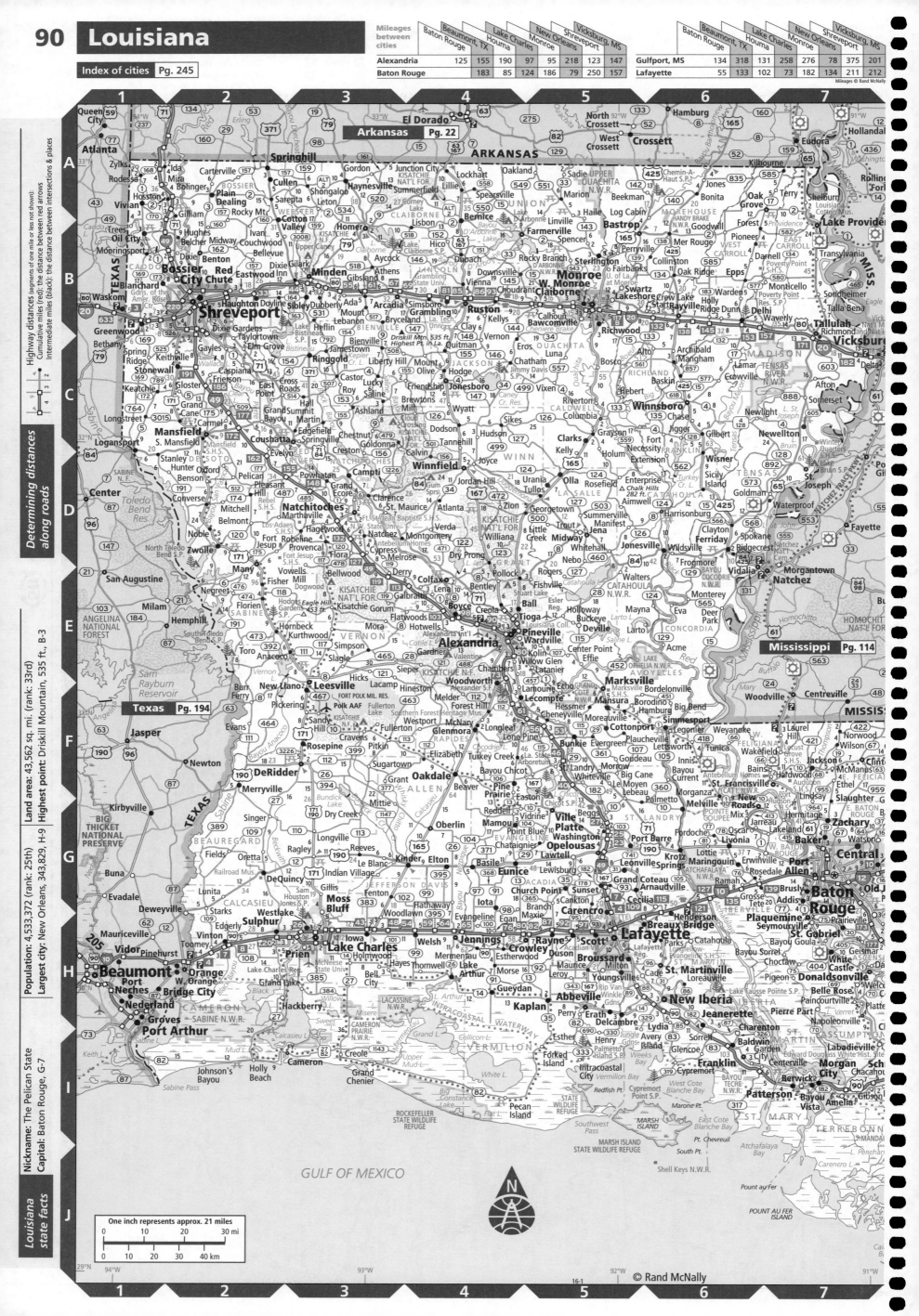

Mileages between cities	Beaumont, TX	Baton Rouge	Lake Charles	Houma	Monroe	New Orleans	Shreveport	Vicksburg, MS
Lake Charles	124	60		177	190	203	184	243
New Orleans	79	262	56		203	281	340	207

	Beaumont, TX	Baton Rouge	Lake Charles	Houma	Monroe	New Orleans	Shreveport	Vicksburg, MS
Shreveport	250	206	314	184	98	340		171
Vicksburg, MS	157	301	234	243	74	207	171	

Mileages © Rand McNally

Total mileages through Louisiana
More mileages at www.randmcnally.com/MC

10 274 miles 49 208 miles
20 190 miles 55 66 miles

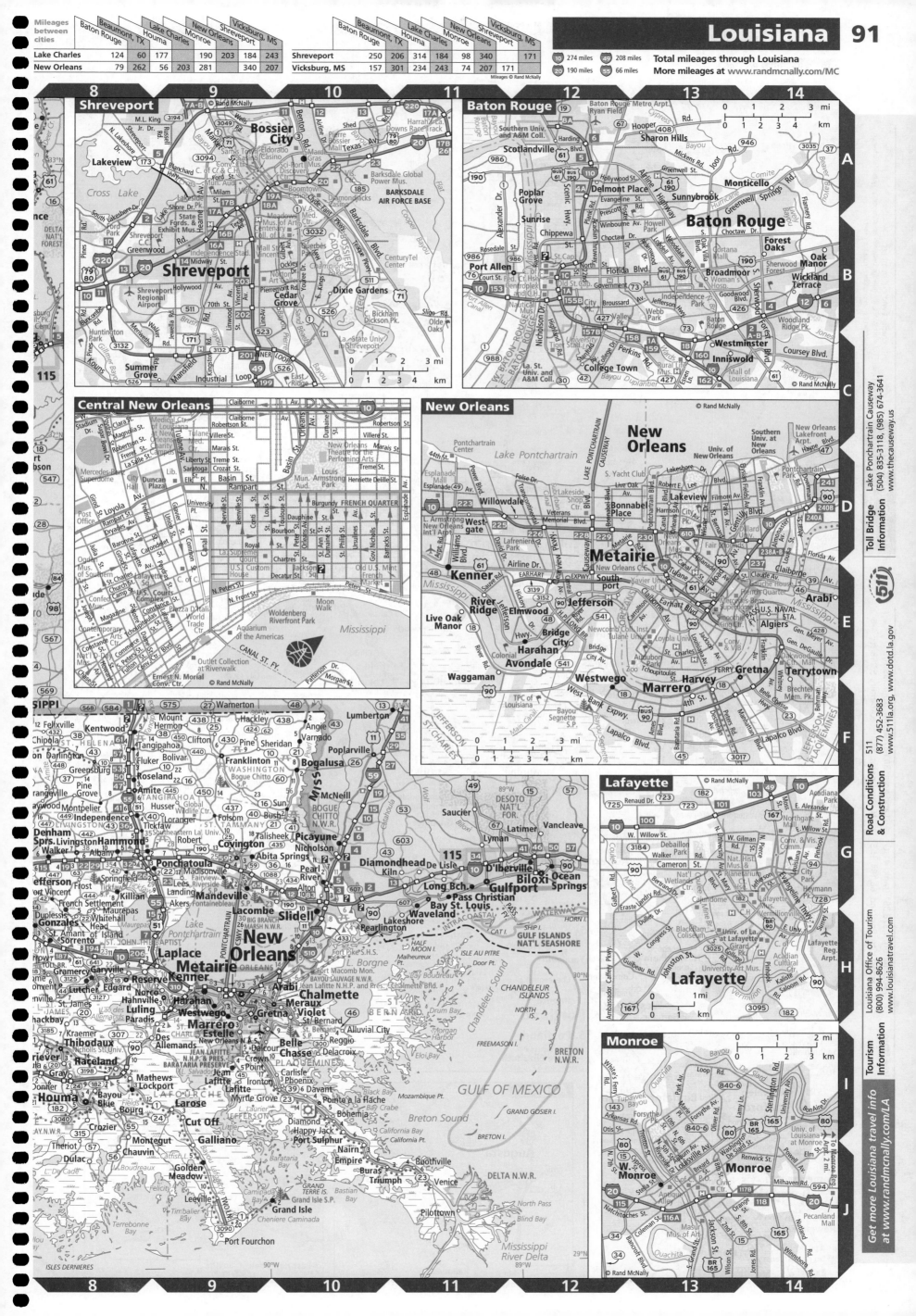

Index of cities Pg. 246

Mileages between cities

	Auburn	Bangor	Bar Harbor	Eastport	Houlton	Millinocket	Portland	Rangeley
Bangor	107		47	120	118	72	128	120
Eastport	226	120	118		115	125	247	242
Houlton	225	118	167	115		69	246	238
Madawaska	326	219	267	218	102	170	347	339

Mileages © Rand McNally

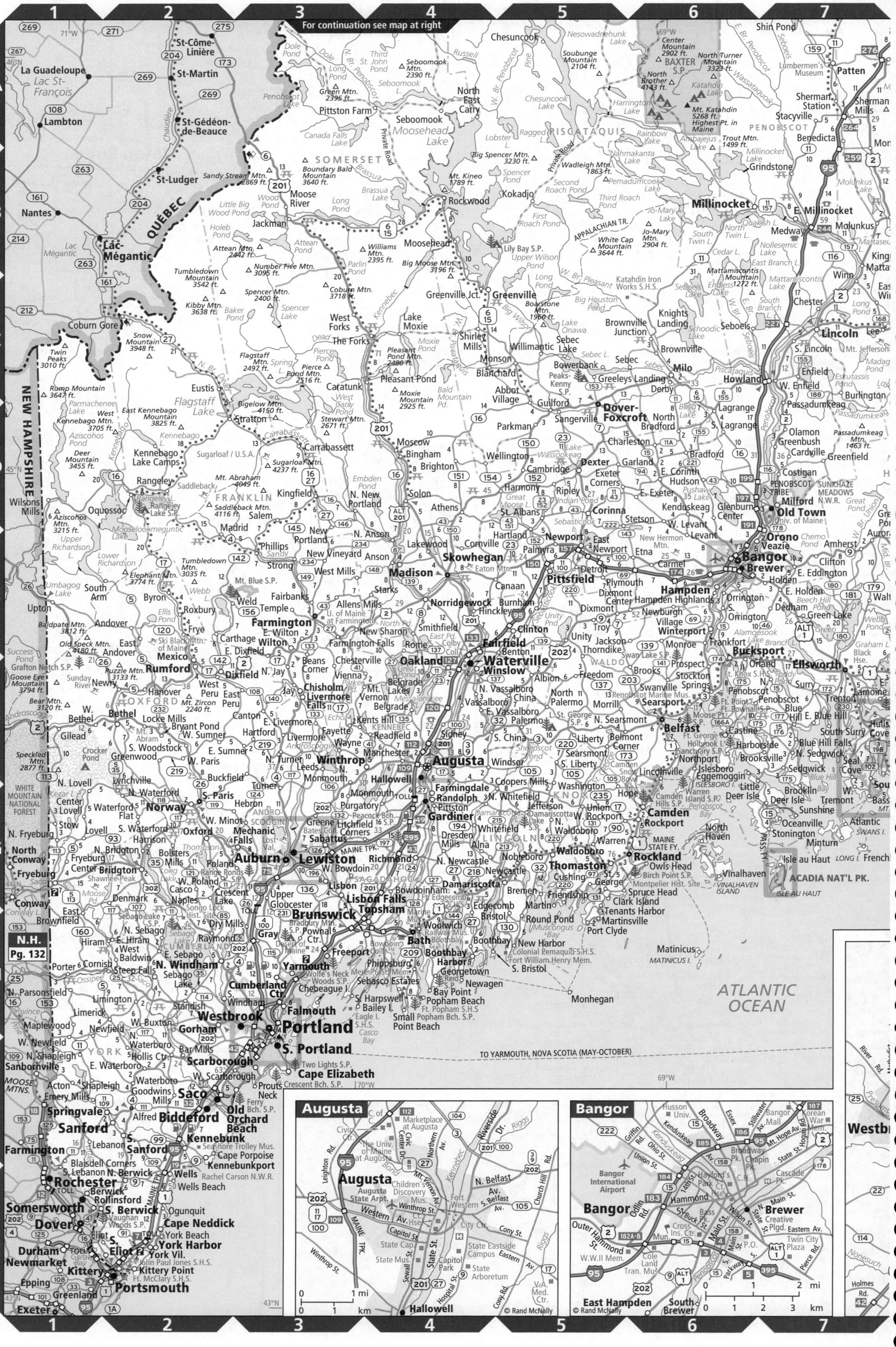

Maine state facts

Nickname: The Pine Tree State
Capital: Augusta, F-4

Population: 1,328,361 (rank: 41st)
Largest city: Portland, 66,194, H-3

Land area: 30,862 sq. mi. (rank: 39th)
Highest point: Mount Katahdin, 5,268 ft., A-6

Determining distances along roads

Interchanges and exit numbers
For most states, the mileage between interchanges may be determined by subtracting one number from the other.

Mileages between cities

	Auburn	Bangor	Bar Harbor	Eastport	Houlton	Millinocket	Portland	Rangeley
Portland	35	128	174	247	246	181		118
Portsmouth, NH	81	180	225	301	298	231	51	165
Rangeley	84	120	165	242	238	153	118	
Waterville	53	55	101	174	173	107	75	77

Mileages © Rand McNally

Total mileages through Maine: 95 299 miles; 1 315 miles; 2 273 miles; 201 164 miles

More mileages at www.randmcnally.com/MC

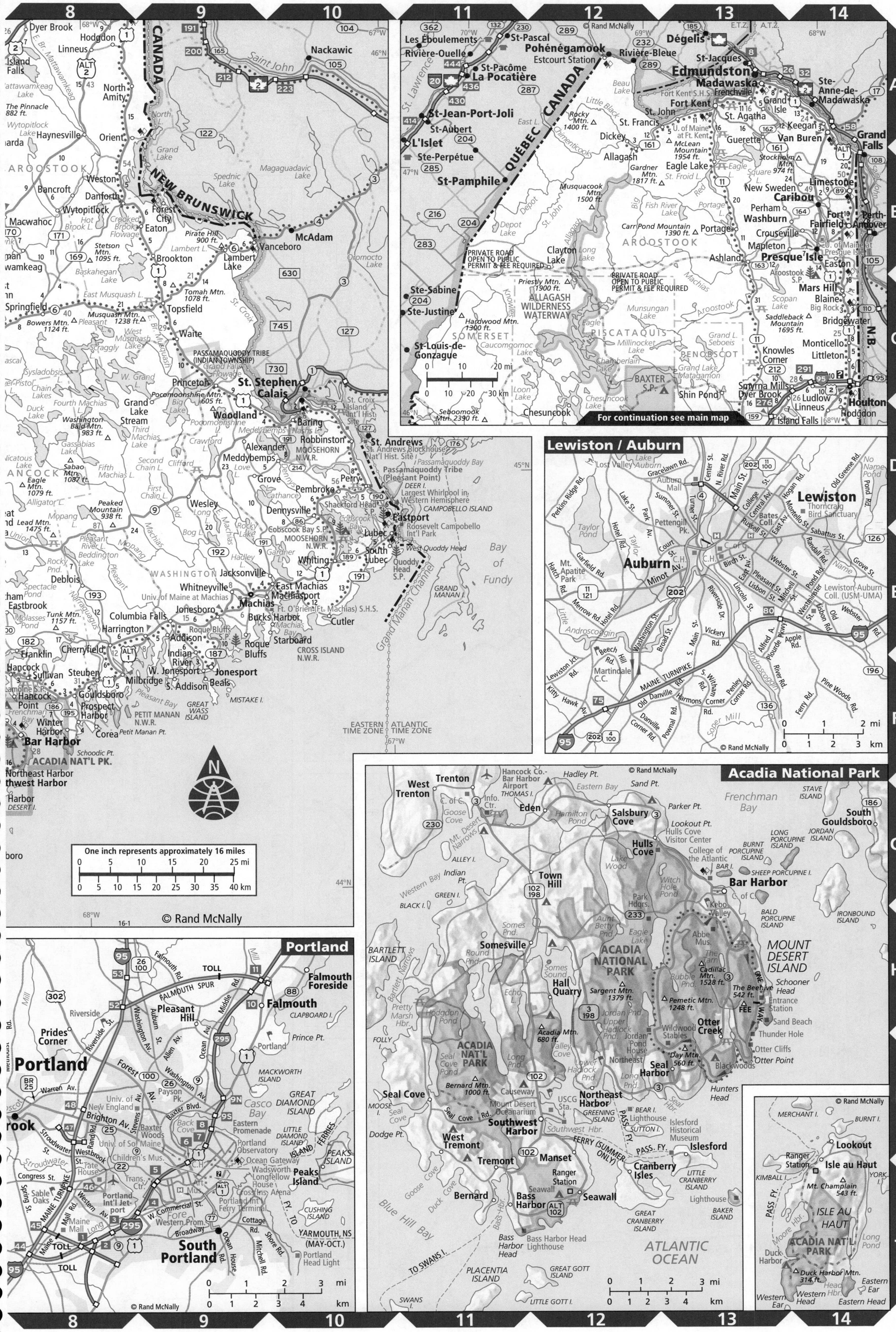

Toll Road Information: Maine Turnpike Authority (E-ZPass) (888) 682-7277 www.maineturnpike.com

Road Conditions & Construction: 511 (866) 282-7578, (207) 624-3595 www.511maine.gov, www.maine.gov/mdot

Tourism Information: Maine Office of Tourism (888) 624-6345 www.visitmaine.com

Plan a Maine trip at www.randmcnally.com/ME

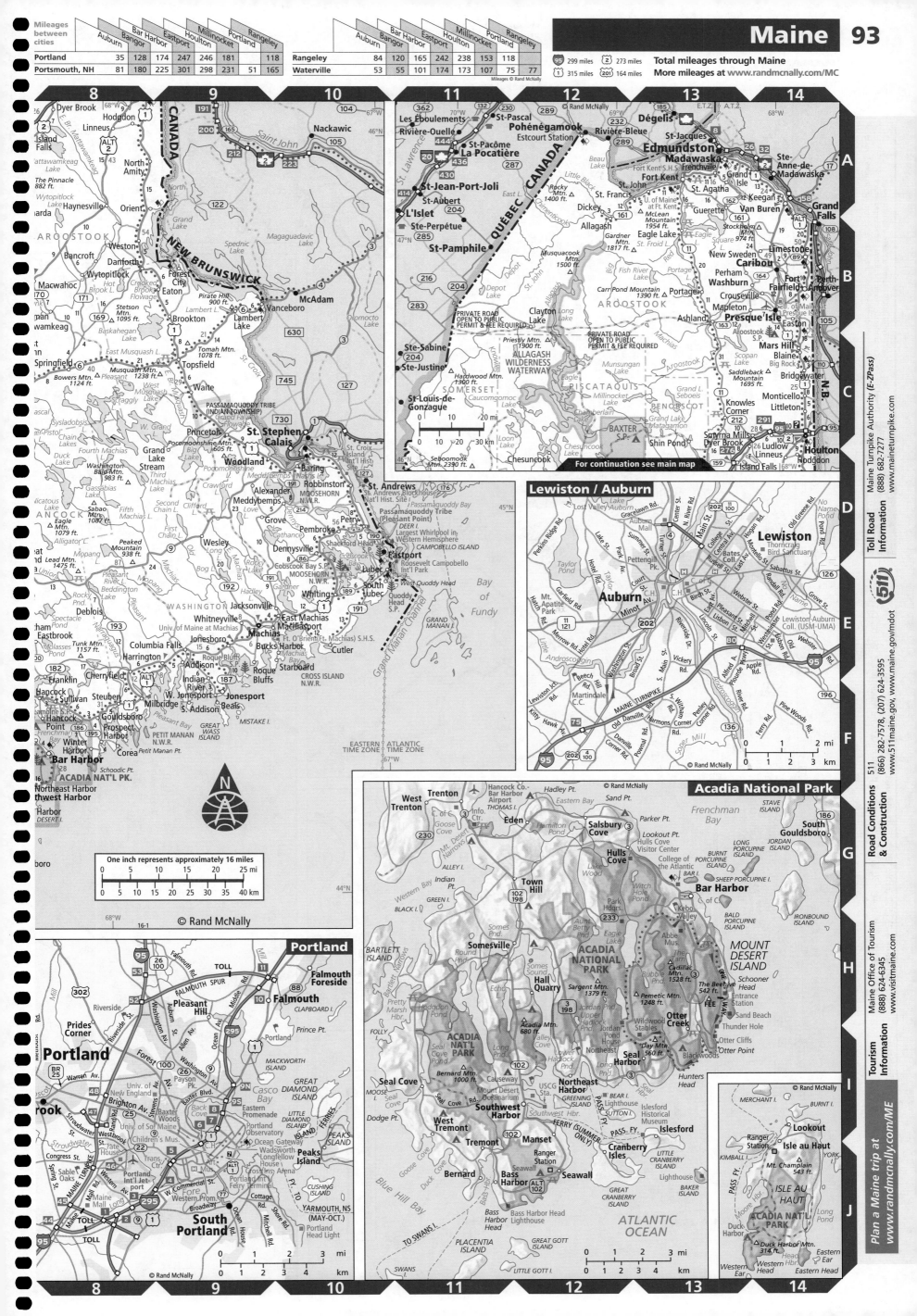

Mileages between cities	Aberdeen	Annapolis	Baltimore	Cambridge	Chestertown	Cumberland	Frederick	Hagerstown	Lexington Park	Ocean City	Pocomoke City	Rockville	St. Charles	Salisbury	Washington, DC	Wilmington, DE
Aberdeen		58	31	113	65	171	83	107	122	134	152	74	90	122	70	42
Annapolis	58		28	57	47	157	68	93	73	108	120	42	41	89	30	96

Mileages © Rand McNally

Maryland state facts

Nickname: The Old Line State
Capital: Annapolis, E-14
Population: 5,773,552 (rank: 19th)
Largest city: Baltimore, 620,961, C-13
Land area: 9,774 sq. mi. (rank: 42nd)
Highest point: Backbone Mountain, 3,360 ft, D-1

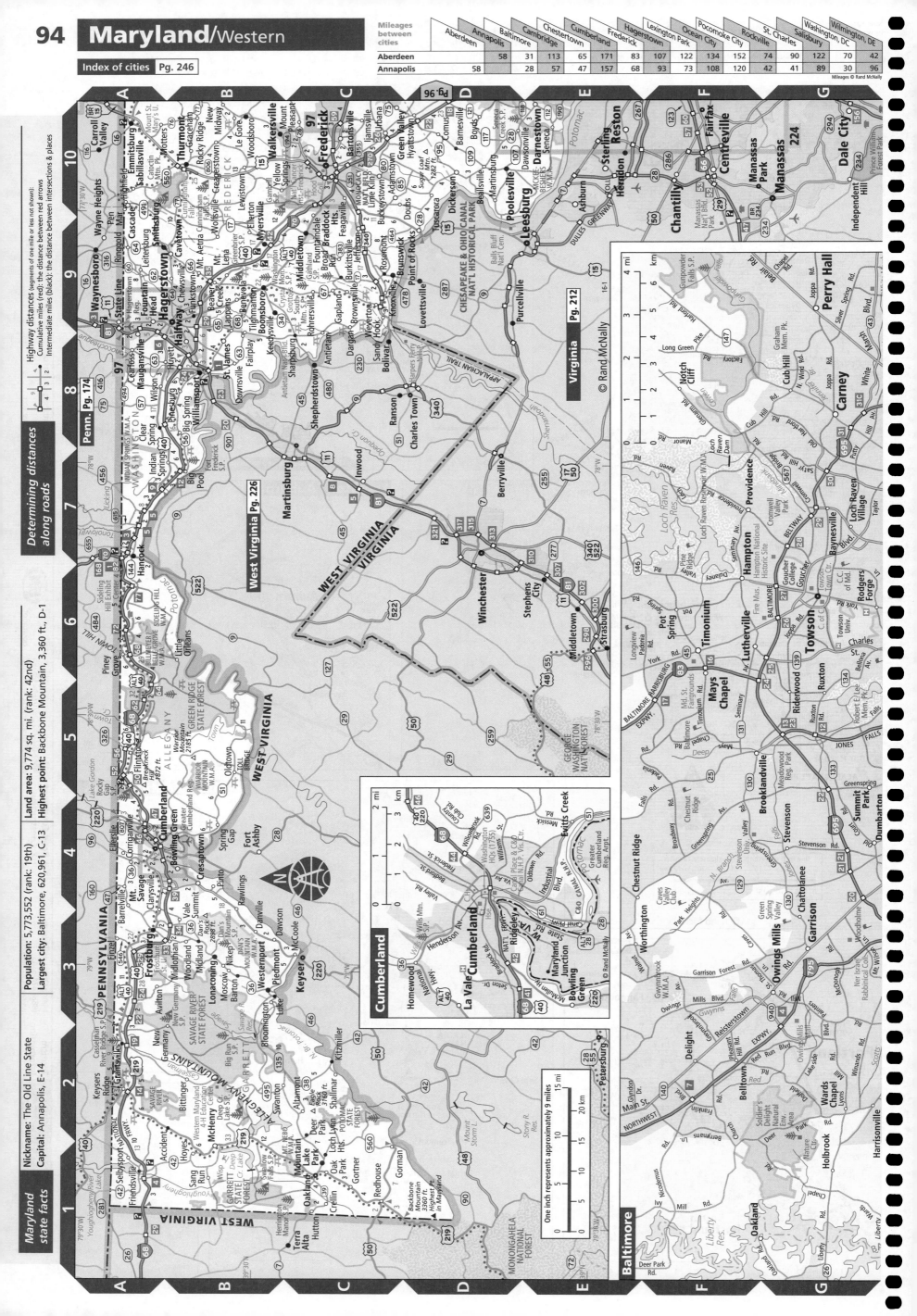

© Rand McNally

Mileages between cities	Aberdeen	Annapolis	Baltimore	Cambridge	Chestertown	Cumberland	Frederick	Hagerstown	Lexington Park	Ocean City	Pocomoke City	Rockville	St. Charles	Salisbury	Washington, DC	Wilmington, DE
Baltimore	31	28		84	73	136	47	72	93	136	146	42	59	116	39	70
Cumberland	171	157	136	212	203		88	67	200	263	275	116	166	244	134	209

Mileages © Rand McNally

Total mileages through Maryland

68	81 miles	81 — 12 miles
70	94 miles	95 — 110 miles

More mileages at www.randmcnally.com/MC

continued p. 96

Pg. 97

Explore Maryland at
www.randmcnally.com/MD

Tourism Information	Maryland Office of Tourism (866) 639-3526 www.visitmaryland.org
Road Conditions & Construction	511, (855) 466-9511, (410) 582-5650 www.md511.org www.roads.maryland.gov
Toll Road Information	Maryland Transportation Authority (E-ZPass) (866) 713-1596, In Maryland: (410) 537-1000 www.mdta.maryland.gov

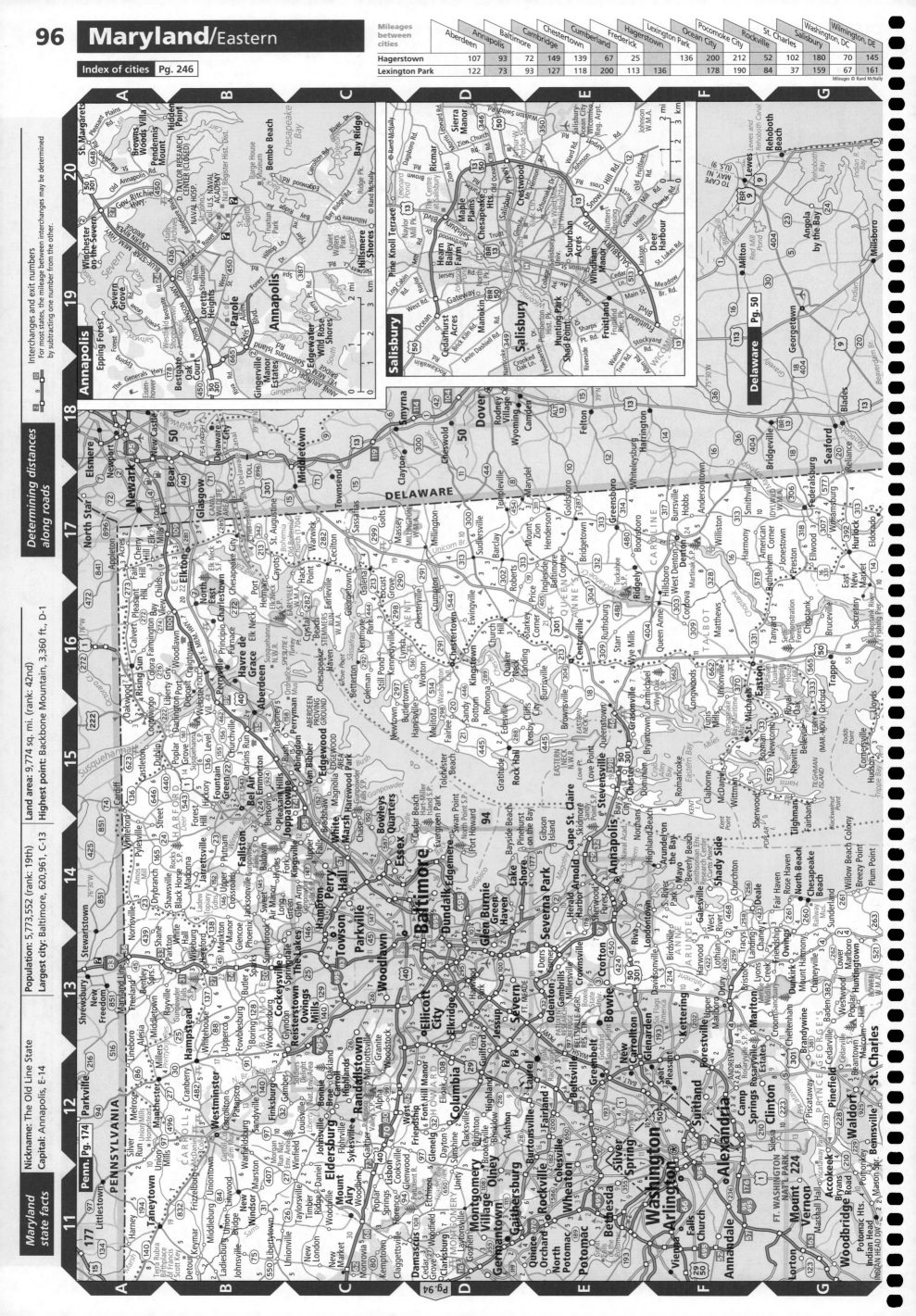

Mileages between cities

Mileages between cities	Aberdeen	Annapolis	Baltimore	Cambridge	Chestertown	Cumberland	Frederick	Hagerstown	Lexington Park	Ocean City	Pocomoke City	Rockville	St. Charles	Salisbury	Washington, DC	Wilmington, DE
Salisbury	122	89	116	32	78	244	156	180	159	29	26	130	128		118	107
Washington, DC	70	30	39	86	76	134	48	70	67	139	148	19	30	118		109

Mileages © Rand McNally

68 81 miles · 70 94 miles · 81 12 miles · 95 110 miles

Total mileages through Maryland

More mileages at www.randmcnally.com/MC

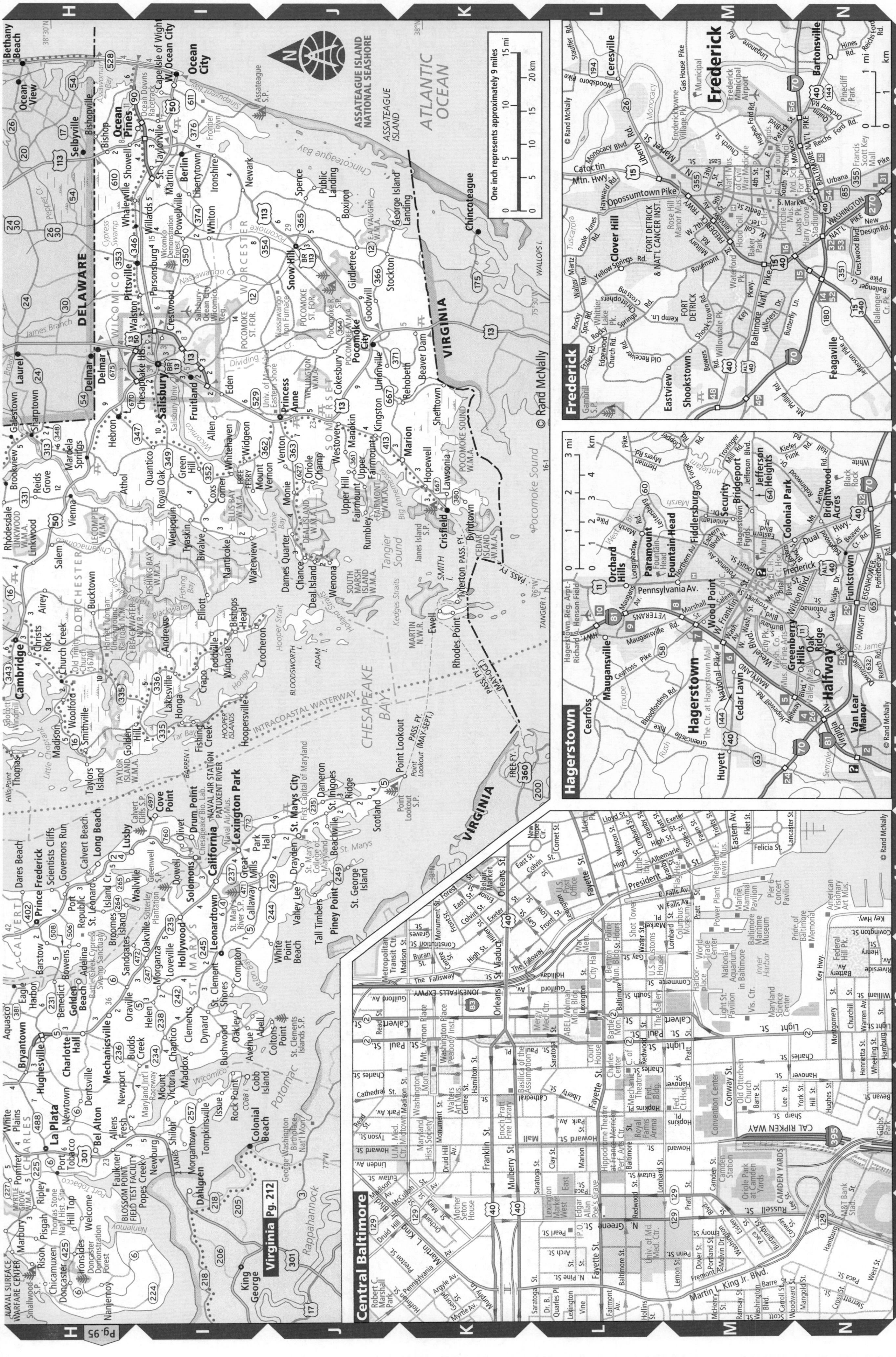

Tourism Information Maryland Office of Tourism (866) 639-3526 www.visitmaryland.org

Road Conditions & Construction 511, (855) 466-9511, (410) 582-5650 www.md511.org www.roads.maryland.gov

Toll Road Information Maryland Transportation Authority (*E-ZPass*) (866) 713-1596, In Maryland: (410) 537-1000 www.mdta.maryland.gov

Explore Maryland at www.randmcnally.com/MD

Index of cities Pg. 246

Mileages between cities	Boston	Brockton	Falmouth	Fitchburg	Gloucester	Greenfield	Lowell	Nantucket	New Bedford	North Adams	Pittsfield	Plymouth	Providence, RI	Provincetown	Springfield	Worcester
Boston		24	76	47	39	94	29	101*	58	157	136	40	50	116	90	43
Gloucester	39	63	114	74		120	47	140*	97	157	169	78	90	154	122	75

*via ferry

Mileages © Rand McNally

Massachusetts state facts

Nickname: The Bay State
Capital: Boston, E-14

Population: 6,547,629 (rank: 14th)
Largest city: Boston, 617,594, E-14

Land area: 7,840 sq. mi. (rank: 45th)
Highest point: Mount Greylock, 3,491 ft., C-2

Determining distances along roads

Highway distances (segments of one mile or less not shown):
Cumulative miles (red): the distance between red arrows
Intermediate miles (black): the distance between intersections & places

One inch represents approximately 7 miles

© Rand McNally

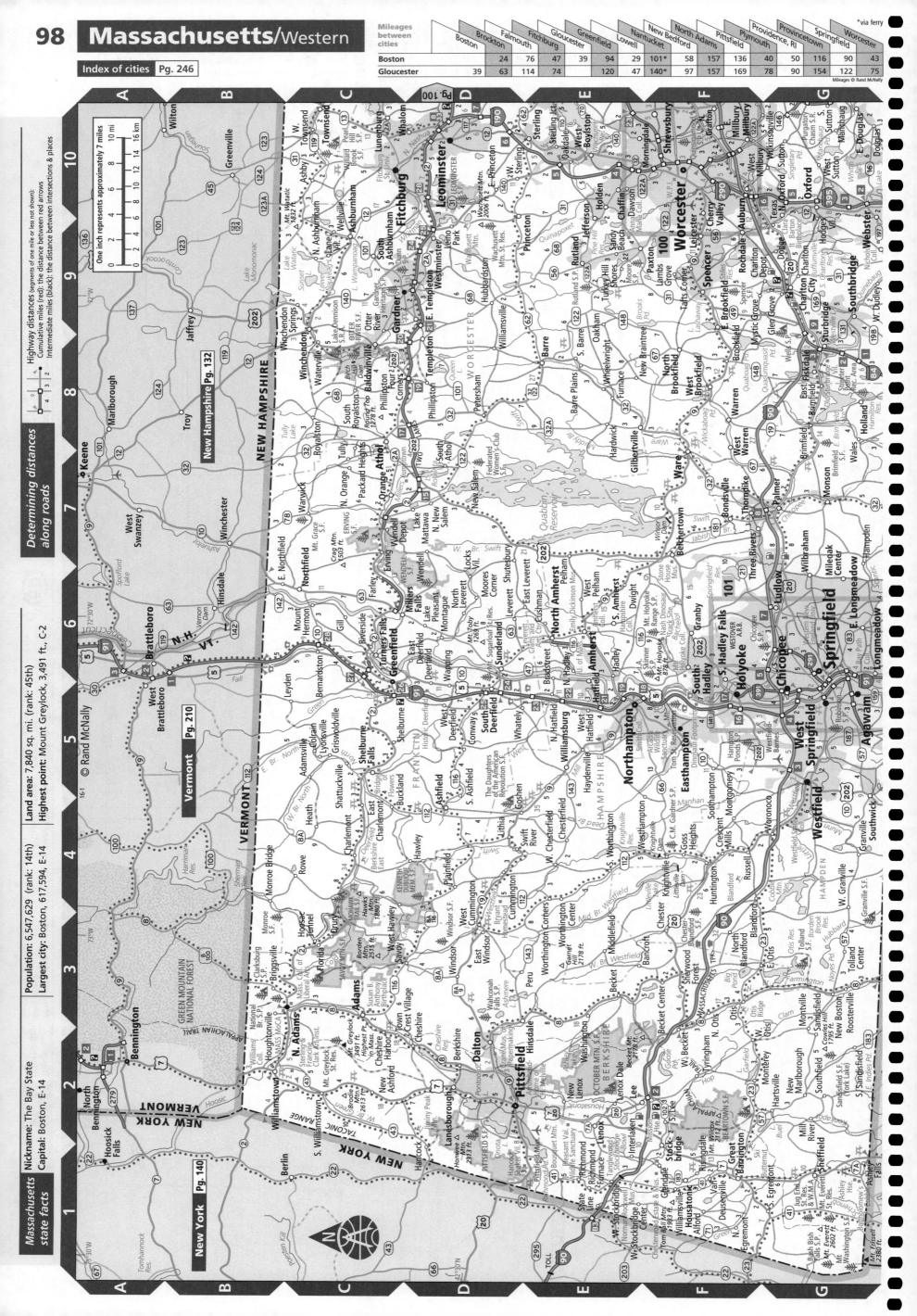

continued p. 100

Mileages between cities	Boston	Brockton	Falmouth	Fitchburg	Gloucester	Greenfield	Lowell	Nantucket	New Bedford	North Adams	Pittsfield	Plymouth	Providence, RI	Provincetown	Springfield	Worcester
Lowell	29	50	102	32	47	78		130*	84	115	139	69	69	145	92	41
New Bedford	58	37	40	94	97	148	84	77*		182	161	37	31	91	114	71

Mileages © Rand McNally

Total mileages through Massachusetts

| 90 | 136 miles | 93 | 47 miles |
| 91 | 55 miles | 95 | 92 miles |

More mileages at www.randmcnally.com/MC

Boston & Vicinity

Central Boston

Index of cities Pg. 246

Mileages between cities	Boston	Brockton	Falmouth	Fitchburg	Gloucester	Greenfield	Lowell	Nantucket	New Bedford	North Adams	Pittsfield	Plymouth	Providence, RI	Provincetown	Springfield	Worcester
Pittsfield	136	150	189	124	169	79	139	226*	161	22		167	130	240	51	98
Provincetown	116	106	69	162	154	208	145	78*	91	262	240	77	119		194	146

*via ferry

Mileages © Rand McNally

Massachusetts state facts

Nickname: The Bay State
Capital: Boston, E-14

Population: 6,547,629 (rank: 14th)
Largest city: Boston, 617,594, E-14

Land area: 7,840 sq. mi. (rank: 45th)
Highest point: Mount Greylock, 3,491 ft., C-2

Determining distances along roads

Interchanges and exit numbers
For most states, the mileage between interchanges may be determined by subtracting one number from the other.

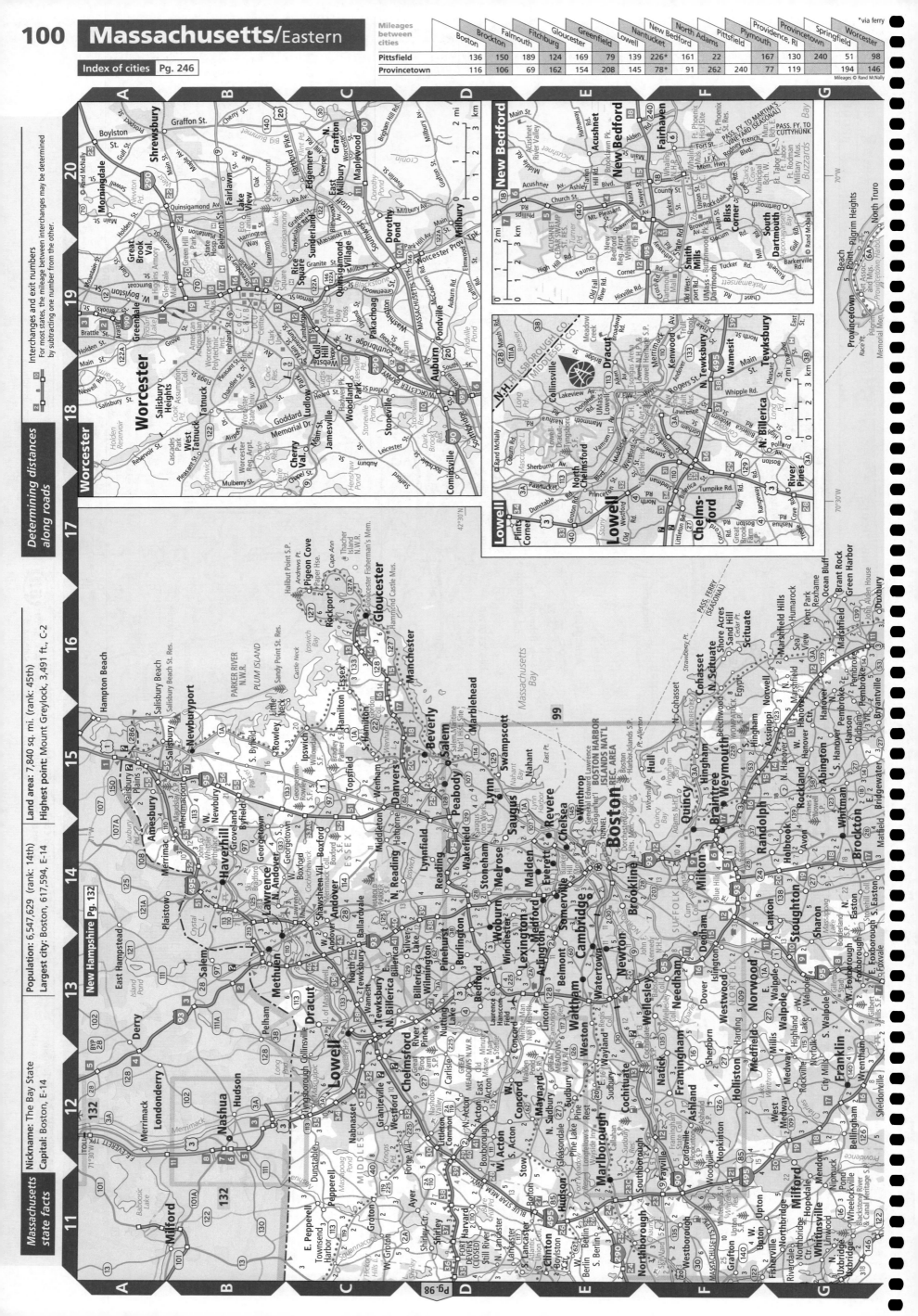

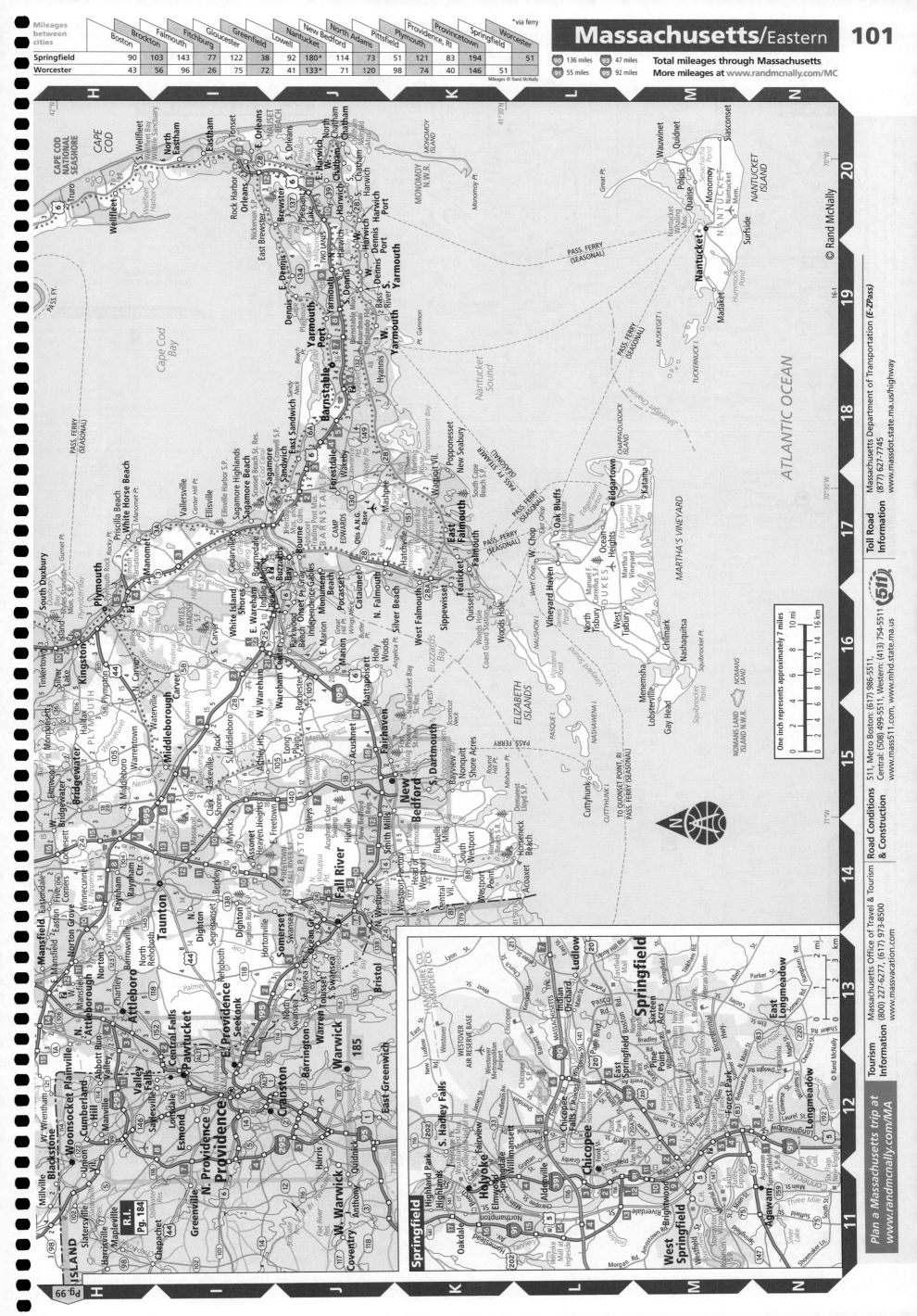

Mileages between cities	Boston	Brockton	Falmouth	Fitchburg	Gloucester	Greenfield	Lowell	Nantucket	New Bedford	North Adams	Pittsfield	Plymouth	Providence, RI	Provincetown	Springfield	Worcester
Springfield	90	103	143	77	122	38	92	180*	114	73	51	121	83	194		51
Worcester	43	56	96	26	75	72	41	133*	71	120	98	74	40	146	51	

*via ferry

Mileages © Rand McNally

Total mileages through Massachusetts
More mileages at www.randmcnally.com/MC

| 90 | 136 miles | 93 | 47 miles |
| 91 | 55 miles | 95 | 92 miles |

Index of cities Pg. 247

Mileages between cities	Alpena	Chicago, IL	Detroit	Grand Rapids	Houghton	Ironwood	Kalamazoo	Ludington	Mackinaw City	Menominee	Muskegon	Port Huron	Saginaw	Sault Ste. Marie	Toledo, OH	Traverse City
Ann Arbor	227	240	43	132	538	584	98	228	272	473	172	102	86	329	51	238
Detroit	244	280		157	553	599	140	252	290	488	197	62	102	345	59	255

Mileages © Rand McNally

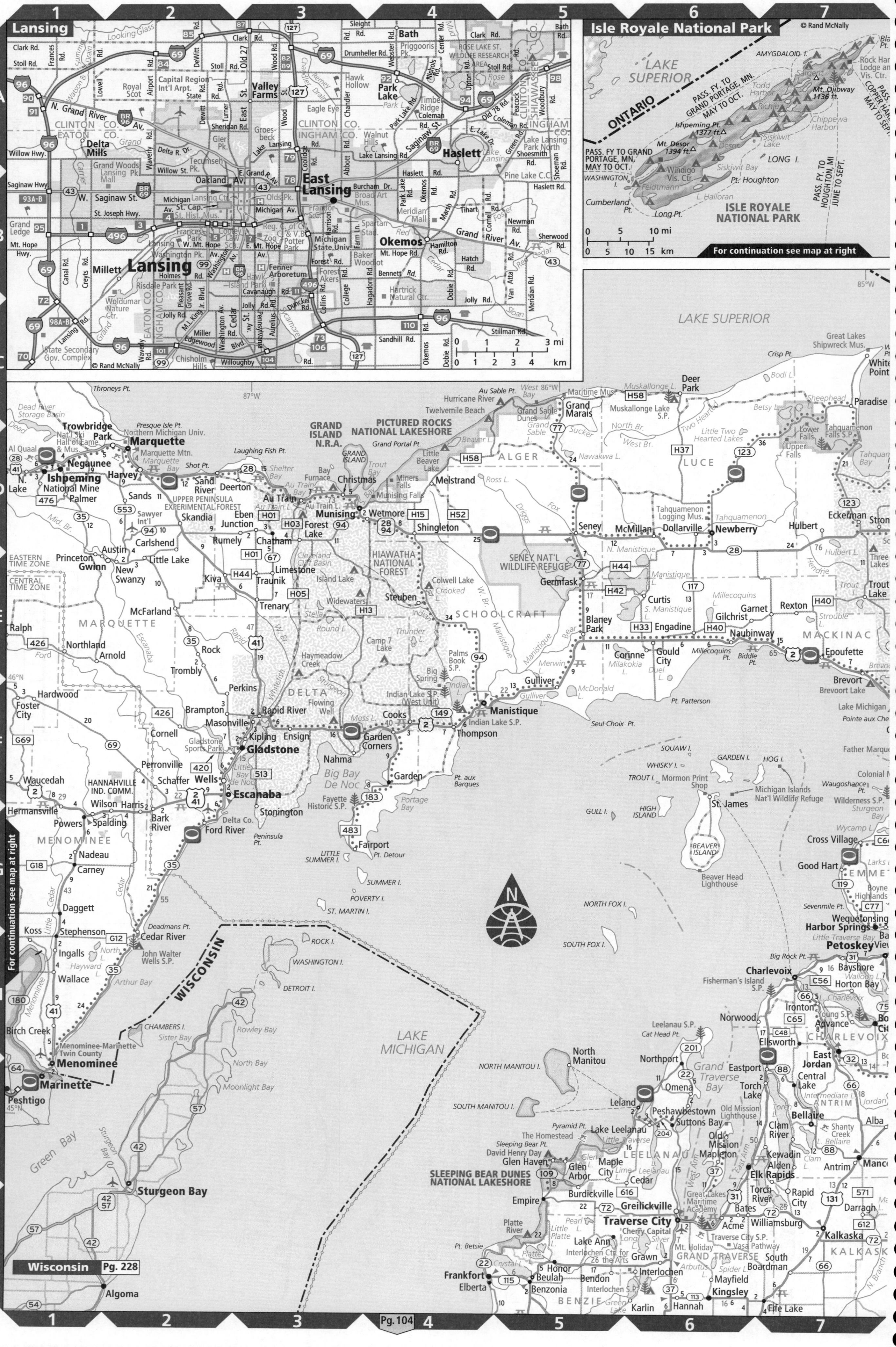

Determining distances along roads

Highway distances (segments of one mile or less not shown):
Cumulative miles (red): the distance between red arrows
Intermediate miles (black): the distance between intersections & places

Michigan state facts

Nickname: The Great Lake State
Capital: Lansing, Q-9
Population: 9,883,640 (rank: 8th)
Largest city: Detroit, 713,777, R-12
Land area: 56,804 sq. mi. (rank: 22nd)
Highest point: Mount Arvon, 1,979 ft., B-13

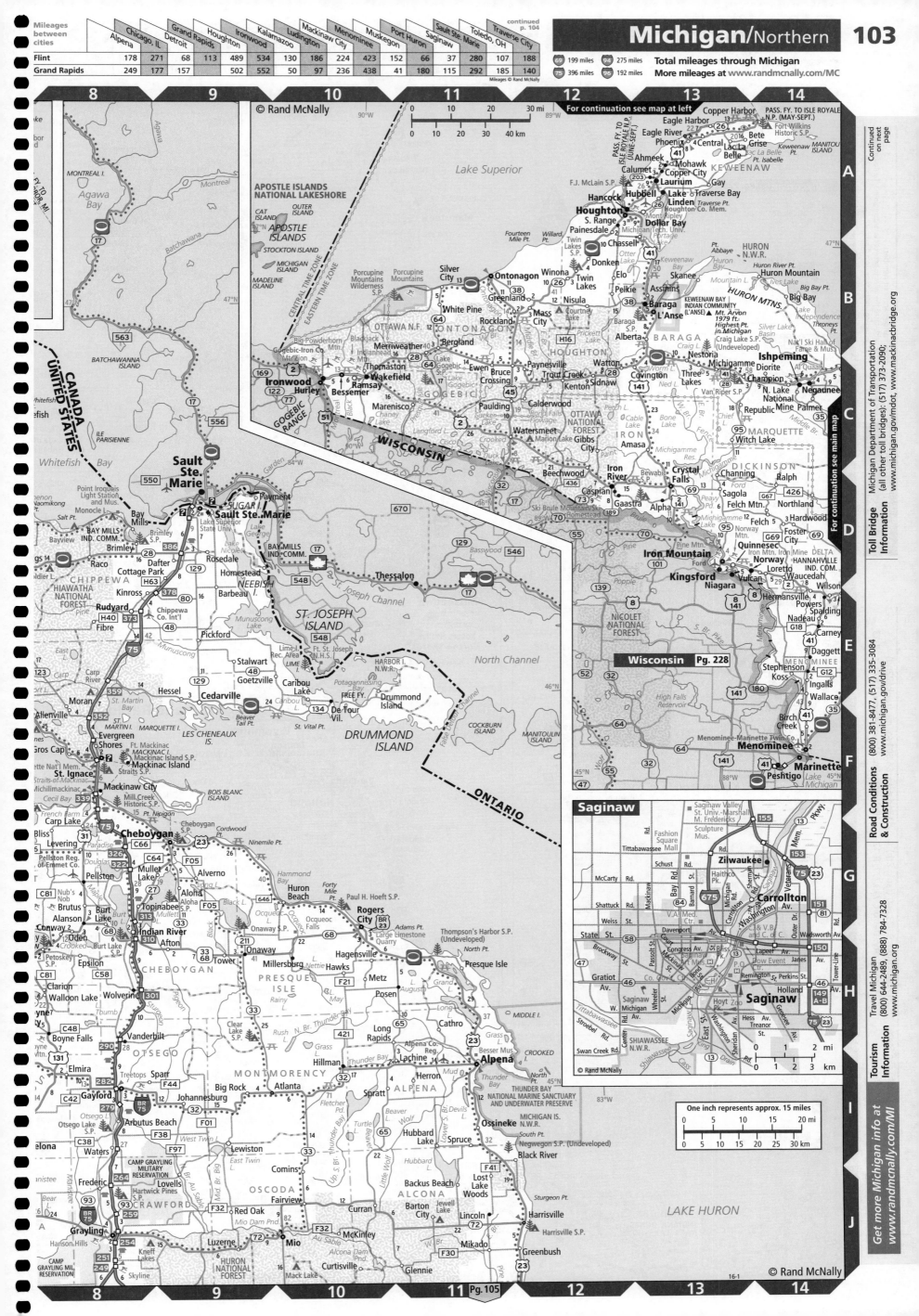

Mileages between cities	Alpena	Chicago, IL	Detroit	Grand Rapids	Houghton	Ironwood	Kalamazoo	Ludington	Mackinaw City	Menominee	Muskegon	Port Huron	Saginaw	Sault Ste. Marie	Toledo, OH	Traverse City
Flint	178	271	68	113	489	534	130	186	224	423	152	66	37	280	107	188
Grand Rapids	249	177	157		502	552	50	97	236	438	41	180	115	292	140	

Mileages © Rand McNally

Total mileages through Michigan
69 199 miles 94 275 miles
75 396 miles 96 192 miles
More mileages at www.randmcnally.com/MC

Toll Bridge Information: Michigan Department of Transportation (all other toll bridges): (517) 373-2090; www.michigan.gov/mdot; www.mackinacbridge.org

Road Conditions & Construction: (800) 381-8477, (517) 335-3084 www.michigan.gov/drive

Tourism Information: Travel Michigan (800) 644-2489, (888) 784-7328 www.michigan.org

Get more Michigan info at www.randmcnally.com/MI

Index of cities Pg. 247

Mileages between cities

	Alpena	Chicago, IL	Detroit	Grand Rapids	Houghton	Ironwood	Kalamazoo	Ludington	Mackinaw City	Menominee	Muskegon	Port Huron	Saginaw	Sault Ste. Marie	Toledo, OH	Traverse City
Ironwood	405	403	599	552	109		544	319	311	195	586	600	499	307	636	413
Kalamazoo	298	145	140	50	556	544		146	287	408	91	197	161	344	150	190

Mileages © Rand McNally

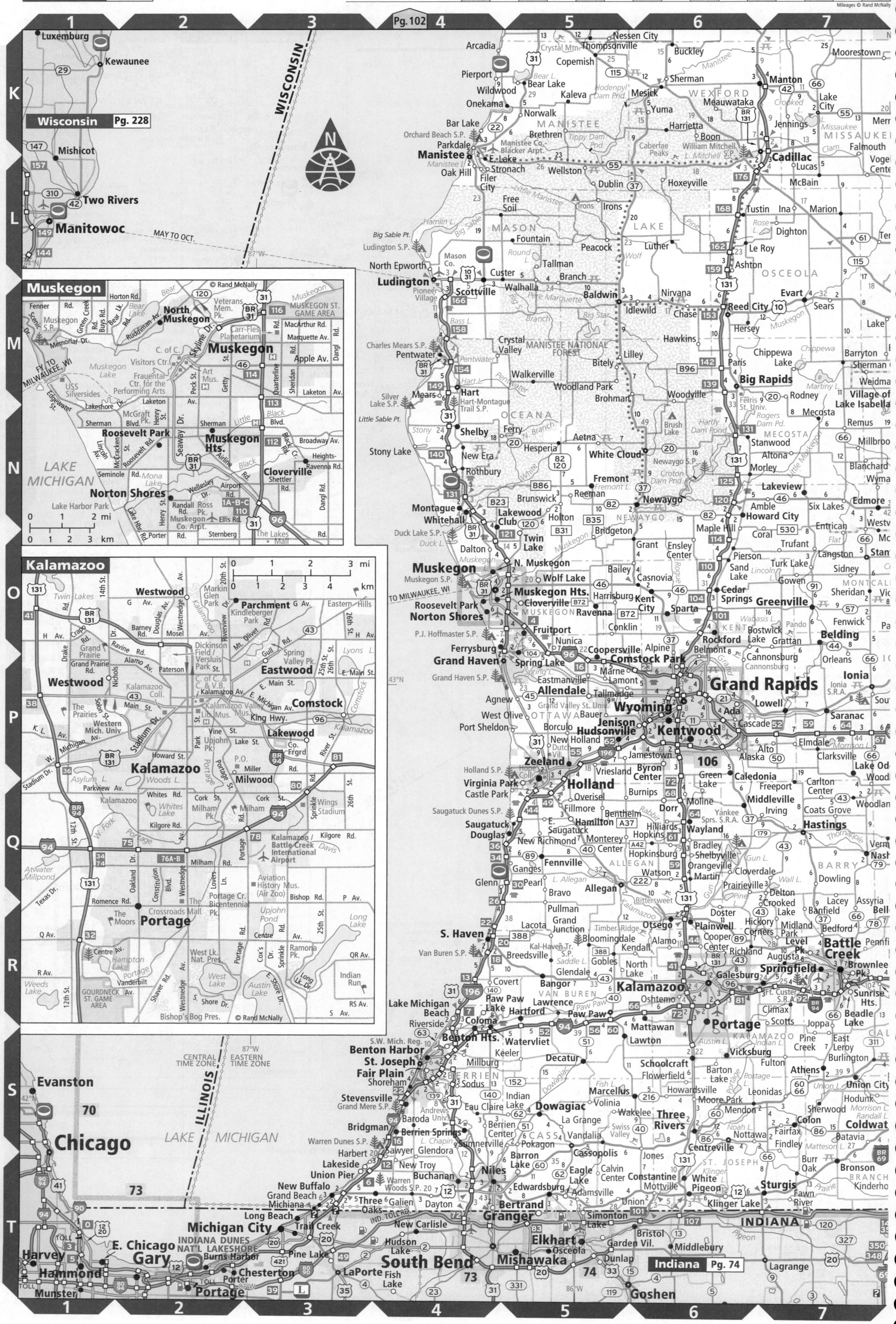

Interchanges and exit numbers
For most states, the mileage between interchanges may be determined by subtracting one number from the other.

Determining distances along roads

Land area: 56,804 sq. mi. (rank: 22nd)
Highest point: Mount Arvon, 1,979 ft., B-13

Population: 9,883,640 (rank: 8th)
Largest city: Detroit, 713,777, R-12

Nickname: The Great Lake State
Capital: Lansing, Q-9

Michigan state facts

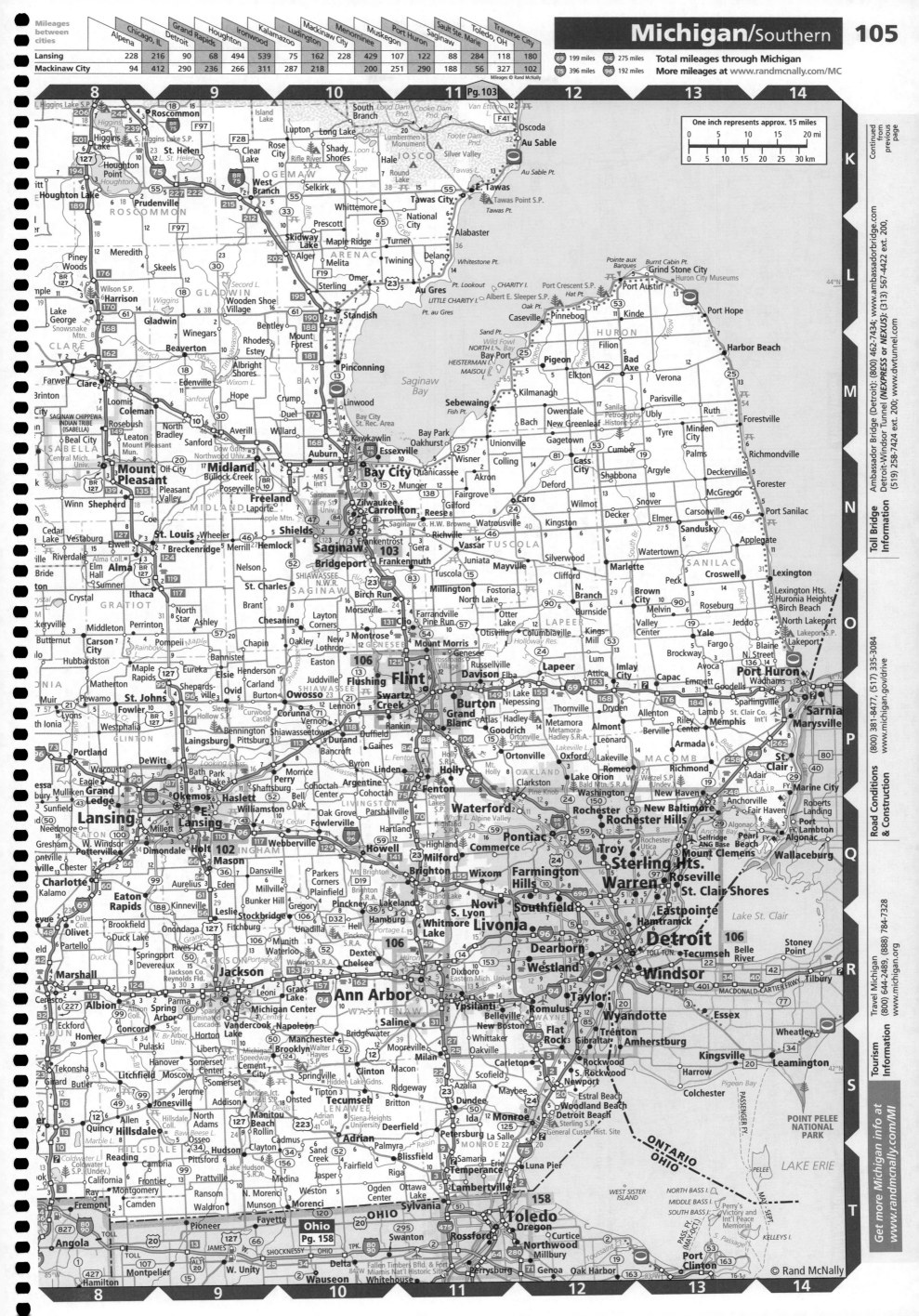

Mileages between cities

	Alpena	Chicago, IL	Detroit	Grand Rapids	Houghton	Ironwood	Kalamazoo	Ludington	Mackinaw City	Menominee	Muskegon	Port Huron	Saginaw	Sault Ste. Marie	Toledo, OH	Traverse City
Lansing	228	216	90	68	494	539	75	162	228	429	107	122	88	284	118	180
Mackinaw City	94	412	290	236	266	311	287	218		200	251	290	188	56	327	102

Mileages © Rand McNally

Total mileages through Michigan
More mileages at www.randmcnally.com/MC

| 69 | 199 miles | 94 | 275 miles |
| 75 | 396 miles | 96 | 192 miles |

One inch represents approx. 15 miles

Continued from previous page
Pg. 103
106
102
103
106
Ohio Pg. 158
158

© Rand McNally

City sights to see
- Arab American National Museum, Dearborn, K-6
- Cranbrook Art Museum, Bloomfield Hills, G-5
- Detroit Zoo, Royal Oak, H-6
- Edsel & Eleanor Ford House, Grosse Pointe Shores, I-9
- Frederik Meijer Gardens, Grand Rapids, A-3
- Gerald R. Ford Museum, Grand Rapids, B-2

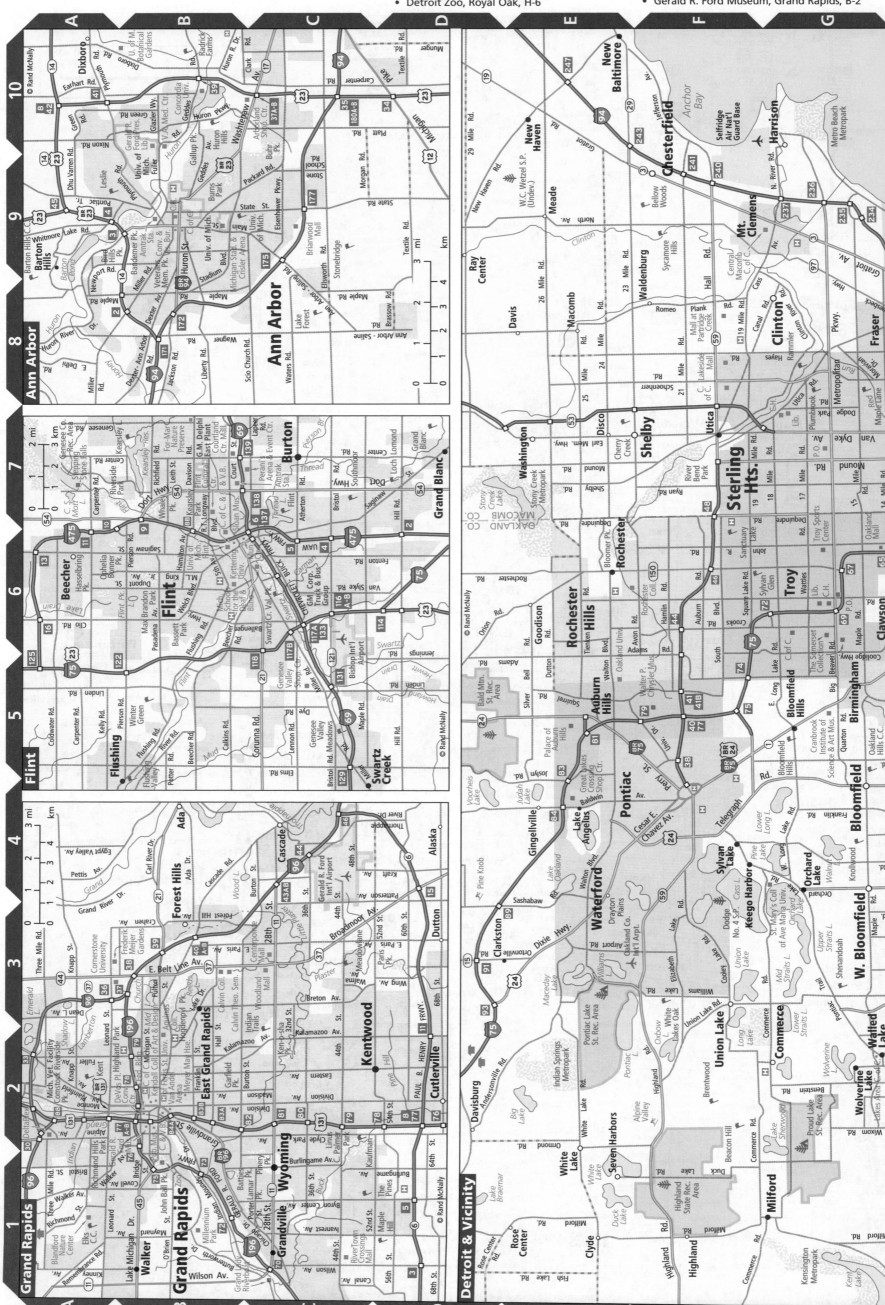

- Gerald R. Ford Presidential Library, Ann Arbor, B-10
- Henry Ford Museum, Dearborn, K-5
- Motown Historical Museum, Detroit, J-7
- New Detroit Science Center, Detroit, J-7
- Renaissance Center, Detroit, N-10
- Sloan Musuem, Flint, B-7
- University of Michigan, Ann Arbor, B-9

Mileages between cities	Albert Lea	Bemidji	Brainerd	Duluth	Grand Forks, ND	Grand Marais	Hibbing	Int'l Falls	Mankato	Marshall	Minneapolis	Moorhead	Rochester	St. Cloud	Sioux Falls, SD	Willmar
Bemidji	316		97	151	114	259	105	112	290	258	222	135	306	151	380	188
Duluth	247	151	113		266	110	76	162	233	273	152	250	226	141	390	204

Mileages © Rand McNally

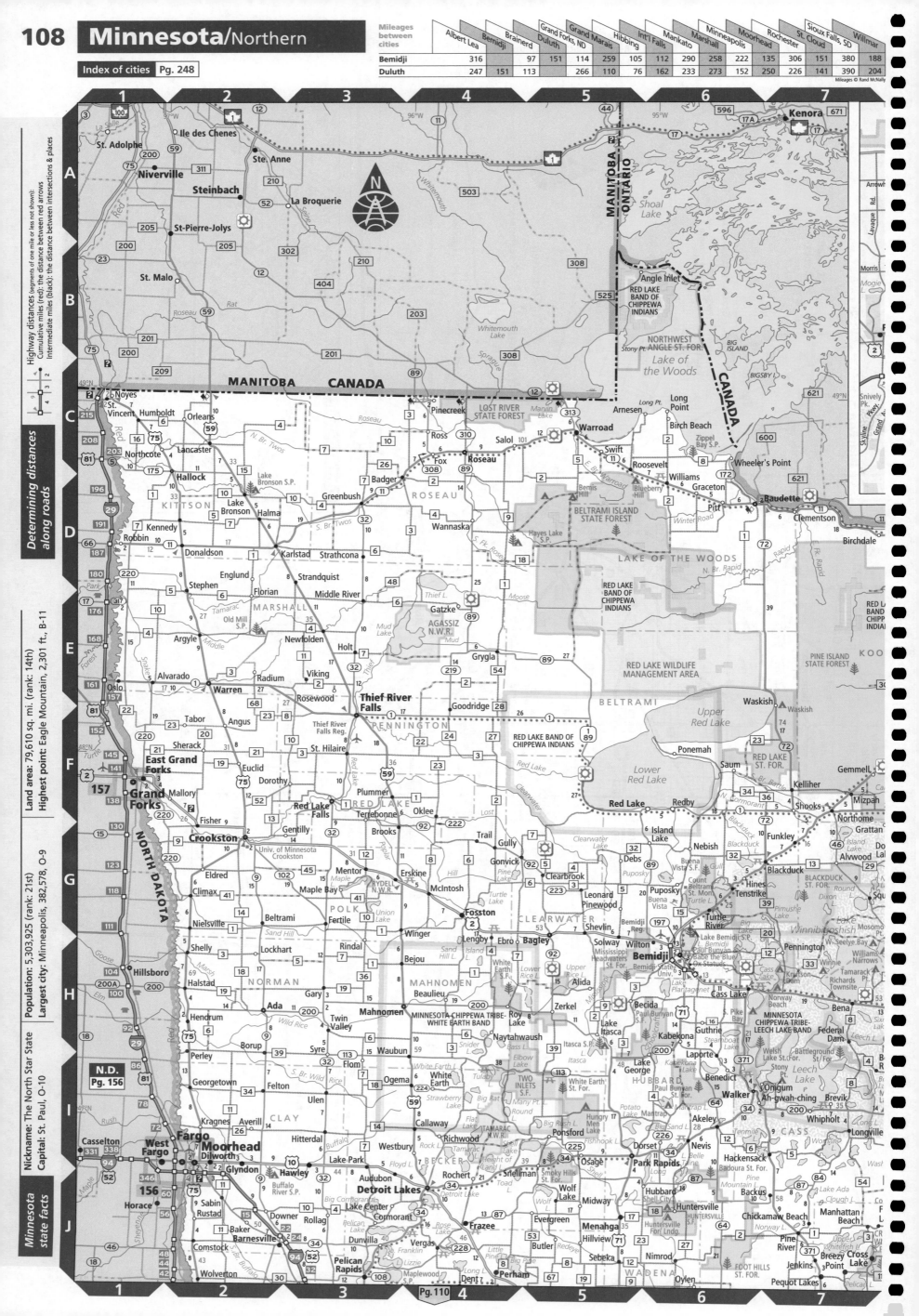

continued p. 110

Mileages between cities	Albert Lea	Bemidji	Brainerd	Grand Forks Duluth	Grand Marais	Hibbing	Int'l Falls	Mankato	Marshall	Minneapolis	Moorhead	Rochester	St. Cloud	Sioux Falls, SD	Willmar
Minneapolis	96	222	130	152	314	262	208	293	80	153		233	86	65	236	93
Moorhead	328	135	136	250	82	361	212	249	303	206	233		321	170	244	172

Mileages © Rand McNally

Total mileages through Minnesota
More mileages at www.randmcnally.com/MC

35 260 miles   94 260 miles
90 276 miles   2 255 miles

© Rand McNally

Toll Road Information
No toll roads

511
Road Conditions 511 & Construction (651) 296-3000, In MN: (800) 657-3774 www.511mn.org, www.dot.state.mn.us

Tourism Information
Explore Minnesota Tourism (888) 868-7476, (651) 296-5029, (651) 757-1845 www.exploreminnesota.com

Explore Minnesota at www.exploreminnesota.com/MN
www.randmcnally.com/MN

One inch represents approx. 16 miles
0 5 10 15 20 25 mi
0 5 10 15 20 25 30 35 40 km

For continuation see main map
For continuation see map above
Pg. 228
Pg. 111
102

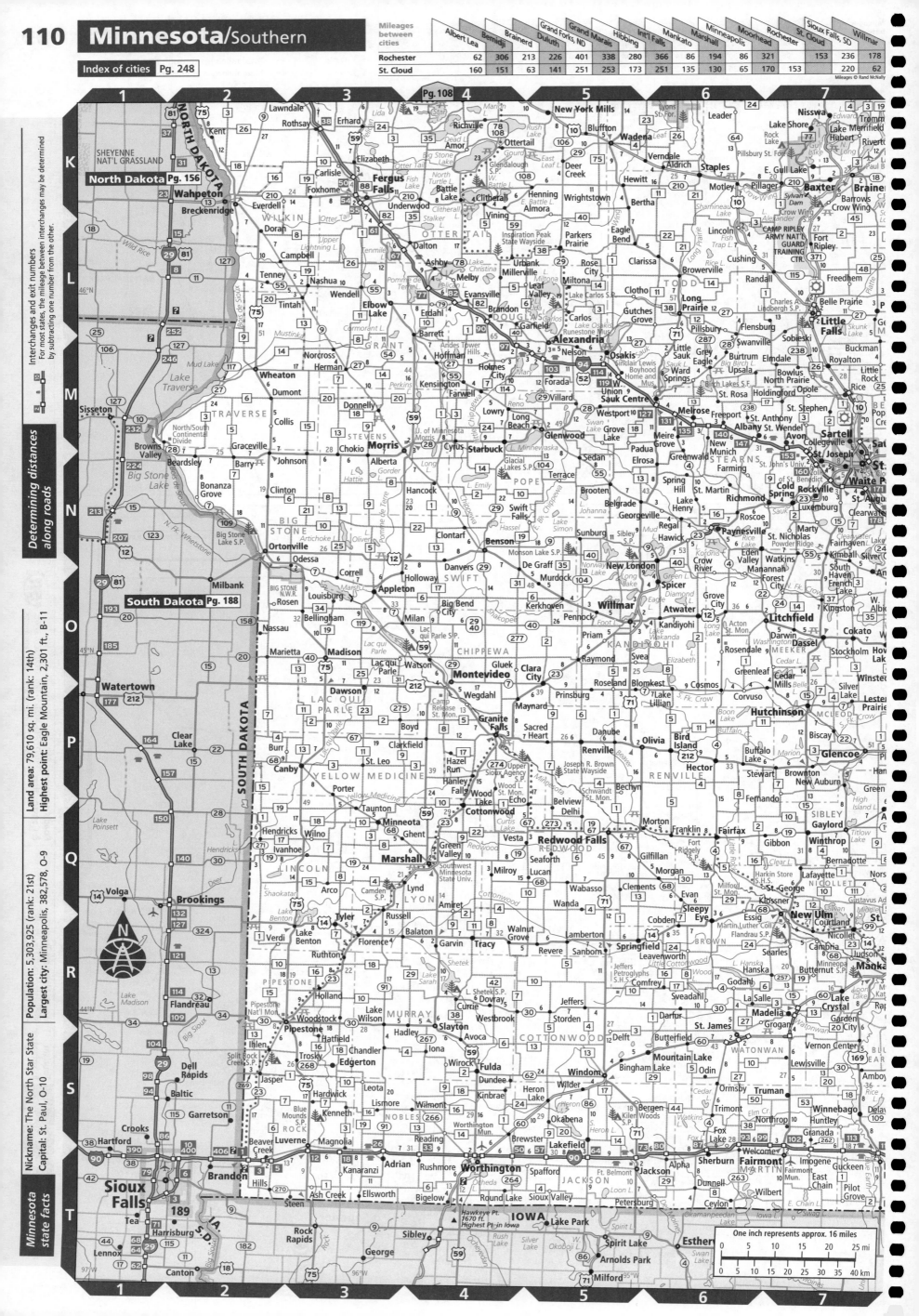

Mileages between cities	Albert Lea	Bemidji	Brainerd	Duluth	Grand Forks, ND	Grand Marais	Hibbing	Int'l Falls	Mankato	Marshall	Minneapolis	Moorhead	Rochester	St. Cloud	Sioux Falls, SD	Willmar
Rochester	62	306	213	226	401	338	280	366	86	194	86	321		153	236	178
St. Cloud	160	151	63	141	251	253	173	251	135	130	65	170	153		220	62

Mileages © Rand McNally

Minnesota state facts

Nickname: The North Star State
Capital: St. Paul, O-10

Population: 5,303,925 (rank: 21st)
Largest city: Minneapolis, 382,578, O-9

Land area: 79,610 sq. mi. (rank: 14th)
Highest point: Eagle Mountain, 2,301 ft., B-11

Determining distances along roads

Interchanges and exit numbers
For most states, the mileage between interchanges may be determined by subtracting one number from the other.

North Dakota Pg. 156

South Dakota Pg. 188

One inch represents approx. 16 miles

0 5 10 15 20 25 mi
0 10 20 30 40 km

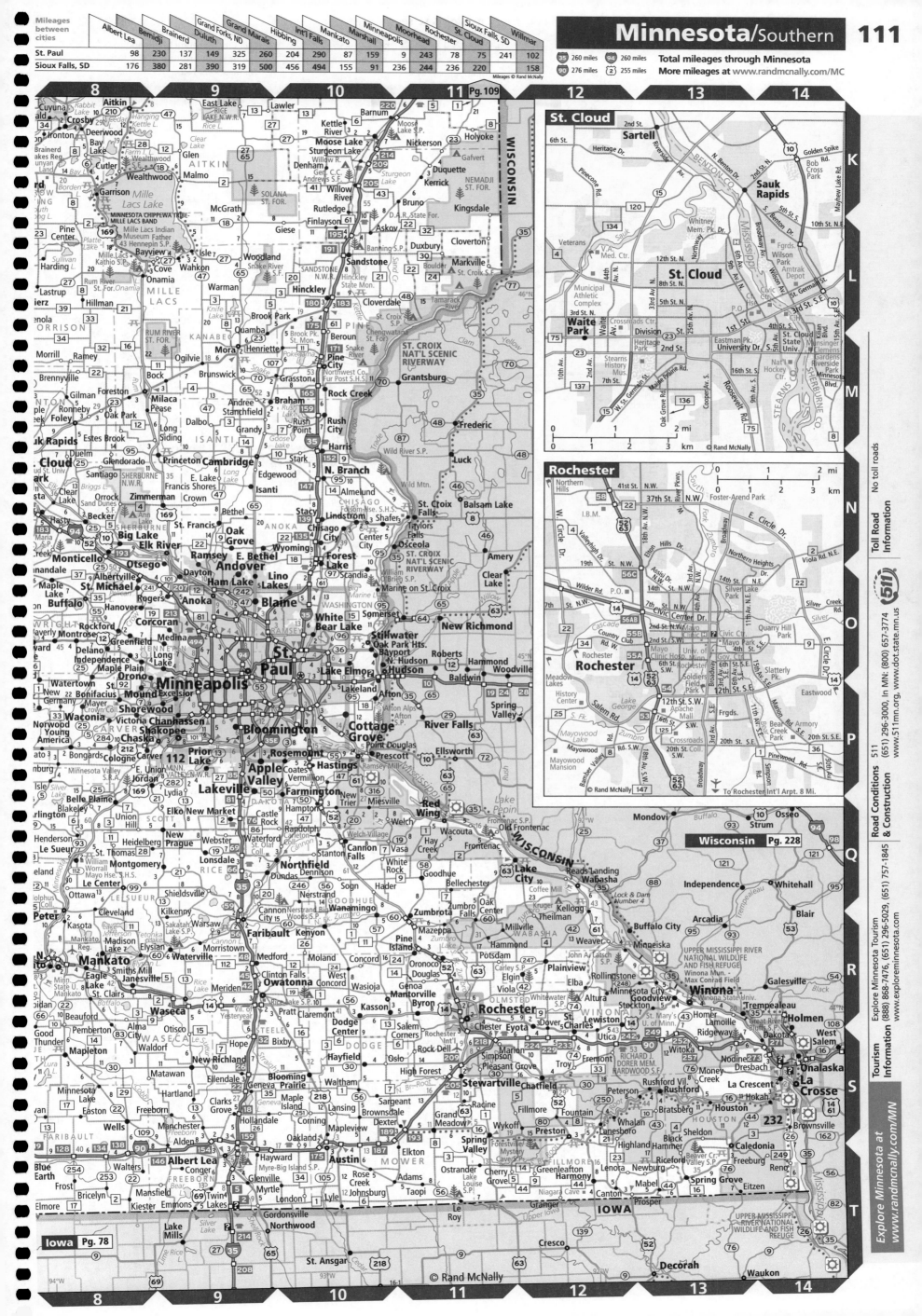

Mileages between cities

	Albert Lea	Bemidji	Brainerd	Duluth	Grand Forks, ND	Grand Marais	Hibbing	Int'l Falls	Mankato	Marshall	Minneapolis	Moorhead	Rochester	St. Cloud	Sioux Falls, SD	Willmar
St. Paul	98	230	137	149	325	260	204	290	87	159	9	243	78	75	241	102
Sioux Falls, SD	176	380	281	390	319	500	456	494	155	91	236	244	236	220		158

Mileages by Rand McNally

Total mileages through Minnesota
More mileages at www.randmcnally.com/MC

- 35 · 260 miles
- 94 · 260 miles
- 90 · 276 miles
- 2 · 255 miles

St. Cloud

Rochester

Tourism · Explore Minnesota Tourism · (888) 868-7476, (651) 296-5029, (651) 296-5029 · www.exploreminnesota.com

Road Conditions & Construction · 511 · (651) 296-3000, In MN: (800) 657-3774 · 511mn.org, www.dot.state.mn.us

Toll Road Information · No toll roads

Explore Minnesota at www.exploreminnesota.com/MN

© Rand McNally

City sights to see
- Bell Mus. of Natural History, Minneapolis, L-4
- Cathedral of St. Paul, St. Paul, M-7
- Frederick R. Weisman Art Museum, Minneapolis, M-4
- Mall of America, Bloomington, I-5
- Mill City Museum, Minneapolis, L-3
- Minneapolis Institute of the Arts, Minneapolis, N-2

Minneapolis / St. Paul & Vicinity

• Minneapolis Sculpture Garden, Minneapolis, M-1
• Minnesota History Center, St. Paul, M-7
• Minnesota State Capitol, St. Paul, L-7
• Ordway Center for the Performing Arts, St. Paul, M-7
• Science Museum of Minnesota, St. Paul, M-7
• Walker Art Center, Minneapolis, M-1

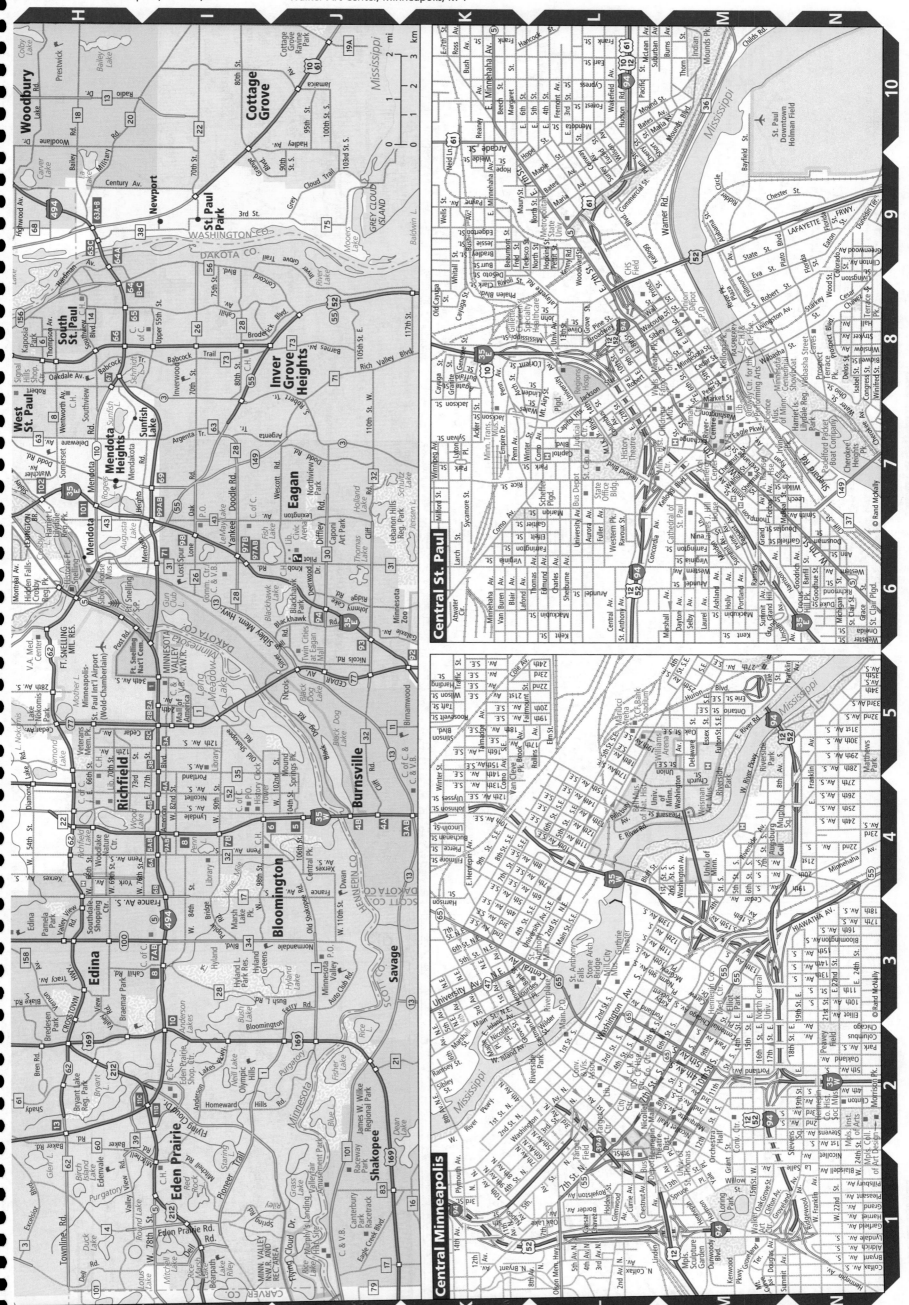

Mileages between cities	Batesville	Biloxi	Hattiesburg	Jackson	Memphis, TN	Natchez	Tupelo	Vicksburg
Biloxi	320		80	172	379	228	315	214
Greenville	112	293	210	121	152	152	177	91

Mileages between cities	Batesville	Biloxi	Hattiesburg	Jackson	Memphis, TN	Natchez	Tupelo	Vicksburg
Jackson	149	172	89		209	103	190	44
Memphis, TN	61	379	297	209		304	105	245

Mileages © Rand McNally

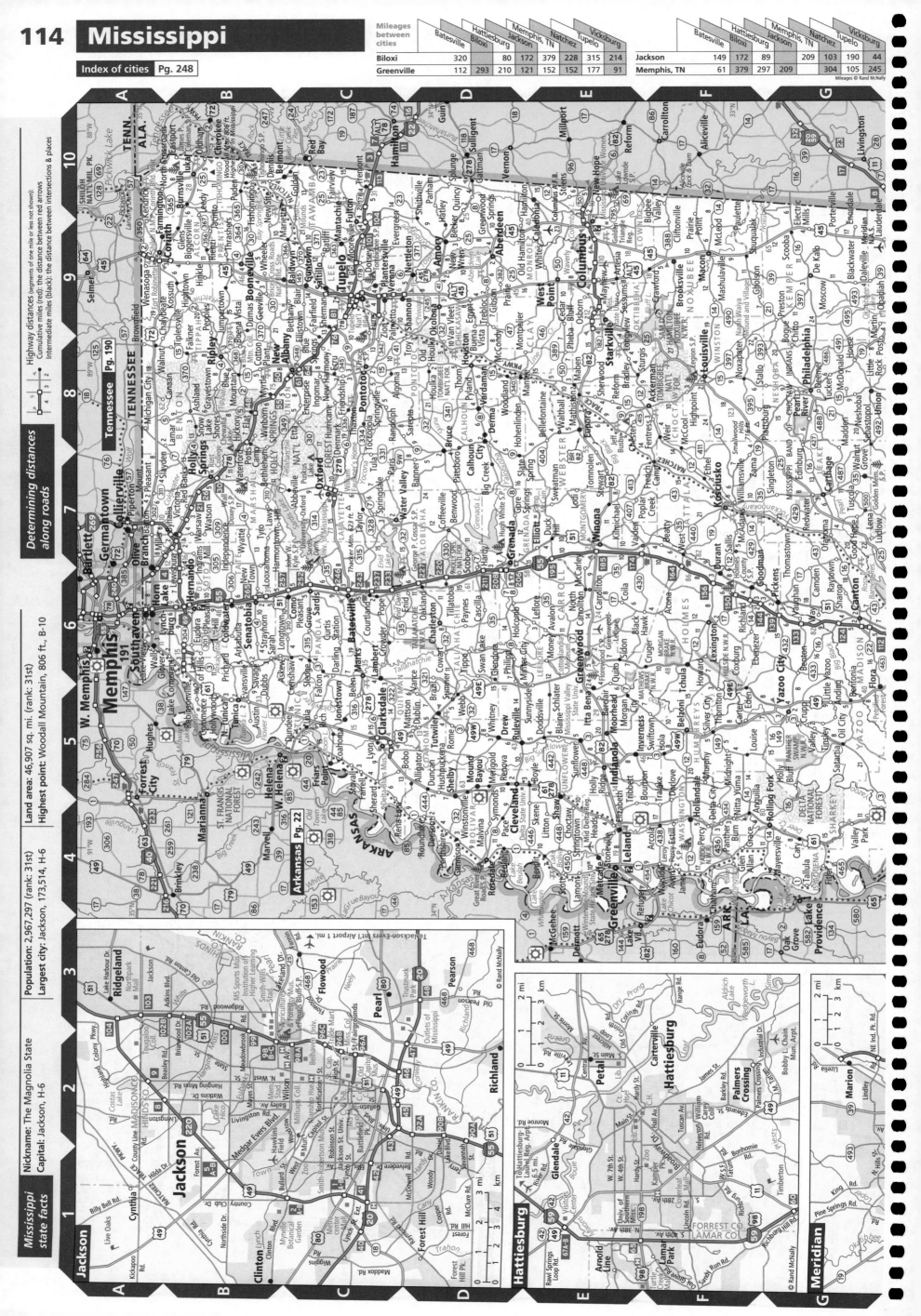

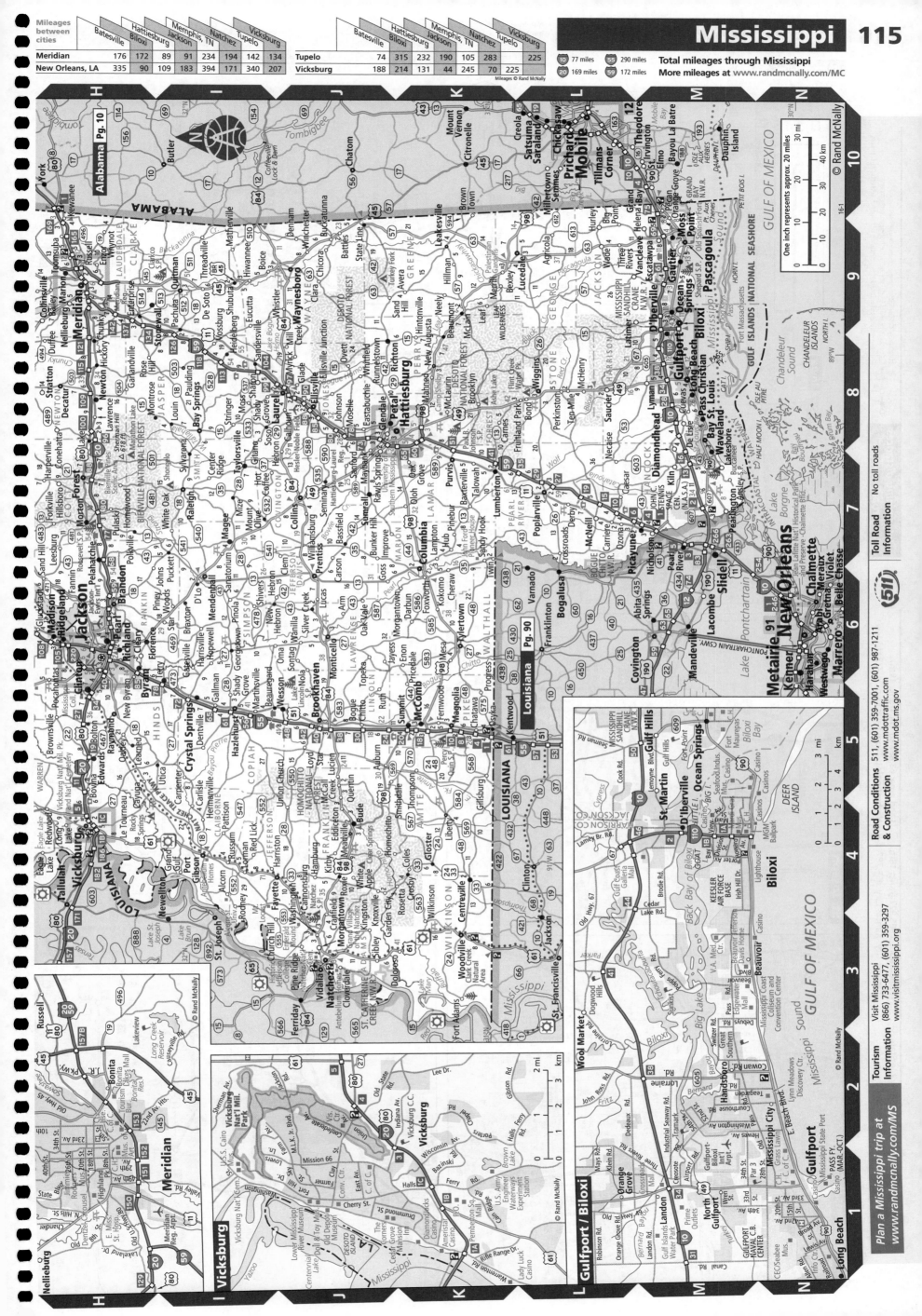

Mileages between cities	Batesville	Biloxi	Hattiesburg	Memphis, Jackson TN	Natchez	Tupelo	Vicksburg
Meridian	176	172	89	91	234	194	142	134
New Orleans, LA	335	90	109	183	394	171	340	207

	Batesville	Biloxi	Hattiesburg	Memphis, Jackson TN	Natchez	Tupelo	Vicksburg
Tupelo	74	315	232	190	105	283		225
Vicksburg	188	214	131	44	245	70	225	

Mileages © Rand McNally

Total mileages through Mississippi
More mileages at www.randmcnally.com/MC

10	77 miles	55	290 miles
20	169 miles	59	172 miles

© Rand McNally

Plan a Mississippi trip at www.randmcnally.com/MS

Tourism Information Visit Mississippi (866) 733-6477, (601) 359-3297 www.visitmississippi.org

Road Conditions & Construction 511, (601) 359-7001, (601) 987-1211 www.mdottraffic.com www.mdot.ms.gov

511

Toll Road · Information

No toll roads

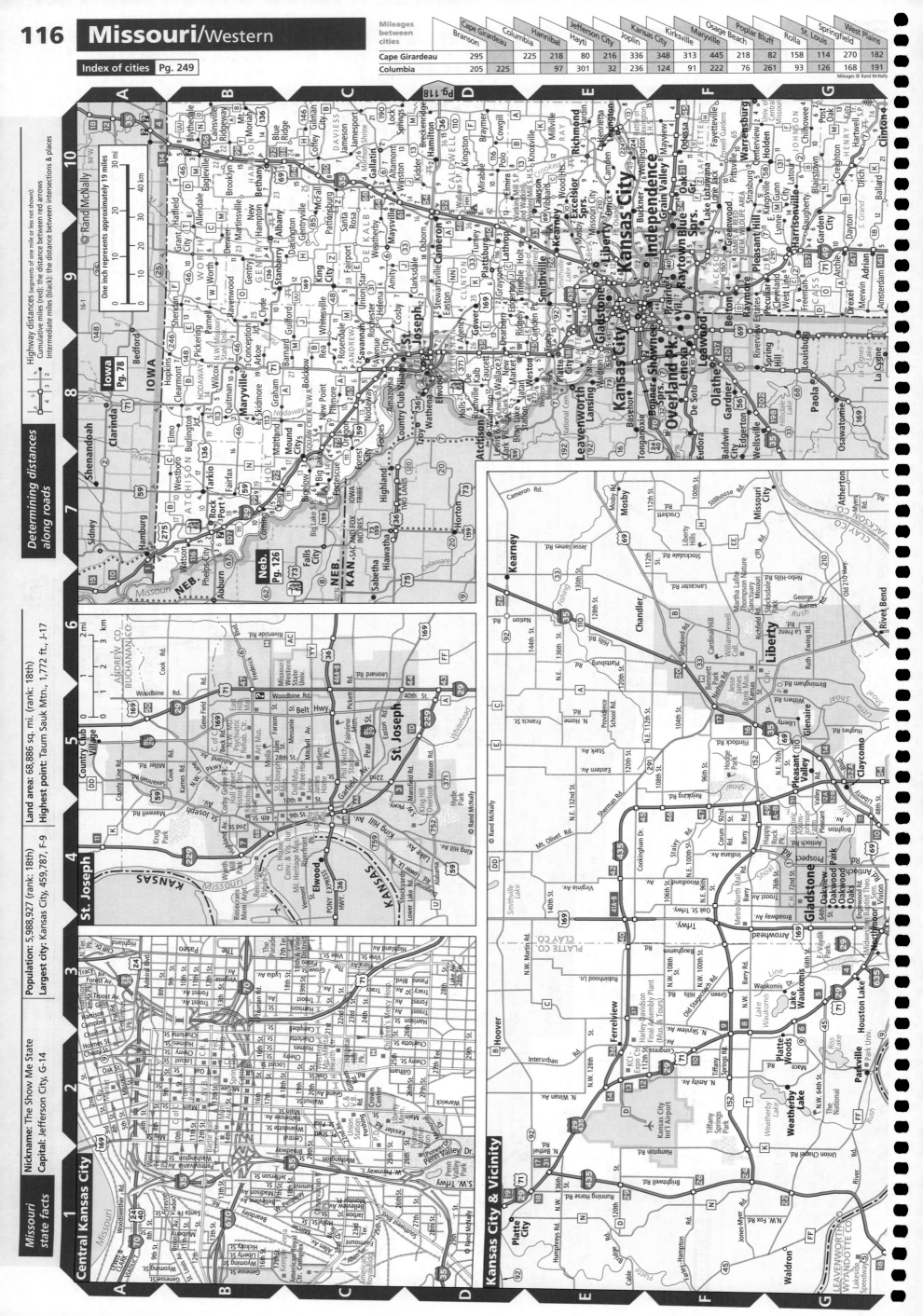

Mileages between cities	Branson	Cape Girardeau	Columbia	Hannibal	Hayti	Jefferson City	Joplin	Kansas City	Kirksville	Maryville	Osage Beach	Poplar Bluff	Rolla	St. Louis	Springfield	West Plains
Joplin	109	336	236	312	319	206		157	312	243	161	256	178	282	70	176
Kansas City	209	348	124	209	424	156	157		157	93	164	356	219	250	166	275

Mileages © Rand McNally

continued p. 118

p. 119
p. 118
Kansas Pg. 82
Kansas Pg. 22
Ark. Pg. 22
Okla. Pg. 166
Okla. Pg. 166

Total mileages through Missouri
More mileages at www.randmcnally.com/MC

| 35 | 115 miles | 55 | 210 miles |
| 44 | 290 miles | 70 | 252 miles |

Tourism Information Missouri Division of Tourism
(573) 751-4133
www.visitmo.org

Road Conditions & Construction (888) 275-6636
(573) 751-2551
www.modot.org

Toll Road Information No toll roads

Explore Missouri at www.randmcnally.com/MO

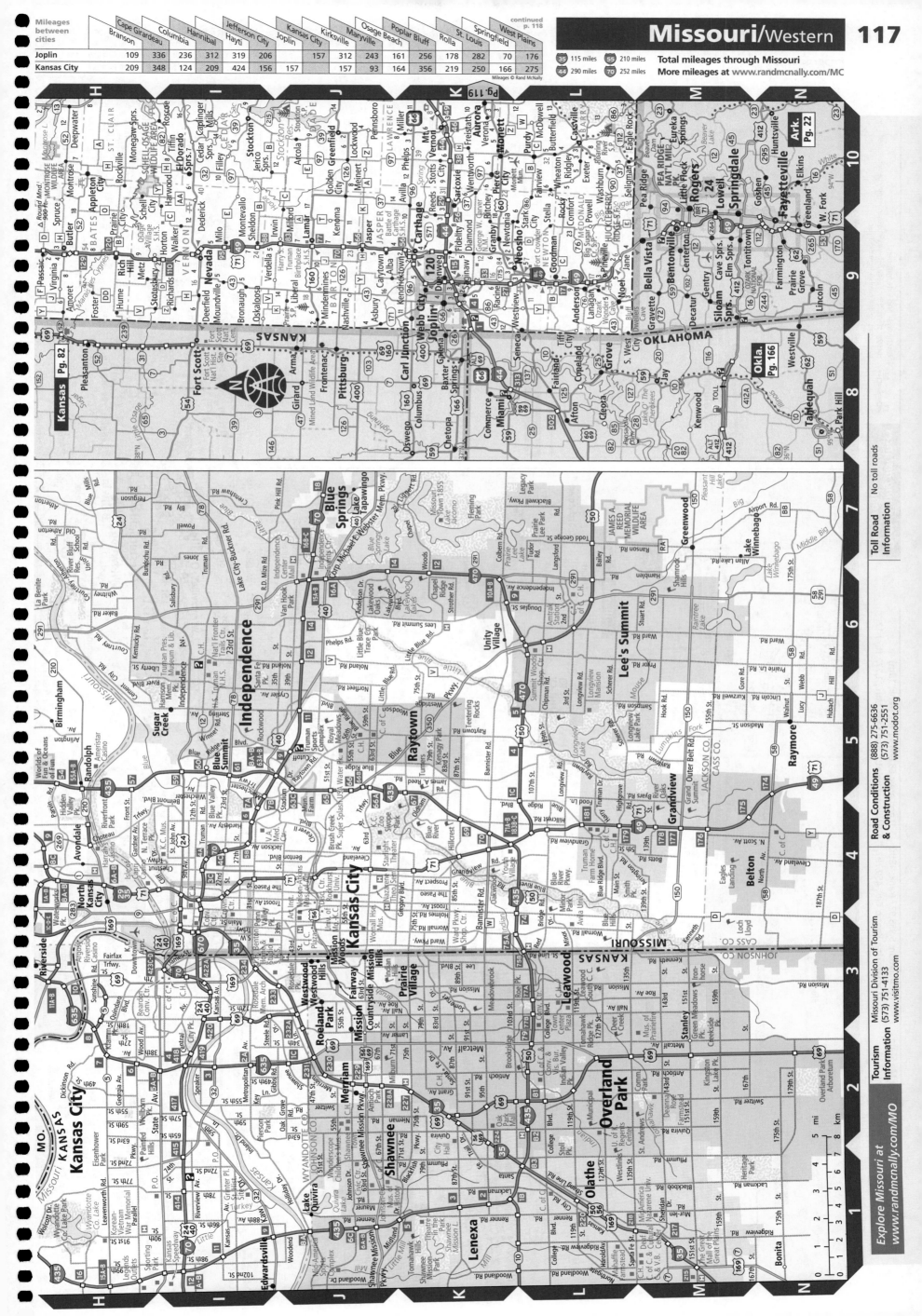

Index of cities Pg. 249

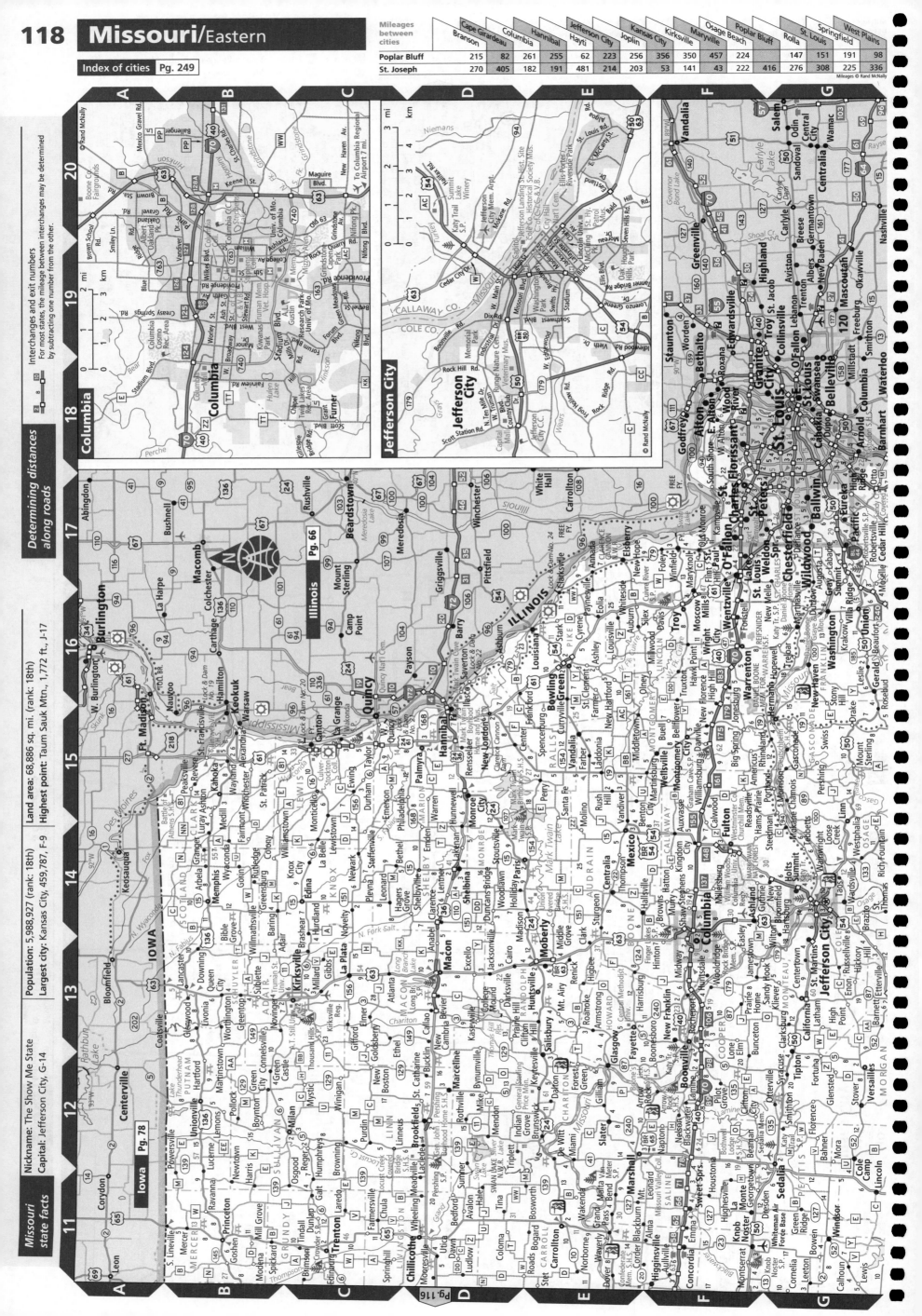

Mileages between cities	Branson	Cape Girardeau	Columbia	Hannibal	Hayti	Jefferson City	Joplin	Kansas City	Kirksville	Maryville	Osage Beach	Poplar Bluff	Rolla	St. Louis	Springfield	West Plains
Poplar Bluff	215	82	261	255	62	223	256	356	350	457	224		147	151	191	98
St. Joseph	270	405	182	191	481	214	203	53	141	43	222	416	276	308	225	336

Mileages © Rand McNally

Missouri state facts

Nickname: The Show Me State
Capital: Jefferson City, G-14

Population: 5,988,927 (rank: 18th)
Largest city: Kansas City, 459,787, F-9

Land area: 68,886 sq. mi. (rank: 18th)
Highest point: Taum Sauk Mtn., 1,772 ft., J-17

Determining distances along roads

Mileages between cities	Branson	Cape Girardeau	Columbia	Hannibal	Hayti	Jefferson City	Joplin	Kansas City	Kirksville	Maryville	Osage Beach	Poplar Bluff	Rolla	St. Louis	Springfield	West Plains
St. Louis	249	114	126	120	192	124	282	250	217	347	164	151	104		213	202
Springfield	42	270	168	242	253	136	70	166	259	266	91	191	108	213		108

Mileages © Rand McNally

35	115 miles	55	210 miles	**Total mileages through Missouri**
44	290 miles	70	252 miles	**More mileages at www.randmcnally.com/MC**

Explore Missouri at
www.randmcnally.com/MO

Tourism Information — Missouri Division of Tourism (573) 751-4133 www.visitmo.com

Road Conditions & Construction — (888) 275-6636 (573) 751-2551 www.modot.org

Toll Road — No toll roads
Information

Arkansas Pg. 22

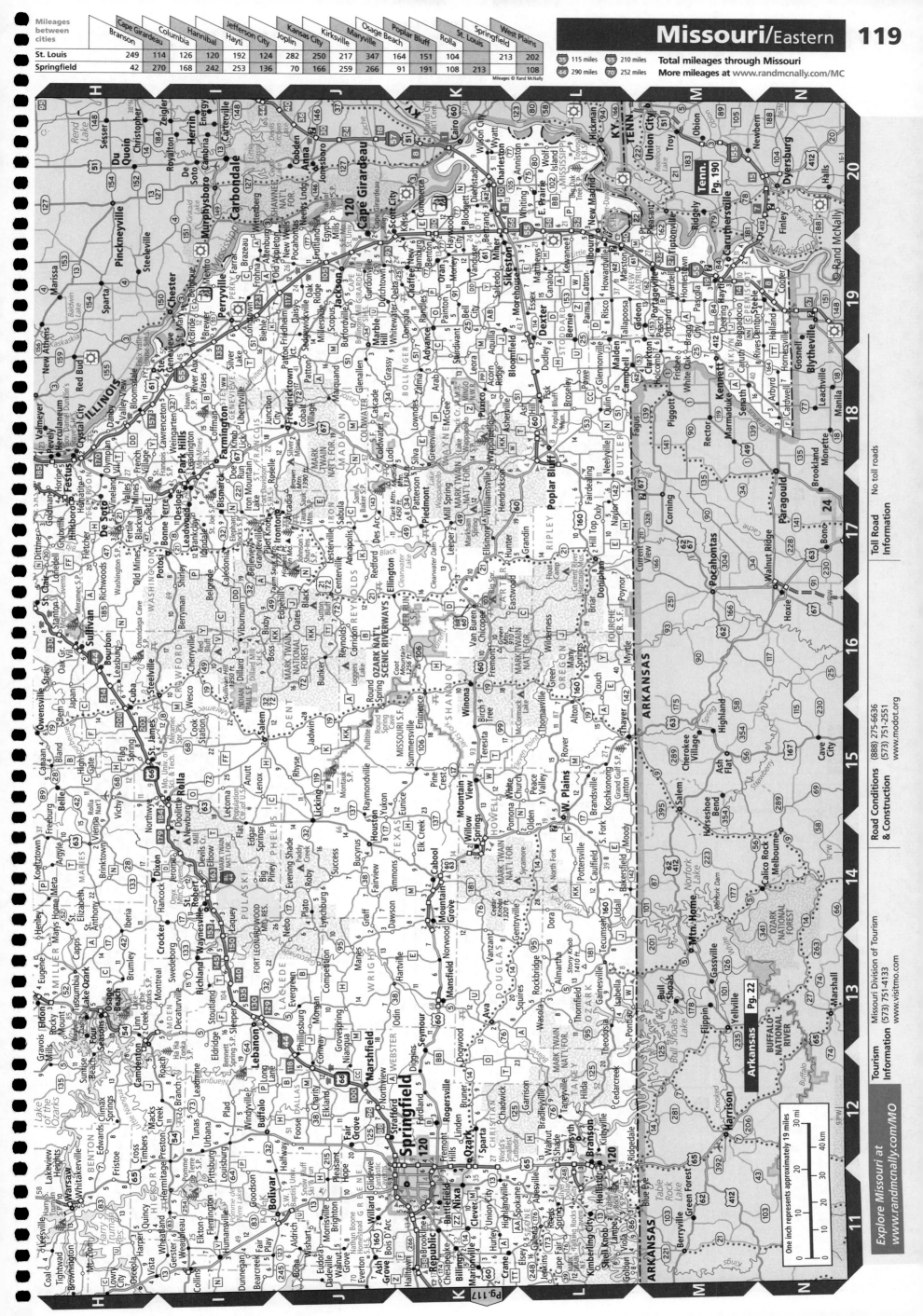

City sights to see
- Andy Williams Moon River Theatre, Branson, M-8
- Anheuser-Busch Brewery, St. Louis, I-7
- Bass Pro Shops® Outdoor World®, Springfield, C-3
- Dolly Parton's Dixie Stampede, Branson, M-9
- Gateway Arch, St. Louis, L-4
- Laumeier Sculpture Park, St. Louis, J-4
- Magic House, Kirkwood, I-4

Cape Girardeau

Joplin

Springfield

St. Louis & Vicinity

- Missouri Botanical Garden, St. Louis, I-6
- Shoji Tabuchi Theatre, Branson, L-7
- St. Louis Art Museum, St. Louis, H-6
- St. Louis Science Center, St. Louis, H-6
- St. Louis Zoo, St. Louis, H-6
- Shepherd of the Hills Homestead & Outdoor Theatre, Branson, K-6
- White Water, Branson, M-7

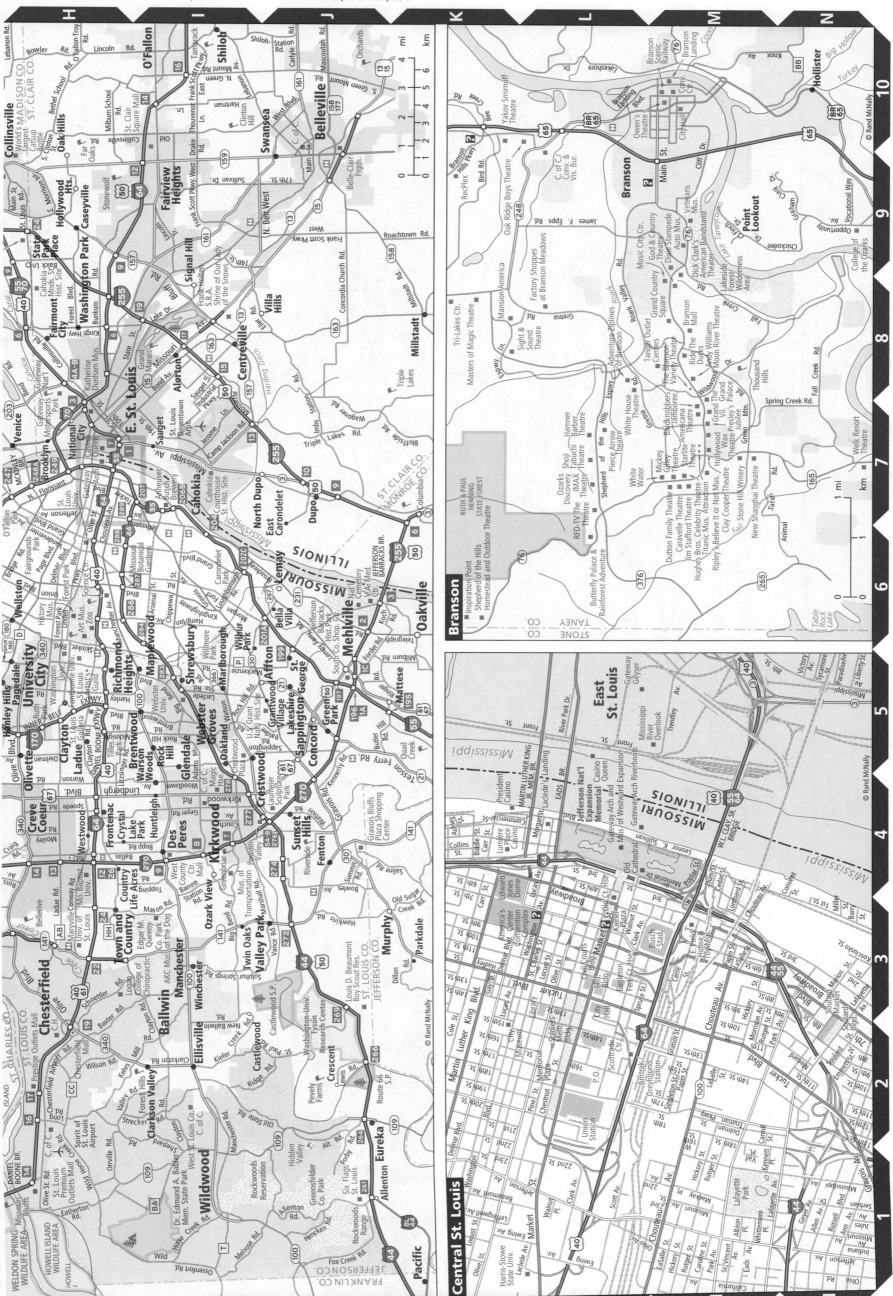

Mileages between cities	Belle Fourche, SD	Billings	Bozeman	Butte	Dillon	Glasgow	Great Falls	Havre	Kalispell	Lewistown	Libby	Miles City	Missoula	St. Mary	W. Yellowstone Sidney
Billings	261		143	223	256	276	218	247	451	125	536	144	343	375	269	232
Butte	486	223	82		54	425	154	267	224	244	309	367	120	269	494	149

Mileages © Rand McNally

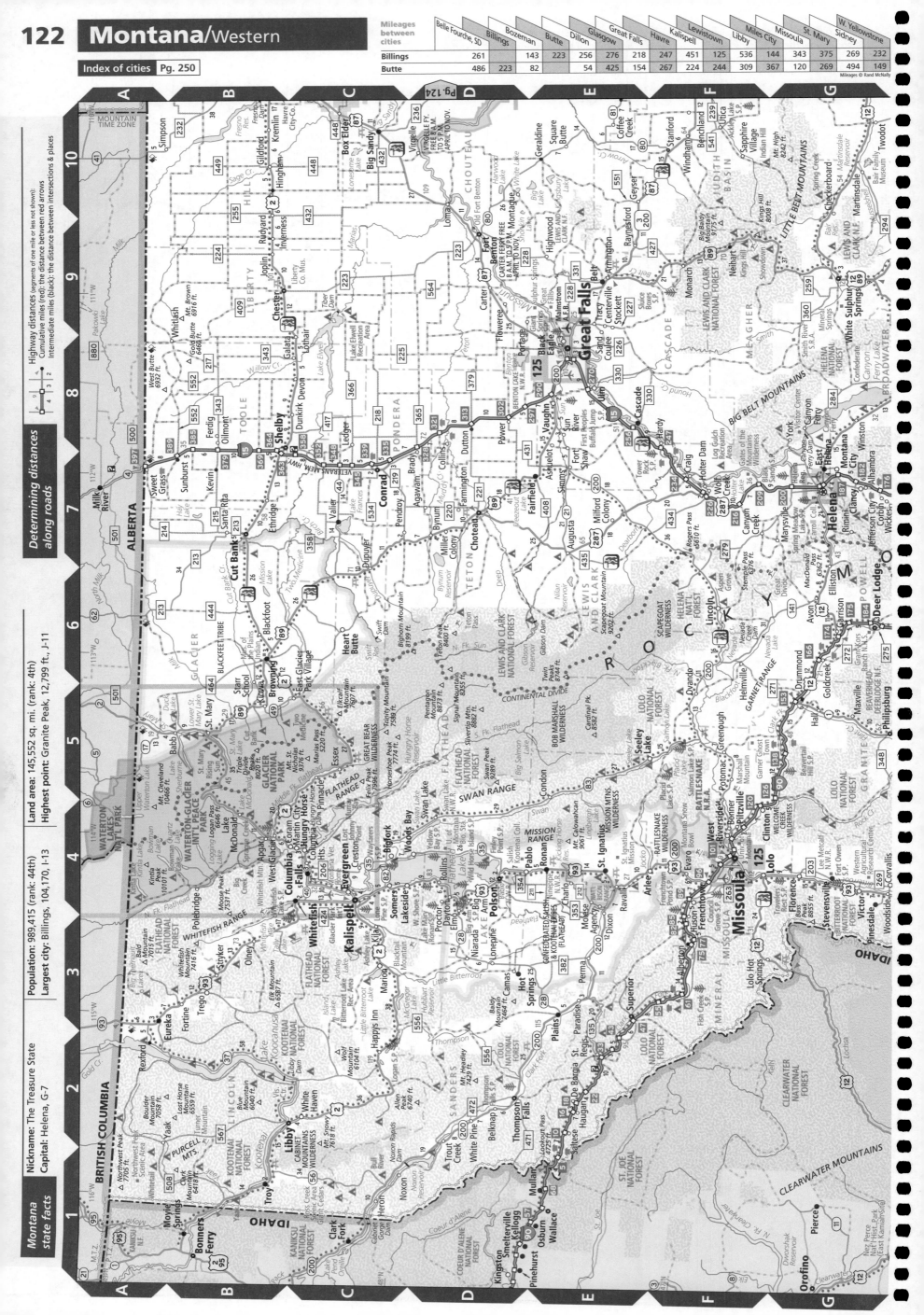

Pg. 124
Pg. 124

Mileages between cities	Belle Fourche, SD	Billings	Bozeman	Butte	Dillon	Glasgow	Great Falls	Havre	Kalispell	Lewistown	Libby	Miles City	Missoula	St. Mary	Sidney	W. Yellowstone
Great Falls	481	218	186	154	219	271		113	224	106	312	317	166	158	375	264
Helena	500	238	98	66	132	360	90	202	193	193	281	383	113	205	463	177

continued p. 124

Mileages © Rand McNally

Total mileages through Montana

15 396 miles   94 249 miles

90 552 miles

More mileages at www.rand mcnally.com/MC

Map of western Montana, including Yellowstone National Park, Waterton-Glacier Int'l Peace Park inset, and Helena inset.

Tourism Information — Montana Office of Tourism (800) 847-4868 www.visitmt.com

Road Conditions & Construction — 511 (800) 226-7623, (406) 444-6200 www.mtd511.com, www.mdt.mt.gov

511

Toll Road Information — No toll roads

Get more Montana info at www.randmcnally.com/MT

© Rand McNally

Montana state facts

Nickname: The Treasure State
Capital: Helena, G-7

Population: 989,415 (rank: 44th)
Largest city: Billings, G-7

Land area: 145,552 sq. mi. (rank: 4th)
Highest point: Granite Peak, 12,799 ft., J-11

Determining distances along roads

Interchanges and exit numbers

For most states, the mileage between interchanges may be determined by subtracting one number from the other.

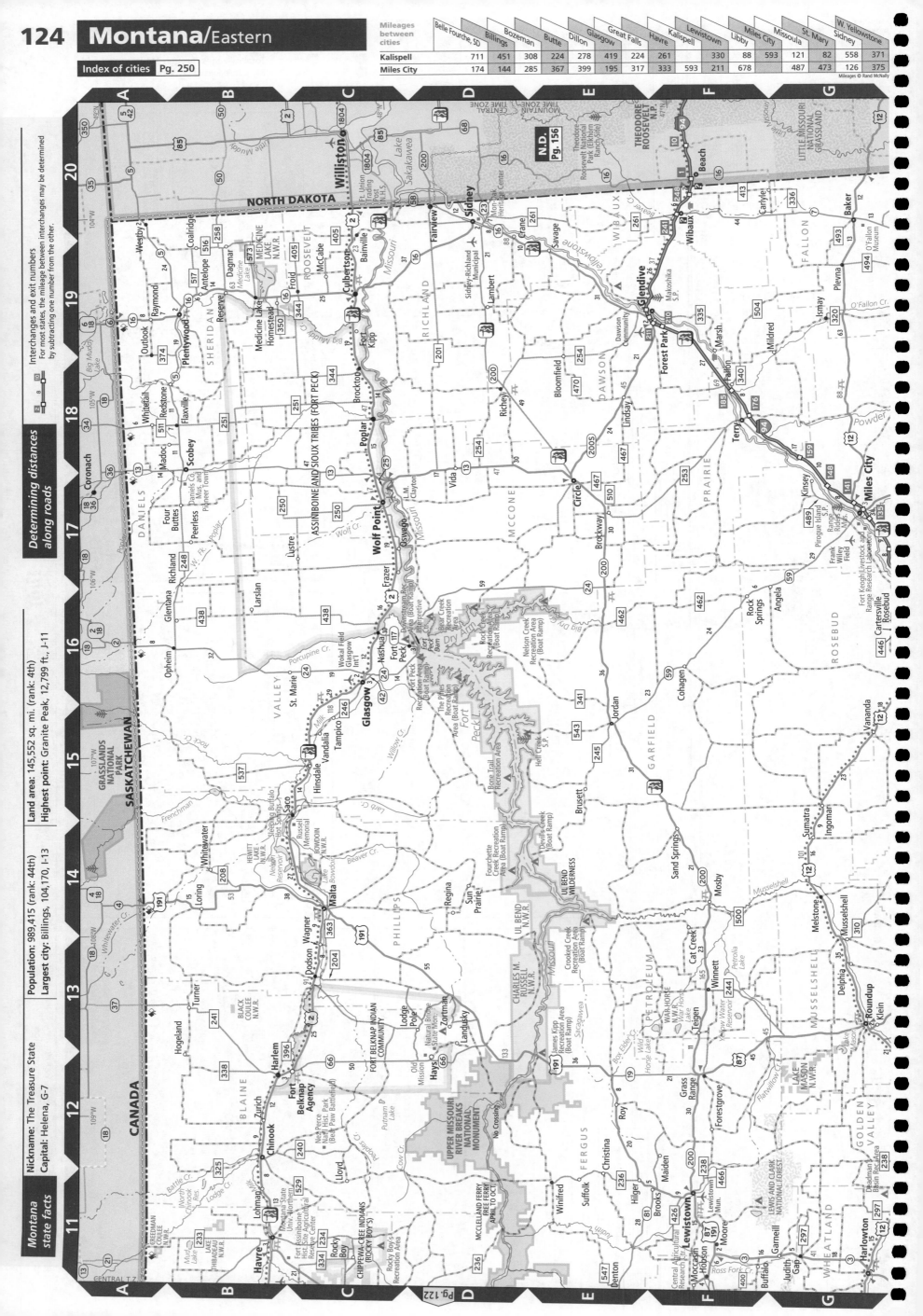

Mileages between cities	Belle Fourche, SD	Billings	Bozeman	Butte	Dillon	Glasgow	Great Falls	Havre	Kalispell	Lewistown	Libby	Miles City	Missoula	St. Mary	W. Yellowstone	Sidney
Missoula	606	343	202	120	172	437	166	280	121	272	191	487		203	614	267
Sidney	298	269	411	494	524	140	375	298	558	270	646	126	614	490	501	

Mileages © Rand McNally

15 396 miles   94 249 miles   **Total mileages through Montana**
15 396 miles   94 552 miles   **More mileages at** www.randmcnally.com/MC

Maps of Montana (Eastern) including insets for Billings, Great Falls, Butte, and Missoula.

Index of cities Pg. 250

Mileages between cities	Beatrice	Chadron	Columbus	Falls City	Grand Island	Kearney	Lincoln	McCook	Norfolk	North Platte	Ogallala	Omaha	O'Neill	Scottsbluff	Sioux City, IA	Valentine
Grand Island	131	326	64	196		50	93	152	105	145	194	147	112	323	187	210
Lincoln	41	450	79	102	93	129		232	124	224	274	55	208	402	151	304

Mileages © Rand McNally

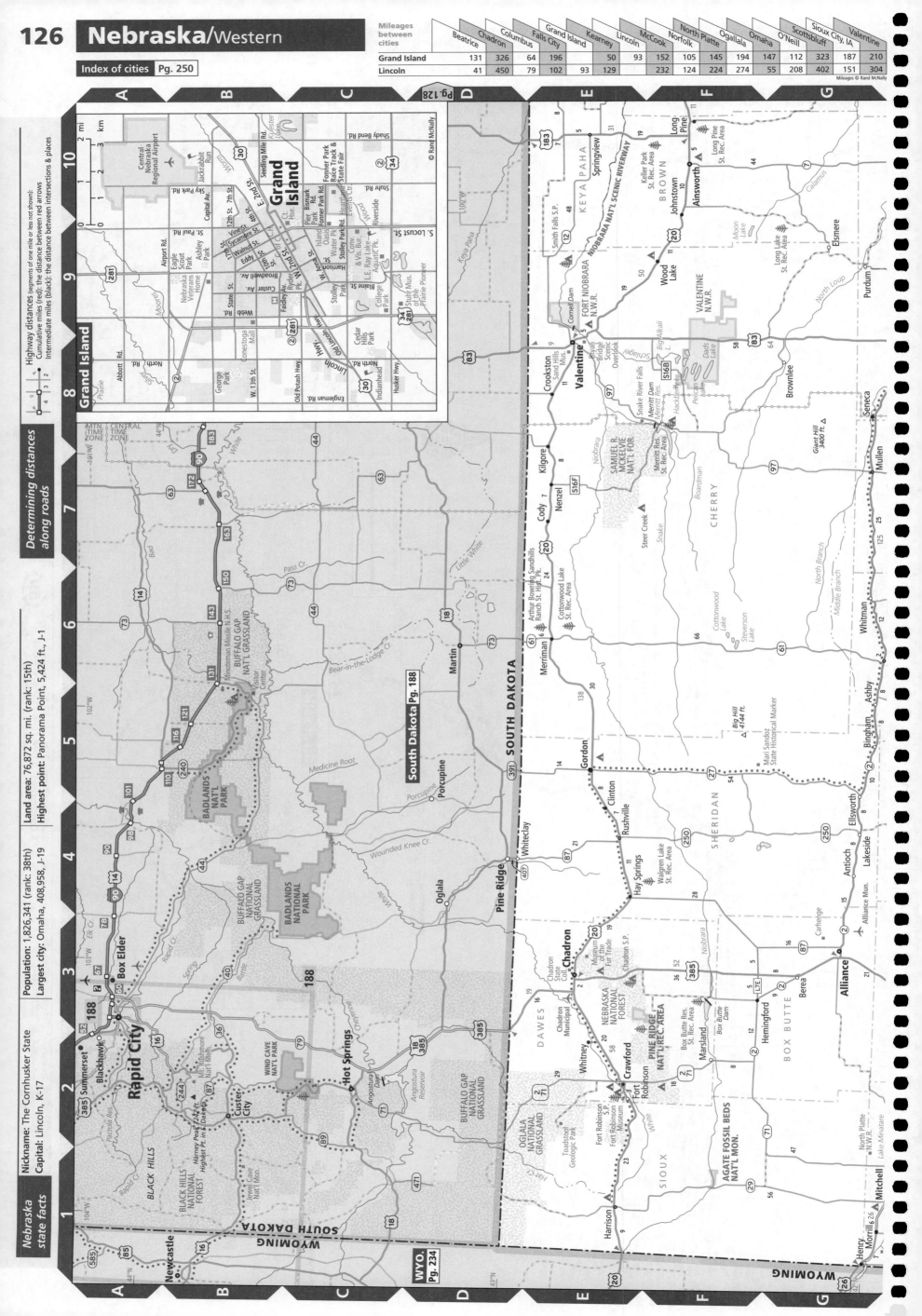

Nebraska state facts

Nickname: The Cornhusker State
Capital: Lincoln, K-17

Population: 1,826,341 (rank: 38th)
Largest city: Omaha, 408,958, J-19

Land area: 76,872 sq. mi. (rank: 15th)
Highest point: Panorama Point, 5,424 ft., J-1

Determining distances along roads

Highway distances (segments of one mile or less not shown):
Cumulative miles (red): the distance between red arrows
Intermediate miles (black): the distance between intersections & places
Highway distances: the distance between intersections & places

continued p. 128

Mileages between cities

	Beatrice	Chadron	Columbus	Falls City	Grand Island	Kearney	Lincoln	McCook	North Platte	Norfolk	Ogallala	Omaha	O'Neill	Scottsbluff	Sioux City, IA	Valentine
Norfolk	162	322	45	218	105	155	124	259	250		300	109	75	417	82	186
North Platte	262	229	210	327	145	99	224	67		250	53	276	189	182	373	129

Mileages © Rand McNally

Total mileages through Nebraska

| 80 | 455 miles | 83 | 226 miles |
| 81 | 219 miles | 20 | 436 miles |

More mileages at www.randmcnally.com/MC

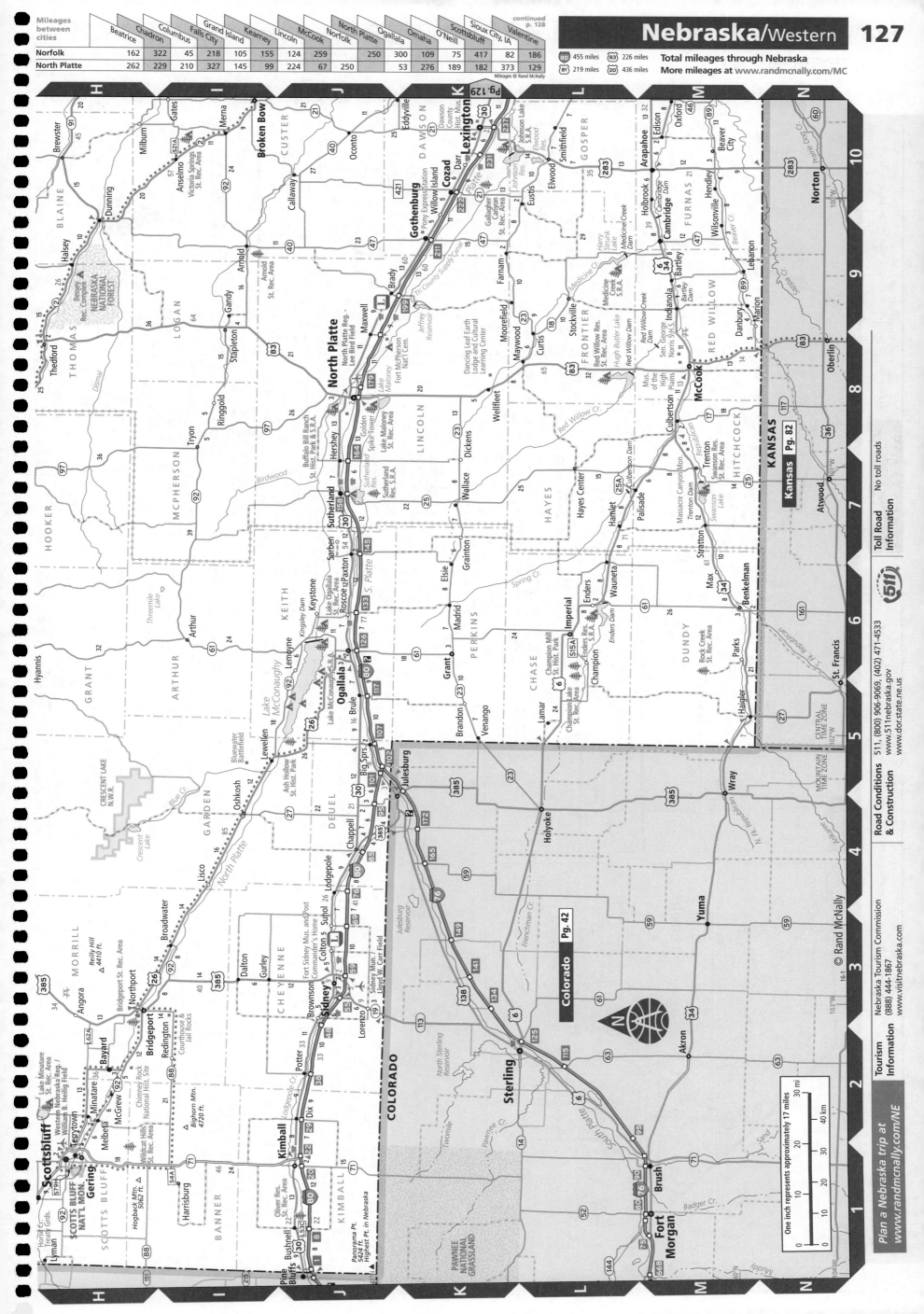

Tourism Information — Nebraska Tourism Commission (888) 444-1867 www.visitnebraska.com

Road Conditions & Construction — 511, (800) 906-9069, (402) 471-4533 www.511nebraska.gov www.dor.state.ne.us

Toll Road Information — No toll roads

Plan a Nebraska trip at www.randmcnally.com/NE

One inch represents approximately 17 miles

Mileages between cities

	Beatrice	Chadron	Columbus	Falls City	Grand Island	Kearney	Lincoln	McCook	Norfolk	North Platte	Ogallala	Omaha	O'Neill	Scottsbluff	Sioux City, IA	Valentine
Omaha	95	431	83	104	147	181	55	283	109	276	325		184	458	97	294
Scottsbluff	440	99	388	505	323	277	402	245	417	182	129	458	322		467	216

Mileages © Rand McNally

Nebraska state facts

Nickname: The Cornhusker State
Capital: Lincoln, K-17

Land area: 76,872 sq. mi. (rank: 38th)
Highest point: Panorama Point, 5,424 ft., J-1

Population: 1,826,341 (rank: 15th)
Largest city: Omaha, 408,958, J-19

Determining distances along roads

Interchanges and exit numbers
For most states, the mileage between interchanges may be determined by subtracting one number from the other.

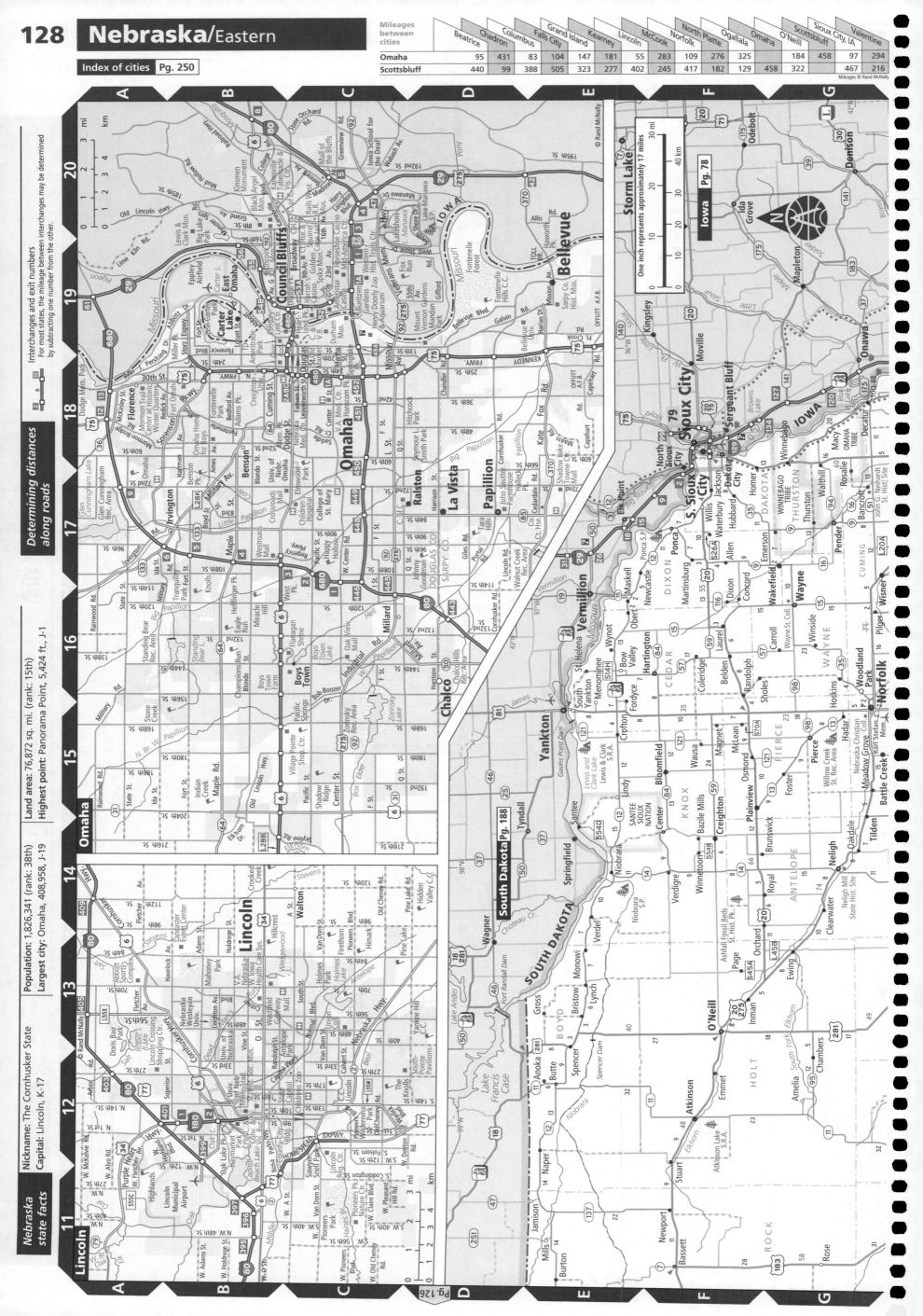

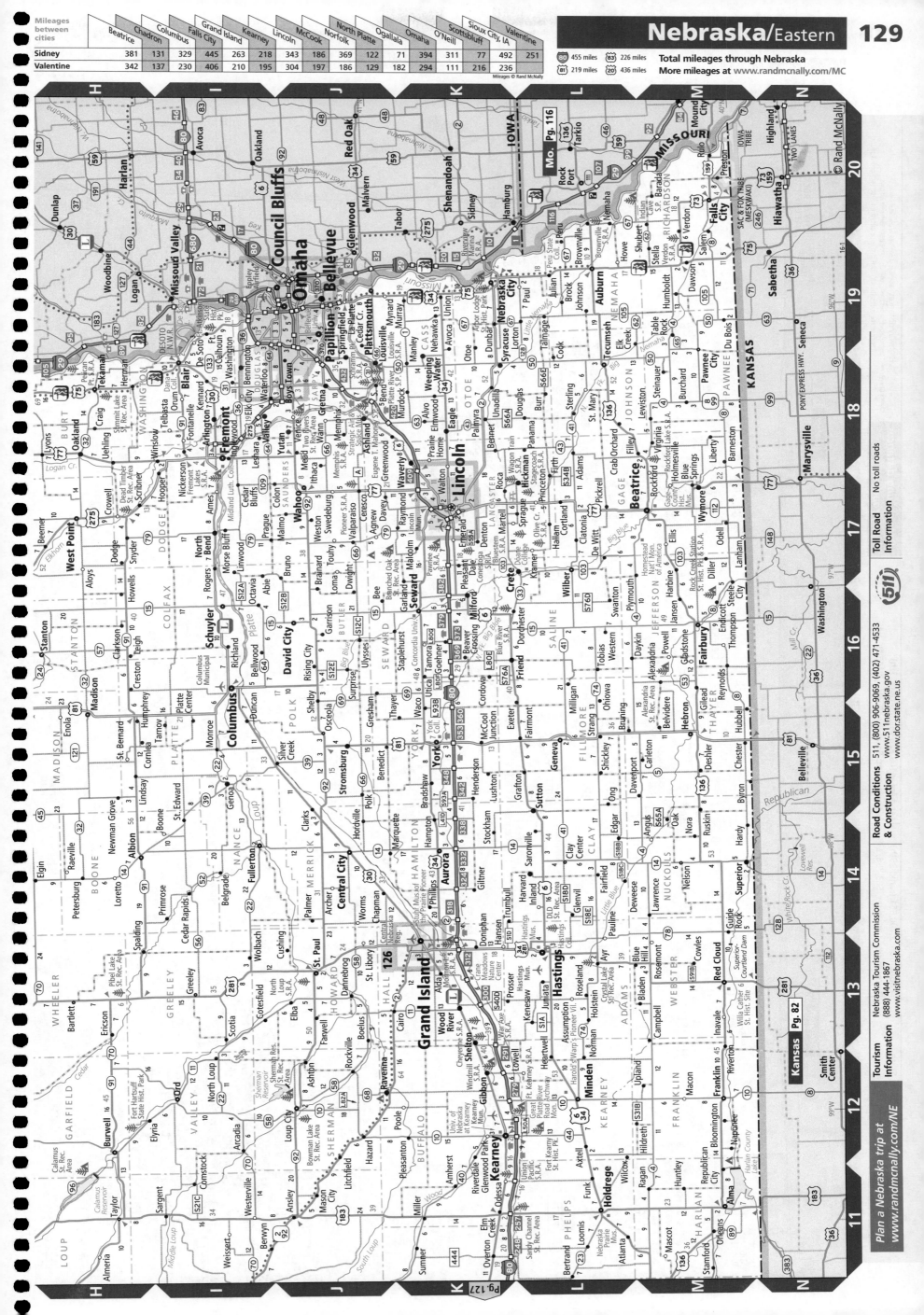

Mileages between cities

	Beatrice	Chadron	Columbus	Falls City	Grand Island	Kearney	Lincoln	McCook	Norfolk	North Platte	Ogallala	Omaha	O'Neill	Scottsbluff	Sioux City, IA	Valentine
Sidney	381	131	329	445	263	218	343	186	369	122	71	394	311	77	492	251
Valentine	342	137	230	406	210	195	304	197	186	129	182	294	111	216	236	

Mileages © Rand McNally

Total mileages through Nebraska
80 455 miles 83 226 miles
80 219 miles 20 436 miles
More mileages at www.randmcnally.com/MC

Plan a Nebraska trip at
www.randmcnally.com/NE

Tourism Information
Nebraska Tourism Commission
(888) 444-1867
www.visitnebraska.com

Road Conditions & Construction
511, (800) 906-9069, (402) 471-4533
511nebraska.gov
www.dor.state.ne.us

Toll Road Information
No toll roads

Kansas Pg. 82
Kansas Pg. 82
Mo. Pg. 116
Pg.126
Pg.127

Nevada state facts

Nickname: The Silver State
Capital: Carson City, F-2

Population: 2,700,551 (rank: 7th)
Largest city: Las Vegas, 583,756, L-8

Land area: 109,826 sq. mi. (rank: 35th)
Highest point: Boundary Peak, 13,143 ft., I-4

Determining distances along roads

Highway distances (segments of one mile or less not shown):
Cumulative miles (red): the distance between red arrows
Intermediate miles (black): the distance between intersections & places

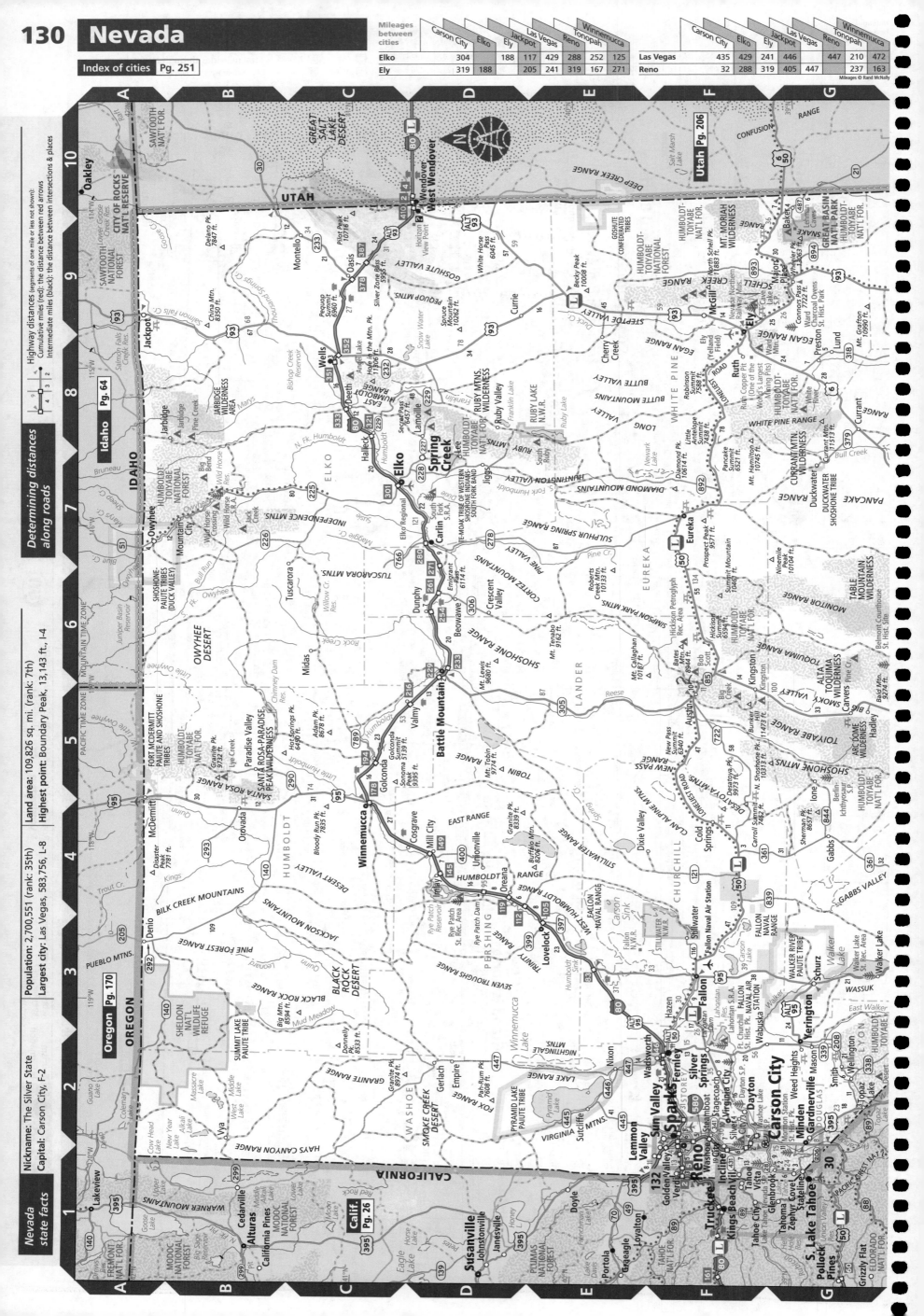

Oregon Pg. 170
Idaho Pg. 64
Utah Pg. 206
Calif. Pg. 26

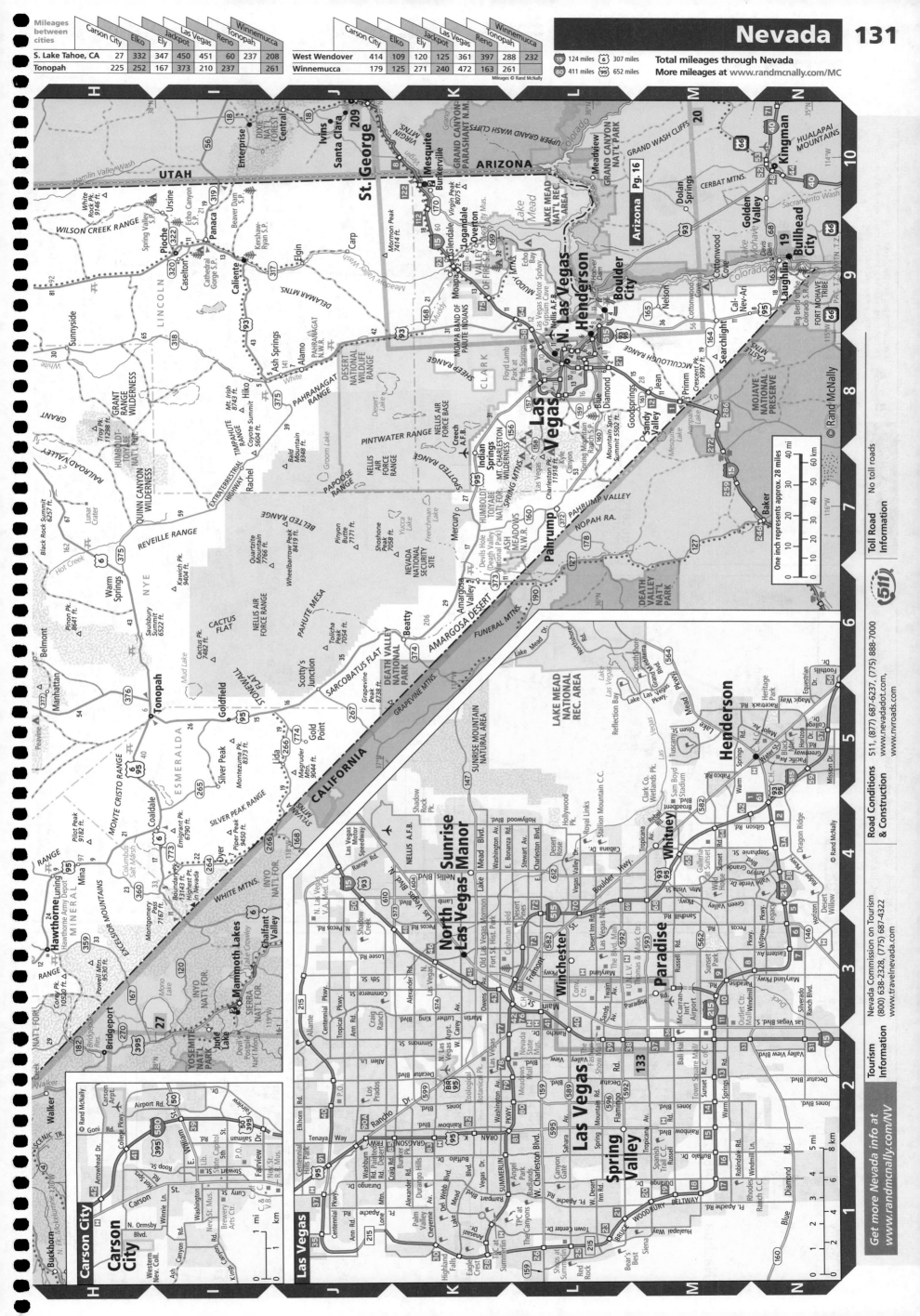

Mileages between cities	Carson City	Elko	Ely	Jackpot	Las Vegas	Reno	Winnemucca	Tonopah
S. Lake Tahoe, CA	27	332	347	450	451	60	237	208
Tonopah	225	252	167	373	210	237	261	

	Carson City	Elko	Ely	Jackpot	Las Vegas	Reno	Winnemucca	Tonopah
West Wendover	414	109	120	125	361	397	288	232
Winnemucca	179	125	271	240	472	163		261

Mileages © Rand McNally

Total mileages through Nevada
More mileages at www.randmcnally.com/MC

15 — 124 miles   6 — 307 miles
80 — 411 miles   95 — 652 miles

Tourism Information
Nevada Commission on Tourism
(800) 638-2328, (775) 687-4322
www.travelnevada.com

Road Conditions & Construction
511, (877) 687-6237, (775) 888-7000
www.nevadadot.com
www.nvroads.com

Toll Road Information
No toll roads

Get more Nevada info at
www.randmcnally.com/NV

Index of cities Pg. 251

Mileages between cities	Colebrook	Concord	Conway	Keene	Laconia	Littleton	Portsmouth	Nashua		Colebrook	Concord	Conway	Keene	Laconia	Littleton	Portsmouth	Nashua
Berlin	49	115	40	168	97	42	151	117	Keene	181	51	130		80	136	50	99
Concord	137		77	51	27	87	36	44	Lebanon	128	57	88	64	58	82	89	111

Mileages © Rand McNally

New Hampshire state facts

Nickname: The Granite State
Capital: Concord, K-7

Population: 1,316,470 (rank: 42nd)
Largest city: Manchester, K-7

Land area: 8,968 sq. mi. (rank: 44th)
Highest point: Mount Washington, 6,288 ft., F-8

Determining distances along roads

Interchanges and exit numbers
For most states, the mileage between interchanges may be determined by subtracting one number from the other.

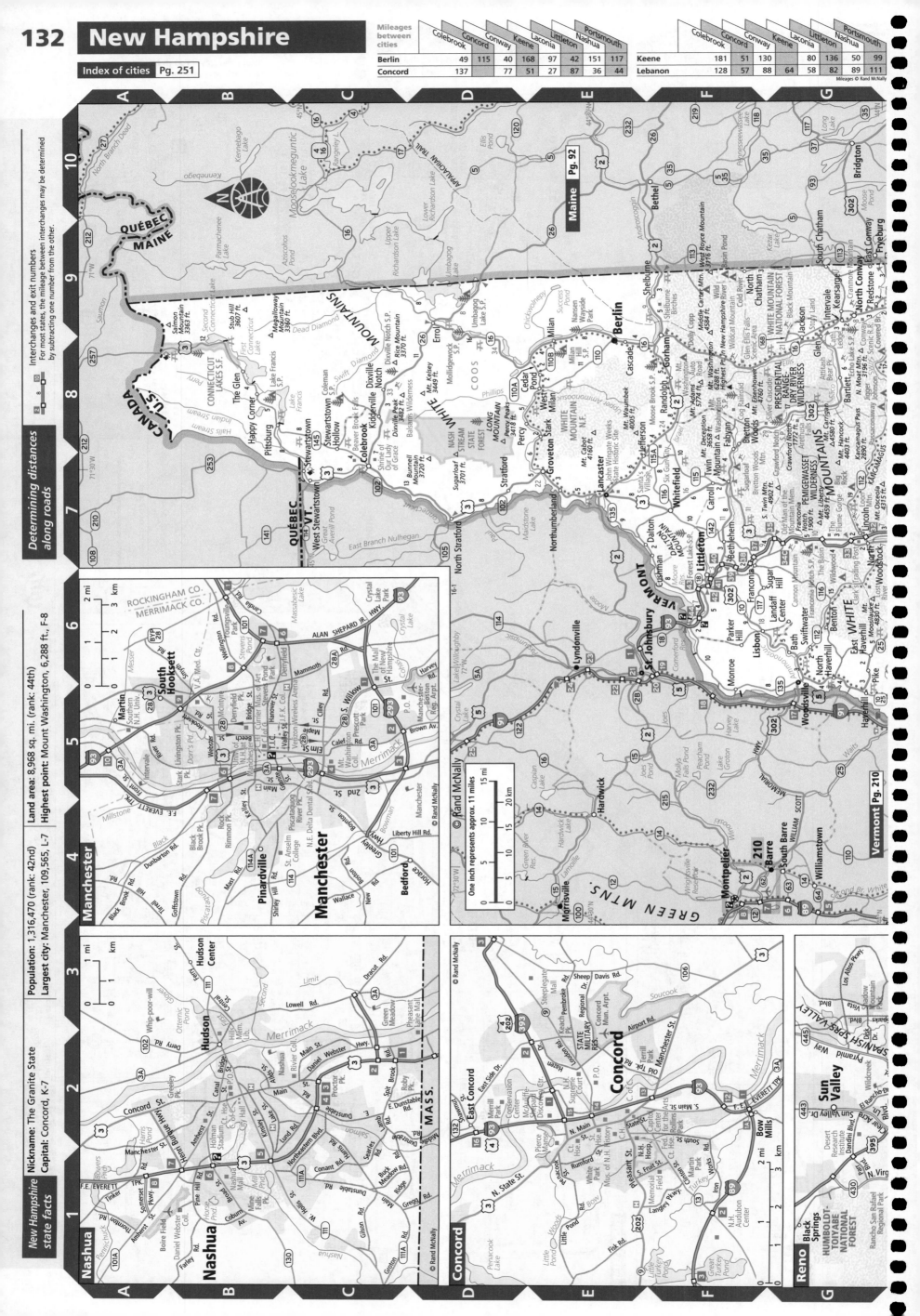

Mileages between cities	Colebrook	Concord	Conway	Keene	Laconia	Littleton	Nashua	Portsmouth
Littleton	56	87	54	136	66		121	129
Manchester	155	18	95	55	45	105	18	43
Nashua	172	36	113	50	63	121		54
Portsmouth	180	44	77	99	57	129	54	

Mileages © Rand McNally

Total mileages through New Hampshire
More mileages at www.randmcnally.com/MC

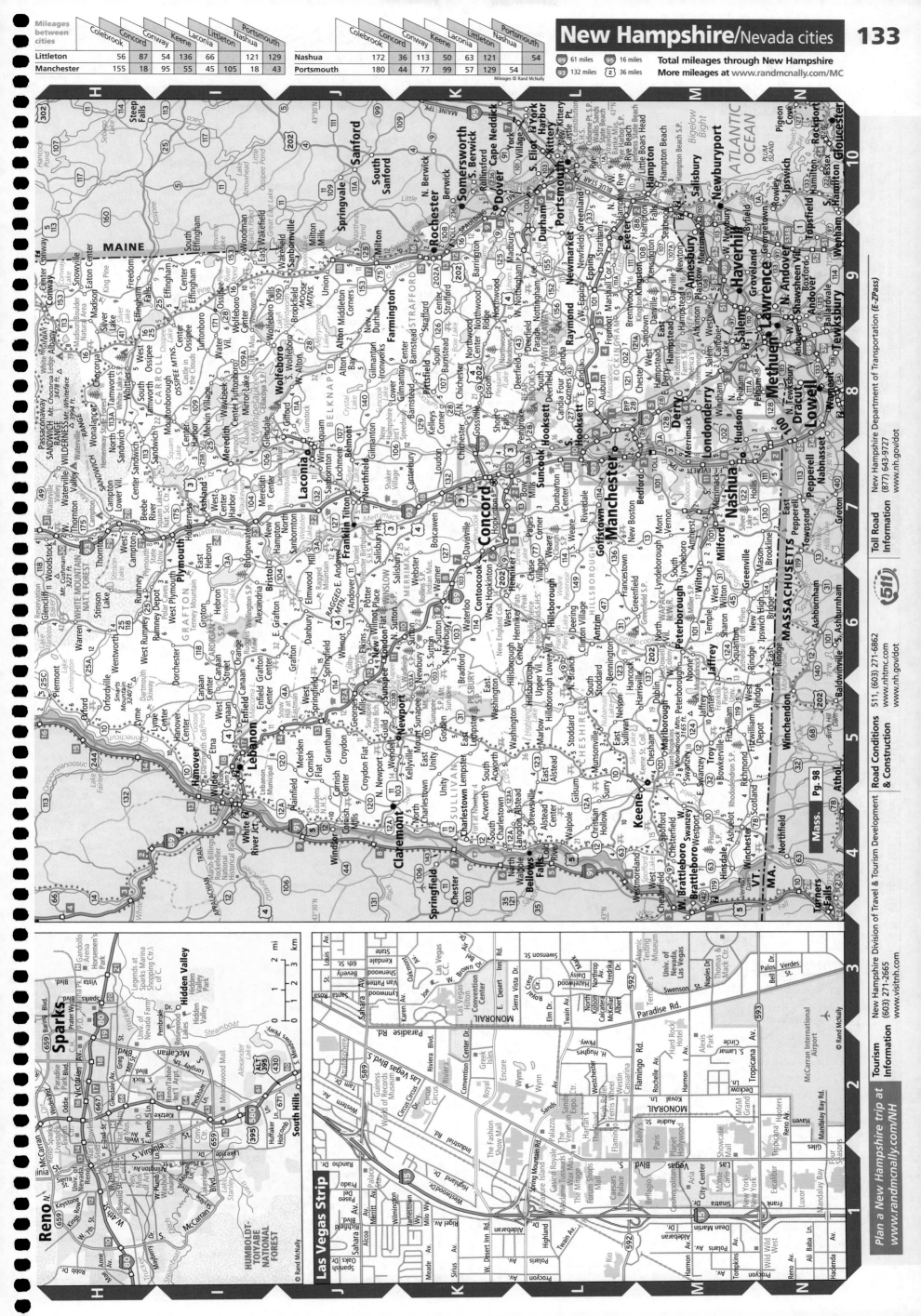

Mileages between cities	Atlantic City	Camden	Cape May	Jersey City	Long Branch	New Brunswick Newark	New York, NY	Paterson	Phillipsburg	Port Jervis, NY	Princeton	Toms River	Trenton	Vineland	Wilmington, DE
Atlantic City		58	47	120	82	115	94	126	129	138	182	99	52	90	36	82
Camden	58		88	86	76	80	61	96	94	80	143	45	55	34	36	31

Mileages © Rand McNally

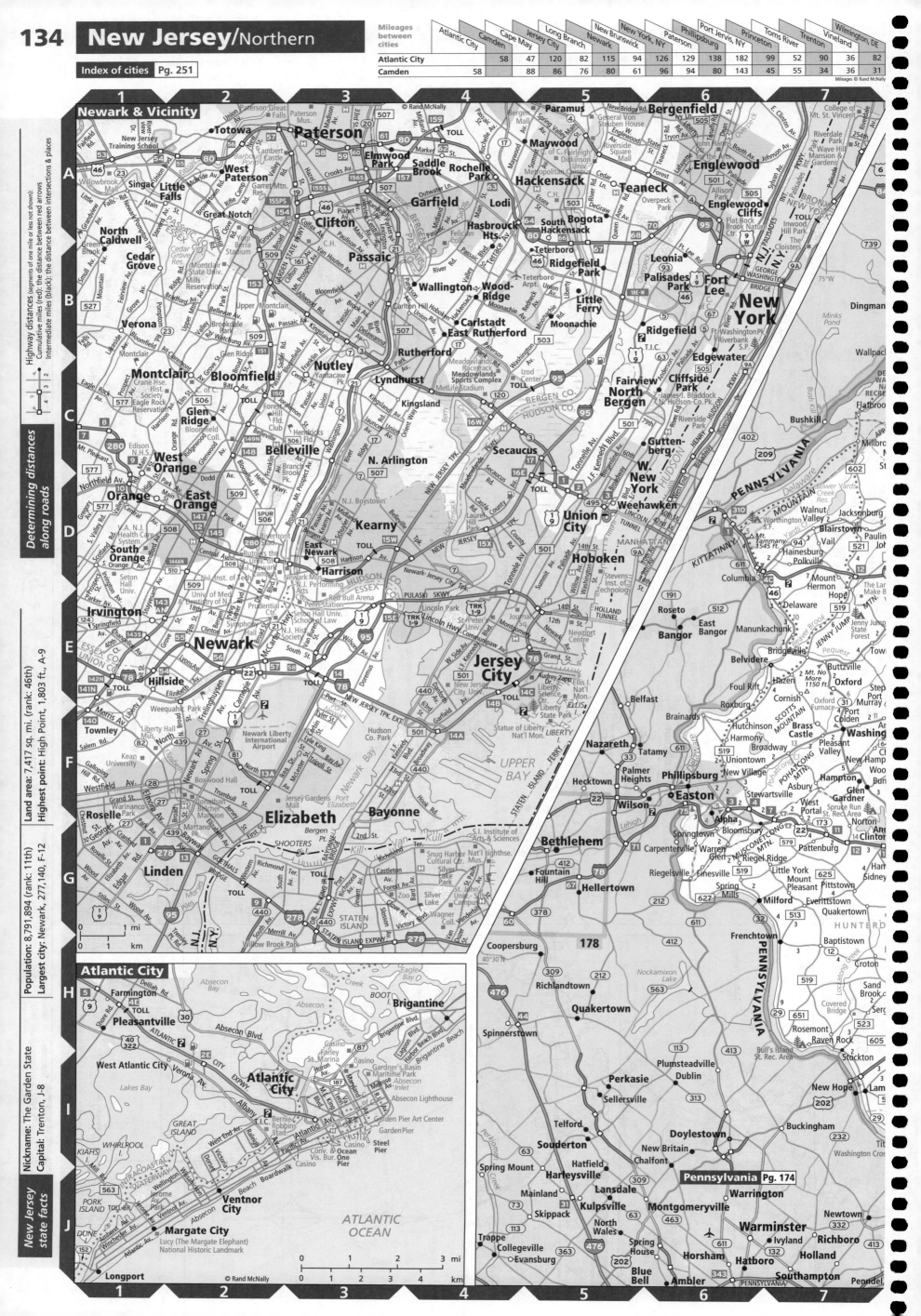

Newark & Vicinity

Atlantic City

178

Pennsylvania Pg. 174

New Jersey state facts

Nickname: The Garden State
Capital: Trenton, J-8
Population: 8,791,894 (rank: 11th)
Largest city: Newark, 277,140, F-12
Land area: 7,417 sq. mi. (rank: 46th)
Highest point: High Point, 1,803 ft., A-9

Determining distances along roads

Mileages between cities	Atlantic City	Camden	Cape May	Jersey City	Long Branch	Newark	New Brunswick	New York, NY	Paterson	Phillipsburg	Port Jervis, NY	Princeton	Toms River	Trenton	Vineland	Wilmington, DE
Cape May	47	88		151	114	147	126	157	161	170	214	131	84	121	48	98
Newark	115	80	147	6	43		25	10	15	58	74	41	63	55	114	112

Mileages © Rand McNally

continued p. 136

Total mileages through New Jersey
More mileages at www.randmcnally.com/MC

One inch represents approximately 6 miles

NEW YORK

New York Pg. 140

Pg. 137

16-1 © Rand McNally

Burlington Co. Bridge Comm. (E-ZPass): (856) 829-1900, (609) 387-1480; www.bcbridges.org
Del. River & Bay Authority (Del. Mem. Br., Cape May/Lewes Fy.) (E-ZPass): (302) 571-6300; www.drba.net
Delaware River Port Authority (Phila. area bridges) (E-ZPass): (877) 567-3772; www.drpa.org

Toll Road Information

Road Conditions & Construction
511, (866) 511-6538
www.state.nj.us/transportation
511, (866) 511-6538
www.511.nj.org

Tourism Information
New Jersey Division of Travel & Tourism
(609) 599-6540
www.visitnj.us

Explore New Jersey at
www.randmcnally.com/NJ

Continued on next page

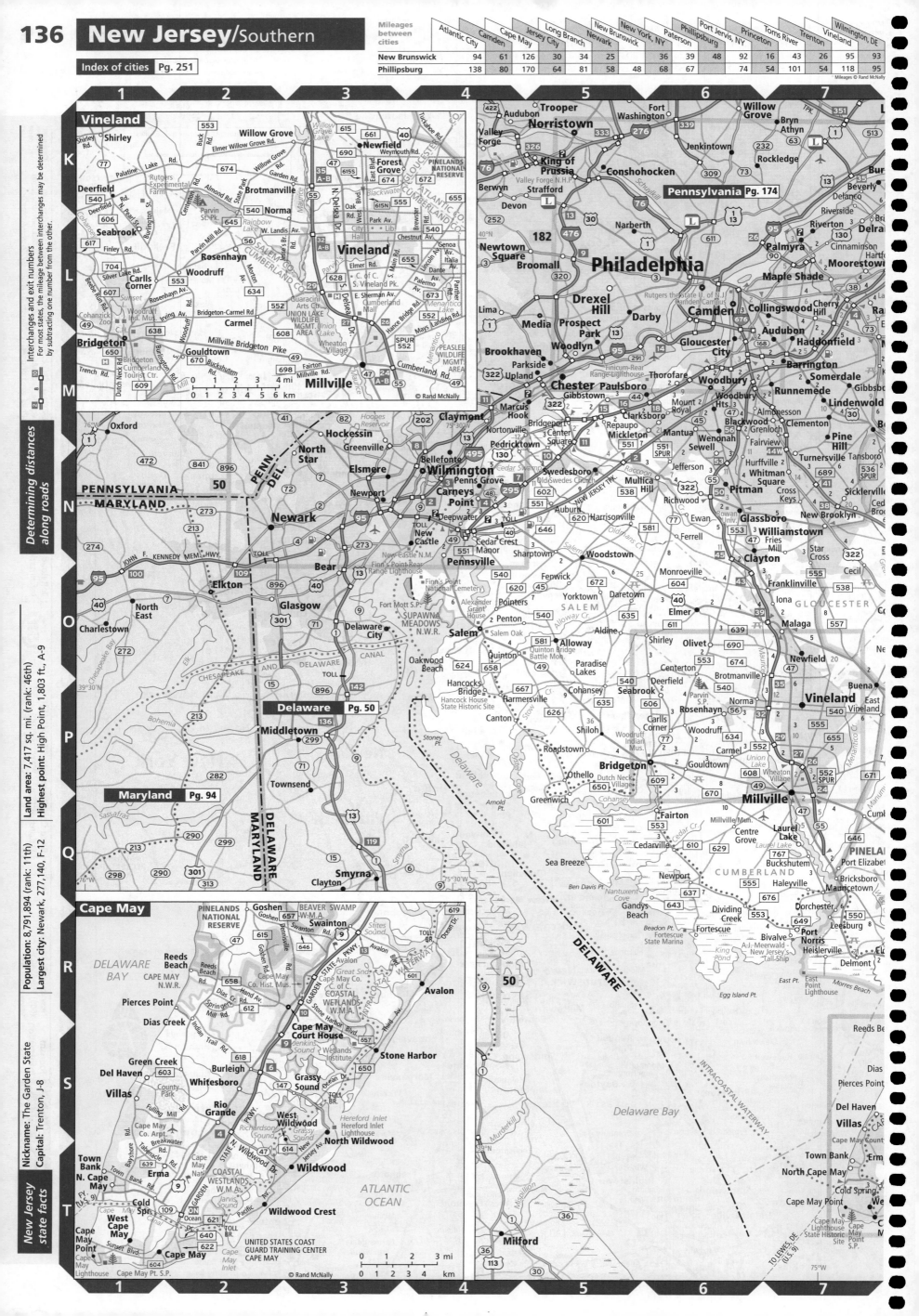

Mileages between cities	Atlantic City	Camden	Cape May	Jersey City	Long Branch	Newark	New Brunswick	New York, NY	Paterson	Phillipsburg	Port Jervis, NY	Princeton	Toms River	Trenton	Vineland	Wilmington, DE
Port Jervis, NY	182	143	214	89	110	74	92	95	73	74		94	130	122	180	158
Trenton	90	34	121	61	52	55	26	66	69	54	122	11	47		69	61

Mileages © Rand McNally

Total mileages through New Jersey
More mileages at www.randmcnally.com/MC

76 68 miles	95 98 miles	
80 68 miles		

N.J. Turnpike Authority (N.J. Turnpike, Gdn. St. Pkwy.) (E-ZPass): (732) 750-5300; www.state.nj.us
Port Authority of N.Y. & N.J. (N.Y. City area bridges & tunnels) (E-ZPass): (800) 221-9903; www.panynj.gov
South Jersey Transportation Authority (Atlantic City Expressway) (E-ZPass): (609) 965-6060; www.sjta.com

Toll Road Information

511, (866) 511-6538
www.state.nj.us/transportation
www.511.nj.org

Road Conditions & Construction

New Jersey Division of Travel & Tourism
(609) 599-6540
www.visitnj.org

Tourism Information

Explore New Jersey at
www.randmcnally.com/NJ

Continued from previous page

ATLANTIC OCEAN

Pinelands National Reserve

Burlington

Camden

Ocean

Atlantic

Cape May

Trenton (inset)

One inch represents approximately 6 miles
0   5   10 mi
0   5   10   15 km

© Rand McNally

16-1

Selected place names: Bordentown, Florence, Roebling, Mansfield, Columbus, New Egypt, Cream Ridge, Jacksons Mills, Candlewood, Ramtown, Spring Lake Hts., Manasquan, Brielle, Lakewood, Point Pleasant, Point Pleasant Beach, Bay Head, Lakehurst, Whitesville, Ridgeway, Crestwood Village, Toms River, Beachwood, Pine Beach, Island Heights, Seaside Heights, Seaside Park, Browns Mills, Medford, Medford Lakes, Tabernacle, Chatsworth, Indian Mills, Warren Grove, Barnegat, Barnegat Light, Loveladies, Harvey Cedars, Surf City, Ship Bottom, Beach Haven, Manahawkin, Tuckerton, Mystic Island, New Gretna, Hammonton, Batsto, Egg Harbor City, Port Republic, Smithville, Pomona, Mays Landing, McKee City, Absecon, Brigantine, Atlantic City, Pleasantville, Northfield, Linwood, Ventnor City, Margate City, Longport, Somers Point, Ocean City, Marmora, Woodbine, Sea Isle City, Avalon, Stone Harbor, Cape May Court House, Rio Grande, Wildwood, Wildwood Crest, Cape May

Trenton inset: Princeton, Princeton Jct., Lawrenceville, Pennington, Titusville, Washington Crossing, Ewing, Ewingville, Yardley, Morrisville, Levittown, Fallsington, Fairless Hills, Trenton, White Horse, Mercerville, Hamilton Square, Robbinsville, Yardville, Bordentown, Groveville

One inch represents approximately 6 miles (inset scale varies)

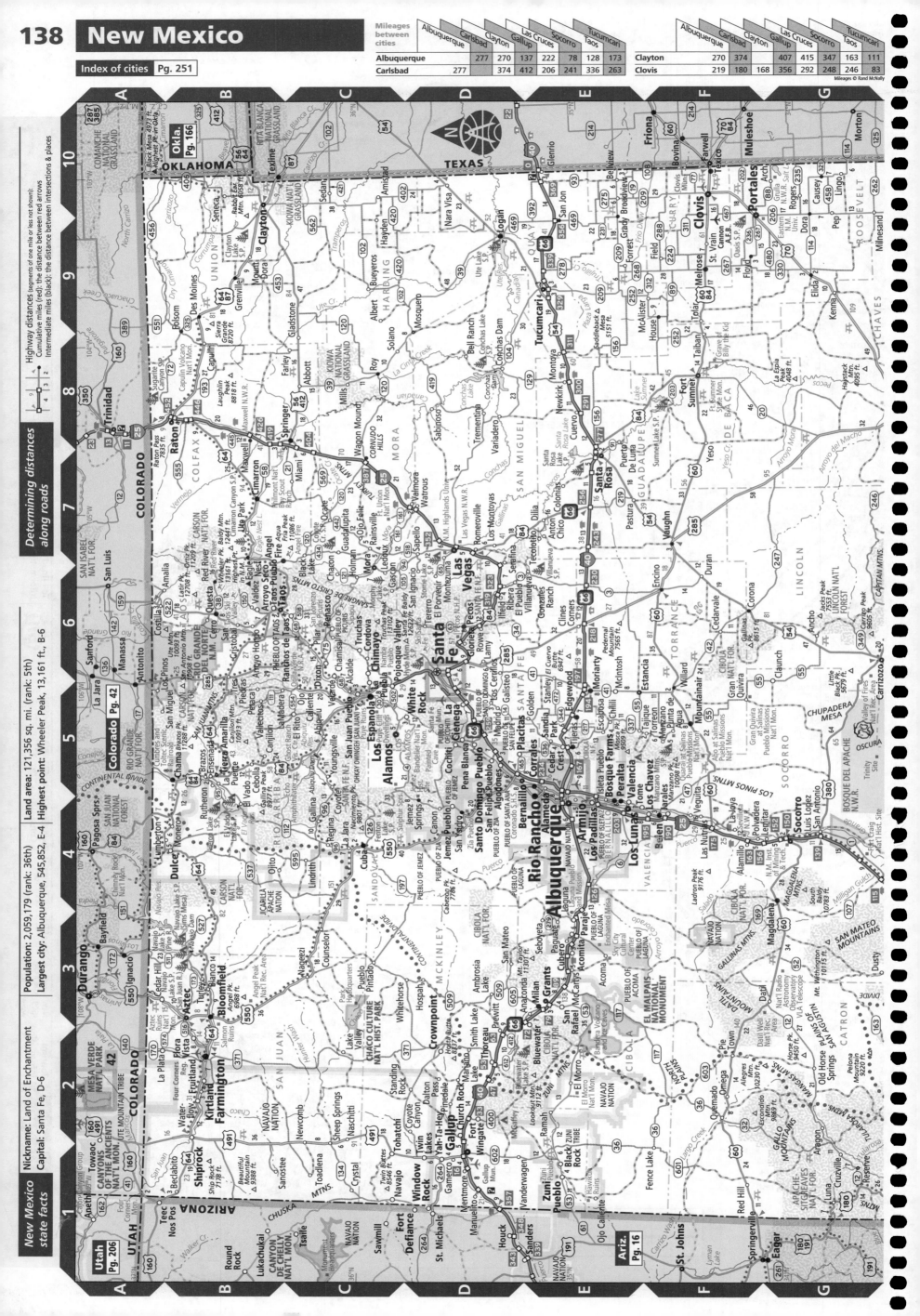

Okla. Pg. 166

Colorado Pg. 42

Ariz. Pg. 16

Utah Pg. 206

New Mexico state facts

Nickname: Land of Enchantment
Capital: Santa Fe, D-6
Population: 2,059,179 (rank: 36th)
Land area: 121,356 sq. mi. (rank: 5th)
Largest city: Albuquerque, 545,852, E-4
Highest point: Wheeler Peak, 13,161 ft., B-6

Determining distances along roads

Highway distances (segments of one mile or less not shown):
Cumulative miles (red); the distance between red arrows
Intermediate miles (black); the distance between intersections & places

Mileages between cities	Albuquerque	Carlsbad	Clayton	Gallup	Las Cruces	Socorro	Tucumcari	Taos		Albuquerque	Carlsbad	Clayton	Gallup	Las Cruces	Socorro	Tucumcari	Taos
Albuquerque		277	270	137	222	78	128	173	Clayton	270	374		407	415	347	163	111
Carlsbad	277		374	412	206	241	336	263	Clovis	219	180	168	356	292	248	246	83

Mileages © Rand McNally

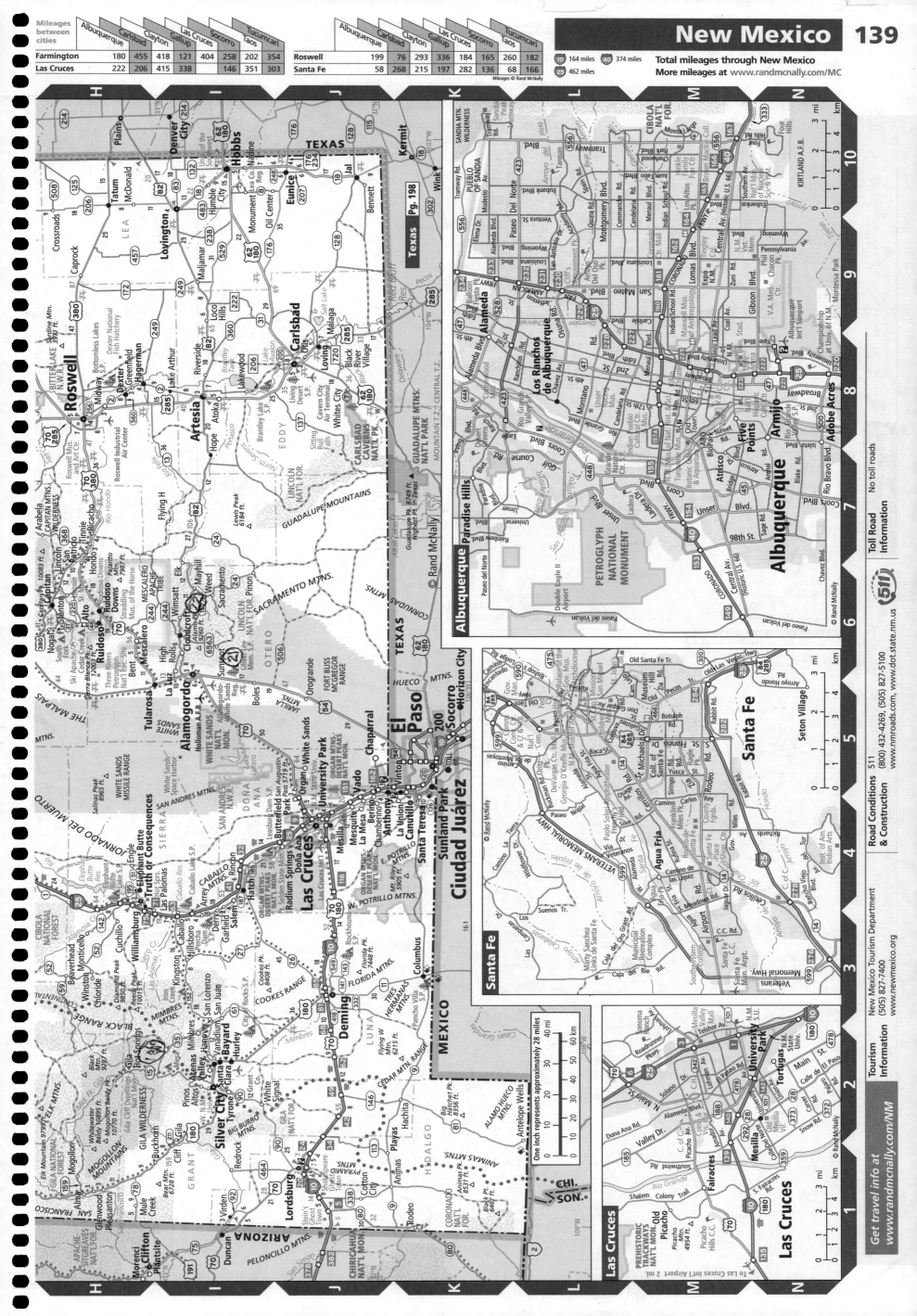

Mileages between cities	Albuquerque	Carlsbad	Clayton	Gallup	Las Cruces	Socorro	Taos	Tucumcari		Albuquerque	Carlsbad	Clayton	Gallup	Las Cruces	Socorro	Taos	Tucumcari
Farmington	180	455	418	121	404	258	202	354	Roswell	199	76	293	336	184	165	260	182
Las Cruces	222	206	415	338		146	351	303	Santa Fe	58	268	215	197	282	68	166	

Mileages © Rand McNally

Total mileages through New Mexico
10 164 miles   40 374 miles
25 462 miles
More mileages at www.randmcnally.com/MC

Tourism Information
New Mexico Tourism Department
(505) 827-7400
www.newmexico.org

Road Conditions & Construction   511
(800) 432-4269, (505) 827-5100
www.nmroads.com, www.dot.state.nm.us

Toll Road Information

No toll roads

Get travel info at
www.randmcnally.com/NM

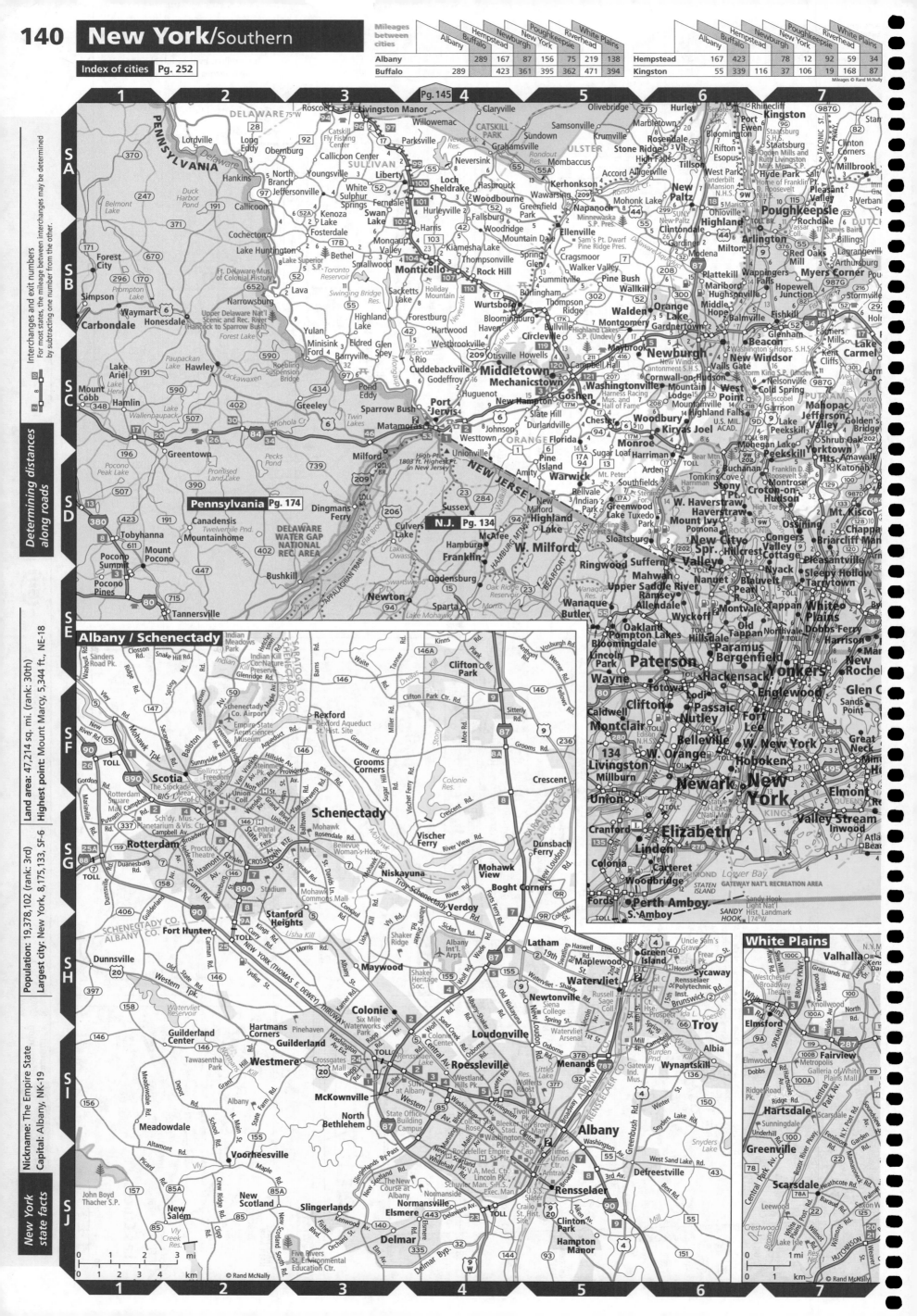

Determining distances along roads

Interchanges and exit numbers: For most states, the mileage between interchanges may be determined by subtracting one number from the other.

New York state facts

Nickname: The Empire State
Capital: Albany, NK-19
Population: 19,378,102 (rank: 3rd)
Largest city: New York, 8,175,133, SF-6
Land area: 47,214 sq. mi. (rank: 30th)
Highest point: Mount Marcy, 5,344 ft., NE-18

Pg. 145

Pennsylvania Pg. 174

N.J. Pg. 134

Albany / Schenectady

White Plains

© Rand McNally

Mileages between cities

	Albany	Buffalo	Hempstead	Newburgh	New York	Poughkeepsie	Riverhead	White Plains
Montauk	260	513	97	172	107	184	42	126
Newburgh	87	361	78		72	19	130	49
New York	156	395	12	72		84	66	26
Poughkeepsie	75	362	92	19	84		143	60

Mileages © Rand McNally

84: 72 miles; 95: 24 miles; 87: 334 miles; 495: 66 miles

Total mileages through New York
More mileages at www.randmcnally.com/MC

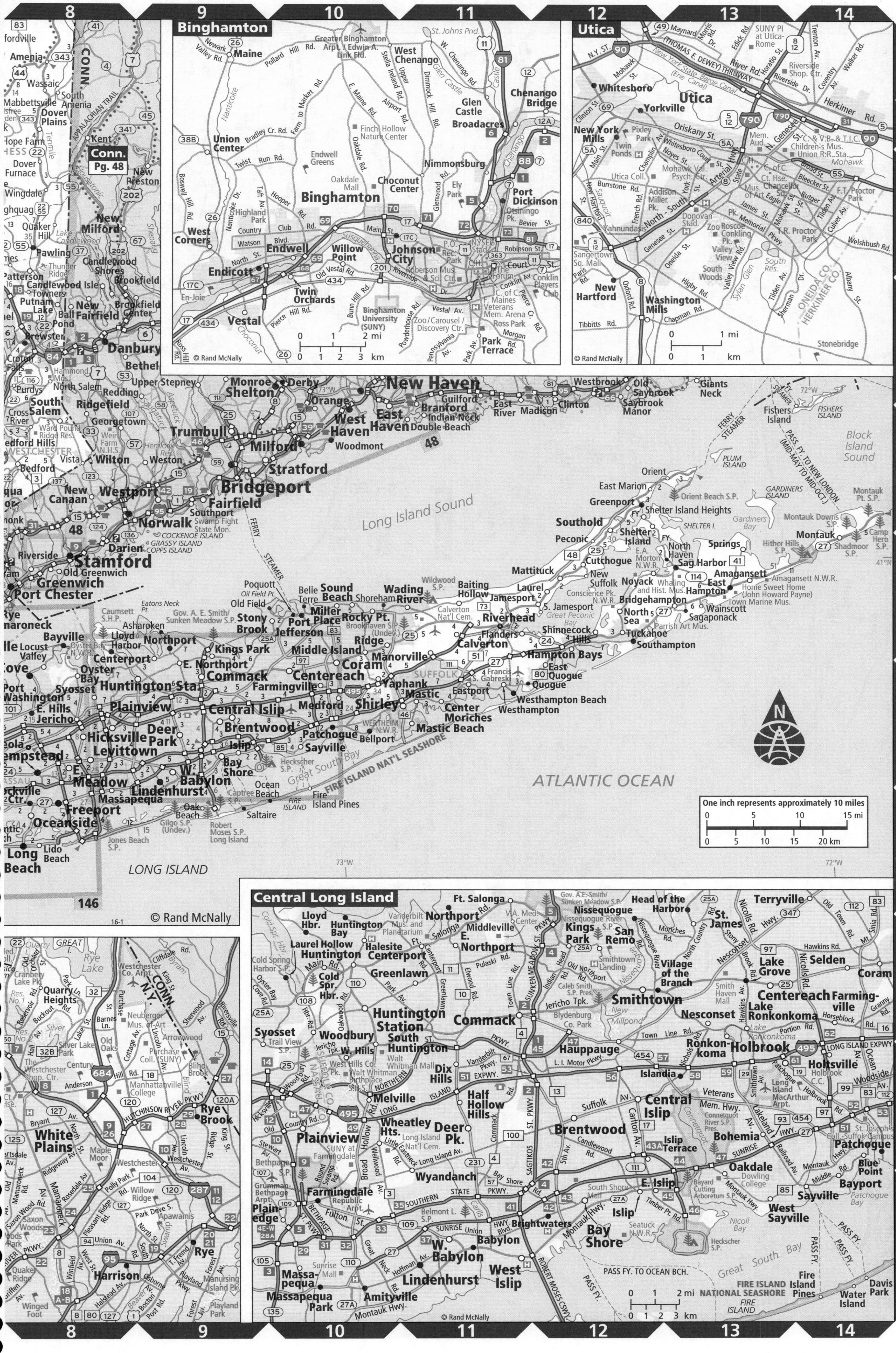

Continued on next 2 pages

Toll Road Information (all use E-ZPass)
MTA (N.Y. City in-state bridges & tunnels): 511, say "Bridges & Tunnels"; web.mta.info
N.Y. State Bridge Authority (Hudson R. bridges): (845) 691-7245; www.nysba.state.ny.us
Port Authority of N.Y. & N.J. (N.Y.C. inter-state bridges & tunnels): (800) 221-9903; www.panynj.gov

Road Conditions & Construction
511, (888) 465-1169, (518) 457-6195
www.511ny.org, www.dot.ny.gov
Thruway: (800) 847-8929, www.thruway.ny.gov

Tourism Information
New York State Division of Tourism
(800) 225-5697
www.iloveny.com

Explore New York at www.randmcnally.com/NY

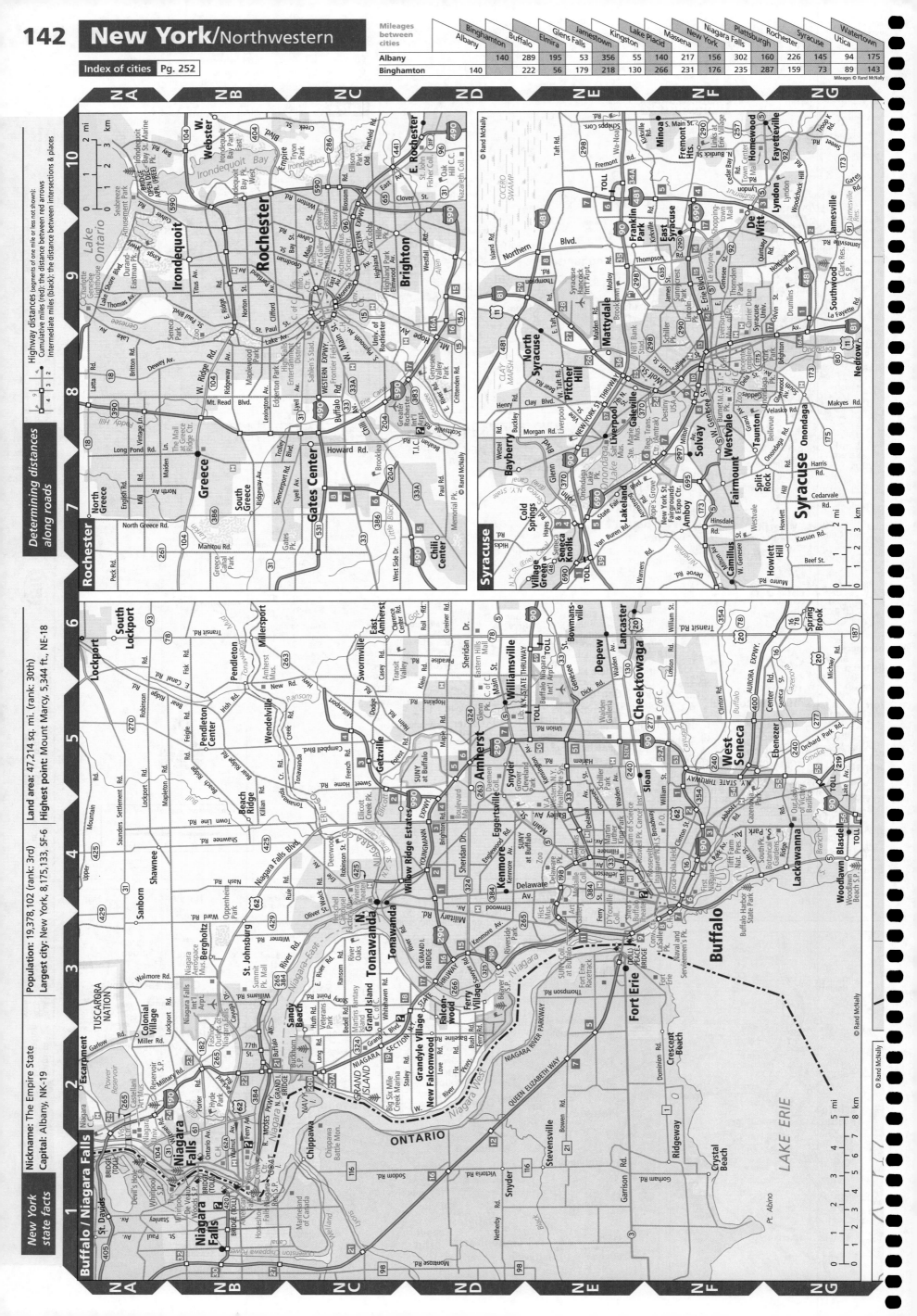

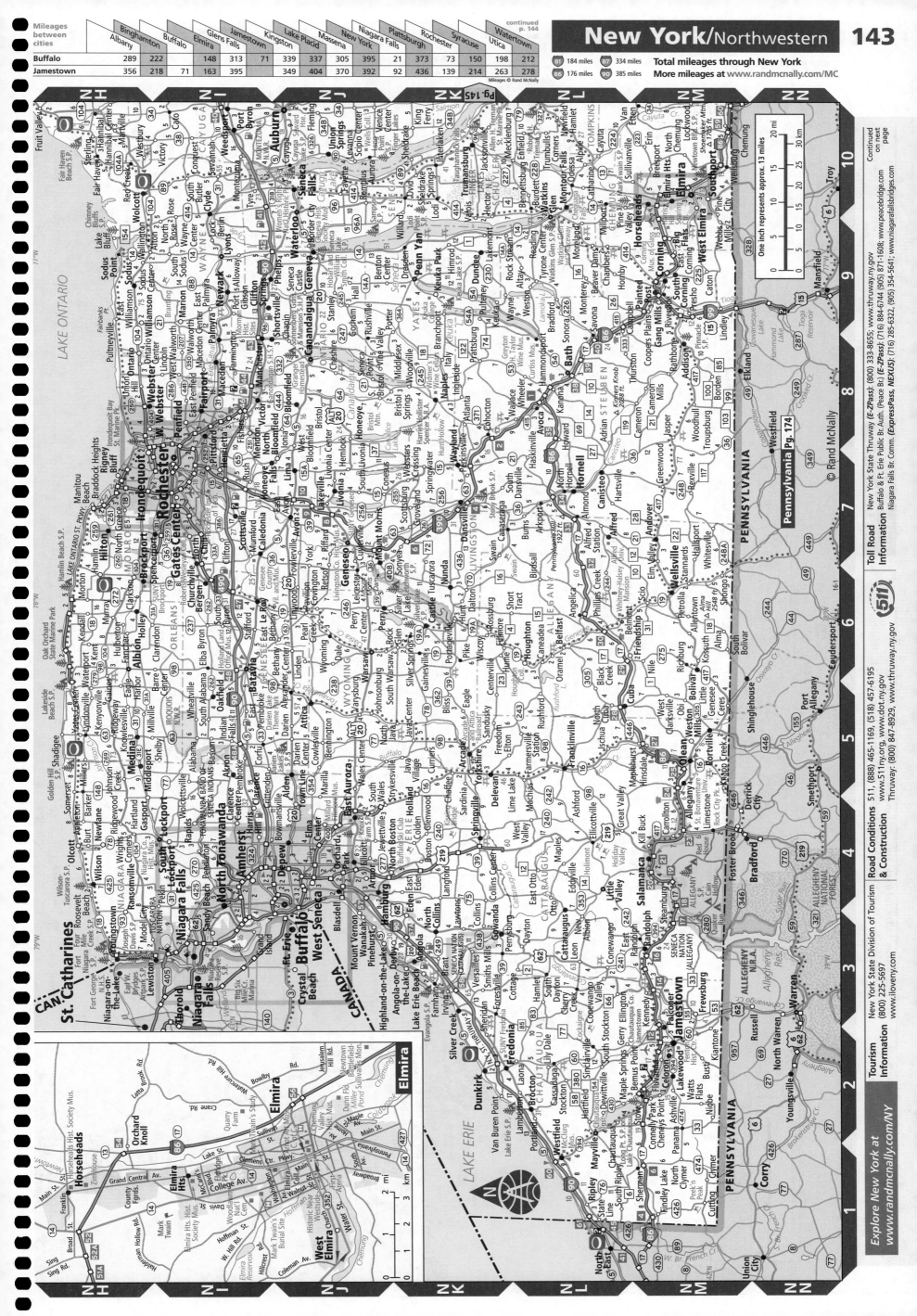

continued p. 144

Mileages © Rand McNally

Total mileages through New York
More mileages at www.randmcnally.com/MC

81	184 miles	87	334 miles
86	176 miles	90	385 miles

Toll Road Information
New York State Thruway (E-ZPass): (800) 333-8655; www.thruway.ny.gov
Buffalo & Ft. Erie Public Br. Auth. (Peace Br.) (E-ZPass): (716) 884-6744 (905) 871-1608; www.peacebridge.com
Niagara Falls Br. Comm. (ExpressPass, NEXUS): (716) 285-6322, (905) 354-5641; www.niagarafallsbridges.com

Road Conditions & Construction
511, (888) 465-1169, (518) 457-6195
511ny.org, www.511ny.org, www.dot.ny.gov
Thruway: (800) 847-8929, www.thruway.ny.gov

Tourism Information
New York State Division of Tourism
(800) 225-5697
www.iloveny.com

Continued on next page

© Rand McNally

Explore New York at www.randmcnally.com/NY

Pennsylvania Pg. 174

Index of cities Pg. 252

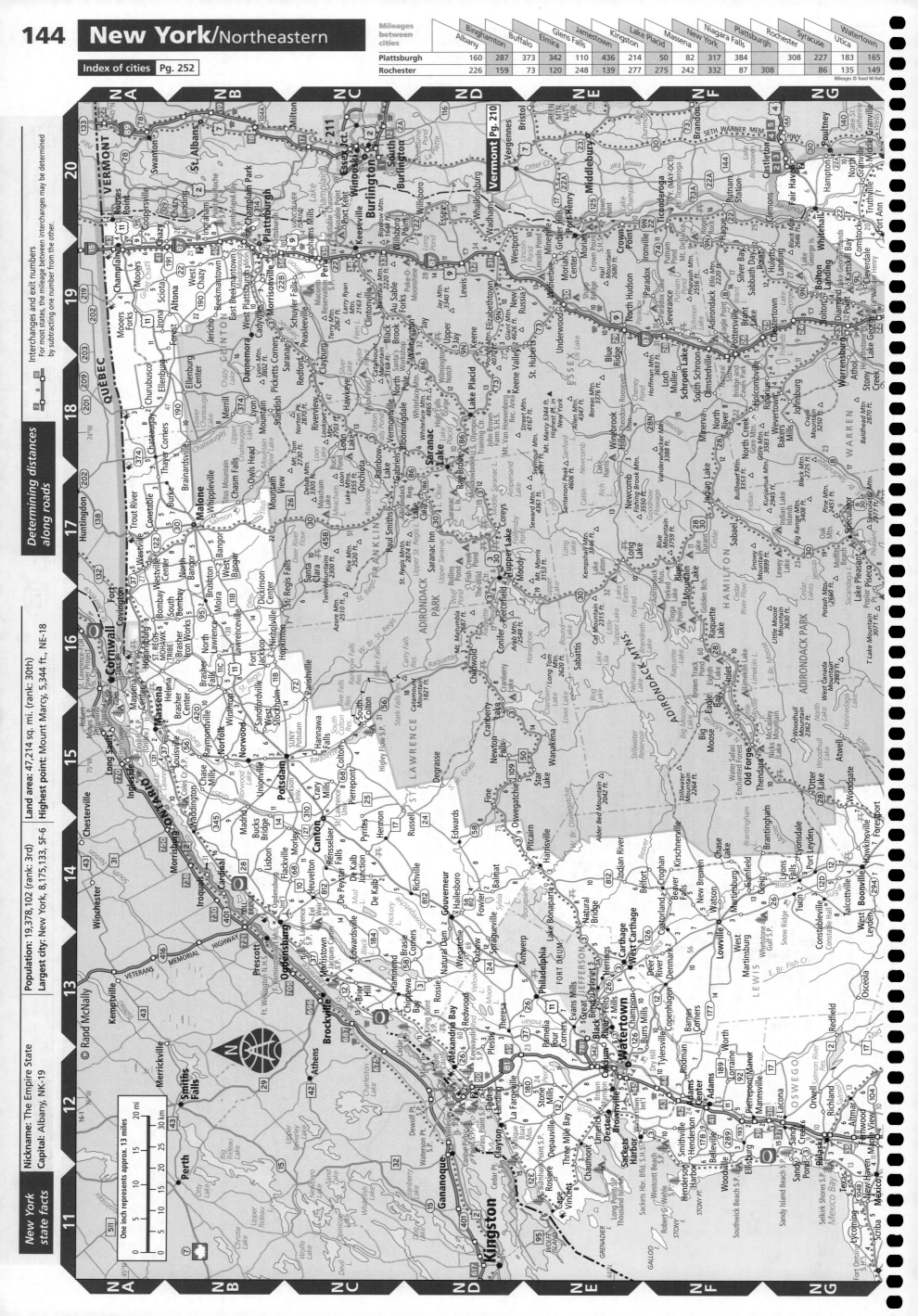

Mileages between cities	Albany	Binghamton	Buffalo	Elmira	Glens Falls	Jamestown	Kingston	Lake Placid	Massena	New York	Niagara Falls	Plattsburgh	Rochester	Syracuse	Utica	Watertown
Plattsburgh	160	287	373	342	110	436	214	50	82	317	384		308	227	183	165
Rochester	226	159	73	120	248	139	277	275	242	332	87	308		86	129	149

Mileages © Rand McNally

New York state facts

Nickname: The Empire State
Capital: Albany, NK-19

Population: 19,378,102 (rank: 3rd)
Largest city: New York, NK-19

Land area: 47,214 sq. mi. (rank: 30th)
Highest point: Mount Marcy, 5,344 ft., NE-18

Determining distances along roads

Interchanges and exit numbers

For most states, the mileage between interchanges may be determined by subtracting one number from the other.

One inch represents approx. 13 miles

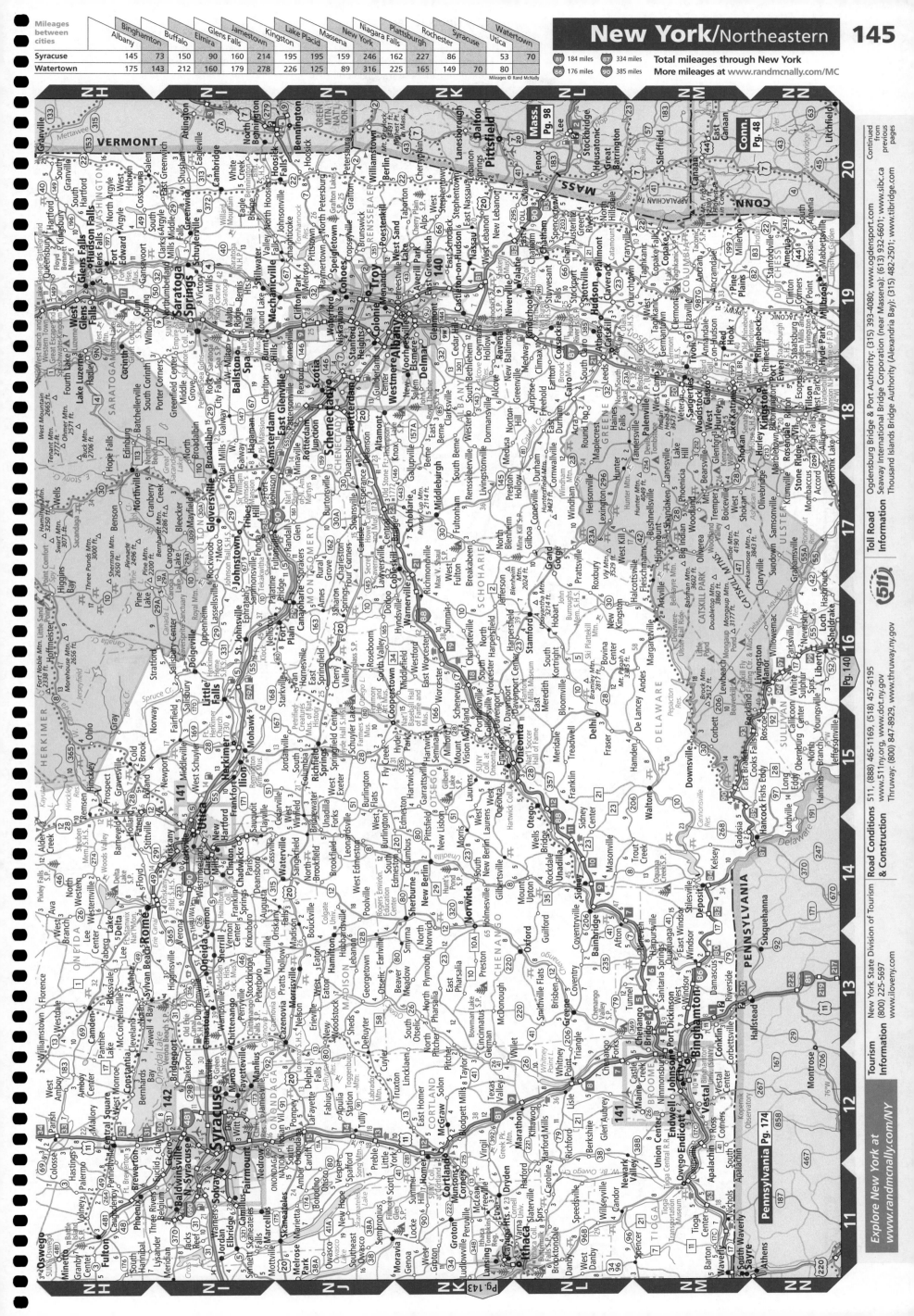

Mileages between cities

	Albany	Binghamton	Buffalo	Elmira	Glens Falls	Jamestown	Kingston	Lake Placid	Massena	New York	Niagara Falls	Plattsburgh	Rochester	Syracuse	Utica	Watertown
Syracuse	145	73	150	90	160	214	195	195	159	246	162	227	86		53	70
Watertown	175	143	212	160	179	278	226	125	89	316	225	165	149	70	80	

Mileages © Rand McNally

Total mileages through New York

81 184 miles   87 334 miles
86 176 miles   90 385 miles

More mileages at www.randmcnally.com/MC

Tourism Information
New York State Division of Tourism (800) 225-5697
www.iloveny.com

Road Conditions & Construction
511; (888) 465-1169, (518) 457-6195
511ny.org, www.511ny.org
www.dot.ny.gov
Thruway: (800) 847-8929, www.thruway.ny.gov

Toll Road Information
Ogdensburg Bridge & Port Authority: (315) 393-4080; www.ogdensport.com
Seaway International Bridge Corporation (near Massena): (613) 932-6601; www.sibc.ca
Thousand Islands Bridge Authority (Alexandria Bay): (315) 482-2501; www.tibridge.com

Continued from previous pages

Pennsylvania Pg. 174
Pg. 143
Pg. 140
Pg. 98
Pg. 48

City sights to see
- American Museum of Natural History, Manhattan, A-4
- Battery Park, Manhattan, I-1
- Belmont Park Race Track, Elmont, H-16
- Bronx Zoo, Bronx, E-12
- Brooklyn Bridge, New York, H-2
- Carnegie Hall, Manhattan, C-4
- Central Park, Manhattan, B-4

New York City & Vicinity

- Chrysler Building, Manhattan, D-4
- Coney Island, Brooklyn, L-10
- Edison Nat'l Historic Site, W. Orange, N.J., F-5
- Ellis Island, Jersey City, N.J./Manhattan, I-9
- Empire State Building, Manhattan, D-3
- Greenwich Village, Manhattan, H-10
- Grand Central Terminal, Manhattan, D-4

continued p.148

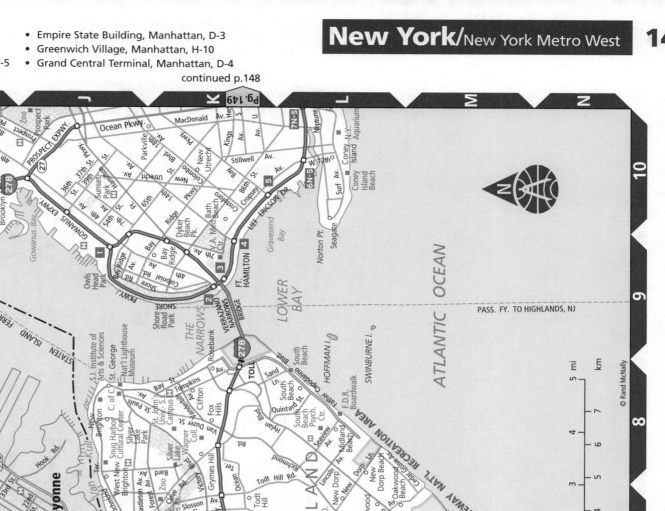

City sights to see—continued
- Guggenheim Museum, Manhattan, A-5
- Intrepid Sea-Air Space Mus., Manhattan, C-2
- Lincoln Center, Manhattan, B-3
- Madison Square Garden, Manhattan, D-2
- Meadowlands Sports Complex, East Rutherford, N.J., F-8
- Metropolitan Museum of Art, Manhattan, B-5

- National Sept. 11 Memorial, Manhattan, H-1
- New York Stock Exchange and Wall Street, Manhattan, H-1
- Rockefeller Center, Manhattan, C-4
- Staten Island Ferry, New York, J-9
- Statue of Liberty, Manhattan, I-9
- Times Square, Manhattan, D-3
- Yankee Stadium, Bronx, E-11

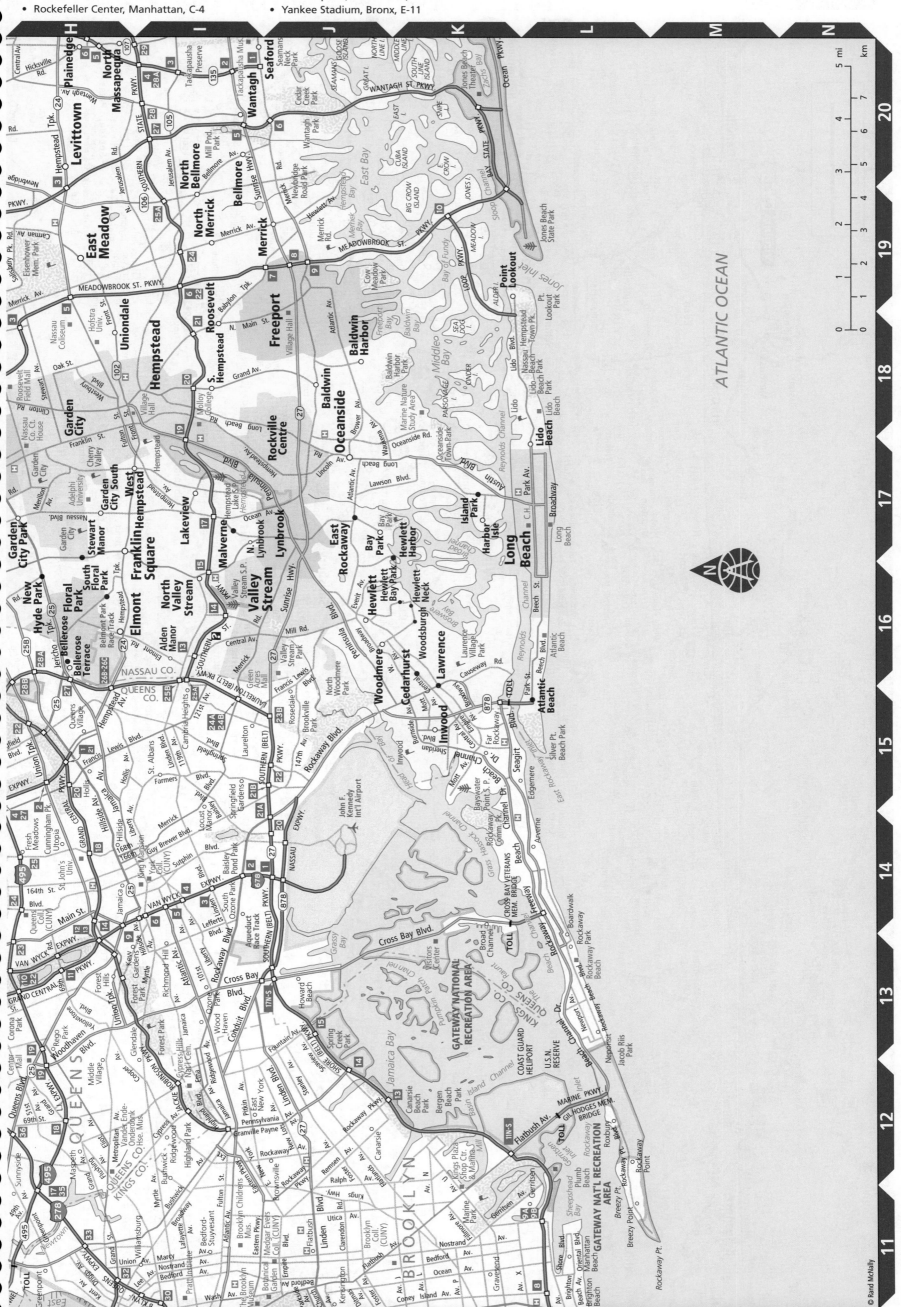

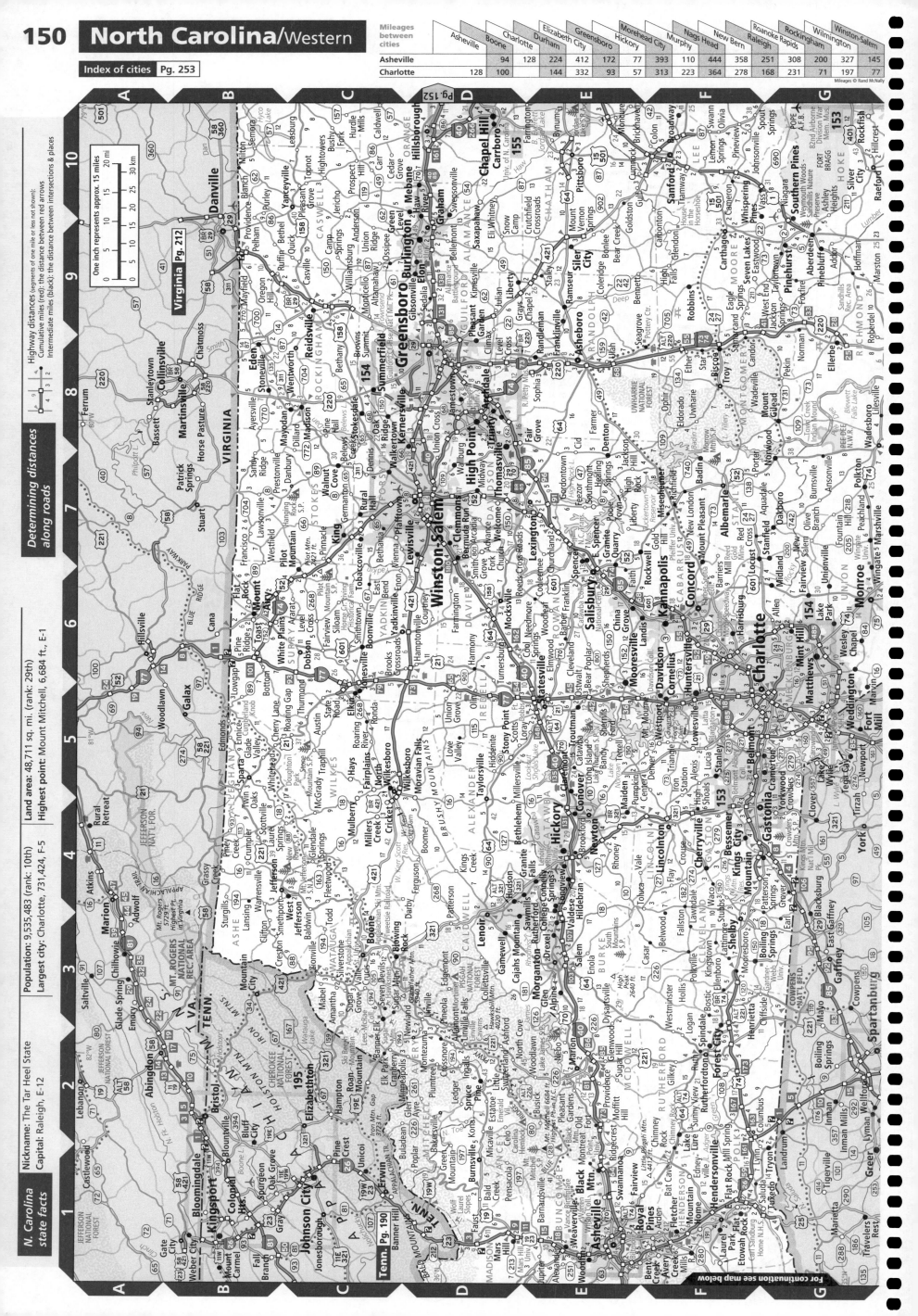

Mileages between cities	Asheville	Boone	Charlotte	Durham	Elizabeth City	Greensboro	Hickory	Morehead City	Murphy	Nags Head	New Bern	Raleigh	Roanoke Rapids	Rockingham	Wilmington	Winston-Salem
Asheville		94	128	224	412	172	77	393	110	444	358	251	308	200	327	145
Charlotte	128		100	144	332	93	57	313	223	364	278	168	231	71	197	77

Mileages © Rand McNally

N. Carolina state facts

Nickname: The Tar Heel State
Capital: Raleigh, E-12

Population: 9,535,483 (rank: 10th)
Largest city: Charlotte, 731,424, F-5

Land area: 48,711 sq. mi. (rank: 29th)
Highest point: Mount Mitchell, 6,684 ft., E-1

Determining distances along roads

Highway distances (segments of one mile or less are not shown):
Cumulative miles (red): the distance between red arrows
Intermediate miles (black): the distance between intersections & places

One inch represents approx. 15 miles

Virginia Pg. 212

continued p. 152

Mileages between cities	Asheville	Boone	Charlotte	Durham	Elizabeth City	Greensboro	Hickory	Morehead City	Murphy	Nags Head	New Bern	Raleigh	Roanoke Rapids	Rockingham	Wilmington	Winston-Salem
Elizabeth City	412	354	332	185		241	338	152	520	56	119	164	97	259	208	269
Fayetteville	261	202	137	89	203	94	189	138	369	234	130	63	127	64	89	119

Mileages © Rand McNally

40 419 miles	85 233 miles	**Total mileages through North Carolina**
77 102 miles	95 182 miles	More mileages at www.randmcnally.com/MC

Map of Western North Carolina including Asheville inset.

© Rand McNally

Plan a North Carolina trip at www.randmcnally.com/NC

Tourism Information — North Carolina Division of Tourism (800) 847-4862, (919) 733-4171 www.visitnc.com

Road Conditions & Construction — 511, (877) 511-4662 www.ncdot.gov/travel/511 www.ncdot.gov

Toll Road Information — North Carolina Turnpike Authority (NC Quick Pass) (877) 769-7277 www.ncdot.gov/turnpike

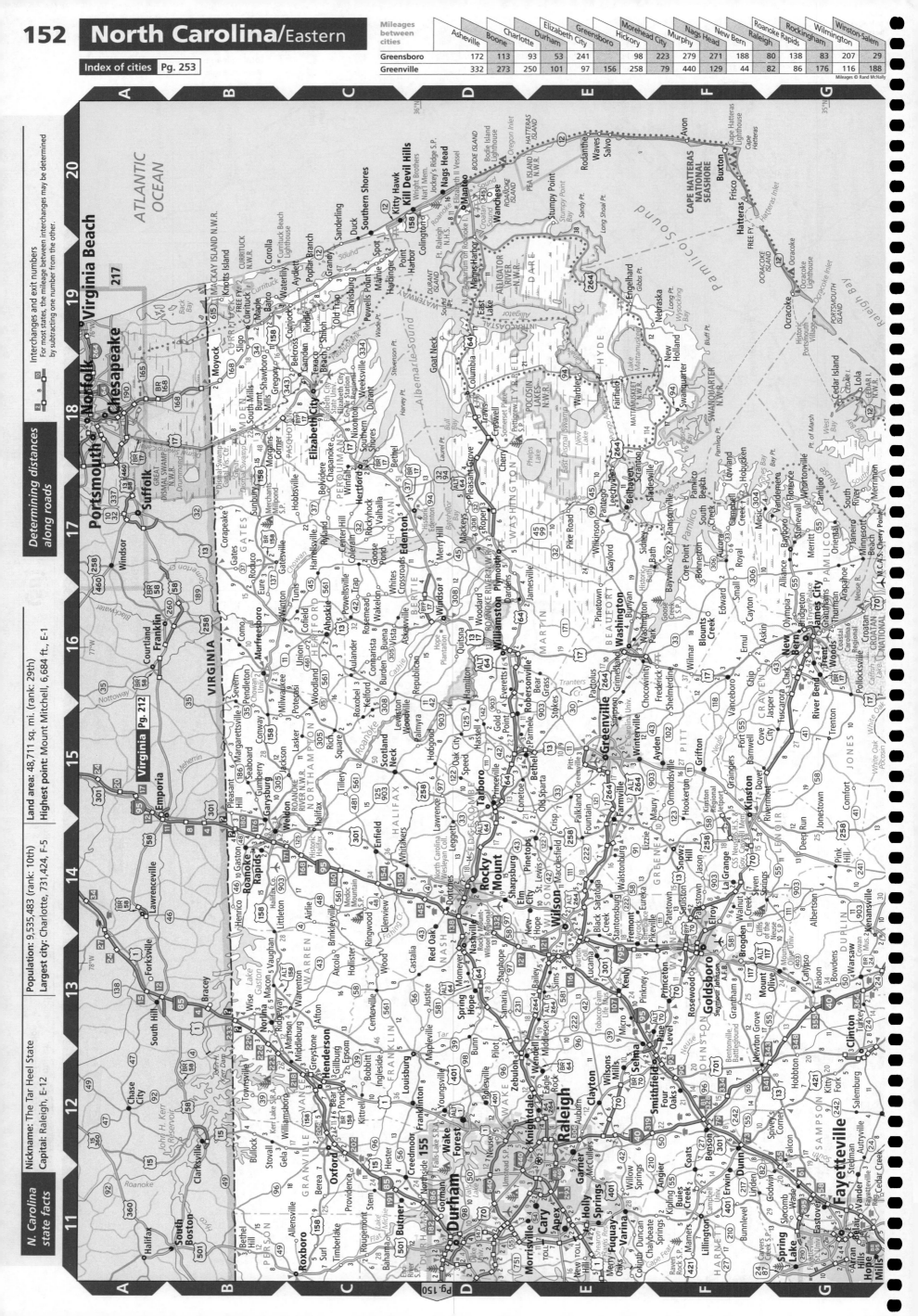

Mileages between cities	Asheville	Boone	Charlotte	Durham	Elizabeth City	Greensboro	Hickory	Morehead City	Murphy	Nags Head	New Bern	Raleigh	Roanoke Rapids	Rockingham	Wilmington	Winston-Salem
Greensboro	172	113	93	53	241		98	223	279	271	188	80	138	83	207	29
Greenville	332	273	250	101	97	156	258	79	440	129	44	82	86	176	116	188

Mileages © Rand McNally

N. Carolina state facts

Nickname: The Tar Heel State
Capital: Raleigh, E-12

Land area: 48,711 sq. mi. (rank: 29th)
Largest city: Charlotte, 731,424, F-5
Highest point: Mount Mitchell, 6,684 ft., E-1

Population: 9,535,483 (rank: 10th)

Determining distances along roads

Interchanges and exit numbers

For most states, the mileage between interchanges may be determined by subtracting one number from the other.

Mileages between cities	Asheville	Boone	Charlotte	Durham	Elizabeth City	Greensboro	Hickory	Morehead City	Murphy	Nags Head	New Bern	Roanoke Rapids	Raleigh	Rockingham	Wilmington	Winston-Salem
Raleigh	251	192	168	22	164	80	177	146	358	195	111	89		98	130	107
Wilmington	327	319	197	156	208	207	259	91	428	230	90	130	178	127		236

Mileages © Rand McNally

Total mileages through North Carolina

40	419 miles	85	233 miles
77	102 miles	95	182 miles

More mileages at www.randmcnally.com/MC

City sights to see
- Discovery Place, Charlotte, H-4
- Dollywood, Pigeon Forge, Tenn., B-11
- Duke Homestead State Historic Site, Durham, F-9
- Guilford Courthouse National Military Park, Greensboro, B-6
- Historic Bethabara Park, Winston-Salem, A-1
- Mint Museum of Art, Charlotte, H-5

Greensboro / Winston-Salem / High Point

Walkertown · Summerfield · Oak Ridge · The Old Mill of Guilford · Kernersville · Colfax · Friendship · Piedmont Triad Int'l Arpt. · Greensboro · Winston-Salem · Guilford College · Starmount · Sedgefield · Sandy Ridge · Union Cross · Wallburg · Jamestown · High Point · Grandover Resort · Midway · Arcadia · Enterprise · Welcome · Arnold · Thomasville · Archdale · Trinity · Glenola · Level Cross

© Rand McNally

Scale: 0 1 2 3 mi / 0 1 2 3 4 km

Charlotte & Vicinity

Concord · Charlotte Motor Speedway · Harrisburg · Mountain Island · Latta Plantation Nature Preserve · Metrolina Expo. · University Research Park · Univ. of N.C. at Charlotte · Verizon Wireless Amphitheater · Pine Ridge · Mount Holly · U.S. National Whitewater Ctr. · Charlotte · Hickory Grove · Belmont Abbey Coll. · McAdenville · Cramerton · Belmont · Charlotte Douglas Int'l Airport · Carolinas Aviation Mus. · Bank of America Stad. · Johnson C. Smith Univ. · Discovery Place · Time Warner Cable Arena · NoDa · Albemarle · Eastland Mall · Mint Museum of Art · Paradise Point · Green Acres · Shopton · Charlotte Premium Outlets · Mint Hill · Myers Park · South Park Mall · Matthews · Daniel J. Stowe Botanical Garden · Lake Wylie · Carowinds Theme Park · Pineville · James K. Polk S.H.S. · Carolina Place Mall · Wm. R. Davie Park · Stallings · Indian Trail · Hemby Bridge · Lake Park

S. CAR. / S. CAROLINA

MECKLENBURG CO. · YORK CO. · GASTON CO. · UNION CO. · CABARRUS CO.

N

Scale: 0 1 2 3 mi / 0 1 2 3 4 km

© Rand McNally

- Morehead Planetarium and Science Center, Chapel Hill, H-8
- North Carolina Museum of Life and Science, Durham, F-10
- North Carolina Museum of History, Raleigh, I-12
- North Carolina State Capitol, Raleigh, I-13
- Old Salem, Winston-Salem, B-2
- Reynolda House, Winston-Salem, B-1

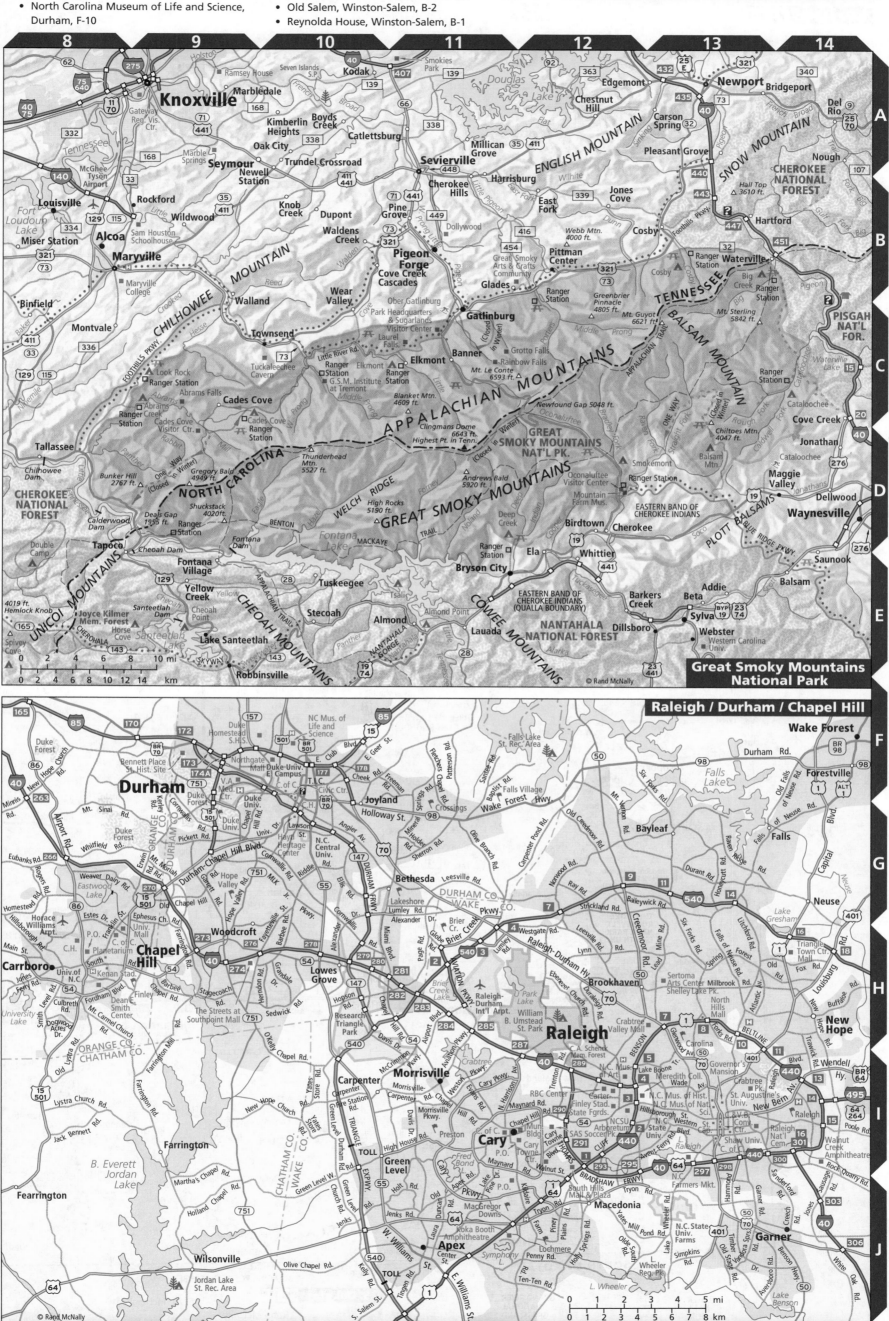

Great Smoky Mountains National Park

Raleigh / Durham / Chapel Hill

© Rand McNally

North Dakota

Index of cities Pg. 254

Mileages between cities

	Bismarck	Bowman	Fargo	Garrison	Grand Forks	Jamestown	Williston	Winnipeg, MB
Bismarck		174	195	75	272	102	228	413
Devils Lake	180	354	165	167	89	99	245	230
Dickinson	97	78	292	149	368	198	132	509
Fargo	195	368		266	80	94	422	222

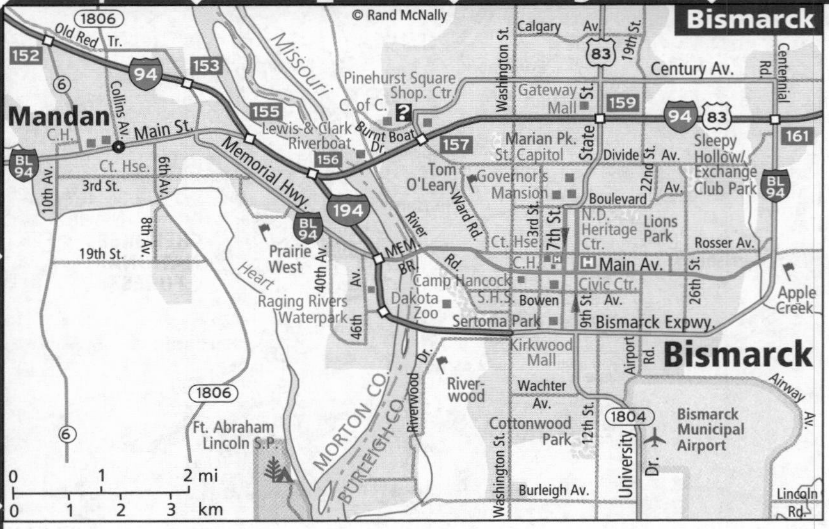

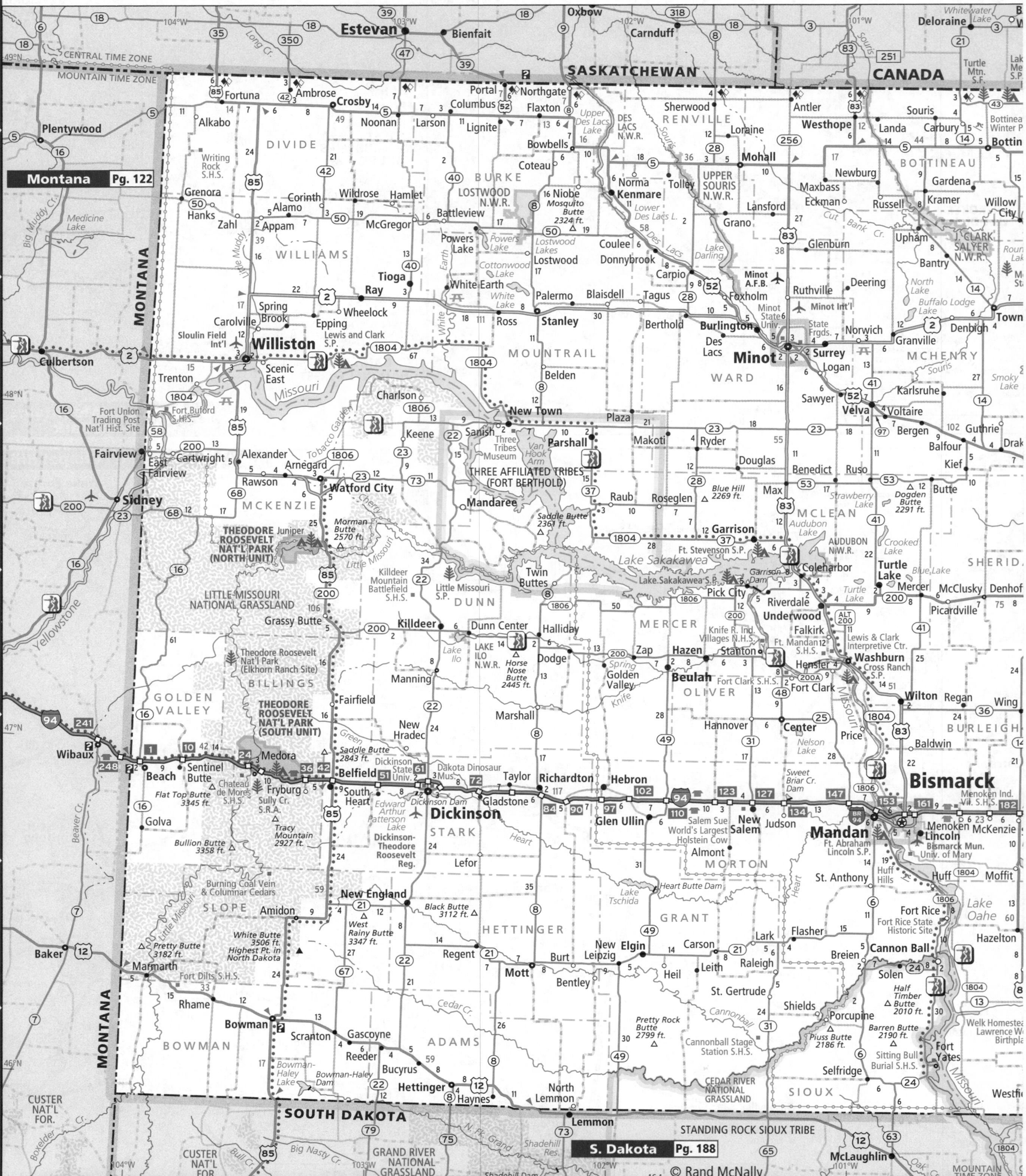

Interchanges and exit numbers
For most states, the mileage between interchanges may be determined by subtracting one number from the other.

Determining distances along roads

Land area: 68,976 sq. mi. (rank: 17th)
Highest point: White Butte, 3,506 ft., I-3

Population: 672,591 (rank: 48th)
Largest city: Fargo, 105,549, H-13

Nickname: The Peace Garden State
Capital: Bismarck, H-7

N. Dakota state facts

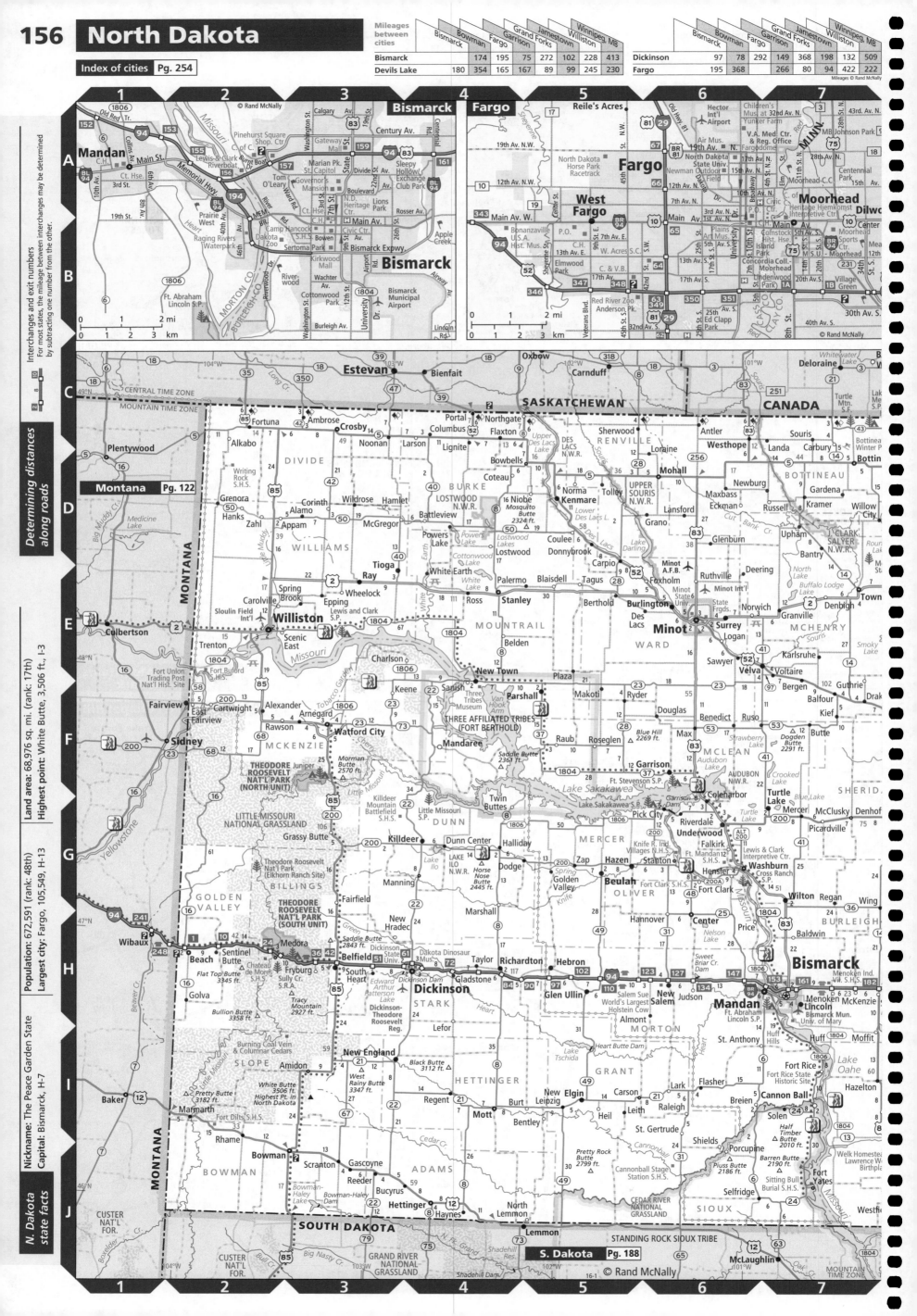

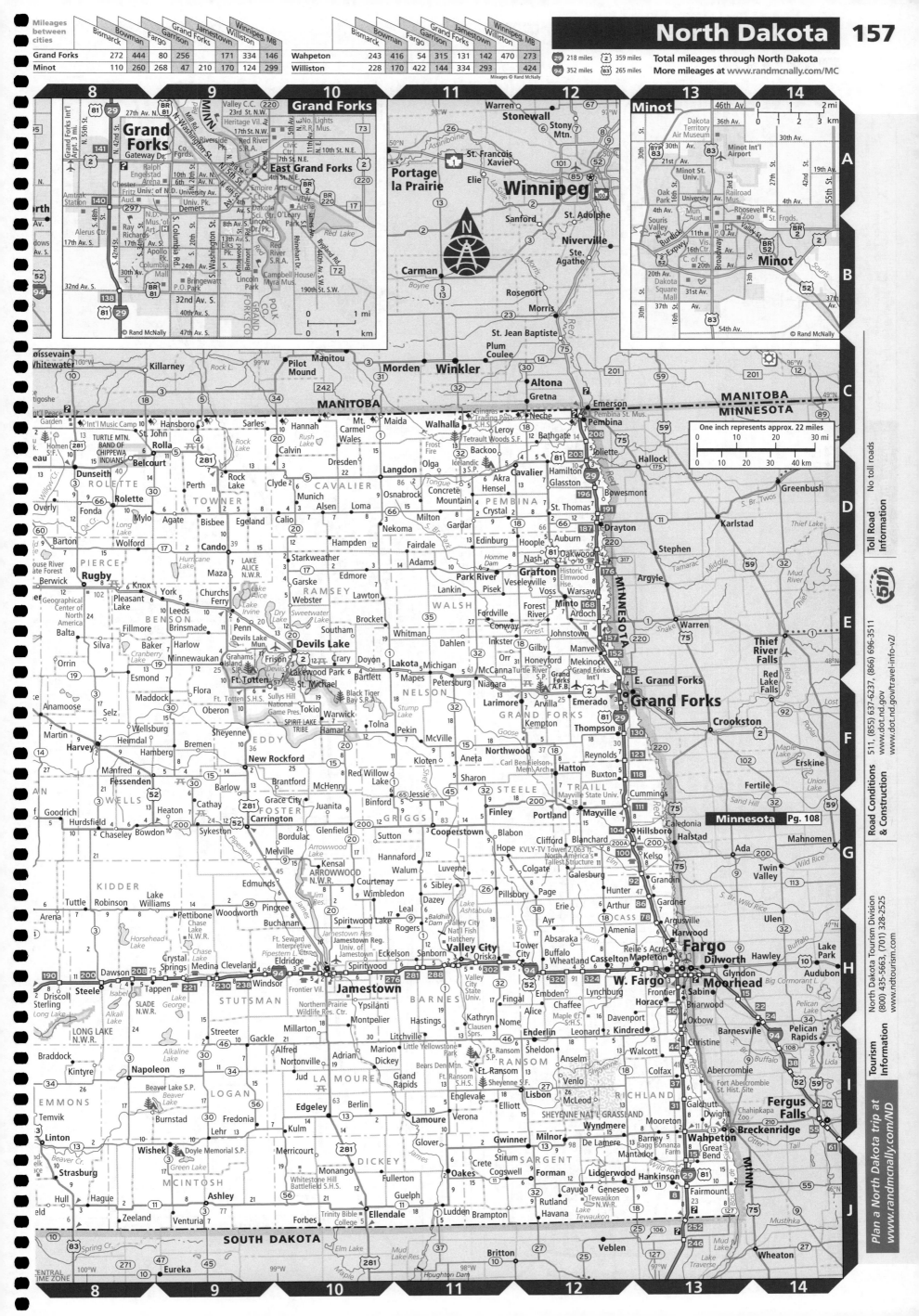

Mileages between cities	Bismarck	Bowman	Fargo	Garrison	Grand Forks	Jamestown	Williston	Winnipeg, MB
Grand Forks	272	444	80	256		171	334	146
Minot	110	260	268	47	210	170	124	299

	Bismarck	Bowman	Fargo	Garrison	Grand Forks	Jamestown	Williston	Winnipeg, MB
Wahpeton	243	416	54	315	131	142	470	273
Williston	228	170	422	144	334	293		424

Mileages © Rand McNally

Total mileages through North Dakota
More mileages at www.randmcnally.com/MC

29 218 miles   2 359 miles
94 352 miles   83 265 miles

Toll Road Information — No toll roads

One inch represents approx. 22 miles

Road Conditions & Construction
511, (855) 637-6237, (866) 696-3511
www.dot.nd.gov
www.dot.nd.gov/travel-info-v2/

Tourism Information
North Dakota Tourism Division
(800) 435-5663, (701) 328-2525
www.ndtourism.com

Plan a North Dakota trip at www.randmcnally.com/ND

Mileages between cities	Ashtabula	Canton	Cincinnati	Cleveland	Columbus	Coshocton	Findlay	Lima	Mansfield	New Philadelphia	Pittsburgh, PA	Sandusky	Steubenville	Toledo	Youngstown
Akron	81	20	232	39	124	80	132	154	62	47	107	85	82	133	48
Cleveland	39	58	58	248	142	102	121	156	80	85	131	62	124	111	72

Mileages © Rand McNally

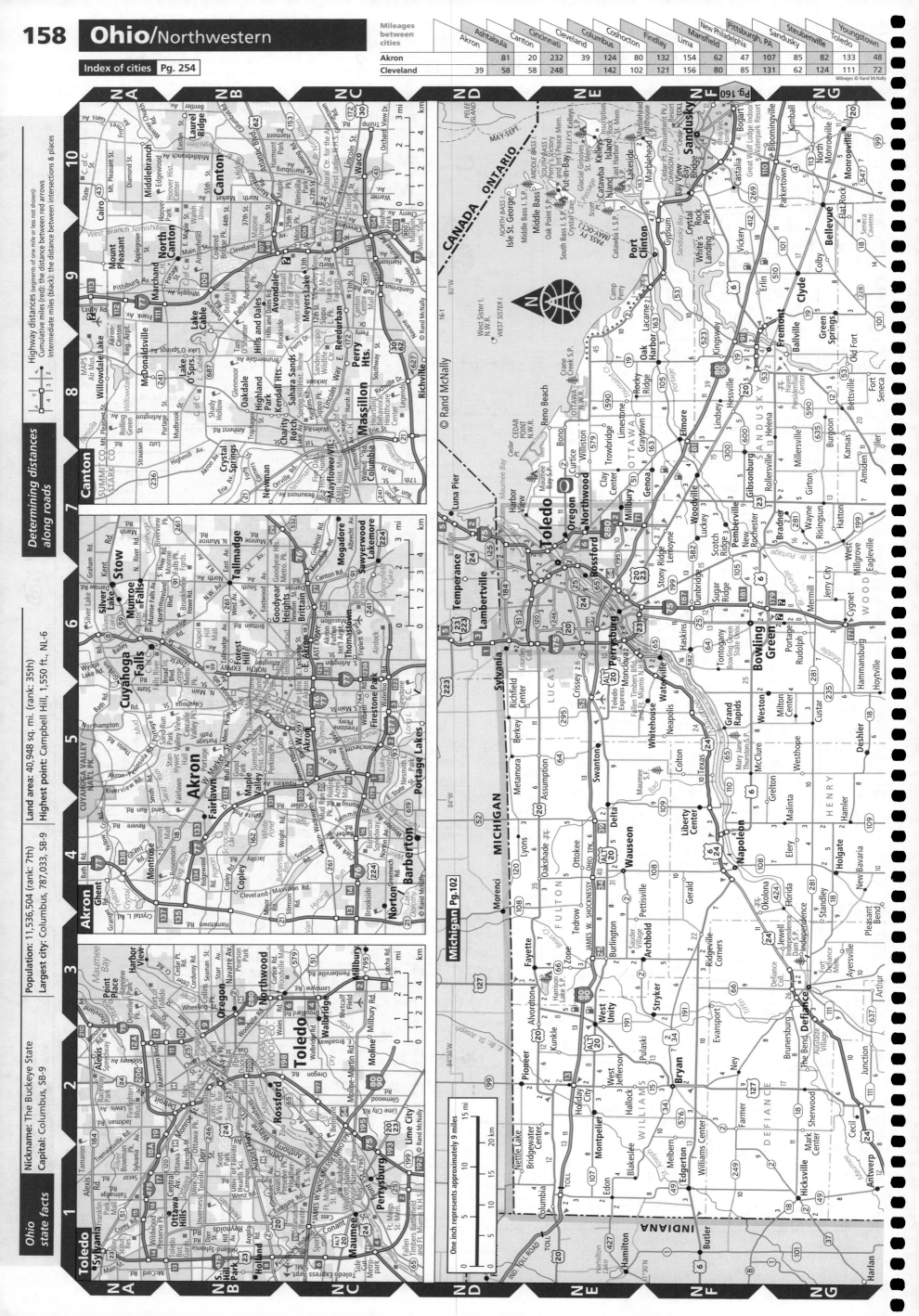

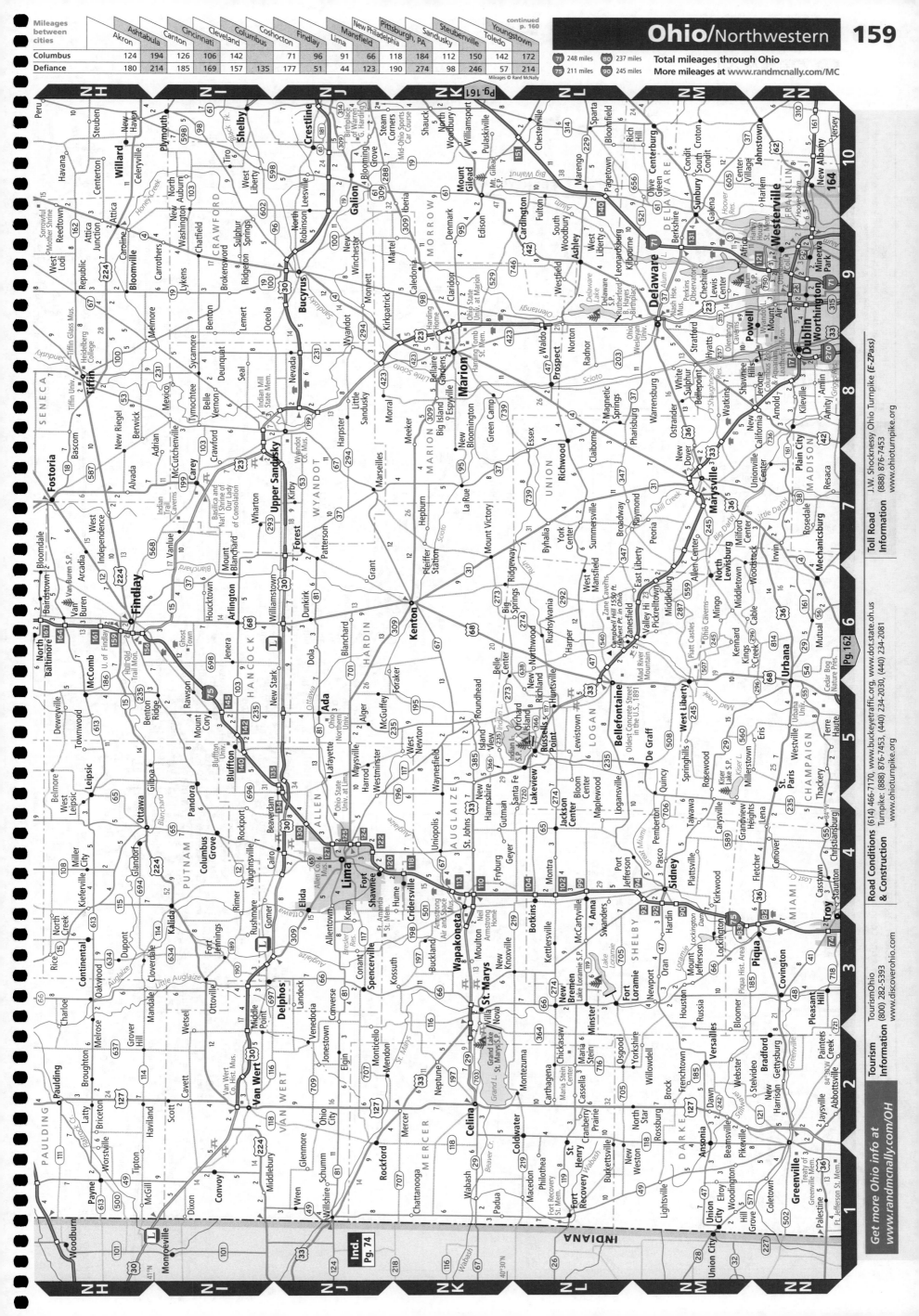

Mileages between cities	Akron	Ashtabula	Canton	Cincinnati	Cleveland	Columbus	Coshocton	Findlay	Lima	Mansfield	New Philadelphia	Pittsburgh, PA	Sandusky	Steubenville	Toledo	Youngstown
Columbus	124	194	126	106	142		71	96	91	66	118	184	112	150	142	172
Defiance	180	214	185	169	157	135	177	51	44	123	190	274	98	246	57	214

continued p. 160

Total mileages through Ohio

71 — 248 miles	80 — 237 miles		
75 — 211 miles	90 — 245 miles		

Mileages © Rand McNally

More mileages at www.randmcnally.com/MC

Toll Road Information
J.W. Shocknessy Ohio Turnpike (E-ZPass)
(888) 876-7453
www.ohioturnpike.org

Road Conditions & Construction
TurnpikeOhio: (888) 876-7453, www.dot.state.oh.us
(614) 466-7170, www.buckeyetraffic.org, Turnpike: (888) 876-7453, (440) 234-2030, (440) 234-2081
www.ohioturnpike.org

Tourism Information
TourismOhio (800) 282-5393
www.discoverohio.com

Get more Ohio info at
www.randmcnally.com/OH

Pg. 161
Pg. 162
Ind. Pg. 74

Mileages between cities	Akron	Ashtabula	Canton	Cincinnati	Cleveland	Columbus	Coshocton	Findlay	Lima	Mansfield	New Philadelphia	Pittsburgh, PA	Sandusky	Steubenville	Toledo	Youngstown
Lima	154	216	156	124	156	91	134	34		94	162	261	96	217	77	202
Mansfield	62	132	64	172	80	66	62	72	94		67	170	53	124	99	110

Mileages © Rand McNally

Ohio state facts

Nickname: The Buckeye State
Capital: Columbus, 5B-9

Population: 11,536,504 (rank: 7th)
Largest city: Columbus, 787,033, SB-9

Land area: 40,948 sq. mi. (rank: 35th)
Highest point: Campbell Hill, 1,550 ft., NL-6

Determining distances along roads

One inch represents approximately 9 miles

Interchanges and exit numbers
For most states, the mileage between interchanges may be determined by subtracting one number from the other.

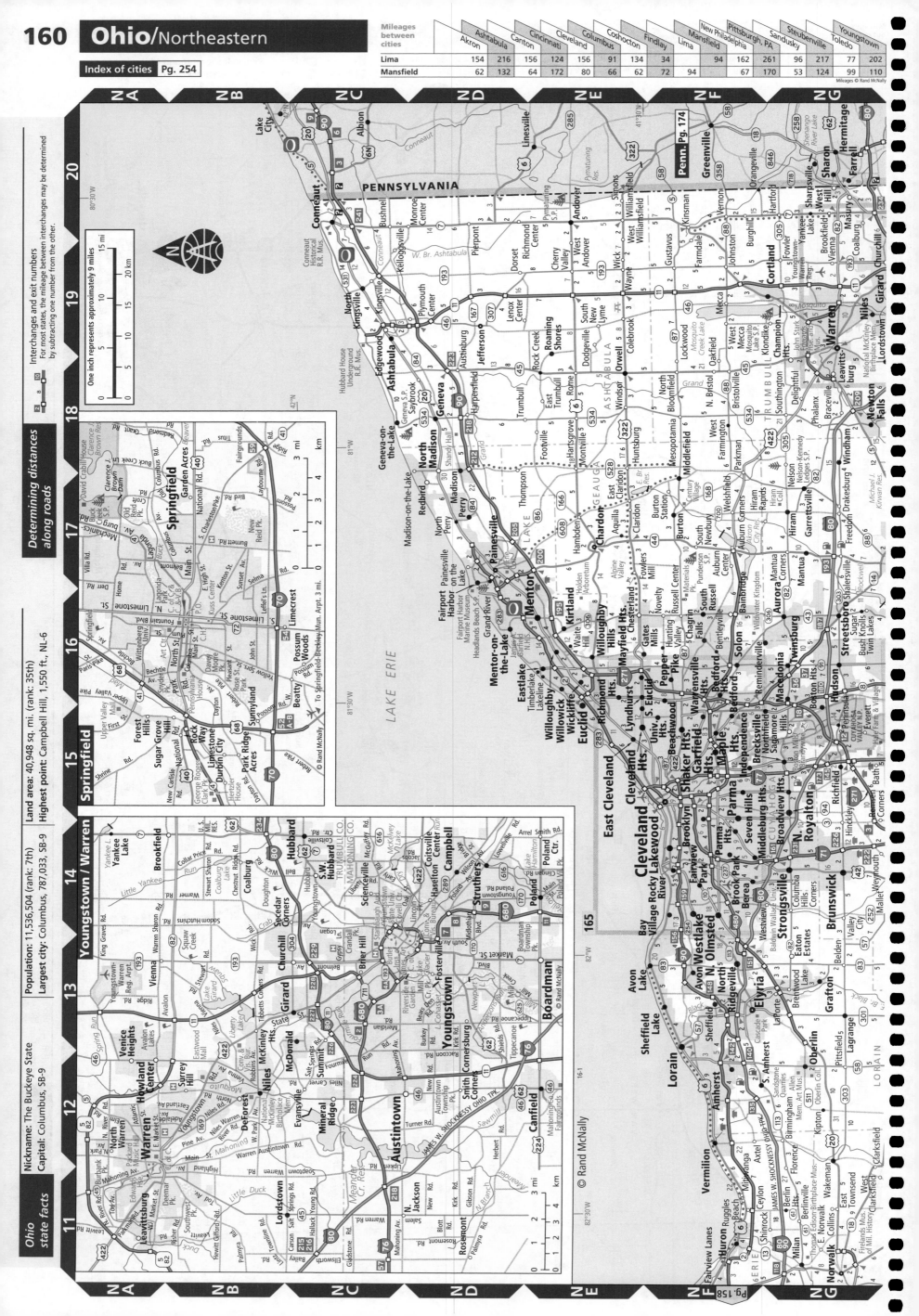

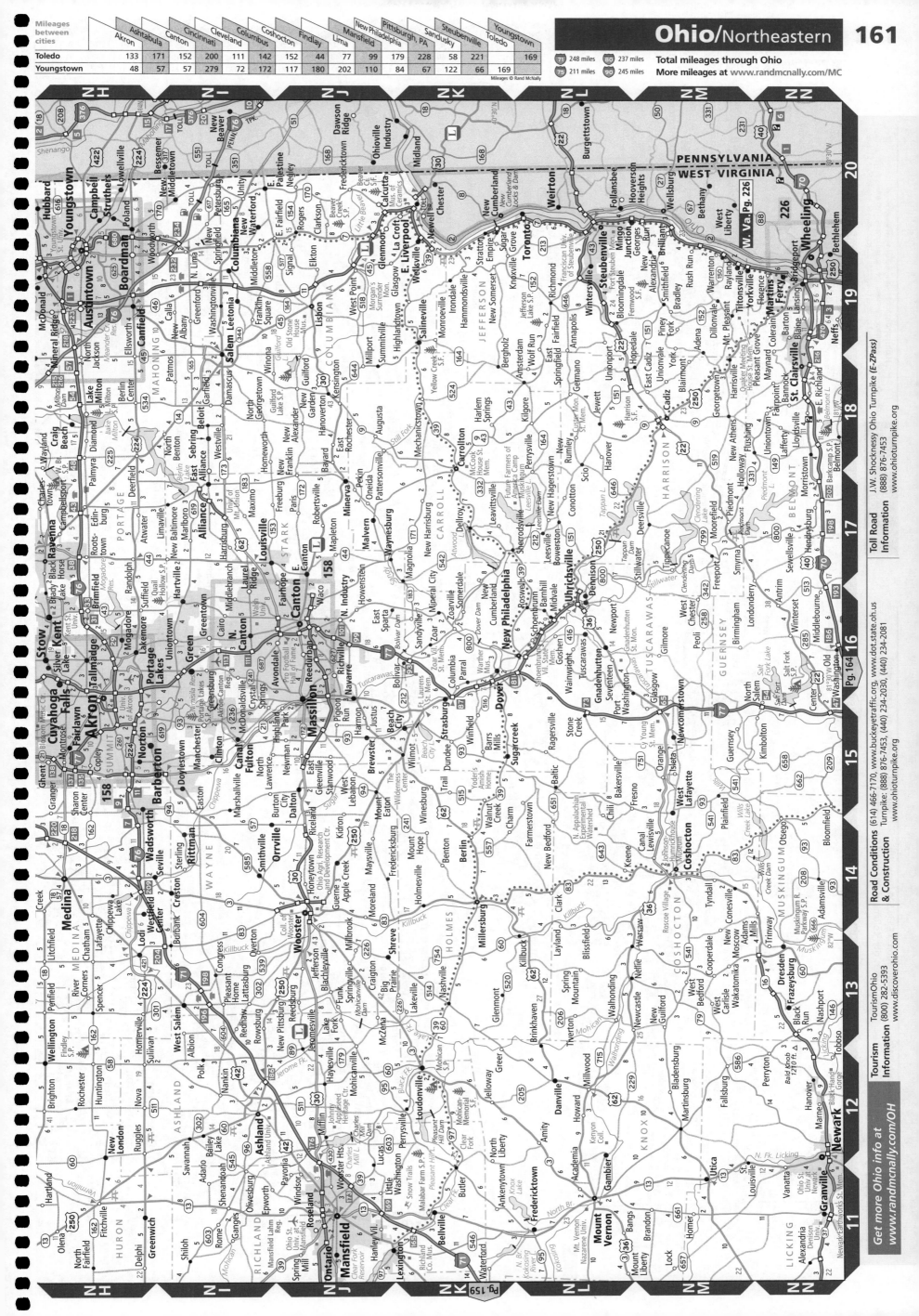

Mileages between cities		Ashtabula	Canton	Cincinnati	Cleveland	Columbus	Coshocton	Findlay	Mansfield	New Philadelphia	Pittsburgh, PA	Sandusky	Steubenville	Youngstown
			Akron						Lima				Toledo	
Toledo	133	171	152	200	111	142	152	44	77	99	179	228	58	221	169
Youngstown	48	57	57	279	72	172	117	180	202	110	84	67	122	66	169

Mileages © Rand McNally

Total mileages through Ohio
More mileages at www.randmcnally.com/MC

71 248 miles   80 237 miles
75 211 miles   90 245 miles

Get more Ohio info at www.randmcnally.com/OH

Tourism Information TourismOhio (800) 282-5393 www.discoverohio.com

Road Conditions & Construction (614) 466-7170, www.buckeyetraffic.org, www.dot.state.oh.us Turnpike: (888) 876-7453, (440) 234-2030, (440) 234-2081 www.ohioturnpike.org

Toll Road Information J.W. Shocknessy Ohio Turnpike (E-ZPass) www.ohioturnpike.org (888) 876-7453

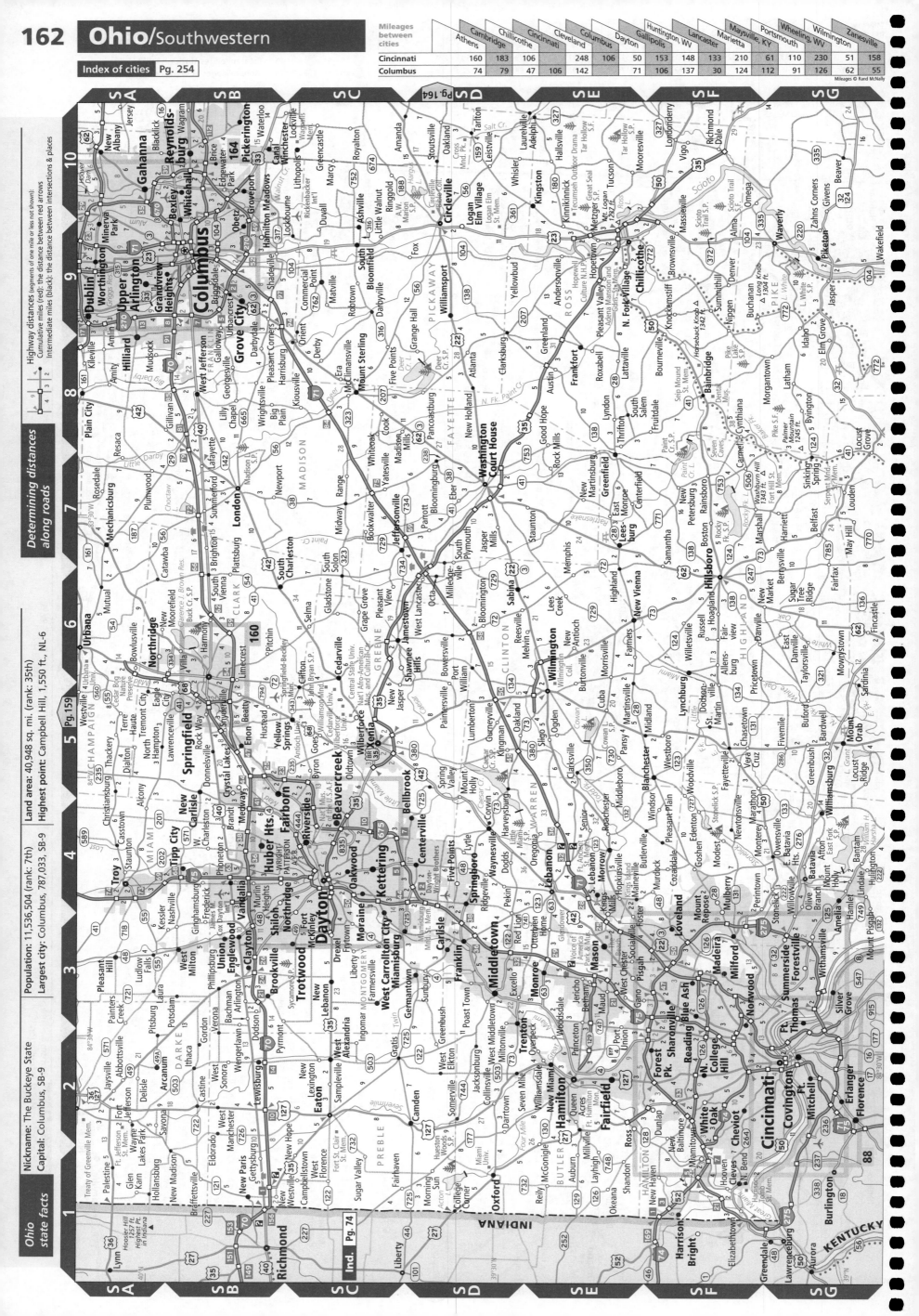

Ohio state facts

Nickname: The Buckeye State
Capital: Columbus, SB-9

Population: 11,536,504 (rank: 7th)
Largest city: Columbus, 787,033, SB-9

Land area: 40,948 sq. mi. (rank: 35th)
Highest point: Campbell Hill, 1,550 ft., NL-6

Determining distances along roads

Highway distances (segments of one mile or less not shown)
Cumulative miles (red): the distance between red arrows
Intermediate miles (black): the distance between intersections & places

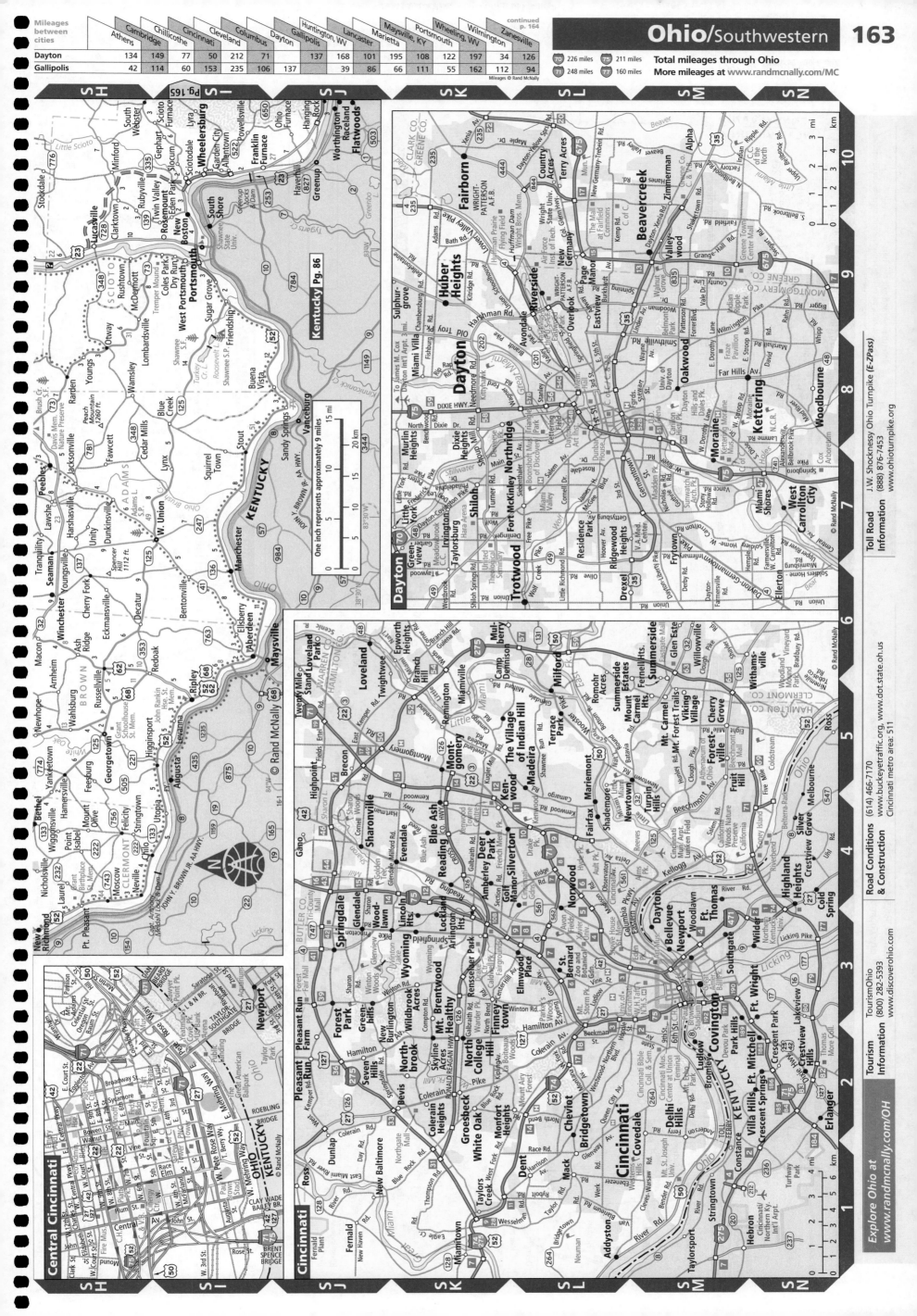

continued p. 164

Mileages between cities	Athens	Cambridge	Chillicothe	Cincinnati	Cleveland	Columbus	Dayton	Gallipolis	Huntington, WV	Lancaster	Marietta	Maysville, KY	Portsmouth	Wheeling, WV	Wilmington	Zanesville
Dayton	134	149	77	50	212	71		137	168	101	195	108	122	197	34	126
Gallipolis	42	114	60	153	235	106	137		39	86	66	111	55	162	112	94

Mileages © Rand McNally

Total mileages through Ohio

70	226 miles	75	211 miles
71	248 miles	77	160 miles

More mileages at www.randmcnally.com/MC

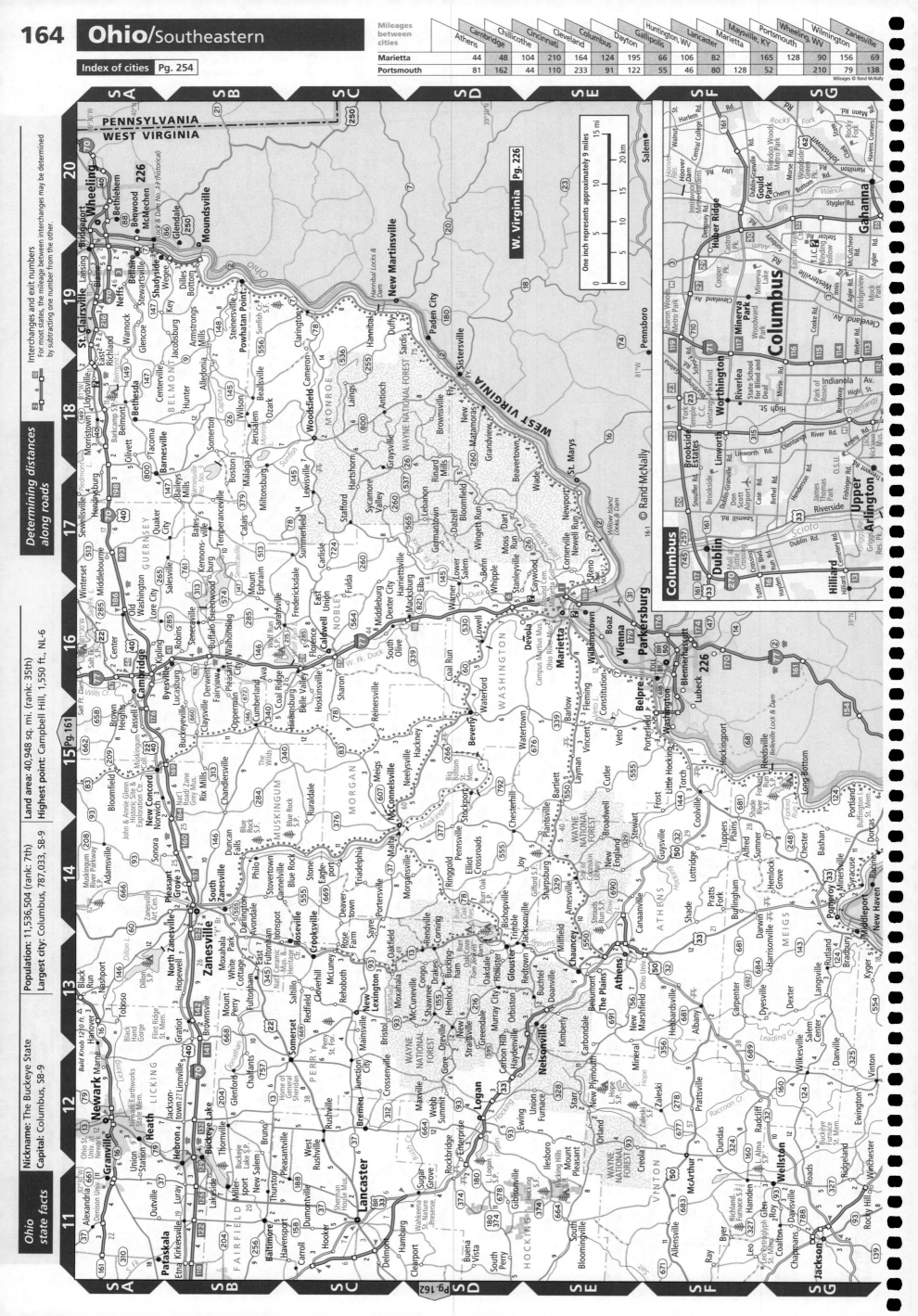

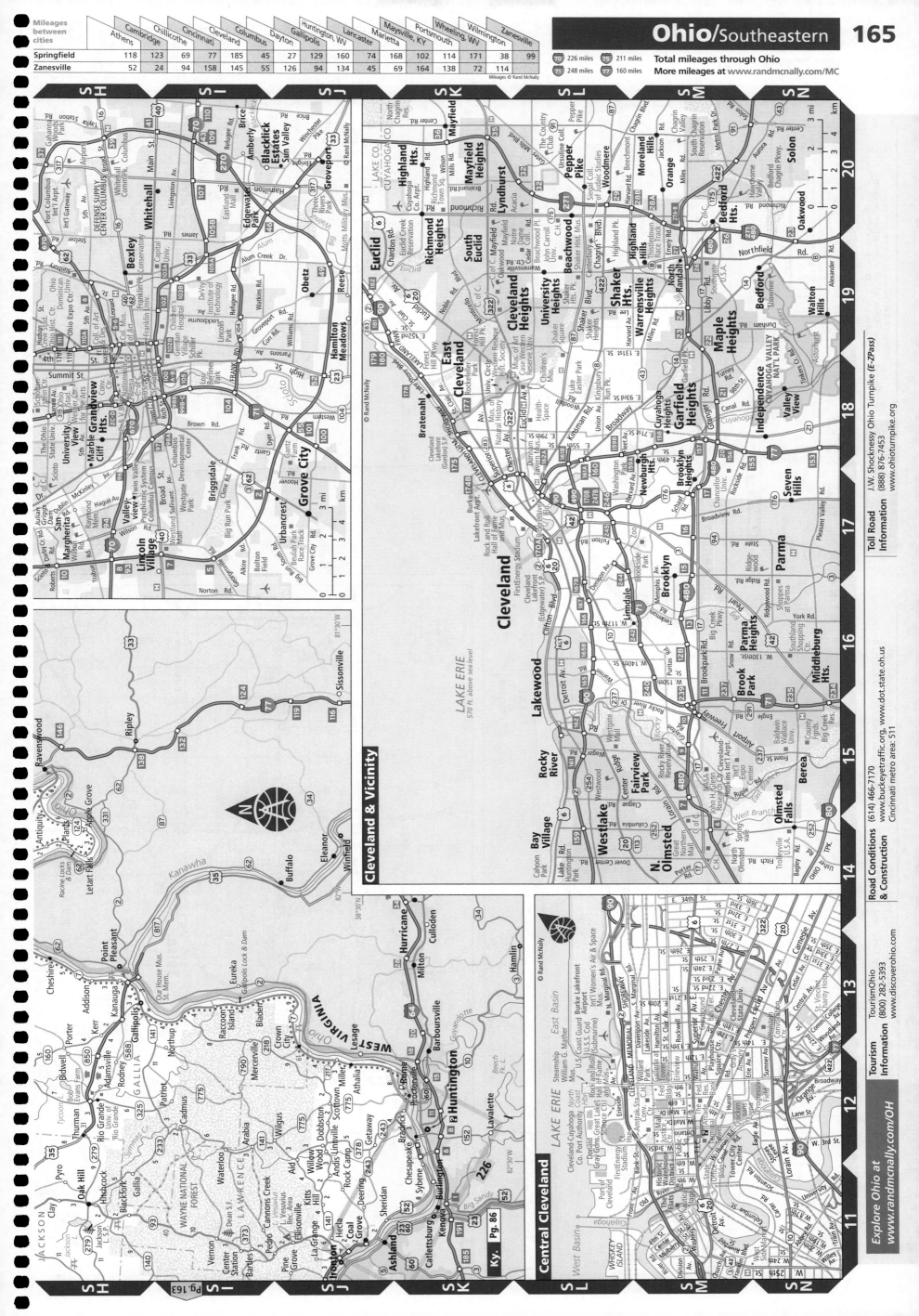

Mileages between cities	Athens	Cambridge	Chillicothe	Cincinnati	Cleveland	Columbus	Dayton	Gallipolis	Huntington, WV	Lancaster	Marietta	Maysville, KY	Portsmouth	Wheeling, WV	Wilmington	Zanesville
Springfield	118	123	69	77	185	45	27	129	160	74	168	102	114	171	38	99
Zanesville	52	24	94	158	145	55	126	94	134	45	69	164	138	72	114	

Mileages © Rand McNally

Total mileages through Ohio

| 70 | 226 miles | 75 | 211 miles |
| 71 | 248 miles | 77 | 160 miles |

More mileages at www.randmcnally.com/MC

Cleveland & Vicinity

Central Cleveland

Ky. 86

Ky. 163

Pg. 163

Toll Road Information J.W. Shockness ey Ohio Turnpike (E-ZPass) (888) 876-7453 www.ohioturnpike.org

Road Conditions & Construction www.buckeyetraffic.org, www.dot.state.oh.us Cincinnati metro area: 511 (614) 466-7170

Tourism Information TourismOhio (800) 282-5393 www.discoverohio.com

Explore Ohio at www.randmcnally.com/OH

Oklahoma state facts

Nickname: The Sooner State
Capital: Oklahoma City, F-13

Population: 3,751,351 (rank: 28th)
Largest city: Oklahoma City, 579,999, F-13

Land area: 68,667 sq. mi. (rank: 19th)
Highest point: Black Mesa, 4,973 ft., B-1

Determining distances along roads

Highway distances (segments of one mile or less not shown)
Cumulative miles (red): the distance between red arrows
Intermediate miles (black): the distance between intersections & places

Mileages between cities	Ardmore	Bartlesville	Dallas, TX	Elk City	Enid	Ft. Smith, AR	Guymon	Joplin, MO	Lawton	McAlester	Muskogee	Oklahoma City	Ponca City	Tulsa	Wichita Falls, TX	Woodward
Ardmore		246	109	208	195	223	360	312	99	116	180	97	200	201	86	236
Elk City	208	260	303		148	292	184	327	108	240	249	112	216	215	143	77

Mileages © Rand McNally

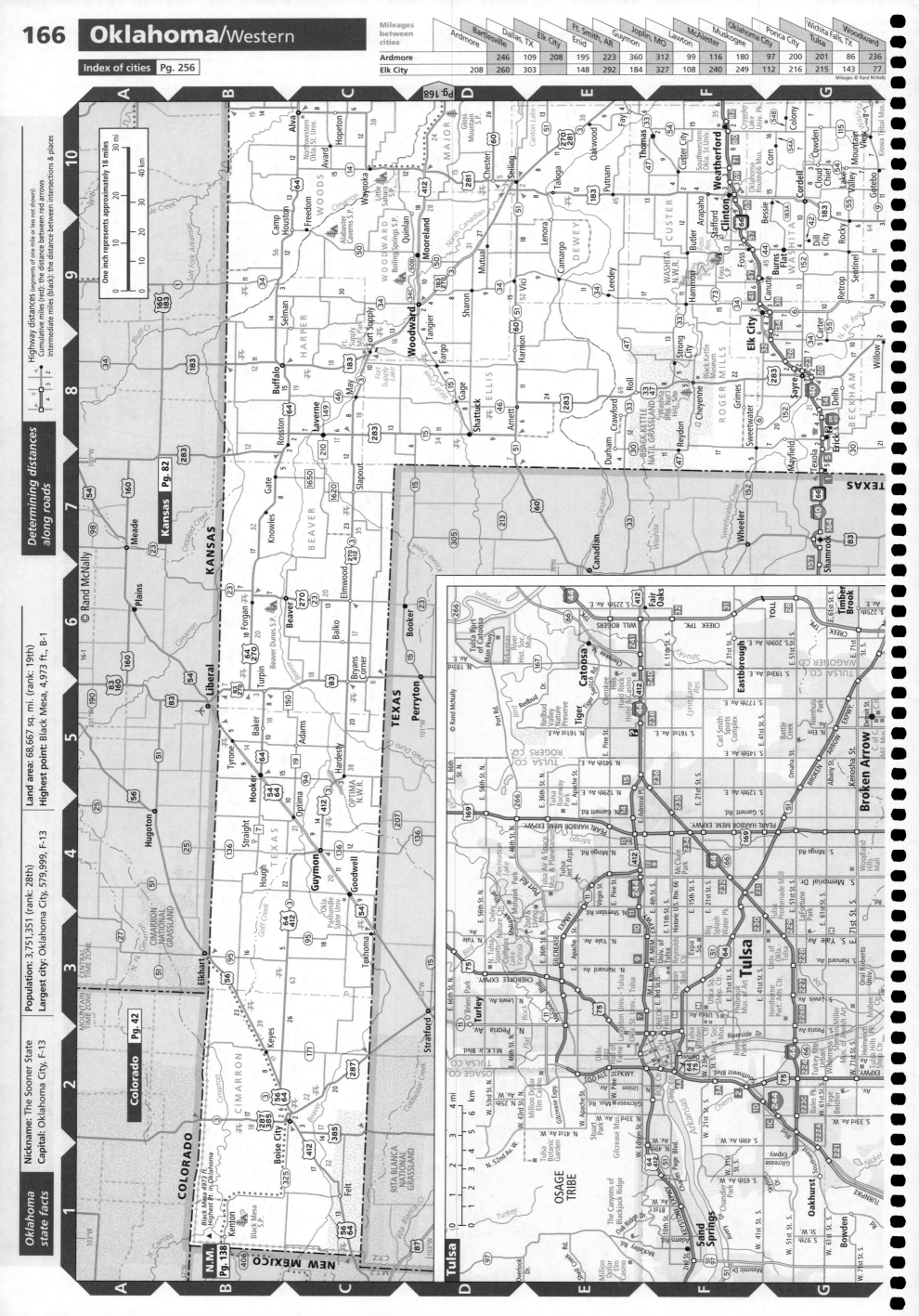

continued p. 168

Mileages between cities	Ardmore	Bartlesville	Dallas, TX	Elk City	Enid	Ft. Smith, AR	Guymon	Joplin, MO	Lawton	McAlester	Muskogee	Oklahoma City	Ponca City	Tulsa	Wichita Falls, TX	Woodward
Enid	195	134	302	148		232	211	227	142	204	164	99	67	114	196	87
Guymon	360	344	459	184	211	443		438	294	391	375	263	278	326	317	124

Mileages © Rand McNally

Total mileages through Oklahoma
More mileages at www.randmcnally.com/MC

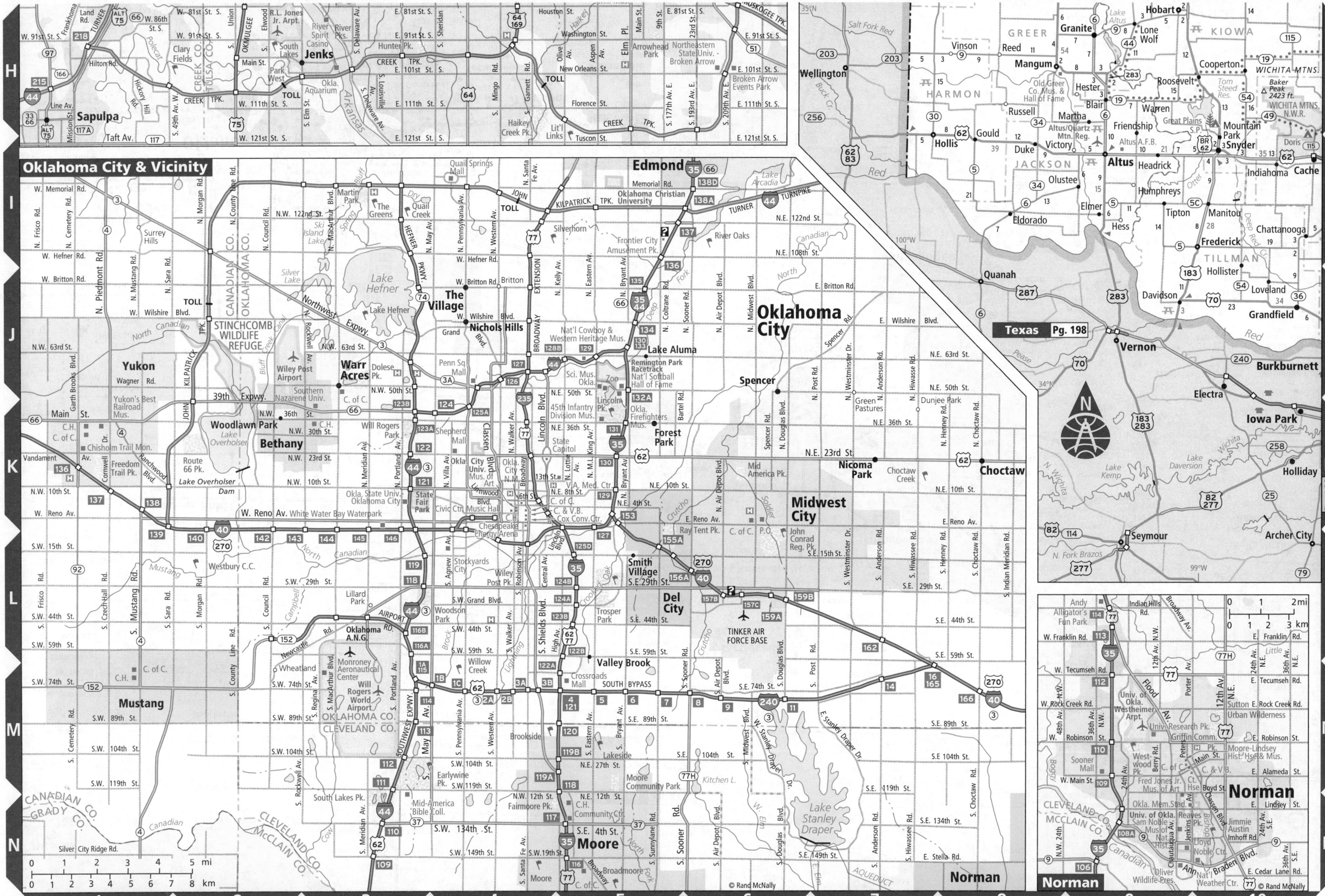

35 236 miles   44 329 miles
40 331 miles   75 227 miles

Oklahoma City & Vicinity

Texas Pg. 198

Pg. 169

Tinker Air Force Base

Norman

Plan an Oklahoma trip at www.randmcnally.com/OK

Tourism Information Oklahoma Tourism & Recreation Department (800) 652-6552 www.travelok.com

Road Conditions & Construction Oklahoma Tourism & Recreation Department (877) 403-7623 (405) 425-2385 www.okladot.state.ok.us

Toll Road Information Oklahoma Turnpike Authority (PIKEPASS) (405) 425-3600 www.pikepass.com

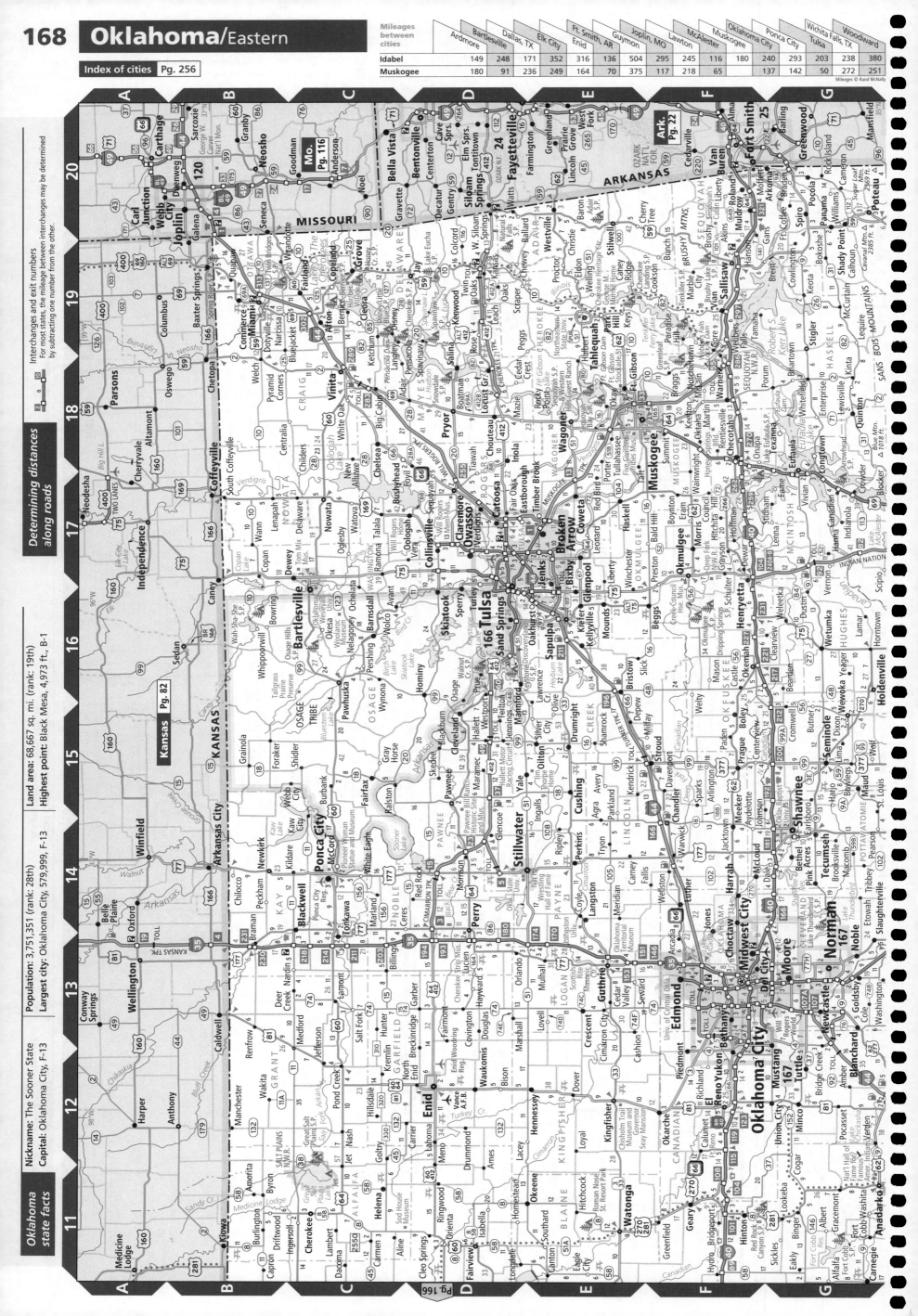

Mileages between cities	Ardmore	Bartlesville	Dallas, TX	Elk City	Enid	Ft. Smith, AR	Guymon	Joplin, MO	Lawton	McAlester	Muskogee	Oklahoma City	Ponca City	Tulsa	Wichita Falls, TX	Woodward
Oklahoma City	97	149	204	112	99	180	263	216	86	128	137		105	104	140	139
Tulsa	201	45	258	215	114	118	326	113	191	91	50	104	91		244	202

Mileages © Rand McNally

Total mileages through Oklahoma
More mileages at www.randmcnally.com/MC

| 35 | 236 miles | 44 | 329 miles |
| 40 | 331 miles | 75 | 227 miles |

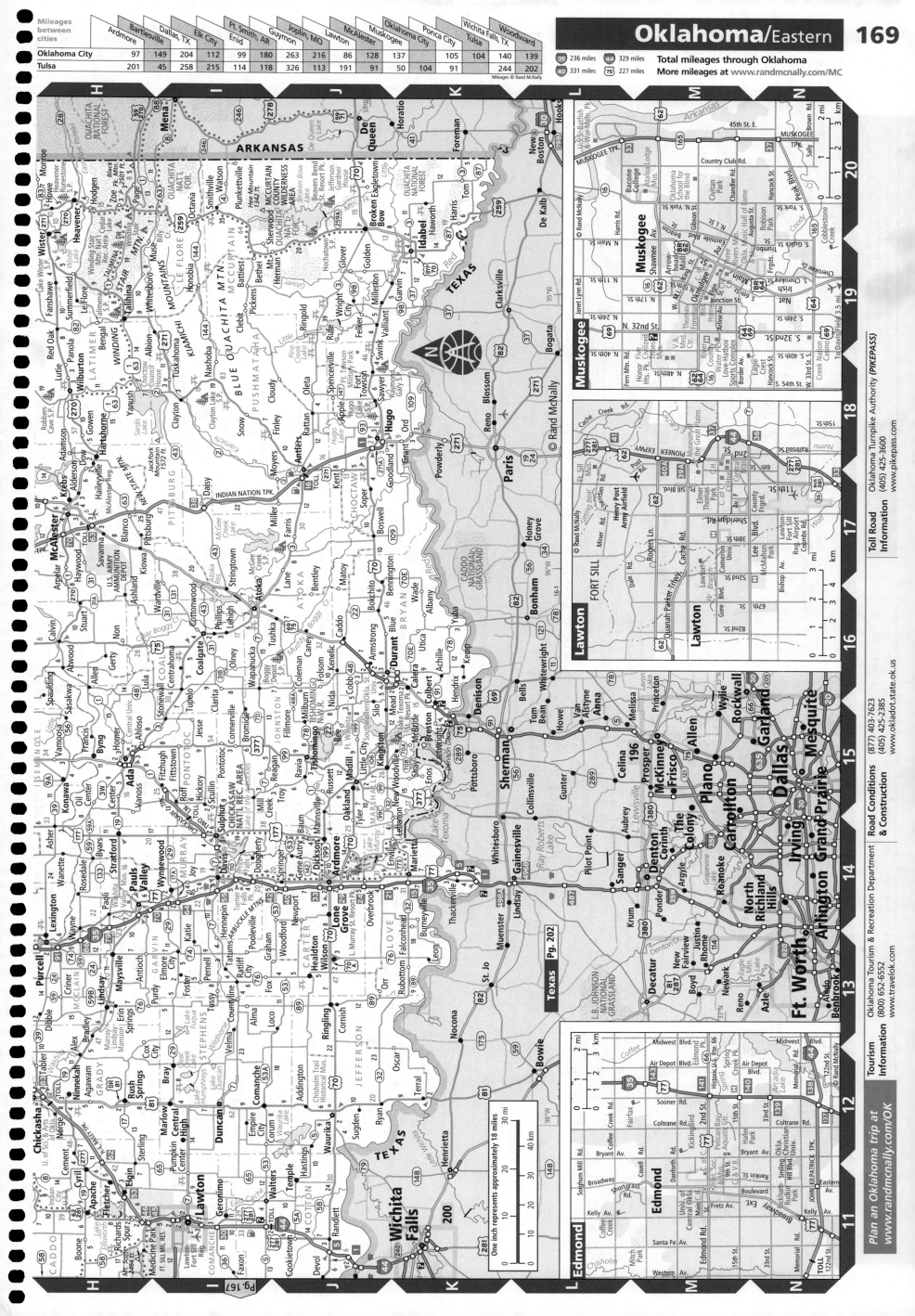

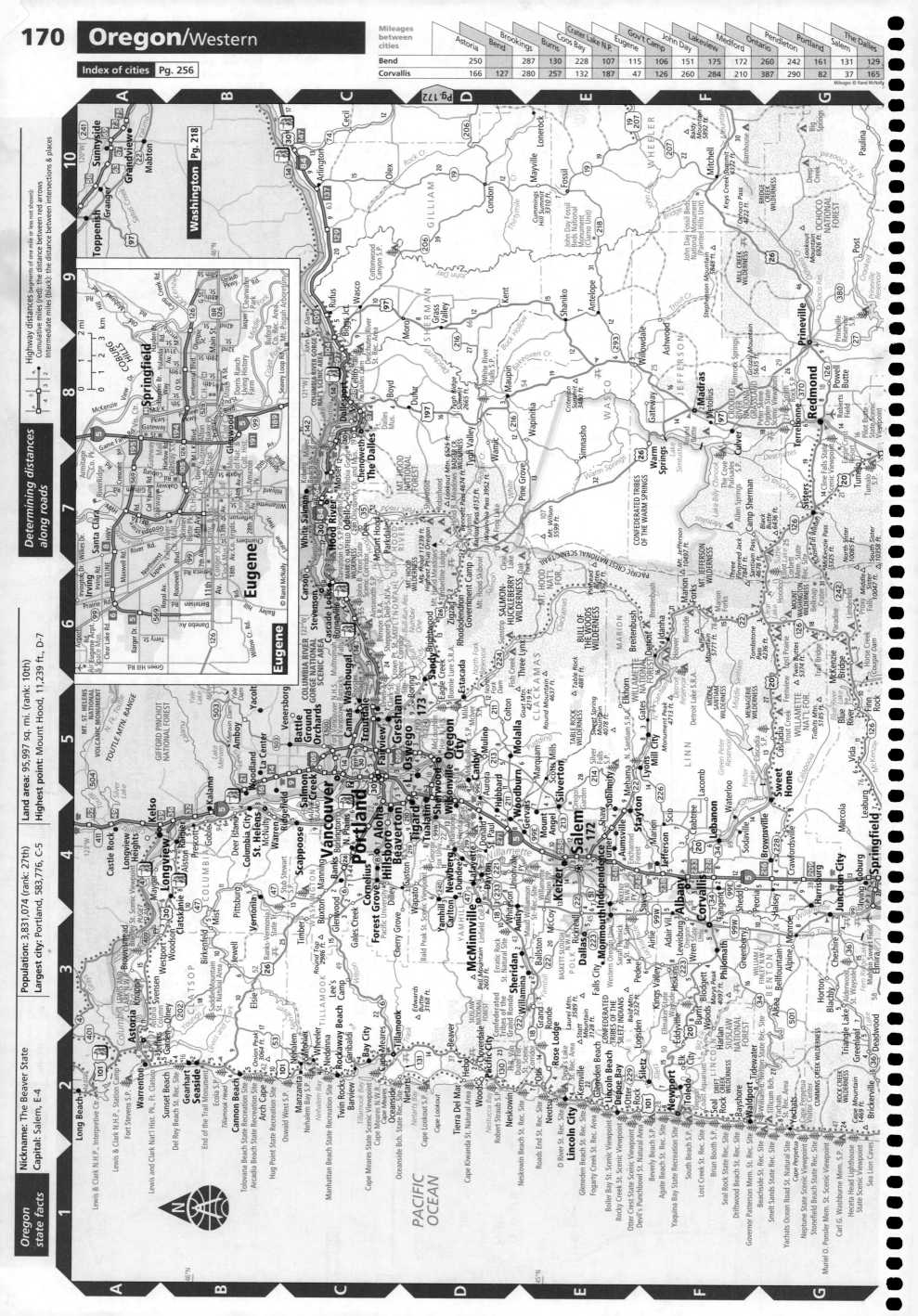

Oregon state facts

Nickname: The Beaver State
Capital: Salem, E-4
Population: 3,831,074 (rank: 27th)
Land area: 95,997 sq. mi. (rank: 10th)
Largest city: Portland, 583,776, C-5
Highest point: Mount Hood, 11,239 ft., D-7

Determining distances along roads

Highway distances (segments of one mile or less not shown)
Cumulative miles (red): the distance between red arrows
Intermediate miles (black): the distance between intersections & places

Mileages between cities	Astoria	Bend	Brookings	Burns	Coos Bay	Crater Lake N.P.	Eugene	Gov't Camp	John Day	Lakeview	Medford	Ontario	Pendleton	Portland	Salem	The Dalles
Bend	250		287	130	228	107	115	106	151	175	172	260	242	161	131	129
Corvallis	166	127	280	257	132	187	47	126	260	284	210	387	290	82	37	165

Mileages © Rand McNally

Mileages between cities	Astoria	Bend	Brookings	Burns	Coos Bay	Crater Lake N.P.	Eugene	Gov't Camp	John Day	Lakeview	Medford	Ontario	Pendleton	Portland	Salem	The Dalles
Eugene	193	115	234	245	109	142		154	249	241	166	375	318	110	66	193
McDermitt, NV	525	277	525	147	505	356	392	380	218	222	400	187	354	436	408	405

Mileages © Rand McNally

continued p. 172

Total mileages through Oregon

5	308 miles	84	375 miles
82	11 miles	101	348 miles

More mileages at www.randmcnally.com/MC

California Pg. 26

© Rand McNally

Index of cities **Pg. 256**

Mileages between cities	Astoria	Bend	Brookings	Burns	Coos Bay	Crater Lake N.P.	Eugene	Gov't Camp	John Day	Lakeview	Medford	Ontario	Pendleton	Portland	Salem	The Dalles
Medford	356	172	125	305	169	74	166	317	328	171		432	481	273	228	356
Ontario	464	260	547	130	488	367	375	354	131	269	432		167	374	420	291

Mileages © Rand McNally

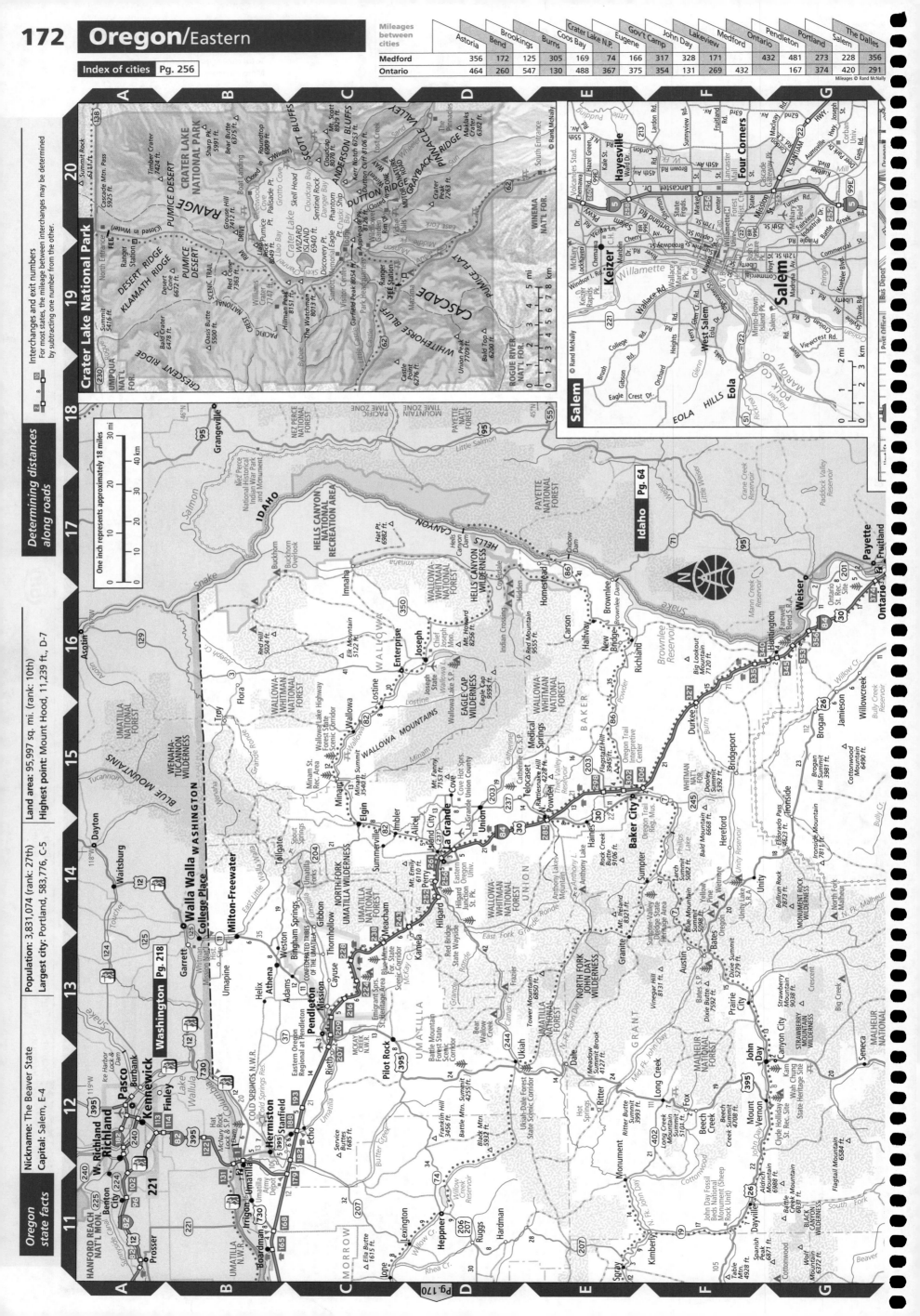

Pg.171
Nevada Pg. 130

Mileages between cities

	Astoria	Bend	Brookings	Burns	Coos Bay	Crater Lake N.P.	Eugene	Gov't Camp	John Day	Lakeview	Medford	Ontario	Pendleton	Portland	Salem	The Dalles
Pendleton	298	242	550	196	428	349	318	188	126	335	481	167		208	254	125
Portland	96	161	342	281	220	250	110	55	265	336	273	374	208		47	83

Mileages © Rand McNally

Total mileages through Oregon

5 308 miles 84 375 miles
82 11 miles 101 348 miles

More mileages at www.randmcnally.com/MC

Central Portland

© Rand McNally

Portland & Vicinity

© Rand McNally

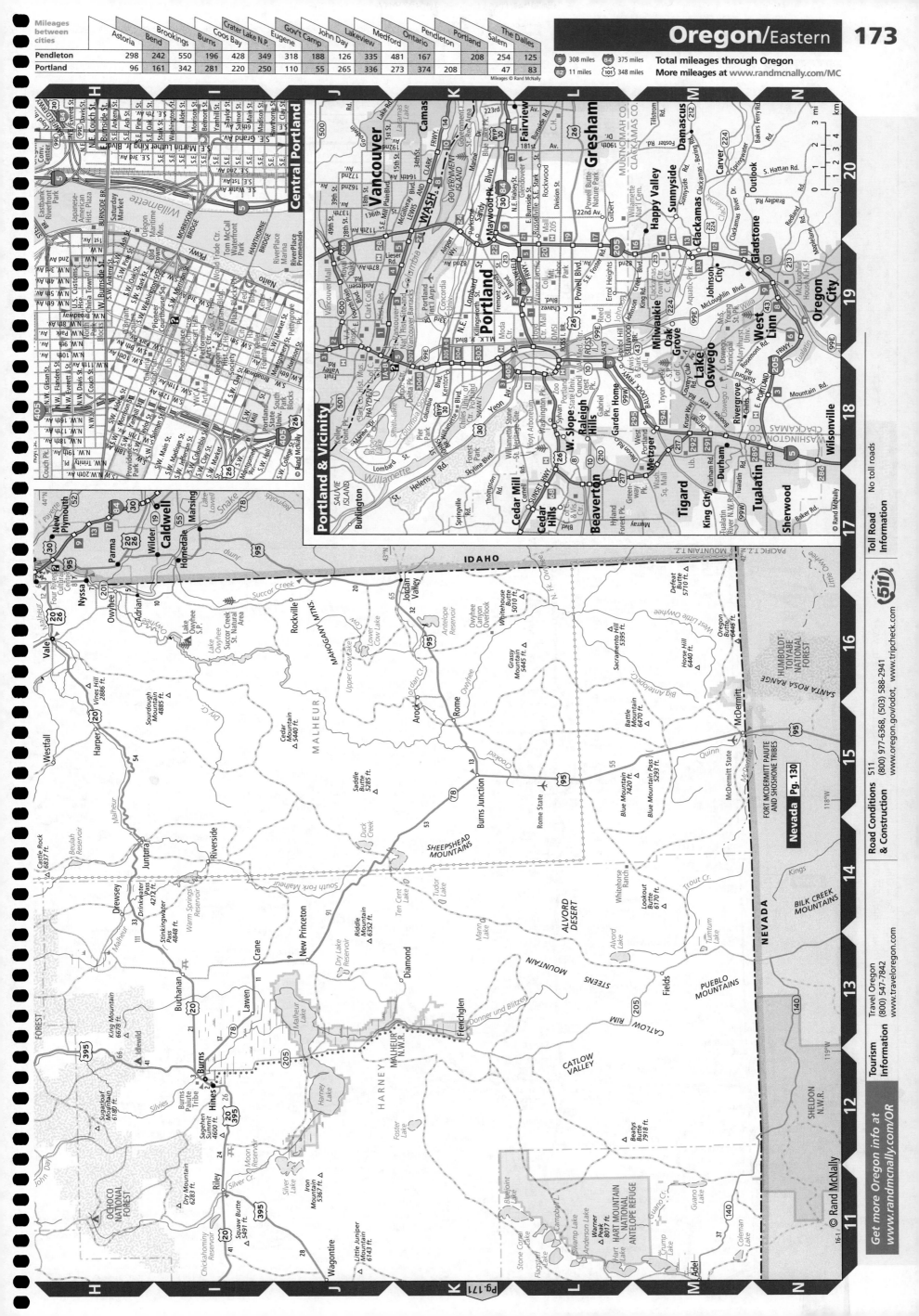

© Rand McNally

Tourism Information
Travel Oregon
(800) 547-7842
www.traveloregon.com

Road Conditions & Construction
511
(800) 977-6368, (503) 588-2941
www.oregon.gov/odot, www.tripcheck.com

511

Toll Road Information
No toll roads

Mileages between cities	Altoona	Chambersburg	Cumberland, MD	Du Bois	Erie	Galeton	Harrisburg	Johnstown	Kittanning	Meadville	New Castle	Philadelphia	Pittsburgh	State College	Uniontown	Warren
Altoona		90	66	71	202	135	134	46	79	165	127	234	96	41	112	130
Chambersburg	90		87	153	282	215	54	94	160	246	206	157	160	101	149	218

Mileages © Rand McNally

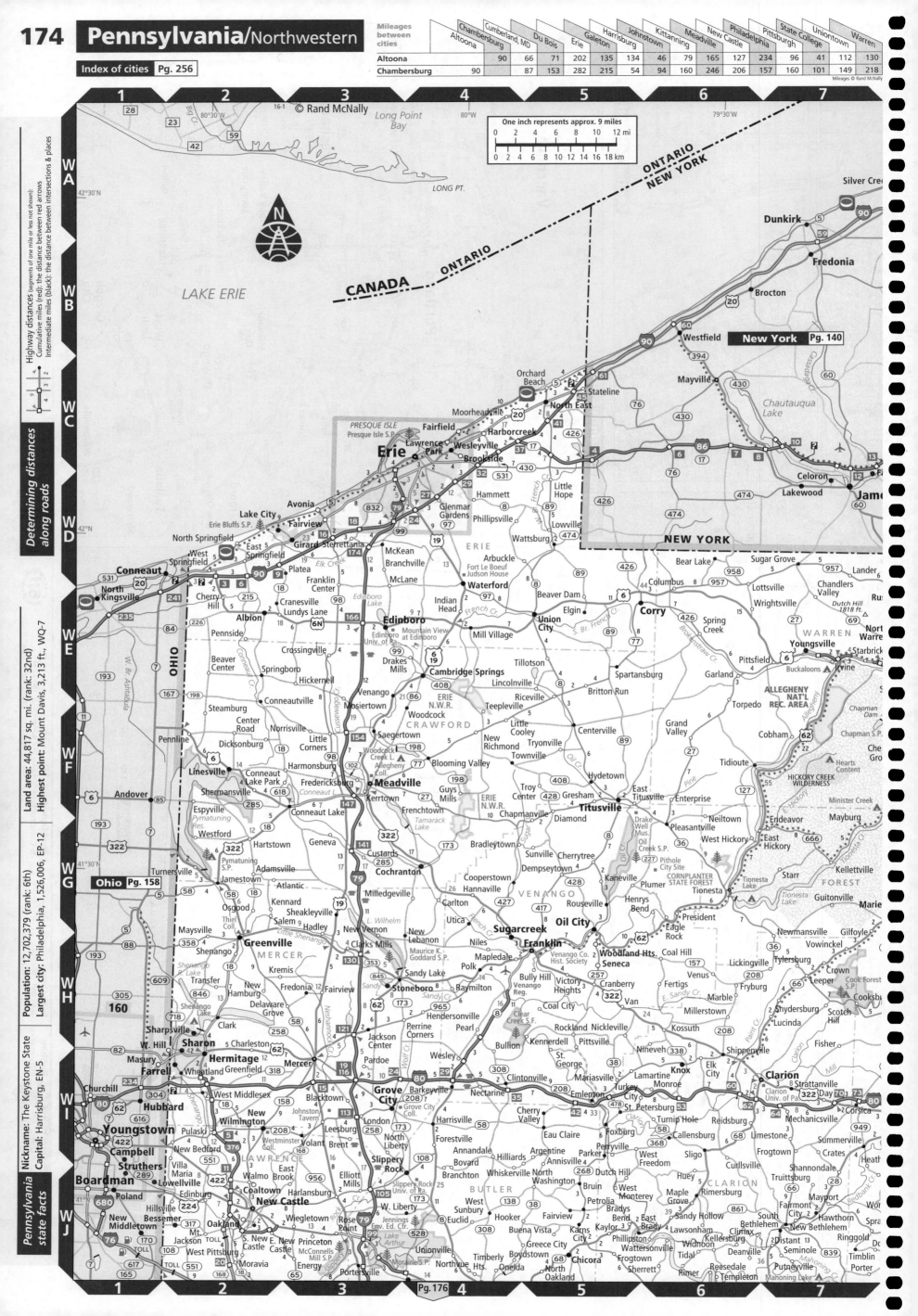

Mileages between cities	Altoona	Chambersburg	Cumberland, MD	Du Bois	Erie	Galeton	Harrisburg	Johnstown	Kittanning	Meadville	New Castle	Philadelphia	Pittsburgh	State College	Uniontown	Warren
Erie	202	282	232	148		159	297	177	123	41	88	419	127	208	184	66
Johnstown	46	94	70	77	177	179	137		53	141	102	238	67	85	80	135

continued p. 176

Mileages © Rand McNally

Route	Miles
70	168 miles
79	183 miles
80	311 miles
90	46 miles

Total mileages through Pennsylvania
More mileages at www.randmcnally.com/MC

Toll Road Information
Delaware River Port Authority (Philadelphia area bridges) (E-ZPass): (877) 567-3772; www.drpa.org
Pennsylvania Turnpike Commission (E-ZPass): (800) 331-3414; www.paturnpike.com

Road Conditions & Construction
511 (888) 783-6783 www.dot.state.pa.us

Tourism Information
Pennsylvania Tourism Office (800) 847-4872 www.visitpa.com

Explore Pennsylvania at
www.randmcnally.com/PA

Rand McNally road map of Northwestern Pennsylvania, including inset maps of Erie and Altoona.

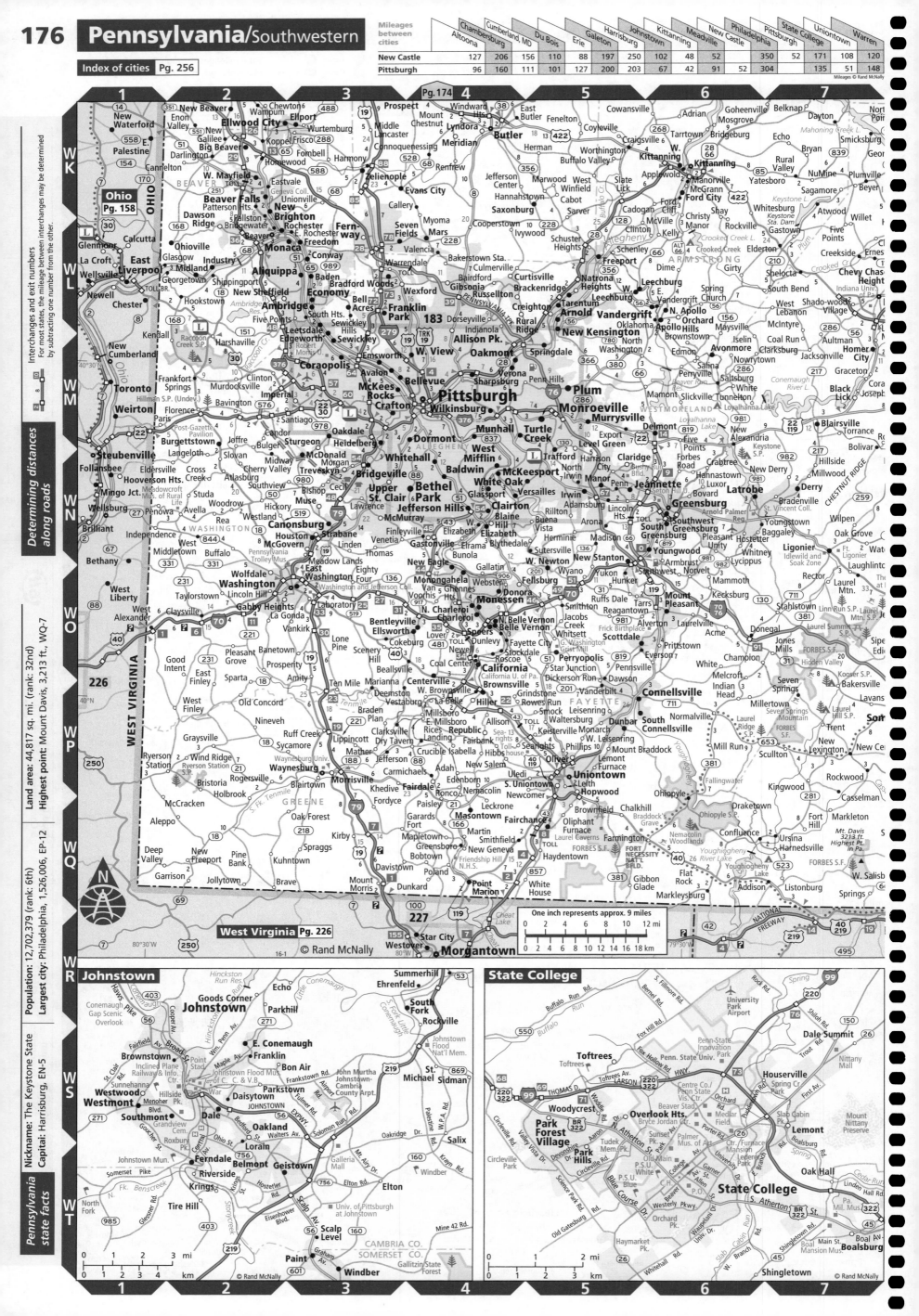

Index of cities Pg. 256

Pennsylvania state facts

Determining distances along roads — Interchanges and exit numbers: For most states, the mileage between interchanges may be determined by subtracting one number from the other.

Land area: 44,817 sq. mi. (rank: 32nd)
Highest point: Mount Davis, 3,213 ft., WQ-7
Population: 12,702,379 (rank: 6th)
Largest city: Philadelphia, 1,526,006, EP-12
Nickname: The Keystone State
Capital: Harrisburg, EN-5

Ohio Pg. 158

West Virginia Pg. 226

Pg. 174

One inch represents approx. 9 miles

© Rand McNally

Johnstown

State College

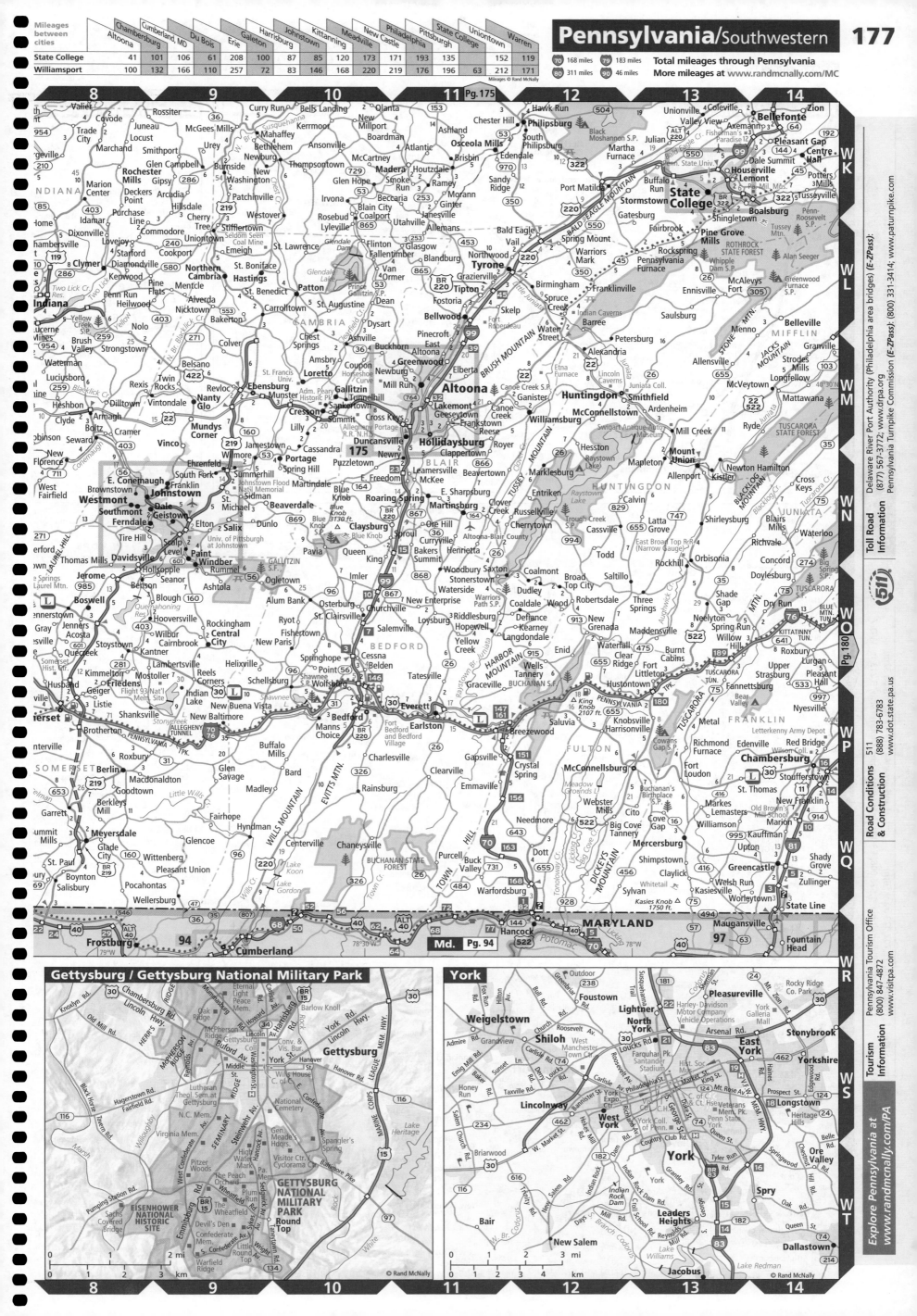

Mileages between cities	Altoona	Chambersburg	Cumberland, MD	Du Bois	Erie	Galeton	Harrisburg	Johnstown	Kittanning	Meadville	New Castle	Philadelphia	Pittsburgh	State College	Uniontown	Warren
State College	41	101	106	61	208	100	87	85	120	173	171	193	135		152	119
Williamsport	100	132	166	110	257	72	83	146	168	220	219	176	196	63	212	171

Mileages © Rand McNally

Total mileages through Pennsylvania

70	168 miles	79	183 miles
80	311 miles	90	46 miles

More mileages at www.randmcnally.com/MC

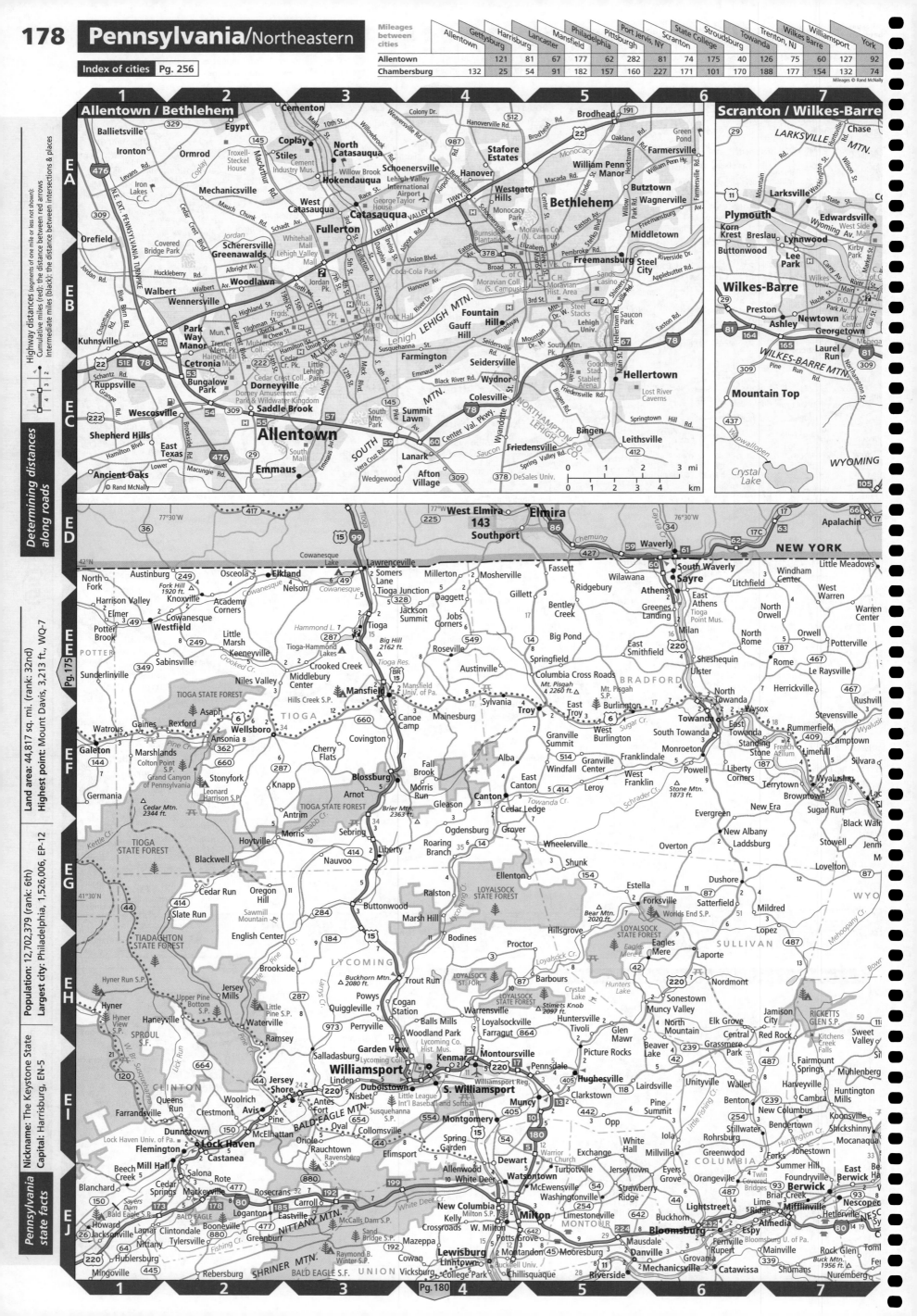

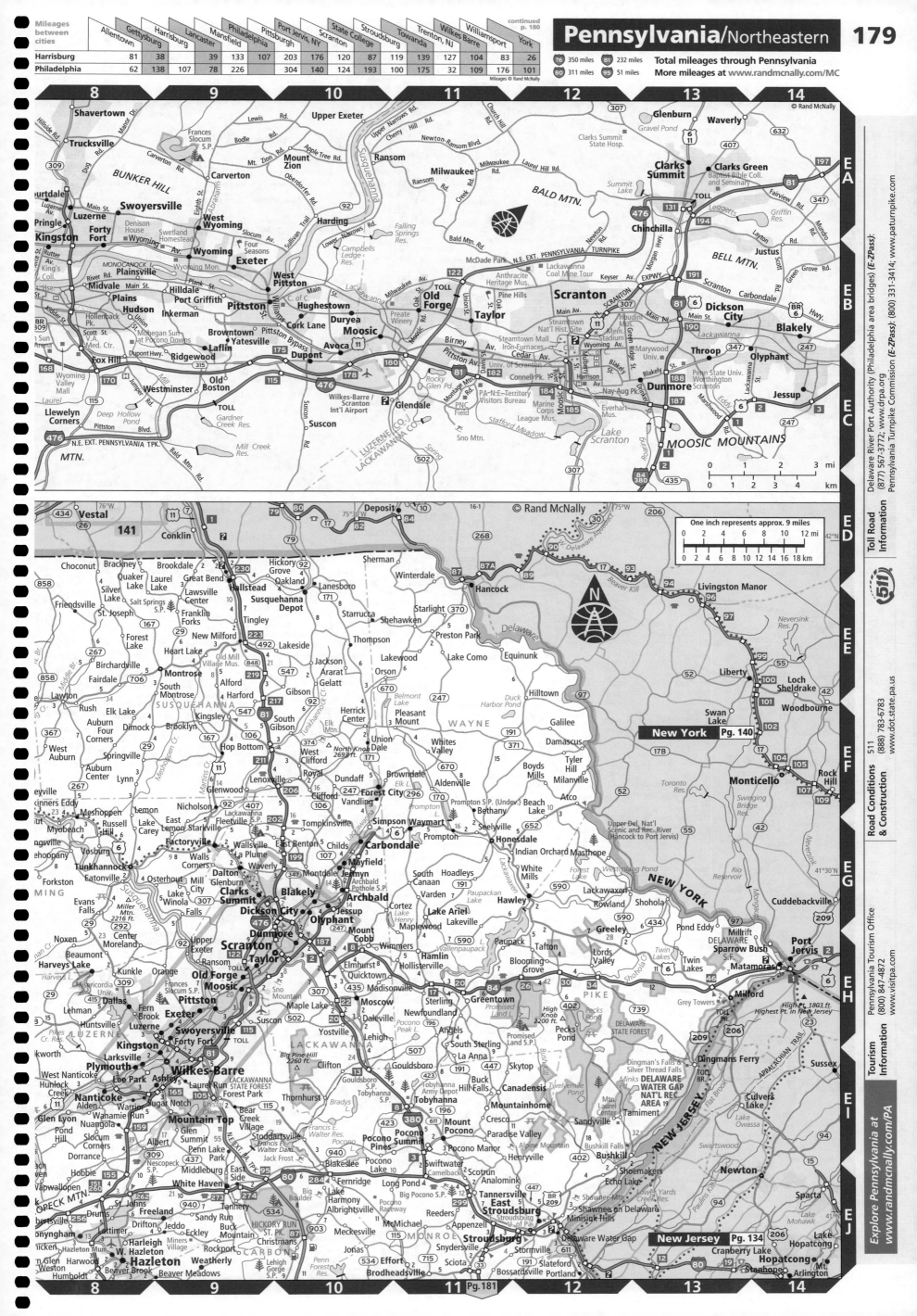

Delaware River Port Authority (Philadelphia area bridges) (E-ZPass)
(877) 567-3772; www.drpa.org
Pennsylvania Turnpike Commission (E-ZPass); (800) 331-3414; www.paturnpike.com

Toll Road Information

Road Conditions & Construction
511
(888) 783-6783
www.dot.state.pa.us

Tourism Information
Pennsylvania Tourism Office
(800) 847-4872
www.visitpa.com

Explore Pennsylvania at
www.randmcnally.com/PA

Mileages between cities

	Allentown	Gettysburg	Harrisburg	Lancaster	Mansfield	Philadelphia	Pittsburgh	Port Jervis, NY	Scranton	State College	Stroudsburg	Towanda	Trenton, NJ	Wilkes Barre	Williamsport	York
Harrisburg	81	38		39	133	107	203	176	120	87	119	139	127	104	83	26
Philadelphia	62	138	107	78	226		304	140	124	193	100	175	32	109	176	101

Mileages © Rand McNally

Total mileages through Pennsylvania

76	350 miles	81	232 miles
80	311 miles	95	51 miles

More mileages at www.randmcnally.com/MC

continued p. 180

Pg. 181

New York Pg. 140

New Jersey Pg. 134

© Rand McNally

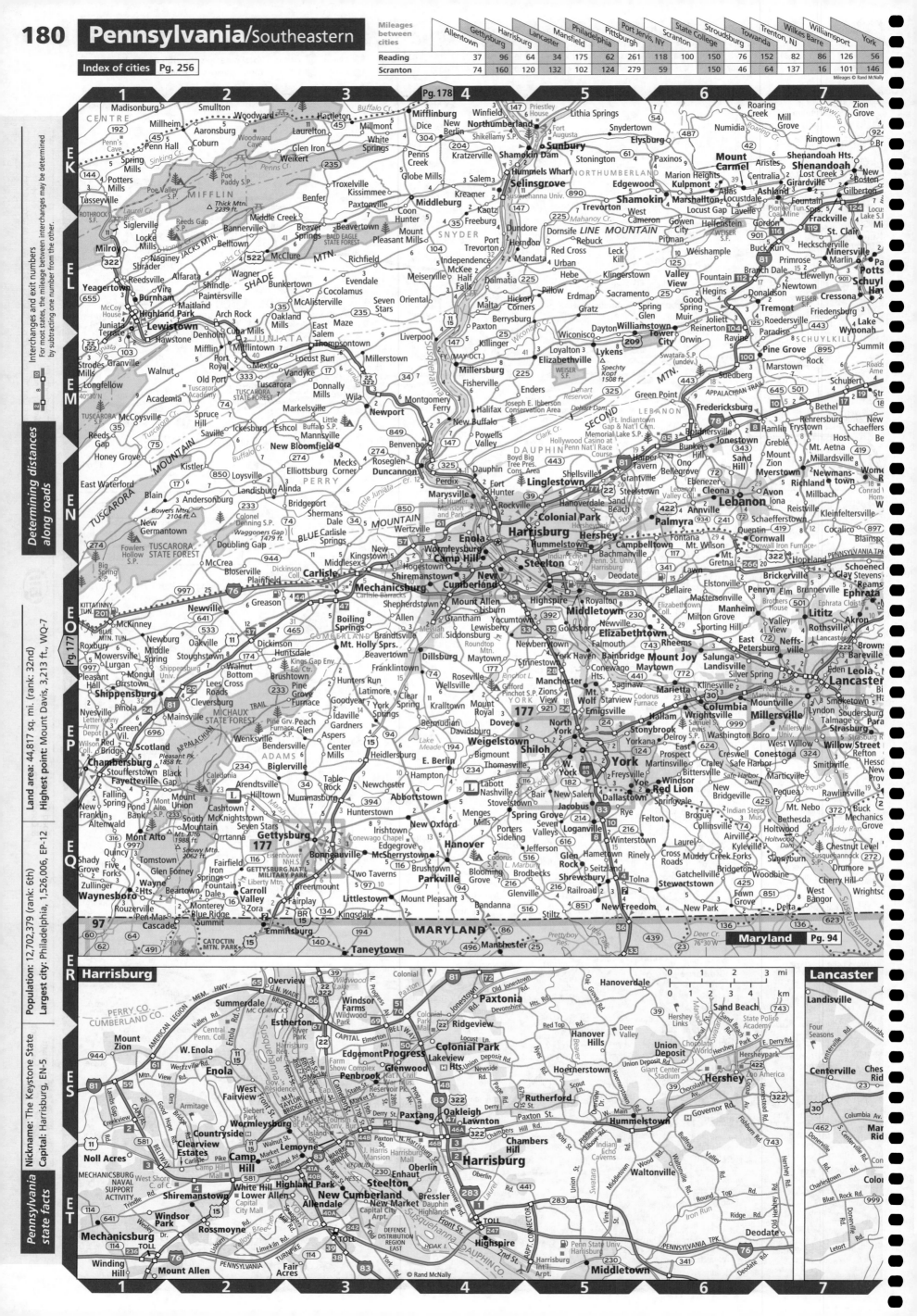

Mileages © Rand McNally

Pennsylvania state facts

Nickname: The Keystone State
Capital: Harrisburg, EN-5
Largest city: Philadelphia, EP-12
Population: 12,702,379 (rank: 6th)
Land area: 44,817 sq. mi. (rank: 32nd)
Highest point: Mount Davis, 3,213 ft., WQ-7

Determining distances along roads

Interchanges and exit numbers
For most states, the mileage between interchanges may be determined by subtracting one number from the other.

Harrisburg

Lancaster

© Rand McNally

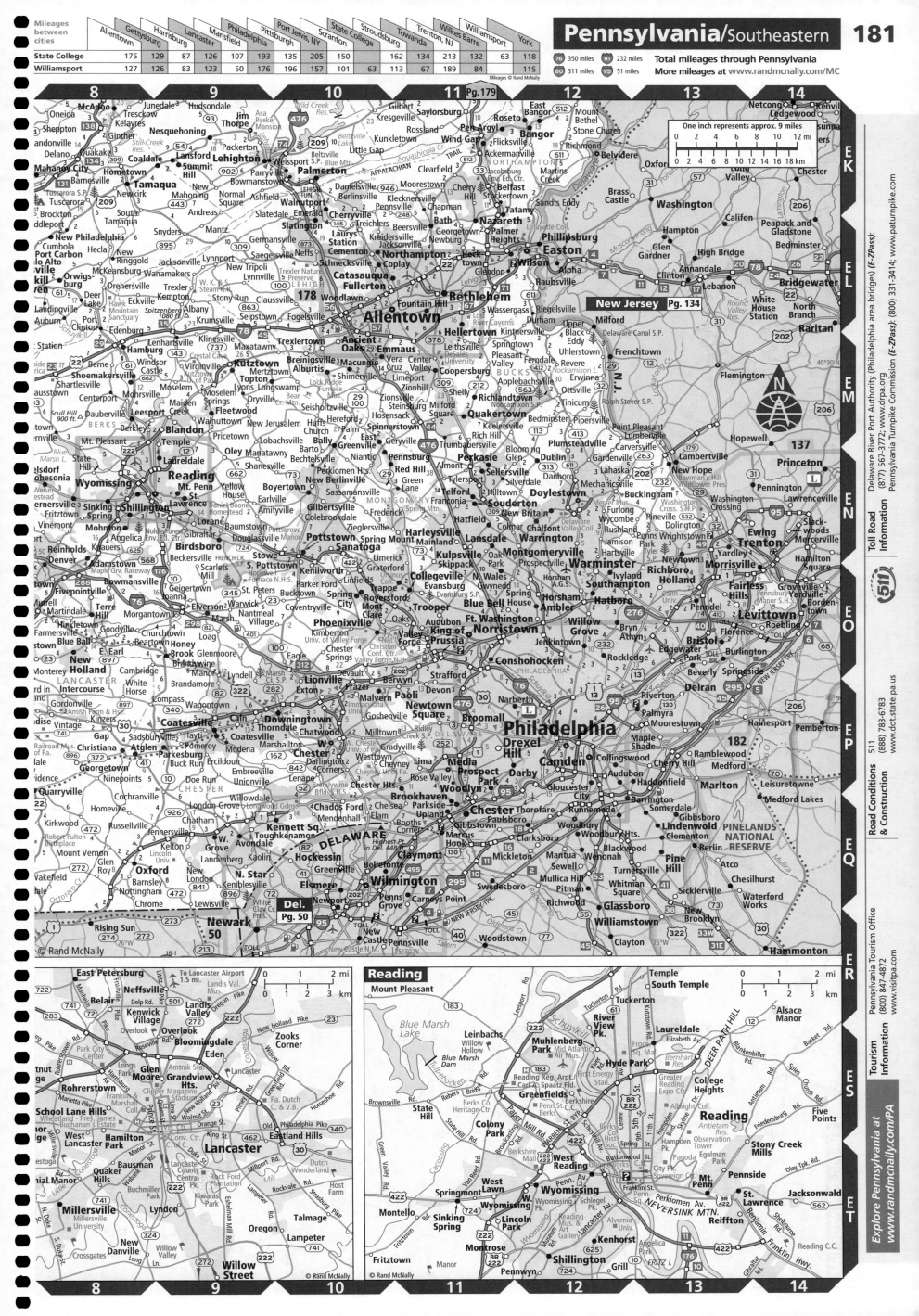

Total mileages through Pennsylvania
More mileages at www.randmcnally.com/MC

Mileages between cities	Allentown	Gettysburg	Harrisburg	Lancaster	Mansfield	Philadelphia	Pittsburgh	Port Jervis, NY	Scranton	State College	Stroudsburg	Towanda	Trenton, NJ	Wilkes Barre	Williamsport	York
State College	175	129	87	126	107	193	135	205	150		162	134	213	132	63	118
Williamsport	127	126	83	123	50	176	196	157	101	63	113	67	189	84		115

Mileages © Rand McNally

76	350 miles
80	311 miles
81	232 miles
95	51 miles

One inch represents approx. 9 miles

137

182

City sights to see

- Adventure Aquarium, Camden, N.J., E-5
- The Andy Warhol Museum, Pittsburgh, L-2
- Betsy Ross House, Philadelphia, F-10
- Carnegie Science Center, Pittsburgh, L-1
- Duquesne & Monongahela Inclines, Pittsburgh, M-1 & N-2
- Franklin Institute Science Museum, Philadelphia, F-6

Philadelphia & Vicinity

Central Philadelphia

- Independence Hall, Philadelphia, G-9
- Liberty Bell, Philadelphia, G-9
- National Constitution Center, Philadelphia, F-9
- Philadelphia Museum of Art, Philadelphia, E-4
- Point State Park, Pittsburgh, M-1
- The Strip District, Pittsburgh, L-3
- The U.S. Mint, Philadelphia, F-9
- USS *Olympia,* Philadelphia, E-5

Pittsburgh & Vicinity
Central Pittsburgh
© Rand McNally

Rhode Island state facts

Nickname: The Ocean State
Capital: Providence, D-6

Population: 1,052,567 (rank: 43rd)
Largest city: Providence, 178,042, D-6

Land area: 1,045 sq. mi. (rank: 50th)
Highest point: Jerimoth Hill, 812 ft., C-3

Determining distances along roads

Interchanges and exit numbers
For most states, the mileage between interchanges may be determined by subtracting one number from the other.

Mileages between cities

	Fall River, MA	Kingston	Newport	Providence	Warwick	Woonsocket	Westerly	Worcester, MA
Chepachet	35	41	45	19	23	54	13	37
Fall River, MA		35	20	16	25	58	31	56
Newport	20	16		33	26	39	47	72
Providence	16	29	33		10	42	14	40

Mileages © Rand McNally

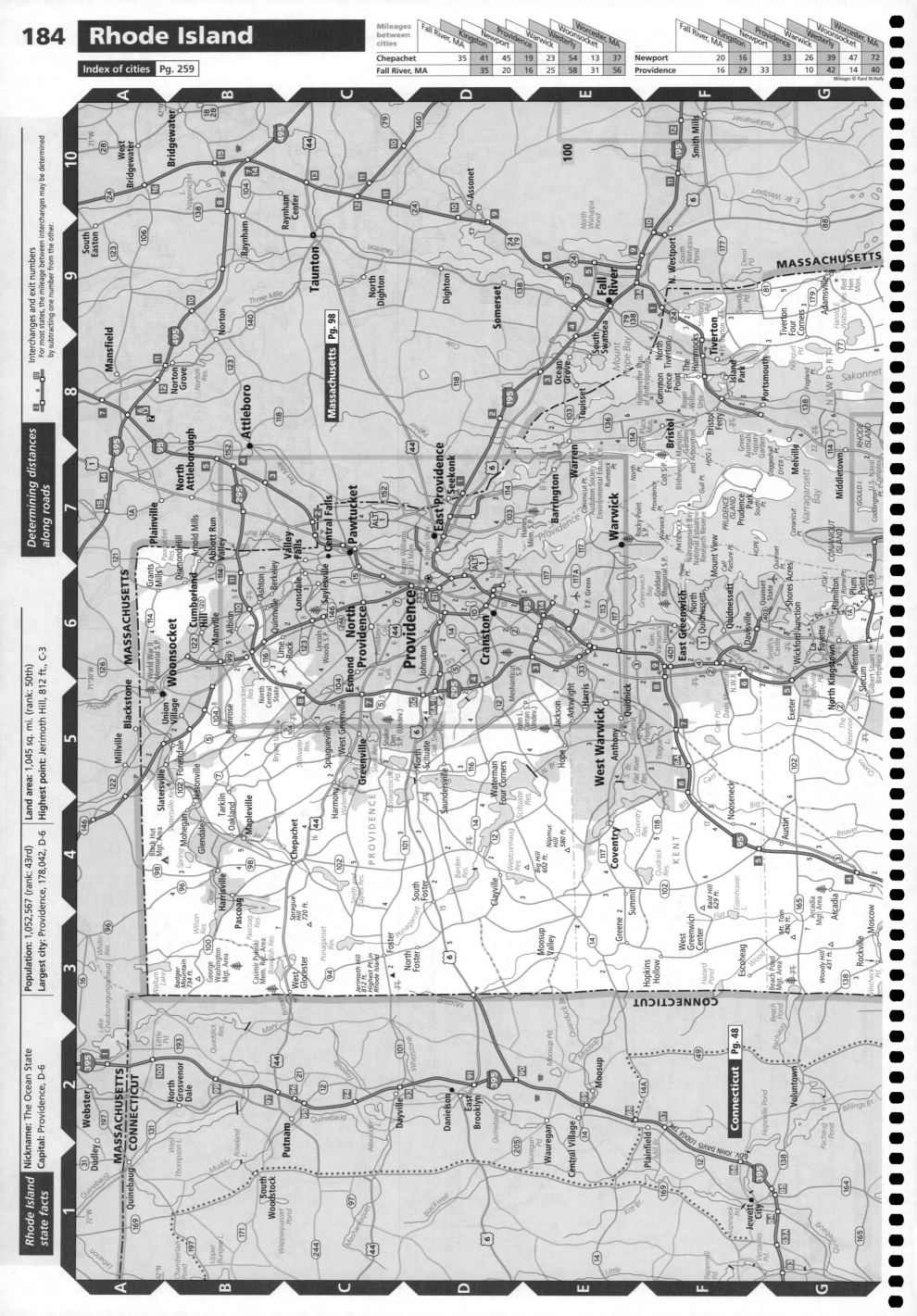

Massachusetts Pg. 98

Connecticut Pg. 48

Mileages between cities	Fall River, MA	Kingston	Newport	Providence	Warwick	Westerly	Woonsocket	Worcester, MA
Warwick	25	23	26	10		37	24	50
Westerly	58	23	39	42	37		56	82
Woonsocket	31	43	47	14	24	56		27
Worcester, MA	56	68	72	40	50	82	27	

Mileages © Rand McNally

Total mileages through Rhode Island
More mileages at www.randmcnally.com/MC

95 42 miles   6 31 miles
1 60 miles

Toll Road Information: R.I. Turnpike & Bridge Authority (E-ZPass) (877) 743-9727 www.ritba.org

Road Conditions 511: Rhode Island Tourism Division (401) 278-9100 www.dot.ri.gov/travel

Tourism Information: Rhode Island Tourism Division (401) 278-9100 (888) 401-4511, (401) 222-2450 www.visitrhodeisland.com

Plan a Rhode Island trip at www.randmcnally.com/RI

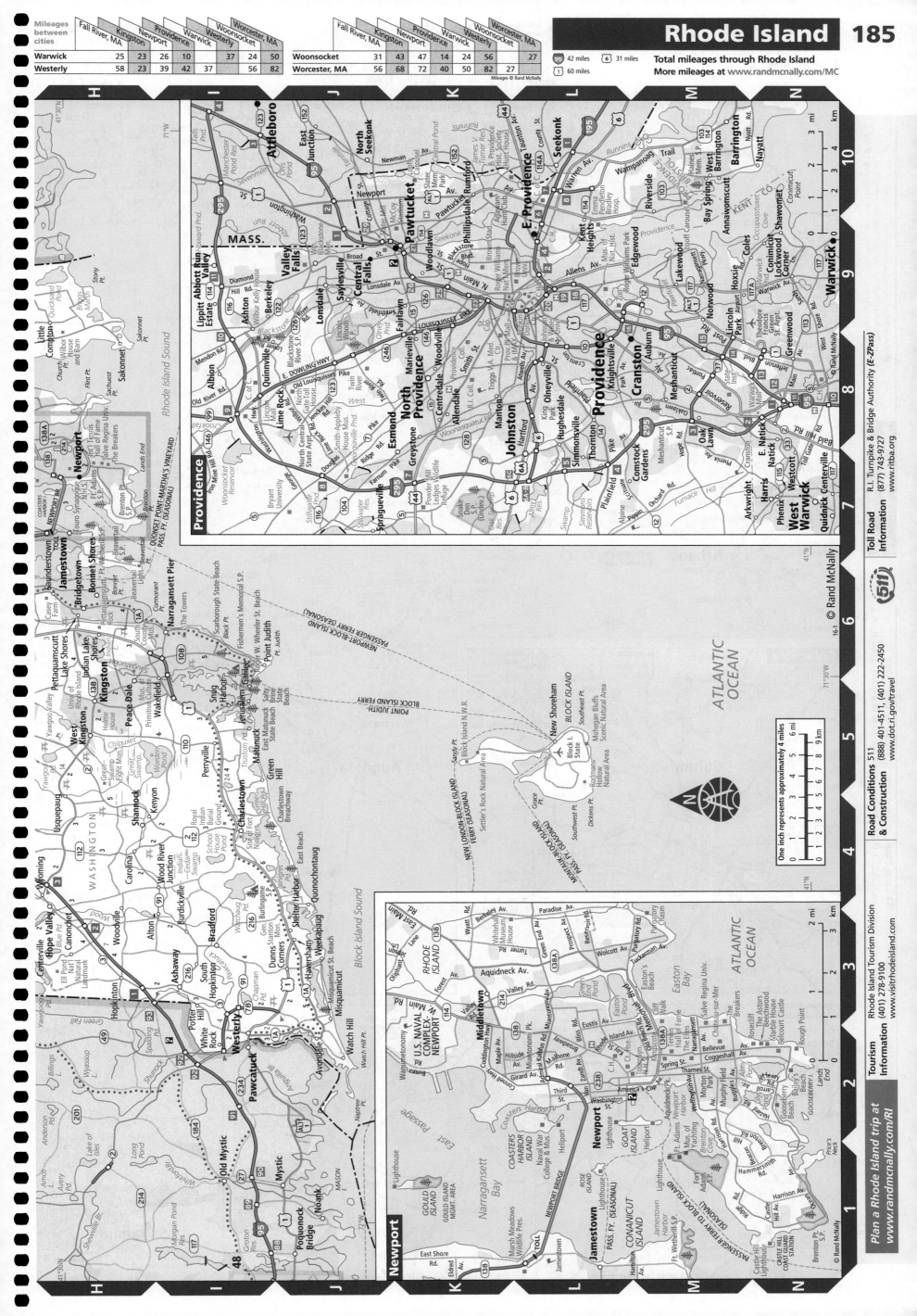

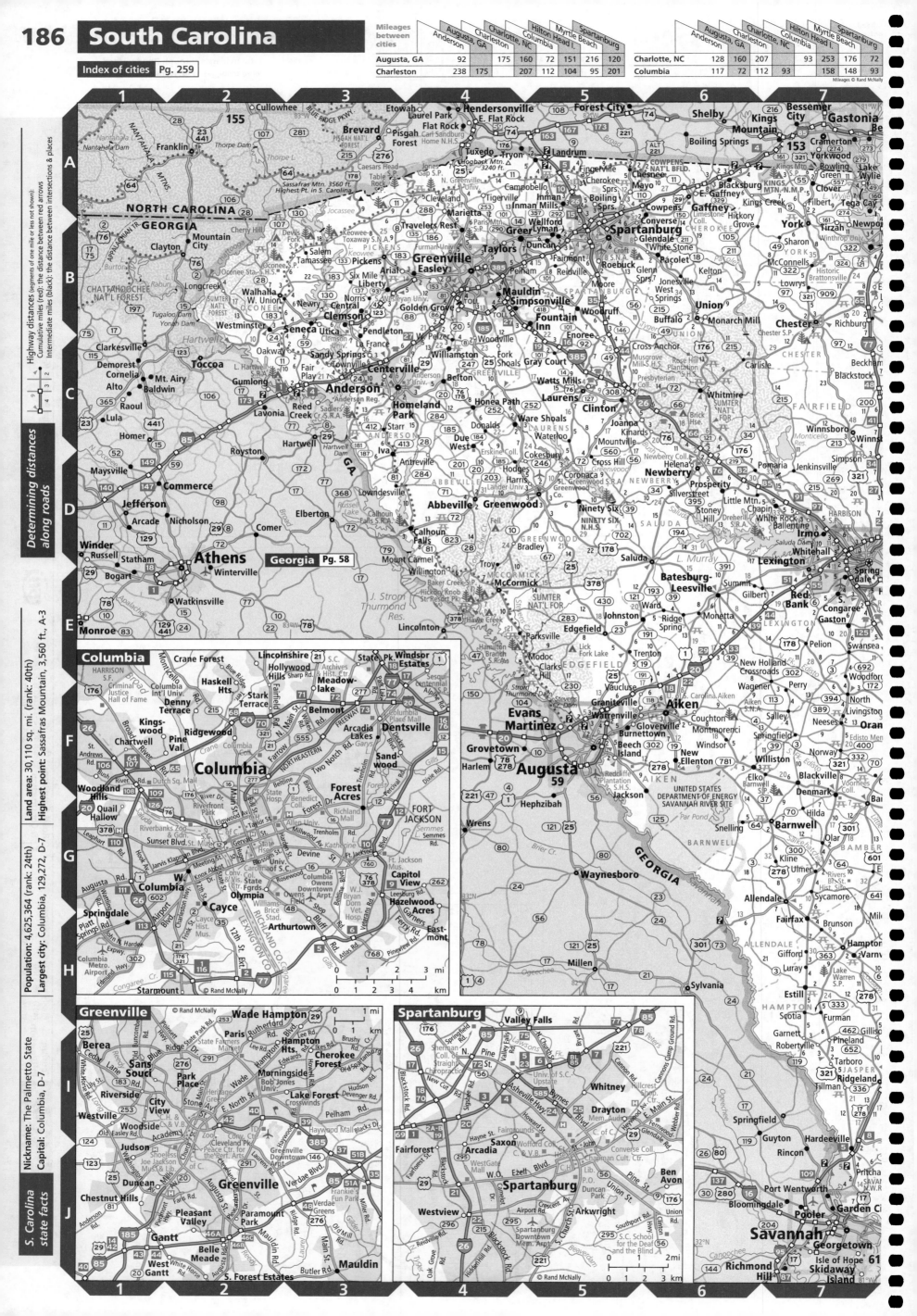

Mileages between cities

	Anderson	Augusta, GA	Charlotte, NC	Columbia	Hilton Head I.	Myrtle Beach	Spartanburg
Augusta, GA	92		175	160	72	151	216	120
Charleston	238	175		207	112	104	95	201
Charlotte, NC	128	160	207		93	253	176	72
Columbia	117	72	112	93		158	148	93

Mileages © Rand McNally

Determining distances along roads

Highway distances (segments of one mile or less not shown):
Cumulative miles (red): the distance between red arrows
Intermediate miles (black): the distance between intersections & places

S. Carolina state facts
Nickname: The Palmetto State
Capital: Columbia, D-7
Population: 4,625,364 (rank: 24th)
Land area: 30,110 sq. mi. (rank: 40th)
Largest city: Columbia, 129,272, D-7
Highest point: Sassafras Mountain, 3,560 ft., A-3

Columbia

Greenville

Spartanburg

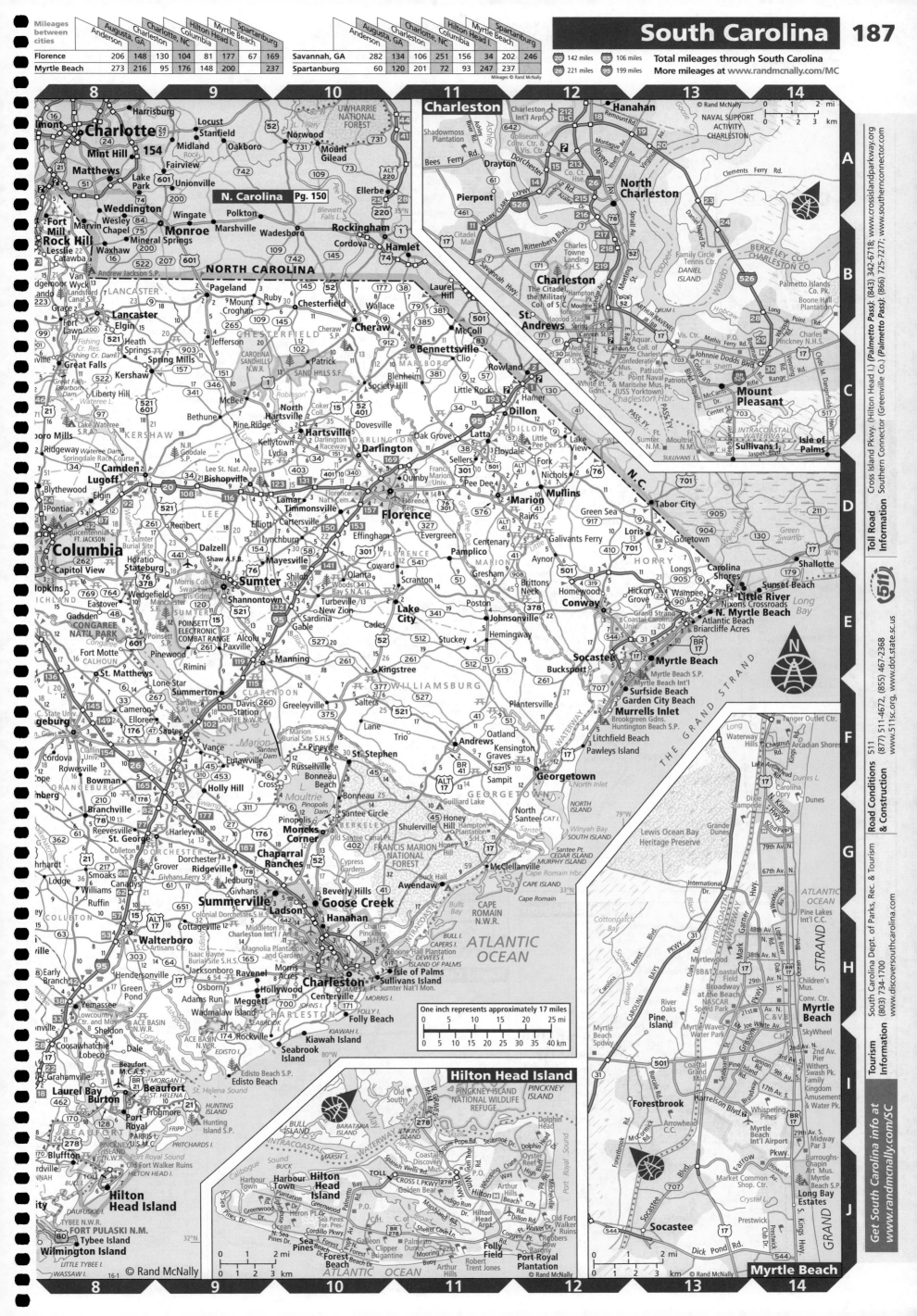

Mileages between cities

	Anderson	Augusta, GA	Charlotte, NC	Columbia	Hilton Head I.	Myrtle Beach	Spartanburg
Florence	206	148	130	104	81	177	67	169
Myrtle Beach	273	216	95	176	148	200		237

	Anderson	Augusta, GA	Charlotte, NC	Columbia	Hilton Head I.	Myrtle Beach	Spartanburg
Savannah, GA	282	134	106	251	156	34	202	246
Spartanburg	60	120	201	72	93	247	237	

Mileages © Rand McNally

Total mileages through South Carolina

| 20 | 142 miles | 85 | 106 miles |
| 26 | 221 miles | 95 | 199 miles |

More mileages at www.randmcnally.com/MC

Charleston

Hilton Head Island

Myrtle Beach

One inch represents approximately 17 miles

0 5 10 15 20 25 mi
0 5 10 15 20 25 30 35 40 km

© Rand McNally

Toll Road Information
Cross Island Pkwy. (Hilton Head I.) (Palmetto Pass): (843) 342-6718; www.crossislandparkway.org
Southern Connector (Greenville Co.) (Palmetto Pass): (866) 725-7277; www.southernconnector.com

Road Conditions & Construction 511
(877) 511-4672, (855) 467-2368
www.511sc.org, www.dot.state.sc.us

Tourism Information
South Carolina Dept. of Parks, Rec. & Tourism
(803) 734-1700
www.discoversouthcarolina.com

Get South Carolina info at
www.randmcnally.com/SC

South Dakota

Index of cities Pg. 259

Mileages between cities

	Aberdeen	Mobridge	Pierre	Pine Ridge	Rapid City	Sioux Falls	Watertown	Yankton
Aberdeen		100	160	360	333	203	96	236
Belle Fourche	312	212	206	172	60	403	362	421
Mobridge	100		108	308	243	303	196	332
Pierre	160	108		200	173	224	188	242

Mileages © Rand McNally

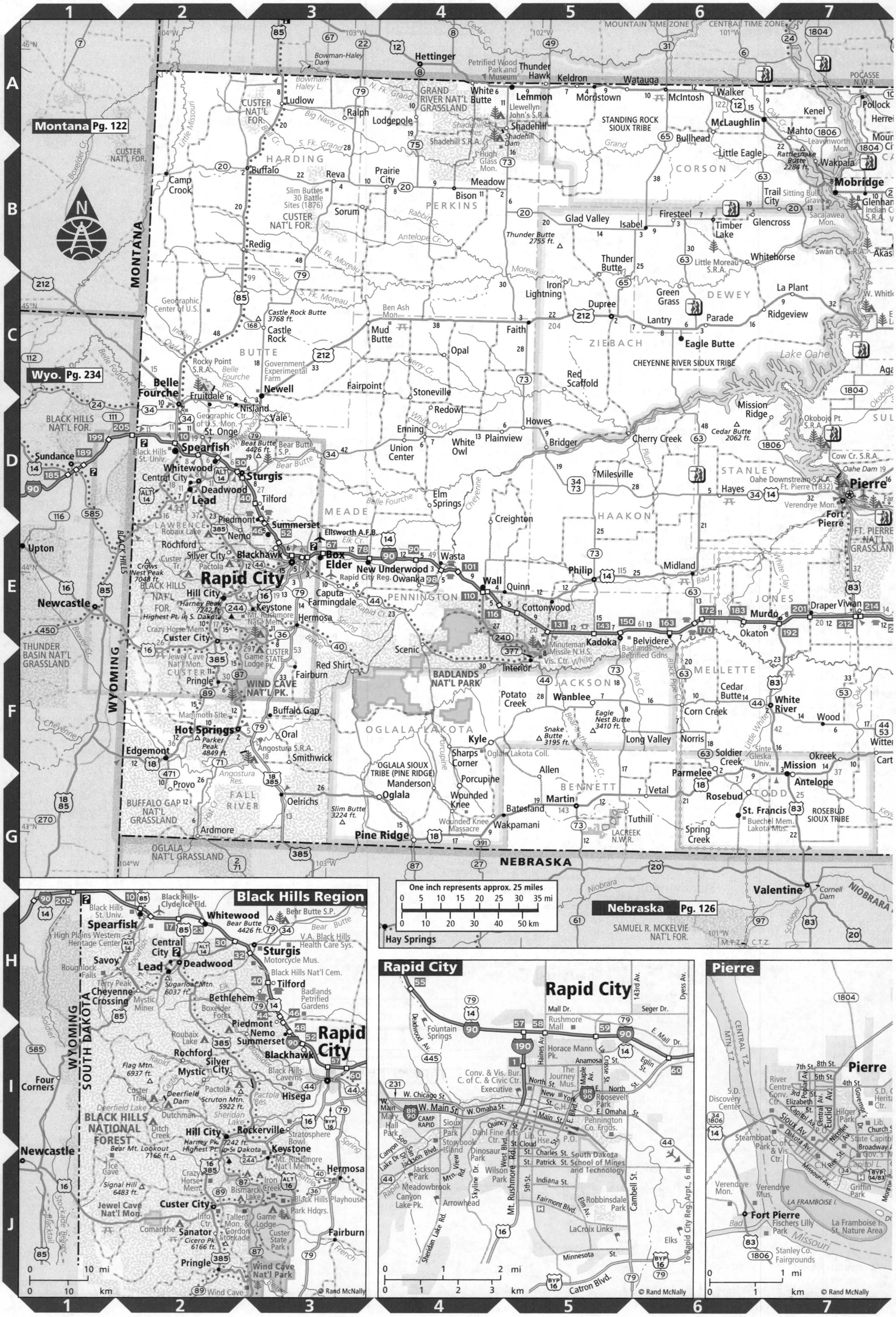

Interchanges and exit numbers
For most states, the mileage between interchanges may be determined by subtracting one number from the other.

Determining distances along roads

Land area: 75,885 sq. mi. (rank: 16th)
Highest point: Harney Peak, 7,242 ft., E-2

Population: 814,180 (rank: 46th)
Largest city: Sioux Falls, 153,888, F-13

Nickname: The Mount Rushmore State
Capital: Pierre, D-7

S. Dakota state facts

Mileages between cities

	Aberdeen	Mobridge	Pierre	Pine Ridge	Rapid City	Sioux Falls	Watertown	Yankton
Rapid City	333	243	173	111		347	403	365
Sioux City, IA	285	384	305	358	428	85	184	63

	Aberdeen	Mobridge	Pierre	Pine Ridge	Rapid City	Sioux Falls	Watertown	Yankton
Sioux Falls	203	303	224	356	347		103	81
Watertown	96	196	188	415	403	103		155

Mileages © Rand McNally

Total mileages through South Dakota

29 — 253 miles	12 — 317 miles		
90 — 413 miles	83 — 242 miles		

More mileages at www.randmcnally.com/MC

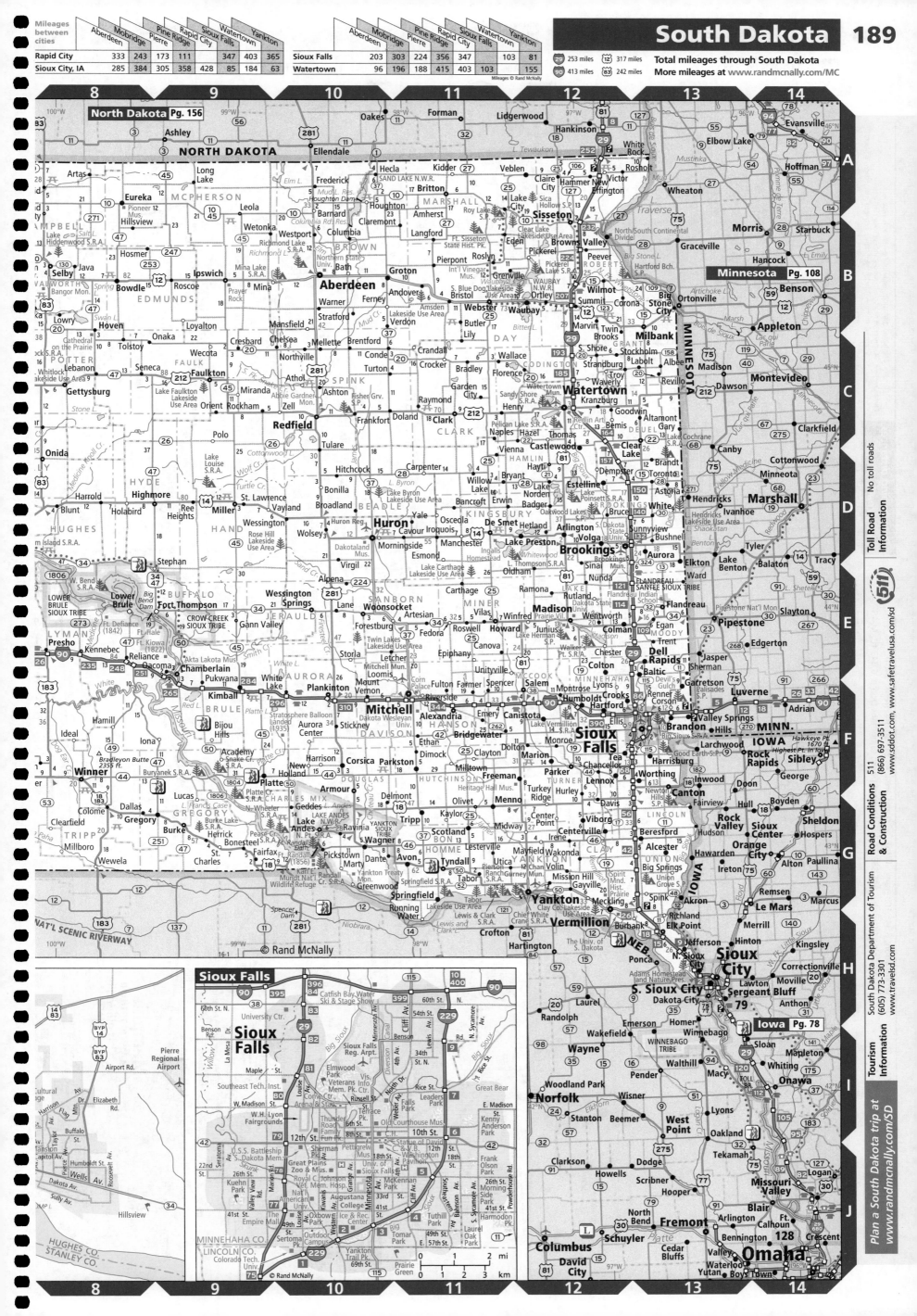

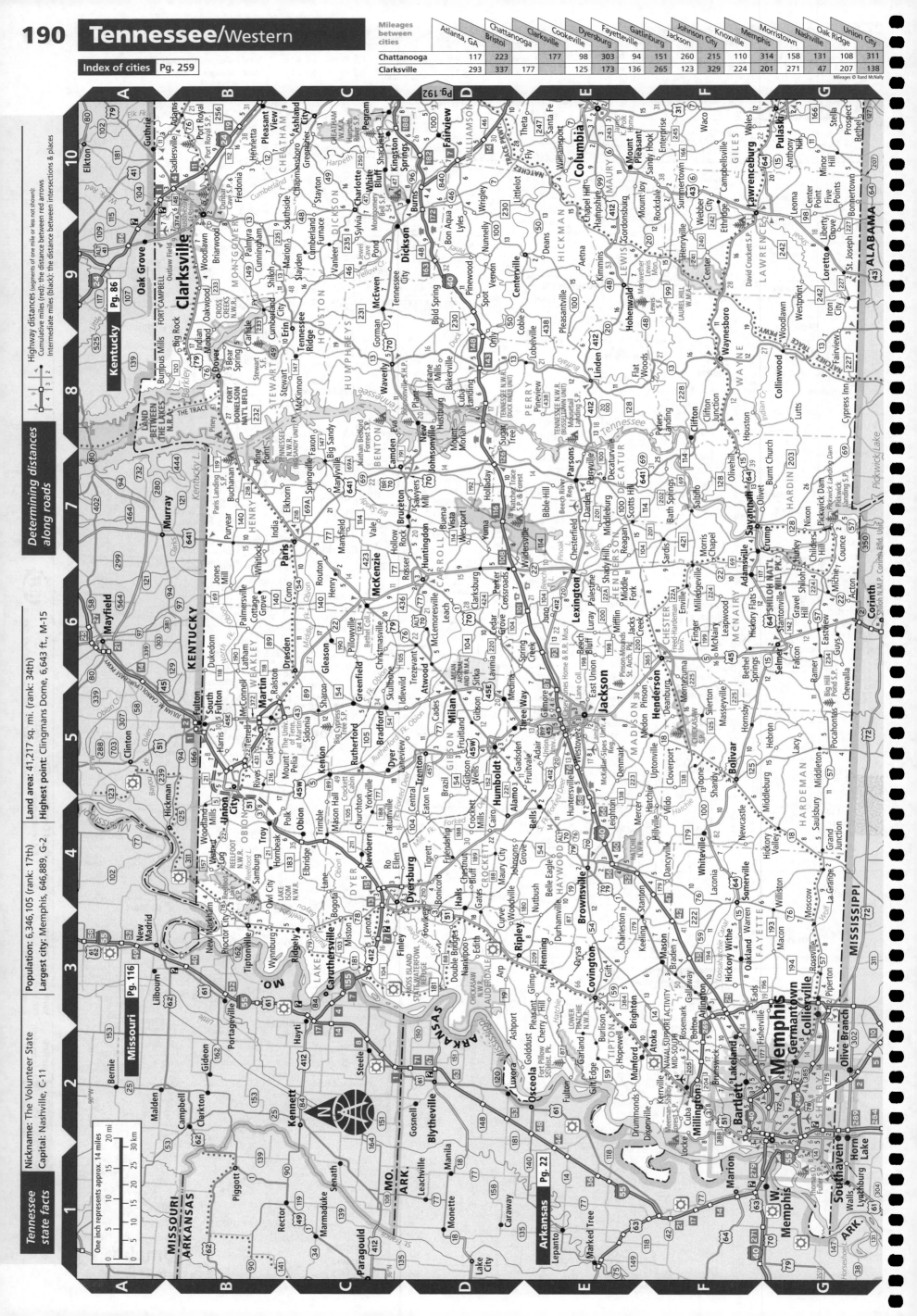

Mileages between cities	Atlanta, GA	Chattanooga	Bristol	Clarksville	Cookeville	Dyersburg	Fayetteville	Gatlinburg	Jackson	Johnson City	Knoxville	Memphis	Morristown	Nashville	Oak Ridge	Union City
Chattanooga	117		223	177	98	303	94	151	260	215	110	314	158	131	108	311
Clarksville	293	337		177	125	173	136	265	123	329	224	201	271	47	209	138

Mileages © Rand McNally

Tennessee state facts

Nickname: The Volunteer State
Capital: Nashville, C-11

Population: 6,346,105 (rank: 17th)
Largest city: Memphis, C-11

Land area: 41,217 sq. mi. (rank: 34th)
Highest point: Clingmans Dome, 6,643 ft., M-15

Determining distances along roads

Highway distances (segments of one mile or less not shown)
Cumulative miles (red): the distance between red arrows
Intermediate miles (black): the distance between intersections & places

continued p. 192

Mileages between cities	Atlanta, GA	Chattanooga Bristol	Clarksville	Cookeville	Dyersburg	Fayetteville	Gatlinburg	Johnson City Jackson	Knoxville	Memphis	Morristown	Nashville	Oak Ridge	Union City
Dyersburg	418	463	303	173	252		229	392	47	455	351	76	398	172	334	34
Fayetteville	211	317	94	136	109	229		246	167	308	204	243	252	90	189	224

Mileages © Rand McNally

Total mileages through Tennessee

40	455 miles	75	161 miles
65	121 miles	81	76 miles

More mileages at www.randmcnally.com/MC

Nashville

Memphis & Vicinity

Alabama Pg. 10

Mississippi Pg. 114

Memphis

Bartlett

Germantown

Southaven

Brentwood

Hendersonville

Goodlettsville

Florence

Explore Tennessee at www.randmcnally.com/TN

Tourism Information	Tennessee Department of Tourist Development (615) 741-2159 www.tnvacation.com
Road Conditions & Construction	511 (877) 244-0065 www.tn511.com, www.tdot.state.tn.us
Toll Road Information	No toll roads

511

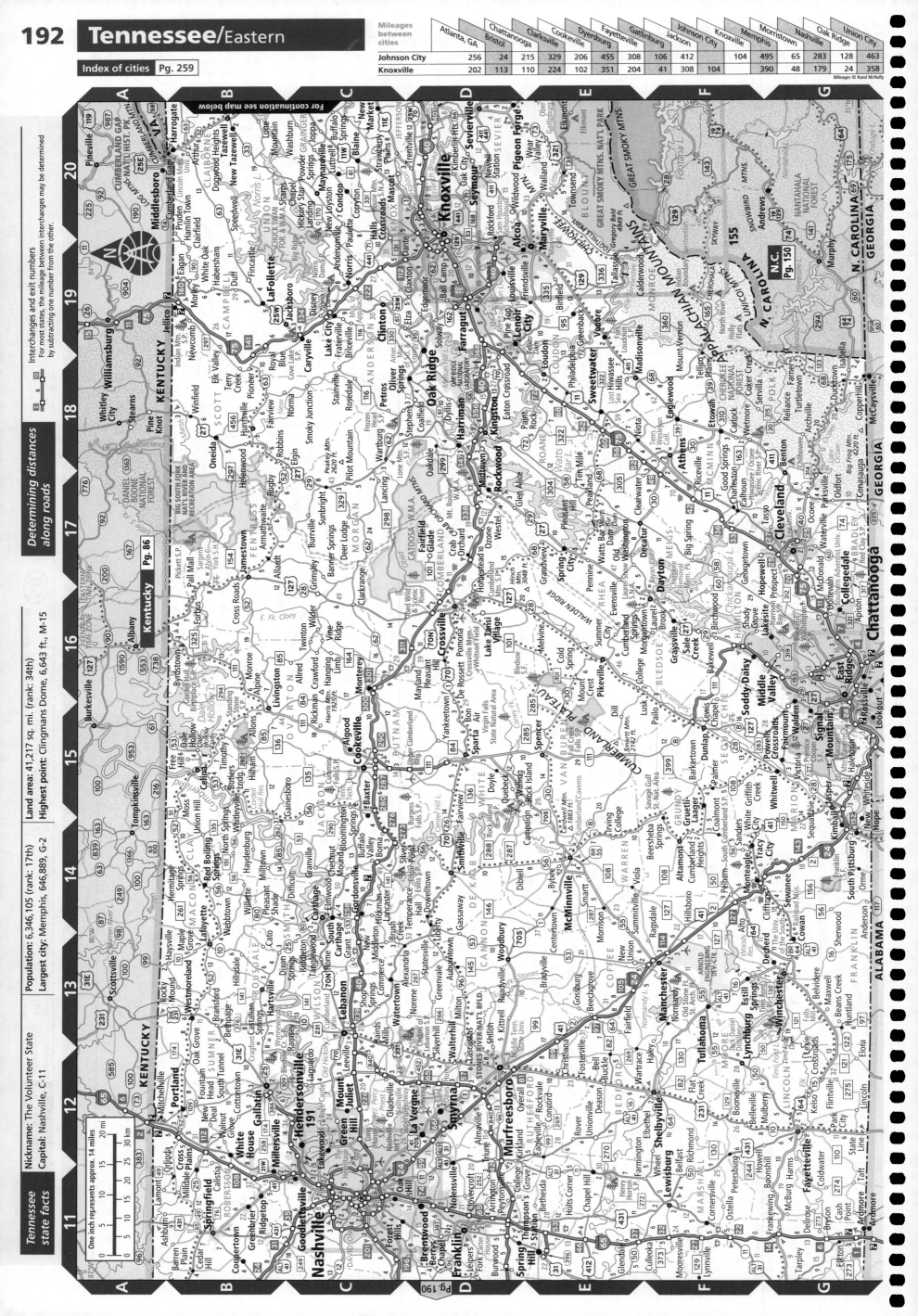

Mileages between cities	Atlanta, GA	Bristol	Chattanooga	Clarksville	Cookeville	Dyersburg	Fayetteville	Gatlinburg	Jackson	Johnson City	Knoxville	Memphis	Morristown	Nashville	Oak Ridge	Union City
Johnson City	256	24	215	329	206	455	308	106	412		104	495	65	283	128	463
Knoxville	202	113	110	224	102	351	204	41	308	104		390	48	179	24	358

Mileages © Rand McNally

Mileages between cities	Atlanta, GA	Bristol	Chattanooga	Clarksville	Cookeville	Dyersburg	Fayetteville	Gatlinburg	Jackson	Johnson City	Knoxville	Memphis	Morristown	Nashville	Oak Ridge	Union City
Memphis	380	502	314	201	291	76	243	431	87	495	390		437	212	373	113
Nashville	249	292	131	47	80	172	90	220	129	283	179	212	226		162	168

Mileages © Rand McNally

Total mileages through Tennessee

40	455 miles	75	161 miles
65	121 miles	81	76 miles

More mileages at www.randmcnally.com/MC

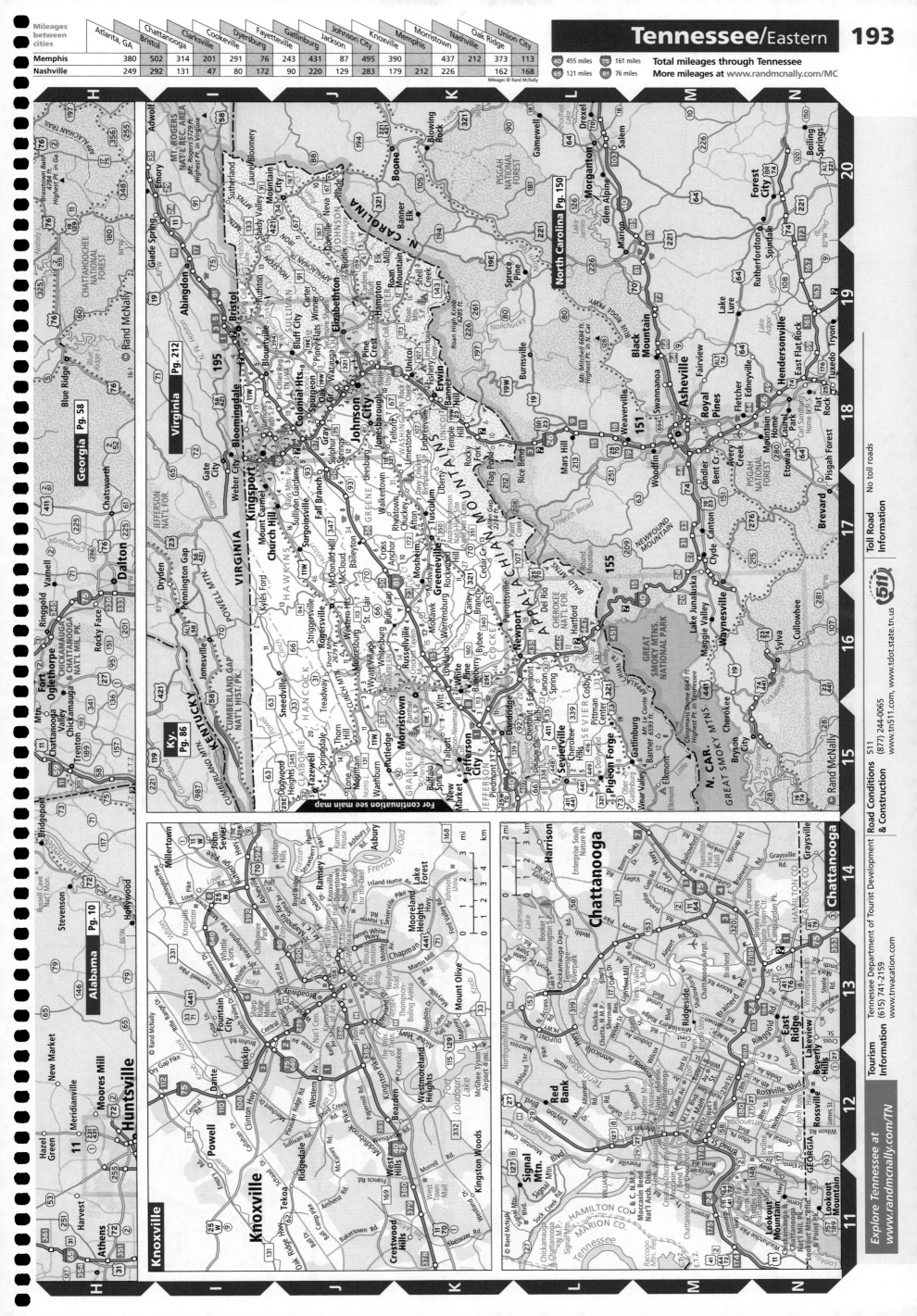

City sights to see

- Appalachian Caverns, Blountville, Tenn., K-3
- Battleship USS *Texas*, La Porte, D-9
- Bayou Place, Houston, K-8
- Bishop's Palace, Galveston, B-10
- Bristol Caverns, Bristol, Tenn., J-6
- Bristol Motor Speedway, Bristol, Tenn., K-4
- Contemporary Arts Museum, Houston, E-5
- Houston Fire Museum, Houston, E-5

Houston & Vicinity

- Houston Zoo, Houston, E-5
- Minute Maid Park, L-9
- Moody Gardens, Galveston, B-9
- Museum of Natural Science, Houston, E-5
- Reliant Stadium, Houston, E-5
- Rocky Mount Museum, Piney Flats, Tenn., L-3
- Space Center Houston, Houston, G-8
- Wortham Theatre Center, Houston, K-8

City sights to see
- AT&T Stadium, Arlington, H-7
- Dallas Arts District, Dallas, B-2
- Dallas Museum of Art, Dallas, B-2
- Dallas Zoo, Dallas, H-10
- Fair Park (Cotton Bowl), Dallas, G-11
- Heard Natural Science Museum & Sanctuary, McKinney, B-13
- Old City Park, Dallas, C-3

Central Dallas

Central Fort Worth

© Rand McNally

Denton, Ponder, Dish, Northlake, Corral City, Justin, Argyle, Lantana, Bartonville, Double Oak, Copper Canyon, Highland Vill., Corinth, Hickory Creek, Shadyshores, Flower Mound, Grapevine, Southlake, Keller, Roanoke, Trophy Club, Westlake, Colleyville, Bedford, Euless, Hurst, N. Richland Hills, Watauga, Richland Hills, Haltom City, Lake Worth, Lakeside, Sansom Park, River Oaks, White Settlement, Westworth, Westover Hills, Fort Worth, Arlington, Pantego, Dalworthington Gardens, Benbrook, Edgecliff Village, Forest Hill, Everman, Kennedale, Mansfield, St. Francis Village, Wheatland, Crowley, Rendon, Burleson

TARRANT CO. / JOHNSON CO.

0 1 2 3 4 5 mi
0 1 2 3 4 5 6 7 8 km

© Rand McNally

- Ripley's Believe It or Not! & Louis Tussaud's Palace of Wax, Grand Prairie, G-8
- The Sixth Floor Museum at Dealey Plaza, Dallas, B-1
- Stockyards Historic District, Fort Worth, G-4
- Sundance Square, Fort Worth, E-1
- Texas Civil War Museum, Fort Worth, G-2
- Will Rogers Memorial Center, Fort Worth, H-3

Dallas / Fort Worth & Vicinity

© Rand McNally

Index of cities Pg. 260

Mileages between cities	Abilene	Amarillo	Big Bend N.P.	Big Spring	Childress	Clovis, NM	Dallas	Eagle Pass	El Paso	Fort Stockton	Lubbock	Odessa	Perryton	San Angelo	San Antonio	Van Horn
Abilene		268	380	108	155	267	179	304	454	255	163	168	306	88	250	332
Amarillo	268		470	226	112	104	363	510	407	344	120	258	115	318	510	423

Mileages © Rand McNally

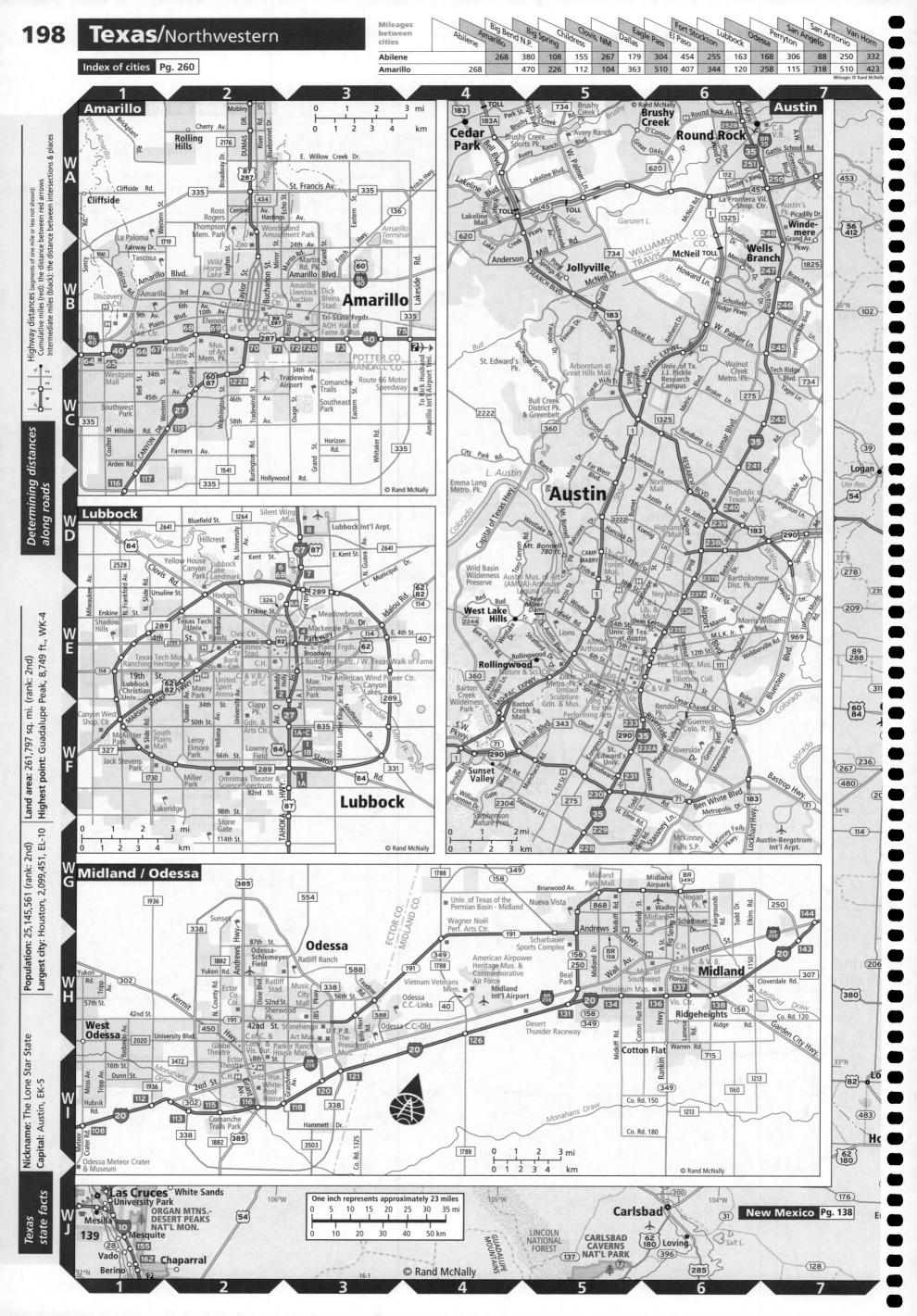

Texas state facts

Nickname: The Lone Star State
Capital: Austin, EK-5

Population: 25,145,561 (rank: 2nd)
Largest city: Houston, 2,099,451, EL-10

Land area: 261,797 sq. mi. (rank: 2nd)
Highest point: Guadalupe Peak, 8,749 ft., WK-4

Determining distances along roads

Highway distances (segments of one mile or less not shown)
Cumulative miles (red): the distance between red arrows
Intermediate miles (black): the distance between intersections & places

© Rand McNally

One inch represents approximately 23 miles

New Mexico Pg. 138

Mileages between cities	Abilene	Amarillo	Big Bend N.P.	Big Spring	Childress	Clovis, NM	Dallas	Eagle Pass	El Paso	Fort Stockton	Lubbock	Odessa	Perryton	San Angelo	San Antonio	Van Horn
Del Rio	241	454	242	240	383	425	426	56	428	184	333	258	534	154	151	303
El Paso	454	407	325	346	482	301	635	484		240	343	284	516	404	554	121

Mileages © Rand McNally

continued p. 200

Total mileages through Texas

10 — 881 miles 40 — 177 miles 20 — 636 miles

More mileages at www.randmcnally.com/MC

NOTE: list extends from pp. 199-205

Cameron Co. Regional Mobility Auth. (TX 550, Brownsville) (TxTag): (956) 982-5414; www.cameroncountyrma.org
Central Texas Regional Mobility Authority (TX 183A, Austin) (TxTag): (512) 996-9778; www.mobilityauthority.com

Toll Road Information — www.txdot.gov   www.drivetexas.org

Road Conditions & Construction — (800) 452-9292, (512) 463-8588

Tourism Information — Texas Tourism (800) 452-9292   www.traveltex.com

Explore Texas at www.randmcnally.com/TX

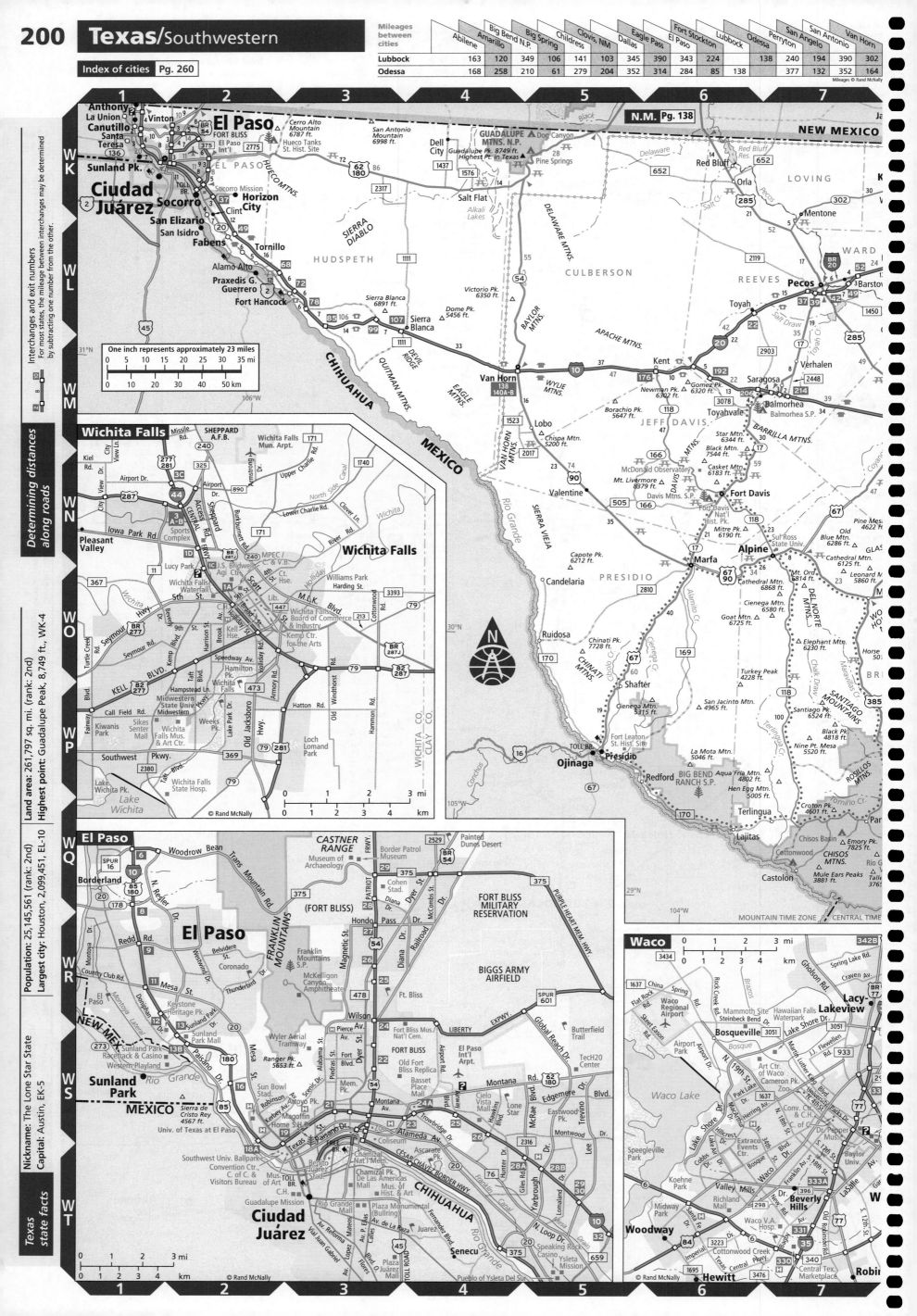

Mileages between cities	Abilene	Amarillo	Big Bend N.P.	Big Spring	Childress	Clovis, NM	Dallas	Eagle Pass	El Paso	Fort Stockton	Lubbock	Odessa	Perryton	San Angelo	San Antonio	Van Horn
Lubbock	163	120	349	106	141	103	345	390	343	224		138	240	194	390	302
Odessa	168	258	210	61	279	204	352	314	284	85	138		377	132	352	164

Mileages © Rand McNally

One inch represents approximately 23 miles

N.M. Pg. 138

NEW MEXICO

Wichita Falls

El Paso

Waco

© Rand McNally

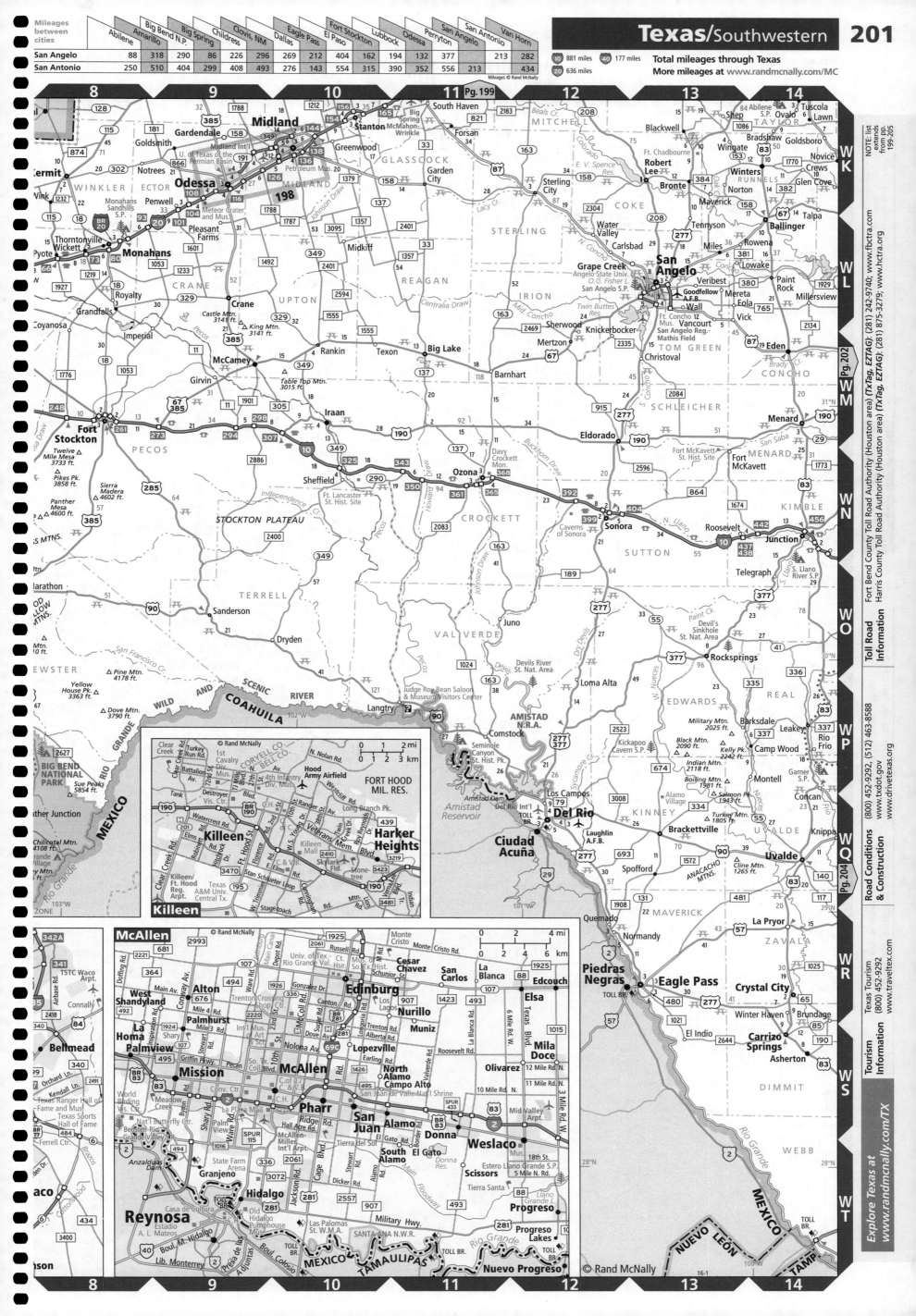

Mileages between cities

	Abilene	Amarillo	Big Bend N.P.	Big Spring	Childress	Clovis, NM	Dallas	Eagle Pass	El Paso	Fort Stockton	Lubbock	Odessa	Perryton	San Angelo	San Antonio	Van Horn
San Angelo	88	318	290	86	226	296	269	212	404	162	194	132	377		213	282
San Antonio	250	510	404	299	408	493	276	143	554	315	390	352	556	213		434

Mileages © Rand McNally

Total mileages through Texas

10	881 miles	40	177 miles
20	636 miles		

More mileages at www.randmcnally.com/MC

Index of cities Pg. 260

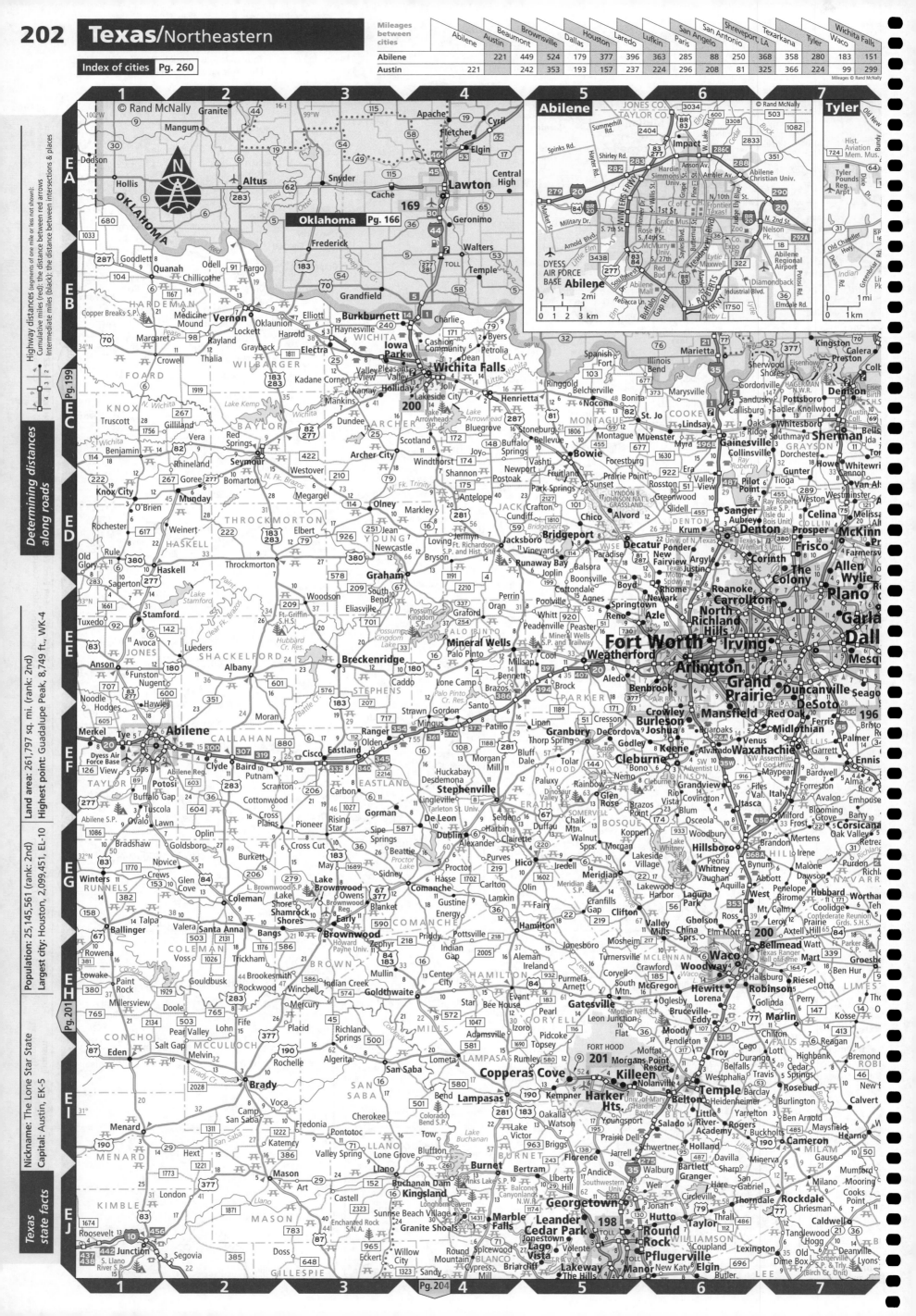

Mileages between cities	Abilene	Austin	Beaumont	Brownsville	Dallas	Houston	Laredo	Lufkin	Paris	San Angelo	San Antonio	Shreveport, LA	Texarkana	Tyler	Waco	Wichita Falls
Abilene		221	449	524	179	377	396	363	285	88	250	368	358	280	183	151
Austin	221		242	353	193	157	237	224	296	208	81	325	366	224	99	299

Mileages © Rand McNally

Abilene 5

Tyler 7

Texas state facts

Nickname: The Lone Star State
Capital: Austin, EK-5

Population: 25,145,561 (rank: 2nd)
Largest city: Houston, 2,099,451, EL-10

Land area: 261,797 sq. mi. (rank: 2nd)
Highest point: Guadalupe Peak, 8,749 ft., WK-4

Determining distances along roads

Highway distances (segments of one mile or less not shown):
Cumulative miles (red): the distance between red arrows
Intermediate miles (black): the distance between intersections & places

Mileages between cities	Abilene	Austin	Beaumont	Brownsville	Dallas	Houston	Laredo	Lufkin	San Angelo	Paris	San Antonio	Shreveport, LA	Texarkana	Tyler	Waco	Wichita Falls
Brownsville	524	353	439		547	354	204	473	622	491	274	596	650	530	435	614
Corpus Christi	387	217	292	156	410	207	138	328	496	355	138	449	504	392	316	477

Mileages © Rand McNally

continued p. 204

Total mileages through Texas
10 811 miles 30 223 miles
20 636 miles 35 504 miles
More mileages at www.randmcnally.com/MC

NOTE: list extends from pp. 199-205

One inch represents approximately 23 miles
0 5 10 15 20 25 30 35 mi
0 10 20 30 40 50 km

Toll Road Information
North East Regional Mobility Authority (TX, 49, Tyler) (TxTag): (903) 594-4834; www.ntta.org www.toll49.org
North Texas Tollway Authority (Dallas Metroplex) (TxTag, TollTag): (972) 818-6882; www.ntta.org

Road Conditions & Construction
(800) 452-9292, (512) 463-8588
www.txdot.gov
www.drivetexas.org

Tourism Information
Texas Tourism
(800) 452-9292
www.traveltex.com

Explore Texas at
www.randmcnally.com/TX

Mileages between cities	Abilene	Austin	Beaumont	Brownsville	Dallas	Houston	Laredo	Lufkin	Paris	San Angelo	San Antonio	Shreveport, LA	Texarkana	Tyler	Waco	Wichita Falls
Dallas	179	193	282	547		228	428	183	106	269	276	187	177	100	96	139
Houston	377	157	85	354	228		348	118	299	368	197	242	295	199	184	375

Mileages © Rand McNally

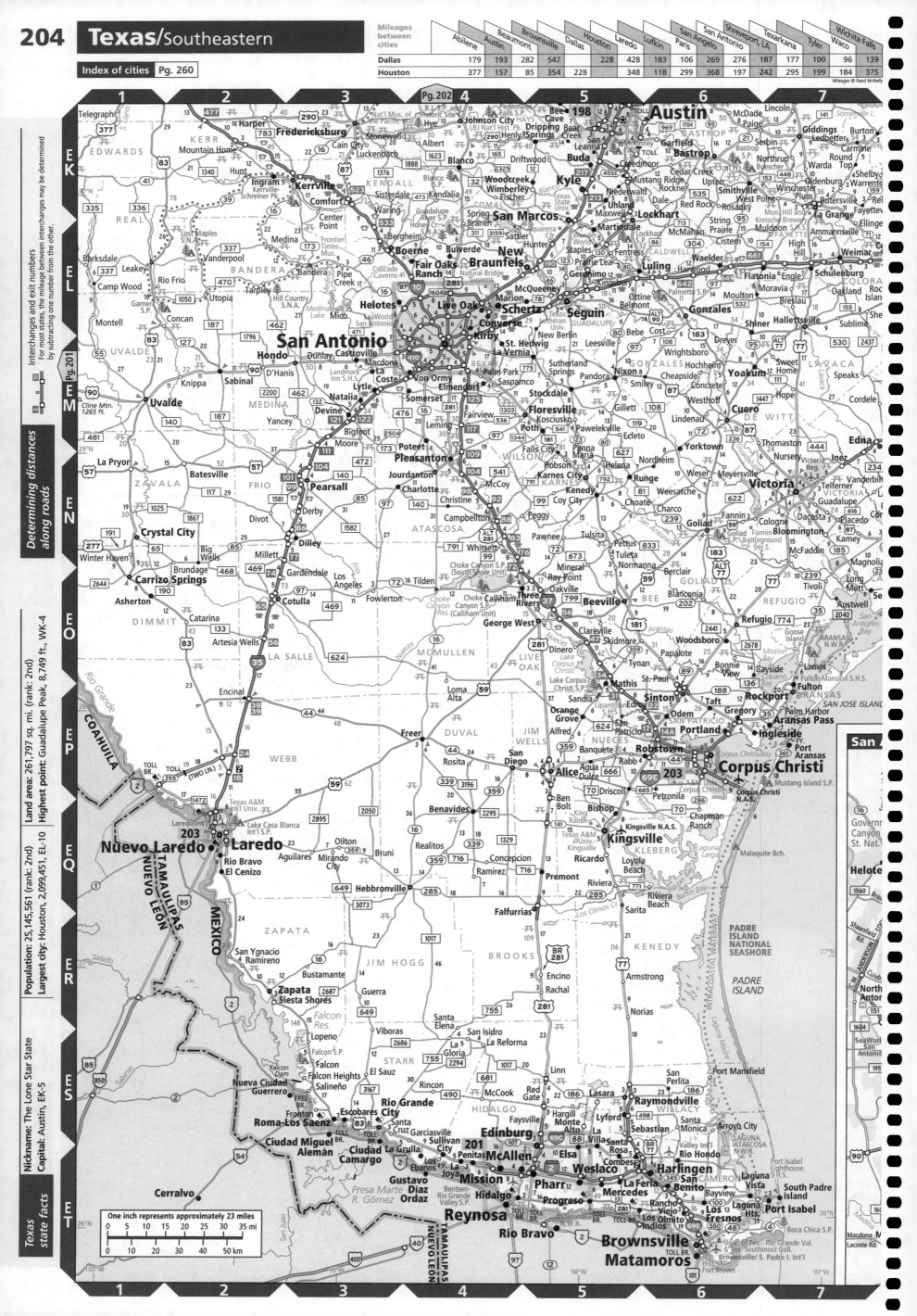

One inch represents approximately 23 miles
0 5 10 15 20 25 30 35 mi
0 10 20 30 40 50 km

Mileages between cities	Abilene	Austin	Beaumont	Brownsville	Dallas	Houston	Laredo	Lufkin	Paris	San Angelo	San Antonio	Shreveport, LA	Texarkana	Tyler	Waco	Wichita Falls
San Antonio	250	81	280	274	276	197	154	314	380	213		406	451	309	180	341
Shreveport, LA	368	325	206	596	187	242	565	120	154	455	406		72	98	226	324

Mileages in color

Total mileages through Texas

| 10 | 811 miles | 30 | 223 miles |
| 20 | 636 miles | 35 | 504 miles |

More mileages at www.randmcnally.com/MC

Central San Antonio
© Rand McNally

Bryan / College Station

Beaumont / Port Arthur

© Rand McNally

Index of cities Pg. 262

Mileages © Rand McNally

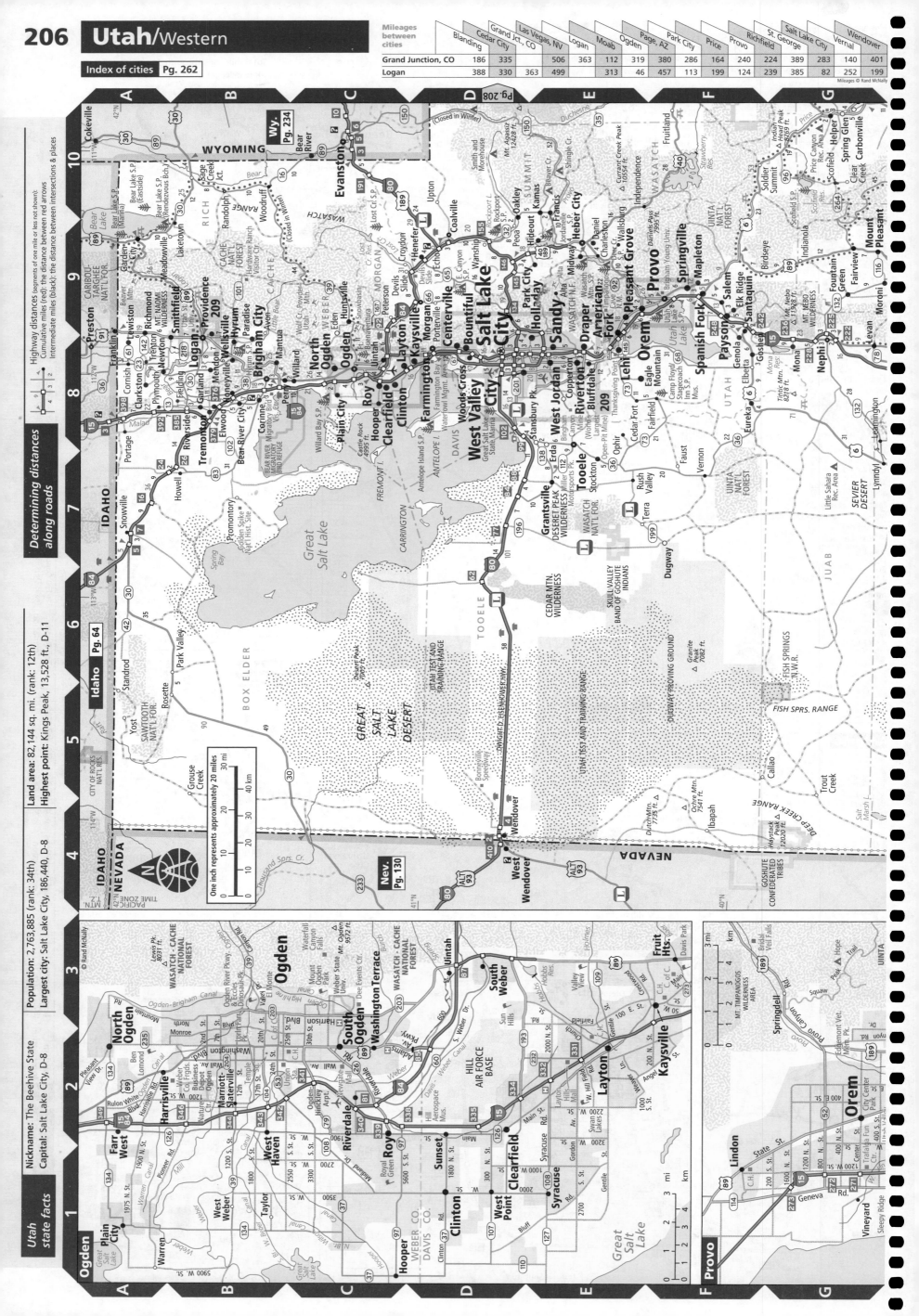

Utah state facts

Nickname: The Beehive State
Capital: Salt Lake City, D-8

Population: 2,763,885 (rank: 34th)
Largest city: Salt Lake City, D-8

Land area: 82,144 sq. mi. (rank: 12th)
Highest point: Kings Peak, 13,528 ft., D-11

Determining distances along roads

Highway distances (segments of one mile or less not shown)
Cumulative miles (red): the distance between red arrows
Intermediate miles (black): the distance between intersections & places

Mileages between cities	Blanding	Cedar City	Grand Jct., CO	Las Vegas, NV	Logan	Moab	Ogden	Page, AZ	Park City	Price	Provo	Richfield	St. George	Salt Lake City	Vernal	Wendover
Moab	74	287	112	456	313		269	268	238	115	190	174	341	234	207	352
Richfield	249	114	224	282	239	174	194	219	166	121	115		169	159	232	270

Mileages © Rand McNally

Total mileages through Utah

15 — 401 miles 80 — 196 miles
70 — 232 miles 84 — 119 miles

More mileages at www.randmcnally.com/MC

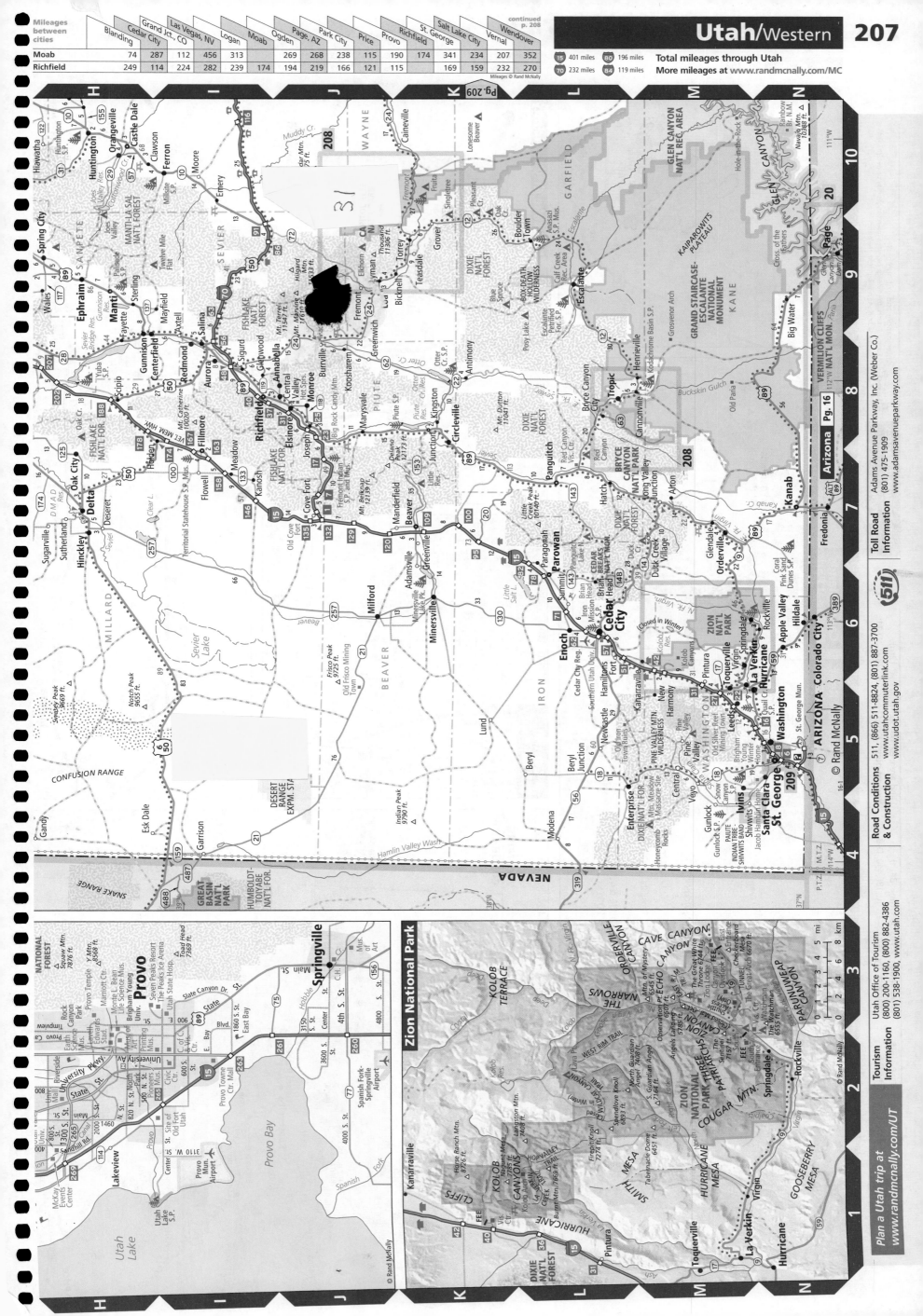

Pg. 209
continued p. 208

Zion National Park

Provo

Springville

Arizona Pg. 16

Tourism Information Utah Office of Tourism (800) 200-1160, (800) 882-4386 (801) 538-1900, www.utah.com

Road Conditions & Construction 511, (866) 511-8824, (801) 887-3700 www.utahcommuterlink.com www.udot.utah.gov

Toll Road Information Adams Avenue Parkway, Inc. (Weber Co.) (801) 475-1909 www.adamsavenueparkway.com

Plan a Utah trip at www.randmcnally.com/UT

Index of cities Pg. 262

Mileages © Rand McNally

Mileages between cities	Blanding	Cedar City	Grand Jct, CO	Las Vegas, NV	Logan	Moab	Ogden	Page, AZ	Park City	Price	Provo	Richfield	St. George	Salt Lake City	Vernal	Wendover
St. George	415	55	389	117	385	341	341	154	308	286	261	169		304	401	333
Salt Lake City	308	250	283	419	82	234	37	377	30	119	43	159	304		172	121

Utah state facts

Nickname: The Beehive State
Capital: Salt Lake City, D-8

Population: 2,763,885 (rank: 34th)
Largest city: Salt Lake City, D-8

Land area: 82,144 sq. mi. (rank: 12th)
Highest point: Kings Peak, 13,528 ft., D-11

Determining distances along roads

Interchanges and exit numbers
For most states, the mileage between interchanges may be determined by subtracting one number from the other.

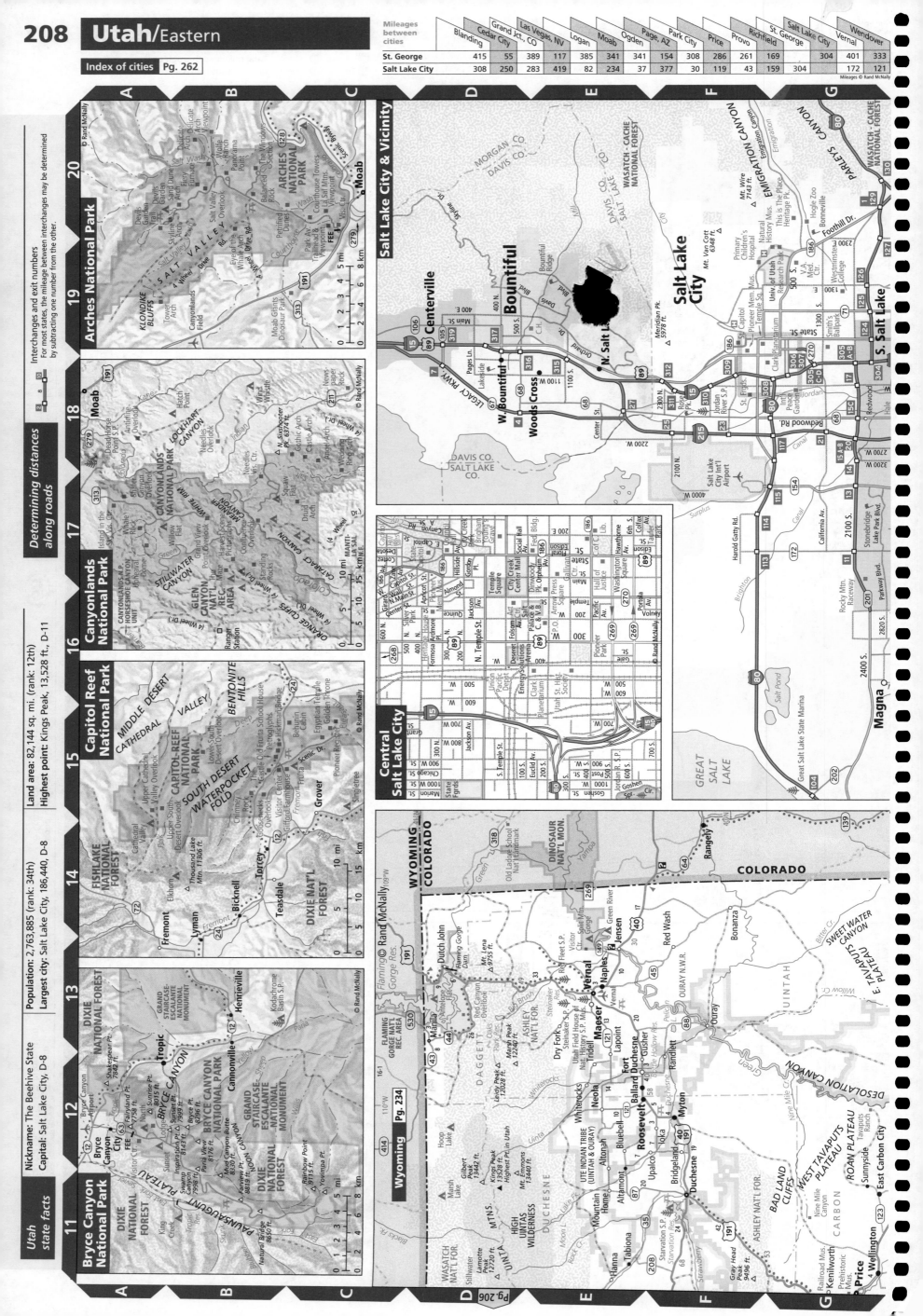

Mileages between cities	Blanding	Cedar City	Grand Jct., CO	Las Vegas, NV	Logan	Moab	Ogden	Page, AZ	Park City	Price	Provo	Richfield	St. George	Salt Lake City	Vernal	Wendover
Vernal	281	345	140	514	252	207	207	450	145	112	154	232	401	172		291
Wendover	426	317	401	361	199	352	154	503	150	237	161	270	333	121	291	

Mileages © Rand McNally

Total mileages through Utah
15 — 401 miles   80 — 196 miles
70 — 232 miles   84 — 119 miles

More mileages at www.randmcnally.com/MC

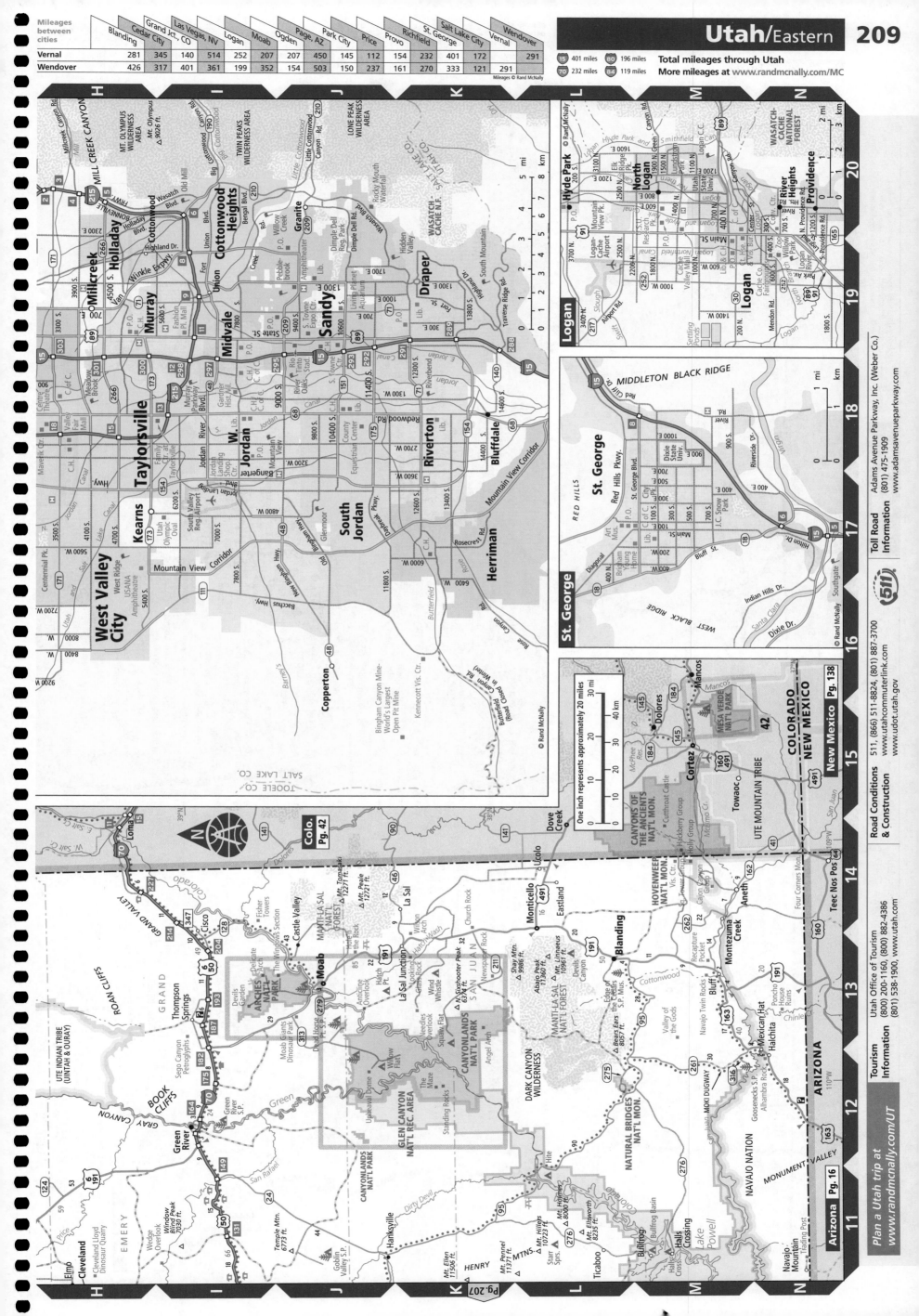

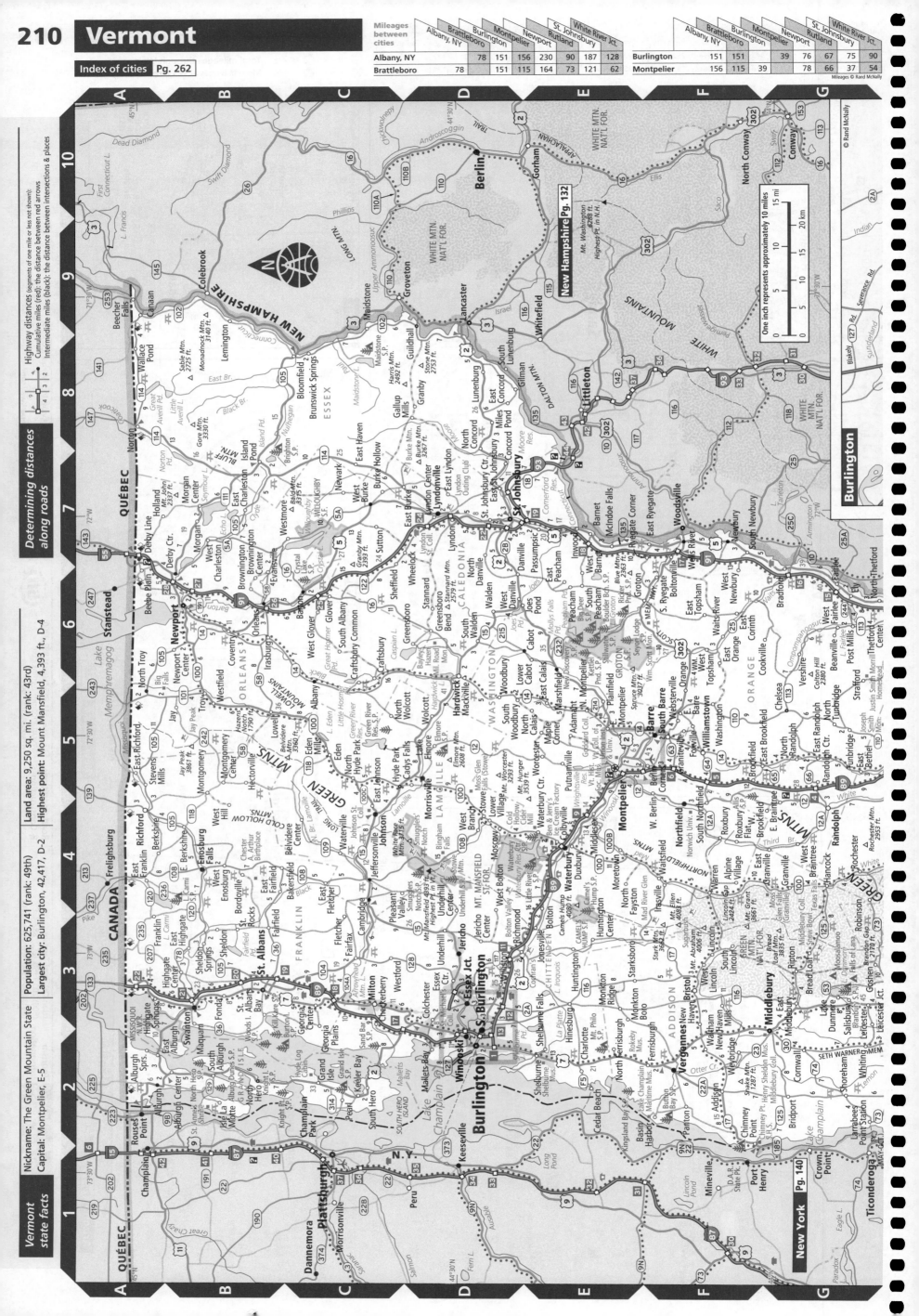

Mileages between cities	Albany, NY	Brattleboro	Burlington	Montpelier	Newport	St. Johnsbury Rutland	White River Jct.
Albany, NY		78	151	156	230	90	187	128
Brattleboro	78		151	115	164	73	121	62

	Albany, NY	Brattleboro	Burlington	Montpelier	Newport	St. Johnsbury Rutland	White River Jct.
Burlington	151	151		39	76	67	75	90
Montpelier	156	115	39		78	66	37	54

Mileages by Rand McNally

© Rand McNally

New Hampshire Pg. 132

Burlington

New York Pg. 140

Mileages between cities	Albany, NY	Brattleboro	Burlington	Montpelier	Newport	Rutland	St. Johnsbury	White River Jct.
Newport	230	164	76	78		147	43	102
Rutland	90	73	67	66	147		105	45

	Albany, NY	Brattleboro	Burlington	Montpelier	Newport	Rutland	St. Johnsbury	White River Jct.
St. Johnsbury	187	121	75	37	43	105		60
White River Jct.	128	62	90	54	102	45	60	

Mileages © Rand McNally

Total mileages through Vermont
More mileages at www.randmcnally.com/MC

89 130 miles 93 11 miles
177 miles 4 64 miles
91

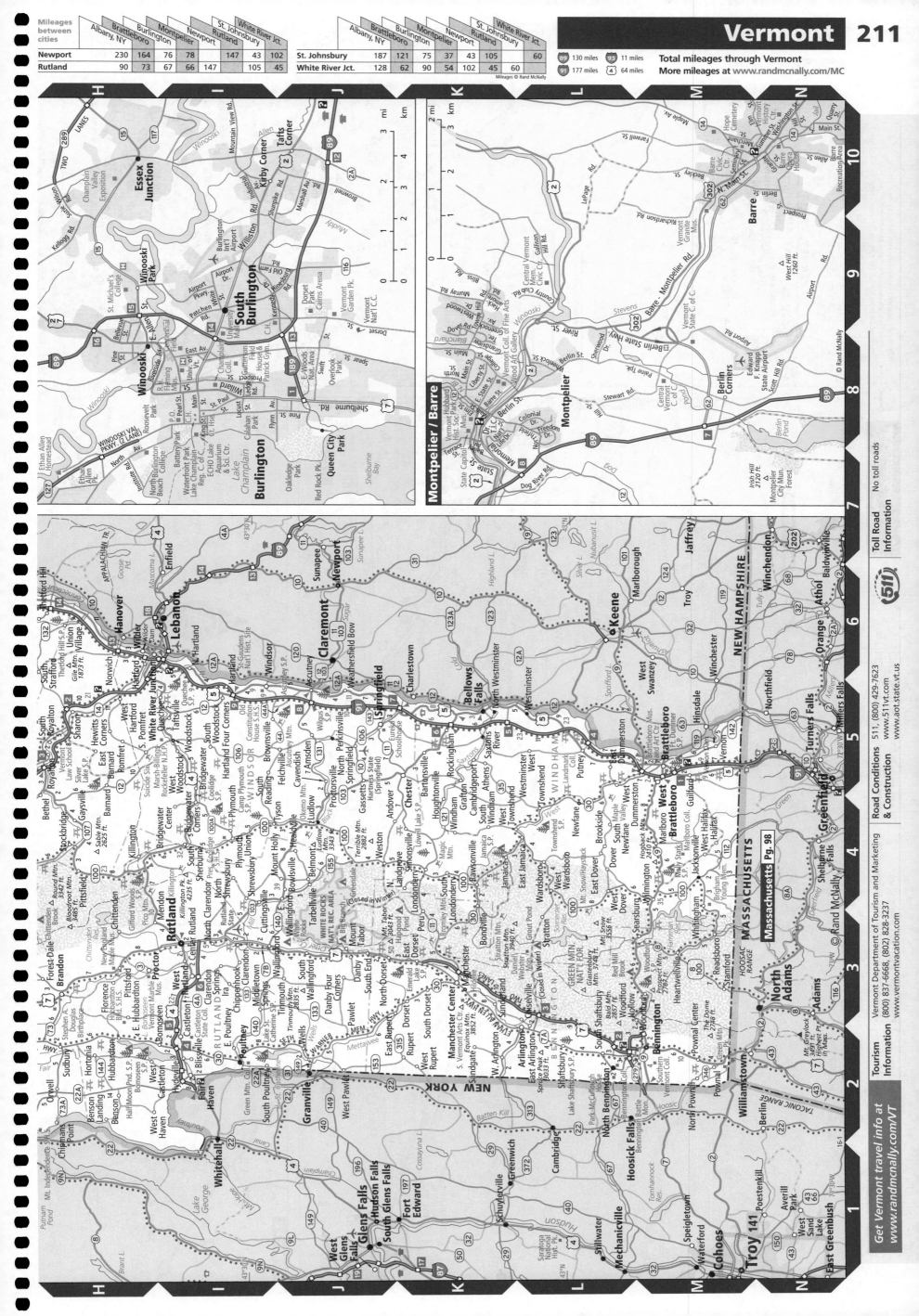

Toll Road
Information

No toll roads

511 511, (800) 429-7623
www.511vt.state.vt.us

Road Conditions & Construction
511, (800) 429-7623
www.511vt.com

Tourism Information
Vermont Department of Tourism and Marketing
(800) 837-6668, (802) 828-3237
www.vermontvacation.com

Get Vermont travel info at
www.randmcnally.com/VT

Index of cities Pg. 262

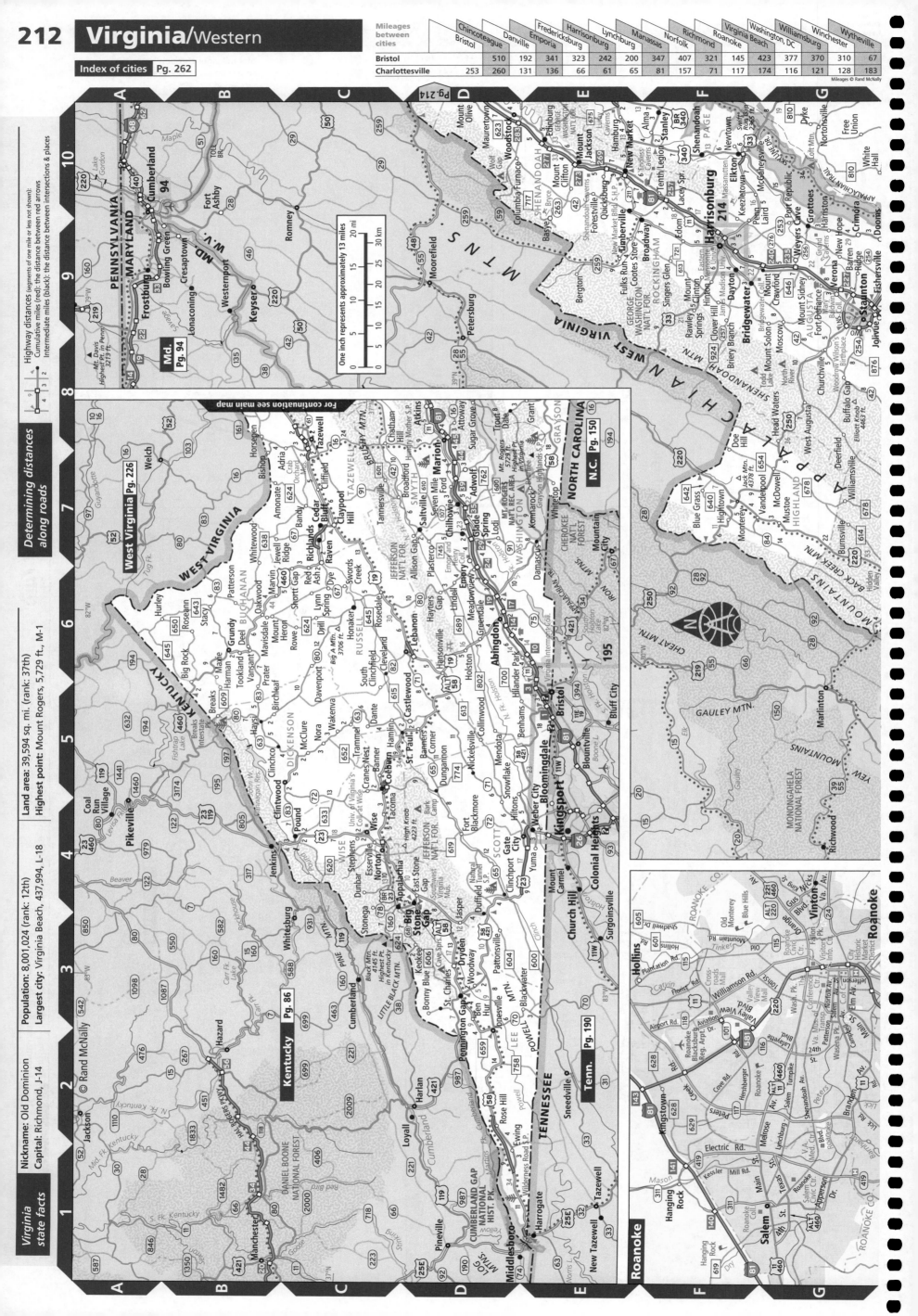

	Bristol	Chincoteague	Danville	Emporia	Fredericksburg	Harrisonburg	Lynchburg	Manassas	Norfolk	Richmond	Roanoke	Virginia Beach	Washington, DC	Williamsburg	Winchester	Wytheville
Bristol		510	192	341	323	242	200	347	407	321	145	423	377	370	310	67
Charlottesville	253	260	131	136	66	61	65	81	157	71	117	174	116	121	128	183

Mileages © Rand McNally

Virginia state facts

Nickname: Old Dominion
Capital: Richmond, J-14

Population: 8,001,024 (rank: 12th)
Largest city: Virginia Beach, 437,994, L-18

Land area: 39,594 sq. mi. (rank: 37th)
Highest point: Mount Rogers, 5,729 ft., M-1

© Rand McNally

Determining distances along roads

Highway distances (segments of one mile or less not shown):
Cumulative miles (red): the distance between red arrows
Intermediate miles (black): the distance between intersections & places

West Virginia Pg. 226

Kentucky Pg. 86

Roanoke

For continuation see main map

One inch represents approximately 13 miles

0 5 10 15 20 mi
0 5 10 15 20 25 30 km

North Carolina N.C. Pg. 150

Tennessee Tenn. Pg. 190

Pg. 214

Md. Pg. 94

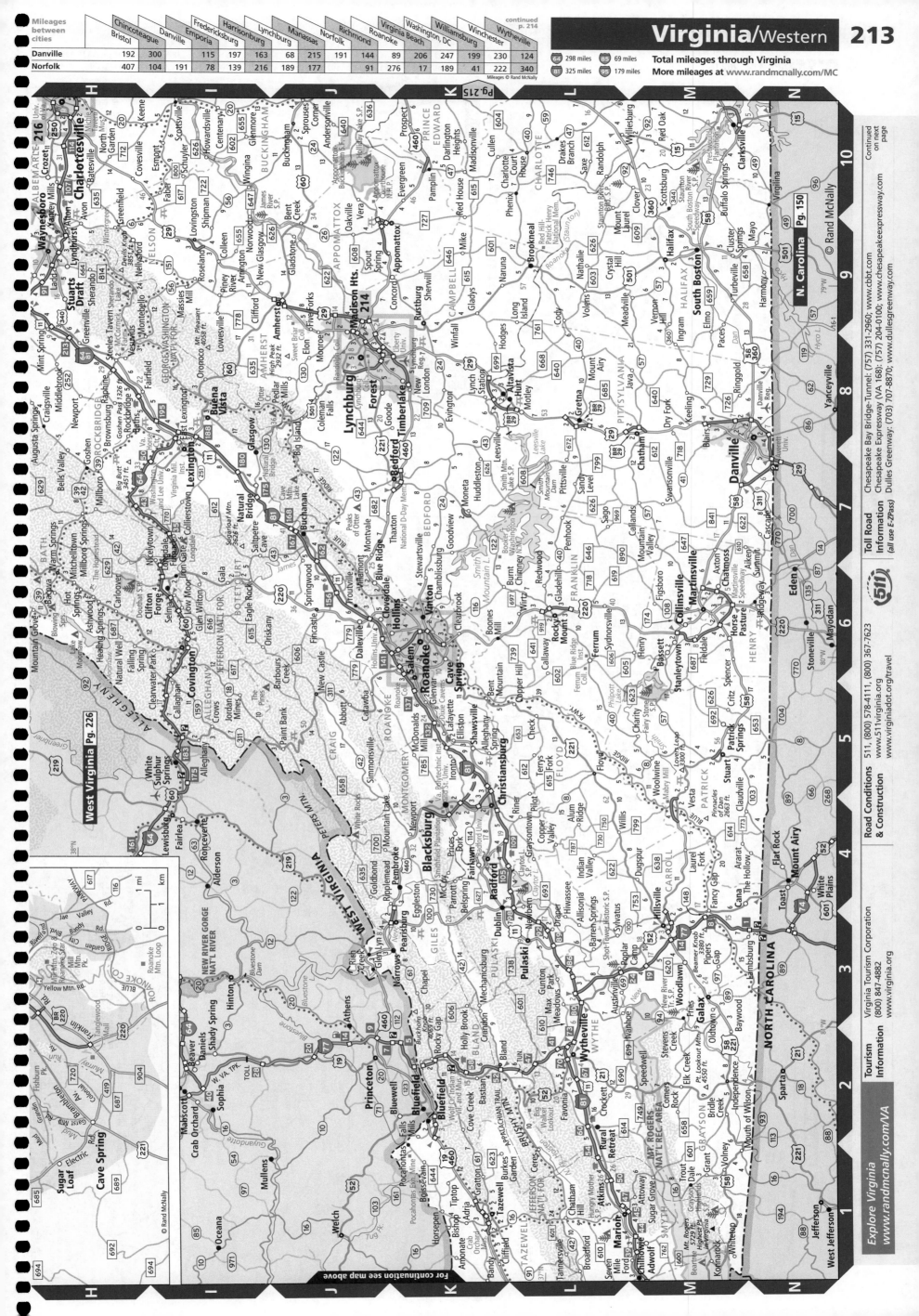

Mileages between cities	Chincoteague	Danville	Fredericksburg	Emporia	Harrisonburg	Lynchburg	Manassas	Norfolk	Richmond	Virginia Beach	Roanoke	Washington, DC	Williamsburg	Winchester	Wytheville
Danville	192	300		115	197	163	68	215	191		144	89	206	247	199	230	124
Norfolk	407	104	191	78	139	216	189	177		91	276	17	189	41	222	340

Mileages © Rand McNally

continued p. 214

Total mileages through Virginia

| 64 | 298 miles | 85 | 69 miles |
| 81 | 325 miles | 95 | 179 miles |

More mileages at www.randmcnally.com/MC

© Rand McNally

Continued on next page

Toll Road Information (all use E-ZPass)
Chesapeake Bay Bridge-Tunnel: (757) 331-2960; www.cbbt.com
Chesapeake Expressway (VA 168): (757) 204-0100; www.chesapeakeexpressway.com
Dulles Greenway: (703) 707-8870; www.dullesgreenway.com

Road Conditions & Construction 511, (800) 578-4111, (800) 367-7623
www.511virginia.org
www.virginiadot.org/travel

Tourism Information Virginia Tourism Corporation (800) 847-4882
www.virginia.com/VA
www.virginia.org

Explore Virginia
www.randmcnally.com/VA

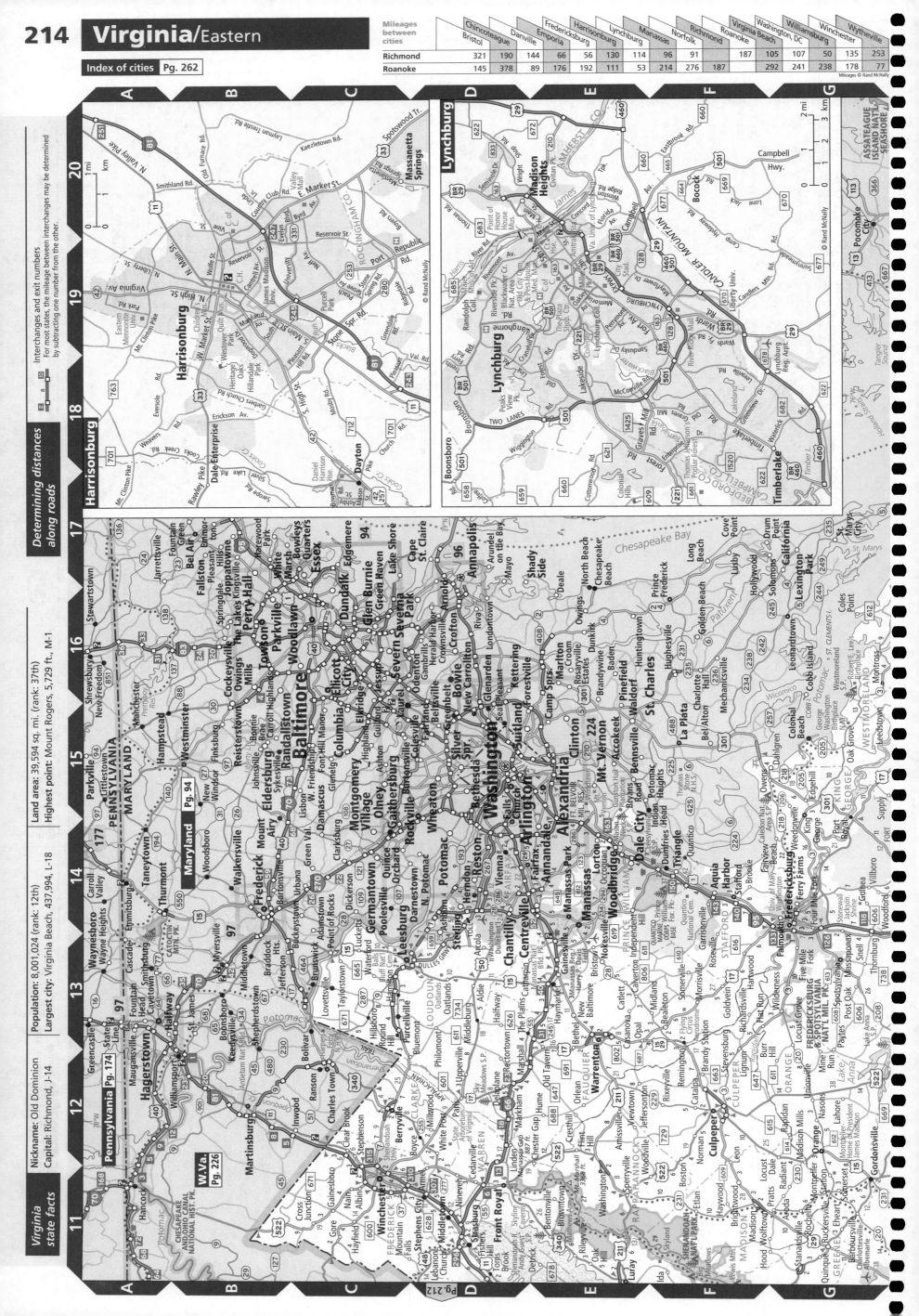

Virginia state facts

Nickname: Old Dominion
Capital: Richmond, J-14

Population: 8,001,024 (rank: 12th)
Largest city: Virginia Beach, J-14

Land area: 39,594 sq. mi. (rank: 37th)
Highest point: Mount Rogers, 5,729 ft, M-1

Pennsylvania Pg. 174

Maryland Pg. 94

W.Va. Pg. 226

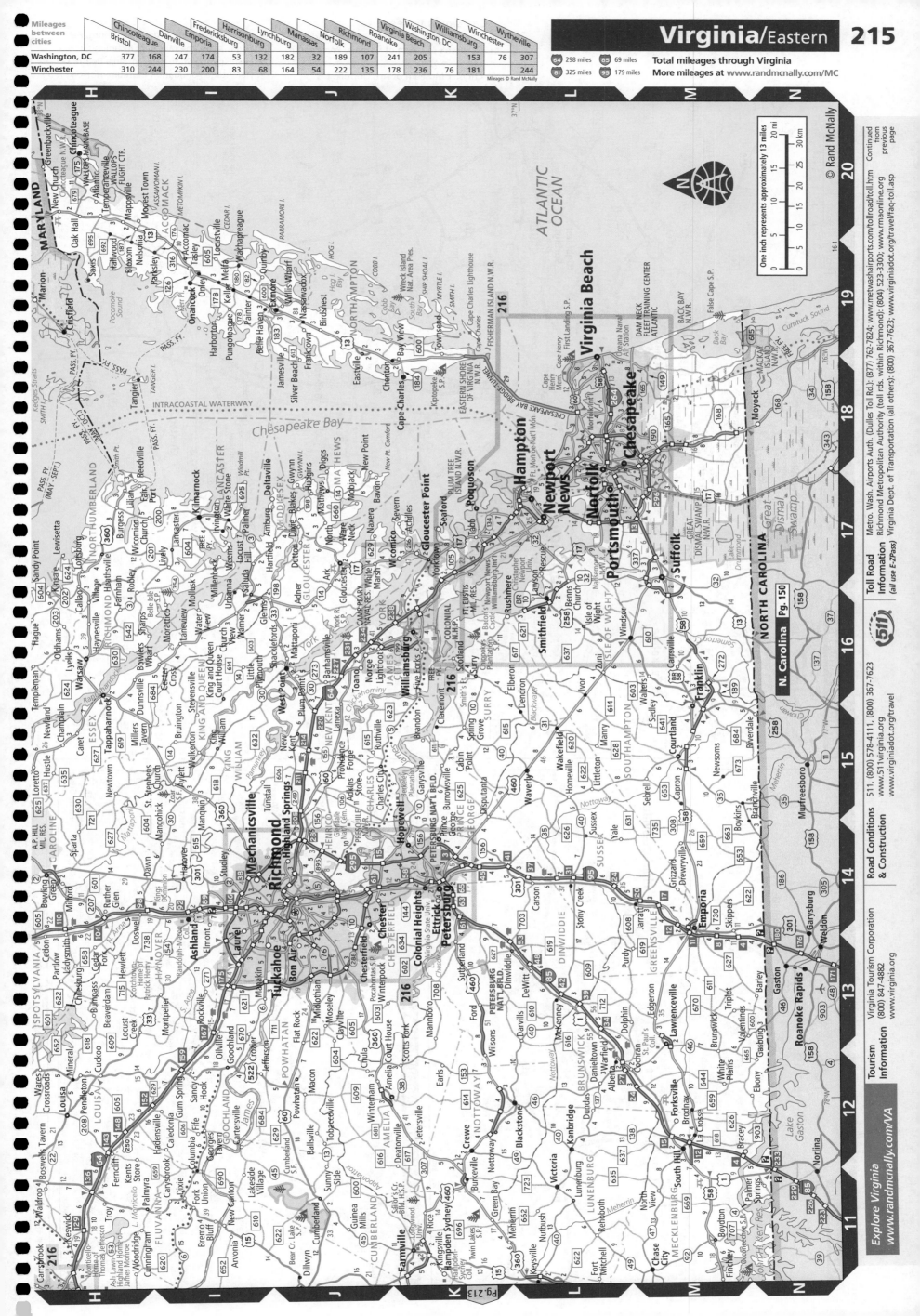

Mileages between cities	Chincoteague	Bristol	Danville	Fredericksburg	Emporia	Harrisonburg	Lynchburg	Manassas	Norfolk	Richmond	Roanoke	Virginia Beach	Washington, DC	Williamsburg	Winchester	Wytheville
Washington, DC	377	168	247	174	53	132	182	32	189	107	241	205		153	76	307
Winchester	310	244	230	200	83	68	164	54	222	135	178	236	76	181		244

Mileages © Rand McNally

Total mileages through Virginia
More mileages at www.randmcnally.com/MC

| 64 | 298 miles | 85 | 69 miles |
| 81 | 325 miles | 95 | 179 miles |

One inch represents approximately 13 miles

© Rand McNally

Metro. Wash. Airports Auth. (Dulles Toll Rd.): (877) 762-7824; www.metwashairports.com/tollroad/toll.htm
Richmond Metropolitan Authority (toll rds. within Richmond): (804) 523-3300; www.rmaonline.org
Virginia Dept. of Transportation (all others): (800) 367-7623; www.virginiadot.org/travel/faq-toll.asp

Toll Road Information (all use *E-ZPass*)

Road Conditions & Construction   511, (800) 578-4111, (800) 367-7623
www.511virginia.org
www.virginiadot.org/travel

Tourism Information   Virginia Tourism Corporation (800) 847-4882
www.virginia.org

Explore Virginia   www.randmcnally.com/VA

Continued from previous page

N. Carolina   Pg. 150

Pg. 213

City sights to see

- Agecroft Hall and Gardens, Richmond, C-7
- Children's Museum of Virginia, Portsmouth, M-6
- Chrysler Museum of Art, Norfolk, L-6
- Colonial Williamsburg, Williamsburg, F-2
- Edgar Allan Poe Museum, Richmond, C-8
- First Landing State Park, Virginia Beach, L-9
- Hermitage Foundation Museum, Norfolk, K-5

- Historic Jamestowne, Williamsburg, G-1
- Monticello, Charlottesville, D-4
- Nauticus, Norfolk, L-6
- Ocean Breeze Waterpark, Virginia Beach, M-10
- Old Cape Henry Lighthouse, Virginia Beach, K-9
- Three Lakes Nature Center and Aquarium, Richmond, B-8
- Virginia State Capitol, Richmond, C-8

Mileages between cities	Aberdeen	Bellingham	Colville	Kennewick	Longview	Olympia	Omak	Port Angeles	Portland, OR	Seattle	Spokane	Tacoma	The Dalles, OR	Vancouver, BC	Wenatchee	Yakima
Bellingham	198		317	306	216	149	201	118	261	89	361	121	326	52	182	224
Kennewick	312	306	209		254	263	189	340	213	223	138	235	130	359	132	82

Mileages © Rand McNally

Washington state facts

Nickname: The Evergreen State
Capital: Olympia, H-6

Land area: 66,544 sq. mi. (rank: 20th)
Highest point: Mount Rainier, 14,411 ft., I-8

Population: 6,724,540 (rank: 13th)
Largest city: Seattle, 608,660, F-7

Determining distances along roads

Highway distances (segments of one mile or less not shown):
- Cumulative miles (red): the distance between cities
- Intermediate miles (black): the distance between intersections & places

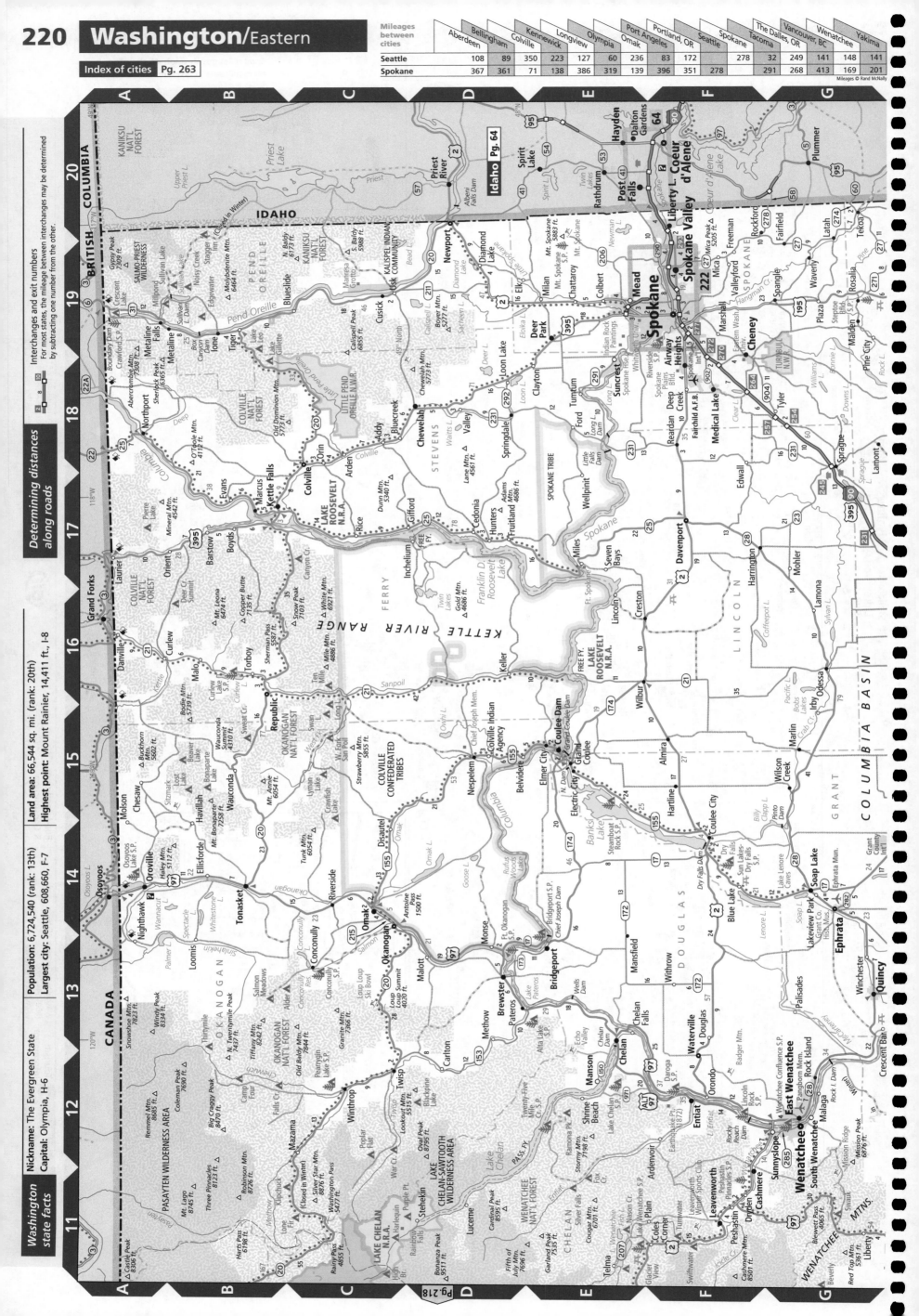

Mileages between cities	Aberdeen	Bellingham	Colville	Kennewick	Longview	Olympia	Omak	Port Angeles	Portland, OR	Seattle	Spokane	Tacoma	The Dalles, OR	Vancouver, BC	Wenatchee	Yakima
Seattle	108	89	350	223	127	60	236	83	172		278	32	249	141	148	141
Spokane	367	361	71	138	386	319	139	396	351	278		291	268	413	169	201

Mileages © Rand McNally

Washington state facts

Nickname: The Evergreen State
Capital: Olympia, H-6

Population: 6,724,540 (rank: 13th)
Largest city: Seattle

Land area: 66,544 sq. mi. (rank: 20th)
Highest point: Mount Rainier, 14,411 ft., F-7

Determining distances along roads

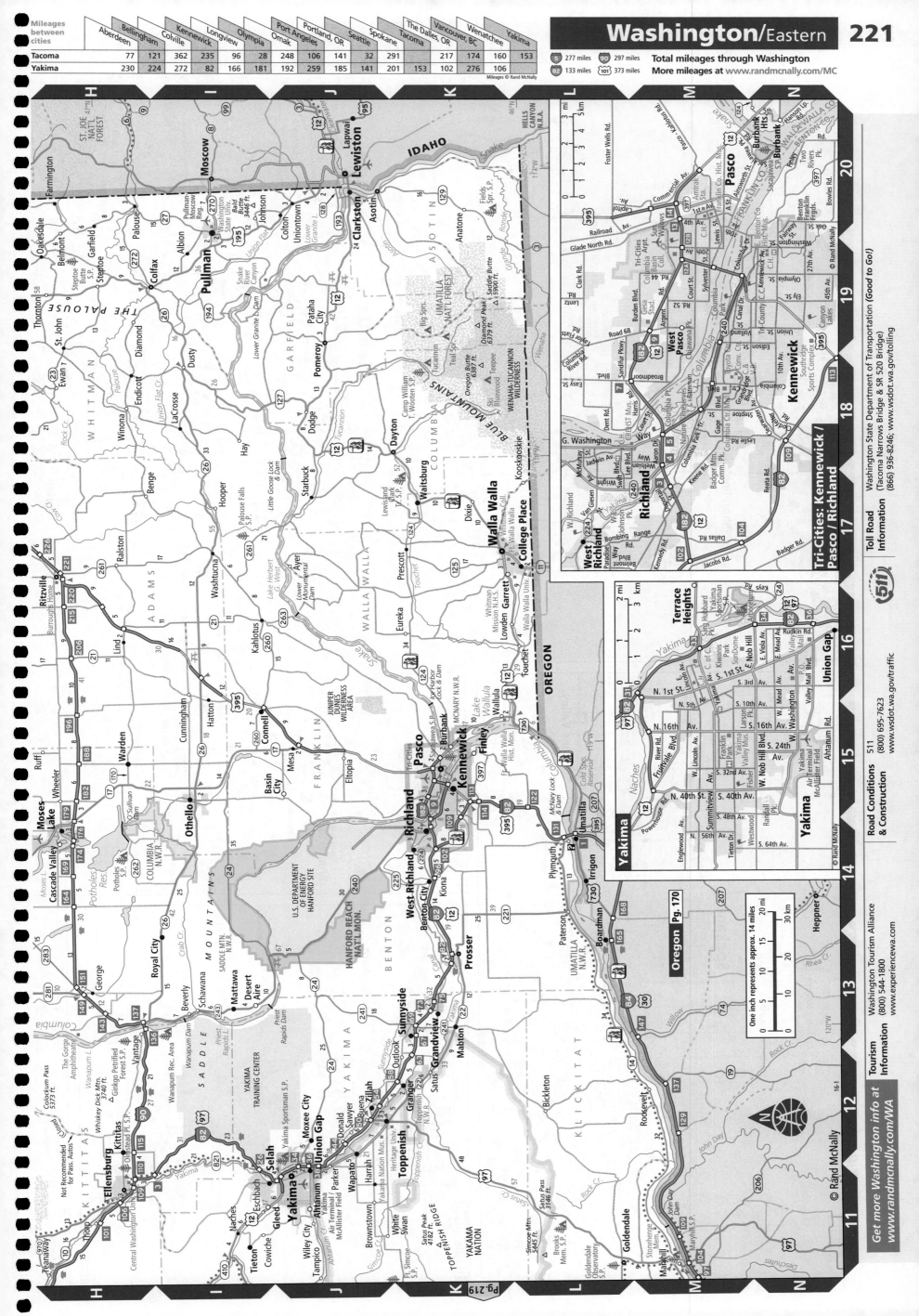

Mileages between cities	Aberdeen	Bellingham	Colville	Kennewick	Longview	Olympia	Omak	Port Angeles	Portland, OR	Seattle	Spokane	Tacoma	The Dalles, OR	Vancouver, BC	Wenatchee	Yakima
Tacoma	77	121	362	235	96	28	248	106	141	32	291		217	174	160	153
Yakima	230	224	272	82	166	181	192	259	185	141	201	153	102	276	106	

Mileages © Rand McNally

Total mileages through Washington
5 277 miles   90 297 miles
82 133 miles   101 373 miles
More mileages at www.randmcnally.com/MC

Tri-Cities: Kennewick / Pasco / Richland

Yakima

Oregon Pg. 170

One inch represents approx. 14 miles

Tourism Information — Washington Tourism Alliance (800) 544-1800 www.experiencewa.com

Road Conditions & Construction — 511 (800) 695-7623 www.wsdot.wa.gov/traffic

Toll Road Information — Washington State Department of Transportation (Good to Go!) (Tacoma Narrows Bridge & SR 520 Bridge) (866) 936-8246; www.wsdot.wa.gov/tolling

Get more Washington info at www.randmcnally.com/WA

© Rand McNally

City sights to see

- Experience Music Project, Seattle, H-1
- Frye Art Museum, Seattle, J-3
- Klondike Gold Rush National Historical Park, Seattle, K-2
- Logmire Museum, Logmire, N-1
- Museum of Glass, Tacoma, L-6
- Nordic Heritage Museum, Seattle, C-7
- Pacific Science Center, Seattle, H-1

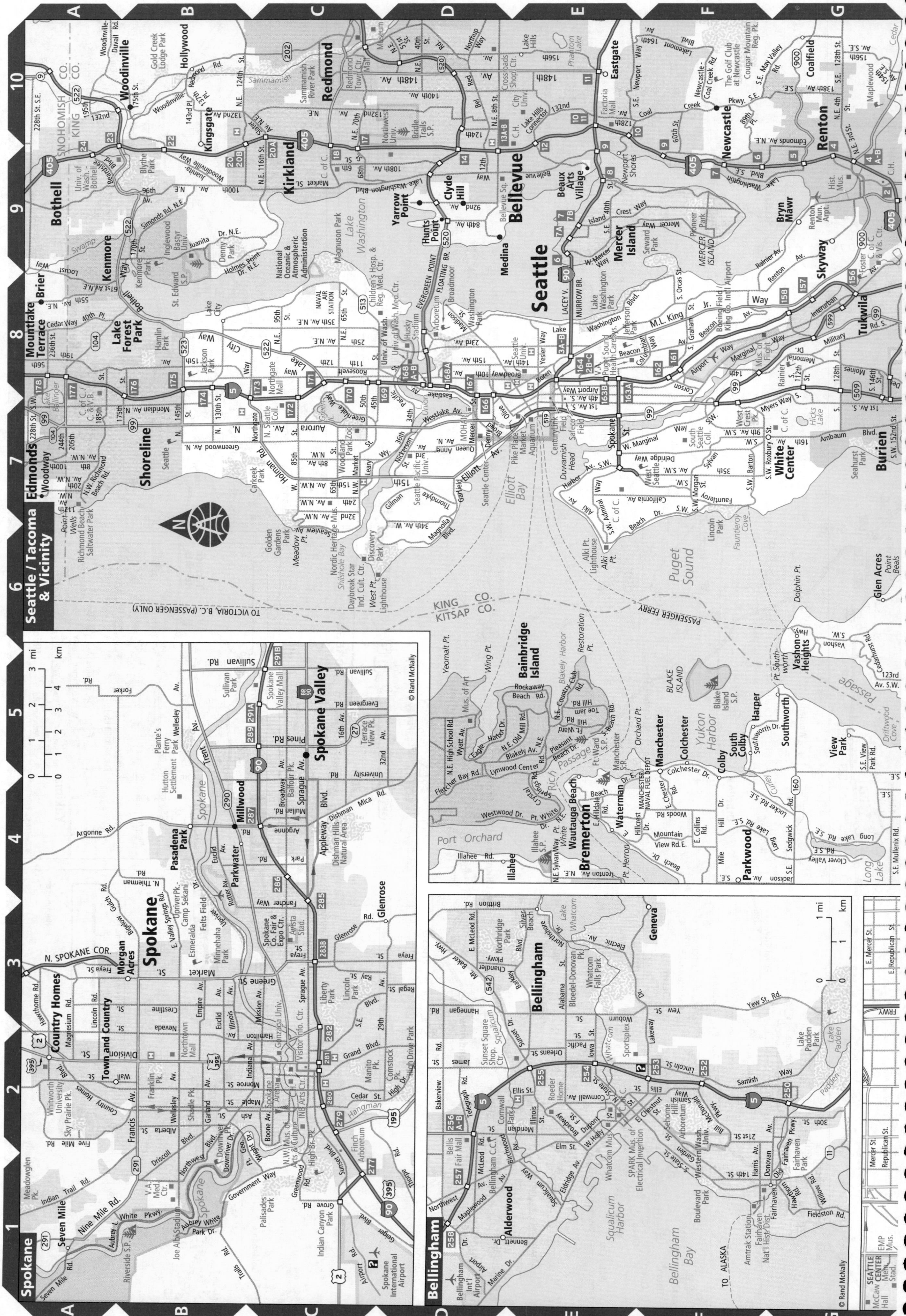

Seattle / Tacoma & Vicinity

Spokane

Bellingham

© Rand McNally

- Pike Place Market, Seattle, J-2
- Point Defiance Zoo & Aquarium, Tacoma, K-5
- Seattle Aquarium, Seattle, J-1
- Space Needle, Seattle, H-1
- Washington State History Mus., Tacoma, L-6
- Whatcom Museum of History and Art, Bellingham, E-2
- Woodland Park Zoo, Seattle, C-7

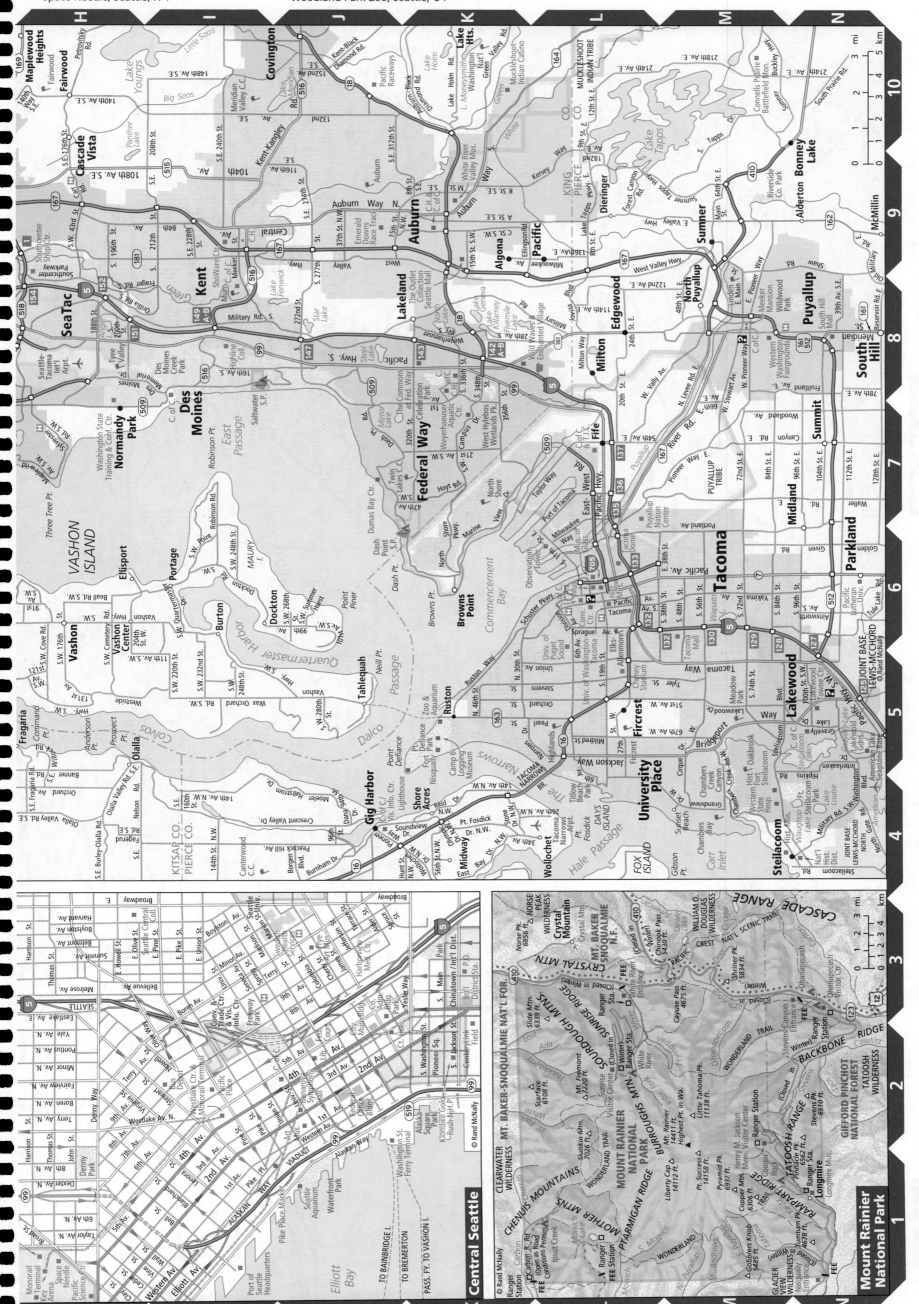

Central Seattle

Mount Rainier National Park

City sights to see
- Arlington National Cemetery, Arlington, Va., G-6
- Frederick Douglass National Historic Site, G-7
- Freedom Park, Arlington, Va., G-5
- John F. Kennedy Ctr. for the Performing Arts, K-3
- Martin Luther King Jr. Memorial, M-4
- National Arboretum, F-7
- National Mall, M-7

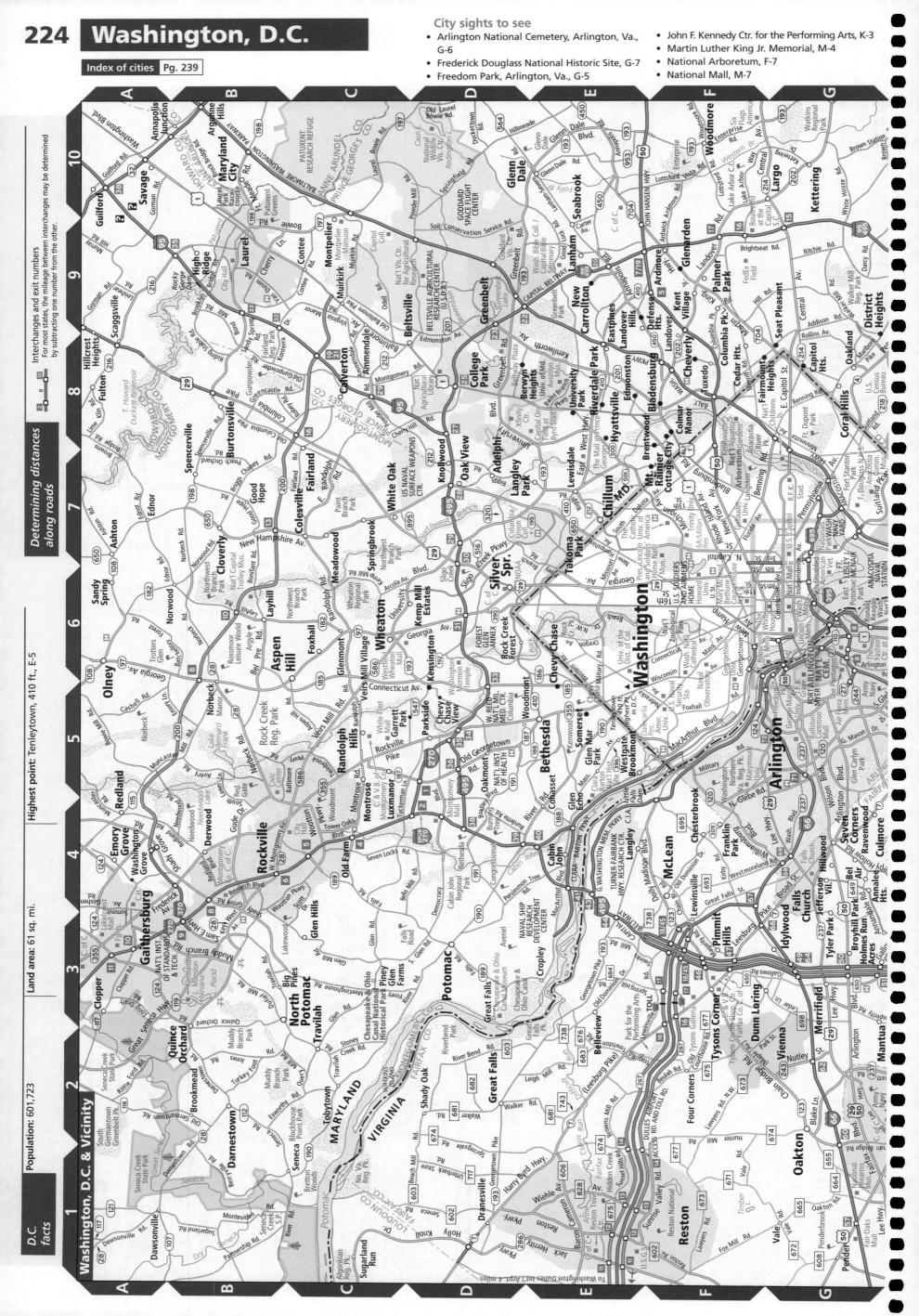

- National Zoological Park, F-6
- Patuxent Research Refuge National Wildlife Visitor Center, Laurel, Md., D-10
- The Pentagon, Arlington, Va., G-6
- Supreme Court of the United States, M-10
- United States Botanic Garden, M-8
- Wolf Trap National Park for the Performing Arts, Vienna, Va., E-2

Central Washington, D.C.

Tourism Information	Destination DC (800) 422-8644, (202) 789-7000 www.washington.org
Road Conditions & Construction	311, (202) 737-4404 (202) 673-6813 www.ddot.dc.gov
Toll Road Information	No toll roads in D.C.; see Maryland and Virginia for toll road information

Get D.C. travel info at www.randmcnally.com/DC

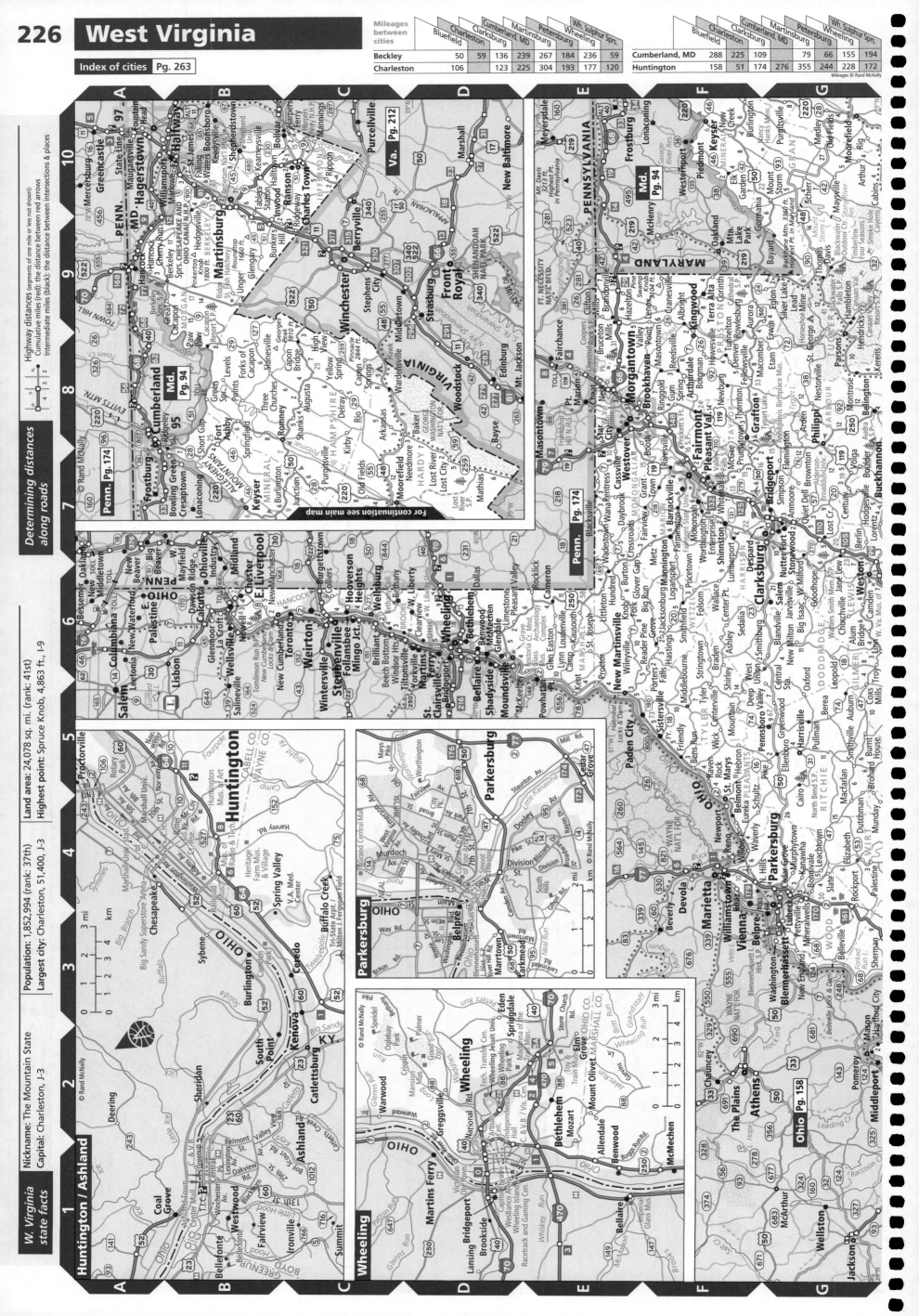

W. Virginia state facts

Nickname: The Mountain State
Capital: Charleston, J-3

Population: 1,852,994 (rank: 37th)
Largest city: Charleston, 51,400, J-3

Land area: 24,078 sq. mi. (rank: 41st)
Highest point: Spruce Knob, 4,863 ft., I-9

Determining distances along roads

Highway distances (segments of one mile or less not shown):
Cumulative miles (red): the distance between red arrows
Intermediate miles (black): the distance between intersections & places

Mileages between cities	Bluefield	Charleston	Clarksburg	Cumberland, MD	Martinsburg	Petersburg	Wheeling	Wh. Sulphur Sprs.
Morgantown	218	154	38	73	151	103	78	187
Parkersburg	183	76	72	181	259	172	104	198

	Bluefield	Charleston	Clarksburg	Cumberland, MD	Martinsburg	Petersburg	Wheeling	Wh. Sulphur Sprs.
Wheeling	283	177	114	155	225	179		262
White Sulphur Sprs.	79	120	155	194	208	125	262	

Mileages © Rand McNally

Total mileages through West Virginia

64	189 miles	77	187 miles
70	14 miles	79	161 miles

More mileages at www.randmcnally.com/MC

Map of West Virginia © Rand McNally

Insets: Morgantown; Charleston; South Charleston

For continuation see map above

Tourism Information — West Virginia Division of Tourism (800) 225-5982, (304) 558-2200 www.wvtourism.com

Road Conditions & Construction — 511, (877) 982-7623 www.wv511.org www.transportation.wv.gov

Toll Road Information — West Virginia Parkways Auth. (E-ZPass) (304) 926-1900 www.transportation.wv.gov/turnpike

Plan a West Virginia trip at www.randmcnally.com/WV

One inch represents approx. 15 miles

Mileages between cities	Beloit	Chicago, IL	Dubuque, IA	Eau Claire	Green Bay	Hayward	La Crosse	Madison	Milwaukee	Oshkosh	Rhinelander	Sheboygan	Sturgeon Bay	Superior	Wausau	Wisconsin Dells
Chicago, IL	96		177	315	206	420	281	146	90	175	338	145	245	462	281	195
Eau Claire	223	315	192		192	106	86	177	243	181	155	228	237	149	98	124

Mileages © Rand McNally

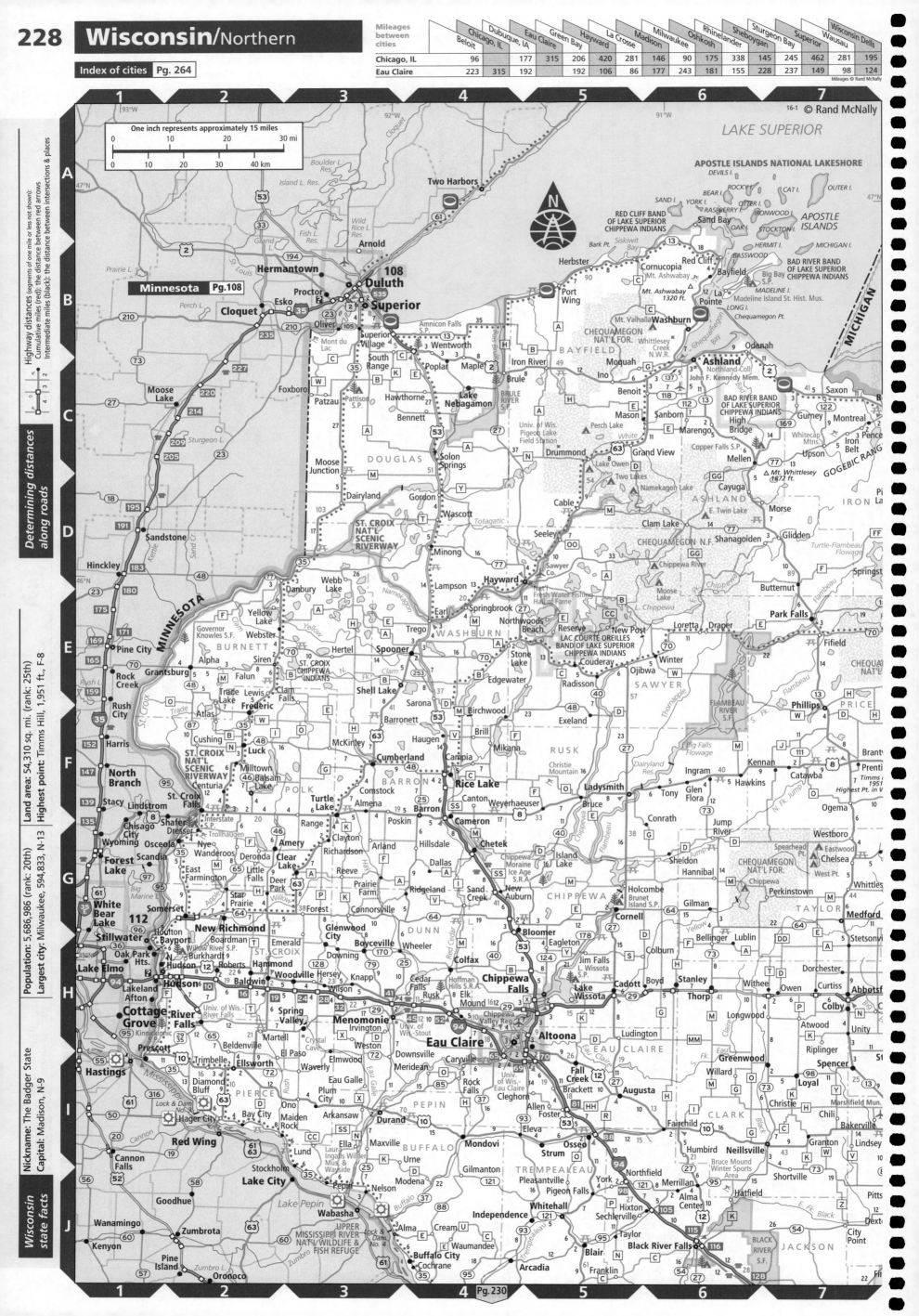

Mileages between cities

	Beloit	Chicago, IL	Dubuque, IA	Eau Claire	Green Bay	Hayward	La Crosse	Madison	Milwaukee	Oshkosh	Rhinelander	Sheboygan	Sturgeon Bay	Superior	Wausau	Wisconsin Dells
Green Bay	184	206	233	192		283	203	138	116	52	136	64	44	326	96	132
La Crosse	188	281	119	86	203	190		143	209	153	214	195	248	233	170	90

continued p. 230

Total mileages through Wisconsin: 39 182 miles; 43 192 miles; 90 189 miles; 94 341 miles

More mileages at www.randmcnally.com/MC

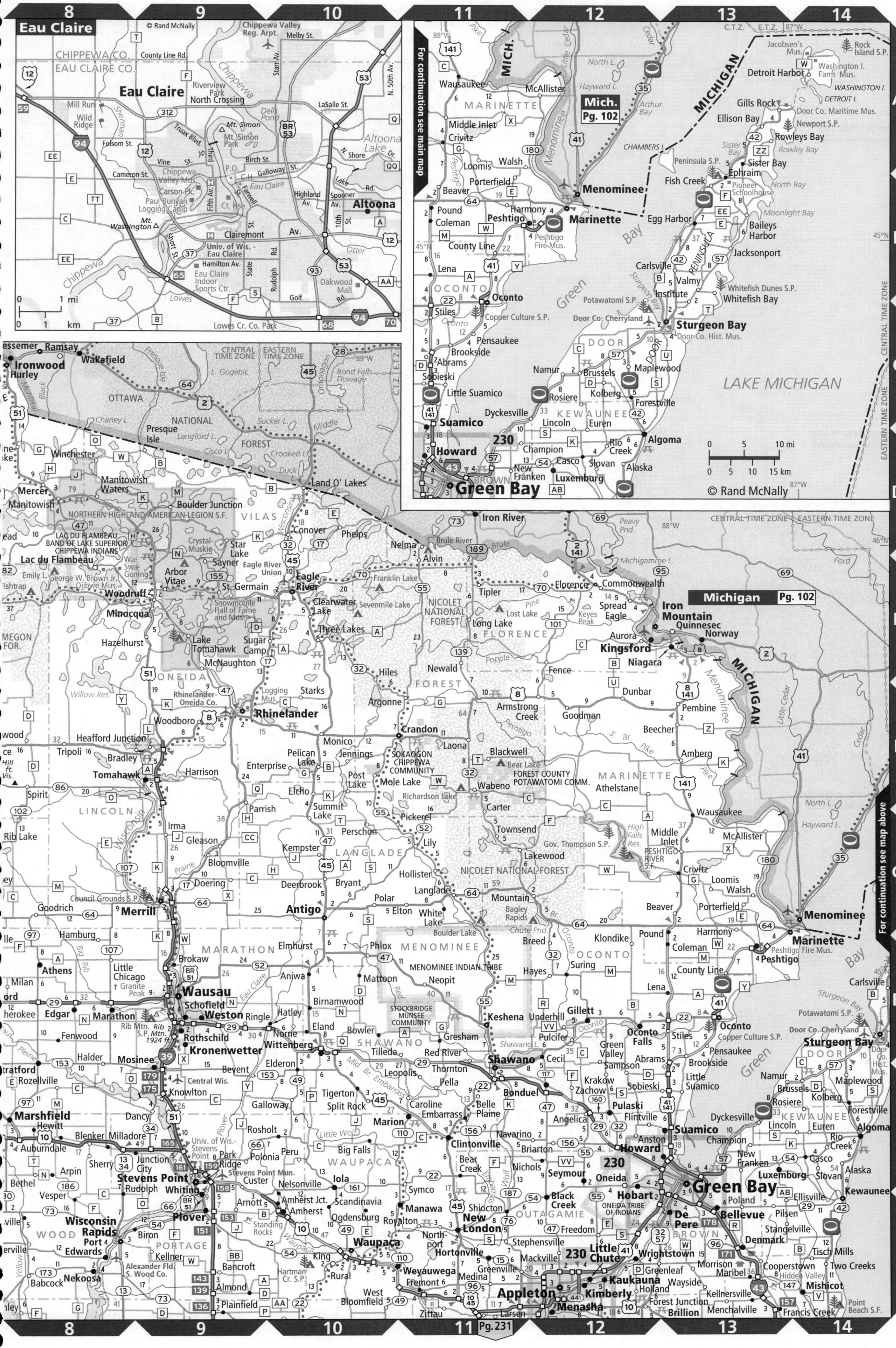

Tourism Information: Wisconsin Department of Tourism (800) 432-8747, (608) 266-2161 www.travelwisconsin.com

Road Conditions & Construction: 511 (866) 511-9472 www.511wi.gov

Toll Road Information: No toll roads

Explore Wisconsin at www.randmcnally.com/WI

Index of cities Pg. 264

Mileages between cities

	Beloit	Chicago, IL	Dubuque, IA	Eau Claire	Green Bay	Hayward	La Crosse	Madison	Milwaukee	Oshkosh	Rhinelander	Sheboygan	Sturgeon Bay	Superior	Wausau	Wisconsin Dells
Madison	54	146	93	177	138	282	143		78	87	200	117	185	325	143	57
Milwaukee	74	90	171	243	116	348	209	78		86	244	54	155	390	187	123

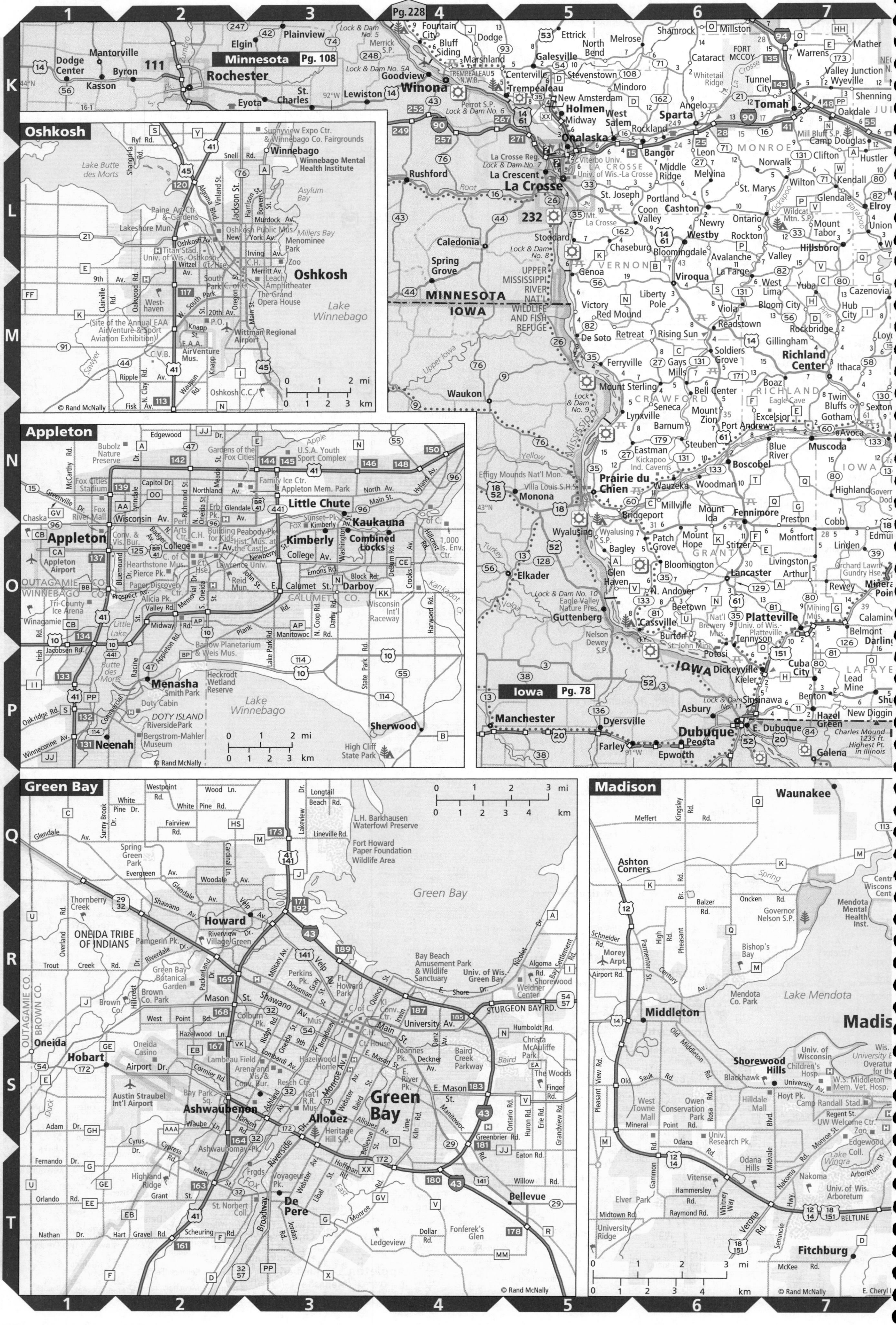

Determining distances along roads

Interchanges and exit numbers
For most states, the mileage between interchanges may be determined by subtracting one number from the other.

Wisconsin state facts

Nickname: The Badger State
Capital: Madison, N-9

Population: 5,686,986 (rank: 20th)
Largest city: Milwaukee, 594,833, N-13

Land area: 54,310 sq. mi. (rank: 25th)
Highest point: Timms Hill, 1,951 ft., F-8

Mileages between cities	Beloit	Chicago, IL	Dubuque, IA	Eau Claire	Green Bay	Hayward	La Crosse	Madison	Milwaukee	Oshkosh	Rhinelander	Sheboygan	Sturgeon Bay	Superior	Wausau	Wisconsin Dells
Superior	370	462	339	149	326	70	233	325	390	332	182	388	370		232	271
Wausau	189	281	239	98	96	189	170	143	187	103	59	158	141	232		112

Mileages © Rand McNally

Total mileages through Wisconsin

39	182 miles	90	189 miles
43	192 miles	94	341 miles

More mileages at www.randmcnally.com/MC

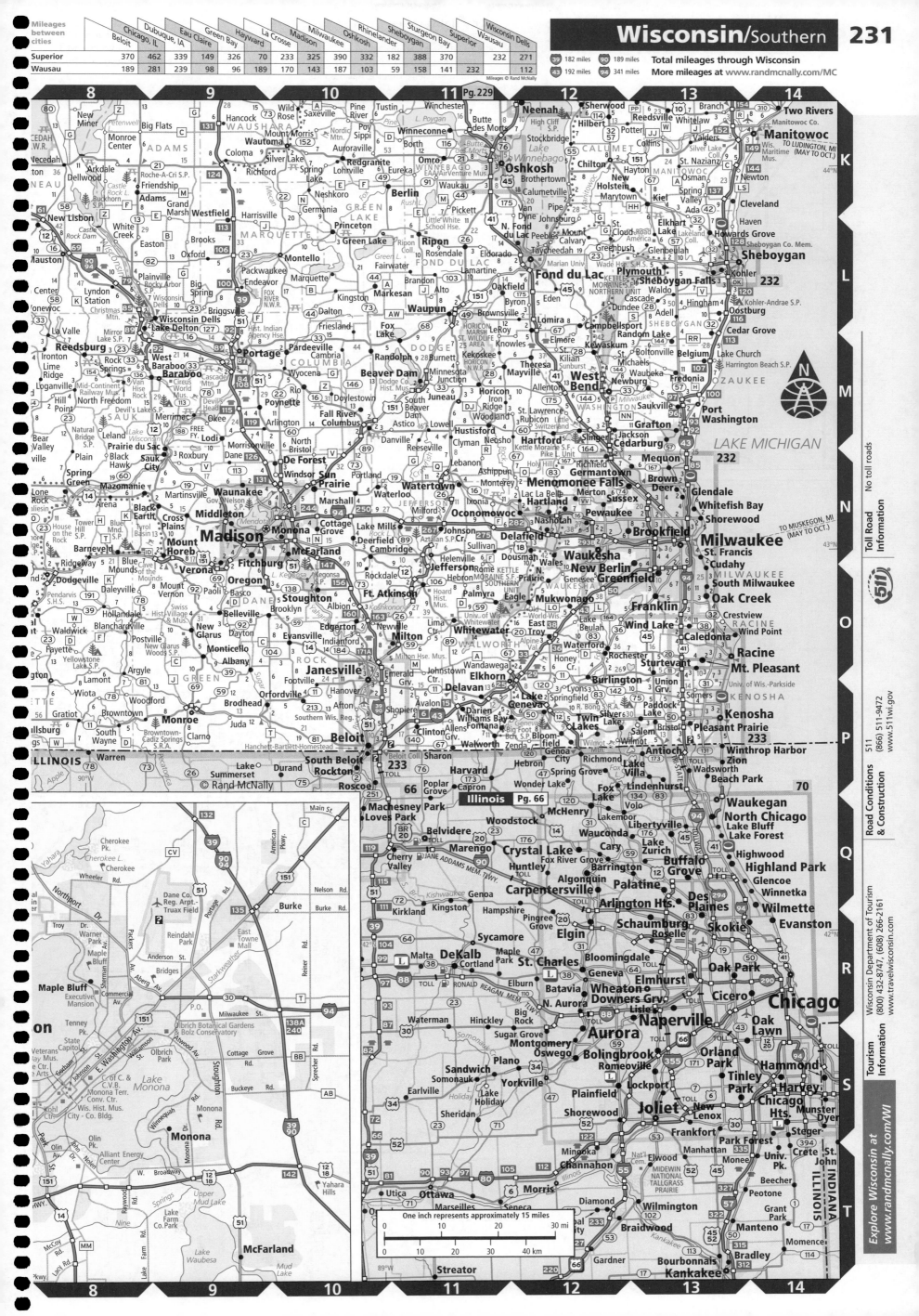

City sights to see
- Angel Museum, Beloit, N-6
- Betty Brinn Children's Museum, Milwaukee, L-3
- Golden Rondelle Theatre, Racine, J-10
- Harley Davidson Museum, Milwaukee, M-2
- Henry Maier Festival Park, Milwaukee, M-3
- J.M. Kohler Arts Center, Sheboygan, F-10

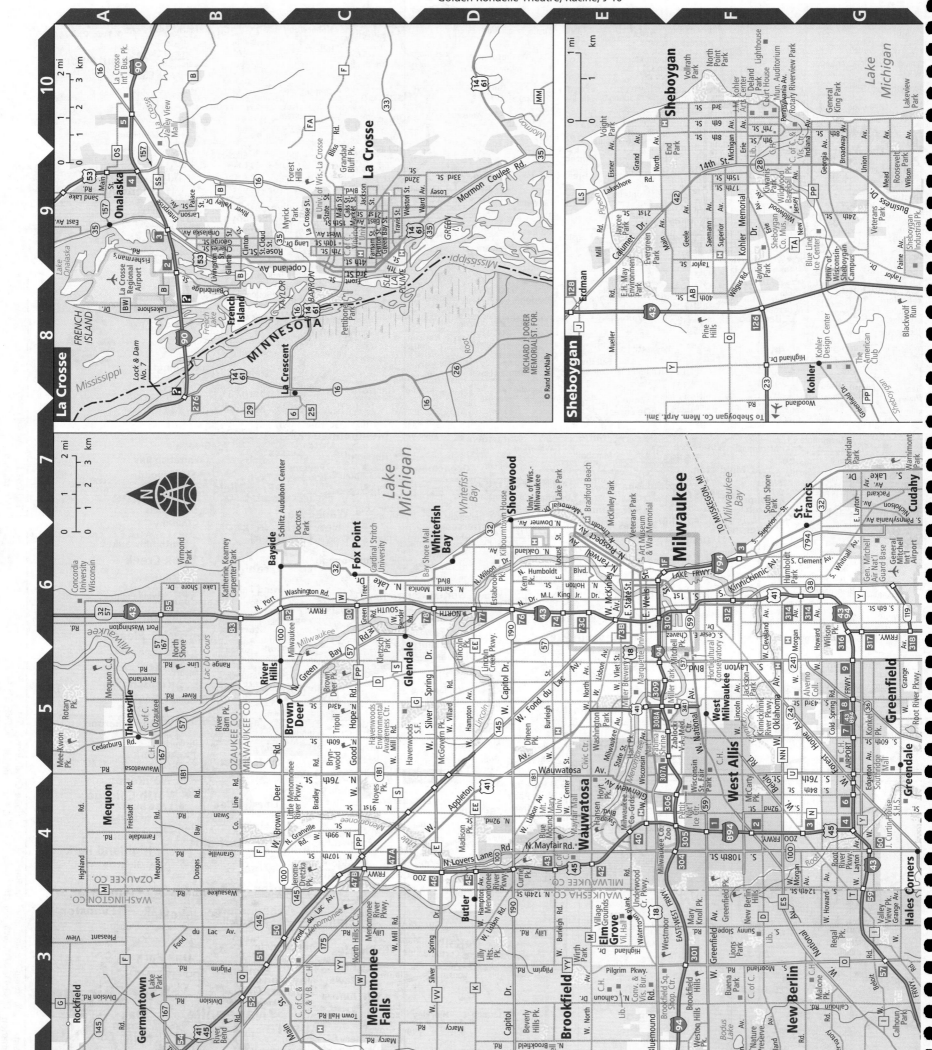

- Kenosha History Center, Kenosha, L-10
- Miller Brewery, Milwaukee, E-5
- Milwaukee Art Museum & War Memorial, Milwaukee, L-3
- Milwaukee Public Museum, Milwaukee, L-2
- Mitchell Park Horticultural Conservatory, Milwaukee, F-5
- Petit National Ice Center, Milwaukee, F-4

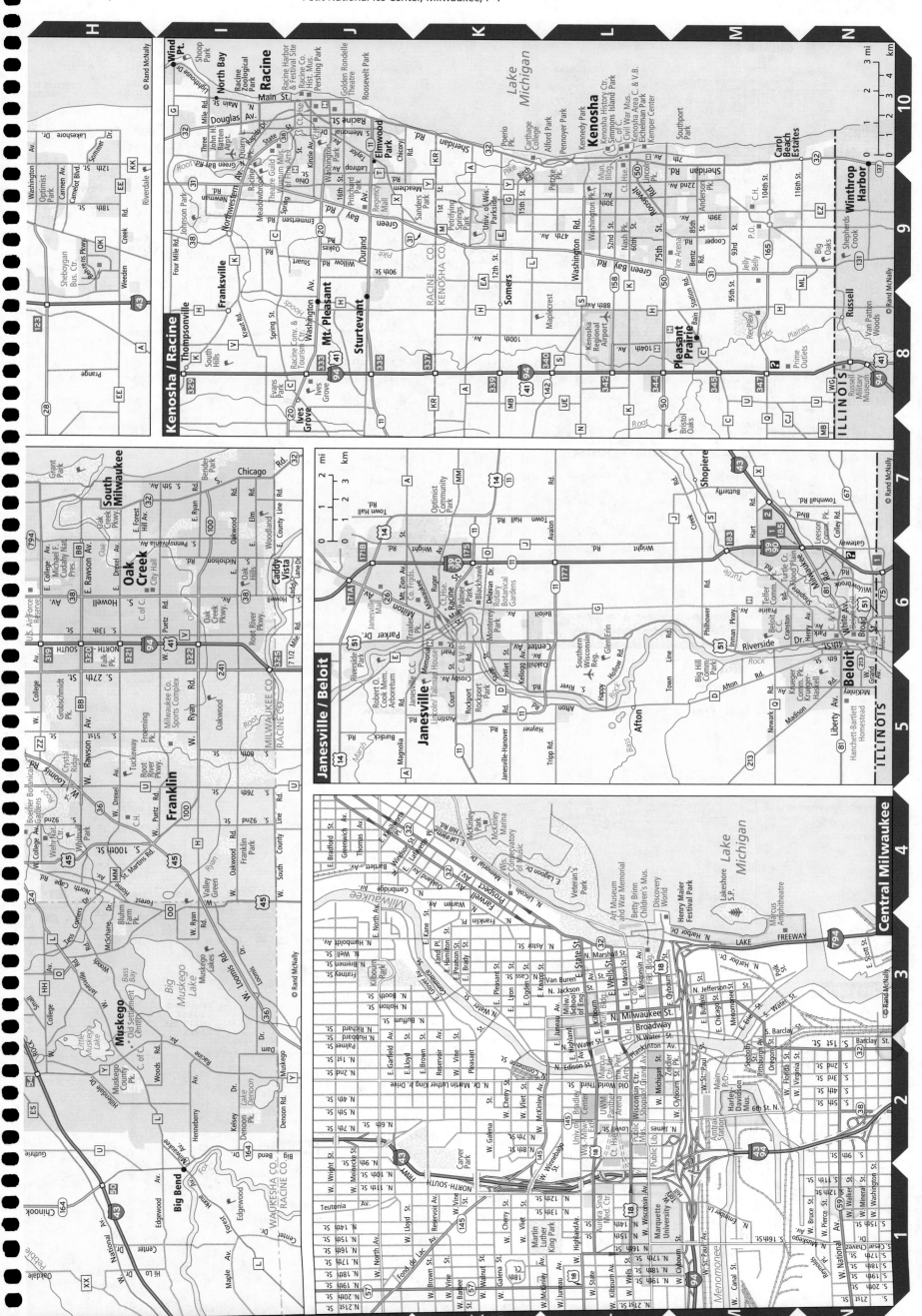

Mileages between cities	Casper	Cheyenne	Cody	Evanston	Gillette	Laramie	Sheridan	Spearfish, SD
Casper		178	213	325	126	147	148	219
Cheyenne	178		392	357	244	49	324	290
Cody	213	392		376	250	363	148	344
Jackson	283	432	177	190	411	383	325	504

Mileages © Rand McNally

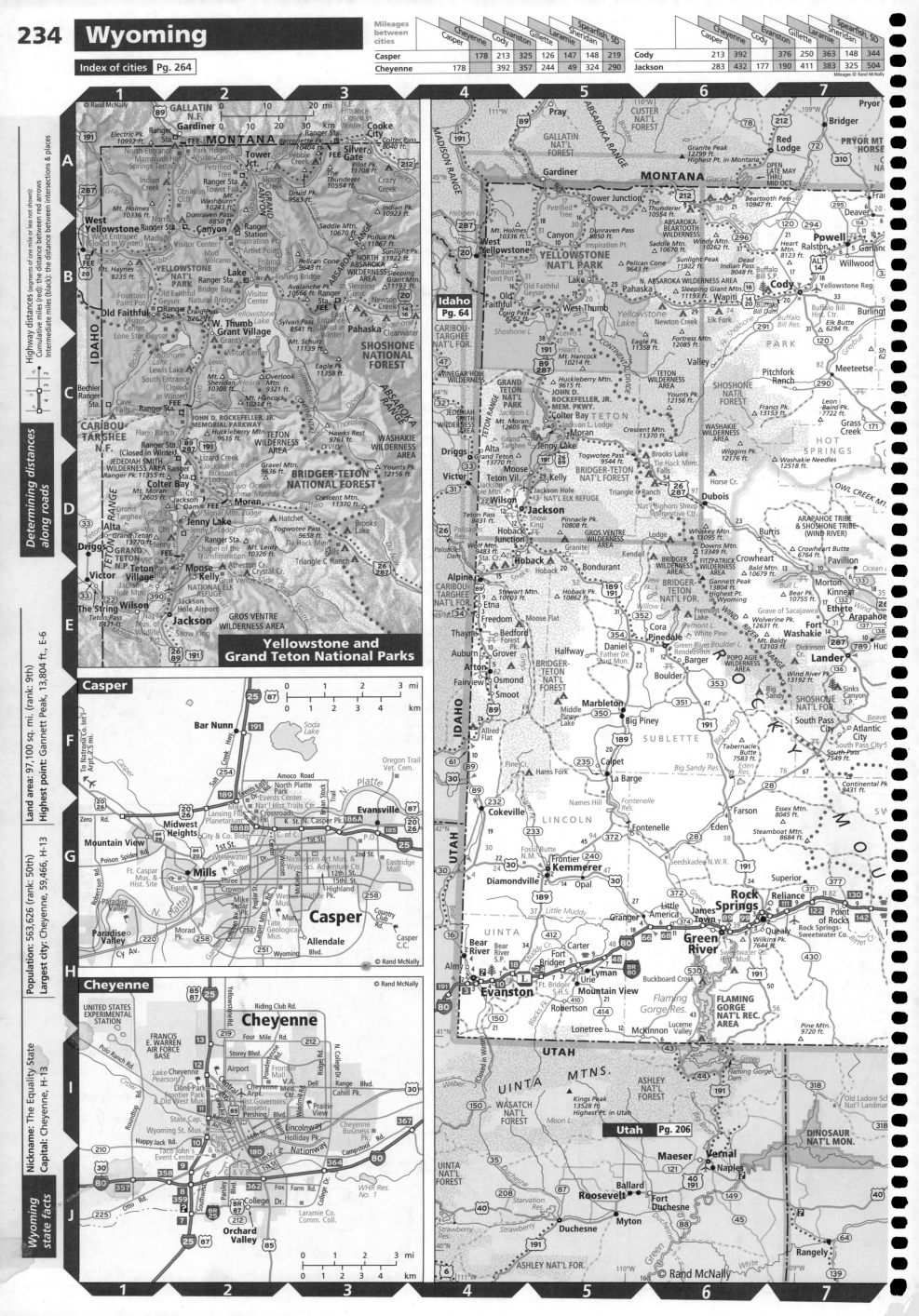

Yellowstone and Grand Teton National Parks

Casper

Cheyenne

Determining distances along roads

Highway distances (segments of one mile or less not shown): the distance between red arrows — Cumulative miles (red); the distance between intersections & places — Intermediate miles (black).

Wyoming state facts

Nickname: The Equality State
Capital: Cheyenne, H-13
Population: 563,626 (rank: 50th)
Largest city: Cheyenne, 59,466, H-13
Land area: 97,100 sq. mi. (rank: 9th)
Highest point: Gannett Peak, 13,804 ft., E-6

Idaho Pg. 64

Utah Pg. 206

© Rand McNally

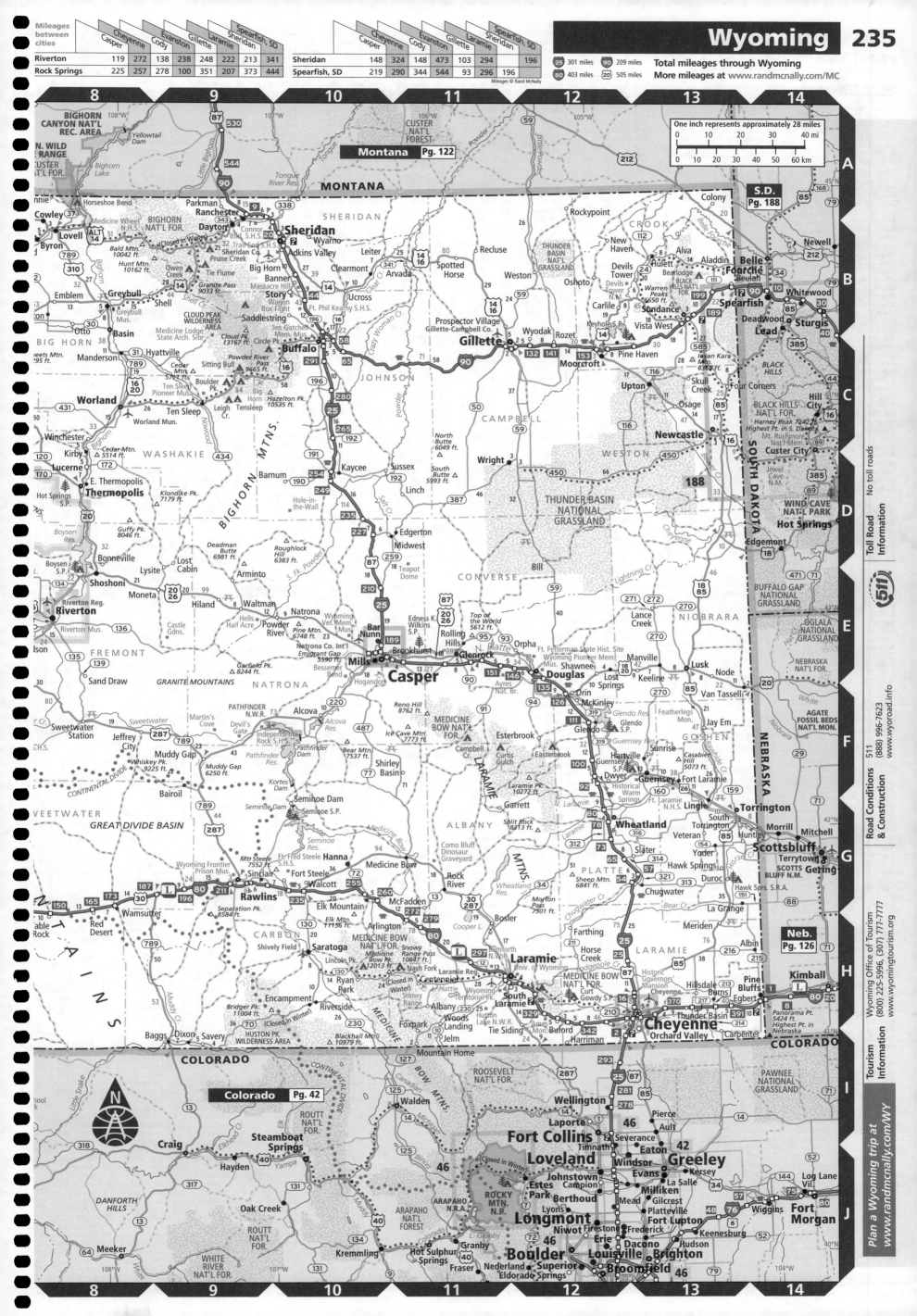

Mileages between cities	Casper	Cheyenne	Cody	Evanston	Gillette	Laramie	Sheridan	Spearfish, SD
Riverton	119	272	138	238	248	222	213	341
Rock Springs	225	257	278	100	351	207	373	444

	Casper	Cheyenne	Cody	Evanston	Gillette	Laramie	Sheridan	Spearfish, SD
Sheridan	148	324	148	473	103	294		196
Spearfish, SD	219	290	344	544	93	296	196	

Mileages © Rand McNally

Total mileages through Wyoming
More mileages at www.randmcnally.com/MC

| 25 | 301 miles | 90 | 209 miles |
| 80 | 403 miles | 20 | 505 miles |

Tourism Information
Wyoming Office of Tourism
(800) 225-5996, (307) 777-7777
www.wyomingtourism.org

Road Conditions & Construction
511
(888) 996-7623
www.wyoroad.info

Toll Road Information
No toll roads

Plan a Wyoming trip at
www.randmcnally.com/WY

One inch represents approximately 28 miles

Montana Pg. 122
Colorado Pg. 42
S.D. Pg. 188
Neb. Pg. 126

United States Counties, cities, towns & places

Populations are from the 2010 U.S. Census or are Rand McNally estimates

Oracle, 3686 ... L-10
Oro Valley, 41011 ... M-10
Overgaard, 400 ... H-11
Page, 7247 ... A-9
Palo Verde, 155 ... J-6
Palominas, 212 ... O-12
Pan Tak ... N-9
Paradise, 60 ... N-14
Paradise Valley, 12820 ... *H-6
Parker, 3083 ... H-3
Parks, 1188 ... E-8
Patagonia, 913 ... O-10
Paul Spur ... O-12
Paulden, 5231 ... F-7
Payson, 15301 ... H-9
Peach Sprs., 1090 ... E-5
Pearce ... N-12
Peeples Valley, 428 ... H-6
Peoria, 154065 ... J-7
Peridot, 1350 ... J-11
Perryville ... *J-2
Phoenix, 1445632 ... J-7
Picacho, 471 ... L-9
Picture Rocks, 9563 ... M-9
Pima, 2387 ... K-12
PIMA CO., 980263 ... M-8
PINAL CO., 375770 ... L-9
Pine, 1963 ... H-9
Pinedale, 487 ... H-11
Pinetop-Lakeside, 4282 ... H-12
Pinon, 904 ... C-11
Pirtleville, 1744 ... O-13
Pisinemo, 321 ... N-7
Plantsite, 600 ... K-13
Polacca, 700 ... D-11
Portal ... N-14
Poston, 285 ... H-3
Prescott, 39843 ... G-7
Prescott Valley, 38822 ... G-7
Punkin Ctr., 100 ... I-9
Quartzsite, 3677 ... I-3
Queen Creek, 26361 ... J-8
Queen Valley, 788 ... J-9
Red Lake, 100 ... C-10
Red Mesa, 480 ... A-13
Red Rock, 2169 ... L-9
Red Rock, 169 ... B-14
Redington ... M-11
Rillito, 97 ... M-9
Rio Rico, 18962 ... O-10
Rio Verde, 1811 ... *G-9
Rock Pt., 642 ... B-13
Rock Sprs. ... H-7
Roll ... L-3
Roosevelt, 28 ... I-9
Rough Rock, 414 ... B-12
Round Rock, 789 ... B-13
Sacaton, 2672 ... K-8
Safford, 9566 ... K-13
Sahuarita, 25259 ... N-10
St. David, 1699 ... N-11
St. Johns, 3480 ... G-13
St. Michaels, 1443 ... D-14
Salina ... C-12
Salome, 1530 ... I-4
San Carlos, 4038 ... J-11
San Luis, 25505 ... L-2
San Manuel, 3551 ... L-11
San Miguel, 197 ... O-8
San Simon, 165 ... M-14
San Tan Valley, 81321 ... K-9
San Xavier, 70 ... N-10
Sanders, 630 ... E-13
SANTA CRUZ CO., 47420 ... O-11
Santa Rosa, 628 ... M-8
Santan, 650 ... K-8
Sasabe ... O-9
Sawmill, 748 ... D-14
Schuchuli ... M-6
Scottsdale, 217385 ... J-8
Second Mesa, 962 ... D-11
Sedona, 10031 ... F-8
Seligman, 445 ... E-6
Sells, 2495 ... N-8
Sentinel ... K-5
Shongopovi, 831 ... D-11
Shonto, 591 ... B-10
Show Low, 10660 ... H-12
Shumway, 200 ... G-12
Sierra Vista, 43888 ... O-11
Sil Nakya ... M-8
Skull Valley ... G-6
Snowflake, 5590 ... G-12
Solomon, 426 ... K-13
Somerton, 14287 ... L-2
Sonoita, 818 ... N-11
S. Tucson, 5652 ... R-3
Springerville, 1961 ... H-13
Stanfield, 740 ... K-8
Star Valley, 2310 ... H-9
Steamboat, 284 ... D-12
Strawberry, 961 ... G-9
Summerhaven, 40 ... L-10
Summit, 5372 ... T-3
Sun City, 37499 ... J-7
Sun City West, 24535 ... I-7
Sun Lakes, 13975 ... K-8
Sun Valley, 316 ... F-12
Sunnyslope ... *H-5
Supai, 208 ... C-6
Superior, 2837 ... J-10
Surprise, 117517 ... I-7
Swift Trail Jct., 2935 ... L-13
Tacna, 602 ... L-3
Tanque Verde, 16901 ... Q-7
Taylor, 4112 ... G-12
Teec Nos Pos, 730 ... A-14
Tempe, 161719 ... J-8
Temple Bar, 100 ... C-3
Thatcher, 4865 ... K-12
The Gap, 100 ... C-9
Theba, 158 ... K-6
Three Points, 5581 ... M-9
Three Way ... K-14
Tolleson, 6545 ... *J-3
Tombstone, 1380 ... N-12
Tonopah, 60 ... J-6
Topawa, 299 ... N-8
Topock, 10 ... G-3
Tortilla Flat ... J-9
Tortolita, 3740 ... N-2
Truxton, 134 ... E-4
Tsaile, 1205 ... C-13
Tuba City, 8611 ... C-9
Tubac, 1191 ... O-10
Tucson, 520116 ... M-10
Tucson Estates, 12192 ... M-10
Turkey Flat ... L-12
Tusayan, 558 ... D-7
Upper Greasewood Trading Post, 10 ... C-13
Vail, 10208 ... M-10
Valentine, 38 ... E-4
Valle, 832 ... *E-8
Vamori ... N-8
Vaya Chin ... M-7
Ventana, 49 ... L-7
Verde Vil., 11605 ... G-8
Vernon, 122 ... H-13
Vicksburg, 597 ... I-4
Waddell, 500 ... *H-2
Wahweap, 200 ... *A-10
Walker, 80 ... G-7
Wellton, 2882 ... L-3
Wenden, 728 ... I-4
White Hills, 323 ... *E-2
Whiteriver, 4104 ... I-12
Why, 167 ... M-6
Wickenburg, 6363 ... I-6
Wide Ruins, 176 ... E-13
Wikieup, 133 ... G-4
Wilhoit, 868 ... G-6
Willcox, 3757 ... M-12
Williams, 3023 ... E-7
Willow Bch. ... D-2
Window Rock, 2712 ... D-14
Winkelman, 353 ... K-10
Winona ... E-9
Winslow, 9655 ... F-10
Wittmann, 763 ... I-7
Woodruff, 191 ... G-12
Yarnell, 649 ... H-6
YAVAPAI CO., 211033 ... F-6
Young, 666 ... H-10
Youngtown, 6156 ... *H-3
Yucca, 126 ... F-3
Yuma, 93064 ... L-2
YUMA CO., 195751 ... K-4

Arkansas

Page locator

Map keys	Atlas pages
1–10	22–23
11–20	24–25

Abbott, 50 ... F-2
Acorn, 70 ... H-2
Adona, 209 ... F-6
Albion, 60 ... E-9
Alco, 30 ... C-7
Alexander, 2901 ... H-7
Algoa, 50 ... E-11
Alicia, 124 ... C-11
Alix, 200 ... E-3
Alleene, 120 ... K-1
Allison ... C-8
Allport, 115 ... H-9
Alma, 5419 ... E-2
Almyra, 283 ... I-10
Alpena, 392 ... B-4
Alpine, 120 ... I-4
Alread ... D-6
Altheimer, 984 ... I-9
Altus, 758 ... E-3
Aly ... G-4
Amagon, 98 ... E-11
Amboy ... K-15
Amity, 723 ... I-4
Amy, 50 ... K-6
Anthonyville, 161 ... F-13
Antioch ... F-8
Antoine, 117 ... J-4
Aplin, 60 ... G-5
Appleton, 200 ... E-6
Apt ... C-17
Arkadelphia, 10714 ... J-5
Arkansas City, 366 ... K-10
ARKANSAS CO., 19019 ... I-10
Arkinda, 50 ... K-1
Armorel, 70 ... C-14
Ash Flat, 1082 ... B-9
Ashdown, 4723 ... K-2
ASHLEY CO., 21853 ... L-9
Athens, 100 ... I-2
Atkins, 3016 ... F-5
Atlanta, 50 ... M-5
Attica ... B-11
Aubrey, 170 ... G-11
Augusta, 2199 ... E-10
Austin, 2038 ... G-8
Austin ... E-7
Auvergne, 75 ... E-10
Avant, 40 ... H-4
Back Gate, 30 ... J-10
Bald Knob, 2897 ... E-9
Banks, 124 ... K-7
Barber, 55 ... F-2
Barling, 4649 ... E-2
Barton, 200 ... H-12
Bates, 125 ... G-1
Batesville, 10248 ... D-9
Bauxite, 487 ... H-7
BAXTER CO., 41513 ... B-7
Bay, 1801 ... D-12
Bayou Meto ... I-9
Bear Creek Sprs., 25 ... B-5
Bearden, 966 ... K-6
Beaver, 100 ... A-3
Bee Branch, 130 ... E-7
Beebe, 7315 ... F-8
Beech Grv. ... B-12
Beedeville, 107 ... E-11
Beirne, 50 ... J-5
Bella Vista, 26461 ... A-2
Bellefonte, 454 ... B-5
Belleville, 441 ... F-4
Ben ... D-8
Ben Hur ... D-5
Ben Lomond, 145 ... J-2
Benton, 30681 ... H-6
BENTON CO., 221339 ... B-1
Bentonville, 35301 ... B-2
Bergman, 439 ... B-5
Berlin ... M-9
Berryville, 5356 ... B-4
Bethel Hts., 2372 ... D-20
Beulah ... G-10
Bexar, 10 ... B-8
Big Flat, 105 ... C-7
Big Fork ... H-2
Bigelow, 315 ... F-6
Biggers, 347 ... B-11
Billstown ... J-4
Birdeye ... E-12
Birdsong, 41 ... E-13
Birta ... F-5
Biscoe, 363 ... G-10
Bismarck, 410 ... I-5
Black Oak, 262 ... D-13
Black Rock, 662 ... C-11
Black Sprs., 99 ... H-3
Blackton, 30 ... H-11
Blackwell, 200 ... F-6
Blakemore ... H-8
Blevins, 315 ... J-3
Blue Ball ... G-3
Blue Eye, 30 ... A-4
Blue Mtn., 124 ... F-3
Bluff City, 124 ... K-5
Bluffton, 60 ... G-3
Blytheville, 15620 ... C-14
Board Camp, 90 ... H-2
Bodcaw, 138 ... L-4
Boles, 120 ... G-2
Bonanza, 575 ... F-1
Bonnerdale, 70 ... I-4
Bono, 2131 ... C-11
Booker ... K-16
BOONE CO., 36903 ... B-5
Booneville, 3990 ... F-3
Boswell ... C-8
Botkinburg ... D-7
Bowman ... D-12
Boxley ... C-4
Boydell, 85 ... L-10
Boydsville, 30 ... B-13
Bradford, 759 ... E-10
Bradley, 628 ... M-3
BRADLEY CO., 11508 ... L-7
Branch, 367 ... E-2
Brashears ... D-3
Brentwood ... C-2
Briarcliff, 236 ... B-7
Brickeys, 60 ... G-12
Briggsville, 100 ... G-4
Brighton ... C-13
Brightstar, 30 ... M-2
Brinkley, 3188 ... G-10
Brockwell ... C-8
Brookland, 1642 ... C-12
Bruins ... G-13
Bruno ... C-6
Bryant, 16688 ... H-7
Buckner, 275 ... L-4
Buena Vista, 50 ... L-5
Buffalo City, 40 ... B-7
Bull Shoals, 1950 ... B-6
Burdette, 191 ... D-14
Burlington, 70 ... B-5
Bussey ... M-4
Butlerville, 180 ... G-9
Byron ... B-8
Cabot, 23776 ... G-8
Caddo Gap, 70 ... I-3
Caddo Valley, 635 ... I-5
Calamine ... C-10
Caldwell, 555 ... F-11
Cale, 79 ... K-4
Calhoun, 30 ... M-5
CALHOUN CO., 5368 ... K-6
Calico Rock, 1545 ... C-8
Calion, 494 ... L-6
Camden, 12183 ... K-6
Cammack Vil., 768 ... L-14
Camp, 200 ... B-9
Campbell Sta., 255 ... D-10
Canaan ... C-6
Canfield, 40 ... M-3
Caraway, 1279 ... D-13
Carlisle, 2214 ... G-9
CARROLL CO., 27446 ... B-4
Carrollton, 75 ... B-4
Carthage, 343 ... J-6
Casa, 171 ... F-5
Cash, 342 ... D-11
Cass, 140 ... D-3
Casscoe, 130 ... H-10
Caulksville, 213 ... E-3
Cauthron, 50 ... G-1
Cavanaugh ... K-19
Cave City, 1904 ... C-9
Cave Sprs., 1729 ... B-2
Cecil, 300 ... E-3
Cedar Creek, 30 ... G-3
Cedarville, 1394 ... D-1
Center, 100 ... C-9
Center Pt., 120 ... J-2
Center Ridge, 388 ... E-6
Centerton, 9515 ... B-2
Centerville, 200 ... F-5
Central, 90 ... I-6
Central City, 502 ... E-2
Charleston, 2494 ... E-2
Charlotte, 100 ... D-10
Chatfield, 40 ... F-13
Cherokee Vil., 4671 ... B-9
Cherry Valley, 651 ... E-12
Chester, 159 ... D-2
CHICOT CO., 11800 ... M-10
Chicot Jct., 40 ... M-10
Chidester, 287 ... K-5
Chismville, 50 ... F-3
Choctaw, 230 ... E-7
Cincinnati, 250 ... C-1
Clarendon, 1664 ... H-10
CLARK CO., 22995 ... J-5
Clarkedale, 371 ... E-13
Clarkridge, 50 ... A-7
Clarksville, 9178 ... E-4
CLAY CO., 16083 ... B-12
CLEBURNE CO., 25970 ... D-8
Cleveland, 150 ... E-6
CLEVELAND CO., 8689 ... J-7
Clifty, 60 ... B-3
Clinton, 2602 ... D-7
Clow, 30 ... J-3
Coal Hill, 1012 ... E-3
College Sta., 600 ... M-16
Collins, 60 ... L-9
Colt, 378 ... F-11
COLUMBIA CO., 24552 ... M-5
Columbus, 60 ... K-3
Cominto, 30 ... L-9
Compton, 30 ... C-4
Concord, 244 ... D-9
Congo, 60 ... H-6
Conway, 58908 ... F-7
CONWAY CO., 21273 ... F-6
Cord, 200 ... D-10
Cornerstone ... I-9
Cornerville, 50 ... K-8
Corning, 3377 ... B-12
Cotter, 970 ... B-7
Cotton Plant, 649 ... F-10
Cove, 382 ... H-1
Cowell ... D-5
Coy, 96 ... H-8
Cozahome, 40 ... C-7
Crabtree ... D-6
CRAIGHEAD CO., 96443 ... C-12
CRAWFORD CO., 61948 ... D-1
Crawfordsville, 479 ... F-13
CRITTENDEN CO., 50902 ... F-13
Crocketts Bluff, 50 ... H-10
CROSS CO., 17870 ... E-11
Cross Roads ... I-7
Crosses ... C-3
Crossett, 5507 ... M-8
Crumrod, 30 ... I-11
Crystal Sprs. ... H-4
Curtis, 300 ... J-5
Cushman, 452 ... C-9
Cypert ... H-11
Daisy, 115 ... I-3
Dalark, 70 ... J-6
DALLAS CO., 8116 ... J-6
Dalton ... B-10
Damascus, 382 ... E-7
Danville, 2409 ... F-4
Dardanelle, 4745 ... F-5
Datto, 100 ... B-12
De Queen, 6594 ... J-1
De Valls Bluff, 619 ... G-10
De Witt, 3292 ... I-10
Decatur, 1699 ... B-1
Deer, 120 ... D-5
Delaney ... C-3
Delaplaine, 116 ... B-12
Delaware, 100 ... E-4
Delight, 279 ... J-4
Dell, 223 ... C-14
Denmark ... E-9
Dennard, 530 ... D-7
Denning, 314 ... E-3
Dermott, 2316 ... L-10
Des Arc, 1717 ... G-10
Desha, 750 ... D-9
DESHA CO., 13008 ... K-10
Dewey ... E-9
Diamond City, 782 ... A-5
Diamondhead, 600 ... H-5
Diaz, 1318 ... D-10
Dierks, 1133 ... J-2
Dixie, 30 ... F-10
Doddridge, 40 ... M-2
Donaldson, 301 ... I-5
Dora, 150 ... I-18
Dover, 1378 ... E-5
Dowdy ... D-10
Drasco, 125 ... D-8
DREW CO., 18509 ... L-9
Driver, 50 ... D-14
Dumas, 4706 ... J-10
Durham ... C-2
Dutch Mills ... C-1
Dutton ... D-3
Dyer, 876 ... E-2
Dyess, 410 ... D-13
Eagle Mills, 50 ... K-6
Eagleton ... H-1
Earle, 2414 ... F-12
E. Camden, 931 ... K-6
E. End, 6998 ... H-7
Edgemont, 140 ... D-8
Edmondson, 427 ... F-13
Egypt, 112 ... C-11
El Dorado, 18884 ... M-6
El Paso, 300 ... F-8
Elaine, 636 ... I-11
Elkins, 2648 ... C-2
Elm Sprs., 1535 ... B-2
Elm Store ... A-10
Emerson, 368 ... M-5
Emmet, 518 ... K-4
England, 2825 ... H-8
Enola, 338 ... F-7
Ethel, 40 ... I-10
Etowah, 351 ... D-13
Eudora, 2269 ... M-10
Eureka Sprs., 2073 ... B-3
Evansville, 100 ... D-1
Evening Shade, 432 ... C-9
Everton, 133 ... B-6
Fair Oaks, 100 ... F-11
Fairfield Bay, 2338 ... D-7
Fairview, 140 ... B-6
Fairview, 40 ... M-10
Falcon, 40 ... L-4
Fallsville ... D-4
Fannie, 30 ... H-4
Fargo, 98 ... G-10
Farmington, 5974 ... C-2
FAULKNER CO., 113237 ... F-7
Fayetteville, 73580 ... C-2
Felsenthal, 150 ... M-8
Felton ... G-12
Ferguson Crossroads, 100 ... L-2
Ferndale ... G-6
Fiftysix, 173 ... C-7
Fisher, 223 ... E-11
Fitzhugh ... E-10
Flippin, 1355 ... B-6
Floral, 160 ... D-9
Florence, 30 ... K-9
Floyd, 130 ... F-8
Fomby ... K-2
Fontaine ... C-11
Fordyce, 4300 ... K-7
Foreman, 1011 ... K-1
Formosa, 90 ... E-7
Forrest City, 15371 ... F-12
Ft. Lynn ... M-3
Ft. Smith, 86209 ... E-1
Forum, 40 ... B-3
Fouke, 859 ... M-3
Fountain Hill, 175 ... L-9
Fountain Lake, 503 ... H-5
Fox, 100 ... D-7
Franklin, 198 ... B-9
FRANKLIN CO., 18125 ... D-3
Frenchmans Bayou, 100 ... E-13
Fulton, 201 ... K-3
FULTON CO., 12245 ... B-8
Furlow, 80 ... G-8
Galloway ... L-17
Gamaliel, 200 ... A-7
Gardner, 200 ... M-7
Garfield, 502 ... A-2
Garland, 242 ... L-3
GARLAND CO., 96024 ... G-5
Garner, 284 ... F-9
Gassville, 2078 ... B-7
Gateway, 405 ... A-3
Genoa, 250 ... L-2
Gentry, 3158 ... B-1
Georgetown, 124 ... F-10
Gethsemane ... I-8
Gibson, 3543 ... J-16
Gieseck ... F-12
Gilbert, 28 ... C-6
Gillett, 691 ... J-10
Gillham, 160 ... I-1
Gilmore, 188 ... E-13
Gin City, 30 ... M-3
Glencoe, 200 ... B-9
Glendale, 60 ... J-8
Glenwood, 2228 ... I-4
Goodwin, 80 ... G-11
Goshen, 1071 ... C-2
Gosnell, 3548 ... C-14
Gould, 837 ... J-9
Grady, 449 ... J-9
Grannis, 554 ... I-1
GRANT CO., 17853 ... I-7
Grapevine, 90 ... I-7
Gravel Ridge, 3232 ... J-16
Gravelly, 210 ... G-3
Gravette, 2325 ... A-1
Grays, 30 ... F-10
Green Forest, 2761 ... B-4
Greenbrier, 4706 ... F-7
GREENE CO., 42090 ... C-12
Greenfield, 60 ... D-12
Greenland, 1259 ... C-2
Greenway, 209 ... B-13
Greenwood, 8952 ... F-2
Greers Ferry, 891 ... E-8
Gregory, 50 ... F-10
Griffithtown, 120 ... J-5
Griffithville, 225 ... F-9
Grubbs, 386 ... D-11
Guion, 86 ... C-8
Gum Sprs., 120 ... J-5
Gurdon, 2212 ... J-5
Guy, 708 ... E-7
Hackett, 812 ... F-1
Hagarville, 129 ... E-4
Halley ... L-10
Halliday, 100 ... C-12
Hamburg, 2857 ... M-9
Hampton, 1324 ... L-7
Hardy, 772 ... B-10
Harmony ... E-4
Harrell, 254 ... L-7
Harriet, 50 ... C-7
Harrisburg, 2288 ... E-12
Harrison, 12943 ... B-5
Hartford, 642 ... F-1
Hartman, 519 ... E-3
Harvey, 30 ... G-3
Haskell, 3990 ... H-6
Hasty, 50 ... C-5
Hatfield, 413 ... H-1
Hattieville, 150 ... E-6
Hatton, 100 ... I-1
Havana, 375 ... F-4
Haynes, 150 ... G-12
Hazen, 1468 ... G-9
Heber Sprs., 7165 ... E-8
Hector, 450 ... E-5
Helena-West Helena, 12282 ... H-12
HEMPSTEAD CO., 22609 ... K-3
Hempwallace ... H-5
Henderson, 130 ... B-7
Hermitage, 830 ... L-8
Hickory Plains, 90 ... G-9
Hickory Ridge, 272 ... E-11
Higden, 120 ... E-7
Higgins ... N-16
Higginson, 621 ... F-9
Highfill, 583 ... B-1
Highland, 1045 ... B-9
Hillemann, 30 ... F-11
Hindsville, 61 ... B-3
Hiwasse, 125 ... A-2
Holland, 557 ... F-7
Hollis ... G-5
Holly Grv., 602 ... H-10
Holly Sprs., 30 ... K-6
Hollywood, 75 ... J-4
Hon, 70 ... G-2
Hooker ... B-12
Hope, 10095 ... K-3
Horatio, 1044 ... J-1
Horseshoe Bend, 2184 ... B-9
Horseshoe Lake, 292 ... G-13
HOT SPRING CO., 32923 ... I-5
Hot Sprs., 35193 ... H-5
Hot Sprs. Vil., 12807 ... H-5
Houston, 173 ... F-6
HOWARD CO., 13789 ... I-2
Howell, 30 ... F-10
Hoxie, 2780 ... C-11
Hughes, 1441 ... G-12
Humnoke, 284 ... H-9
Humphrey, 557 ... I-9
Hunt, 80 ... E-3
Hunter, 105 ... F-11
Huntington, 635 ... F-2
Huntsville, 2346 ... C-3
Hurricane Grv. ... H-4
Huttig, 597 ... M-8
Ida, 60 ... D-8
Imboden, 677 ... B-10
Immanuel ... I-10
INDEPENDENCE CO., 36647 ... C-9
Indian Bay, 40 ... I-11
Ingalls, 40 ... L-8
Ink ... H-2
Ione ... F-2
Ivan, 50 ... J-7
IZARD CO., 13696 ... C-8
JACKSON CO., 17997 ... E-10
Jacksonville, 28364 ... G-8
Japton ... C-3
Jasper, 466 ... C-5
JEFFERSON CO., 77435 ... I-8
Jennette, 115 ... F-13
Jennie, 120 ... M-10
Jerome, 39 ... L-10
Jersey, 30 ... L-7
Jerusalem, 200 ... E-6
Jessieville, 100 ... H-5
Johnson, 3354 ... F-19
JOHNSON CO., 25540 ... E-4
Johnsville, 50 ... L-8
Joiner, 576 ... E-13
Jonesboro, 67263 ... D-12
Joplin ... H-4
Jordan, 50 ... B-8
Joy ... E-8
Judsonia, 2019 ... F-9
Junction City, 581 ... M-6
Keiser, 759 ... D-13
Kelso, 30 ... K-10
Kensett, 1648 ... F-9
Keo, 256 ... H-8
Kibler, 961 ... E-2
King, 90 ... I-1
Kingsland, 447 ... J-7
Kingston, 60 ... C-4
Kirby, 786 ... I-3
Knobel, 287 ... B-12
Knoxville, 731 ... E-4
La Grange, 89 ... H-12
Lacey, 110 ... L-9
Ladd ... J-8
Ladelle, 75 ... L-9
LAFAYETTE CO., 7645 ... M-3
Lafe, 458 ... B-12
L. Catherine, 870 ... H-5
Lake City, 2082 ... D-13
L. Hamilton, 2135 ... H-5
Lake Vil., 2575 ... L-10
Lakeview, 741 ... B-7
Lakeview, 443 ... I-12
Lamar, 1605 ... E-4
Lamartine, 30 ... L-4
Lambrook, 50 ... I-11
Laneburg, 80 ... K-4
Langley, 30 ... I-3
Lavaca, 2289 ... E-2
LAWRENCE CO., 17415 ... C-10
Lawson, 100 ... M-7
Leachville, 1993 ... C-13
Lead Hill, 271 ... B-6
LEE CO., 10424 ... G-11
Leola, 501 ... I-6
Leonard ... B-13
Lepanto, 1893 ... D-13
Leslie, 441 ... D-6
Letona, 255 ... E-9
Lewisville, 1280 ... L-3
Lexa, 286 ... H-12
Light, 80 ... C-12
Limestone ... D-4
Lincoln, 2249 ... C-1
LINCOLN CO., 14134 ... J-9
Lisbon ... M-6
Little Flock, 2585 ... B-2
LITTLE RIVER CO., 13171 ... K-1
Little Rock, 193524 ... G-7
Locke, 30 ... D-2
Lockesburg, 739 ... J-2
Locust Bayou, 140 ... L-6
Locust Grv., 85 ... D-9
Lodge Corner ... I-9
LOGAN CO., 22353 ... F-3
London, 1039 ... E-4
Lono ... I-6
Lonoke, 4245 ... G-8
LONOKE CO., 68356 ... G-8
Lorado, 120 ... C-12
Louann, 164 ... L-6
Lowell, 7327 ... B-2
Lurton ... D-5
Luxora, 1178 ... D-14
Lynn, 288 ... C-10
Mabelvale ... N-13
Macedonia ... M-4
Macon, 960 ... G-8
Madison, 769 ... F-12
MADISON CO., 15717 ... C-3
Magazine, 847 ... F-3
Magness, 202 ... D-10
Magnet Cove, 5 ... H-6
Magnolia, 11577 ... M-4
Malvern, 10318 ... I-6
Mammoth Spr., 977 ... A-9
Mandeville, 520 ... L-2
Manila, 3342 ... C-13
Manning, 70 ... J-6
Mansfield, 1139 ... F-2
Manson ... B-11
Marble, 60 ... C-4
Marcella, 80 ... D-8
Marianna, 4115 ... G-12
Marie, 84 ... D-14
Marion, 12345 ... F-13
MARION CO., 16653 ... B-6
Marked Tree, 2566 ... E-13
Marmaduke, 1111 ... B-13
Marshall, 1355 ... C-6
Marvell, 1186 ... H-11
Masonville, 60 ... K-10
Massard ... J-20
Maumelle, 17163 ... G-7
Mayfield ... C-3
Mayflower, 2234 ... G-7
Maynard, 426 ... B-11
Maysville, 130 ... B-1
McAlmont, 1873 ... K-16
McArthur ... K-10
McCaskill, 96 ... J-3
McCrory, 1729 ... F-10
McDougal, 186 ... A-13
McGehee, 4219 ... K-10
McKamie ... M-4
McMilan Cor., 40 ... L-10
McNab, 68 ... K-3
McNeil, 516 ... L-5
McRae, 682 ... F-9
Melbourne, 1848 ... C-8
Mellwood, 100 ... I-11
Mena, 5737 ... H-2
Menifee, 302 ... F-6
Metalton ... B-4
Middlebrook ... A-11
Midland, 325 ... F-1
Midway, 389 ... I-5
Midway ... E-4
MILLER CO., 43462 ... L-3
Mineral Sprs., 1208 ... J-2
Minturn, 109 ... C-11
MISSISSIPPI CO., 46480 ... D-13
Mist ... M-9
Mitchell ... B-8
Mitchellville, 360 ... J-10
Moko, 30 ... A-9
Monette, 1501 ... C-13
Monroe, 110 ... G-11
MONROE CO., 8149 ... H-10
MONTGOMERY CO., 9487 ... H-3
Monticello, 9467 ... K-9
Montrose, 354 ... L-10
Moorefield, 137 ... D-9
Moreland, 210 ... E-5
Morganton ... E-7
Morning Star ... E-17
Moro, 216 ... G-11
Morrilton, 6767 ... F-6
Morrow, 150 ... C-1
Morton, 140 ... F-11
Moscow, 200 ... J-9
Mt. George ... F-5
Mt. Holly, 150 ... L-5
Mt. Ida, 1076 ... H-3
Mt. Judea, 530 ... C-5
Mt. Pleasant, 414 ... C-9
Mt. Pleasant ... N-20
Mt. Vernon, 145 ... F-8
Mountain Home, 12448 ... B-7
Mountain Pine, 770 ... H-5
Mountain View, 2748 ... D-8
Mountainburg, 631 ... D-2
Mulberry, 1655 ... E-2
Murfreesboro, 1641 ... J-3
Nail ... D-4
Nashville, 4627 ... J-3
Natural Dam, 75 ... D-1
Naylor, 110 ... F-8
Nebo ... J-9
Needmore, 40 ... G-2
NEVADA CO., 8997 ... K-4
New Blaine, 174 ... E-4
New Edinburg, 127 ... K-7
Newark, 1176 ... D-10
Newell, 50 ... M-6
Newhope, 80 ... I-3
Newport, 7879 ... D-10
NEWTON CO., 8330 ... C-4
Nimmons, 69 ... B-13
Nimrod, 50 ... G-5
Noland ... B-11
Norfork, 511 ... B-7
Norman, 378 ... H-3
Norphlet, 844 ... L-6
N. Crossett, 3119 ... M-8
N. Little Rock, 62304 ... G-7
Number Nine, 30 ... C-14
Nunley ... H-2
Oak Grv. Hts., 889 ... C-12
Oakgrove, 369 ... A-4
Oakhaven, 63 ... K-3
Oakland, 60 ... A-6
Oark, 50 ... D-4
Oden, 232 ... H-3
Ogden, 180 ... K-2
Ogemaw, 50 ... L-5
Oil Trough, 260 ... D-10
O'Kean, 194 ... B-11
Okolona, 147 ... J-4
Ola, 1281 ... F-5
Old Jenny Lind, 240 ... F-1
Old Milo ... L-8
Omaha, 169 ... A-5
Onia ... C-7
Onyx ... G-4
Oppelo, 781 ... F-6
Osage, 20 ... B-4
Osceola, 7757 ... D-14
Otter Creek ... M-13
Otto ... F-8
Otwell, 140 ... D-11
Ouachita, 30 ... K-6
OUACHITA CO., 26120 ... K-6
Overcup, 50 ... F-6
Owensville, 100 ... H-6
Oxford, 670 ... B-8
Oxley ... D-7
Ozan, 85 ... J-3
Ozark, 3684 ... E-3
Ozark Acres, 760 ... B-10
Ozone, 120 ... D-4
Palatka ... A-12
Palestine, 681 ... G-11
Pangburn, 601 ... E-9
Pansy ... K-8
Paragould, 26113 ... C-12
Paris, 3532 ... E-3
Parkdale, 277 ... M-9
Parkers Chapel, 500 ... M-6
Parkin, 1105 ... F-12
Parks, 90 ... G-2
Paron, 80 ... G-6
Parthenon, 300 ... C-5
Patmos, 64 ... L-3
Patterson, 452 ... F-10
Payneway ... E-12
Pea Ridge, 4794 ... A-2
Pea Ridge, 30 ... J-10
Peach Orchard, 135 ... B-12
Pearcy, 175 ... H-4
Pearson ... E-8
Peel, 85 ... A-6
Pencil Bluff, 150 ... H-3
Pennys, 110 ... J-2
Perry, 270 ... F-6
PERRY CO., 10445 ... G-5
Perrytown, 272 ... K-4
Perryville, 1460 ... F-6
Pettigrew ... D-3
Pettus ... H-8
PHILLIPS CO., 21757 ... H-11
Pickens, 55 ... K-10
Pickens ... E-8
Piggott, 3849 ... B-13
Pike City, 250 ... J-3
PIKE CO., 11291 ... I-4
Pindall, 112 ... C-6
Pine Bluff, 49083 ... I-8
Pine Grv. ... J-6
Pine Ridge, 50 ... H-3
Pineville, 238 ... B-8
Piney, 4699 ... E-15
Plainview, 608 ... G-4
Pleasant Grv., 220 ... D-8
Pleasant Grv. ... A-18
Pleasant Plains, 349 ... E-9
Plumerville, 826 ... F-6
Pocahontas, 6608 ... B-11
POINSETT CO., 24583 ... E-12
Pt. Cedar ... I-4
POLK CO., 20662 ... H-2
Pollard, 222 ... A-13
Ponca, 30 ... C-4
POPE CO., 61754 ... E-5
Poplar Grv., 200 ... H-11
Portia, 437 ... C-11
Portland, 430 ... M-10
Possum Grape, 130 ... E-10
Postelle, 30 ... H-11
Pottsville, 2838 ... F-5
Poughkeepsie, 200 ... C-10
Powhatan, 72 ... C-11
Poyen, 290 ... I-6
PRAIRIE CO., 8715 ... G-9
Prairie Grv., 4380 ... C-2
Prattsville, 305 ... I-6
Prescott, 3296 ... K-4
Prim ... D-8
Princeton, 50 ... J-6
Providence, 100 ... E-9
Provo, 90 ... J-2
Pruitt, 30 ... C-5
PULASKI CO., 382748 ... H-8
Pyatt, 221 ... B-6
Quitman, 762 ... E-7
Ralph ... B-6
RANDOLPH CO., 17969 ... B-11
Ranger ... F-4
Ratcliff, 202 ... E-3
Ratio, 30 ... I-11
Ravanna, 35 ... M-2
Ravenden, 470 ... B-10
Ravenden Sprs., 118 ... B-10
Rea Valley ... B-7
Reader, 66 ... K-5
Readland, 25 ... M-10
Rector, 1977 ... B-13
Redfield, 1297 ... H-8
Reed, 141 ... K-10
Relfs Bluff ... K-9
Rena ... E-1
Reydell, 50 ... I-9
Reyno, 456 ... B-12
Rich ... G-11
Rison, 1344 ... J-7
Rixey ... K-16
Roe, 114 ... H-10
Rogers, 55964 ... B-2
Rohwer, 75 ... K-10
Roland, 746 ... G-7
Romance, 60 ... F-8
Rondo, 198 ... H-11
Rose Bud, 482 ... E-8
Rose City ... L-16
Rosie, 300 ... D-9
Rosston, 261 ... K-4
Rover, 260 ... G-4
Royal ... H-4
Rudd ... B-4
Rudy, 61 ... E-2
Rupert ... D-6
Rushing ... D-7
Russell, 216 ... E-9
Russellville, 27920 ... F-5
Rye, 146 ... K-8
Saddle ... B-9
Saffell, 150 ... C-10
Sage, 80 ... C-9
St. Charles, 230 ... I-11
St. Francis, 250 ... A-13
ST. FRANCIS CO., 28258 ... F-11
St. James ... D-8
St. Joe, 132 ... C-6
St. Paul, 113 ... D-3
St. Vincent, 60 ... E-6
Salem, 2607 ... H-6
Salem, 1635 ... B-9
Salem, 40 ... I-3
Salesville, 450 ... B-7
SALINE CO., 107118 ... G-6
Salus, 20 ... D-4
Sand Gap, 30 ... D-5
Saratoga, 200 ... K-3
Sardis ... H-7
Savoy ... C-1
Scotland, 130 ... E-6
Scott, 72 ... G-8
SCOTT CO., 11233 ... G-2
Scottsville, 60 ... E-5
Scranton, 224 ... E-4
Searcy, 22858 ... F-9
SEARCY CO., 8195 ... D-6
SEBASTIAN CO., 125744 ... F-1
Sedgwick, 152 ... C-11
Selma, 50 ... K-9
SEVIER CO., 17058 ... J-1
Shannon Hills, 3143 ... H-7
SHARP CO., 17264 ... C-9
Shell Lake, 50 ... F-12
Sheridan, 4603 ... I-7
Sherrill, 84 ... I-8
Sherwood, 29523 ... G-7
Shirley, 291 ... D-7
Shover Sprs., 30 ... K-4
Sidney, 181 ... C-9
Siloam Sprs., 15039 ... B-1
Silver Hill, 30 ... C-6
Sims, 250 ... H-3
Slovak, 50 ... H-9
Smackover, 1865 ... L-6
Smithville, 78 ... C-10
Snow Hill, 50 ... L-6
Snow Lake ... J-11
Snowball, 60 ... C-6
Snyder, 170 ... L-9
Social Hill ... I-5
Soudan ... G-12
S. Lead Hill, 102 ... B-6
Southside, 565 ... D-9
Sparkman, 427 ... J-6
Spring Hill, 90 ... K-3
Spring Valley ... B-3
Springdale, 69797 ... B-2
Springfield, 185 ... F-6
Stacy, 30 ... D-12
Stamps, 1693 ... L-4
Star City, 2274 ... J-9
Staves, 116 ... J-7
Stephens, 891 ... L-5
STONE CO., 12394 ... D-8
Story, 100 ... H-4
Strawberry, 302 ... C-10
Strickler ... D-2
Strong, 558 ... M-7
Sturkie, 35 ... A-8
Stuttgart, 9326 ... H-9
Subiaco, 572 ... E-3
Success, 149 ... A-12
Sulphur City ... C-2
Sulphur Rock, 456 ... D-9
Sulphur Sprs., 1101 ... I-8
Sulphur Sprs., 511 ... A-1
Summers, 250 ... C-1
Summit, 604 ... B-6
Sumpter ... L-8
Sunset, 198 ... F-13
Swain ... D-4
Sweet Home, 849 ... H-7
Swifton, 798 ... D-11
Tarry ... J-9
Taylor, 566 ... M-4
Texarkana, 29919 ... L-2
Thida, 110 ... E-10
Thornburg, 120 ... G-6
Thornton, 407 ... K-7
Three Brothers ... A-7
Three Creeks, 50 ... M-5
Tichnor, 85 ... I-10
Tillar, 225 ... K-10
Tilly, 50 ... D-6
Tilton, 70 ... E-11
Timbo, 240 ... C-7
Tinsman, 54 ... K-7
Tokio, 50 ... J-3
Tollette, 240 ... K-3
Tollville ... G-9
Tomato, 30 ... C-14
Tontitown, 2460 ... B-2
Traskwood, 518 ... H-6
Trumann, 7243 ... D-12
Tucker, 285 ... H-8
Tuckerman, 1862 ... D-10
Tulip ... J-6
Tull, 448 ... H-6
Tumbling Shoals, 978 ... E-8
Tupelo, 180 ... E-10
Turner, 50 ... H-11
Turrell, 615 ... E-13
Twin Groves, 335 ... E-7
Twist, 50 ... E-12
Tyro, 30 ... K-9
Tyronza, 762 ... E-13
Ulm, 170 ... H-10
Umpire, 210 ... I-2
UNION CO., 41639 ... M-6
Uniontown, 250 ... D-1
Urbana, 300 ... M-7
Valley Sprs., 183 ... B-5
Valley View ... C-16
Van Buren, 22791 ... E-1
VAN BUREN CO., 17295 ... D-6
Vandervoort, 87 ... I-1
Vanndale, 225 ... E-12
Vendor, 30 ... C-5
Vesta ... E-2
Vick, 30 ... L-8
Victoria, 37 ... D-14
Vilonia, 3815 ... F-8
Viola, 337 ... B-8
Wabash, 60 ... I-11
Wabbaseka, 255 ... I-9
Waldenburg, 61 ... E-11
Waldo, 1372 ... L-4
Waldron, 3618 ... G-2
Walker ... F-9
Walnut Ridge, 4890 ... C-11
Ward, 4067 ... F-8
Warm Sprs., 30 ... A-11
Warren, 6003 ... K-8
Washington, 180 ... K-3
WASHINGTON CO., 203065 ... C-1
Washita, 90 ... H-4
Waterloo, 50 ... L-4
Watson, 211 ... J-10
Waveland ... F-3
Weber, 30 ... I-10
Weddington ... C-1
Weiner, 716 ... D-11
Welcome, 50 ... M-4
Weldon, 75 ... E-10
Wesley, 50 ... C-3
Wesson, 125 ... M-6
W. Crossett, 1256 ... M-8
W. Fork, 2317 ... C-2
W. Memphis, 26245 ... F-13
West Pt., 185 ... F-9
Western Grv., 384 ... C-5
Wheatley, 355 ... G-11
Whelen Sprs., 92 ... K-5
White, 30 ... M-8
WHITE CO., 77076 ... E-8
White Hall, 5526 ... I-8
Whitehall, 50 ... E-12
Wickes, 754 ... I-1
Widener, 273 ... F-12
Wilburn, 75 ... E-8
Williford, 75 ... B-10
Willisville, 152 ... L-4
Willow, 50 ... J-6
Wilmar, 511 ... K-8
Wilmot, 550 ... M-9
Wilson, 903 ... D-14
Wilton, 374 ... K-2
Winchester, 167 ... K-10
Winfield, 30 ... G-2
Wing ... G-4
Winslow, 391 ... D-2
Winthrop, 192 ... J-1
Wirth ... A-10
Wiseman, 50 ... B-9
Witcherville, 200 ... F-2
Witter, 30 ... C-3
Witts Sprs., 60 ... D-6
Woodberry, 40 ... K-7
Woodland Hts. ... K-13
WOODRUFF CO., 7260 ... F-10
Woodson, 403 ... H-7
Wooster, 860 ... F-7
Worden, 100 ... E-10
Wright, 350 ... H-8
Wrightsville, 2114 ... H-7
Wynne, 8367 ... F-12
Y City, 60 ... G-2
Yarbro, 200 ... C-14
YELL CO., 22185 ... F-4
Yellville, 1204 ... B-6
Yorktown, 30 ... J-9
Zion, 135 ... C-9

California

Page locator

Map keys	Atlas pages
NA1–NN10	26–27
NA11–NN20	28–29
SA1–SN10	34–35
SA11–SN20	36–37

* City keyed to pp. 30–31
† City keyed to pp. 32–33
‡ City keyed to pp. 38–39
§ City keyed to pp. 40–41

Aberdeen, 100 ... SJ-4
Acampo, 341 ... NL-7
Acton, 7596 ... SI-11
Adelanto, 31765 ... SH-13
Adin, 272 ... NC-8
Aetna Sprs., 5 ... NJ-5
Agoura Hills, 20330 ... SJ-10
Agua Dulce, 3342 ... ‡N-6
Aguanga, 1128 ... SL-14
Ahwahnee, 2246 ... NN-11
Alameda, 73812 ... NM-5
ALAMEDA CO., 1510271 ... NM-6
Alamo, 14570 ... NE-17
Alamo Oaks ... NE-18
Alberhill, 200 ... §J-18
Albion, 168 ... NI-2
Alderpoint, 186 ... NF-3
Alhambra, 83089 ... ‡E-8
Aliso Viejo, 47823 ... §L-13
Alleghany, 58 ... NH-8
Allendale, 1506 ... NK-6
Allensworth, 471 ... SE-8
Almanor ... NF-8
Almonte ... NE-12
Alpaugh, 1026 ... SE-8
Alpine, 14236 ... SM-15
ALPINE CO., 1175 ... NK-11
Alta Loma ... §D-15
Alta Sierra, 6911 ... NI-8
Alta Sierra, 70 ... SE-10
Altadena, 42777 ... ‡C-9
Alturas, 2827 ... NC-9
Alum Rock, 15536 ... NL-20
Amador City, 185 ... NK-8
AMADOR CO., 38091 ... NK-10
Ambler Pk., 600 ... *N-4
Amboy ... SH-17
American Canyon, 19454 ... NL-5
Anaheim, 336265 ... SK-12
Anchor Bay, 340 ... NJ-3
Anderson, 9932 ... NE-5
Angels Camp, 3836 ... NL-9
Angwin, 3051 ... NK-5
Annapolis ... NJ-3
Antelope, 45770 ... *F-4
Antioch, 102372 ... NL-6
Anza, 3014 ... SK-15
Apple Valley, 69135 ... SI-13
Applegate, 970 ... NI-8
Aptos, 6220 ... SB-3
Arbuckle, 3028 ... NI-6
Arcade, 42000 ... *G-4
Arcadia, 56364 ... ‡D-10
Arcata, 17231 ... ND-2
Arden Town, 55000 ... *H-4
Argus ... SE-13
Arleta ... ‡C-5
Armona, 4156 ... SD-8
Arnold, 3843 ... NL-9
Arrowhead Highlands, 1900 ... §C-19
Arroyo Grande, 17252 ... SG-6
Artesia, 16522 ... ‡H-9
Artois, 295 ... NH-6
Arvin, 19304 ... SG-10
Ashland, 21925 ... NG-16
Aspendell ... SH-2
Asti ... NJ-4
Atascadero, 28310 ... SF-6
Atherton, 6914 ... NK-15
Atwater, 28168 ... NN-9
Atwood ... §H-12
Auberry, 2369 ... SB-8
Auburn, 13330 ... NJ-8
August, 8390 ... *L-10
Avalon, 3728 ... SL-11
Avenal, 15505 ... SE-7
Avery, 646 ... NL-9
Avila Bch., 1627 ... SG-5
Avocado Hts., 15411 ... ‡E-10
Azusa, 46361 ... §D-11
Badger ... SC-9
Baker, 735 ... SF-16
Bakersfield, 347483 ... SF-9
Balboa ... §L-11
Baldwin Pk., 75390 ... ‡D-10
Ballico, 406 ... NN-9
Bangor, 646 ... NH-7
Banning, 29603 ... SJ-14
Banta, 550 ... NM-7
Bard, 230 ... SM-20
Barrett Jct., 180 ... SN-15
Barstow, 22639 ... SH-14
Bass Lake, 527 ... SA-8
Baxter, 100 ... NI-9
Bay Pt., 21349 ... NC-18
Bayliss ... NH-6
Bayside, 600 ... ND-2
Bayview, 2510 ... ND-2
Baywood Pk., 6000 ... SF-5
Bear Valley, 125 ... NM-10
Bear Valley, 121 ... NK-10
Beaumont, 36877 ... SJ-14
Beckwourth, 432 ... NG-9
Bel Air ... ‡E-5
Bel Marin Keys, 1650 ... NB-12
Belden, 22 ... NG-8
Bell, 35477 ... ‡F-8
Bell Gdns., 42072 ... ‡F-8
Bella Vista, 2781 ... NE-6
Bellflower, 76616 ... ‡H-9
Belmont, 25835 ... NJ-14
Belvedere, 2068 ... NE-12
Ben Lomond, 6234 ... SA-2
Benbow, 321 ... NF-2
Bend, 619 ... NF-6
Benicia, 26997 ... NL-6
Benton, 280 ... NM-14
Berenda ... SB-7
Berkeley, 112580 ... NM-5
Berry Creek, 1424 ... NH-7
Bethel Island, 2137 ... NL-7
Beverly Glen ... ‡E-5
Beverly Hills, 34109 ... SJ-11
Bieber, 312 ... ND-8
Big Bar ... NE-3
Big Bear City, 12304 ... SI-14
Big Bear Lake, 5019 ... SI-14
Big Bend, 102 ... ND-6
Big Creek, 175 ... SA-9
Big Oak Flat, 300 ... NM-10
Big Pine, 1756 ... SA-11
Big River, 1327 ... SI-20
Big Sur, 275 ... SD-3
Biggs, 1707 ... NH-7
Biola, 1623 ... SB-7
Birds Lndg. ... NL-6
Bishop, 3879 ... NN-14
Bitterwater ... SC-5
Black Pt., 470 ... NA-12
Blackhawk, 9354 ... NF-19
Blackwells Cor., 110 ... SF-7
Blairsden, 39 ... NG-9
Blocksburg, 50 ... NF-3
Bloomfield, 345 ... NK-4
Bloomington, 23851 ... §E-17
Blue Canyon, 75 ... NI-9
Blue Jay, 700 ... §B-20
Blue Lake, 1253 ... ND-2
Blythe, 20817 ... SK-19
Bodega, 220 ... NK-4
Bodega Bay, 1077 ... NK-4
Bodfish, 1956 ... SF-10
Bolinas, 1620 ... NL-4
Bolsa ... §J-11
Bolsa Knolls, 1950 ... SB-3
Bombay Bch., 295 ... SL-17
Bonita, 12538 ... †L-4
Bonsall, 3982 ... SL-13
Boonville, 1035 ... NI-3
Bootjack, 960 ... NN-1
Boron, 2253 ... SG-12
Borrego Sprs., 3429 ... SL-15
Bostonia, 15379 ... †H-6
Boulder Creek, 4923 ... SA-2
Boulevard, 315 ... SN-16
Bowman, 1100 ... NJ-8
Boyes Hot Sprs., 6656 ... NK-5
Bradbury, 1048 ... §D-11
Bradley, 93 ... SE-5
Branscomb, 100 ... NH-3
Brawley, 24953 ... SM-17
Bray ... NB-6
Brea, 39282 ... §G-11
Brentwood, 51481 ... NL-7
Briceland, 90 ... NF-2
Bridgeport, 575 ... NL-12
Bridgeville ... NE-2
Brisbane, 4282 ... NH-13
Broadmoor, 4176 ... NG-12
Brockway, 370 ... *F-9
Broderick ... *H-2
Brooks, 100 ... NJ-6
Brooktrails, 3235 ... NH-3
Browns Valley, 150 ... NI-7
Brownsville, 700 ... NH-8
Bryn Mawr ... §E-20
Bryson, 30 ... SE-5
Bryte ... *H-1
Buck Meadows, 31 ... NM-10
Buckhorn, 2429 ... NK-9
Buellton, 4828 ... SH-7
Buena ... †I-10
Buena Pk., 80530 ... ‡H-10
Buena Vista, 429 ... NK-8
Burbank, 103340 ... SJ-11
Burbank, 4926 ... NM-19
Burlingame, 28806 ... NI-14
Burney, 3154 ... ND-7
Burnt Ranch, 281 ... ND-3
Burrel ... SC-7
Burson ... NL-8
Butte City, 250 ... NH-6
BUTTE CO., 220000 ... NH-7
Butte Meadows, 40 ... NG-7
Buttonwillow, 1508 ... SF-8
Byron, 1277 ... NM-7
Cabazon, 2535 ... SJ-14
Cadiz ... SH-17
Cajon Jct. ... §A-17
Calabasas, 23058 ... ‡D-2
CALAVERAS CO., 45578 ... NK-10
Calexico, 38572 ... SN-18
Caliente ... SG-10
California City, 14120 ... SG-12
California Hot Sprs., 37 ... SE-10
California Pines, 520 ... NC-9
Calimesa, 7879 ... SJ-14
Calipatria, 7705 ... SL-17
Calistoga, 5155 ... NK-5
Callahan, 150 ... NC-4
Callender, 1262 ... SG-6
Calpella, 679 ... NI-3
Calpine, 205 ... NH-9
Calwa ... SC-19
Camarillo, 65201 ... SI-9
Cambria, 6032 ... SF-5
Cambrian Pk., 3282 ... NN-19
Cameron Pk., 18228 ... NJ-8
Camino, 1750 ... NJ-9
Camino Tassajara, 2197 ... NF-19
Camp Nelson, 97 ... SD-10
Camp Richardson ... NJ-10
Campbell, 39349 ... SA-3
Campo, 2684 ... SN-15
Campo Seco ... NL-8
Camptonville, 158 ... NH-8
Canby, 315 ... NC-8
Canoga Pk. ... ‡C-3
Cantil ... SF-12
Cantua Creek, 466 ... SC-6
Canyon ... NE-16
Canyon Lake, 10561 ... SK-13
Canyondam, 31 ... NF-8
Capay, 200 ... NJ-6
Capistrano Bch. ... §N-14
Cardiff-by-the-Sea ... †D-1
Caribou ... NG-8
Carlotta, 375 ... NE-2
Carlsbad, 105328 ... SL-13
Carmel Highlands, 940 ... SC-3
Carmel Pt., 500 ... *N-1
Carmel Valley Vil., 4407 ... SC-3
Carmel-by-the-Sea, 3722 ... SC-3
Carmichael, 61762 ... NK-7
Carpinteria, 13040 ... SI-8
Carson, 91714 ... ‡H-7
Cartago, 92 ... SD-11
Caruthers, 2497 ... SC-7
Casa de Oro, 12000 ... †J-6
Casitas Sprs., 800 ... SI-9
Caspar, 509 ... NH-2
Cassel, 207 ... ND-7
Castaic, 19015 ... SI-10
Castella ... ND-5
Castro Valley, 61388 ... NM-6
Castroville, 6481 ... SB-3
Cathedral City, 51200 ... SK-15
Catheys Valley, 825 ... NN-10
Cayucos, 2592 ... SF-5
Cazadero, 354 ... NK-4
Cecilville ... NC-4
Cedar Glen, 2100 ... §B-20
Cedar Grv. ... SK-2
Cedar Ridge, 600 ... NI-8
Cedarpines Pk., 850 ... §B-18
Cedarville, 514 ... NC-10
Centerville, 392 ... SC-8
Ceres, 45417 ... NM-8
Cerritos, 49041 ... ‡H-9
Chalfant Valley, 651 ... NN-14
Challenge, 250 ... NH-8
Charter Oak, 9310 ... §D-12
Chatsworth ... ‡B-3
Chatsworth Lake Manor, 1100 ... ‡C-2
Cherokee, 69 ... NH-7
Cherokee Strip, 227 ... SF-9
Cherryland, 14728 ... NG-17
Chester, 2144 ... NF-8
Chico, 86187 ... NG-6
Chilcoot, 230 ... NG-10
Chinese Camp, 126 ... NM-9
Chino, 77983 ... §F-14
Chino Hills, 74799 ... SJ-12
Chiriaco Summit ... SK-17
Cholame ... SE-6
Chowchilla, 18720 ... SA-7
Chualar, 1190 ... SC-4
Chula Vista, 243916 ... SN-14
Cima ... SF-17
Citrus, 10866 ... §D-11
Citrus Hts., 83301 ... NJ-7
Clairemont ... †H-2
Claremont, 34926 ... §D-13
Clarksburg, 418 ... NK-7
Clay, 1195 ... NK-8
Clayton, 10897 ... NL-6
Clear Creek, 30 ... NB-3
Clearlake, 15250 ... NJ-5
Clearlake Oaks, 2359 ... NI-5
Clements, 200 ... NL-8
Cleone, 618 ... NH-2
Clio, 66 ... NG-9
Clipper Gap, 330 ... NJ-8
Clipper Mills, 142 ... NH-8
Cloverdale, 8618 ... NJ-4
Cloverdale ... NE-5
Clovis, 95631 ... SB-8
Clyde, 678 ... NC-17
Coachella, 40704 ... SK-16
Coalinga, 13380 ... SD-6
Coarsegold, 1840 ... SA-8
Cobb, 1778 ... NJ-4
Codora, 30 ... NH-6
Coffee Creek, 100 ... ND-5
Cohasset, 847 ... NG-7
Cold Sprs., 181 ... NL-10
Coleville, 495 ... NK-11
Colfax, 1963 ... NI-8
College City, 290 ... NI-6
Collierville, 1934 ... NL-7
Collinsville, 90 ... NL-6
Colma, 1792 ... NH-12
Coloma, 529 ... NJ-8
Colton, 52154 ... SJ-13
Columbia, 2297 ... NL-9
Colusa, 5971 ... NI-6
COLUSA CO., 21419 ... NI-5
Commerce, 12823 ... ‡F-8
Comptche, 159 ... NI-3
Compton, 96455 ... ‡H-7
Concord, 122067 ... NL-6
Conejo, 300 ... SC-8
CONTRA COSTA CO., 1049025 ... NM-6
Cool, 1200 ... NJ-8
Copco, 80 ... NA-5
Copperopolis, 3671 ... NL-9
Corcoran, 24813 ... SD-8
Cordelia, 170 ... NL-6
Cornell ... ‡D-1
Corning, 7663 ... NG-6
Corona, 152374 ... SJ-13
Corona Del Mar ... §L-12
Coronado, 18912 ... SN-14
Coronita, 2608 ... §H-15
Corte Madera, 9253 ... ND-12
Coso Jct., 20 ... SD-12
Costa Mesa, 109960 ... §K-11
Cotati, 7265 ... NK-4
Coto de Caza, 14866 ... §L-15
Cottonwood, 3316 ... NF-6
Coulterville, 201 ... NM-10
Country Club, 9379 ... *L-9
Courtland, 355 ... NK-7
Covelo, 1255 ... NG-3
Covina, 47796 ... §E-12
Covington Mill, 30 ... ND-4
Cowan Hts., 4000 ... §I-13
Crescent City, 7643 ... NB-2
Crescent Mills, 196 ... NF-8
Cressey, 394 ... NN-9
Crest Pk., 600 ... §B-20
Crestline, 10770 ... §B-19
Crestmore, 4500 ... §E-17
Creston, 94 ... SF-6
Crestview ... NM-12
Crockett, 3094 ... NB-15
Cromberg, 261 ... NG-9
Crows Lndg., 355 ... NN-8
Cudahy, 23805 ... ‡G-8
Culver City, 38883 ... ‡F-5
Cummings ... NG-3
Cupertino, 58302 ... NM-17
Cutler, 5000 ... SC-9
Cuyama ... SH-8
Cypress, 47802 ... ‡I-9
Daggett, 450 ... SH-14
Dairyville, 1000 ... NF-6
Dales ... NF-6
Daly City, 101123 ... NG-12
Dana, 100 ... ND-7
Dana Pt., 33351 ... §N-14
Danville, 42039 ... NM-6
Dardanelle ... NK-11
Darrah, 500 ... NN-11
Darwin, 43 ... SD-12
Davenport, 408 ... SB-2
Davis, 65622 ... NK-7
Davis Creek, 110 ... NB-10
Day, 50 ... NC-7
Dayton, 250 ... NH-6
De Luz ... §N-19
Death Valley Jct., 20 ... SD-15
Deep Sprs. ... NN-15
Del Aire, 10001 ... ‡G-6
Del Dios, 355 ... †C-3
Del Mar, 4161 ... SM-13
Del Monte Forest, 4514 ... *M-1
DEL NORTE CO., 28610 ... NB-2
Del Rey, 1639 ... SC-8
Del Rey Oaks, 1624 ... SC-3
Delano, 53041 ... SE-9
Delevan ... NH-6
Delhi, 10755 ... NN-8
Denair, 4404 ... NN-8
Denny, 30 ... ND-3
Derby Acres, 322 ... SG-8
Descanso, 1423 ... SM-15
Desert Ctr., 204 ... SK-18
Desert Hot Sprs., 25938 ... SJ-15
Desert Shores, 1104 ... SL-16
Desert View Highlands, 2360 ... SH-11
Devore ... SI-13
Di Giorgio, 450 ... SG-10
Diablo, 1158 ... NE-18
Diamond Bar, 55544 ... §F-12
Diamond Sprs., 11037 ... NJ-8
Dillon Bch., 283 ... NK-4
Dinsmore, 50 ... NE-3
Dinuba, 21453 ... SC-8
Dixon, 18351 ... NK-6
Dobbins, 624 ... NH-8
Dollar Pt., 1215 ... *F-8
Dorrington, 609 ... NK-10
Dorris, 939 ... NA-6
Dos Palos, 4950 ... SB-6
Dos Rios, 100 ... NG-3
Douglas City, 713 ... NE-4
Douglas Flat, 200 ... NL-9
Downey, 111772 ... SJ-11
Downieville, 282 ... NH-8
Doyle, 678 ... NG-10
Drakesbad ... NF-7
Drytown, 167 ... NK-8
Duarte, 21321 ... §D-11
Dublin, 46036 ... NM-6
Ducor, 612 ... SE-9
Dulzura, 220 ... SN-15
Dunlap, 300 ... SC-9
Dunmovin ... SD-12
Dunnigan, 1416 ... NJ-6
Dunsmuir, 1650 ... NC-6
Durham, 5518 ... NH-6
Dutch Flat, 160 ... NI-9
Eagle Mtn., 580 ... SJ-17
Eagleville, 59 ... NC-10
Earlimart, 8537 ... SE-9
Earp, 70 ... SI-20
E. Blythe ... SK-20
E. Foothills, 8269 ... NL-20
E. Highlands ... §D-20
E. La Mirada, 9757 ... ‡G-10
E. Los Angeles, 126496 ... ‡F-8
E. Nicolaus, 225 ... NJ-7
E. Palo Alto, 28155 ... NK-16
E. Pasadena, 6144 ... ‡D-9
E. Quincy, 2489 ... NG-8
E. Richmond Hts., 3280 ... ND-14
Easton, 2083 ... SC-8
Edgewood, 43 ... NC-5
Edison, 400 ... SF-10
Eel Rock ... NF-2
El Cajon, 99478 ... SM-14
El Centro, 42598 ... SM-17
El Cerrito, 23549 ... NL-5
El Cerrito, 5100 ... §H-16
El Dorado, 1300 ... NJ-8
EL DORADO CO., 181058 ... NK-9
El Granada, 5467 ... NJ-12
El Modena ... §I-12
El Monte, 113475 ... ‡E-10
El Nido, 330 ... SA-6
El Portal, 474 ... NM-11
El Rio, 7198 ... SI-9
El Segundo, 16654 ... ‡G-5
El Sobrante, 12669 ... NC-14
El Sueno, 2000 ... †B-3
Elk ... NI-2
Elk Creek, 163 ... NH-5
Elk Grv., 153015 ... NK-7
Ellwood, 7800 ... †B-1
Elmira, 188 ... NK-6
Elverta, 5492 ... *F-2
Emerald Bay, 1100 ... §L-13
Emerald L. Hills, 4278 ... NK-15
Emeryville, 10080 ... NE-14
Emigrant Gap ... NI-9
Empire, 4189 ... NM-8
Encinitas, 59518 ... SM-13
Encino ... ‡D-4
Escalon, 7132 ... NM-8
Escondido, 143911 ... SL-14
Esparto, 3108 ... NJ-6
Essex ... SH-18
Estrella ... SE-6
Etiwanda ... §D-16
Etna, 737 ... NC-4
Ettersburg ... NF-2
Eucalyptus Hills, 5313 ... †G-6
Eugene ... NM-8
Eureka, 27191 ... ND-2
Exeter, 10334 ... SD-9
Fair Oaks, 30912 ... *G-5
Fairbanks Ranch, 3148 ... †E-2
Fairfax, 7441 ... NL-5
Fairfax, 991 ... SM-8
Fairfield, 105321 ... NL-6
Fairmead, 1447 ... SB-7
Fairmont Ter., 4000 ... NG-16
Fairview, 10003 ... NH-17
Fairview, 10 ... SE-10
Fall River Mills, 573 ... ND-7
Fallbrook, 30534 ... SL-13
Farmersville, 10588 ... SD-9
Farmington, 207 ... NL-8
Fawnskin, 500 ... SI-14
Feather Falls ... NH-8
Fellows, 106 ... SG-8
Felton, 4057 ... SB-3
Fernbridge, 200 ... NE-1
Fernbrook ... †E-7
Ferndale, 1371 ... NE-1
Fernwood, 500 ... ‡E-3
Fiddletown, 235 ... NK-9
Fieldbrook, 859 ... ND-2
Fig Gdn. ... SA-17
Fillmore, 15002 ... SI-10
Finley ... NI-4
Firebaugh, 7549 ... SB-6
Fish Camp, 59 ... NN-11
Five Pts., 110 ... SC-7
Florence, 25000 ... ‡G-7
Florin, 47513 ... *I-3
Flournoy, 101 ... NG-5
Folsom, 72203 ... NJ-8
Fontana, 196069 ... §D-17
Foothill Farms, 33121 ... *F-4
Forbestown, 320 ... NH-8
Ford City, 4278 ... SG-8
Forest, 50 ... NH-8
Forest Falls, 550 ... SJ-14
Forest Glen, 5 ... NF-3
Forest Meadows, 1249 ... NL-9
Forest Ranch, 1184 ... NG-7
Foresthill, 1483 ... NI-8
Forestville, 3293 ... NK-4
Forks of Salmon, 70 ... NC-3
Ft. Bidwell, 173 ... NB-10
Ft. Bragg, 7273 ... NH-2
Ft. Dick, 200 ... NA-2
Ft. Jones, 839 ... NB-4
Ft. Seward, 160 ... NF-3
Fortuna, 11926 ... NE-2
Foster City, 30567 ... NI-15
Fountain Valley, 55313 ... ‡J-10
Fouts Sprs. ... NH-5
Fowler, 5570 ... SC-8
Frazier Pk., 2691 ... SH-9

***, †, ‡, §, ◊ See explanation under state title in this index.**
County and parish names are listed in capital letters & boldface type.
Independent cities (not included in a county) are listed in italics.

Freedom, 3070 SB-3
Freeport, 38 *J-2
Fremont, 214089 NM-6
French Camp, 3376 NM-7
French Gulch, 346 NE-5
Freshwater, 300 ND-2
Fresno, 494665 SC-8
FRESNO CO., 930450 SC-7
Friant, 509 SB-8
Fruitridge Manor *I-3
Fruto NH-5
Fullerton, 135161 SJ-12
Fulton, 541 NK-4
Furnace Creek, 24 SC-14
Galt, 23647 NL-7
Garberville, 913 NF-2
Garden Acres, 10648 *L-10
Garden Grv., 170883 SK-12
Garden Valley, 700 NJ-8
Gardena, 58829 ‡H-6
Garey, 68 SH-6
Gas Pt., 30 NF-5
Gasquet, 661 NA-2
Gaviota, 70 SI-7
Gazelle, 70 NC-5
Genesee, 150 NG-9
Georgetown, 2367 NJ-8
Gerber, 1060 NG-6
Geyserville, 862 NJ-4
Gilroy, 48821 SB-4
Glamis SM-18
Glen Ellen, 784 NK-5
Glencoe, 300 NK-9
Glendale, 191719 SJ-11
Glendora, 50073 §D-12
Glenhaven, 360 NI-4
Glenn, 110 NH-6
GLENN CO., 28122 NH-5
Glennville, 210 SE-10
Glenview, 160 ‡D-3
Goffs SG-18
Gold River, 7912 *G-5
Gold Run, 200 NI-8
Golden Hills, 8656 SG-10
Goleta, 29888 SI-7
Gonzales, 8187 SC-4
Goodyears Bar, 68 NH-8
Gorman, 50 SH-10
Goshen, 3006 SD-8
Graeagle, 737 NG-9
Granada Hills ‡B-4
Grand Ter., 12040 §E-18
Grangeville, 469 SD-8
Granite Bay, 20402 *E-6
Granite Hills, 3035 †I-7
Graniteville, 11 NH-9
Grass Valley, 12860 NI-8
Graton, 1707 NK-4
Grayson, 952 NM-8
Greeley Hill, 915 NM-10
Green Brae, 3400 ND-12
Greenacres, 5566 SL-5
Greenfield, 16330 SD-4
Greenview, 201 NB-4
Greenville, 1129 NF-8
Greenwood, 600 NJ-8
Grenada, 367 NB-5
Gridley, 6584 NH-7
Grimes, 391 NI-6
Grizzly Flat, 1066 NK-9
Groveland, 601 NM-10
Grover Bch., 13156 SG-6
Guadalupe, 7080 SG-6
Gualala, 1500 NJ-3
Guasti §E-15
Guerneville, 4534 NK-4
Guernsey SD-8
Guinda, 254 NJ-6
Gustine, 5520 SA-5
Hacienda Hts., 54038 ‡F-10
Half Moon Bay, 11324 NN-5
Hamburg, 140 NB-4
Hamilton Branch, 537 NF-8
Hamilton City, 1759 NG-6
Hammond SM-1
Hanford, 53967 SD-8
Happy Camp, 1190 NB-3
Harbor City ‡I-6
Hardwick, 138 SC-8
Harmony SF-5
Harris NF-3
Harvard SG-15
Hat Creek, 309 ND-7
Havasu Lake, 410 SH-20
Havilah SF-10
Hawaiian Gdns., 14254 ‡H-9
Hawkinsville, 20 NB-5
Hawthorne, 84293 ‡G-6
Hayfork, 2368 NE-4
Hayward, 144186 NM-6
Healdsburg, 11254 NJ-4
Heber, 4275 SM-17
Helena NE-4
Helendale, 700 SH-13
Helm SC-7
Hemet, 78657 SK-14
Henderson Vil., 200 NL-7
Herald, 1184 NK-8
Hercules, 24060 NC-15
Herlong, 298 NF-10
Hermosa Bch., 19506 ‡H-5
Herndon SA-17
Hesperia, 90173 SI-13
Hi Vista SH-12
Hickman, 641 NM-9
Hidden Hills, 1856 ‡D-2
Hidden Valley, 1400 NJ-8
Hidden Valley Lake, 5579 NJ-5
Highgrove, 3988 §F-18
Highland, 53104 SJ-13
Highway City SB-17
Hillsborough, 10825 NI-14
Hilt, 30 NA-5
Hinkley, 1000 SG-13
Hobart Mills NH-10
Hodge SH-13
Hollister, 34928 SB-4
Hollywood ‡E-6
Hollywood by the Sea †C-8
Holt NL-7
Holtville, 5939 SM-18
Home Gdns., 11570 §H-16
Homewood, 350 NI-10
Honcut, 370 NI-7
Honeydew, 80 NF-2
Hooker NF-5
Hoopa, 1200 ND-3
Hope Ranch, 1600 †B-3
Hopeton NN-9
Hopland, 756 NI-4
Hornbrook, 248 NA-5
Hornitos, 75 NN-10
Horse Creek NB-4
Hughson, 6640 NM-8
HUMBOLDT CO., 134623 NE-2
Humboldt Hill, 3414 NE-2
Hume SB-10
Humphreys Sta. SB-8
Huntington Bch., 189992 SK-12
Huntington Pk., 58114 ‡F-7
Huron, 6754 SD-7
Hyampom, 241 NE-3
Hydesville, 1237 NE-2
Idlewild, 43 SE-10
Idria SC-6
Idyllwild, 2200 SK-15
Igo NE-5
Imperial, 14758 SM-17
Imperial Bch., 26324 SN-14
IMPERIAL CO., 174528 SM-18
Incline, 60 NM-1
Independence, 669 SB-11
Indian Wells, 4958 SK-16
Indio, 76036 SK-16
Indio Hills, 972 SG-2
Industry, 219 §F-11
Inglenook, 50 NH-2
Inglewood, 109673 SJ-11
Ingot NE-6
Inverness, 1304 NL-4
INYO CO., 18546 SC-13
Inyokern, 1099 SF-12
Ione, 7918 NK-8
Iowa Hill NI-8
Irvine, 212375 SK-12
Irwin, 1050 NN-8
Irwindale, 1422 §D-11
Isla Vista, 23096 SI-7
Island Mtn. NG-3
Isleton, 804 NL-7
Ivanhoe, 4495 SD-9
Ivanpah SF-18
Jackson, 4651 NK-9
Jacumba, 561 SN-16
Jamesburg SC-4
Jamestown, 3433 NL-9
Jamul, 6163 SN-14
Janesville, 1408 NF-9
Jenner, 136 NK-3
Johannesburg, 172 SF-12
Johnsondale SE-10
Johnstonville, 1024 NF-9
Johnsville, 20 NG-9
Jonesville NF-7
Joshua Tree, 7414 SJ-16
Julian, 1502 SM-15
Junction City, 680 NE-4
June Lake, 629 NM-12
Jurupa Valley, 94235 §F-16
Kaweah SM-1
Keddie, 66 NG-8
Keeler, 66 SC-12
Keene, 431 SG-10
Kelsey, 250 NJ-8
Kelseyville, 3353 NI-4
Kelso SG-17
Kennedy, 3254 *M-10
Kensington, 5077 ND-14
Kentfield, 6485 ND-11
Kenwood, 1028 NK-5
Kerman, 13544 SC-7
KERN CO., 839631 SF-10
Kernville, 1395 SE-11
Keswick, 451 NE-5
Kettleman City, 1439 SE-7
Keyes, 5601 NM-8
King City, 12874 SD-5
Kings Bch., 3796 NI-10
KINGS CO., 152982 SD-7
Kingsburg, 11382 SC-8
Kirkville NJ-6
Kirkwood, 158 NJ-10
Kirkwood, 100 NG-6
Kit Carson NJ-10
Klamath, 779 NB-2
Klamath Glen, 290 NB-2
Klamath River NB-4
Kneeland, 30 ND-2
Knights Ferry, 700 NM-9
Knights Lndg., 995 NJ-7
Knightsen, 1568 NL-7
Kramer Jct., 200 SG-13
Kyburz, 150 NJ-10
La Cañada Flintridge, 20246 ‡C-7
La Crescenta, 13000 ‡C-7
La Grange NM-9
La Habra, 60239 §G-11
La Habra Hts., 5325 §G-11
La Honda, 928 SA-2
La Jolla †H-1
La Mesa, 57065 †I-5
La Mirada, 48527 ‡G-10
La Palma, 15568 ‡H-10
La Porte, 26 NH-8
La Presa, 34169 †J-5
La Puente, 39816 ‡E-10
La Quinta, 37467 SK-16
La Riviera, 10802 *H-4
La Verne, 31063 SJ-12
Ladera, 1426 NL-16
Ladera Hts., 6498 ‡F-6
Ladera Ranch, 350 §L-15
Lafayette, 23893 ND-16
Laguna Bch., 22723 SK-12
Laguna Hills, 30344 §L-14
Laguna Niguel, 62979 §M-14
Laguna Woods, 16192 §L-13
L. Alpine NK-10
L. Arrowhead, 12424 §B-20
Lake City, 61 NB-10
LAKE CO., 64665 NI-4
L. Elsinore, 51821 SK-13
L. Forest, 77264 SK-12
L. Hughes, 649 SH-11
L. Isabella, 3466 SF-11
L. Los Angeles, 12328 SH-12
L. Nacimiento, 2411 SE-5
Lake of the Pines, 3917 NI-8
Lake View Ter. ‡B-5
L. Wildwood, 4991 NI-8
Lakehead, 461 ND-5
Lakeland Vil., 11541 §K-18
Lakeport, 4753 NI-4
Lakeshore SA-9
Lakeside, 20648 SM-14
Lakeview, 2104 SJ-14
Lakewood, 80048 ‡H-9
Lamont, 15120 SG-10
Lanare, 589 SC-7
Lancaster, 156633 SH-11
Landers, 2300 SI-15
Larkspur, 11926 ND-11
Las Cruces, 70 SI-7
Las Flores, 5971 §L-15
LASSEN CO., 34895 NE-9
Lathrop, 18023 NM-7
Laton, 1824 SC-8
Lawndale, 32769 ‡H-5
Laytonville, 1227 NG-3
Le Grand, 1659 SA-7
Lebec, 1468 SH-10
Lee Vining, 222 NL-12
Leggett, 122 NG-2
Lemon Cove, 308 SC-9
Lemon Cove SN-1
Lemon Grv., 25320 †J-5
Lemon Hts., 2800 §I-13
Lemoore, 24531 SD-8
Lennox, 22753 ‡G-6
Lenwood, 3543 SH-14
Leona Valley, 1607 ‡M-6
Lewiston, 1193 NE-4
Likely, 63 NC-9
Lincoln, 42819 NJ-7
Lincoln Acres, 1650 †K-4
Lincoln Vil., 4381 *K-9
Linda, 17773 NI-7
Linden, 1784 NL-8
Lindsay, 11768 SD-9
Litchfield, 195 NF-9
Little Lake, 50 SE-12
Little River, 117 NI-2
Little Valley ND-8
Littlerock, 1377 SI-12
Live Oak, 8392 NI-7
Live Oak Sprs., 240 SN-16
Livermore, 80968 NM-6
Livingston, 13058 NN-9
Loch Lomond, 300 NJ-4
Lockeford, 3233 NL-8
Lockwood, 379 SE-5
Lodgepole SL-2
Lodi, 62134 NL-7
Lodoga, 197 NI-5
Logan Hts. †J-3
Loleta, 783 NE-1
Loma Linda, 23261 SJ-13
Loma Rica, 2368 NI-7
Lomita, 20256 ‡I-6
Lompoc, 42434 SH-6
London, 1869 SC-8
Lone Pine, 2035 SC-11
Long Barn, 155 NL-10
Long Bch., 462257 SK-11
Longvale, 50 NH-3
Lookout, 84 NC-8
Loomis, 6430 NJ-8
Loraine SF-11
Los Alamitos, 11449 ‡I-9
Los Alamos, 1890 SH-6
Los Altos, 28976 NN-6
Los Altos Hills, 7922 NL-16
Los Angeles, 3792621 SJ-11
LOS ANGELES CO., 9818605 SI-12
Los Banos, 35972 SB-5
Los Gatos, 29413 SA-3
Los Molinos, 2037 NG-6
Los Nietos, 8200 ‡F-9
Los Olivos, 1132 SH-7
Los Osos, 14276 SF-5
Los Ranchitos, 425 NC-11
Los Serranos §F-14
Lost Hills, 2412 SF-8
Lost Lake, 110 SJ-20
Lotus, 700 NJ-8
Lower Lake, 1294 NJ-5
Loyalton, 769 NH-10
Loyola, 3261 NL-17
Lucas Valley, 4000 NC-11
Lucerne, 3067 NI-4
Lucerne Valley, 5811 SI-14
Ludlow SH-16
Lynwood, 69772 ‡G-7
Lytle Creek, 701 §B-16
Macdoel, 133 NB-6
Mad River, 420 NE-3
Madeline ND-9
Madera, 61416 SB-7
Madera Acres, 9163 SB-7
MADERA CO., 150865 SB-7
Madison, 503 NJ-6
Magalia, 11310 NG-7
Malibu, 12645 SJ-10
Mammoth Lakes, 8234 NM-12
Manchester, 195 NI-2
Manhattan Bch., 35135 SJ-11
Manteca, 67096 NM-8
Manton, 347 NF-6
Maricopa, 1154 SG-8
Marin City, 2666 NE-12
MARIN CO., 252409 NL-4
Marina, 19718 SC-3
Marina del Rey, 8866 ‡F-5
Marinwood, 2300 NB-11
Mariposa, 2173 NN-10
MARIPOSA CO., 18251 SA-7
Markleeville, 210 NJ-11
Marshall NL-4
Martell, 282 NK-9
Martinez, 35824 NL-6
Marysville, 12072 NI-7
Massack NG-8
Maxwell, 1103 NI-6
Maywood, 27395 ‡F-8
McArthur, 338 ND-7
McCloud, 1101 NC-6
McFarland, 12707 SE-9
McKinleyville, 15177 ND-2
McKittrick, 115 SF-8
Mead Valley, 18510 §H-19
Meadow Valley, 464 NG-8
Meadow Vista, 3217 NI-8
Mecca, 8577 SK-16
Meeks Bay NI-10
Meiners Oaks, 3571 SI-9
Mendocino, 894 NH-2
MENDOCINO CO., 87841 NH-3
Mendota, 11014 SB-6
Menifee, 77519 SK-14
Menlo Pk., 32026 NN-5
Merced, 78958 SA-6
MERCED CO., 255793 SA-6
Meridian, 358 NI-6
Mesa Verde, 1023 SK-19
Mettler, 136 SG-9
Middletown, 1323 NJ-5
Midpines, 1204 NN-10
Midway City, 8485 ‡J-10
Milford, 167 NF-9
Mill Creek, 20 NF-7
Mill Valley, 13903 NL-5
Millbrae, 21532 NI-13
Millville, 727 NE-6
Milo SD-10
Milpitas, 66790 NN-6
Milton NL-8
Mineral, 123 NF-7
Mineral King SC-10
Minkler, 1003 SC-8
Mira Mesa †F-3
Mira Monte, 6854 SI-9
Miracle Hot Sprs. SF-10
Miranda, 520 NF-2
Mission Bch. †I-1
Mission Hills ‡B-4
Mission Viejo, 93305 SK-12
Mi-Wuk Vil., 941 NL-10
Moccasin NM-10
Modesto, 201165 NM-8
Modjeska, 500 §J-15
MODOC CO., 9686 NB-8
Mojave, 4238 SG-11
Mokelumne Hill, 646 NK-9
Mono City, 170 NL-12
MONO CO., 14202 NL-13
Mono Hot Sprs. SA-9
Mono Vil. NK-2
Monrovia, 36590 ‡D-10
Montague, 1443 NB-5
Montalvin Manor, 2876 NC-14
Montalvo †B-9
Montara, 2909 NJ-12
Montclair, 36664 §E-14
Monte Nido, 850 ‡E-2
Monte Rio, 1152 NK-4
Monte Sereno, 3341 NN-18
Montebello, 62500 ‡F-9
Montecito, 8965 SI-8
Monterey, 27810 SC-3
MONTEREY CO., 415057 SD-4
Monterey Pk., 60269 ‡E-8
Montgomery Creek, 163 ND-6
Montrose, 4100 ‡C-7
Moorpark, 34421 SI-10
Morada, 3828 *K-10
Moraga, 16016 NE-16
Moreno Valley, 193365 SJ-14
Morgan Hill, 37882 SA-3
Mormon Bar, 130 NN-10
Morongo Valley, 3552 SJ-15
Morro Bay, 10234 SF-5
Moss Bch., 3103 NJ-12
Mt. Baldy, 200 §B-14
Mt. Bullion NN-10
Mt. Hebron, 95 NB-6
Mt. Helix, 6400 †I-6
Mt. Shasta, 3394 NC-6
Mountain Ctr., 63 SK-15
Mountain Gate, 943 NE-5
Mountain Mesa, 777 SF-11
Mountain Pass SF-17
Mountain Ranch, 1628 NL-9
Mountain View, 74066 NL-17
Mountain View, 1500 NC-16
Mugginsville, 50 NB-4
Murphys, 2213 NL-9
Murrieta, 103466 SK-14
Murrieta Hot Sprs., 2948 §L-20
Muscoy, 10644 §D-18
Myers Flat, 146 NF-2
Napa, 76915 NK-5
NAPA CO., 136484 NK-5
National City, 58582 SN-14
Navarro, 250 NI-3
Needles, 4844 SH-19
Nelson, 150 NH-6
Nevada City, 3068 NI-8
NEVADA CO., 98764 NH-9
New Cuyama, 517 SG-8
New Pine Creek, 98 NA-10
Newark, 42573 NM-6
Newberry Sprs., 1500 SH-15
Newcastle, 1224 NJ-8
Newell, 449 NB-7
Newman, 10224 SA-5
Newport Bch., 85186 SK-12
Newville NG-5
Nicasio, 96 NL-4
Nice, 2731 NI-4
Nicolaus, 211 NJ-7
Niland, 1006 SL-17
Nipomo, 16714 SG-6
Nipton, 25 SF-18
Norco, 27063 SJ-13
Nord, 320 NG-6
Norden NI-9
N. Bloomfield NH-8
N. Edwards, 1058 SG-12
N. Fair Oaks, 14687 NK-15
N. Fork, 500 SA-8
N. Highlands, 42694 *F-4
N. Hills ‡C-4
N. Hollywood ‡D-6
N. Richmond, 3717 ND-13
N. San Juan, 269 NH-8
N. Shore, 3477 SK-16
N. Tustin, 24044 §I-13
Northridge ‡C-4
Norwalk, 105549 ‡H-9
Novato, 51904 NL-5
Nubieber, 50 ND-8
Nuevo, 6447 §I-20
Nyland, 2200 †B-9
Oak Grv., 100 SL-14
Oak Hills, 8879 SI-13
Oak Pk., 13811 ‡C-1
Oak Run, 250 NE-6
Oak View, 4066 SI-9
Oakdale, 20675 NM-8
Oakhurst, 2829 NN-11
Oakland, 390724 NM-5
Oakley, 35432 NL-6
Oakville, 71 NK-5
Oasis, 6890 SK-16
O'Brien, 30 ND-5
Occidental, 1115 NK-4
Ocean Bch. †J-1
Oceano, 7286 SG-6
Oceanside, 167086 SL-13
Ocotillo, 266 SM-16
Ocotillo Wells, 200 SL-16
Oildale, 32684 SF-9
Ojai, 7461 SI-9
Olancha, 192 SD-12
Old River, 200 SG-9
Old Sta., 51 NE-7
Olinda NE-5
Olinda §G-12
Olive §H-12
Olivehurst, 13656 NI-7
Olympic Valley *F-8
Omo Ranch NK-9
O'Neals SA-8
Ono, 60 NE-5
Ontario, 163924 SJ-12
Onyx, 475 SE-11
Orange, 136416 §I-12
ORANGE CO., 3010232 SK-12
Orange Cove, 9078 SC-9
Orange Pk. Acres §I-13
Orangevale, 33960 *F-6
Orcutt, 28905 SH-6
Ordbend, 80 NH-6
Oregon House, 300 NI-8
Orick, 357 NC-2
Orinda, 17643 NE-16
Orland, 7291 NG-6
Orleans, 375 NC-3
Oro Fino, 30 NB-4
Oro Grande, 310 SH-13
Orosi, 8770 SC-9
Oroville, 15546 NH-7
Otay †M-4
Outingdale, 400 NK-9
Oxnard, 197899 SJ-9
Pacheco, 3685 NC-17
Pacific NJ-9
Pacific Bch. †H-1
Pacific Grv., 15041 SC-3
Pacific Palisades ‡E-4
Pacifica, 37234 NM-5
Pacoima ‡B-5
Paicines SB-4
Pajaro, 3070 SB-3
Pala, 1050 SL-14
Palermo, 5382 NH-7
Palm City †M-4
Palm Desert, 48445 SK-15
Palm Sprs., 44552 SJ-15
Palmdale, 152750 SH-11
Palo Alto, 64403 NN-5
Palo Cedro, 1269 NE-6
Palo Verde, 171 SK-19
Paloma, 300 NL-9
Palomar Pk., 530 NJ-15
Palos Verdes Estates, 13438 ‡I-5
Paradise, 26218 NG-7
Paramount, 54098 ‡H-8
Park Vil., 100 SC-14
Parkfield SE-6
Parkway, 14670 *I-2
Parkwood, 2268 SB-7
Parlier, 14494 SC-8
Pasadena, 137122 SJ-11
Paskenta, 112 NG-5
Paso Robles, 29793 SF-6
Patrick Creek NA-2
Patterson, 20413 NN-8
Pauma Valley, 800 SL-14
Paxton, 14 NG-8
Paynes Creek, 57 NF-6
Paynesville NJ-11
Peanut NE-4
Pearblossom, 700 SI-12
Pearland ‡M-9
Pearsonville, 17 SE-12
Pebble Bch. SC-3
Penn Valley, 1621 NI-8
Penngrove, 2522 NK-4
Pennington NI-6
Penryn, 831 NJ-8
Pepperwood, 60 NE-2
Perris, 68386 SK-13
Pescadero, 643 SA-2
Petaluma, 57941 NL-4
Peters, 672 NL-8
Petrolia NF-1
Phelan, 14304 SI-13
Phillipsville, 140 NF-2
Philo, 349 NI-3
Piñon Hills, 7272 SI-12
Pico Rivera, 62942 ‡F-9
Piedmont, 10667 NE-15
Piedra, 270 SB-8
Piercy NG-2
Pilot Hill, 800 NJ-8
Pine Grv., 2219 NK-9
Pine Hills, 3131 ND-2
Pine Mtn. Club, 2315 SH-9
Pine Valley, 1510 SM-15
Pinehurst, 150 SC-9
Pineridge, 200 SB-9
Pinole, 18390 NC-14
Pioneer Pt. SE-13
Piru, 2063 SI-10
Pismo Bch., 7655 SG-6
Pittsburg, 63264 NL-6
Pittville ND-7
Pixley, 3310 SE-9
Placentia, 50533 §H-12
PLACER CO., 348432 NI-9
Placerville, 10389 NJ-9
Plainview, 945 SD-9
Planada, 4584 SA-6
Plantation, 65 NJ-3
Plaster City, 60 SM-17
Platina, 100 NF-4
Playa Del Rey ‡G-5
Pleasant Grv., 250 NJ-7
Pleasant Hill, 33152 NL-6
Pleasanton, 70285 NM-6
PLUMAS CO., 20007 NF-9
Plymouth, 1005 NK-8
Point Arena, 449 NJ-2
Point Reyes Sta., 848 NL-4
Pollock Pines, 6871 NJ-9
Pomona, 149058 SJ-12
Pond, 200 SE-9
Pondosa NC-7
Pope Valley, 250 NK-5
Port Costa, 190 NB-16
Port Hueneme, 21723 SJ-9
Porter Ranch ‡B-3
Porterville, 54165 SD-9
Portola, 2104 NG-9
Portola Hills, 6391 §K-15
Portola Valley, 4353 NL-15
Potrero, 656 SN-15
Potter Valley, 646 NH-4
Poway, 47811 SM-14
Pozo SF-6
Prather SB-8
Princeton, 303 NH-6
Proberta, 267 NF-6
Prunedale, 17560 SB-3
Pulga, 30 NG-7
Pumpkin Ctr., 520 SG-9
Quartz Hill, 10912 SH-11
Quincy, 1728 NG-8
Rackerby, 350 NH-7
Rail Road Flat, 475 NK-9
Rainbow, 1832 SL-14
Raisin City, 380 SC-7
Ramona, 20292 SM-14
Ranchita, 300 SL-15
Rancho Calaveras, 5325 NL-8
Rancho Cordova, 64776 NK-7
Rancho Cucamonga, 165269 §D-15
Rancho Mirage, 17218 SK-15
Rancho Murieta, 5488 NK-8
Rancho Palos Verdes, 41643 ‡J-6
Rancho Rinconada NM-18
Rancho San Diego, 21208 †J-6
Rancho Santa Fe, 3117 SM-14
Rancho Santa Margarita, 47853 §K-16
Randsburg, 69 SF-12
Ravendale NE-10
Raymond, 200 SA-7
Red Bank NF-5
Red Bluff, 14076 NF-6
Red Hill, 2800 §J-13
Red Mtn., 100 SF-12
Redcrest, 89 NE-2
Redding, 89861 NE-5
Redlands, 68747 SJ-14
Redondo Bch., 66748 SJ-11
Redway, 1225 NF-2
Redwood City, 76815 NN-5
Redwood Valley, 1729 NI-3
Reedley, 24194 SC-8
Requa, 180 NB-2
Rescue, 1200 NJ-8
Reseda ‡C-4
Rialto, 99171 SJ-13
Rice SJ-19
Richardson Sprs., 100 NG-6
Richfield, 306 NG-6
Richgrove, 2882 SE-9
Richmond, 103701 ND-13
Richvale, 244 NH-7
Ridgecrest, 27616 SF-12
Rimforest, 700 §B-19
Rio del Mar, 9216 SB-3
Rio Dell, 3368 NE-2
Rio Linda, 15106 *F-3
Rio Oso, 356 NJ-7
Rio Vista, 7360 NL-7
Ripley, 692 SK-19
Ripon, 14297 NM-8
Ripperdan, 350 SB-7
River Pines, 379 NK-9
Riverbank, 22678 NM-8
Riverdale, 3153 SC-7
Riverdale Pk., 1128 *J-8
Riverside, 303871 SJ-13
RIVERSIDE CO., 2189641 SJ-16
Robbins, 323 NJ-7
Rocklin, 56974 NJ-8
Rodeo, 8679 NB-15
Rohnert Pk., 40971 NK-4
Rolinda, 200 SC-7
Rolling Hills, 1860 ‡I-6
Rolling Hills Estates, 8067 ‡I-6
Rollingwood, 2969 NC-14
Romoland, 1684 §I-20
Rosamond, 18150 SH-11
Rosedale, 14058 SF-9
Roseland, 6325 *L-6
Rosemead, 53764 ‡E-9
Rosemont, 22681 *H-4
Rosemont, 800 †E-6
Roseville, 118788 NJ-7
Ross, 2415 NC-11
Rossmoor, 10244 ‡I-9
Rough And Ready, 963 NI-8
Round Mtn., 155 NE-6
Rovana NN-13
Rowland Hts., 48993 §F-11
Rumsey, 200 NJ-5
Running Sprs., 4862 SI-14
Ruth, 195 NF-3
Rutherford, 164 NK-5
Ryde, 200 NL-7
Sacramento, 466488 NK-7
SACRAMENTO CO., 1418788 NK-8
Sage SK-14
St. Helena, 5814 NK-5
Salida, 13722 NM-8
Salinas, 150441 SC-3
Salmon Creek, 86 NK-4
Salton City, 3763 SL-16
Salton Sea Bch., 422 SL-16
Salyer, 500 ND-3
Samoa, 258 ND-2
San Andreas, 2783 NL-9
San Anselmo, 12336 NC-11
San Antonio Hts., 3371 §D-14
San Ardo, 517 SD-5
SAN BENITO CO., 55269 SC-5
San Bernardino, 209924 SJ-13
SAN BERNARDINO CO., 2035210 SG-16
San Bruno, 41114 NM-5
San Carlos, 28406 NN-5
San Clemente, 63522 SL-13
San Diego, 1307402 SN-14
SAN DIEGO CO., 3095313 SM-15
San Dimas, 33371 §D-12
San Fernando, 23645 SI-11
San Francisco, 805235 NM-5
San Gabriel, 39718 ‡E-9
San Gregorio, 200 NN-5
San Jacinto, 44199 SK-14
San Joaquin, 4001 SC-7
SAN JOAQUIN CO., 685306 NL-8
San Jose, 945942 NN-6
San Juan Bautista, 1862 SB-4
San Juan Capistrano, 34593 SK-12
San Leandro, 84950 NM-6
San Lorenzo, 23452 NH-16
San Lucas, 269 SD-5
San Luis Obispo, 45119 SG-6
SAN LUIS OBISPO CO., 269637 SG-6
San Luis Rey †H-8
San Marcos, 83781 SL-14
San Marino, 13147 ‡D-9
San Martin, 7027 SB-4
San Mateo, 97207 NI-14
SAN MATEO CO., 718451 SA-2
San Miguel, 2336 SE-6
San Pablo, 29139 NL-5
San Pedro ‡J-7
San Quentin, 100 ND-12
San Rafael, 57713 NL-5
San Ramon, 72148 NM-6
San Simeon, 462 SE-4
San Ysidro †N-4
Sand City, 334 *M-2
Sanger, 24270 SC-8
Santa Ana, 324528 SK-12
Santa Barbara, 88410 SI-8
SANTA BARBARA CO., 423895 SH-8
Santa Clara, 116468 NL-18
SANTA CLARA CO., 1781642 SA-4
Santa Clarita, 176320 SI-10
Santa Cruz, 59946 SB-3
SANTA CRUZ CO., 262382 SB-3
Santa Fe Sprs., 16223 ‡G-9
Santa Margarita, 1259 SF-6
Santa Maria, 99553 SG-6
Santa Monica, 89736 SJ-11
Santa Nella Vil., 1380 SB-5
Santa Paula, 29321 SI-9
Santa Rita Pk., 170 SB-6
Santa Rosa, 167815 NK-4
Santa Susana, 1037 ‡B-2
Santa Venetia, 4292 NC-12
Santa Ynez, 4418 SH-7
Santa Ysabel, 100 SL-15
Santee, 53413 SM-14
Saranap, 5202 NE-17
Saratoga, 29926 SA-3
Saticoy, 1029 †A-9
Sattley, 49 NH-9
Sausalito, 7061 NE-12
Sawyers Bar, 100 NC-4
Schellville, 200 NK-5
Scotia, 850 NE-2
Scotland, 285 §B-16
Scott Bar, 150 NB-4
Scotts Valley, 11580 SB-3
Sea Ranch, 1305 NJ-3
Seal Bch., 24168 ‡J-9
Searles Valley, 1739 SE-13
Seaside, 33025 SC-3
Sebastopol, 7379 NK-4
Sedco Hills, 3078 §K-19
Seeley, 1739 SM-17
Seiad Valley, 270 NB-4
Selma, 23219 SC-8
Seneca NF-8
Seven Pines SK-4
Shackelford, 3371 *J-9
Shafter, 16988 SF-9
Shandon, 1295 SF-6
Shasta, 1771 NE-5
SHASTA CO., 177223 NE-6
Shasta Lake, 10164 NE-5
Shaver Lake, 634 SB-9
Sheep Ranch, 110 NL-9
Shelter Cove, 693 NF-2
Sheridan, 1238 NJ-7
Sherman Oaks ‡D-5
Sherwood Forest, 2600 ND-14
Shingle Sprs., 4432 NJ-8
Shingletown, 2283 NE-6
Shively, 110 NE-2
Shore Acres, 4000 NB-18
Shoshone, 31 SE-15
Sierra City, 221 NH-9
SIERRA CO., 3240 NH-9
Sierra Madre, 10917 ‡D-9
Sierraville, 200 NH-9
Signal Hill, 11016 ‡I-8
Silver City SM-2
Silver Strand, 1200 †C-8
Silverado, 800 §J-15
Simi Valley, 124237 SI-10
Simmler SF-7
SISKIYOU CO., 44900 NC-5
Sisquoc, 183 SH-6
Sites NI-5
Sky Valley, 2406 SG-1
Skyforest, 750 §B-20
Sleepy Hollow §G-13
Sloat, 100 NG-9
Sloughhouse, 350 NK-8
Smartville, 177 NI-7
Smith River, 866 NA-2
Smithflat, 250 NJ-9
Snelling, 231 NN-9
Soda Sprs., 81 NI-9
Solana Bch., 12867 SM-13
SOLANO CO., 413344 NK-6
Soledad, 25738 SC-4
Solvang, 5245 SH-7
Somerset, 160 NK-9
Somes Bar, 150 NC-3
Somis, 1000 SI-9
Sonoma, 10648 NK-5
SONOMA CO., 483878 NJ-3
Sonora, 4903 NL-9
Soquel, 9644 SB-3
Sorensens, 50 NJ-10
Soulsbyville, 2215 NL-10
S. Dos Palos, 1620 SB-6
S. El Monte, 20116 ‡E-10
S. Fontana §E-16
S. Gate, 94396 ‡G-8
S. Laguna §M-13
S. L. Tahoe, 21403 NJ-10
S. Los Angeles ‡G-7
S. Pasadena, 25619 ‡D-8
S. San Francisco, 63632 NM-5
S. San Gabriel, 8070 ‡E-9
S. San Jose Hills, 20551 §F-11
S. Taft, 2169 SG-8
S. Whittier, 57156 ‡G-10
Spalding Tract, 178 NE-9
Spanish Ranch, 170 NG-8
Spreckels, 673 *N-5
Spring Gdn., 16 NG-9
Spring Valley, 28205 SN-14
Springville, 934 SD-10
Squaw Valley, 3162 SC-9
Stallion Sprs., 2488 SG-10
Standish, 180 NF-9
STANISLAUS CO., 514453 SA-4
Stanton, 38186 ‡I-10
Stevinson, 313 NN-8
Stewarts Pt., 100 NJ-3
Stinson Bch., 632 NL-4
Stirling City, 295 NG-7
Stockton, 291707 NL-7
Stonyford, 149 NH-5
Storrie, 4 NG-7
Stovepipe Wells, 30 SC-13
Stratford, 1277 SD-7
Strathmore, 2819 SD-9
Strawberry, 5393 ND-12
Strawberry, 86 NL-10
Strawberry Valley, 100 NH-8
Studio City ‡D-5
Suisun City, 28111 NL-6
Sultana, 775 SC-9
Summerland, 1448 SI-8
Sun Valley ‡C-6
Sunfair SF-2
Sunland ‡B-6
Sunnyside, 4235 SC-20
Sunnyside, 1000 †K-5
Sunnyvale, 140081 NL-17
Sunol, 913 NI-19
Sunset Bch., 971 ‡J-9
Surf SH-6
Surfside ‡J-9
Susanville, 17947 NF-9
Sutter, 2904 NI-6
SUTTER CO., 94737 NI-6
Sutter Creek, 2501 NK-8
Swanton SB-2
Sycamore NI-6
Sylmar ‡B-4
Sylvia Pk., 600 ‡D-3
Taft, 9327 SG-8
Taft Hts., 1949 SG-8
Tahoe City, 700 NI-10
Tahoe Pines, 110 NI-10
Tahoe Vista, 1433 NI-10
Tahoma, 1191 NI-10
Talmage, 1130 NI-3
Tamalpais Valley, 7000 NE-12
Tara Hills, 5126 NC-14
Tarpey Vil., 3888 SB-20
Tarzana ‡D-4
Tassajara Hot Sprs. SD-4
Taylorsville, 140 NG-8
Tecopa, 150 SE-16
Tecopa Hot Sprs., 50 SE-16
Tehachapi, 14414 SG-11
Tehama, 418 NG-6
TEHAMA CO., 63463 NG-5
Temecula, 100097 SK-14
Temescal Valley, 22535 §I-16
Temple City, 35558 ‡E-9
Templeton, 7674 SF-6
Tennant, 41 NB-6
Terminous, 381 NL-7
Termo ND-9
Terra Bella, 3310 SE-9
Thermal, 2865 SK-16
Thermalito, 6646 NH-7
Thornton, 1131 NL-7
Thousand Oaks, 126683 SJ-10
Thousand Palms, 7715 SJ-15
Three Rivers, 2182 SC-10
Three Rocks, 246 SC-6
Tiburon, 8962 NM-5
Tionesta, 30 NB-8
Tipton, 2543 SD-9
Tollhouse, 400 SB-8
Tomales, 204 NK-4
Toms Place, 170 NM-13
Topanga, 8289 ‡E-3
Topanga Pk., 600 ‡D-2
Topaz, 50 NK-11
Torrance, 145438 SK-11
Trabuco Canyon, 800 §K-15
Tracy, 82922 NM-7
Tranquillity, 799 SC-7
Traver, 713 SC-8
Tres Pinos, 476 SB-4
Trimmer SB-9
Trinidad, 367 ND-2
Trinity Ctr., 267 ND-5
TRINITY CO., 13786 NE-4
Trinity Vil., 297 ND-3
Truckee, 16180 NI-10
Tujunga ‡B-7
Tulare, 59278 SD-9
TULARE CO., 442179 SD-9
Tulelake, 1010 NA-7
Tuolumne, 1779 NL-10
TUOLUMNE CO., 55365 NM-9
Turlock, 68549 NN-8
Tustin, 75540 §J-12
Tuttle, 103 SA-6
Tuttletown, 668 NL-9
Twain, 82 NG-8
Twain Harte, 2226 NL-10
Twentynine Palms, 25048 SJ-16
Twin Bridges NJ-10
Twin Peaks, 2100 §B-19
Ukiah, 16075 NI-3
Union City, 69516 NI-16
University City †G-2
Upland, 73732 SJ-12
Upper Lake, 1052 NI-4
Vacaville, 92428 NK-6
Valinda, 22822 §E-11
Valle Vista, 14578 SK-14
Vallecito, 442 NL-9
Vallejo, 115942 NL-5
Valley Acres, 527 SG-8
Valley Ctr., 9277 SL-14
Valley Ford, 147 NK-4
Valley Home, 228 NM-8
Valley Sprs., 3553 NL-8
Valyermo, 100 SI-12
Van Nuys ‡C-5
Vandenberg Vil., 6497 SH-6
Venice ‡F-4
Ventucopa, 50 SH-8
Ventura, 106433 SI-9
VENTURA CO., 823318 SH-9
Verdemont §C-18
Vernalis NM-7
Vernon, 112 ‡F-7
Victor, 293 NL-8
Victorville, 115903 SI-13
Vidal SI-20
Vidal Jct. SI-19
View Pk., 5500 ‡F-6
Villa Pk., 5812 §I-12
Vina, 237 NG-6
Vincent, 15922 SI-11
Vine Hill, 3761 NC-16
Vineyard, 24836 *J-4
Vinton, 155 NG-10
Viola, 30 NE-7
Visalia, 124442 SD-9
Vista, 93834 SL-13
Volcano, 115 NK-9
Volta, 246 SB-5
Vorden NK-7
Walker, 721 NK-11
Wallace, 403 NL-8
Walnut, 29172 §E-12
Walnut Creek, 64173 NL-6
Walnut Grv., 1542 NL-7
Walnut Pk., 15966 ‡F-7
Warner Sprs. SL-15
Wasco, 25545 SF-9
Washington, 185 NI-9
Waterford, 8456 NM-9
Waterloo, 572 NL-8
Watsonville, 51199 SB-3
Watts ‡G-7
Wawona, 169 NN-11
Weaverville, 3600 NE-4
Weed, 2967 NC-5
Weimar, 850 NI-8
Weitchpec, 30 NC-3
Weldon, 2642 SE-11
Wendel NF-10
Weott, 288 NF-2
W. Athens, 8729 ‡G-7
W. Carson, 21699 ‡I-7
W. Covina, 106098 §E-11
W. Hollywood, 34399 ‡E-6
W. Los Angeles ‡E-5
W. Menlo Pk., 3659 NK-15
W. Park, 1157 SC-18
W. Point, 674 NK-9
W. Puente Valley, 22636 §E-11
W. Sacramento, 48744 NK-7
Westhaven, 370 ND-2
WestL. Vil., 8270 SJ-10
Westley, 603 NN-8
Westminster, 89701 ‡J-10
Westmorland, 2225 SM-17
Westport, 160 NH-2
Westwood, 1647 NF-8
Wheatland, 3456 NI-7
Whiskeytown, 100 NE-5
Whispering Pines, 100 NJ-4
White River SE-10
White Water SJ-15
Whitethorn, 300 NF-2
Whitley Gdns., 285 SE-6
Whitmore, 100 NE-6
Whittier, 85331 SJ-12
Wilbur Sprs. NI-5
Wildomar, 32176 SK-13
Wildwood, 50 NF-4
Williams, 5123 NI-6
Willits, 4888 NH-3
Willow Creek, 1710 ND-3
Willow Ranch NB-10
Willows, 6166 NH-6
Wilmington ‡I-7
Wilseyville, 350 NK-9
Wilsonia, 5 SK-1
Wilton, 5363 NK-7
Winchester, 2534 SK-14
Windsor, 26801 NK-4
Windsor Hills, 5000 ‡F-6
Winter Gdns., 20631 †H-6
Winterhaven, 394 SM-20
Winters, 6624 NK-6
Winton, 10613 NN-9
Wofford Hts., 2200 SE-11
Woodcrest, 14347 §H-18
Woodfords, 100 NJ-11
Woodlake, 7279 SC-9
Woodland, 55468 NJ-6
Woodland Hills ‡D-3
Woodside, 5287 NK-15
Woodville, 1740 SD-9
Woody SE-10
Wrightwood, 4525 SI-12
Wyandotte, 110 NH-7
Yermo, 1000 SH-14
Yettem, 211 SC-9
Yolano NK-7
Yolo, 450 NJ-6
YOLO CO., 200849 NJ-6
Yorba Linda, 64234 §G-13
Yorkville, 130 NJ-3
Yosemite Forks, 210 NN-11
Yosemite Lakes, 4952 SA-8
Yosemite Vil., 1035 NM-11
Yountville, 2933 NK-5
Yreka, 7765 NB-5
Yuba City, 64925 NI-7
YUBA CO., 72155 NI-7
Yucaipa, 51367 SJ-14
Yucca Valley, 20700 SJ-15
Zamora, 100 NJ-6
Zenia, 40 NF-3

Colorado

Page locator

Map keys	Atlas pages
1–10	42–43
11–20	44–45

* City keyed to pp. 46–47

ADAMS CO., 441603 E-15
Agate, 80 F-16
Aguilar, 538 L-14
Akron, 1702 D-17
Alamosa, 8780 L-11
ALAMOSA CO., 15445 L-11
Allenspark, 528 D-12
Allison, 110 N-7
Alma, 270 G-11
Almont, 70 I-9
Amherst, 58 B-20
Anton, 40 E-17
Antonito, 781 M-11
Arapahoe, 100 H-20
ARAPAHOE CO., 572003 F-14
Arboles, 280 N-7
ARCHULETA CO., 12084 M-8
Arlington, 40 J-17
Aroya H-18
Arriba, 193 G-17
Arriola, 240 L-4
Arvada, 106433 E-13
Aspen, 6658 G-9
Atwood, 133 C-17
Ault, 1519 C-14
Aurora, 325078 E-14
Avon, 6447 F-10
Avondale, 674 J-15
BACA CO., 3788 L-19
Bailey, 150 F-12
Barnesville C-14
Barr Lake, 100 *F-9
Bartlett L-20
Basalt, 3857 F-8
Bayfield, 2333 M-7
Bedrock J-4
Beecher Island E-20
Bellvue, 400 C-13
Bennett, 2308 E-15
BENT CO., 6499 K-18
Berthoud, 5105 D-13
Bethune, 237 G-19
Beulah, 280 J-13
Black Forest, 13116 H-14
Black Hawk, 118 E-12
Blakeland, 700 *L-6
Blanca, 385 L-12
Blende, 878 J-14
Blue Mtn., 15 D-4
Blue River, 849 F-11
Bonanza, 16 J-10
Boncarbo, 70 M-14
Bond E-9
Bondad M-6
Boone, 339 J-15
Boulder, 97385 D-13
BOULDER CO., 294567 D-12
Bow Mar, 866 *K-6
Bowie, 40 H-7
Boyero H-17
Brandon, 21 I-19
Branson, 74 N-16
Breckenridge, 4540 F-11
Breen M-6
Briggsdale, 110 C-15
Brighton, 33352 E-14
Bristol, 130 J-20
Broadmoor *I-1
Brookvale, 280 F-12
Broomfield, 55889 E-13
Brush, 5463 D-16
Buena Vista, 2617 H-11
Buffalo Creek F-13
Buford E-7
Burlington, 4254 G-20
Burns E-9
Byers, 1160 E-15
Caddoa J-18
Cahone, 50 L-4
Calhan, 780 H-15
Camp Bird K-7
Campion, 1830 D-13
Campo, 109 M-19
Cañon City, 16400 I-13
Capulin, 200 M-11
Carbondale, 6427 F-8
Carr, 60 B-13
Cascade, 500 H-13
Castle Pines North, 12390 *M-8
Castle Rock, 48231 F-14
Cattle Creek, 641 F-8
Cedaredge, 2253 H-6
Centennial, 100377 F-13
Center, 2230 K-11
Central City, 663 E-12
CHAFFEE CO., 17809 I-11
Chama, 245 M-12
Cheraw, 252 J-17
Cherry Creek, 11120 *J-8
Cherry Hills Vil., 5987 *J-7
CHEYENNE CO., 1836 H-19
Cheyenne Wells, 846 H-20
Chimney Rock M-8
Chipita Pk., 465 H-13
Chivington, 40 I-19
Chromo N-9
Cimarron I-7
Clark B-9
Clarkville C-19
CLEAR CREEK CO., 9088 F-12
Clifton, 19889 G-5
Coal Creek, 343 J-13
Coaldale, 255 J-11
Coalmont, 50 C-10
Cokedale, 129 M-14
Collbran, 708 G-6
Colona, 30 J-7
Colorado City, 2193 K-14
Colorado Sprs., 416427 H-14
Columbine B-9
Columbine Valley, 1256 *K-6
Commerce City, 45913 *H-7
Como G-11
Conejos, 58 M-11
CONEJOS CO., 8256 M-10
Conifer, 200 F-12
Cope, 100 F-18
Cortez, 8482 L-5
COSTILLA CO., 3524 M-12
Cotopaxi, 47 J-12
Cowdrey, 100 B-10
Craig, 9464 C-7
Crawford, 431 H-7
Creede, 290 K-9
Crested Butte, 1487 H-8
Crestone, 127 K-11
Cripple Creek, 1189 H-13
Crook, 110 B-18
Crowley, 176 J-16
CROWLEY CO., 5823 J-16
Crystola, 160 H-13
Cuchara M-13
CUSTER CO., 4255 J-12
Dacono, 4152 D-13
Dailey C-18
De Beque, 504 F-6
Deckers G-13
Deer Trail, 546 F-15
Del Norte, 1686 L-10
Delhi L-16
Delta, 8915 H-6
DELTA CO., 30952 H-6
Denver, 600158 E-13
Devine J-15
Dillon, 904 F-11
Dinosaur, 339 D-4
Divide, 127 H-13
Dolores, 936 L-5
DOLORES CO., 2064 K-5
DOUGLAS CO., 285465 G-13
Dove Creek, 735 K-4
Doyleville I-9
Drake C-12
Dupont, 3650 *G-7
Durango, 16887 M-6
Eads, 609 I-19
Eagle, 6508 F-9
EAGLE CO., 52197 E-9
E. Portal E-12
Eastlake *F-7
Eaton, 4365 C-14
Eckley, 257 D-19
Edgewater, 5170 *I-6
Edwards, 10266 F-9
Egnar K-4
El Jebel, 3801 F-8
El Moro, 221 M-15
EL PASO CO., 622263 H-14
Elbert, 230 G-14
ELBERT CO., 23086 F-15
Eldora, 142 E-12
Eldorado Sprs., 585 E-13
Elizabeth, 1358 G-14
Elk Sprs., 25 C-5
Ellicott, 1131 H-15
Empire, 282 E-12
Englewood, 30255 F-13
Erie, 18135 D-13
Estes Pk., 5858 C-12
Estrella M-11
Evans, 18537 C-14
Evergreen, 9038 F-12
Fairplay, 679 G-11
Falcon, 255 H-14
Falfa, 100 M-6
Farisita K-13
Federal Hts., 11467 *G-6
Ferncliff, 70 D-12
Firestone, 10147 D-13
Flagler, 561 G-18
Fleming, 408 B-18
Florence, 3881 J-13
Florissant, 104 H-13
Ft. Carson, 13813 *I-2
Ft. Collins, 143986 C-13
Ft. Garland, 433 L-12
Ft. Lupton, 7377 D-14
Ft. Lyon J-18
Ft. Morgan, 11315 D-16
Fountain, 25846 I-14
Fowler, 1182 J-16
Foxfield, 685 F-14
Foxton F-13
Franktown, 395 F-14
Fraser, 1224 E-11
Frederick, 8679 D-13
FREMONT CO., 46824 I-12
Frisco, 2683 F-11
Fruita, 12646 G-4
Fruitvale, 7675 G-5
Galeton, 225 C-14
Garcia, 110 N-12
Garden City, 234 F-2
Gardner, 100 K-13
GARFIELD CO., 56389 F-6
Gateway H-4
Gem Vil. M-7
Genoa, 139 G-17
Georgetown, 1034 E-12
Gilcrest, 1034 D-14
Gilman F-10
GILPIN CO., 5441 E-12
Glade Pk., 40 G-4
Glen Haven, 130 C-12
Glendale, 4184 *I-7
Glendevey B-11
Glenwood Sprs., 9614 F-8
Golden, 18867 E-13
Goldfield, 49 H-13
Goodnight, 1400 I-1
Goodrich, 35 D-15
Gould, 50 C-11
Granada, 517 J-20
Granby, 1864 D-11
GRAND CO., 14843 D-10
Grand Jct., 58566 G-5
Grand Lake, 471 D-11
Grand Mesa, 30 G-6
Grand View Estates, 528 *L-9
Granite H-10
Grant F-12
Greeley, 92889 C-14
Green Mtn. Camp E-10
Green Mtn. Falls, 640 H-13
Greenwood, 140 J-13
Greenwood Vil., 13925 *K-7
Grover, 137 B-15
Guffey, 98 H-12
Gulnare, 100 M-14
Gunbarrel, 9263 *A-7
Gunnison, 5854 I-9
GUNNISON CO., 15324 H-8
Gypsum, 6477 F-9
Hahns Peak, 40 B-9
Hale F-20
Hamilton, 30 C-7
Hardin D-15
Harris Pk., 200 F-12
Hartman, 81 J-20
Hartsel, 80 H-11
Hasty, 144 J-18
Haswell, 68 I-18
Hawley K-16
Haxtun, 946 C-19
Hayden, 1810 C-8
Heeney, 76 E-10
Henderson, 600 *F-8
Hereford, 60 B-15
Hermosa, 260 L-6
Hesperus M-6
Hiawatha, 10 A-5
Highland Pk., 300 F-12
Highlands Ranch, 96713 *L-7
Hillrose, 264 D-17
Hillside J-12
HINSDALE CO., 843 K-7
Hoehne, 111 M-15
Holly, 802 J-20
Holyoke, 2313 C-19
Homelake, 260 L-11
Hooper, 103 K-11
Hot Sulphur Sprs., 663 D-11
Hotchkiss, 944 H-7
Howard, 723 I-11
Hoyt, 30 E-15
Hudson, 2356 D-14
HUERFANO CO., 6711 L-13
Hugo, 730 G-17
Hygiene, 400 D-13
Idaho Sprs., 1717 E-12
Idalia, 88 E-20
Ignacio, 697 M-7
Iliff, 266 B-18
Indian Hills, 1280 F-13
Irondale *G-8
Ivywild *H-2
JACKSON CO., 1394 B-10
Jamestown, 274 D-12
Jansen, 112 M-14
Jaroso, 60 N-12
Jefferson, 40 F-11
JEFFERSON CO., 534543 F-12
Joes, 80 F-19
Johnson Vil., 246 H-11
Johnstown, 9887 D-13
Julesburg, 1225 B-20
Karval, 65 H-17
Kassler *M-5
Keenesburg, 1127 D-14
Kelim, 90 C-13
Keota B-15
Kersey, 1454 C-14
Kim, 74 M-17
Kiowa, 723 G-14
KIOWA CO., 1398 I-18
Kirk, 59 F-19
Kit Carson, 233 H-18
KIT CARSON CO., 8270 F-19
Knob Hill *H-2
Kremmling, 1444 D-10
La Garita K-10
La Jara, 818 M-11
La Junta, 7077 K-17
LA PLATA CO., 51334 L-6
La Salle, 1955 D-14
La Valley, 160 M-12
La Veta, 800 L-13
Lafayette, 24453 *D-5
Laird, 47 D-20
Lake City, 408 K-8
LAKE CO., 7310 G-10
L. George, 120 H-12
Lakeside, 8 *H-6
Lakewood, 142980 *I-5
Lamar, 7804 J-19
Laporte, 2450 *A-8
LARIMER CO., 299630 C-12
Larkspur, 183 G-13
Las Animas, 2410 J-17
LAS ANIMAS CO., 15507 M-15
Las Mesitas, 60 N-10
Last Chance, 25 E-17
Lawson, 320 E-12
Lay C-7
Lazear, 140 H-7
Leadville, 2602 G-10
Lebanon, 160 L-5
Lewis, 302 L-4
Limon, 1880 G-16
LINCOLN CO., 5467 H-17
Lincoln Pk., 3546 I-13
Lindon, 120 E-17
Littleton, 41737 F-13
Livermore, 60 B-13
Lochbuie, 4726 *E-10
Log Lane Vil., 873 D-16
LOGAN CO., 22709 B-17
Loma, 1293 G-4
Lombard Vil., 600 I-2
Lone Tree, 10218 *L-8
Longmont, 86270 D-13
Louisville, 18376 E-13
Louviers, 269 F-13
Loveland, 66859 C-13
Lucerne, 160 C-14
Ludlow M-14
Lyons, 2033 D-13
Mack, 240 G-4
Maher, 100 I-7
Manassa, 991 M-11
Mancos, 1336 M-5
Manitou Sprs., 4992 H-13
Manzanola, 434 J-16
Marble, 131 G-8
Marvel, 65 M-6
Masonville, 140 C-13
Matheson G-16
Maybell, 72 C-6
Maysville, 135 I-10
McClave, 190 J-18
McCoy, 24 E-9
Mead, 3405 D-13
Meeker, 2475 D-6
Meeker Pk., 120 D-12
Meredith F-9
Merino, 284 C-17
Mesa, 240 G-6
MESA CO., 146723 H-5
Mesita, 50 M-12
Milliken, 5610 D-14
Milner, 200 C-9
MINERAL CO., 712 L-8
Minturn, 1027 F-10
Model, 110 M-15
Moffat, 116 K-11
MOFFAT CO., 13795 C-6
Mogote, 85 N-11
Molina, 90 G-6
Monte Vista, 4444 L-10
Montezuma, 65 F-11
MONTEZUMA CO., 25535 M-4
Montrose, 19132 I-6
MONTROSE CO., 41276 I-6
Monument, 5530 G-13
MORGAN CO., 28159 D-16
Morrison, 428 F-13
Mosca, 130 L-11
Mt. Crested Butte, 801 H-9
Mountain View, 1700 *B-8
Mountain View, 507 *H-6
Mountain Vil., 1320 K-6
Nathrop, 200 H-11
Naturita, 546 J-5
Nederland, 1445 E-12
New Castle, 4518 F-7
Ninaview L-17
Niwot, 4006 D-13
N. Avondale, 50 J-15
Northglenn, 35789 *F-7
Norwood, 518 J-5
Nucla, 711 J-5
Nunn, 416 B-14
Oak Creek, 884 D-9
Oak Grv., 175 I-6
Ohio, 40 I-9
Olathe, 1849 I-6
Olney Sprs., 345 J-16
Ophir, 159 K-6
Orchard, 90 D-15
Orchard City, 3119 H-6
Orchard Mesa, 6836 G-5
Ordway, 1080 J-16
Ortiz, 60 N-11
OTERO CO., 18831 K-16
Otis, 475 D-18
Ouray, 1000 K-7
OURAY CO., 4436 J-6
Ovid, 318 B-19
Oxford, 90 M-7
Padroni, 76 B-17
Pagosa Jct., 25 N-8
Pagosa Sprs., 1727 M-8
Palisade, 2692 G-5
Palmer Lake, 2420 G-13
Pandora K-7
Paoli, 34 C-19
Paonia, 1451 H-7
Parachute, 1085 F-6
Paradox, 70 I-4
Paragon Estates, 380 *D-7
PARK CO., 16206 G-11
Parker, 45297 F-14
Parlin, 50 I-9
Parshall, 47 D-10
Pearl B-10
Peckham, 135 D-14
Peetz, 238 B-18
Penrose, 3582 I-13
Peyton, 250 H-14
PHILLIPS CO., 4442 C-19
Phippsburg, 204 D-9
Pierce, 834 C-14
Pikeview *F-2
Pine Grv., 150 F-12
Pitkin, 66 I-10
PITKIN CO., 17148 G-9
Placerville, 250 K-6
Platner, 35 D-18
Platoro, 100 M-9
Platteville, 2485 D-14
Pleasant View, 80 L-4
Poncha Sprs., 737 I-11
Poudre Pk., 100 C-13
Powder Wash, 55 B-6
Powderhorn J-8
Pritchett, 140 M-18
Proctor B-18

***, †, ‡, §, ◊ See explanation under state title in this index.**
County and parish names are listed in capital letters & boldface type.
Independent cities (not included in a county) are listed in italics.

Colorado (continued)

Prospect Valley, 70 ... D-15
Prowers ... J-19
PROWERS CO.,
  12551 ... K-19
Pryor ... J-14
Pueblo, 106595 ... J-14
PUEBLO CO.,
  159063 ... J-14
Pueblo West, 29637 ... J-14
Punkin Ctr., H-16
Purcell ... C-10
Ramah, 123 ... G-15
Rand ... D-4
Rangely, 2365 ... D-4
Raymer, 96 ... C-16
Raymond, 60 ... D-12
Red Cliff, 267 ... G-9
Red Feather Lakes,
  343 ... B-12
Red Wing, 40 ... K-13
Redlands, 8685 ... G-5
Redmesa, 40 ... M-5
Redstone, 130 ... G-8
Redvale, 236 ... J-5
Rico, 265 ... K-6
Ridgway, 924 ... J-7
Rifle, 9172 ... F-7
RIO BLANCO CO.,
  6666 ... E-6
RIO GRANDE CO.,
  11982 ... L-10
Rockvale, 487 ... J-13
Rocky Ford, 3957 ... K-16
Roggen, 130 ... E-15
Rollinsville, 181 ... E-12
Romeo, 404 ... M-11
Roswell ... *G-2
ROUTT CO.,
  23509 ... C-8
Rush, 80 ... H-15
Rustic ... J-4
Rye, 153 ... K-13
Saguache, 485 ... J-10
SAGUACHE CO.,
  6108 ... K-9
St. Petersburg ... C-18
Salida, 5236 ... J-11
Salt Creek, 587 ... J-13
San Acacio, 40 ... M-12
San Antonio, 190 ... N-11
San Isabel, 50 ... K-13
SAN JUAN CO., 699 ..L-7
San Luis, 629 ... M-12
SAN MIGUEL CO.,
  7359 ... K-5
San Pablo, 170 ... M-12
Sanford, 879 ... M-11
Sapinero ... J-8
Sargents, 40 ... J-10
Sawpit, 40 ... K-6
Security, 4400 ... *I-3
Sedalia, 276 ... F-13
Sedgwick, 146 ... B-19
SEDGWICK CO.,
  2379 ... B-19
Segundo, 98 ... M-14
Seibert, 181 ... G-18
Severance, 3165 ... C-14
Shawnee, 100 ... *J-2
Sheridan, 5664 ... *J-6
Sheridan Lake, 88 ... J-20
Silt, 2930 ... F-7
Silver Cliff, 587 ... J-12
Silver Plume, 170 ... F-12
Silverthorne, 3887 ... F-11
Silverton, 637 ... K-7
Simla, 616 ... G-15
Singleton, 40 ... *J-2
Slater, 50 ... A-8
Slick Rock ... J-5
Snowmass ... G-9
Snowmass Vil., 2826 ... G-9
Snyder, 132 ... D-16
Somerset ... H-7
S. Fork, 386 ... L-9
S. Platte ... *J-2
Springfield, 1451 ... L-19
Starkville, 59 ... M-14
Steamboat Sprs.,
  12088 ... C-9
Sterling, 14777 ... C-17
Stoneham, 90 ... C-16
Stoner ... K-6
Stonewall, 80 ... M-20
Stonington, 30 ... M-20
Strasburg, 2447 ... E-15
Stratmoor Hills,
  2350 ... *I-2
Stratton, 658 ... G-19
Stratton Meadows ... *I-2
Stringtown, 140 ... G-10
Sugar City, 258 ... J-16
SUMMIT CO.,
  27994 ... F-11
Sunbeam ... C-7
Superior, 12483 ... E-13
Swink, 617 ... K-16
Tabernash, 417 ... E-11
TELLER CO.,
  23350 ... H-13
Telluride, 2325 ... K-6
Texas Creek ... J-12
Thatcher, 15 ... L-15
Thornton, 118772 ... J-13
Thurman, 40 ... F-17
Tiffany ... N-7
Timnath, 625 ... C-13
Timpas ... K-16
Tincup, 10 ... H-10
Toonerville ... D-9
Toponas ... D-9
Torres ... M-14
Towaoc, 1087 ... M-4
Tower, 22 ... *J-2
Trinchera, 80 ... N-16
Trinidad, 9096 ... M-14
Twin Lakes, 171 ... G-10
Two Buttes, 43 ... L-19
Tyrone ... L-15
Uravan ... J-4
Vail, 5305 ... F-10
Vancorum ... J-5
Vernon, 29 ... F-19
Victor, 390 ... J-13
Viejo San Acacio ... M-12
Vilas, 114 ... M-19
Vila Grv., 40 ... M-17
Villegreen, 30 ... M-17
Vineland, 500 ... J-14
Virginia Dale ... B-12
Vona, 106 ... G-18
Walden, 608 ... B-10
Walsenburg, 3068 ... L-14
Walsh, 646 ... L-20
Ward, 150 ... D-12
WASHINGTON CO.,
  4814 ... D-17
Watkins, 653 ... J-14
Wattenberg, 330 ... E-14
Waverly, 300 ... B-13
Welby, 14846 ... *G-7
WELD CO.,
  252825 ... B-15
Weldona, 139 ... D-16
Wellington, 6289 ... B-13
Westcliffe, 568 ... J-12
Western Hills, 2600 ... *G-6
Westminster,
  106114 ... D-13
Weston, 55 ... M-14
Wetmore, 60 ... J-13
Wheat Ridge,
  30166 ... *H-5
Whitepine ... J-10
Whitewater, 70 ... H-5
Widefield, 4200 ... *J-4
Wiggins, 893 ... D-15
Wild Horse, 25 ... H-18
Wiley, 405 ... J-19
Willard, 40 ... C-17
Williamsburg, 662 ... J-13
Windsor, 18644 ... C-13
Winter Pk., 999 ... E-11
Wolcott, 15 ... E-9
Woodland Pk.,
  7200 ... H-14
Woodrow, 20 ... E-17
Woody Creek, 263 ... G-9
Wray, 2342 ... D-20
Yampa, 429 ... D-9
Yellow Jacket, 60 ... L-4
Yoder ... H-15
Yuma, 3524 ... D-19
YUMA CO.,
  10043 ... D-19

Connecticut
Page locator
Map keys | Atlas pages
A–J | 48–49

Abington, 750 ... B-13
Addison, 800 ... C-4
Almyville ... C-10
Amenia Union, 100 ... B-4
Amesville, 120 ... A-4
Amston, 780 ... D-11
Andover, 600 ... C-11
Ansonia, 19249 ... F-5
Ashford, 230 ... B-12
Attawan Bch., 280 ... G-12
Attawaugan, 660 ... B-13
Atwoodville, 200 ... C-12
Avery Hill, 160 ... E-12
Avon, 1800 ... C-8
Bakersville, 400 ... B-6
Ball Pond, 2400 ... E-3
Ballouville, 600 ... A-14
Baltic, 1250 ... D-12
Barkhamsted, 4 ... B-7
Bashan, 420 ... D-10
Beacon Falls, 1650 ... E-6
Berkshire Estates,
  220 ... F-3
Berlin, 1230 ... D-8
Bethany, 1280 ... E-6
Bethel, 9549 ... E-4
Bethlehem, 2021 ... D-5
Birch Hill, 230 ... C-14
Birchwood, 380 ... D-11
Black Pt., 20 ... G-12
Bloomfield, 7500 ... B-8
Blue Hills, 2901 ... A-13
Boardman Br., 100 ... D-4
Bolton, 230 ... C-10
Botsford, 490 ... F-5
Bozrah Street ... C-5
Branchville, 350 ... G-4
Branford, 5819 ... G-8
Branford Ctr., 5819 ... J-11
Bridgeport, 144229 ... H-5
Bridgewater, 500 ... E-4
Bristol, 60477 ... D-7
Broad Brook, 4069 ... B-9
Brookfield, 1650 ... E-4
Brookfield Ctr., 1550 ... E-4
Brooklyn, 981 ... C-13
Buckingham, 200 ... C-10
Bulls Br., 100 ... D-4
Bunker Hill ... A-2
Burlington, 500 ... C-7
Burnside ... H-14
Byram, 4144 ... I-3
Canaan, 1212 ... A-5
Candlewood Isle,
  1260 ... E-4
Candlewood Knolls,
  560 ... E-4
Candlewood Shores,
  1800 ... E-4
Cannondale, 141 ... G-4
Canterbury, 200 ... C-13
Canton, 680 ... C-7
Canton Ctr., 380 ... B-7
Cedar Br. ... C-2
Centerbrook, 1000 ... F-10
Centerville ... A-14
Central Vil., 1800 ... C-13
Chaplin, 230 ... C-12
Cheshire, 5786 ... E-7
Chester, 1558 ... F-10
Chesterfield ... E-11
Clarks Corner ... B-13
Clarks Falls, 170 ... E-14
Clinton, 3368 ... G-10
Cobalt, 500 ... D-9
Colchester, 4781 ... D-11
Colebrook, 40 ... A-6
Collinsville, 3746 ... C-7
Columbia, 800 ... C-11
Cornwall, 330 ... B-5
Cornwall Br., 500 ... B-4
Cos Cob, 6770 ... I-3
Coventry, 600 ... C-11
Cromwell, 2500 ... D-9
Crystal Lake, 1945 ... B-10
Danbury, 80893 ... F-4
Danielson, 4051 ... C-13
Darien, 20732 ... H-4
Dayville, 1650 ... B-13
Deep River, 1700 ... F-10
Derby, 12902 ... F-6
Devon ... F-6
Dodgingtown, 300 ... F-5
Double Bch., 1100 ... G-8
Durham, 2933 ... E-9
Eagleville, 460 ... C-11
E. Berlin, 1900 ... D-8
E. Bridgeport ... H-13
E. Brooklyn, 1638 ... C-13
E. Canaan, 1000 ... A-5
E. Farms, 500 ... C-9
E. Glastonbury, 300 ... C-10
E. Haddam, 800 ... E-10
E. Hampton, 2691 ... D-10
E. Hartford, 51252 ... C-9
E. Hartland, 1200 ... A-7
E. Haven, 29257 ... G-7

(Connecticut, col. 2)
E. Litchfield, 180 ... C-6
E. Morris ... D-6
E. Mountain ... B-3
E. River, 3800 ... G-9
E. Thompson, 640 ... A-14
East Vil., 100 ... F-6
E. Willington ... B-11
E. Windsor Hill, 400 ... H-14
E. Woodstock, 470 ... A-13
Eastford, 1000 ... B-13
Easton, 480 ... G-5
Ebbs Corner, 620 ... A-8
Ellington, 1700 ... B-9
Elmville, 330 ... B-13
Elmwood ... C-8
Enfield ... A-9
Essex, 1270 ... F-10
N. Ashford ... A-12
N. Bloomfield ... B-8
N. Branford, 7400 ... F-8
N. Canton, 270 ... B-7
N. Granby, 1944 ... A-8
N. Grosvenor Dale,
  1530 ... A-14
N. Guilford ... F-9
N. Haven, 24093 ... F-7
N. Kent, 170 ... C-4
N. Madison ... F-9
N. Stonington, 350 ... F-14
N. Westchester, 300 ... D-10
N. Wilton, 100 ... G-4
N. Windham, 1000 ... C-12
N. Woodstock ... A-13
Northfield, 710 ... C-6
Northford, 3600 ... F-8
Northville, 400 ... D-4
Norwalk, 85603 ... H-4
Norwich, 40493 ... D-12
Oakdale, 910 ... E-12
Oakdale Mnr., 400 ... E-12
Oakland Gdns., 300 ... I-11
Oakville, 9007 ... D-6
Old Greenwich, 6611 ... I-3
Old Lyme, 480 ... G-11
Old Lyme Shores,
  300 ... G-11
Old Mystic, 3554 ... F-13
Old Saybrook, 2039 ... G-11
Oneco, 750 ... C-14
Orange, 13956 ... G-7
Orcutts, 240 ... B-7
Oronoque ... J-7
Oswegatchie, 150 ... F-12
Oxford, 2100 ... F-6
Pachaug ... D-13
Palmertown, 610 ... E-12
Pawcatuck, 5624 ... F-14
Pequabuck ... B-7
Phoenixville ... B-12
Pine Br., 1000 ... F-4
Pine Meadow, 530 ... B-7
Pine Orchard, 950 ... G-8
Pine Rock Pk. ... J-7
Plainfield, 2557 ... D-13
Plainville, 17400 ... D-7
Plantsville, 6000 ... D-7
Platts Mills ... J-2
Pleasant Valley, 460 ... B-7
Plymouth, 1200 ... D-6
Pt. O'Woods, 740 ... G-11
Pomfret, 670 ... B-13
Pomfret Ctr., 390 ... B-13
Pomfret, 160 ... F-9
Poquetanuck, 220 ... E-13
Poquonock, 1700 ... B-8
Poquonock Br.,
  1727 ... F-13
Portland, 5862 ... D-9
Preston City, 220 ... E-13
Prospect, 7770 ... E-7
Putnam, 7214 ... A-13
Putnam Hts., 210 ... B-14
Quaddick, 540 ... A-14
Quaker Hill, 500 ... F-12
Quarryville, 410 ... C-10
Quinebaug, 1133 ... A-13
Redding, 100 ... F-4
Redding Ridge, 550 ... F-5
Ridgebury, 220 ... F-4
Ridgefield, 7645 ... G-4
Riverbend ... G-4
Riverside, 8416 ... I-3
Riverton, 580 ... A-7
Robertsville, 280 ... A-6
Rockfall, 980 ... D-9
Rockville, 7474 ... B-10
Rocky Hill, 16500 ... D-9
Rogers, 660 ... B-13
Roxbury, 500 ... D-5
Roxbury Falls, 130 ... E-5
Sachem Head, 500 ... G-8
Salem, 40 ... E-11
Salmon, 264 ... D-9
Sandy Hook, 1200 ... F-5
Saybrook Mnr.,
  1052 ... G-11
Scantic, 400 ... B-9
Scotland, 900 ... C-12
Seymour, 14300 ... F-6
Shady Rest, 270 ... E-9
Shailerville ... E-10
Sharon, 729 ... B-4
Sharon Valley, 300 ... B-4
Shelton, 39559 ... G-6
Sherman, 150 ... D-3
Short Bch., 200 ... G-8
Simsbury, 5836 ... B-8
Somers, 1789 ... A-10
Somersville, 1300 ... A-10
Sound View, 230 ... G-11
S. Britain, 1060 ... E-5
S. Canaan, 400 ... A-5
S. Chaplin ... C-12
S. End ... C-9
S. Glastonbury, 2000 ... D-9
S. Kent, 300 ... D-4
S. Killingly, 220 ... C-14
S. Lyme, 320 ... G-11
S. Norwalk, 9100 ... H-4
S. Wilton, 400 ... G-4
S. Windham, 1421 ... D-12
S. Windsor, 14000 ... B-9
S. Woodstock, 1291 ... A-13
Southbury, 800 ... E-5
Southford ... E-6
Southington, 22000 ... D-7
Southport, 1585 ... H-5
Spring Glen ... H-10
Spring Grove ... C-5

(Connecticut, col. 3)
Moodus, 1413 ... E-10
Moosup, 3231 ... C-13
Morris, 300 ... D-6
Morris Cove ... J-10
Mt. Hope, 200 ... B-12
Mystic, 4205 ... F-13
Naugatuck, 31862 ... E-6
Nepaug, 300 ... B-7
New Britain, 73206 ... D-8
New Canaan, 17900 ... H-4
New Fairfield, 5200 ... E-4
New Hartford, 620 ... B-7
New Haven, 129779 ... G-7
NEW HAVEN CO.,
  862477 ... E-7
New London, 27620 ... F-12
NEW LONDON CO.,
  274055 ... E-13
New Milford, 6523 ... D-4
New Preston, 1182 ... D-5
Newent, 230 ... D-13
Newington, 30562 ... C-8
Newtown, 1941 ... F-5
Niantic, 3114 ... F-12
Nichols ... I-6
Noank, 1796 ... F-13
Norfolk, 553 ... A-5
N. Ashford ... A-12
Stafford Sprs.,
  4988 ... A-11
Staffordville, 760 ... A-11
Stamford, 122643 ... I-3
Stepney, 750 ... G-5
Sterling, 660 ... C-14
Sterling Hill ... C-14
Stevenson, 1500 ... F-5
Stonington, 929 ... F-13
Stony Creek, 830 ... G-8
Storrs, 15344 ... C-11
Stratford, 51384 ... G-6
Suffield Depot, 1325 ... A-9
Taconic, 350 ... A-4
Tariffville, 1324 ... B-8
Terryville, 5387 ... D-7
Thomaston, 1910 ... D-6
Thompson, 960 ... A-14
Thompsonville, 8577 ... A-9
Tolland, 1350 ... B-11
TOLLAND CO.,
  152691 ... B-10
Torrington, 36383 ... C-6
Town Plot Hill ... B-2
Trumbull, 36018 ... G-5
Tylerville ... E-10
Union, 60 ... A-12
Union City ... J-2
Unionville, 4400 ... C-7
Upper Stepney, 1000 ... F-5
Vernon, 28100 ... B-10
Versailles, 580 ... D-12
Voluntown, 520 ... D-14
Wallingford, 18209 ... E-8
Warehouse Pt., 2100 ... B-9
Warren, 240 ... C-5
Warrenville, 140 ... B-12
Washington, 700 ... D-5
Washington Depot,
  700 ... D-5
Waterbury, 110366 ... E-6
Waterford ... G-11
Watertown, 3574 ... D-6
Waterville ... A-2
Watrous, 1205 ... C-13
Wauregan, 1205 ... C-13
Welles Vil. ... I-14
Wequetequock, 850 ... F-14
W. Avon, 100 ... C-8
W. Cornwall, 330 ... B-4
W. Goshen, 700 ... C-6
W. Granby, 700 ... A-8
W. Hartford, 63268 ... C-8
W. Hartland, 400 ... A-7
W. Haven, 55564 ... G-7
W. Mystic ... F-13
W. Norfolk ... A-6
W. Redding, 200 ... F-4
W. Shore ... J-9
W. Side Hill ... B-2
W. Simsbury, 2447 ... B-8
W. Stafford, 860 ... A-11
W. Suffield, 860 ... A-9
W. Thompson, 210 ... A-13
W. Woodstock ... A-12
Westbrook, 2413 ... G-10
Westchester, 200 ... E-10
Westford, 100 ... B-12
Weston, 1460 ... G-4
Westport, 26391 ... H-4
Westville ... H-9
Wethersfield, 26668 ... C-9
Whigville, 450 ... C-7
Willimantic, 17737 ... C-11
Willington, 470 ... B-11
Wilsonville, 640 ... A-13
Wilton, 732 ... G-4
Winchester Ctr., 200 ... B-6
Windham, 1150 ... C-12
WINDHAM CO.,
  118428 ... C-13
Windsor, 18800 ... B-9
Windsor Locks,
  12498 ... B-9
Winnville, 350 ... B-9
Winsted, 7712 ... B-6
Winthrop, 490 ... F-10
Wolcott, 6400 ... D-7
Woodbridge, 7860 ... F-7
Woodbury, 1294 ... E-5
Woodmont, 1488 ... G-7
Woodstock, 410 ... A-13
Woodstock Valley,
  350 ... A-12
Woodville, 740 ... D-7
Woodville ... D-5

Delaware
Page locator
Map keys | Atlas pages
A–N | 50–51

Adamsville ... J-2
Andrewville ... I-2
Anglesey, 125 ... C-7
Argo by the Bay,
  1200 ... K-5
Arden, 439 ... C-3
Ardencroft, 231 ... B-9
Ardentown, 264 ... B-9
Argos Cor., 50 ... J-4
Ashland ... B-2
Atlanta, 425 ... K-2
Bay View Bch., 50 ... E-2
Bayard ... F-5
Bear, 19371 ... D-2
Bellefonte, 1193 ... C-3
Bellevue Mnr., 200 ... C-2
Belvidere, 800 ... B-7
Bethany Bch., 1060 ... I-5
Bethel, 171 ... L-3
Big Stone Bch., 15 ... I-4
Birchwood Pk., 400 ... D-6
Blackbird ... F-2
Blades, 1241 ... K-3
Bowers Bch., 335 ... H-5
Brandywine, 1400 ... B-8
Brandywood, 800 ... B-9
Bridgeville, 2048 ... K-3
Broadkill Bch., 100 ... I-5
Camden, 3464 ... H-4
Cannon, 400 ... L-2
Carrcroft, 1500 ... C-3
Carrcroft Crest, 900 ... B-3
Castle Hills, 2000 ... D-8
Centerville, 500 ... B-8
Chalfonte, 1680 ... C-9
Cheswold, 1380 ... G-2

(Delaware, col. 2)
Christiana, 500 ... D-2
Clarksville, 200 ... I-5
Claymont, 8253 ... C-3
Clayton, 2139 ... F-1
Cleland Hts., 900 ... D-8
Collins Pk., 1500 ... D-8
Concord, 750 ... K-2
Cool Spr., 50 ... K-4
Coventry, 1500 ... C-7
Crossroads ... G-6
Darley Woods, 1300 ... B-9
Delaware City, 1695 ... D-2
Delaware Hts., 40 ... C-7
Delmar, 1597 ... M-2
Delpark Mnr., 1100 ... D-7
Devonshire, 200 ... C-9
Dewey Bch., 341 ... K-5
Dover, 36047 ... G-3
Downs Chapel, 25 ... H-3
Dunleith, 3400 ... D-8
Dupont Mnr., 300 ... G-2
Edgemoor, 5677 ... C-9
Ellendale, 381 ... J-3
Elsmere, 6131 ... C-9
Fairfield Farms, 700 ... H-8
Fairthorne, 1600 ... B-8
Farmington, 110 ... I-3
Faulkland, 1300 ... C-7
Felton, 1298 ... I-2
Fenwick Island, 379 ... M-5
Forest Brook Glen,
  200 ... C-8
Fox Hall ... C-7
Frankford, 847 ... L-4
Frederica, 714 ... I-3
Garfield Pk., 400 ... D-8
Georgetown, 6422 ... K-3
Glasgow, 14303 ... D-1
Gravel Hill, 75 ... K-4
Graylyn Crest, 450 ... B-9
Green Acres, 1100 ... B-8
Greenville, 2326 ... C-2
Greenwood, 973 ... J-2
Guyencourt, 100 ... B-8
Gwinhurst, 400 ... B-9
Hamilton Pk., 200 ... D-8
Harrington, 3562 ... I-2
Hartly, 74 ... G-1
Hazlettville, 400 ... G-2
Hearns Crossroads ... L-3
Hearns Mill, 130 ... L-2
Henlopen Acres, 122 ... K-5
Hickman, 100 ... J-1
Hillcrest, 1500 ... C-9
Hitchens Crossroads ... L-3
Hockessin, 13527 ... C-2
Holloway Ter., 1200 ... D-8
Hollyville ... K-4
Houston, 374 ... I-3
Huntley, 100 ... H-9
Indian Bch., 10 ... K-5
Ivy Ridge, 1800 ... C-9
Jefferson Farms,
  2300 ... D-8
Jimtown, 45 ... K-4
Kenton, 302 ... G-2
Keen-Wik, 400 ... M-5
Kent Acres, 2000 ... H-3
KENT CO., 162310...H-3
Kenton, 261 ... G-2
Kirkwood, 150 ... D-2
Kitts Hummock, 300 ... H-4
L. Pines, 125 ... L-4
Lancaster Vil. ... C-8
Laurel, 3708 ... L-2
Lebanon, 120 ... H-3
Leipsic, 183 ... G-3
Lewes, 2747 ... J-5
Lincoln, 500 ... J-3
Little Creek, 224 ... G-3
Little Heaven, 250 ... H-3
Llangollen Estates,
  1200 ... E-7
Lynch Hts., 125 ... I-3
Magnolia, 226 ... H-3
Marshallton, 1300 ... C-7
Masseys, 80 ... H-3
Mastens Cor., 60 ... H-2
Maypearl, 125 ... J-4
Meadowood, 600 ... D-8
Mechanicsville, 400 ... L-3
Middleford, 150 ... K-3
Middlesex Bch., 25 ... I-5
Middletown, 18871 ... E-1
Midway, 600 ... K-5
Milford, 9559 ... I-3
Milford Crossroads ... I-3
Millsboro, 3877 ... L-4
Millville, 544 ... L-5
Milton, 2576 ... J-4
Minquadale, 650 ... D-8
Montchanin, 300 ... B-8
Mt. Pleasant, 100 ... F-2
Nassau, 125 ... J-4
New Castle, 5285 ... D-2
NEW CASTLE CO.,
  538479 ... E-3
Newark, 31454 ... C-1
Newport, 1055 ... C-2
N. Shores, 100 ... J-5
N. Star, 7480 ... D-1
Oak Orchard, 500 ... L-5
Oakley ... J-3
Ocean View, 1882 ... I-5
Odessa, 364 ... E-2
Ogletown, 600 ... C-7
Omar ... L-4
Pearsons Corner, 40 ... G-2
Penn Acres, 2000 ... D-8
Pennyhill, 600 ... C-9
Pepper, 40 ... L-4
Petersburg, 250 ... H-2
Pine Tree Cors. ... J-2
Pleasanton Acres, 50 ... D-8
Port Penn, 250 ... E-2
Portsville, 100 ... L-2
Primehook Bch., 50 ... J-4
Rambleton Acres ... D-7

District of Columbia
Page locator
Map keys | Atlas pages
A–N | 224–225

Georgetown, 601723 ... E-6

Florida
Page locator
Map keys | Atlas pages
A–J | 52–53
K–T | 54–55

* City keyed to p. 51
† City keyed to pp. 56–57

Adamsville, 280 ... *D-8
Alachua, 9059 ... D-7
Alafaya, 78113 ... H-10
Alford, 400 ... R-7
Allentown, 894 ... Q-3
Alligator ... D-8
Alton, 100 ... C-5
Altoona, 80 ... G-9
Alturas, 4185 ... J-9
Alva, 2596 ... N-9
Amelia City, 730 ... B-10
Anclote, 260 ... H-6
Anglers Pk., 980 ... R-13
Ankona, 280 ... L-13
Anna Maria, 1503 ... K-6
Anthony, 1150 ... F-8
Apalachicola, 2231 ... T-8
Apopka, 41542 ... H-10
Arcadia, 7637 ... L-9
Archer, 1118 ... E-7
Aripeka, 300 ... G-6
Armstrong, 300 ... D-10
Arran ... C-2
Asbury Lake, 8700 ... C-9
Ashville ... B-4
Astatula, 1810 ... G-9
Astor, 50 ... G-9
Astor Pk., 150 ... F-9
Athena, 60 ... B-1
Atlantic Bch.,
  12655 ... C-10
Atlantis, 2005 ... N-14
Auburndale, 13507 ... I-9
Aucilla, 100 ... B-3
Avalon Bch., 679 ... R-3
Ave Maria, 30 ... O-10
Aventura, 35762 ... P-14
Avon Pk., 8836 ... K-10
Avondale ... *I-1
Azalea Pk., 13556 ... H-10
Babson Park, 1356 ... J-10
Bagdad, 3761 ... R-3
Baker, 300 ... Q-4
BAKER CO., 27115...B-7
Bal Harbour, 3513 ... *K-3
Baldwin, 1425 ... C-8
Balm, 1457 ... I-8
Barberville, 145 ... F-9
Barefoot Bay, 3000 ... J-12
Bartow, 17298 ... J-9
Bascom, 127 ... Q-7
Bay Harbor Islands,
  5628 ... *K-3
Bay Lake, 130 ... H-9
Bay Lake, 25 ... O-9
Bay Pines, 2931 ... *D-1
Bay Ridge, 155 ... K-2
Bay Sprs., 50 ... R-2
Bayou George, 230 ... S-6
Bayport, 43 ... G-6
Bayshore Gdns. ... *F-3

(Florida, col. 2)
Rodric Vil., 100 ... H-9
Roxana, 100 ... L-5
Belle Glade, 17467 ... N-12
Belle Isle, 5988 ... O-4
Bellair, 3869 ... J-6
Bellair Bch., 1560 ... I-6
Bellair Bluffs, 2031 ... *C-1
Belleview, 4492 ... F-8
Bellview, 23355 ... R-2
Bellwood, 500 ... D-12
Benedict, 800 ... E-6
Berrydale, 441 ... Q-3
Bethune Beach ... G-10
Beulah, 800 ... R-2
Beulah, 200 ... N-2
Beverly Bch., 338 ... F-10
Beverly Hills, 8445 ... G-7
Big Coppitt Key,
  2458 ... T-9
Big Pine Key, 4252 ... T-10
Bilmore ... H-1
Biscayne Pk., 3055 ... *K-3
Bithlo, 8268 ... H-11
Blackman ... Q-4
Bloomingdale,
  22711 ... I-8
Blountstown, 2514 ... R-7
Bloxham, 200 ... B-1
Boca Del Mar,
  21800 ... *F-9
Boca Grande, 700 ... N-8
Boca Pointe, 3300 ... *F-9
Boca Raton, 84392 ... O-14
Boca West, 2000 ... *E-9
Bokeelia, 1180 ... N-8
Bonifay, 2793 ... Q-6
Bonita Sprs., 43914 ... O-9
Bostwick, 300 ... E-9
Boulogne, 260 ... A-8
Bowden ... J-2
Bowling Green, 2930 ... K-9
Boyette, 5890 ... *D-5
Boynton Bch.,
  68217 ... N-14
Bradenton, 49546 ... K-7
Bradenton Bch.,
  1171 ... K-6
Bradfordville, 470 ... B-2
Bradley Jct., 686 ... J-8
Brandon, 103483 ... I-7
Branford, 712 ... D-6
Brent, 21804 ... *I-9
Briny Breezes, 601 ... *D-10
Bristol, 996 ... R-7
Broadview Pk., 7125 ... *I-8
Bronson, 1113 ... E-7
Brooker, 338 ... D-7
Brookridge, 4420 ... H-7
Brooksville, 7719 ... H-7
Bruce, 200 ... R-5
Bryant, 180 ... M-12
Bryceville, 180 ... B-8
Buchanan ... C-9
Buckhead Ridge,
  1450 ... L-11
Buckingham, 4036 ... N-9
Buenaventura Lakes,
  26079 ... I-10
Bunnell, 2676 ... E-10
Bushnell, 2418 ... H-8
Callahan, 1123 ... B-9
Callaway, 14405 ... S-6
Cameron City, 180 ... A-5
Campbell, 2479 ... I-10
Campbellton, 202 ... Q-7
Campton, 125 ... Q-4
Campville, 200 ... E-8
Canal Pt., 367 ... M-12
Candler, 370 ... F-8
Canova Bch. ... G-14
Cantonment, 2800 ... R-2
Cape Canaveral,
  9912 ... H-12
Cape Coral, 154305 ... N-8
Cape Haze, 2000 ... M-8
Capitola, 165 ... B-2
Capps, 20 ... B-3
Captiva, 583 ... N-8
Carrabelle, 2778 ... T-1
Carrollwood, 33365 ... *B-3
Carters Cor., 250 ... G-2
Caryville, 411 ... Q-6
Casselberry, 26241 ... I-4
Cassia, 90 ... G-10
Cedar Grv., 4397 ... S-6
Center Hill, 988 ... H-8
Century, 1698 ... Q-2
Chaires, 100 ... B-3
Chapman, 500 ... *A-4
Chaseville ... C-10
Chassahowitzka,
  850 ... G-6
Chattahoochee, 3652 ... R-8
Cherry Lake ... A-4
Chester, 370 ... Q-4
Chiefland, 2245 ... E-6
Chipley, 3605 ... Q-6
Chipola ... Q-7
Chokoloskee, 359 ... P-10
Christmas, 1146 ... H-11
Chuluota, 2483 ... H-11
Chumuckla, 850 ... Q-2
Citra, 1828 ... F-8

(Florida, col. 3)
Bell, 456 ... D-6
Belle Glade, 17467 ... N-12
Compass Lake, 200 ... R-7
Conch Key, 140 ... S-12
Concord, 125 ... B-2
Conway, 13467 ... G-10
Cooper City, 28547 ... *I-8
Copeland, 30 ... P-10
Coral Cove, 1160 ... L-7
Coral Gables,
  46780 ... Q-13
Coral Sprs., 121096 ... O-13
Coral Ter., 24376 ... *M-7
Corkscrew ... N-10
Cornwell ... L-11
Cortez, 4241 ... *G-2
Cottage Hill, 1050 ... R-2
Cottondale, 933 ... Q-7
Crawfordville, 3702 ... C-2
Crescent Bch., 811 ... D-10
Crescent City, 1577 ... E-10
Cresent City, 1577 ... L-10
Crestview, 20978 ... Q-4
Cross City, 1728 ... C-5
Cross Creek, 270 ... E-8
Crystal Bch., 1350 ... *A-1
Crystal Lake, 15 ... R-6
Crystal River, 3108 ... G-7
Crystal Sprs., 1327 ... I-8
Cudjoe Key, 1763 ... T-10
Curlew, 780 ... *B-1
Cutler, 5000 ... *P-3
Cutler Bay, 40286 ... Q-13
Cypress, 250 ... R-7
Cypress Gdns. ... J-9
Cypress Quarters,
  1215 ... L-11
Dade City, 6437 ... H-8
Dalkeith ... T-7
Dania Bch., 29639 ... P-13
Darby, 375 ... H-7
Darsey, 300 ... J-2
Davenport, 2888 ... I-9
Davie, 91992 ... P-13
Day, 116 ... C-5
Daytona Bch.,
  61005 ... F-11
Daytona Bch. Shores,
  4247 ... F-11
De Funiak Sprs.,
  5177 ... R-5
De Soto City, 600 ... K-10
De Soto City, 600 ... K-11
DeBary, 19320 ... G-10
Deer Pk. ... H-12
Deerfield Bch.,
  75018 ... O-14
Dekle Bch., 50 ... C-5
DeLand, 27031 ... F-10
Dellwood, 75 ... Q-7
Delray Bch., 60522 ... N-14
Deltona, 85182 ... G-10
Denaud ... M-9
Destin, 12305 ... R-4
Dinsmore ... C-9
Dixie, 150 ... K-9
Doctors Inlet, 1800 ... C-9
Doral, 45704 ... *L-7
Dorcas ... R-5
Dover, 3702 ... I-8
Dowling Pk., 500 ... C-5
Drifton, 25 ... B-3
Duette, 50 ... K-8
Dukes, 200 ... D-7
Dundee, 3717 ... I-9
Dunedin, 35321 ... I-6
Dunnellon, 1733 ... F-7
Durant, 225 ... I-8
Duval Sprs. ... A-4
DUVAL CO.,
  864263 ... B-8
Eagle Lake, 2255 ... J-9
Earleton, 320 ... E-8
E. Lake Weir, 140 ... G-8
E. Naples, 250 ... O-9
E. Palatka, 1654 ... E-9
E. Tampa, 750 ... I-7
Eastpoint, 2337 ... T-8
Eaton Pk., 900 ... *K-2
Eatonville, 2159 ... H-10
Ebro, 270 ... R-6
Edgar, 50 ... F-9
Edgewater, 20750 ... G-11
Edgewood, 2503 ... N-4
Egypt Lake, 3500 ... *B-3
El Destinado, 550 ... *K-8
El Jobean, 600 ... M-8
El Portal, 2325 ... *K-3
Elfers, 13986 ... I-6
Elkton ... D-9
Ellaville ... B-4
Ellenton, 4275 ... K-7
Ellzey ... E-6
Eloise Woods, 1900 ... *K-5
Emeralda, 96 ... G-9
Ensley, 20602 ... R-2
Enterprise, 2000 ... G-10
Eridu, 60 ... C-4
Estero, 22612 ... N-9
Estiffanulga, 120 ... R-7
Esto, 364 ... Q-6
Eureka, 130 ... F-8
Eustis, 18558 ... G-9

(Florida, col. 4)
Fisher Island, 132 ... *M-9
Five Points, 1265 ... C-7
Flagler Bch., 4484 ... E-11
Flagler ... E-10
FLAGLER CO.,
  95696 ... E-10
Flamingo ... R-11
Flamingo Bay, 880 ... N-8
Flemington ... E-8
Florahome, 430 ... D-9
Floral City, 5217 ... G-7
Florida City, 11245 ... Q-13
Floridana Bch., 200 ... *K-7
Florosa, 1000 ... R-4
Forest City, 13854 ... I-3
Forest Hills, 550 ... G-8
Ft. Drum, 140 ... K-12
Ft. Green, 101 ... K-8
Ft. Green Sprs., 231 ... K-8
Ft. Lauderdale,
  165521 ... O-13
Ft. Lonesome, 400 ... J-8
Ft. McCoy, 300 ... F-8
Ft. Meade, 5626 ... J-9
Ft. Myers, 62298 ... N-9
Ft. Myers Bch., 6277 ... N-8
Ft. Myers Villas,
  5600 ... *F-3
Ft. Ogden, 300 ... L-9
Ft. Pierce, 41590 ... L-13
Ft. Walton Bch.,
  1875 ... R-4
Fountain, 500 ... S-6
Four Corners ... *F-11
Fountainbleau,
  59764 ... *L-7
Fowlers Bluff, 90 ... E-6
Fox Town, 300 ... Q-13
Franklin, 400 ... I-5
FRANKLIN CO.,
  11549 ... D-1
Franklin Pk., 2400 ... *M-2
Franklintown, 500 ... B-10
Freeport, 1787 ... R-5
Frink ... S-7
Frostproof, 2992 ... J-10
Fruit Cove, 29362 ... C-9
Fruitland, 500 ... F-9
Fruitland Pk., 4078 ... G-8
Fruitville, 13224 ... L-7
Fuller Hts., 8758 ... I-8
Gainesville, 124354 ... E-7
Galloway, 150 ... O-9
Gandy Bch., 150 ... D-4
Garden City, 150 ... Q-4
Garden Cove, 674 ... R-7
Gardner, 463 ... L-9
Gaskin, 150 ... Q-5
Gateway, 8401 ... N-9
Geneva, 2940 ... G-11
Georgetown, 480 ... E-9
Gibsonia, 4507 ... I-1
Gibsonton, 14234 ... J-7
Gifford, 9590 ... K-13
GILCHRIST CO.,
  16939 ... E-6
Gilmore ... F-8
GLADES CO.,
  12884 ... M-10
Gladeview, 11535 ... *L-8
Glen Ridge, 219 ... *B-10
Glen St. Mary, 437 ... C-8
Glendale, 100 ... Q-5
Glenvar Hts.,
  16898 ... *M-7
Glenwood, 600 ... F-10
Golden Bch., 919 ... *J-3
Golden Gate, 23961 ... O-9
Golden Gate, 2650 ... L-13
Goldenrod, 12039 ... M-4
Golf, 252 ... *D-9
Gonzalez, 13273 ... R-2
Goodby's ... J-2
Goodland, 267 ... P-9
Gordonville, 1500 ... *L-4
Gotha, 1915 ... N-3
Goulding, 4102 ... *I-9
Graceville, 2278 ... Q-6
Graham, 200 ... D-8
Grand Island, 200 ... G-9
Grand Ridge, 892 ... R-7
Grandin ... D-9
Grant-Valkaria,
  3850 ... J-12
Grayton Bch., 150 ... S-5
Grayvik, 125 ... *F-8
Green Cove Sprs.,
  6908 ... D-9
Greenacres, 37573 ... N-13
Greenacres City,
  37573 ... *E-9
Greensboro, 602 ... R-1
Greenville, 843 ... B-4
Greenwood, 686 ... Q-7
Gretna, 1460 ... R-1
Griffin ... J-1
Grove City, 1804 ... M-7
Grove Pk., 140 ... E-8
Groveland, 8729 ... H-9
Gulf Bch. Hts., 1600 ... *L-7
Gulf Breeze, 5763 ... R-3
Gulf City, 500 ... J-7
Gulf Gate Estates,
  12344 ... *G-13
Gulf Hammock, 250 ... E-6
Gulf Harbors, 800 ... I-6
Gulf Stream, 786 ... *D-10
Gulfport, 12029 ... I-6
Hague, 400 ... E-7
Haines City, 20535 ... I-9
Hall City, 145 ... M-10
Hallandale, 37113 ... *I-9
Hallandale Bch.,
  37113 ... *P-13
HAMILTON CO.,
  14799 ... B-6
Hammond, 140 ... I-8
Hampton, 500 ... D-8
Hampton Sprs. ... C-4
Hanlover ... D-11
Harbin's ... L-3

(Florida, col. 5)
Hawthorne, 1417 ... E-8
Heathrow, 5896 ... G-10
Hedges, 800 ... B-9
Helena ... *L-8
L. Bird, 50 ... J-12
L. Brantley, 3000 ... I-3
L. Buena Vista, 10 ... H-10
L. Butler, 1897 ... D-7
L. Cain Hills, 1600 ... N-3
L. Clarke Shores,
  3376 ... *D-9
L. Como, 500 ... E-9
L. Geneva, 1200 ... D-8
L. Hamilton, 1231 ... I-9
L. Helen, 2624 ... G-10
L. Kathryn, 45 ... G-9
L. Marian Highlands,
  300 ... J-11
L. Mary, 13822 ... G-9
L. Monroe, 250 ... G-10
L. Panasoffkee, 3551 ... G-8
L. Placid, 2223 ... L-10
L. Suzy, 1040 ... M-9
L. Wales, 14225 ... J-9
L. Worth, 34910 ... N-14
LAKE CO., 297052...H-9
Lakeland, 97442 ... I-8
Lakeport, 300 ... M-11
Lakewood Pk.,
  10902 ... L-13
Lamont, 178 ... B-3
Lanark Vil., 50 ... T-1
Land O' Lakes, 31996 ... I-7
Lantana, 10423 ... N-14
Largo, 77648 ... J-6
Lauderdale Lakes,
  32593 ... *H-8
Lauderdale-by-the-Sea,
  6056 ... *H-9
Laurel, 8171 ... L-7
Laurel Hill, 537 ... Q-4
Lawtey, 730 ... C-8
Lazy Lake, 24 ... *H-8
Lealman, 19879 ... *D-2
Lebanon Sta., 30 ... F-7
Lee, 352 ... B-5
LEE CO., 618754...N-9
Leesburg, 20117 ... G-9
Lehigh Acres, 86784 ... N-9
Leisure City, 22655 ... Q-13
Lemon City, 667 ... K-8
LEON CO., 275487...B-3
Leonia, 150 ... Q-5
LEVY CO., 40801...E-6
Liberty, 100 ... J-9
LIBERTY CO., 8365...S-8
Lighthouse Pt.,
  10344 ... O-14
Limestone, 132 ... L-9
Linden, 120 ... H-8
Lisbon, 260 ... G-9
Little Havana ... *L-8
Little River ... J-3
Live Oak, 6850 ... C-6
Lloyd, 215 ... B-3
Lochloosa, 260 ... E-8
Lockmoor, 2300 ... *F-1
L. Key Largo, 1244 ... R-13
Lockhart, 13060 ... M-3
Longboat Key, 6888 ... L-6
Longwood, 13657 ... I-4
Lorida, 340 ... K-10
Loughman, 2680 ... I-10
Lowell, 220 ... F-8
Loxahatchee Groves,
  3180 ... N-13
Lulu, 100 ... C-7
Lumberton, 220 ... J-2
Luraville ... C-5
Lutz, 19344 ... I-7
Lynn Haven, 18493 ... S-6
Macclenny, 6374 ... C-8
Madison, 2843 ... B-4
MADISON CO.,
  19224 ... C-4
Maitland, 15751 ... M-4
Malabar, 2757 ... J-12
Malone, 2088 ... Q-7
Manalapan, 406 ... *C-10
Manatee, 540 ... *M-2
MANATEE CO.,
  322833 ... K-7
Mandarin ... C-9
Mango, 11313 ... I-8
Mangonia Pk.,
  1888 ... *E-9
Manhattan, 40 ... *F-5
Marathon, 8297 ... T-11
Marco Island, 16413 ... P-9
Margate, 53284 ... O-13
Marianna, 6102 ... Q-7
Marietta, 645 ... B-9
MARION CO.,
  331298 ... F-7
Marion Oaks, 1846 ... F-8
Markham ... I-3
Martel, 200 ... F-8
MARTIN CO.,
  146318 ... L-13
Mary Esther, 3851 ... R-4
Mascotte, 5101 ... H-9
Masaryktown, 1000 ... H-7
Matlacha, 735 ... N-8
Maximo ... *D-2
Maxville, 200 ... C-9
Mayo, 1237 ... C-5
McAlpin, 105 ... C-6
McDavid, 100 ... Q-2
McIntosh, 452 ... F-8
Medart, 150 ... C-1
Medley, 838 ... *L-7
Medulla, 8892 ... *K-1
Melbourne, 76068 ... I-12
Melbourne Bch.,
  3101 ... J-12
Melbourne Shores,
  125 ... J-12
Melbourne Vil., 662 ... N-13
Melrose, 1100 ... E-8
Memphis, 7848 ... *F-1
Merritt Island,
  34743 ... H-12
Mexico Bch., 1072 ... S-6
Miakka City ... K-8

(Florida, col. 6)
Miami Lakes, 29361 ... *K-7
Miami Shores,
  10493 ... *K-8
Miami Sprs., 13809 ... *L-7
MIAMI-DADE CO.,
  2496435 ... R-12
Micanopy, 600 ... E-7
Micco, 9052 ... J-12
Miccosukee, 285 ... B-3
Middleburg, 13008 ... C-9
Midway, 3004 ... B-2
Midway, 5350 ... G-10
Milligan, 350 ... Q-4
Milview, 1100 ... *J-7
Milton, 8826 ... R-3
Mims, 7058 ... H-11
Minneola, 9403 ... H-9
Miramar, 122041 ... P-13
Mission Bay, 2900 ... *F-9
Mission City, 1700 ... J-11
Molino, 1772 ... Q-2
MONROE CO.,
  73090 ... Q-11
Montbrook ... E-6
Monticello, 2506 ... B-3
Montverde, 1463 ... M-1
Moore Haven,
  1680 ... M-11
Morningside Pk.,
  500 ... O-3
Morriston, 164 ... *-7
Morse Shores, 3300 ... *L-3
Moss Bluff, 120 ... F-9
Mossy Head, 250 ... Q-5
Mt. Carmel, 227 ... Q-3
Mt. Dora, 12370 ... G-9
Mt. Pleasant, 75 ... Q-7
Mt. Plymouth, 4011 ... G-3
Mulberry, 3817 ... J-8
Munson, 372 ... Q-3
Murdock ... M-8
Myakka City, 170 ... L-8
Myakka Head, 100 ... K-8
Myrtle Grv., 15870 ... R-2
Naples, 19537 ... O-9
Naples Manor, 5562 ... P-9
Naples Pk., 5967 ... O-9
Naranja, 8303 ... Q-13
Narcoossee, 200 ... I-10
NASSAU CO.,
  73314 ... B-9
National Gdns., 400 ... F-11
Navarre, 31378 ... R-3
Neptune Bch., 7037 ... C-10
New Berlin ... C-10
New Hope, 100 ... Q-6
New Port Richey,
  14911 ... I-6
New Smyrna Bch.,
  22464 ... F-11
Newberry, 4950 ... E-7
Newport ... C-2
Niceville, 12749 ... R-4
Nobleton, 282 ... H-8
Nocatee, 4524 ... L-9
Nokomis, 3167 ... L-7
Nonna, 400 ... R-7
N. Bay Vil., 7137 ... *K-9
N. Fort Myers, 39407 ... N-9
N. Key Largo, 1244 ... R-13
N. Lauderdale,
  41203 ... *G-8
N. Miami, 58786 ... P-13
N. Miami Bch.,
  41523 ... P-13
N. Palm Bch.,
  12015 ... M-14
N. Port, 57357 ... M-8
N. Redington Bch.,
  1417 ... *D-1
N. River Shores,
  3079 ... L-13
N. River Shores ... L-13
Northdale, 22079 ... I-7
Oak Grv., 300 ... I-7
Oak Hill, 1792 ... G-11
Oakdale, 50 ... R-7
Oakland, 2538 ... N-1
Oakland Pk., 41363 ... O-14
O'Brien, 100 ... C-6
Ocala, 56315 ... F-8
Ocean Ridge, 1786 ... *C-10
Ocklawaha, 860 ... F-8
Ocoee, 35579 ... M-2
Odessa, 7267 ... I-7
Ojus, 18036 ... *J-2
Okahumpka, 267 ... G-9
OKALOOSA CO.,
  180822 ... R-4
Okeechobee, 5621 ... L-11
OKEECHOBEE CO.,
  39996 ... K-11
Old Myakka, 200 ... K-8
Old Town, 250 ... C-5
Oldsmar, 13591 ... I-6
Oriole Bch., 1420 ... *J-10
Orlando, 238300 ... N-3
Orlovista, 6123 ... N-3
Ormond Bch.,
  38137 ... F-10
Ormond-By-The-Sea,
  7406 ... F-11
Ortona, 314 ... M-11
Oneco, 3200 ... K-7
O'Neil, 455 ... B-3
Opa-locka, 15219 ... P-13
ORANGE CO.,
  1145956 ... H-11
Orange Lake, 700 ... E-8
Orange Mills, 200 ... D-9
Orange Pk., 9402 ... C-9
Orangedale, 400 ... C-9
Orangetree, 4406 ... O-9
Orchid, 415 ... K-13
Oriel ... C-7
Osceola, 80 ... B-6
OSCEOLA CO.,
  268685 ... J-11
Osprey, 6100 ... L-7
Osteen, 500 ... G-10
Otter Creek, 134 ... E-6
Overstreet, 30 ... S-6

Kalapana ... M-10
Kalaupapa, 120 ... J-6
Kalihi, 1900 ... G-7
Kamehameha Hts., 1100 ... G-8
Kāne'ohe, 34597 ... J-5
Kapa'a, 10699 ... I-2
Kapolei, 15186 ... M-2
KAUAI CO., 67091 ... I-2
Kaunakakai, 3425 ... J-6
Kaupakulua, 350 ... I-9
Kaupō ... J-10
Kawailoa ... K-2
Kawailoa Bch., 300 ... K-2
Kawela, 100 ... J-3
Kea'au, 2253 ... M-10
Kealakekua, 2019 ... M-8
Ke'anae, 50 ... K-8
Kekaha, 3537 ... I-2
Keokea, 1612 ... K-7
Kīhei, 20881 ... K-7
Kīlauea, 2803 ... H-2
Kīpahulu ... J-10
Koali ... J-10
Kokomo, 320 ... I-9
Koloa, 2144 ... I-2
Kualapu'u, 2027 ... J-6
Kukuihaele, 336 ... L-9
Kuli'ou'ou, 370 ... N-5
Kunia Camp, 580 ... L-2
Kurtistown, 1298 ... M-10
Lahaina, 11704 ... K-7
Lā'ie, 6138 ... J-4
Lāna'i City, 3102 ... K-6
Laupāhoehoe, 581 ... L-9
Līhu'e, 6455 ... I-2
Lower Paia, 220 ... I-9
Mā'alaea, 352 ... I-8
Mā'ili, 9488 ... M-1
Mākaha, 8278 ... L-1
Makakilo City, 18248 ... M-2
Makawao, 7184 ... I-9
Mākena, 99 ... J-9
Mānā ... I-2
MAUI CO., 154834 ... J-7
Maunalani Hts., 700 ... G-10
Maunaloa, 376 ... J-6
Maunawili, 2040 ... M-5
Mililani Town, 27629 ... L-3
Miloli'i ... N-8
Mountain View, 3924 ... M-9
Nā'ālehu, 866 ... N-9
Nānākuli, 12666 ... J-4
Niu, 570 ... N-5
Olowalu, 80 ... I-8
Ō'ōkala, 150 ... L-9
Pā'auhau, 270 ... L-9
Pa'auilo, 595 ... L-9
Pacific Hts., 650 ... F-8
Pacific Palisades, 5600 ... M-3
Pāhala, 1356 ... N-9
Pāhoa, 945 ... M-10
Paia, 2668 ... I-9
Pāpā ... N-8
Pāpa'aloa, 320 ... L-9
Pāpa'ikou, 1314 ... M-10
Pa'uwela, 500 ... K-7
Pearl City, 47698 ... J-5
Pepe'ekeo, 1789 ... M-10
Poamoho ... L-3
Pukalani, 7574 ... K-7
Punalu'u ... K-4
Pu'uanahulu ... M-8
Pu'uiki ... J-10
Pu'ukoli'i, 200 ... I-8
Pu'unēnē ... I-8
Pu'uwai ... I-1
St. Louis Hts., 1000 ... G-10
Spreckelsville ... I-9
Sunset Bch., 660 ... J-3
'Ulupalakua, 75 ... K-7
Volcano, 2575 ... M-9
Wahiawā, 17821 ... J-5
Waiakoa, 900 ... J-9
Waialua, 3860 ... J-7
Wai'anae, 13177 ... J-4
Waiehu, 600 ... I-8
Waikapu, 2965 ... K-7
Waikīkī, 3000 ... H-9
Wailua, 2254 ... I-2
Wailua, 120 ... I-10
Wailuku, 15313 ... K-7
Waimānalo, 5451 ... J-5
Waimānalo Bch., 4481 ... M-6
Waimea, 9212 ... L-9
Waimea, 1855 ... I-2
Waimea, 650 ... J-2
Waipahu, 38216 ... M-3
Waipi'o Acres ... L-3
Whitmore Vil., 4499 ... L-3
Woodlawn, 1200 ... F-9

Idaho

Page locator

Map keys	Atlas pages
A–N	64–65

Aberdeen, 1994 ... L-6
Acequia, 124 ... M-5
ADA CO., 392365 ... K-2
ADAMS CO., 3976 ... H-1
Ahsahka, 150 ... F-2
Albion, 267 ... M-5
Almo ... N-5
American Falls, 4457 ... L-6
Ammon, 13816 ... K-7
Arbon, 35 ... M-7
Arco, 995 ... K-6
Arimo, 355 ... M-7
Ashton, 1127 ... J-8
Athol, 692 ... C-1
Atlanta ... K-3
Atomic City, 29 ... K-6
Bancroft, 377 ... M-8
Banida, 125 ... M-8
Banks, 17 ... J-2
BANNOCK CO., 82839 ... M-7
Basalt, 394 ... K-7
Bayview, 350 ... C-2
BEAR LAKE CO., 5986 ... N-9
Bellevue, 2287 ... K-4
BENEWAH CO., 9285 ... E-1
Bennington, 190 ... M-8
Bern, 60 ... M-8
Big Creek ... H-3
BINGHAM CO., 45607 ... L-6
Blackfoot, 11899 ... L-7
BLAINE CO., 21376 ... K-5
Blanchard, 261 ... C-1
Bliss, 318 ... L-4
Bloomington, 206 ... M-8
Boise, 205671 ... K-2
BOISE CO., 7028 ... J-2
Bone ... K-8
BONNER CO., 40877 ... C-2
Bonners Ferry, 2543 ... B-2
BONNEVILLE CO., 104234 ... K-8
BOUNDARY CO., 10972 ... B-2
Bovill, 260 ... E-2
Bowmont, 150 ... K-1
Bruneau, 100 ... L-2
Buhl, 4122 ... M-4
Burgdorf ... H-2
Burley, 10345 ... M-5
Butte City, 74 ... K-6
BUTTE CO., 2891 ... K-6
Cabinet ... C-2
Calder ... D-2
Caldwell, 46237 ... K-1
CAMAS CO., 1117 ... K-4
Cambridge, 328 ... I-1
CANYON CO., 188923 ... K-1
Carey, 604 ... K-5
Careywood ... C-2
CARIBOU CO., 6963 ... L-7
Carmen, 25 ... H-5
Cascade, 939 ... I-2
CASSIA CO., 22952 ... M-5
Castleford, 226 ... M-4
Cataldo, 260 ... D-2
Cavendish, 30 ... F-2
Challis, 1081 ... I-4
Chatcolet ... D-1
Chester, 350 ... J-8
Chilco ... C-1
Chubbuck, 13922 ... L-7
CLARK CO., 982 ... J-7
Clark Fork, 536 ... C-2
Clarkia, 80 ... E-2
Clayton, 7 ... J-4
Clearwater, 50 ... G-2
CLEARWATER CO., 8761 ... E-3
Clifton, 259 ... M-7
Cobalt ... H-4
Cocolalla, 140 ... C-2
Coeur d'Alene, 44137 ... D-1
Colburn, 100 ... B-2
Conda ... L-8
Coolin, 200 ... B-1
Corral ... K-4
Cottonwood, 900 ... G-2
Council, 839 ... I-2
Craigmont, 501 ... F-2
Crouch, 162 ... J-2
Culdesac, 380 ... F-1
CUSTER CO., 4368 ... J-4
Dalton Gdns., 2335 ... C-1
Darlington, 50 ... K-6
Dayton, 463 ... N-7
Deary, 506 ... E-2
Declo, 343 ... M-5
Dietrich, 332 ... L-4
Dingle, 200 ... M-8
Dixie, 25 ... G-3
Donnelly, 152 ... I-2
Dover, 556 ... C-2
Downey, 625 ... M-7
Driggs, 1660 ... K-9
Drummond, 16 ... J-8
Dubois, 677 ... J-7
Eagle, 19908 ... K-2
E. Hope, 210 ... C-2
Eastport ... A-2
Eden, 405 ... M-4
Elba ... M-5
Elk City, 200 ... G-3
Elk River, 125 ... E-2
Ellis, 40 ... I-5
Elmira ... B-2
ELMORE CO., 27038 ... L-3
Emida, 100 ... E-2
Emmett, 6557 ... J-2
Fairfield, 416 ... K-4
Featherville ... K-3
Felt ... J-8
Fenn, 30 ... G-2
Ferdinand, 159 ... F-2
Fernan Lake Vil., 169 ... D-1
Fernwood, 425 ... E-2
Filer, 2508 ... M-4
Firth, 477 ... L-7
Fish Haven, 50 ... N-8
Franklin, 641 ... N-8
FRANKLIN CO., 12786 ... M-8
FREMONT CO., 13242 ... J-8
Fruitland, 4684 ... J-1
Fruitvale, 100 ... I-2
Gannett ... K-5
Garden City, 10972 ... B-6
Garden Valley, 394 ... J-2
GEM CO., 16719 ... J-2
Genesee, 955 ... F-1
Georgetown, 476 ... M-8
Gibbonsville ... G-5
Gifford ... F-2
Givens Hot Sprs., 120 ... K-1
Glenns Ferry, 1319 ... L-3
Golden ... G-3
Gooding, 3567 ... L-4
GOODING CO., 15464 ... L-4
Grace, 915 ... M-8
Grand View, 452 ... L-2
Grangeville, 3141 ... G-2
Grasmere ... M-2
Greencreek, 30 ... F-2
Greenleaf, 846 ... K-1
Greer ... F-2
Hagerman, 872 ... L-4
Hailey, 7960 ... K-4
Hamer, 48 ... J-7
Hammett, 300 ... L-3
Hansen, 1144 ... M-4
Harpster, 50 ... G-2
Harrison, 203 ... D-1
Harvard, 55 ... E-1
Hayden, 13294 ... C-1
Hayden Lake, 574 ... C-1
Hazelton, 753 ... M-5
Headquarters, 35 ... F-3
Heise ... K-8
Helmer ... E-2
Henry ... L-8
Heyburn, 3089 ... M-5
Hill City ... L-3
Holbrook ... N-7
Hollister, 272 ... M-4
Homedale, 2633 ... K-1
Hope, 86 ... C-2
Horseshoe Bend, 707 ... J-2
Howe, 80 ... K-6
Hoyt, 40 ... D-2
Huetter, 100 ... E-9
Idaho City, 485 ... K-2
IDAHO CO., 16267 ... G-2
Idaho Falls, 56813 ... K-7
Indian Valley, 75 ... I-2
Inkom, 854 ... L-7
Iona, 1803 ... K-7
Irwin, 219 ... K-8
Island Pk., 286 ... I-8
JEFFERSON CO., 26140 ... K-7
Jerome, 10890 ... M-4
JEROME CO., 22374 ... L-4
Joel, 100 ... E-1
Juliaetta, 579 ... F-1
Kamiah, 1295 ... F-2
Kellogg, 2120 ... D-2
Kendrick, 303 ... F-1
Ketchum, 2689 ... K-4
Kilgore ... I-7
Kimberly, 3264 ... M-4
King Hill, 100 ... L-3
Kingston, 800 ... D-2
Kooskia, 607 ... F-2
Kootenai, 678 ... B-2
KOOTENAI CO., 138494 ... C-1
Kuna, 15210 ... K-2
Laclede, 400 ... C-1
L. Fork, 120 ... I-2
Lakeview, 40 ... C-2
Lapwai, 1137 ... F-1
LATAH CO., 37244 ... E-2
Lava Hot Sprs., 407 ... M-7
Leadore, 105 ... I-6
Lemhi, 30 ... I-5
LEMHI CO., 7936 ... H-4
Lenore ... F-2
Leslie ... J-5
Letha, 240 ... J-1
LEWIS CO., 3821 ... F-2
Lewiston, 31894 ... F-1
Lewisville, 458 ... K-7
Liberty ... M-8
Lincoln, 3647 ... K-7
LINCOLN CO., 5208 ... L-5
Lorenzo, 100 ... K-8
Lost River, 68 ... K-5
Lowell, 25 ... F-3
Lowman, 42 ... J-3
Lucile, 100 ... G-2
Mackay, 517 ... J-5
MADISON CO., 37536 ... K-8
Magic City ... L-4
Malad City, 2095 ... M-7
Malta, 193 ... M-6
Marley, 100 ... L-4
Marsing, 1031 ... K-1
Marysville, 180 ... J-8
May, 50 ... I-5
McCall, 2991 ... I-2
McCammon, 809 ... M-7
McGuires ... E-7
Meadows, 190 ... I-2
Medimont ... D-2
Melba, 513 ... K-1
Menan, 741 ... K-7
Meridian, 75092 ... K-2
Mesa, 65 ... I-2
Middleton, 5524 ... K-1
Midvale, 171 ... I-1
Minidoka, 112 ... L-5
MINIDOKA CO., 20069 ... L-5
Mink Creek ... M-8
Monteview ... J-7
Montpelier, 2597 ... M-8
Moore, 189 ... K-6
Moreland, 1278 ... L-7
Moscow, 23800 ... E-1
Mt. Idaho ... G-2
Mountain Home, 14206 ... L-3
Moyie Sprs., 718 ... B-2
Mud Lake, 358 ... K-7
Mullan, 692 ... D-3
Murphy, 97 ... L-1
Murray, 75 ... D-2
Murtaugh, 115 ... M-5
Nampa, 81557 ... K-1
Naples, 450 ... B-2
New Centerville ... J-2
New Meadows, 496 ... H-2
New Plymouth, 1538 ... J-1
Newdale, 323 ... J-8
NEZ PERCE CO., 39265 ... F-1
Nezperce, 466 ... F-2
Nordman ... B-1
N. Fork ... H-5
Oakley, 763 ... M-5
Ola ... J-2
Onaway, 187 ... E-1
ONEIDA CO., 4286 ... N-6
Oreana ... L-2
Orofino, 3142 ... F-2
Orogrande ... G-3
Osburn, 1555 ... D-2
Ovid ... M-8
OWYHEE CO., 11526 ... M-2
Oxford, 48 ... M-7
Palisades, 100 ... K-8
Paris, 513 ... M-8
Parker, 305 ... J-8
Parma, 1983 ... K-1
Patterson, 5 ... I-5
Paul, 1169 ... M-5
Payette, 7433 ... J-1
PAYETTE CO., 22623 ... J-1
Peck, 197 ... F-2
Picabo, 100 ... K-5
Pierce, 508 ... F-3
Pine ... K-3
Pinehurst, 1619 ... D-2
Pingree, 150 ... L-7
Pioneerville ... J-2
Placerville, 53 ... J-2
Pleasant View ... F-6
Pleasantview, 220 ... N-7
Plummer, 1044 ... D-1
Pocatello, 54255 ... L-7
Pollock, 140 ... H-2
Ponderay, 1137 ... B-2
Porthill ... A-2
Post Falls, 27574 ... C-1
Potlatch, 804 ... E-1
POWER CO., 7817 ... M-6
Preston, 5204 ... N-8
Prichard ... D-2
Priest River, 1751 ... C-1
Princeton, 148 ... E-1
Rathdrum, 6826 ... C-1
Red River Hot Sprs. ... G-3
Reubens, 71 ... F-2
Rexburg, 25484 ... K-8
Reynolds ... L-1
Richfield, 482 ... L-5
Rigby, 3945 ... K-7
Riggins, 419 ... H-2
Ririe, 656 ... K-8
Riverside, 838 ... L-7
Roberts, 580 ... K-7
Rockland, 295 ... M-6
Rocky Bar ... K-3
Rogerson, 100 ... M-4
Rose Lake ... D-2
Rupert, 5554 ... M-5
St. Anthony, 3542 ... J-8
St. Charles, 131 ... N-8
St. Joe ... D-2
St. Maries, 2402 ... D-2
Salmon, 3112 ... H-5
Samaria, 100 ... N-7
Samuels, 150 ... B-2
Sanders ... E-1
Sandpoint, 7365 ... C-2
Santa, 100 ... E-2
Shelley, 4409 ... K-7
Shoshone, 1461 ... L-4
SHOSHONE CO., 12765 ... D-2
Shoup, 60 ... H-4
Silver City ... L-1
Silverton, 300 ... D-2
Smelterville, 627 ... D-2
Smiths Ferry, 75 ... J-2
Soda Sprs., 3058 ... M-8
Southwick, 40 ... F-2
Spalding ... F-1
Spencer, 37 ... J-7
Spirit Lake, 1945 ... C-1
Springfield, 100 ... L-7
Stanley, 63 ... J-4
Star, 5793 ... K-2
Sterling ... L-6
Stites, 221 ... G-2
Stone ... N-6
Sugar City, 1514 ... J-8
Sun Valley, 1406 ... K-4
Sunbeam, 40 ... J-4
Swan Valley, 204 ... K-8
Swanlake ... M-7
Sweet, 200 ... J-2
Syringa, 30 ... F-3
Tendoy ... I-5
Tensed, 123 ... E-1
Terreton ... K-7
Teton, 735 ... J-8
TETON CO., 10170 ... K-8
Tetonia, 269 ... K-8
Thatcher ... M-8
The String, 100 ... K-9
Thornton, 100 ... K-8
Triumph ... K-4
Troy, 862 ... E-1
Twin Falls, 44125 ... M-4
TWIN FALLS CO., 77230 ... M-4
Tyhee, 1123 ... L-7
Ucon, 1108 ... K-7
Ustick ... B-5
VALLEY CO., 9862 ... I-3
Victor, 1928 ... K-9
Viola, 150 ... E-1
Virginia ... M-7
Waha ... F-1
Wallace, 784 ... D-2
Warm Lake ... I-3
Warm River, 3 ... J-8
Warren, 45 ... H-3
WASHINGTON CO., 10198 ... I-1
Wayan, 35 ... L-8
Weippe, 441 ... F-2
Weiser, 5507 ... J-1
Wendell, 2782 ... L-4
Weston, 437 ... N-7
White Bird, 91 ... G-2
Whitney, 200 ... N-8
Wilder, 1533 ... K-1
Winchester, 340 ... F-1
Worley, 257 ... D-1
Yellow Pine, 32 ... I-3

Illinois

Page locator

Map keys	Atlas pages
A–J	66–67
K–T	68–69

* City keyed to pp. 70–71
† City keyed to pp. 72–73
‡ City keyed to pp. 120–121
§ City keyed to p. 233

Abingdon, 3319 ... G-6
Adair, 210 ... H-5
Adams, 50 ... J-3
ADAMS CO., 67103 ... J-3
Addieville, 252 ... O-8
Addison, 36942 ... *H-5
Adeline, 85 ... B-8
Aden ... P-11
Adrian, 60 ... H-4
Akin, 110 ... Q-10
Albany, 891 ... C-6
Albers, 1190 ... O-8
Albion, 1988 ... P-12
Alden, 250 ... A-11
Aledo, 3640 ... E-5
Alexander, 300 ... K-7
ALEXANDER CO., 8238 ... T-8
Alexis, 831 ... F-5
Algonquin, 30046 ... B-11
Alhambra, 681 ... N-7
Allendale, 475 ... O-13
Allenville, 148 ... K-11
Allerton, 291 ... J-12
Alma, 320 ... N-10
Alorton, 2002 ... ‡I-8
Alpha, 671 ... E-6
Alsey, 227 ... K-5
Alsip, 19277 ... *K-8
Alta, 400 ... G-8
Altamont, 2319 ... M-10
Alto Pass, 391 ... R-9
Alton, 27865 ... N-6
Altona, 531 ... F-6
Alvin, 279 ... I-13
Amboy, 2500 ... D-9
Anchor, 146 ... H-11
Ancona, 80 ... F-10
Andalusia, 1178 ... E-5
Andover, 578 ... E-6
Anna, 4442 ... S-9
Annapolis, 55 ... M-13
Annawan, 878 ... E-7
Antioch, 14430 ... A-12
Apple Canyon Lake, 558 ... A-6
Apple River, 366 ... A-7
Aptakisic ... *D-6
Arbury Hills, 1770 ... *M-7
Archer ... †M-15
Arcola, 2916 ... K-11
Arenzville, 409 ... J-6
Argenta, 947 ... J-10
Argo Fay, 100 ... C-7
Argyle, 100 ... A-10
Arlington, 193 ... D-9
Arlington Hts., 75101 ... B-12
Armington, 343 ... I-9
Armstrong, 200 ... I-12
Aroma Pk., 743 ... F-13
Arrowsmith, 294 ... H-10
Arthur, 2288 ... K-11
Ashburn ... *J-8
Ashkum, 761 ... G-12
Ashland, 1333 ... J-7
Ashley, 536 ... P-9
Ashmore, 785 ... K-12
Ashton, 972 ... C-9
Assumption, 1168 ... K-9
Astoria, 1141 ... I-6
Athens, 1988 ... J-7
Athensville, 50 ... L-6
Atkinson, 972 ... E-7
Atlanta, 1692 ... I-9
Atlas, 50 ... K-4
Atterberry, 120 ... J-7
Atwater, 100 ... L-7
Atwood, 1224 ... J-11
Auburn, 4771 ... K-7
Augusta, 587 ... I-4
Aurora, 197899 ... C-11
Austin ... *H-8
Ava, 654 ... Q-8
Aviston, 1945 ... O-8
Avon, 799 ... G-6
Avondale ... *G-9
Balcom, 70 ... S-9
Baldwin, 373 ... P-7
Banner, 189 ... H-7
Bannockburn, 1583 ... *D-7
Bardolph, 251 ... H-5
Barnhill, 80 ... P-11
Barrington, 10327 ... B-12
Barrington Hills, 4209 ... *E-3
Barry, 1318 ... K-4
Barstow, 140 ... S-6
Bartelso, 595 ... O-8
Bartlett, 41208 ... *G-3
Bartonville, 6471 ... H-8
Basco, 98 ... H-3
Batavia, 26045 ... C-11
Batchtown, 214 ... M-5
Bath, 333 ... I-6
Bay City ... T-11
Baylis, 205 ... K-4
Beach Pk., 13638 ... A-12
Beardstown, 6123 ... J-6
Beason, 189 ... I-9
Beaucoup, 80 ... P-9
Beaverville, 362 ... F-13
Bedford Pk., 580 ... *J-7
Beecher, 4359 ... E-13
Beecher City, 463 ... M-10
Beecreek ... L-5
Belgium, 404 ... I-13
Belknap, 104 ... S-10
Bellair, 25 ... M-12
Belle Prairie City, 54 ... P-11
Belle Rive, 361 ... P-10
Belleview, 25 ... L-4
Belleville, 44478 ... O-7
Bellevue, 1978 ... G-8
Bellflower, 357 ... I-11
Bellmont, 276 ... O-12
Belltown, 40 ... L-6
Bellwood, 19071 ... *H-7
Belvidere, 25585 ... B-10
Bement, 1730 ... J-11
Benld, 1556 ... M-7
Bensenville, 18352 ... *G-6
Benson, 423 ... G-9
Bentley, 35 ... H-4
Benton, 7087 ... Q-10
Berdan, 50 ... L-6
Berkeley, 5209 ... *H-6
Berlin, 180 ... K-7
Bernadotte, 100 ... H-6
Berry, 70 ... K-8
Berryville, 30 ... O-12
Berwick, 160 ... G-5
Berwyn, 56657 ... *I-8
Bethalto, 9521 ... N-7
Bethany, 1352 ... K-10
Beverly, 30 ... J-4
Beverly ... *K-9
Bible Grv., 100 ... N-11
Big Foot Prairie, 75 ... A-10
Big Rock, 1126 ... C-11
Biggsville, 304 ... G-4
Bingham, 83 ... M-9
Birds, 50 ... N-13
Bishop Hill, 128 ... E-6
Bismarck, 579 ... I-13
Bissell ... †L-17
Blackstone, 100 ... F-10
Blandinsville, 651 ... H-4
Bloomfield ... S-10
Bloomingdale, 22018 ... C-12
Bloomington, 76610 ... H-9
Blue Island, 23706 ... *K-9
Blue Mound, 1158 ... K-9
Blue Ridge ... I-11
Bluff City, 300 ... M-9
Bluff Sprs., 120 ... J-6
Bluffs, 715 ... K-5
Bluford, 688 ... P-10
Blyton, 25 ... H-6
Boaz ... S-10
Boden, 100 ... E-5
Bogota, 60 ... N-12
Bolingbrook, 73366 ... D-12
BOND CO., 17768 ... N-8
Bondville, 443 ... I-11
Bone Gap, 246 ... O-12
Bonfield, 382 ... F-12
Bonnie, 397 ... P-10
Boody, 276 ... K-9
BOONE CO., 54165 ... B-10
Boos ... N-12
Borton, 60 ... K-12
Boskydell, 30 ... R-9
Boulder, 100 ... N-9
Bourbon, 140 ... K-11
Bourbonnais, 18631 ... F-12
Bowen, 494 ... I-4
Braceville, 793 ... E-11
Bradford, 768 ... F-8
Bradley, 15895 ... F-13
Braidwood, 6191 ... E-12
Breese, 4442 ... O-8
Bremen, 50 ... Q-7
Bridgeport, 1886 ... N-13
Bridgeport ... *I-9
Bridgeview, 16446 ... *J-7
Brighton, 2254 ... M-6
Brighton Pk. ... *I-9
Brimfield, 868 ... G-7
Bristol, 500 ... D-11
Broadlands, 349 ... J-12
Broadview, 7932 ... *I-7
Broadwell, 145 ... I-8
Brocton, 322 ... K-12
Brookfield, 18978 ... *I-7
Brooklyn, 749 ... ‡H-7
Brooklyn, 100 ... I-5
Brookport, 984 ... T-10
Brookville, 80 ... B-8
Broughton, 194 ... Q-11
BROWN CO., 6937 ... J-5
Brownfield, 75 ... S-11
Browning, 137 ... I-6
Browns, 134 ... O-12
Brownstown, 759 ... M-10
Brownsville, 50 ... Q-12
Bruce, 50 ... K-11
Brussels, 141 ... M-5
Bryant, 220 ... H-6
Buckingham, 300 ... F-12
Buckley, 600 ... H-12
Buckner, 462 ... Q-9
Buda, 538 ... E-8
Buffalo, 503 ... J-8
Buffalo Grv., 41496 ... B-12
Buffalo Hart, 25 ... J-8
Bull Valley, 1077 ... *B-2
Buncombe, 203 ... S-9
Bungay, 45 ... P-11
Bunker Hill, 1774 ... M-7
Burbank, 28925 ... *J-8
BUREAU CO., 34978 ... E-8
Burgess, 50 ... F-5
Burksville, 80 ... P-6
Burlington, 618 ... B-11
Burnham, 4206 ... *L-10
Burnt Prairie, 52 ... P-11
Burr Ridge, 10559 ... *J-6
Burtons Br., 700 ... *B-3
Bushnell, 3117 ... H-5
Bushton, 100 ... K-12
Butler, 180 ... M-8
Butterfield, 3750 ... *I-5
Byron, 3753 ... B-9
Cabery, 266 ... F-12
Cable, 120 ... E-5
Cache, 50 ... T-9
Cahokia, 15241 ... O-6
Cairo, 2831 ... T-9
Caledonia, 197 ... A-10
Calhoun, 172 ... O-12
CALHOUN CO., 5089 ... L-5
Calumet City, 37042 ... *L-10
Calumet Pk., 7835 ... *L-9
Calvin, 30 ... P-12
Camargo, 445 ... J-12
Cambria, 1228 ... R-9
Cambridge, 2160 ... E-6
Camden, 86 ... I-5
Cameron, 200 ... G-5
Camp Grv., 120 ... F-8
Camp Pt., 1132 ... J-4
Campbell Hill, 336 ... Q-8
Campton Hills, 11131 ... *H-1
Campus, 166 ... F-11
Canton, 14704 ... H-7
Cantrall, 139 ... J-8
Capron, 1376 ... A-10
Carbon Cliff, 2134 ... S-5
Carbondale, 25902 ... R-9
Carlinville, 5917 ... L-7
Carlock, 552 ... H-9
Carlyle, 3281 ... O-8
Carman, 100 ... G-4
Carmi, 5240 ... Q-12
Carol Stream, 39711 ... *H-4
Carpenter, 100 ... ‡D-10
Carpentersville, 37691 ... B-11
Carrier Mills, 1653 ... R-10
CARROLL CO., 15387 ... C-7
Carrollton, 2484 ... L-6
Carterville, 5496 ... R-9
Carthage, 2605 ... H-4
Cary, 18271 ... B-11
Casey, 2769 ... L-12
Caseyville, 4245 ... ‡H-9
Casner, 50 ... J-10
CASS CO., 13642 ... J-6
Castleton, 130 ... F-7
Catlin, 2040 ... I-13
Cave-In-Rock, 318 ... S-12
Cazenovia, 100 ... G-9
Cedar Pt., 277 ... E-9
Cedarville, 741 ... A-8
Centerville, 50 ... P-12
Central City, 1172 ... O-9
Centralia, 13032 ... O-9
Centreville, 5309 ... ‡I-8
Cerro Gordo, 1403 ... J-10
Chadwick, 551 ... C-7
Chambersburg, 100 ... J-5
Champaign, 81055 ... I-11
CHAMPAIGN CO., 201081 ... J-12
Chana, 200 ... C-9
Chandlerville, 553 ... J-6
Channahon, 12560 ... E-11
Chapin, 512 ... K-6
Charleston, 21838 ... L-12
Charlotte, 25 ... G-11
Chatham, 11500 ... K-7
Chatham ... *J-10
Chatsworth, 1205 ... G-11
Chauncey, 80 ... N-13
Chebanse, 1062 ... F-12
Chemung, 308 ... A-10
Cheneyville, 80 ... H-13
Chenoa, 1785 ... G-10
Cherry, 482 ... E-9
Cherry Valley, 3162 ... B-10
Chester, 8586 ... Q-7
Chesterfield, 188 ... L-6
Chesterville, 110 ... K-11
Chestnut, 246 ... J-9
Chicago, 2695598 ... C-13
Chicago Hts., 30276 ... D-13
Chicago Lawn ... *J-9
Chicago Ridge, 14305 ... *K-8
Chillicothe, 6097 ... F-8
Chrisman, 1343 ... J-13
CHRISTIAN CO., 34800 ... K-8
Christopher, 2382 ... Q-9
Cicero, 83891 ... C-13
Cisco, 261 ... J-10
Cisne, 672 ... O-11
Cissna Pk., 846 ... H-12
Clare, 75 ... C-10
Claremont, 176 ... N-12
Clarence, 80 ... H-12
Clarendon Hills, 8427 ... *I-6
CLARK CO., 16335 ... L-13
Clarksburg, 50 ... L-10
Clarksville, 100 ... L-13
Clay City, 959 ... N-11
CLAY CO., 13815 ... N-11
Clayton, 709 ... J-4
Claytonville, 130 ... H-13
Clear Lake, 229 ... †L-17
Clearing ... *J-8
Cleveland, 188 ... D-6
Clifton, 1468 ... F-12
Clinton, 7225 ... I-10
CLINTON CO., 37762 ... N-8
Coal City, 5587 ... E-11
Coal Valley, 3743 ... E-6
Coalton, 304 ... L-9
Coatsburg, 147 ... J-4
Cobden, 1157 ... S-9
Coello, 608 ... Q-9
Coffeen, 685 ... M-8
Colchester, 1401 ... H-5
COLES CO., 53873 ... K-11
Coleta, 164 ... C-7
Colfax, 1061 ... H-10
Collinsville, 25579 ... N-7
Collison, 100 ... I-13
Colmar, 70 ... H-4
Colona, 5099 ... T-6
Columbia, 9707 ... O-6
Columbus, 99 ... J-4
Compton, 303 ... D-9
Concord, 167 ... J-6
Congerville, 474 ... H-9
COOK CO., 5194675 ... C-13
Cooks Mills, 200 ... K-11
Cooksville, 182 ... H-10
Cora, 25 ... Q-8
Cordova, 672 ... D-6
Corinth, 30 ... R-10
Cornell, 467 ... F-10
Cornland, 93 ... J-8
Cortland, 4270 ... C-10
Cottage Hills, 980 ... ‡D-8
Coulterville, 945 ... P-8
Country Club Hills, 16541 ... *M-8
Countryside, 5895 ... *J-7
Cowden, 629 ... L-10
Cowling, 120 ... P-12
Crab Orchard, 333 ... R-10
Cragin ... *H-8
CRAWFORD CO., 19817 ... M-13
Creal Sprs., 543 ... R-10
Crescent City, 615 ... G-13
Crest Hill, 20837 ... *M-4
Creston, 662 ... C-10
Crestwood, 10950 ... *L-8
Crete, 8259 ... E-13
Creve Coeur, 5451 ... G-8
Cropsey, 120 ... H-11
Crossville, 745 ... P-12
Crystal Lake, 40743 ... B-11
Cuba, 1294 ... H-6
Cullom, 555 ... G-11
CUMBERLAND CO., 11048 ... L-11
Curran, 212 ... K-7
Custer Pk., 300 ... E-12
Cutler, 441 ... Q-8
Cypress, 234 ... S-9
Dahinda, 150 ... F-6
Dahlgren, 525 ... P-10
Dakota, 506 ... A-8
Dale, 150 ... Q-11
Dallas City, 945 ... G-4
Dalton City, 544 ... K-10
Dalzell, 717 ... E-9
Dana, 159 ... F-10
Danforth, 604 ... G-12
Danvers, 1154 ... H-9
Danville, 33027 ... I-13
Darien, 22086 ... *J-5
Darmstadt, 68 ... P-7
Darwin, 60 ... L-13
Davis, 677 ... A-8
Davis Jct., 2373 ... B-9
Dawson Pk. ... G-13
Daysville, 150 ... C-9
Dayton, 537 ... E-10
De Land, 446 ... I-10
De Soto, 1590 ... R-9
De Witt, 184 ... I-10
DE WITT CO., 16561 ... I-9
Decatur, 76122 ... J-10
Deer Creek, 704 ... G-9
Deer Grv., 48 ... D-8
Deer Pk., 3200 ... *D-4
Deer Plain, 80 ... N-5
Deerfield, 18225 ... *D-7
DeKalb, 43862 ... C-10
DEKALB CO., 105160 ... B-10
Del Mar Woods, 120 ... *D-7
Delafield, 40 ... P-11
Delavan, 1689 ... H-8
Delwood ... R-11
Dennison, 100 ... L-13
Denver, 120 ... I-4
Depue, 1838 ... E-9
Des Plaines, 58364 ... B-12
Deselm ... E-12
Detroit, 83 ... K-5
Devereux Hts. ... †K-17
Dewey, 150 ... I-11
Diamond, 2527 ... E-11
Diamond Lake, 1500 ... *C-5
Dieterich, 617 ... M-11
Dillon, 60 ... H-8
Divernon, 1172 ... K-8
Dix, 461 ... O-10
Dixmoor, 3644 ... *L-9
Dixon, 15733 ... C-8
Dixon Sprs., 50 ... S-10
Dolton, 23153 ... *L-10
Dongola, 726 ... S-9
Donnellson, 210 ... M-8
Donovan, 304 ... G-13
Dorsey, 200 ... M-7
DOUGLAS CO., 19980 ... K-12
Dover, 168 ... E-8
Dowell, 408 ... Q-9
Downers Grv., 47833 ... C-12
Downs, 1005 ... H-10
Druce Lake, 200 ... *A-5
Du Bois, 205 ... P-9
Du Quoin, 6109 ... Q-9
Duck Lake Woods, 400 ... *A-4
Duncans Mills, 60 ... I-6
Dundas, 250 ... N-12
Dunfermline, 300 ... H-7
Dunlap, 1386 ... G-8
Dunning ... *G-7
DUPAGE CO., 916924 ... C-12
Dupo, 4138 ... O-6
Durand, 1443 ... A-9
Dwight, 4260 ... F-11
Eagerville, 127 ... M-7
Earlville, 1701 ... D-10
E. Alton, 6301 ... N-6
E. Cape Girardeau, 385 ... S-8
E. Carondelet, 499 ... ‡J-7
E. Clinton ... C-6
E. Dubuque, 1704 ... A-5
E. Dundee, 2860 ... *E-2
E. Galesburg, 812 ... F-6
E. Hannibal, 35 ... K-3
E. Hardin, 30 ... M-5
E. Hazel Crest, 1543 ... *M-9
E. Lynn, 200 ... H-13
E. Moline, 21302 ... D-6
E. Peoria, 23402 ... G-8
E. St. Louis, 27006 ... O-6
Easton, 321 ... I-7
Eastwood Manor, 950 ... *A-3
Eaton, 100 ... M-13
Echo Lake, 550 ... *C-4
Eddyville, 101 ... S-11
Edelstein, 160 ... F-8
Eden, 220 ... P-8
Edgar, 40 ... K-13
EDGAR CO., 18576 ... K-13
Edgewood, 440 ... N-10
Edgington, 450 ... E-5
Edinburg, 1078 ... K-8
Edison Pk. ... *F-7
Edwards, 350 ... G-7
EDWARDS CO., 6721 ... O-12
Edwardsville, 24293 ... N-7
Effingham, 12328 ... M-11
EFFINGHAM CO., 34242 ... M-11
Egan, 50 ... B-8
El Dara, 78 ... K-4
El Paso, 2810 ... G-9
Elbridge, 80 ... K-13
Elburn, 5602 ... C-11
Elco, 150 ... S-9
Eldorado, 4122 ... R-11
Eldred, 201 ... L-5
Eleroy, 120 ... A-7
Elgin, 108188 ... B-11
Elizabeth, 761 ... A-6
Elizabethtown, 299 ... S-11
Elk Grove Vil., 33127 ... *F-5
Elkhart, 405 ... J-8
Elkville, 928 ... Q-9
Ellery, 50 ... P-12
Elliott, 295 ... H-11
Ellis Grv., 363 ... Q-7
Ellisville, 96 ... G-6
Ellsworth, 195 ... H-10
Elmhurst, 44121 ... C-12
Elmira, 50 ... F-7
Elmwood, 2097 ... G-7
Elmwood Pk., 24883 ... *H-7
Elsah, 673 ... M-6
Elvaston, 165 ... H-3
Elwin, 150 ... K-9
Elwood, 2279 ... E-12
Emden, 485 ... I-8
Emerald Pk., 400 ... *A-3
Emington, 117 ... F-11
Emma, 90 ... Q-12
Energy, 1146 ... R-9
Enfield, 596 ... P-11
Englewood ... *J-9
Enterprise, 40 ... O-11
Eola, 100 ... *J-3
Equality, 595 ... R-11
Erie, 1602 ... D-7
Essex, 802 ... F-12
Etna, 60 ... L-11
Eureka, 5295 ... G-9
Evanston, 74486 ... B-13
Evansville, 701 ... Q-7
Evergreen Pk., 19852 ... *K-8
Ewing, 307 ... Q-10
Exeter, 65 ... K-5
Fair Haven, 30 ... C-7
Fairbury, 3757 ... G-11
Fairdale, 200 ... B-10
Fairfield, 5154 ... P-11
Fairmont, 2459 ... *M-4
Fairmont City, 2635 ... ‡H-8
Fairmount, 642 ... J-13
Fairview, 522 ... G-6
Fairview Hts., 17078 ... ‡I-9
Fall Creek, 40 ... J-3
Fancher, 75 ... L-10
Fancy Prairie, 100 ... J-8
Fandon, 60 ... H-5
Farina, 518 ... N-10
Farmer City, 2037 ... I-10
Farmersville, 724 ... L-8
Farmington, 2448 ... G-7
FAYETTE CO., 22140 ... M-9
Fayetteville, 366 ... P-7
Fenton, 170 ... D-7
Ferris, 156 ... H-4
Fiatt, 200 ... H-6
Fieldon, 239 ... M-5
Fillmore, 330 ... M-9
Findlay, 683 ... K-10
Fisher, 1881 ... I-11
Fishhook, 30 ... J-4
Fithian, 485 ... I-12
Five Islands Pk., 220 ... *G-2
Flag Ctr., 100 ... C-9
Flanagan, 1110 ... G-10
Flat Rock, 331 ... N-13
Flatville, 60 ... I-12
Flora, 5070 ... N-11
Floraville, 53 ... P-6
Florence, 100 ... B-8
Florence, 38 ... K-5
Flossmoor, 9464 ... *M-9
Foosland, 101 ... H-11
FORD CO., 14081 ... H-12
Ford Hts., 2763 ... *N-10
Forest City, 246 ... H-7
Forest Homes, 1700 ... ‡D-8
Forest Lake, 1659 ... *C-5
Forest Pk., 14167 ... *I-7
Forest View, 698 ... *I-7
Forrest, 1220 ... G-11
Forreston, 1446 ... B-8
Forsyth, 3490 ... J-10
Fosterburg, 250 ... M-6
Fountain Green, 120 ... H-4
Fowler, 400 ... J-3
Fox Lake, 10579 ... A-12
Fox River Grv., 4854 ... B-11
Frankfort, 17782 ... D-12
Franklin, 610 ... K-7
FRANKLIN CO., 39561 ... Q-10
Franklin Grv., 1021 ... C-9
Franklin Pk., 18333 ... *G-7
Frederick, 100 ... I-5
Freeburg, 4354 ... O-7
Freeman Spur, 287 ... Q-9
Freeport, 25638 ... B-8
Fulton, 3481 ... C-6
FULTON CO., 37069 ... H-6
Fults, 26 ... P-6
Funks Grv. ... H-9
Future City, 150 ... T-9
Gage Pk. ... *J-9
Galatia, 933 ... Q-11
Gale ... T-8
Galena, 3429 ... A-6
Galesburg, 32195 ... F-6
GALLATIN CO., 5589 ... R-12
Galt, 210 ... C-7
Galton, 20 ... K-11
Galva, 2589 ... F-7
Ganntown, 35 ... S-10
Garden of Eden, 140 ... F-13
Garden Plain, 80 ... C-6
Garden Prairie, 352 ... B-10
Gardner, 1463 ... F-11
Garrett, 162 ... J-11
Gays, 281 ... L-11
Geff, 367 ... O-11
Geneseo, 6586 ... E-6
Geneva, 21495 ... C-11
Genoa, 5193 ... B-10
Georgetown, 3474 ... J-13
Gerlaw, 150 ... F-5
German Valley, 463 ... B-8
Germantown, 1269 ... O-8
Germantown Hills, 3438 ... G-8
Gibson City, 3407 ... H-11
Gibsonia ... R-12
Gifford, 975 ... I-12
Gila, 35 ... M-11
Gilberts, 6879 ... *E-1
Gilead, 30 ... M-5
Gillespie, 3319 ... M-7
Gilman, 1814 ... G-12
Gilson, 190 ... G-6
Girard, 2103 ... L-7
Gladstone, 281 ... G-4
Glasford, 1022 ... H-7
Glasgow, 141 ... K-5
Glen Carbon, 12934 ... ‡F-9
Glen Ellyn, 27450 ... *H-5
Glenarm, 200 ... K-8
Glencoe, 8723 ... B-13
Glendale, 50 ... S-10
Glendale Hts., 34208 ... *G-4
Glenview, 44692 ... *E-7
Glenwood, 8969 ... *M-9
Godfrey, 17982 ... M-6
Godley, 601 ... E-11
Golconda, 668 ... S-11
Golden, 644 ... I-4
Golden Eagle, 50 ... N-5
Golden Gate, 68 ... P-12
Golf, 500 ... *F-8
Good Hope, 396 ... H-5
Goodenow, 140 ... E-13
Goodfield, 860 ... G-9
Goodwine, 80 ... H-13
Gordon, 20 ... M-13
Goreville, 1049 ... R-9
Gorham, 236 ... R-8
Grafton, 674 ... M-5
Grand Detour, 429 ... C-8
Grand Ridge, 560 ... E-10
Grand Tower, 605 ... R-8
Grandview, 1441 ... †L-17
Grandview, 110 ... K-13
Granite City, 29849 ... N-6
Grant Pk., 1331 ... E-13
Grantfork, 337 ... N-8
Grantsburg, 150 ... S-10
Granville, 1427 ... E-9
Graymont, 130 ... G-10
Grayslake, 20957 ... *B-5
Grayville, 1666 ... P-12
Green Oaks, 3866 ... *B-6
Green Valley, 709 ... H-8
Greenbush, 100 ... G-5
GREENE CO., 13886 ... L-5
Greenfield, 1071 ... L-6
Greenup, 1513 ... L-12
Greenview, 778 ... I-7
Greenville, 7000 ... N-8
Gridley, 1432 ... G-10
Griggsville, 1226 ... K-5
Grimsby ... R-8
Groveland, 500 ... H-8
GRUNDY CO., 50063 ... E-11
Gulfport, 54 ... G-4
Gurnee, 31295 ... *A-6
Hagarstown, 100 ... M-9
Hainesville, 3597 ... *A-5
Half Day ... *C-6
Hallsville, 80 ... I-9
Hamburg, 128 ... L-5
Hamburg ... N-9
Hamel, 816 ... N-7
Hamilton, 2951 ... H-3
HAMILTON CO., 8457 ... P-11
Hammond, 509 ... J-10
Hampshire, 5563 ... B-11
Hampton, 1863 ... R-5
HANCOCK CO., 19104 ... H-3
Hanna City, 1225 ... G-7
Hanover, 844 ... B-6
Hanover Pk., 37973 ... *F-4
Harco, 100 ... R-10
Hardin, 967 ... M-5
HARDIN CO., 4320 ... S-11
Harding, 120 ... D-10
Hardinville ... N-13
Harmon, 120 ... D-8
Harper, 30 ... B-8
Harrisburg, 9017 ... R-11
Harrison, 160 ... A-9
Harrisonville ... P-6
Harristown, 1367 ... J-9
Hartford, 1429 ... ‡E-8
Hartsburg, 314 ... I-8
Harvard, 9447 ... A-10
Harvel, 223 ... L-8
Harvey, 25282 ... D-13
Harwood Hts., 8612 ... *G-7
Havana, 3301 ... I-7
Hawthorn Woods, 7663 ... *C-5
Hayes ... J-11
Hazel Crest, 14100 ... *M-9
Hazel Dell, 100 ... M-12
Hebron, 1216 ... A-11
Hecker, 481 ... P-7
Hegeler, 1900 ... I-13
Hegewisch ... *L-10
Henderson, 255 ... F-6
HENDERSON CO., 7331 ... G-4
Hennepin, 757 ... E-9
Henning, 251 ... I-13
Henry, 2464 ... F-8
HENRY CO., 50486 ... E-6
Herald, 80 ... Q-12
Herbert, 100 ... B-10
Hermon, 50 ... G-6
Herod, 70 ... R-11
Herrick, 436 ... M-9
Herrin, 12501 ... R-9
Herscher, 1591 ... F-12
Hersman, 80 ... J-5
Hettick, 181 ... L-7
Hewittville, 450 ... K-9
Heyworth, 2841 ... I-9
Hickory Grv., 400 ... J-3
Hickory Hills, 14049 ... *J-7
Hidalgo, 106 ... M-12
Highland, 9919 ... N-8
Highland Hills ... *I-5
Highland Lake ... *A-5
Highland Pk., 29763 ... B-13
Highway Vil. ... †J-17
Highwood, 5405 ... B-13
Hillcrest, 1326 ... C-9
Hillerman, 35 ... T-10
Hillsboro, 6207 ... M-8
Hillsdale, 523 ... D-6
Hillside, 8157 ... *H-6
Hillview, 193 ... L-5
Hinckley, 2070 ... C-10
Hindsboro, 313 ... K-12
Hinsdale, 16816 ... *J-6
Hodgkins, 1897 ... *J-7
Hoffman, 508 ... O-9
Hoffman Estates, 51895 ... *F-4
Holcomb, 270 ... B-9
Holder, 60 ... H-10
Holiday Hills, 610 ... *B-3
Hollywood Hts., 1060 ... ‡H-9
Homer, 1193 ... J-12
Homer Glen, 24220 ... *L-6
Hometown, 4349 ... *J-8
Homewood, 19323 ... *M-9
Hoopeston, 5351 ... H-13
Hooppole, 204 ... D-7
Hopedale, 865 ... H-8
Hopewell, 410 ... F-8
Hopkins Pk., 603 ... F-13
Hord, 175 ... N-11
Hoyleton, 531 ... O-9
Hudson, 1838 ... H-9
Huey, 169 ... O-9
Hull, 461 ... K-3
Humboldt, 437 ... K-11
Hume, 380 ... J-13
Humm Wye, 25 ... S-11
Hunt City, 90 ... M-12
Huntley, 24291 ... B-11
Hurst, 795 ... Q-9
Hutsonville, 554 ... M-13
Hutton, 50 ... L-12
Hyde Pk. ... *J-10
Illinois City, 250 ... E-4
Illiopolis, 891 ... J-9
Ina, 2338 ... P-10
Indian Creek, 462 ... *C-6
Indian Head Pk., 3809 ... *J-6
Indian Oaks, 500 ... E-13
Indianola, 276 ... J-13
Industry, 478 ... I-5
Ingalls Pk., 3314 ... *N-5
Ingleside, 1700 ... *A-4
Ingraham, 150 ... N-11
Inverness, 7399 ... *E-5
Iola, 141 ... N-10
Ipava, 470 ... H-6
Irene ... B-10
Iroquois, 154 ... G-13
IROQUOIS CO., 29718 ... G-12
Irving, 495 ... M-8
Irving Pk. ... *G-8
Irvington, 659 ... O-9
Irwin, 74 ... F-12
Island Lake, 8080 ... *B-3
Itasca, 8649 ... *G-5
Iuka, 489 ... O-10
Ivanhoe, 100 ... *B-5
Ivesdale, 267 ... J-11
JACKSON CO., 60218 ... Q-8
Jacksonville, 19446 ... K-6
Jamestown, 120 ... N-8
Janesville, 150 ... L-11
JASPER CO., 9698 ... M-12
JEFFERSON CO., 38827 ... O-10
Jefferson Pk. ... *G-8
Jerome, 1656 ... †M-16
JERSEY CO., 22985 ... M-6
Jerseyville, 8465 ... M-6
Jewett, 223 ... M-12
JO DAVIESS CO., 22678 ... B-6
JOHNSON CO., 12582 ... S-10
Johnsonville, 77 ... O-11
Johnston City, 3543 ... R-10
Joliet, 147433 ... D-12
Jonesboro, 1821 ... S-9
Joppa, 360 ... T-10
Joslin, 100 ... D-6
Joy, 417 ... E-4
Junction, 129 ... R-12
Junction City, 482 ... O-9
Justice, 12926 ... *J-7
Kampsville, 328 ... L-5
Kane, 438 ... M-6
KANE CO., 515269 ... C-11
Kaneville, 484 ... C-11
Kangley, 251 ... F-10
Kankakee, 27537 ... F-12
KANKAKEE CO., 113449 ... F-12
Kansas, 787 ... K-12
Kappa, 227 ... G-9
Karbers Ridge, 45 ... R-11
Karnak, 499 ... S-10
Kasbeer, 85 ... D-8
Kaskaskia, 14 ... Q-7
Keenes, 83 ... P-10
Keeneyville, 300 ... *G-4
Keensburg, 210 ... P-13
Keithsburg, 609 ... F-4
Kell, 219 ... O-10
Kellerville, 30 ... J-4
Kemper, 70 ... M-6
Kempton, 231 ... F-11
KENDALL CO., 114736 ... D-11
Kenilworth, 2513 ... *E-8
Kenney, 326 ... I-9
Kent, 100 ... A-7
Keptown, 45 ... M-10
Kewanee, 12916 ... E-7
Keyesport, 421 ... N-9
Kickapoo, 400 ... G-7
Kilbourne, 302 ... I-7
Kildeer, 3968 ... *D-5
Kincaid, 1505 ... K-8
Kinderhook, 216 ... K-3
Kings, 250 ... C-9
Kingston, 1164 ... B-10
Kingston, 30 ... J-4
Kingston Mines, 302 ... H-7
Kinmundy, 796 ... N-10
Kinsman, 99 ... E-11
Kirkland, 1744 ... B-10
Kirksville, 50 ... K-10
Kirkwood, 714 ... G-5
Knollwood, 1747 ... *B-7
KNOX CO., 52919 ... F-6
Knoxville, 2911 ... F-6
La Clede, 100 ... N-10
La Fox, 250 ... *H-1
La Grange, 15550 ... *I-7
La Grange Highlands, 3650 ... *J-6
La Grange Pk., 13579 ... *I-7
La Harpe, 1235 ... H-4
La Hogue, 30 ... G-12
La Moille, 726 ... D-9
La Prairie, 47 ... I-4
La Rose, 144 ... F-9
La Salle, 9609 ... E-9
LA SALLE CO., 113924 ... E-10
Lacon, 1937 ... F-8
Ladd, 1295 ... E-9
Lafayette, 223 ... F-7
L. Barrington, 4973 ... *C-4
L. Bluff, 5722 ... B-12
Lake City, 110 ... K-10
LAKE CO., 703462 ... B-12
L. Forest, 19375 ... B-13
L. Fork, 100 ... J-8
L. Holiday, 4761 ... D-10
Lake in the Hills, 28965 ... *D-2
L. Killarney, 700 ... *C-3
L. Lawrence, 150 ... N-13
L. Mattoon, 1000 ... L-11
L. Summerset, 2048 ... A-8
L. Villa, 8741 ... A-12
L. Wildwood, 500 ... F-9
L. Zurich, 19631 ... B-12
Lakemoor, 6017 ... A-11
Lakeview ... *G-9
Lakewood, 3811 ... *C-1
Lakewood, 100 ... L-10
Lanark, 1457 ... B-7
Lancaster, 150 ... O-13
Landes ... N-13
Lane, 130 ... I-10
Langleyville, 432 ... K-8
Lansing, 28331 ... *M-10
LaPlace, 259 ... J-10
Larchland ... G-5
Latham, 380 ... J-9
Laura, 150 ... F-7
Lawndale, 150 ... I-9
Lawndale ... *I-8
Lawrence, 200 ... A-10
LAWRENCE CO., 16833 ... N-13
Lawrenceville, 4348 ... N-13
Le Roy, 3560 ... H-10
Leaf River, 443 ... B-8
Lebanon, 4418 ... O-7
Lee, 337 ... C-10
Lee Ctr., 250 ... C-9
LEE CO., 36031 ... D-8
Leesville, 100 ... F-13
Leland, 977 ... D-10
Leland Grv., 1503 ... †M-16
Lemont, 16000 ... *K-5
Lena, 2912 ... A-7
Lenzburg, 521 ... P-7
Leonore, 130 ... E-9
Lerna, 286 ... L-11
Lewistown, 2384 ... H-6
Lexington, 2060 ... G-10
Liberty, 516 ... J-4
Libertyville, 20315 ... B-12
Lick Creek, 60 ... S-9
Lily Lake, 993 ... C-11
Lilymoor, 450 ... *A-3
Lima, 163 ... I-3
Lincoln, 14504 ... I-8
Lincolnshire, 7275 ... *D-6
Lincolnwood, 12590 ... *F-8
Lindenhurst, 14462 ... A-12
Lindenwood, 300 ... B-9
Lis ... M-11
Lisbon, 285 ... D-11
Lisbon Ctr. ... *M-1
Lisle, 22390 ... C-12
Litchfield, 6939 ... M-8
Literberry, 100 ... J-6
Little America, 200 ... H-7
Little York, 331 ... F-5
Littleton, 181 ... I-5
Lively Grv., 45 ... P-8
Liverpool, 129 ... H-7
Livingston, 858 ... M-7
LIVINGSTON CO., 38950 ... F-11
Loami, 745 ... K-7
Lockport, 24839 ... D-12
Loda, 407 ... H-12
Lodge, 100 ... I-11
Logan, 327 ... Q-10
Logan ... K-13
LOGAN CO., 30305 ... I-8
Logan Sq. ... *H-9
Lomax, 454 ... G-4
Lombard, 43165 ... *H-5
London Mills, 392 ... G-6
Long Creek, 1328 ... J-10
Long Grv., 8043 ... *D-5
Long Lake, 3515 ... *A-4
Long Pt., 226 ... F-10
Longview, 153 ... J-12
Loogootee, 70 ... N-10
Loop ... *H-9
Loraine, 313 ... I-3
Loran, 40 ... B-7
Lostant, 498 ... F-9
Louisville, 1139 ... N-11
Loves Pk., 23996 ... A-9
Lovington, 1130 ... K-10
Low Pt., 200 ... G-9
Lowder, 100 ... K-7
Lowell, 50 ... E-9
Ludlow, 371 ... H-12
Lyndon, 648 ... D-7
Lynn Ctr., 150 ... E-6
Lynnville, 117 ... K-6
Lynwood, 9007 ... *M-10
Lyons, 10729 ... *I-7
Macedonia, 63 ... Q-10
Machesney Pk., 23499 ... A-9
Mackinaw, 1950 ... H-8
Macomb, 19288 ... H-5
Macon, 1138 ... K-9
MACON CO., 110768 ... J-9
MACOUPIN CO., 47765 ... L-7
Madison, 3891 ... ‡G-7
MADISON CO., 269282 ... N-7
Maeystown, 157 ... P-6
Magnolia, 260 ... F-9
Mahomet, 7258 ... I-11
Makanda, 561 ... R-9
Malta, 1164 ... C-10
Manchester, 292 ... K-6
Manhattan, 7051 ... E-12
Manito, 1642 ... H-7
Manlius, 359 ... E-8
Mansfield, 906 ... I-11
Manteno, 9204 ... E-13
Manville, 50 ... F-10
Maple Pk., 1310 ... C-10
Mapleton, 270 ... H-7
Maquon, 284 ... G-6
Marblehead, 100 ... J-3
Marcelline, 100 ... I-3
Marengo, 7648 ... B-10
Marietta, 112 ... H-6
Marine, 960 ... N-7
Marion, 17193 ... R-10
MARION CO., 39437 ... O-10
Marissa, 1979 ... P-7
Markham, 12508 ... *L-9
Marley, 100 ... *M-6
Maroa, 1801 ... J-10
Marseilles, 5094 ... E-10
Marshall, 3933 ... L-13
MARSHALL CO., 12640 ... F-9
Martinsville, 1167 ... L-13
Martinton, 381 ... F-13
Maryville, 7487 ... ‡G-10
Mascoutah, 7483 ... O-7
Mason, 345 ... N-10
Mason City, 2343 ... I-8
MASON CO., 14666 ... I-7
MASSAC CO., 15429 ... T-10
Matherville, 723 ... E-5
Matteson, 19009 ... *N-8
Mattoon, 18555 ... L-11
Maunie, 139 ... Q-12
Maywood, 24090 ... *H-7
Mazon, 1015 ... E-11
McClure, 402 ... S-8
McConnell, 250 ... A-7
McCook, 228 ... *J-7
McCormick ... R-10
McCullom Lake, 1049 ... *A-2
MCDONOUGH CO., 32612 ... I-5
McHenry, 26992 ... A-11
MCHENRY CO., 308760 ... A-11
McLean, 830 ... I-9
MCLEAN CO., 169572 ... H-10
McLeansboro, 2883 ... Q-11
McNabb, 285 ... F-9
Meadowbrook, 1000 ... ‡D-9
Meadows, 300 ... G-10
Mechanicsburg, 590 ... J-8
Media, 107 ... G-4
Medinah ... *G-5
Medora, 419 ... M-6
Melrose ... L-13
Melrose Pk., 25411 ... *H-7
Melvin, 452 ... H-11
MENARD CO., 12705 ... I-7
Mendon, 953 ... I-3
Mendota, 7372 ... D-9
Menominee, 248 ... A-5
Meppen, 60 ... M-5
MERCER CO., 16434 ... E-5
Meredosia, 1044 ... J-5
Meriden, 50 ... D-9
Mermet ... S-10
Merna, 40 ... H-10
Merrionette Pk., 1900 ... *K-9
Metamora, 3636 ... G-8
Metcalf, 189 ... J-13
Metropolis, 6537 ... T-10
Mettawa, 547 ... *C-6
Meyer, 50 ... I-3
Michael, 50 ... L-5
Middletown, 324 ... I-8
Midlothian, 14819 ... *L-8
Midway, 330 ... H-8
Midway, 25 ... T-10
Milan, 5099 ... T-3
Milford, 1306 ... G-13
Mill Creek, 65 ... S-9
Mill Shoals, 215 ... P-11
Milledgeville, 1032 ... C-7
Millersburg, 100 ... E-5
Millersville, 65 ... L-9
Millington, 665 ... D-10
Millstadt, 4011 ... O-6
Milton, 271 ... K-5
Mineral, 237 ... E-7
Minier, 1252 ... H-9
Minonk, 2078 ... G-9
Minooka, 10924 ... E-11
Mitchell, 1356 ... ‡F-8
Mitchellsville, 100 ... R-11
Modesto, 189 ... L-7
Modoc, 100 ... Q-6
Moecherville ... *J-2
Mokena, 18740 ... *M-7
Moline, 43483 ... D-5
Momence, 3310 ... F-13
Monee, 5148 ... E-13
Monica, 80 ... F-7
Monmouth, 9444 ... F-5
Monroe Ctr., 471 ... B-9
MONROE CO., 32957 ... P-6
Montgomery, 18438 ... D-11
MONTGOMERY CO., 30104 ... L-8
Monticello, 5548 ... J-11
Montrose, 201 ... M-11
Mooseheart, 100 ... *I-2
MORGAN CO., 35547 ... J-6
Morgan Pk. ... *K-9
Morris, 13636 ... E-11
Morrison, 4188 ... C-7
Morrisonville, 1056 ... L-8
Morton, 16267 ... H-8
Morton Grv., 23270 ... *F-7
MOULTRIE CO., 14846 ... K-10
Mound City, 588 ... T-9
Mounds, 810 ... T-9
Mt. Auburn, 480 ... K-9
Mt. Carmel, 7284 ... O-13
Mt. Carroll, 1717 ... B-7
Mt. Erie, 88 ... O-12
Mt. Greenwood ... *K-8
Mt. Morris, 2998 ... B-8
Mt. Olive, 2099 ... M-7
Mt. Pleasant, 50 ... S-9
Mt. Prospect, 54167 ... *E-6
Mt. Pulaski, 1566 ... J-9
Mt. Sterling, 2025 ... J-5
Mt. Vernon, 15277 ... P-10
Mt. Zion, 5833 ... K-10
Moweaqua, 1831 ... K-9
Mozier, 50 ... L-5
Muddy, 68 ... R-11
Mulberry Grv., 634 ... N-9
Mulkeytown, 175 ... Q-9
Mundelein, 31064 ... *C-5
Murdock, 150 ... J-12
Murphysboro, 7970 ... R-8
Murrayville, 587 ... K-6
Nachusa, 270 ... C-8
Naperville, 141853 ... C-12
Naplate, 496 ... E-10
Naples, 130 ... K-5
Nashville, 3258 ... P-8
Nason, 236 ... P-9
National City ... ‡H-7
Nauvoo, 1149 ... H-3
Near North Side ... *H-9
Nebo, 340 ... L-5
Nekoma, 30 ... F-6
Nelson, 170 ... C-8
Neoga, 1636 ... L-11
Neponset, 473 ... E-7
Neunert, 25 ... R-8
New Athens, 2054 ... P-7
New Baden, 3349 ... O-7
New Bedford, 75 ... D-7
New Berlin, 1346 ... K-7
New Boston, 683 ... F-4
New Burnside, 211 ... R-10
New Canton, 359 ... K-4
New Columbia, 150 ... S-10
New Delhi, 40 ... M-6
New Douglas, 319 ... M-8
New Grand Chain, 210 ... T-9
New Hanover, 60 ... O-6
New Haven, 433 ... Q-12
New Hebron, 50 ... M-13
New Holland, 269 ... I-8
New Lenox, 24394 ... D-12
New Liberty, 70 ... T-11
New Memphis, 300 ... O-8
New Milford, 697 ... B-9
New Minden, 215 ... O-8
New Philadelphia, 100 ... H-5
New Salem, 137 ... K-4
New Windsor, 748 ... E-6
Newark, 992 ... D-11
Newbern, 100 ... M-6
Newman, 865 ... J-12
Newton, 2849 ... M-12
Niantic, 707 ... J-9
Niles, 29803 ... *F-7
Nilwood, 239 ... L-7
Niota, 300 ... G-3
Noble, 677 ... N-12
Nokomis, 2256 ... L-9
Nora, 121 ... A-7
Normal, 52497 ... H-9
Normandy, 30 ... D-8
Norridge, 14572 ... *G-7
Norris, 213 ... G-7
Norris City, 1275 ... Q-11
N. Aurora, 16760 ... C-11
N. Barrington, 3047 ... *C-4
N. Chicago, 32574 ... A-12
N. Dupo, 1380 ... ‡J-7
N. Glen Ellyn, 1400 ... *H-5
N. Henderson, 187 ... F-5
N. Riverside, 6672 ... *I-7
Northbrook, 33170 ... *E-7
Northfield, 5420 ... *E-8
Northlake, 12323 ... *H-6
Nortonville, 50 ... K-6
Norway, 300 ... E-10
Norwood Pk. ... *G-7
Nutwood, 120 ... M-5
Oak Brook, 7883 ... *I-6
Oak Forest, 27962 ... *L-8
Oak Grv., 396 ... E-5
Oak Hill, 100 ... G-7
Oak Hills, 1150 ... ‡H-9
Oak Lawn, 56690 ... D-13
Oak Pk., 51878 ... C-13
Oak Run, 547 ... F-6
Oakbrook Ter., 2134 ... *I-6
Oakdale, 221 ... P-8
Oakford, 286 ... I-7
Oakland, 880 ... K-12
Oakwood, 1595 ... I-13
Oakwood Hills, 2083 ... *C-3
Oblong, 1466 ... M-12
Oconee, 180 ... L-9
Odell, 1046 ... F-11

*, †, ‡, §, ◊ See explanation under state title in this index.
County and parish names are listed in capital letters & boldface type.
Independent cities (not included in a county) are listed in italics.

Indiana–Iowa 243

Raglesville, 141 .... O-6
Ragsdale, 129 .... O-4
Rainsville, 50 .... G-4
Raleigh, 80 .... K-12
Ramsey, 200 .... Q-9
RANDOLPH CO., 26171 .... I-13
Raub, 100 .... F-4
Ravenswood *B-18
Ray, 60 .... A-13
Rays Crossing, 60 .... K-11
Reddington, 200 .... N-10
Redkey, 1353 .... H-12
Reelsville, 150 .... K-6
Reiffsburg, 40 .... F-12
Remington, 1185 .... F-5
Rensselaer, 5859 .... E-5
Reynolds, 533 .... F-6
Richland, 50 .... L-12
Richland City, 425 .... S-5
Richmond, 36812 .... J-13
Richvalley, 120 .... F-10
Ridgeville, 803 .... H-13
Rigdon, 60 .... G-10
Riley, 221 .... L-4
Rileysburg, 35 .... I-4
RIPLEY CO., 28818 .... M-12
Rising Sun, 2304 .... N-14
Rivare, 60 .... E-14
Riverside, 75 .... H-5
Riverton, 25 .... N-3
Riverview, 50 .... M-3
Riverwood, 500 .... I-9
Roachdale, 926 .... J-6
Roann, 479 .... E-10
Roanoke, 1722 .... E-12
Rob Roy, 50 .... H-5
Robertsdale *K-11
Robinwood, 150 .... L-3
Rochester, 6218 .... D-8
Rockfield, 300 .... F-7
Rockford, 400 .... N-10
Rockford, 50 .... F-12
Rocklane, 120 .... K-9
Rockport, 2270 .... T-5
Rockville, 2607 .... J-5
Rocky Ripple, 606 .... *C-17
Roll, 100 .... G-12
Rolling Hills, 450 .... H-6
Rolling Hills, 360 .... Q-11
Rolling Prairie, 582 .... A-7
Rome, 40 .... S-7
Rome City, 1361 .... B-12
Romney, 450 .... H-6
Roseburg K-13
Rosedale, 725 .... K-4
Roseland, 630 .... A-8
Roselawn, 4131 .... D-4
Ross, 47890 .... B-4
Rosston, 50 .... I-8
Rossville, 1653 .... G-7
Roth Pk., 150 .... F-7
Royal Ctr., 861 .... E-7
Royalton, 50 .... I-8
Royerton, 900 .... H-12
Rugby, 50 .... M-10
RUSH CO., 17392 .... K-11
Rushville, 6341 .... K-11
Russellville, 358 .... I-6
Russiaville, 1094 .... G-8
St. Anthony, 400 .... R-6
St. Bernice, 646 .... K-4
St. Croix, 60 .... R-7
St. Henry, 130 .... R-6
St. Joe, 460 .... C-13
St. John, 14850 .... B-4
St. Joseph, 75 .... S-3
ST. JOSEPH CO., 266931 .... B-8
St. Leon, 678 .... M-13
St. Louis Crossing, 90 .... M-10
St. Marks, 100 .... R-6
St. Mary-of-the-Woods, 797 .... L-4
St. Meinrad, 706 .... R-6
St. Omer, 75 .... L-11
St. Paul, 1031 .... L-11
St. Peter, 70 .... M-13
St. Philip, 500 .... S-3
St. Wendel, 500 .... R-3
Salamonia, 157 .... G-14
Salem, 6319 .... P-9
Salem, 40 .... H-14
Salem F-14
Saline City, 90 .... L-5
Saltillo, 92 .... P-8
Samaria, 75 .... L-9
San Jacinto N-11
San Pierre, 144 .... C-6
Sandborn, 415 .... O-5
Sandusky, 60 .... L-11
Santa Claus, 2481 .... S-6
Santa Fe, 100 .... F-9
Saratoga, 254 .... H-13
Sardinia, 125 .... M-11
Schererville, 29243 .... B-4
Schneider, 277 .... D-4
Schnellville, 250 .... Q-6
Scipio, 153 .... N-10
Scipio, 30 .... L-14
Scircleville, 140 .... H-8
Scotland, 134 .... O-6
Scott, 60 .... A-11
Scott City, 15 .... M-4
SCOTT CO., 24181 .... P-10
Scottsburg, 6747 .... P-10
Sedalia, 130 .... G-7
Seelyville, 1029 .... L-4
Sellersburg, 6128 .... Q-10
Selma, 866 .... H-12
Selvin, 50 .... R-5
Servia, 180 .... E-10
Sevastopol, 30 .... D-9
Sexton, 60 .... K-11
Seymour, 17503 .... N-10
Shadeland, 1610 .... G-6
Shamrock Lakes, 231 .... G-11
Shannondale, 35 .... I-7
Sharpsville, 607 .... G-9
Shelburn, 1252 .... M-4
Shelby, 539 .... C-4
SHELBY CO., 44436 .... L-10
Shelbyville, 19191 .... L-10
Sheridan, 2665 .... I-8
Shideler, 160 .... H-12
Shipshewana, 658 .... A-11
Shirkieville, 100 .... K-4
Shirley, 830 .... J-11
Shoals, 756 .... P-6
Shore Acres *B-18
Siberia, 50 .... R-6
Sidney, 83 .... D-10
Silver Lake, 915 .... D-10
Silverville O-7
Silverwood, 50 .... J-4
Simonton Lake, 4678 .... A-9
Sitka, 20 .... E-7
Smith Valley, 1800 .... K-8
Smithfield, 30 .... H-12
Smithville, 200 .... N-7
Solitude S-2
Solsberry, 200 .... N-6
Somerset, 401 .... F-10
Somerville, 293 .... R-4
S. Bend, 101168 .... A-8
S. Boston, 75 .... P-9
S. Center, 150 .... B-7
S. Gate, 40 .... M-13
S. Milford, 200 .... B-12
S. Washington, 220 .... P-5
S. Whitley, 1751 .... D-11
Southport, 1712 .... K-9
Southwest, 50 .... B-9
Southwood, 500 .... M-2
Sparksville, 50 .... O-8
Spartanburg, 110 .... I-14
Spearsville, 40 .... M-9
Speed, 300 .... Q-10
Speedway, 11812 .... J-8
Speicherville, 30 .... E-10
Spelterville, 500 .... K-2
Spencer, 2217 .... M-6
SPENCER CO., 20952 .... S-5
Spencerville, 350 .... C-13
Spiceland, 890 .... J-11
Spraytown, 50 .... N-9
Spring Grv., 344 .... J-13
Spring Hills, 98 .... *C-17
Spring Lake, 218 .... J-10
Springport, 149 .... I-12
Springville, 300 .... O-7
Spurgeon, 207 .... R-4
Stacer R-3
Stanford, 100 .... N-7
Star City, 344 .... E-7
STARKE CO., 23363 .... C-7
State Line, 143 .... H-4
Staunton, 534 .... L-5
Stendal, 150 .... R-5
STEUBEN CO., 34185 .... B-13
Stevenson S-4
Stewartsville, 180 .... R-2
Stilesville, 316 .... K-7
Stillwell, 275 .... B-7
Stinesville, 198 .... M-7
Stockdale E-9
Stockwell, 545 .... H-6
Stone Head N-9
Stonebluff, 120 .... I-5
Stones Crossing, 150 .... K-9
Story N-8
Straughn, 222 .... J-12
Stroh, 400 .... B-12
Sullivan, 4249 .... N-4
SULLIVAN CO., 21475 .... N-4
Sulphur, 100 .... R-7
Sulphur Sprs., 399 .... I-11
Sumava Resorts, 300 .... D-4
Summitville, 967 .... H-11
Sunman, 1049 .... M-13
Sunshine Gdns. *F-17
Swan, 55 .... C-12
Swanington, 60 .... F-4
Swayzee, 981 .... G-10
Sweetser, 1229 .... G-10
Switz City, 293 .... N-5
SWITZERLAND CO., 10613 .... O-13
Sycamore, 90 .... G-10
Sycamore Pk., 120 .... K-11
Sylvania J-4
Syracuse, 2810 .... B-10
Tab, 60 .... G-4
Talbot, 40 .... G-4
Talma, 130 .... D-9
Tampico, 60 .... O-9
Tangier, 30 .... J-4
Taswell, 130 .... Q-7
Taylorsville, 919 .... M-9
Taylorville, 104 .... L-1
Teegarden, 160 .... B-8
Tefft, 100 .... D-6
Tell City, 7272 .... S-6
Templeton, 120 .... G-5
Tennyson, 279 .... S-5
Terhune, 90 .... I-8
Terre Haute, 60785 .... L-4
Testersburg, 50 .... H-9
Thayer, 400 .... D-4
Thomaston, 20 .... C-6
Thornhope, 150 .... E-7
Thorntown, 1520 .... I-7
Thurman, 40 .... *L-20
Tilden J-8
Tiosa, 150 .... D-9
Tippecanoe, 350 .... C-9
TIPPECANOE CO., 172780 .... H-6
Tipton, 5106 .... H-9
TIPTON CO., 15936 .... H-9
Toad Hop, 108 .... L-1
Tobinsport T-7
Tocsin, 120 .... E-13
Tolleston *M-12
Topeka, 1153 .... B-11
Toto, 200 .... C-7
Town of Pines, 708 .... A-6
Townley D-13
Tracy, 200 .... B-7
Traders Pt. *B-15
Trafalgar, 1101 .... L-9
Trail Creek, 2052 .... A-6
Travisville, 30 .... F-12
Treaty, 30 .... F-10
Trenton, 35 .... G-12
Trevlac, 150 .... M-8
Tri-Lakes, 1421 .... C-11
Trinity Sprs., 60 .... O-6
Troy, 385 .... S-6
Tunker D-11
Tunnelton, 120 .... O-8
Turner, 100 .... L-5
Twelve Mile, 225 .... E-8
Twin Lakes, 200 .... C-8
Tyner, 250 .... B-8
Ulen, 117 .... I-8
Underwood, 200 .... P-10
Union, 90 .... Q-4
Union City, 3584 .... H-14
UNION CO., 7516 .... K-13
Union Mills, 400 .... B-6
Uniondale, 310 .... E-12
Unionport I-13
Uniontown, 60 .... O-10
Uniontown, 50 .... R-4
Unionville, 150 .... M-8
Universal, 362 .... K-4
Upland, 3845 .... G-11
Urbana, 350 .... E-10
Utica, 776 .... Q-11
Valeene, 130 .... Q-8
Valentine, 50 .... B-11
Valley City, 35 .... S-8
Valley Mills *F-16
Vallonia, 336 .... O-9
Valparaiso, 31730 .... B-5
Van Bibber Lake, 485 .... K-6
Van Buren, 864 .... F-11
Van Buren Pk., 700 .... R-12
Vandalia, 35 .... M-6
VANDERBURGH CO., 179703 .... R-3
Veedersburg, 2180 .... I-5
Velpen, 150 .... Q-5
Vera Cruz, 80 .... F-13
VERMILLION CO., 16212 .... J-4
Vernon, 318 .... N-11
Versailles, 2113 .... N-12
Vevay, 1683 .... O-13
Vicksburg, 200 .... N-5
Vienna, 120 .... P-10
Vigo M-3
VIGO CO., 107848 .... M-4
Vincennes, 18423 .... P-3
Wabash, 10666 .... E-10
WABASH CO., 32888 .... E-10
Wadena, 35 .... F-5
Wadesville, 500 .... R-2
Wakarusa, 1758 .... B-9
Waldron, 804 .... L-10
Walesboro, 125 .... N-10
Walkerton, 2144 .... B-7
Wallace, 105 .... I-5
Walnut D-9
Walton, 1049 .... F-8
Wanamaker *F-20
Wanatah, 1048 .... B-6
Warren, 1239 .... F-11
WARREN CO., 8508 .... G-4
Warren Pk., 1480 .... *D-20
Warrenton, 110 .... R-3
WARRICK CO., 59689 .... R-4
Warrington, 50 .... J-11
Warsaw, 13559 .... C-10
Washington, 11509 .... P-5
WASHINGTON CO., 28262 .... P-9
Waterford, 350 .... A-6
Waterford Mills, 200 .... B-10
Waterloo, 2242 .... B-13
Waterloo K-5
Watson, 500 .... Q-10
Waugh I-8
Waveland, 420 .... J-5
Waverly, 200 .... K-8
Wawaka, 200 .... B-11
Wawpecong, 70 .... F-9
Waymansville, 75 .... N-9
WAYNE CO., 68917 .... J-13
Waynedale *M-18
Waynesburg, 35 .... M-11
Waynesville, 160 .... N-10
Waynetown, 958 .... I-5
Webster, 250 .... J-13
WELLS CO., 27636 .... F-12
W. Baden Sprs., 574 .... P-7
W. College Cor., 676 .... K-14
W. Elwood, 100 .... H-10
W. Fork R-7
W. Franklin, 150 .... T-3
W. Harrison, 289 .... M-14
W. Lafayette, 29596 .... G-6
W. Lebanon, 723 .... H-4
W. Middleton, 225 .... G-8
W. Newton *G-16
W. Terre Haute, 2236 .... L-4
Westfield, 30068 .... I-9
Westlawn, 700 .... D-12
Westphalia, 202 .... O-5
Westpoint, 594 .... H-5
Westport, 1379 .... M-11
Westville, 5853 .... B-6
Westwood, 150 .... J-11
Wheatfield, 853 .... C-5
Wheatland, 480 .... P-4
Wheeler, 443 .... B-5
Wheeling, 100 .... H-5
Wheeling, 30 .... G-8
Whitcomb, 60 .... L-13
Whitcomb Hts., 300 .... L-4
WHITE CO., 24643 .... F-6
Whitehall, 50 .... M-7
Whiteland, 4169 .... L-9
Whitestown, 2867 .... I-8
Whitesville, 60 .... K-6
Whitewater, 83 .... J-14
Whitfield, 100 .... P-6
Whiting, 4997 .... *K-11
WHITLEY CO., 33292 .... D-11
Wilders C-6
Wildwood Lake, 70 .... Q-7
Wilfred, 40 .... M-4
Wilkinson, 449 .... J-11
Williams, 286 .... O-7
Williams E-13
Williams Creek, 407 .... J-9
Williamsburg, 360 .... J-13
Williamsport, 1898 .... H-4
Williamstown, 40 .... L-11
Willow Branch, 150 .... J-10
Wilmington, 150 .... N-13
Wilmot, 60 .... C-11
Winamac, 2490 .... D-7
Winchester, 4935 .... H-13
Windfall, 708 .... H-9
Windsor, 110 .... I-12
Winfield, 4383 .... B-5
Wingate, 263 .... H-5
Winona, 200 .... C-7
Winona Lake, 4908 .... C-10
Winslow, 864 .... Q-5
Wirt, 25 .... O-11
Wolcott, 1001 .... F-5
Wolcottville, 998 .... B-12
Wolflake, 250 .... C-11
Woodburn, 1520 .... D-13
Woodbury, 150 .... J-10
Woodland, 60 .... B-9
Woodland Pk., 200 .... I-3
Woodlawn Hts., 79 .... G-2
Woodridge L-2
Woodruff, 35 .... B-12
Wooster, 35 .... C-10
Worthington, 1463 .... N-6
Wyatt, 400 .... B-9
Wynnedale, 231 .... *C-17
Yankeetown, 250 .... S-4
Yeddo, 110 .... I-5
Yeoman, 139 .... F-7
Yoder, 250 .... E-12
Yorktown, 9405 .... H-11
Young America, 235 .... G-8
Youngstown, 100 .... L-4
Yountsville, 100 .... I-6
Zanesville, 600 .... E-12
Zenas, 40 .... N-11
Zionsville, 14160 .... J-8
Zulu, 40 .... D-13

Iowa

Page locator

Map keys	Atlas pages
1–10	78–79
11–20	80–81

* City keyed to p. 68
† City keyed to p. 128

Abingdon, 80 .... K-14
Ackley, 1589 .... E-11
Ackworth, 83 .... J-10
Adair, 781 .... I-7
ADAIR CO., 7682 .... J-7
ADAMS CO., 4029 .... L-6
Adaza G-7
Adel, 3682 .... I-8
Afton, 845 .... K-8
Agency, 638 .... K-13
Ainsworth, 567 .... J-16
Akron, 1486 .... D-1
Albert City, 699 .... D-6
Albia, 3766 .... K-12
Albion, 505 .... G-11
Alburnett, 673 .... G-15
Alden, 787 .... E-10
Alexander, 175 .... D-10
Algona, 5560 .... C-8
ALLAMAKEE CO., 14330 .... B-16
Alleman, 432 .... H-10
Allendorf, 70 .... B-4
Allerton, 501 .... L-10
Allison, 1029 .... D-12
Alpha, 90 .... C-14
Alta, 1883 .... E-5
Alta Vista, 266 .... C-13
Alton, 1216 .... C-3
Altoona, 14541 .... I-10
Alvord, 196 .... B-2
Amana, 442 .... H-15
Amber, 100 .... G-17
Ames, 58965 .... G-10
Anamosa, 5533 .... G-16
Anderson, 65 .... L-4
Andover, 103 .... G-19
Andrew, 434 .... G-18
Anita, 972 .... J-6
Ankeny, 45582 .... H-10
Anthon, 565 .... F-3
Aplington, 1128 .... E-12
APPANOOSE CO., 12887 .... M-11
Arcadia, 484 .... G-5
Archer, 131 .... C-3
Aredale, 74 .... D-11
Argyle, 100 .... M-16
Arion, 108 .... H-4
Arispe, 100 .... L-8
Arlington, 429 .... D-15
Armstrong, 926 .... B-7
Arnolds Pk., 1126 .... B-5
Artesian E-13
Arthur, 206 .... F-5
Asbury, 4170 .... E-18
Ashton, 458 .... B-3
Aspinwall, 40 .... H-5
Atalissa, 311 .... I-17
Athelstan, 19 .... M-7
Atkins, 1670 .... G-15
Atlantic, 7112 .... J-5
Attica, 80 .... J-11
Auburn, 322 .... F-6
Audubon, 2176 .... H-6
AUDUBON CO., 6119 .... I-6
Augusta, 100 .... L-16
Aurelia, 1036 .... E-4
Aurora, 185 .... E-15
Austinville, 100 .... E-11
Avery, 120 .... K-12
Avoca, 1506 .... I-4
Ayrshire, 143 .... C-6
Badger, 561 .... E-8
Bagley, 303 .... H-7
Baldwin, 109 .... G-18
Balltown, 68 .... E-17
Bancroft, 732 .... B-8
Bangor, 30 .... G-11
Bankston, 25 .... E-17
Barnes City, 176 .... I-13
Barnum, 191 .... E-7
Bartlett, 50 .... L-3
Bassett, 66 .... C-13
Batavia, 499 .... K-14
Battle Creek, 713 .... F-4
Baxter, 1101 .... H-11
Bayard, 471 .... H-7
Beacon, 494 .... J-12
Beaconsfield, 15 .... L-8
Beaman, 191 .... G-12
Beaver, 48 .... G-8
Bedford, 1440 .... M-6
Beebeetown I-3
Beech, 80 .... J-10
Belknap, 75 .... L-13
Belle Plaine, 2534 .... H-13
Bellevue, 2191 .... F-19
Belmond, 2376 .... D-10
Beloit, 70 .... B-1
Bennett, 405 .... H-17
Benton, 41 .... L-7
BENTON CO., 26076 .... G-14
Bentonsport, 40 .... L-15
Berkley, 32 .... H-8
Bernard, 112 .... F-18
Bertram, 294 .... H-16
Berwick, 600 .... C-20
Bethlehem L-11
Bettendorf, 33217 .... I-19
Bevington, 63 .... J-9
Big Rock, 70 .... H-18
Bingham L-4
Birmingham, 448 .... L-14
BLACK HAWK CO., 131090 .... F-13
Bladensburg K-14
Blairsburg, 215 .... F-9
Blairstown, 692 .... H-14
Blakesburg, 296 .... K-12
Blanchard, 38 .... M-5
Blencoe, 224 .... H-2
Blockton, 192 .... M-7
Bloomfield, 2640 .... L-13
Blue Grass, 1452 .... I-18
Bluffton, 50 .... B-14
Bode, 302 .... D-8
Bolan, 33 .... B-11
Bonair B-14
Bonaparte, 433 .... L-15
Bondurant, 3860 .... I-10
Boone, 12661 .... G-9
BOONE CO., 26306 .... H-9
Booneville, 85 .... I-9
Botna I-5
Bouton, 129 .... H-8
Boxholm, 195 .... G-8
Boyd, 30 .... C-13
Boyden, 707 .... C-3
Boyer, 30 .... G-5
Braddyville, 159 .... M-5
Bradford, 99 .... E-11
Bradgate, 86 .... D-7
Brandon, 309 .... F-14
Brayton, 128 .... I-6
Brazil, 90 .... L-12
Breda, 483 .... G-6
Bremer, 30 .... D-13
BREMER CO., 24276 .... D-13
Bridgewater, 182 .... K-6
Brighton, 652 .... K-15
Bristow, 160 .... D-12
Britt, 2069 .... C-9
Bronson, 322 .... F-2
Brooklyn, 1468 .... H-13
Brooks, 60 .... K-6
Brunsville, 151 .... D-2
Bryant, 35 .... G-19
Buchanan, 30 .... H-16
BUCHANAN CO., 20958 .... E-15
Buck Grv., 43 .... H-4
Buckcreek D-14
Buckeye, 108 .... F-10
Buckingham, 40 .... F-13
BUENA VISTA CO., 20260 .... E-5
Buffalo, 1270 .... I-18
Buffalo Ctr., 905 .... B-9
Burchinal, 40 .... C-11
Burlington, 25663 .... L-17
Burnside, 130 .... F-8
Burr Oak, 166 .... B-15
Burt, 533 .... C-8
Bussey, 422 .... K-12
BUTLER CO., 14867 .... E-12
Cairo, 30 .... K-16
Calamus, 439 .... H-18
CALHOUN CO., 9670 .... F-6
California Jct., 85 .... I-3
Callender, 376 .... F-8
Calmar, 978 .... C-15
Calumet, 170 .... D-4
Camanche, 4448 .... H-19
Cambria, 50 .... L-10
Cambridge, 827 .... H-10
Canby J-7
Canton, 40 .... G-17
Cantril, 222 .... M-14
Capitol Hts., 900 .... B-20
Carbon, 34 .... K-6
Carl K-6
Carlisle, 3876 .... I-10
Carmel, 70 .... C-2
Carnarvon, 60 .... E-5
Carpenter, 109 .... B-11
Carroll, 10103 .... G-6
CARROLL CO., 20816 .... G-6
Carson, 812 .... K-4
Carter Lake, 3785 .... †B-19
Cartersville D-11
Cascade, 2159 .... F-17
Casey, 426 .... I-7
CASS CO., 13956 .... J-6
Castalia, 173 .... C-15
Castana, 147 .... G-3
Cedar, 120 .... J-13
Cedar Bluff, 60 .... H-16
CEDAR CO., 18499 .... H-17
Cedar Falls, 39260 .... E-13
Cedar Rapids, 126326 .... G-15
Cedar Valley, 30 .... G-16
Cedar View, 50 .... G-2
Center Jct., 111 .... G-17
Center Pt., 2421 .... G-15
Centerville, 5528 .... L-12
Central City, 1257 .... G-16
Centralia, 134 .... E-18
CERRO GORDO CO., 44151 .... C-11
Chapin, 87 .... D-11
Chariton, 4321 .... K-10
Charles City, 7652 .... C-12
Charleston, 50 .... M-16
Charlotte, 394 .... G-19
Charter Oak, 502 .... G-4
Chatsworth, 79 .... D-1
Chelsea, 267 .... H-13
Cherokee, 5253 .... D-4
CHEROKEE CO., 12072 .... E-3
Chester, 127 .... B-13
Chickasaw, 40 .... C-13
CHICKASAW CO., 12439 .... C-13
Chillicothe, 97 .... K-13
Church B-16
Churchville, 50 .... J-9
Churdan, 386 .... G-7
Cincinnati, 357 .... M-12
Clare, 146 .... E-7
Clarence, 974 .... H-17
Clarinda, 5572 .... L-5
Clarion, 2850 .... E-9
CLARKE CO., 9286 .... L-9
Clarksville, 1439 .... D-12
CLAY CO., 16667 .... C-5
Clayton, 43 .... D-17
Clayton Ctr., 30 .... D-16
CLAYTON CO., 18129 .... D-15
Clear Lake, 7777 .... C-10
Clearfield, 363 .... L-7
Cleghorn, 240 .... D-4
Clemons, 148 .... G-11
Clermont, 632 .... C-15
Cleves, 20 .... F-11
Climbing Hill, 97 .... E-2
Clinton, 26885 .... H-20
CLINTON CO., 49116 .... H-19
Clio, 80 .... M-10
Clive, 15447 .... I-9
Cloverdale B-4
Clutier, 213 .... G-13
Coalville, 610 .... F-8
Coburg, 42 .... L-5
Coggon, 658 .... F-16
Coin, 193 .... M-5
Colesburg, 404 .... E-17
Colfax, 2093 .... I-11
College Sprs., 214 .... M-5
Collins, 495 .... H-10
Colo, 876 .... G-10
Columbia, 100 .... K-11
Columbus City, 391 .... J-16
Columbus Jct., 1899 .... J-16
Colwell, 73 .... C-12
Conesville, 432 .... J-16
Confidence, 25 .... L-11
Conrad, 1108 .... G-12
Conroy, 259 .... H-14
Conway, 41 .... L-7
Coon Rapids, 1305 .... H-6
Cooper, 35 .... H-7
Coppock, 47 .... K-15
Coralville, 18907 .... I-15
Corley, 26 .... I-5
Cornelia, 80 .... D-9
Cornell D-5
Corning, 1635 .... K-6
Correctionville, 821 .... E-3
Corwith, 309 .... D-9
Corydon, 1585 .... L-10
Cotter, 48 .... J-16
Coulter, 281 .... E-10
Council Bluffs, 62230 .... J-3
Covington, 200 .... J-18
Craig, 89 .... D-2
Cranston, 40 .... J-16
CRAWFORD CO., 17096 .... G-5
Crawfordsville, 264 .... J-16
Crescent, 617 .... J-3
Cresco, 3868 .... B-14
Creston, 7834 .... K-7
Cromwell, 107 .... K-7
Croton, 50 .... M-15
Crystal Lake, 250 .... C-9
Cumberland, 262 .... J-6
Cumming, 351 .... I-9
Curlew, 58 .... D-6
Cushing, 220 .... F-4
Cylinder, 88 .... C-7
Dakota City, 843 .... E-8
Dallas Ctr., 1623 .... I-9
DALLAS CO., 66135 .... I-8
Dana, 71 .... G-8
Danbury, 348 .... F-3
Danville, 934 .... L-16
Davenport, 99685 .... I-18
Davis City, 204 .... M-9
DAVIS CO., 8753 .... L-13
Dawson, 131 .... H-8
Dayton, 837 .... F-8
De Soto, 1050 .... I-8
De Witt, 5322 .... H-19
Decatur City, 197 .... L-9
DECATUR CO., 8457 .... M-9
Decorah, 8127 .... B-15
Dedham, 266 .... H-6
Deep River, 279 .... I-13
Defiance, 284 .... H-4
Delaware, 159 .... E-16
DELAWARE CO., 17764 .... F-16
Delhi, 460 .... F-16
Delmar, 525 .... G-18
Deloit, 264 .... G-5
Delphos, 25 .... M-7
Delta, 328 .... J-13
Denison, 8298 .... G-4
Denmark, 423 .... L-16
Denver, 1780 .... E-13
Depew C-7
Derby, 115 .... L-10
Des Moines, 203433 .... I-10
DES MOINES CO., 40325 .... L-16
Dewar, 250 .... E-14
Dexter, 611 .... I-8
Diagonal, 330 .... L-7
Dickens, 185 .... C-6
DICKINSON CO., 16667 .... B-5
Dike, 1209 .... F-12
Dillon, 30 .... H-12
Dinsdale, 50 .... F-13
Dixon, 247 .... H-18
Dolliver, 66 .... B-7
Donahue, 346 .... H-18
Donnan D-15
Donnellson, 912 .... M-16
Doon, 577 .... B-2
Dorchester, 70 .... B-16
Douds, 152 .... L-14
Dougherty, 58 .... D-11
Dow City, 510 .... H-4
Downey, 100 .... I-16
Dows, 538 .... E-10
Drakesville, 184 .... L-13
Dubuque, 57637 .... E-18
DUBUQUE CO., 93653 .... F-17
Dumont, 637 .... E-11
Dunbar, 50 .... H-12
Duncan, 131 .... C-9
Duncombe, 410 .... F-8
Dundee, 174 .... E-16
Dunkerton, 852 .... E-14
Dunlap, 1042 .... H-4
Durango, 22 .... E-18
Durant, 1832 .... I-17
Dyersville, 4058 .... E-17
Dysart, 1379 .... G-13
Eagle Ctr. F-13
Eagle Grv., 3583 .... E-9
Earlham, 1450 .... I-8
Earling, 437 .... H-4
Earlville, 812 .... E-16
Early, 557 .... F-5
E. Amana, 56 .... H-15
E. Peru, 125 .... J-9
Eddyville, 1024 .... K-12
Edgewood, 864 .... E-16
Edna, 20 .... B-3
Elberon, 196 .... G-13
Eldon, 927 .... L-13
Eldora, 2732 .... F-11
Eldorado, 80 .... C-15
Eldridge, 5651 .... I-18
Elgin, 683 .... D-15
Elk Horn, 662 .... I-5
Elk Run Hts., 1117 .... F-13
Elkader, 1273 .... D-16
Elkhart, 683 .... H-10
Elkport, 37 .... D-16
Elliott, 350 .... K-5
Ellston, 43 .... L-8
Ellsworth, 531 .... F-10
Elma, 546 .... C-13
Elvira, 60 .... H-19
Elwood, 100 .... G-18
Ely, 1776 .... H-15
Emerson, 438 .... K-4
Emery C-11
EMMET CO., 10302 .... B-6
Emmetsburg, 3904 .... C-7
Epworth, 1860 .... F-17
Essex, 798 .... L-5
Estherville, 6360 .... B-6
Evans, 30 .... J-12
Evansdale, 4751 .... F-13
Everly, 603 .... C-5
Ewart, 30 .... I-12
Exira, 840 .... I-6
Exline, 160 .... M-12
Fairbank, 1113 .... E-14
Fairfax, 2123 .... H-15
Fairfield, 9464 .... K-14
Fairport, 300 .... J-17
Fairview, 80 .... G-16
Farley, 1537 .... F-17
Farlin, 70 .... G-7
Farmersburg, 302 .... D-16
Farmington, 664 .... M-15
Farnhamville, 371 .... F-7
Farragut, 485 .... L-4
Farson, 40 .... K-14
Faulkner, 30 .... E-11
Fayette, 1338 .... D-15
FAYETTE CO., 20880 .... D-14
Fenton, 279 .... C-7
Ferguson, 126 .... H-12
Fern, 30 .... E-12
Fernald, 90 .... G-10
Fertile, 370 .... B-10
Festina, 150 .... C-15
Finchford, 130 .... E-13
Flagler, 50 .... J-11
Florenceville, 40 .... B-14
Floris, 138 .... L-13
Floyd, 335 .... C-12
FLOYD CO., 16303 .... C-12
Folletts, 100 .... H-19
Fonda, 631 .... E-6
Fontanelle, 672 .... J-7
Forest City, 4151 .... B-9
Ft. Atkinson, 349 .... C-14
Ft. Des Moines D-19
Ft. Dodge, 25206 .... E-8
Ft. Madison, 11051 .... M-16
Fostoria, 231 .... C-5
Franklin, 143 .... M-16
FRANKLIN CO., 10680 .... E-10
Frankville, 150 .... C-15
Fraser, 102 .... G-9
Frederika, 183 .... D-13
Fredericksburg, 931 .... D-14
Fredonia, 244 .... J-16
Freeman C-11
Freeport, 150 .... B-15
Fremont, 743 .... L-13
FREMONT CO., 7441 .... L-4
Froelich C-16
Fruitland, 977 .... J-17
Fulton, 30 .... G-18
Galesburg, 70 .... I-12
Galt, 32 .... E-10
Galva, 434 .... E-4
Garber, 88 .... D-16
Garden City, 89 .... F-10
Garden Grv., 211 .... L-10
Gardiner H-8
Garnavillo, 745 .... D-16
Garner, 3129 .... C-10
Garrison, 371 .... G-14
Garwin, 527 .... G-12
Gaza, 40 .... C-4
Geneva, 165 .... E-11
George, 1080 .... B-3
Georgetown K-11
German Valley B-8
Germantown, 50 .... D-3
Giard, 40 .... C-16
Gibson, 61 .... I-13
Gifford, 100 .... F-11
Gilbert, 1082 .... G-9
Gilbertville, 712 .... F-14
Gillett Grv., 49 .... C-5
Gilman, 509 .... H-12
Gilmore City, 504 .... E-7
Gladbrook, 945 .... G-12
Glasgow, 30 .... L-15
Glendale, 40 .... L-15
Glenwood, 5269 .... K-3
Glidden, 1146 .... G-6
Goldfield, 635 .... E-9
Goodell, 139 .... D-10
Goose Lake, 240 .... G-19
Gowrie, 1037 .... F-8
Graettinger, 844 .... C-6
Graf, 79 .... E-17
Grafton, 252 .... B-11
Grand Jct., 824 .... G-8
Grand Mound, 642 .... H-18
Grand River, 236 .... L-9
Grandview, 556 .... J-17
Granger, 1244 .... H-9
Granger Homesteads, 240 .... H-9
Granite B-1
Grant, 92 .... K-6
Granville, 312 .... C-3
Gravity, 188 .... L-6
Gray, 63 .... H-6
Greeley, 256 .... E-16
Green Castle, 30 .... H-11
Green Island, 50 .... G-19
Green Mtn., 126 .... G-12
Greene, 1130 .... D-12
GREENE CO., 9336 .... H-7
Greenfield, 1982 .... J-7
Greenville, 75 .... C-5
Grimes, 8246 .... I-9
Grinnell, 9218 .... I-12
Griswold, 1036 .... J-5
Grundy Ctr., 2706 .... F-12
GRUNDY CO., 12453 .... F-12
Gruver, 94 .... B-6
Guernsey, 63 .... I-13
Gunder, 50 .... D-15
Guss L-6
Guthrie Ctr., 1569 .... I-7
GUTHRIE CO., 10954 .... I-6
Guttenberg, 1919 .... D-17
Halbur, 246 .... G-6
Hale, 70 .... G-17
Hamburg, 1187 .... M-3
Hamilton, 130 .... K-12
HAMILTON CO., 15673 .... F-9
Hamlin, 70 .... I-6
Hampton, 4461 .... E-11
Hancock, 196 .... J-4
HANCOCK CO., 11341 .... C-9
Hanford, 30 .... C-11
Hanley, 60 .... J-9
Hanlontown, 226 .... B-10
Hanover E-5
Hansell, 98 .... D-11
Harcourt, 303 .... F-8
HARDIN CO., 17534 .... F-11
Hardy, 47 .... D-8
Harlan, 5106 .... I-5
Harper, 114 .... J-14
Harpers Ferry, 328 .... C-17
Harris, 170 .... B-4
HARRISON CO., 14928 .... H-3
Hartford, 771 .... J-10
Hartley, 1672 .... C-4
Hartwick, 86 .... H-13
Harvard, 30 .... M-11
Harvey, 235 .... J-12
Haskins, 40 .... J-16
Hastings, 152 .... K-4
Havelock, 138 .... D-6
Haven H-13
Haverhill, 173 .... H-11
Hawarden, 2546 .... C-1
Hawkeye, 449 .... D-14
Hawleyville L-6
Hawthorne, 30 .... K-4
Hayesville, 50 .... J-14
Hayfield, 43 .... C-9
Hazleton, 823 .... E-14
Hedrick, 764 .... K-13
Henderson, 185 .... K-4
HENRY CO., 20145 .... K-16
Hepburn, 23 .... L-5
Herndon, 40 .... H-7
Hesper, 150 .... B-15
Hiawatha, 7024 .... G-15
Highland Ctr., 40 .... K-13
Highlandville, 40 .... B-15
Highview F-9
Hills, 703 .... I-16
Hillsboro, 180 .... L-15
Hinton, 928 .... E-2
Hiteman, 100 .... K-12
Hobarton C-8
Holbrook I-15
Holiday Lake, 433 .... H-13
Holland, 282 .... F-12
Holly Sprs., 50 .... F-2
Holmes E-9
Holstein, 1396 .... E-4
Holy Cross, 374 .... E-17
Homer F-9
Homestead, 148 .... H-15
Honey Creek, 75 .... I-3
Hopeville, 30 .... L-8
Hopkinton, 628 .... F-16
Hornick, 225 .... F-2
Hospers, 698 .... C-3
Houghton, 146 .... L-16
HOWARD CO., 9566 .... B-13
Hubbard, 845 .... F-10
Hudson, 2282 .... F-13
Hull, 2175 .... C-2
Humboldt, 4690 .... E-8
HUMBOLDT CO., 9815 .... D-8
Humeston, 494 .... L-10
Huntington, 30 .... B-6
Hutchins, 28 .... C-9
Huxley, 3317 .... H-10
Iconium, 40 .... L-12
IDA CO., 7089 .... F-4
Ida Grv., 2142 .... F-4
Imogene, 72 .... L-4
Independence, 5966 .... F-15
Indianola, 14782 .... J-10
Inwood, 814 .... B-2
Ionia, 291 .... C-13
Iowa Ctr., 30 .... H-10
Iowa City, 67862 .... I-16
IOWA CO., 16355 .... I-14
Iowa Falls, 5238 .... E-11
Ira, 50 .... H-11
Ireton, 609 .... C-2
Irving, 30 .... H-13
Irvington, 38 .... C-8
Irwin, 341 .... H-5
JACKSON CO., 19848 .... F-18
Jackson Jct., 58 .... C-14
Jacksonville, 30 .... I-5
Jamaica, 224 .... H-8
James, 50 .... E-2
Jamison, 30 .... K-9
Janesville, 930 .... E-13
JASPER CO., 36842 .... H-11
Jefferson, 4345 .... G-7
JEFFERSON CO., 16843 .... L-14
Jerico, 30 .... C-13
Jerome, 70 .... L-11
Jesup, 2520 .... F-14
Jewell, 1215 .... F-9
JOHNSON CO., 130882 .... I-15
Johnston, 17278 .... I-9
Joice, 222 .... B-10
Jolley, 41 .... F-6
JONES CO., 20638 .... G-17
Jordan G-9
Kalona, 2363 .... I-15
Kamrar, 199 .... F-9
Kanawha, 652 .... D-9
Kellerton, 315 .... L-8
Kelley, 309 .... H-9
Kellogg, 599 .... I-12
Kendallville, 40 .... B-14
Kensett, 266 .... B-11
Kent, 61 .... L-7
Keokuk, 10780 .... N-16
KEOKUK CO., 10511 .... J-14
Keomah Vil., 84 .... J-13
Keosauqua, 1006 .... L-14
Keota, 1009 .... J-14
Kesley, 100 .... E-12
Keswick, 246 .... J-14
Keystone, 622 .... G-14
Killduff, 120 .... I-12
Kimballton, 322 .... I-5
King, 150 .... F-18
Kingsley, 1411 .... E-3
Kingston, 120 .... K-17
Kinross, 73 .... I-14
Kirkman, 64 .... H-5
Kirkville, 167 .... K-13
Kiron, 279 .... G-5
Klemme, 507 .... C-10
Klinger, 30 .... E-14
Knierim, 60 .... F-7
Knoke, 30 .... E-6
Knoxville, 7313 .... J-11
Kossuth, 100 .... K-17
KOSSUTH CO., 15543 .... C-8
Koszta H-14
La Fayette, 60 .... E-15
La Motte, 260 .... F-18
La Porte City, 2285 .... F-14
Lacey, 40 .... J-12
Lacona, 361 .... K-10
Ladora, 283 .... H-14
Lake City, 1727 .... F-6
L. Mills, 2100 .... B-10
Lake Pk., 1105 .... B-5
L. View, 1142 .... F-5
Lakeside, 596 .... E-5
Lakota, 255 .... B-8
Lambs Grv., 172 .... I-11
Lamoille, 50 .... G-11
Lamoni, 2324 .... M-9
Lamont, 461 .... E-15
Lanesboro, 121 .... G-6
Langdon, 70 .... C-5
Langworthy, 50 .... G-16
Lansing, 999 .... B-16
Larchwood, 866 .... B-2
Larrabee, 132 .... D-4
Latimer, 507 .... D-10
Laurel, 239 .... H-12
Laurens, 1258 .... D-6
Lawler, 439 .... C-14
Lawn Hill, 30 .... F-11
Lawton, 908 .... E-2
Le Claire, 3765 .... I-19
Le Grand, 938 .... G-12
Le Mars, 9826 .... D-2
Le Roy, 15 .... L-11
Leando, 115 .... L-14
Lebanon, 40 .... C-2
Lebanon L-14
Ledyard, 130 .... B-8
LEE CO., 35862 .... L-16
Lehigh, 416 .... F-8
Leighton, 162 .... J-12
Leland, 289 .... B-10
Lenox, 1407 .... L-7
Leon, 1977 .... L-9
Lester, 294 .... B-2
Letts, 384 .... J-17
Lewis, 433 .... J-5
Liberty, 30 .... K-9
Liberty Ctr., 100 .... K-10
Libertyville, 315 .... K-14
Lidderdale, 180 .... G-6
Lime Sprs., 505 .... B-13
Linby, 30 .... K-14
Lincoln, 162 .... F-12
Linden, 199 .... I-8
Lineville, 217 .... M-10
LINN CO., 211226 .... F-16
Linn Grv., 154 .... D-5
Lisbon, 2152 .... H-16
Liscomb, 301 .... G-11
Little Cedar, 60 .... B-12
Little Rock, 459 .... B-3
Little Sioux, 170 .... H-3
Little Turkey, 30 .... C-14
Littleport, 20 .... D-16
Littleton, 220 .... E-14
Livermore, 384 .... D-8
Lockridge, 268 .... K-15
Logan, 1534 .... I-3
Logansport, 140 .... G-9
Lohrville, 368 .... F-7
Lone Rock, 146 .... C-8
Lone Tree, 1300 .... I-16
Long Grv., 808 .... H-18
Lorah I-6
Lorimor, 360 .... K-8
Lost Nation, 446 .... G-18
LOUISA CO., 11387 .... K-16
Lourdes, 30 .... B-13
Loveland, 35 .... I-3
Lovilia, 538 .... K-12
Lovington, 700 .... B-19
Low Moor, 288 .... H-19
Lowden, 789 .... H-17
Lowell, 100 .... L-16
Lu Verne, 261 .... D-8
Luana, 269 .... C-16
Lucas, 216 .... K-10
LUCAS CO., 8898 .... K-10
Luther, 122 .... H-9
Luton F-2
Luxemburg, 240 .... E-17
Luzerne, 96 .... H-14
Lyman, 100 .... J-5
Lynnville, 379 .... I-12
LYON CO., 11581 .... B-2
Lytton, 315 .... F-6
Macedonia, 246 .... K-4
Macksburg, 113 .... J-8
MADISON CO., 15679 .... J-9
Madrid, 2543 .... H-9
Magnolia, 183 .... I-3
Maharishi Vedic City, 259 .... K-14
MAHASKA CO., 22381 .... J-12
Malcom, 287 .... I-13
Mallard, 274 .... D-7
Malone, 25 .... H-19
Maloy, 29 .... M-7
Malvern, 1142 .... K-4
Manchester, 5179 .... E-16
Manilla, 776 .... H-5
Manly, 1323 .... B-11
Manning, 1500 .... H-5
Manson, 1690 .... E-7
Maple Hill, 30 .... B-7
Maple River, 80 .... G-6
Mapleton, 1224 .... G-3
Maquoketa, 6141 .... G-18
Marathon, 237 .... D-6
Marble Rock, 307 .... D-12
Marcus, 1117 .... D-3
Marengo, 2528 .... H-14
Marietta, 50 .... G-11
Marion, 34768 .... G-15
MARION CO., 33309 .... J-11
Mark, 30 .... M-13
Marne, 120 .... J-5
Marquette, 375 .... C-17
MARSHALL CO., 40648 .... H-11
Marshalltown, 27552 .... G-12
Martelle, 255 .... G-16
Martensdale, 465 .... J-9
Martinsburg, 112 .... K-14
Marysville, 66 .... K-12
Mason City, 28079 .... C-11
Masonville, 127 .... E-15
Massena, 355 .... J-6
Massey, 120 .... F-18
Massillon, 50 .... H-17
Matlock, 87 .... B-3
Maurice, 275 .... D-2
Maxwell, 920 .... H-10
May City, 110 .... B-4
Maynard, 518 .... D-15
Maysville, 176 .... I-18
McCallsburg, 333 .... G-10
McCausland, 291 .... H-19
McClelland, 151 .... J-3
McGregor, 871 .... C-17
McIntire, 122 .... B-12
McNally D-2
Mechanicsville, 1146 .... H-16
Mederville, 30 .... D-16
Mediapolis, 1560 .... K-17
Medora, 50 .... K-10
Melbourne, 830 .... H-11
Melcher-Dallas, 1288 .... J-11
Melrose, 112 .... K-11
Melvin, 214 .... B-4
Menlo, 353 .... I-7
Meriden, 159 .... D-4
Merrill, 755 .... D-2
Meservey, 256 .... D-10
Meyer, 31 .... B-12
Middleburg, 30 .... C-3
Middletown, 318 .... L-17
Midway, 150 .... G-15
Miles, 445 .... G-19
Milford, 2898 .... B-5
Miller, 60 .... C-10
Millersburg, 159 .... I-14
Millerton, 45 .... L-10
MILLS CO., 15059 .... K-4
Millville, 30 .... E-17
Milo, 775 .... J-10
Milton, 443 .... M-14
Minburn, 365 .... H-8
Minden, 599 .... I-4
Mineola, 166 .... K-3
Mingo, 302 .... H-11
Missouri Valley, 2838 .... I-3
Mitchell, 138 .... B-12
MITCHELL CO., 10776 .... B-12
Mitchellville, 2254 .... I-10
Modale, 283 .... I-3
Moingona, 100 .... G-9
Mona, 34 .... B-11
Mondamin, 402 .... H-3
Moneta C-4
Monmouth, 153 .... G-18
Monona, 1549 .... C-16
MONONA CO., 9243 .... G-3
Monroe, 1830 .... I-11
MONROE CO., 7970 .... K-12
Monteith, 50 .... I-7
Monterey, 30 .... M-13
Montezuma, 1462 .... I-13
Montgomery, 80 .... B-5
MONTGOMERY CO., 10740 .... K-5
Monticello, 3796 .... F-17
Montour, 249 .... G-12
Montpelier, 230 .... I-18
Montrose, 898 .... M-16
Mooar, 80 .... M-16
Moorhead, 226 .... H-3
Moorland, 169 .... F-8
Moran, 50 .... H-9
Moravia, 665 .... L-12
Morley, 115 .... G-16
Morning Sun, 836 .... K-17
Morrison, 94 .... F-12
Morse, 80 .... H-16
Morton Mills, 25 .... K-6
Moscow, 300 .... I-17
Moulton, 605 .... M-12
Mt. Auburn, 150 .... F-14
Mt. Ayr, 1691 .... L-8
Mt. Carmel, 70 .... G-6
Mt. Etna, 30 .... K-6
Mt. Hamill, 30 .... L-16
Mt. Joy, 400 .... I-19
Mt. Pleasant, 8668 .... K-16
Mt. Sterling, 36 .... M-15
Mt. Union, 107 .... K-16
Mt. Vernon, 4506 .... H-16
Mt. Zion, 30 .... L-15
Moville, 1618 .... E-2
Munterville K-12
Murray, 756 .... K-9
Muscatine, 22886 .... J-17
MUSCATINE CO., 42745 .... I-17
Mystic, 425 .... L-12
Napier, 50 .... G-9
Nashua, 1663 .... D-13
Nashville, 30 .... G-18
Nemaha, 85 .... E-5
Neola, 842 .... I-4
Neptune, 30 .... E-2
Nevada, 6798 .... G-10
New Albin, 522 .... A-16
New Boston, 60 .... M-16
New Hampton, 3571 .... C-13
New Hartford, 516 .... E-12
New Haven, 91 .... B-12
New Liberty, 137 .... H-18
New London, 1897 .... L-16
New Market, 415 .... L-6
New Providence, 228 .... F-11
New Sharon, 1293 .... I-12
New Vienna, 407 .... E-17
New Virginia, 489 .... K-9
Newburg, 120 .... H-12
Newell, 876 .... E-6
Newhall, 875 .... G-14
Newkirk, 70 .... C-3
Newton, 15254 .... I-11
Nichols, 374 .... I-16
Noble, 50 .... K-15
Nodaway, 114 .... L-6
Nora Sprs., 1431 .... C-11
N. Buena Vista, 121 .... E-17
N. English, 1041 .... I-14
N. Liberty, 13374 .... H-15
N. Washington, 117 .... C-13
Northboro, 58 .... M-5
Northwood, 1989 .... B-11
Norwalk, 8945 .... I-9
Norway, 545 .... H-14
Norwich, 30 .... L-5
Norwood, 30 .... K-10
Norwoodville, 1200 .... B-20
Numa, 92 .... M-11
Oakland, 1527 .... J-4
Oakland Acres, 156 .... I-12
Oakland Mills, 50 .... L-15
Oakley, 30 .... K-10
Oakville, 173 .... K-17
O'BRIEN CO., 14398 .... C-3
Ocheyedan, 490 .... B-4
Odebolt, 1013 .... F-5
Oelwein, 6415 .... E-14
Ogden, 2044 .... G-8
Okoboji, 807 .... B-5
Olds, 229 .... K-16
Olin, 698 .... G-17
Ollie, 215 .... K-14
Onawa, 2998 .... G-2
Oneida, 40 .... E-16
Onslow, 197 .... G-17
Oran, 150 .... E-14
Orange City, 6004 .... C-3
Orchard, 71 .... C-12
Orient, 408 .... K-7
Orleans, 608 .... B-5
Osage, 3619 .... B-12
Osborne D-16
Osceola, 4929 .... K-9
OSCEOLA CO., 6462 .... B-4
Osgood C-6
Oskaloosa, 11463 .... J-12
Ossian, 845 .... C-15
Osterdock, 59 .... D-17
Otho, 542 .... F-8
Otley, 300 .... J-11
Oto, 108 .... F-3
Otranto, 27 .... B-11
Otter Creek, 100 .... F-18
Otterville, 50 .... E-14
Ottosen, 55 .... D-7
Ottumwa, 25023 .... K-13
Owasa, 43 .... F-11
Oxford, 807 .... H-15
Oxford Jct., 496 .... G-17
Oxford Mills, 100 .... G-17
Oyens, 103 .... D-3
Pacific Jct., 471 .... K-3
Packard D-12
Packwood, 204 .... K-14
PAGE CO., 15932 .... L-5
Palmer, 165 .... E-7
Palmyra, 50 .... J-10
Palo, 1026 .... G-15
PALO ALTO CO., 9421 .... D-7
Panama, 221 .... H-4
Panora, 1124 .... I-7
Panorama Pk., 129 .... *R-4
Paralta, 50 .... G-16
Paris, 60 .... F-15
Paris, 40 .... L-13
Park View, 2389 .... H-19
Parkersburg, 1870 .... E-12
Parnell, 193 .... I-14
Paton, 236 .... G-8
Patterson, 130 .... J-9
Paullina, 1056 .... D-4
Pella, 10352 .... J-12
Peoria, 110 .... J-12
Peosta, 1377 .... F-18
Percival, 87 .... L-3
Perkins, 30 .... C-2
Perry, 7702 .... H-8
Pershing, 300 .... J-11
Persia, 319 .... I-4
Petersburg, 140 .... E-16
Peterson, 334 .... D-5
Pierson, 366 .... E-3
Pilot Grv., 40 .... L-16
Pilot Mound, 173 .... G-8
Pioneer, 23 .... E-7
Piper E-7
Pisgah, 251 .... H-3
Pittsburg L-14
Pitzer I-8
Plainfield, 436 .... D-13
Plainview, 50 .... I-18
Plano, 70 .... L-11
Pleasant Grv., 40 .... K-16
Pleasant Hill, 8785 .... I-10
Pleasant Plain, 93 .... K-15
Pleasant Prairie J-18
Pleasant Valley, 700 .... I-19
Pleasanton, 49 .... M-9
Pleasantville, 1694 .... J-11
Plover, 77 .... D-7
Plymouth, 382 .... C-11
PLYMOUTH CO., 24986 .... E-2
Pocahontas, 1789 .... E-6
POCAHONTAS CO., 7310 .... E-6
Polk City, 3418 .... H-9
POLK CO., 430640 .... H-10
Pomeroy, 662 .... E-6
Popejoy, 79 .... E-10
Portland, 35 .... C-11
Portsmouth, 195 .... I-4
Postville, 2227 .... C-15
POTTAWATTAMIE CO., 93158 .... J-4
Powersville D-12
POWESHIEK CO., 18914 .... H-13
Prairie City, 1680 .... I-11
Prairieburg, 178 .... F-16
Prescott, 257 .... K-7
Preston, 1012 .... G-19
Primghar, 909 .... C-4
Primrose, 30 .... M-15
Princeton, 886 .... I-19
Prole, 50 .... J-9
Promise City, 111 .... L-11
Protivin, 283 .... C-14
Pulaski, 260 .... L-14
Quarry, 60 .... G-12
Quasqueton, 554 .... F-15
Quimby, 319 .... E-4
Radcliffe, 545 .... F-10
Rake, 225 .... B-9
Ralston, 79 .... G-7
Randalia, 68 .... D-15
Randall, 173 .... F-10
Randolph, 168 .... L-4
Rands F-7
Rathbun, 89 .... L-12
Raymond, 788 .... F-14
Readlyn, 808 .... E-14
Reasnor, 152 .... I-11
Red Line H-5
Red Oak, 5742 .... K-5
Redding, 82 .... M-7
Redfield, 835 .... I-8
Reinbeck, 1664 .... F-13
Rembrandt, 203 .... D-5
Remsen, 1663 .... D-3
Renwick, 242 .... D-9
Rhodes, 305 .... H-11
Riceville, 785 .... B-13
Richard, 30 .... F-7
Richland, 584 .... K-14
Richmond, 100 .... I-15
Rickardsville, 182 .... E-17
Ricketts, 145 .... G-4
Ridgeport, 30 .... G-9
Ridgeway, 315 .... B-14
Rinard, 52 .... F-7
RINGGOLD CO., 5131 .... L-7
Ringsted, 422 .... B-7
Rippey, 292 .... H-8
Ritter B-3
River Hts., 580 .... H-16
River Sioux, 59 .... H-2
Riverdale, 405 .... I-19
Riverside, 993 .... I-16
Riverton, 304 .... L-4
Robins, 3142 .... G-15
Rochester, 133 .... I-17
Rock Creek, 30 .... C-12
Rock Falls, 155 .... C-11
Rock Rapids, 2549 .... B-2
Rock Valley, 3354 .... C-2
Rockford, 860 .... C-11
Rockwell, 1039 .... D-11
Rockwell City, 1709 .... F-7
Rodman, 45 .... C-7
Rodney, 60 .... G-3
Roelyn, 30 .... F-7
Roland, 1284 .... G-10
Rolfe, 584 .... D-7
Rome, 117 .... K-15
Rose Hill, 168 .... J-13
Roselle, 60 .... G-6
Ross, 60 .... H-6
Rossie, 70 .... C-5
Rowan, 158 .... E-10
Rowley, 264 .... F-15
Royal, 446 .... C-5
Rudd, 369 .... C-12
Runnells, 507 .... I-10
Russell, 554 .... K-11
Ruthven, 737 .... C-6
Rutland, 126 .... D-8
Ryan, 361 .... F-16
Sabula, 576 .... G-20
Sac City, 2220 .... F-6
SAC CO., 10350 .... F-5
Sageville, 122 .... E-18
St. Ansgar, 1107 .... B-12
St. Anthony, 102 .... G-11
St. Benedict, 39 .... C-8
St. Charles, 653 .... J-9
St. Donatus, 135 .... F-18
St. Joseph, 61 .... D-8
St. Lucas, 143 .... C-14
St. Marys, 127 .... J-9
St. Olaf, 108 .... D-16
St. Paul, 129 .... L-16
Salem, 383 .... L-15
Salina, 25 .... K-15
Salix, 363 .... F-2
Sanborn, 1404 .... C-4
Sand Sprs., 40 .... F-17
Sandusky, 70 .... M-16
Sandyville, 51 .... J-10
Saratoga, 60 .... B-13
Saude C-14
Savannah, 30 .... M-13
Saydel, 3500 .... A-19
Saylorville, 3301 .... A-19
Scarville, 72 .... B-10
Schaller, 772 .... E-5
Schleswig, 882 .... G-4
Schley, 30 .... B-14
Scotch Grv., 60 .... G-17
SCOTT CO., 165224 .... H-19
Scranton, 557 .... G-7
Searsboro, 148 .... I-12
Selma, 80 .... L-14
Seneca, 30 .... B-7
Seney, 80 .... D-2
Sergeant Bluff, 4227 .... F-2
Sewal, 40 .... M-11
Sexton, 37 .... C-8
Seymour, 701 .... M-11
Shambaugh, 191 .... M-5
Sharon Ctr., 120 .... I-15
Sharpsburg, 89 .... L-7
Sheffield, 1172 .... D-11
Shelby, 641 .... I-4
SHELBY CO., 12167 .... I-4
Sheldahl, 319 .... H-9
Sheldon, 5188 .... C-3
Shell Rock, 1296 .... E-13
Shellsburg, 983 .... G-15
Shenandoah, 5150 .... L-4
Sherrill, 177 .... E-18
Sherwood F-6
Shipley G-10
Shueyville, 577 .... H-15
Siam M-6
Sibley, 2798 .... B-3
Sidney, 1138 .... L-4
Sigourney, 2059 .... J-14
Silver City, 245 .... K-4
Sinclair E-12
Sioux Ctr., 7048 .... C-2
Sioux City, 82684 .... E-2
SIOUX CO., 33704 .... C-2
Sioux Rapids, 775 .... D-5
Slater, 1489 .... H-9
Slifer, 30 .... F-7
Sloan, 973 .... F-2
Smithland, 224 .... F-3
Soldier, 174 .... G-3
Solon, 2037 .... H-16
Somers, 113 .... F-7
S. Amana, 159 .... H-14
S. English, 212 .... J-14
Spaulding K-7
Spencer, 11233 .... C-5
Sperry, 70 .... K-17
Spillville, 367 .... C-14
Spirit Lake, 4840 .... B-5
Spragueville, 81 .... G-19
Spring Grv., 100 .... I-17
Spring Hill, 63 .... J-9
Springbrook, 144 .... G-19
Springdale, 50 .... I-16
Springville, 1074 .... G-16
Stacyville, 494 .... B-12
Stanhope, 422 .... F-9
Stanley, 125 .... E-15
Stanton, 689 .... K-5
Stanwood, 684 .... H-17
Stanzel J-8
State Ctr., 1468 .... G-11
Steamboat Rock, 310 .... F-11
Stennett K-5
Stilson C-9
Stockport, 296 .... L-15
Stockton, 197 .... I-18
Stone City, 192 .... G-16
Storm Lake, 10600 .... E-5
Story City, 3431 .... G-10
STORY CO., 89542 .... G-10
Stout, 224 .... E-12
Strahan, 30 .... K-4
Stratford, 743 .... F-9
Strawberry Pt., 1279 .... E-16
Struble, 78 .... D-2
Stuart, 1648 .... I-7
Sully, 821 .... I-12
Sulphur Sprs., 40 .... E-5
Summerset, 150 .... J-10
Summitville, 50 .... M-16
Sumner, 2028 .... D-14
Sunbury, 50 .... I-17
Superior, 130 .... B-6
Sutherland, 649 .... D-4
Swaledale, 165 .... D-10
Swan, 72 .... J-10
Swea City, 536 .... B-8
Swedesburg, 130 .... K-16
Swisher, 879 .... H-15
Tabor, 1040 .... L-3
Taintor, 40 .... I-12
Tama, 2877 .... H-13
TAMA CO., 17767 .... G-13
Tara E-8
TAYLOR CO., 6317 .... M-6
Teeds Grv., 100 .... G-19
Templeton, 362 .... H-6
Ten Mile, 30 .... G-19
Tennant, 68 .... I-4
Tenville Jct., 20 .... K-5
Terril, 367 .... B-6
Thayer, 59 .... K-8
Thirty M-12
Thompson, 502 .... B-9
Thor, 186 .... E-8
Thornburg, 67 .... J-13
Thornton, 422 .... D-10
Thurman, 229 .... L-3
Ticonic G-3
Tiffin, 1947 .... I-15
Tingley, 184 .... L-8
Tipton, 3221 .... H-17
Titonka, 476 .... C-8
Toddville, 200 .... G-15
Toeterville, 48 .... B-12
Toledo, 2341 .... G-13
Toolesboro, 40 .... K-17
Toronto, 124 .... H-18
Tracy, 450 .... J-12
Traer, 1703 .... G-13
Trenton, 120 .... K-15
Treynor, 919 .... J-4
Tripoli, 1313 .... D-13
Troy, 70 .... L-14
Troy Mills, 200 .... F-15
Truesdale, 81 .... E-5
Truro, 485 .... K-9
Turin, 68 .... G-3
Turkey River E-17
Twin View Hts., 350 .... H-16
Udell, 47 .... L-12
Ulmer, 30 .... F-6
Underwood, 917 .... J-3
Union, 397 .... F-11
UNION CO., 12534 .... K-7
Unionville, 102 .... L-12
University Hts., 1051 .... I-16
University Pk., 487 .... J-12
Urbana, 1458 .... G-15
Urbandale, 39463 .... I-9
Ute, 374 .... G-3
Vail, 436 .... G-5
Valeria, 57 .... H-10
VAN BUREN CO., 7570 .... L-14
Van Cleve, 50 .... H-11
Van Horne, 682 .... G-14
Van Meter, 1016 .... I-9
Van Wert, 230 .... L-9
Vandalia, 60 .... I-10
Varina, 71 .... E-6
Ventura, 717 .... C-10
Vernon, 60 .... L-15
Vernon, 30 .... D-11
Vernon Sprs., 40 .... B-14
Vernon View, 120 .... K-20
Victor, 893 .... H-13
Villisca, 1252 .... L-5
Vincennes, 40 .... M-16
Vincent, 174 .... E-8
Vining, 50 .... G-13
Vinton, 5257 .... G-14
Viola, 120 .... G-16
Volga, 208 .... D-16
Volney, 30 .... C-16
Voorhies, 60 .... F-13
Wadena, 262 .... D-15
Wahpeton, 341 .... B-5
Walcott, 1629 .... I-18
Wales, 25 .... K-5
Walford, 1463 .... H-15
Walker, 791 .... F-15
Wall Lake, 819 .... F-5
Wallingford, 197 .... B-6
Walnut, 785 .... I-5
Wapello, 2067 .... K-17
WAPELLO CO., 35625 .... L-13
Ware D-6
WARREN CO., 46225 .... J-10
Washburn, 876 .... F-13
Washington, 7266 .... J-15
WASHINGTON CO., 21704 .... J-15
Washta, 248 .... E-3
Waterloo, 68406 .... E-13
Waterville, 144 .... C-16
Watkins, 118 .... H-14
Waubeek, 100 .... G-16
Waucoma, 257 .... C-14
Waukee, 13790 .... I-9
Waukon, 3897 .... B-16
Waukon Jct., 20 .... C-17
Waverly, 9874 .... E-13
Wayland, 966 .... K-15
WAYNE CO., 6403 .... M-10
Webb, 141 .... D-6
Webster, 88 .... J-14
Webster City, 8070 .... F-9
WEBSTER CO., 38013 .... F-8
Weldon, 125 .... L-9
Wellman, 1408 .... I-15
Wellsburg, 707 .... F-12
Welton, 165 .... H-18
Wesley, 390 .... C-8
W. Amana, 140 .... H-14
W. Bend, 785 .... D-7
W. Branch, 2322 .... I-16
W. Burlington, 2968 .... L-17
W. Chester, 146 .... J-15
W. Des Moines, 56609 .... I-9
W. Grove, 50 .... L-13
W. Lemars, 30 .... D-2
W. Liberty, 3736 .... I-16
W. Okoboji, 289 .... B-5
W. Point, 966 .... L-16
W. Union, 2486 .... D-15
Westfield, 132 .... D-1
Westgate, 211 .... D-14
Weston, 92 .... J-3
Westphalia, 127 .... H-4
Westside, 299 .... G-5

***, †, ‡, §, ◊ See explanation under state title in this index.**
County and parish names are listed in capital letters & boldface type.
Independent cities (not included in a county) are listed in *italics*.

Westwood, 112 .... K-15
Wever, 140 .... L-17
What Cheer, 646 .... J-13
Wheatland, 764 .... I-18
Whiting, 762 .... G-2
Whittemore, 504 .... C-7
Whitten, 149 .... F-11
Whittier, 130 .... G-16
Wick, 40 .... J-9
Willey, 88 .... G-6
Williams, 344 .... F-10
Williamsburg, 3068 .... I-14
Williamson, 152 .... K-11
Williamson K-7
Williamstown, 100 .... I-15
Wilton, 2802 .... I-17
Windsor Hts., 4860 .... B-18
Winfield, 1134 .... K-16

WINNEBAGO CO.,
10866 .... B-9
WINNESHIEK CO.,
21056 .... B-14
Winterset, 5190 .... J-8
Winthrop, 850 .... F-15
Wiota, 116 .... J-6
Wiscotta, 40 .... C-8
Woden, 229 .... C-9
Wood H-16
Woodbine, 1459 .... H-3
Woodburn, 202 .... K-10
WOODBURY CO.,
102172 .... F-3
Woodland M-10
Woodward, 1024 .... I-9
Woolstock, 168 .... E-9
WORTH CO.,
7598 .... B-11
Worthington, 401 .... F-17
Wright, 50 .... J-12
WRIGHT CO.,
13229 .... E-9
Wyman, 30 .... K-16
Wyoming, 515 .... G-17
Yale, 246 .... H-7
Yarmouth, 120 .... K-16
Yetter, 34 .... F-6
Yorktown, 85 .... L-5
Zaneta G-11
Zearing, 554 .... G-11
Zwingle, 91 .... F-17

Kansas

Abbyville, 87 .... H-11
Abilene, 6844 .... E-13
Ada, 100 .... D-11
Adams, 20 .... I-11
Admire, 156 .... F-16
Agenda, 68 .... B-12
Agra, 267 .... B-8
Agricola F-17
Akron E-13
Alamota, 25 .... F-6
Albert, 175 .... F-9
Alden, 148 .... G-10
Alexander, 65 .... F-7
Aliceville, 40 .... F-16
Allen, 177 .... G-15
ALLEN CO.,
13371 .... H-17
Alma, 832 .... D-15
Almena, 408 .... B-7
Alta Vista, 444 .... E-15
Altamont, 1080 .... J-18
Alton, 103 .... C-9
Altoona, 414 .... I-17
Americus, 894 .... F-15
Ames, 40 .... C-12
Amy F-5
Andale, 928 .... H-12
ANDERSON CO.,
8102 .... G-17
Andover, 11791 .... H-13
Angelus, 45 .... D-5
Angola, 50 .... I-12
Anson, 30 .... I-12
Antelope F-14
Anthony, 2269 .... I-11
Antonino, 50 .... E-8
Arcadia, 310 .... H-19
Argonia, 501 .... I-12
Arkansas City,
12415 .... J-13
Arlington, 473 .... H-11
Arma, 1481 .... I-19
Arnold, 50 .... E-8
Arrington, 40 .... C-17
Ash Grv D-10
Asherville, 28 .... C-11
Ashland, 867 .... I-7
Ashton, 25 .... I-13
Assaria, 413 .... E-12
Atchison, 11021 .... C-18
ATCHISON CO.,
16924 .... C-17
Athol, 49 .... B-9
Atlanta, 195 .... I-14
Attica, 626 .... I-11
Atwood, 1194 .... B-4
Aubry, 100 .... E-19
Auburn, 1227 .... E-16
Augusta, 9274 .... H-13
Aulne, 50 .... G-13
Aurora, 50 .... B-15
Axtell, 406 .... B-15
Baileyville, 181 .... B-15
Bala, 30 .... D-13
Baldwin City, 4515 .... E-18
Bancroft C-16
BARBER CO., 4861 .... I-9
Barnard, 70 .... D-11
Barnes, 159 .... B-14
Bartlett, 80 .... J-18
BARTON CO.,
27674 .... F-9
Basehor, 4613 .... D-18
Bassett, 14 .... H-17
Bavaria, 90 .... E-12
Baxter Sprs., 4238 .... J-19
Bazaar, 25 .... G-15
Bazine, 334 .... F-7
Beagle, 70 .... F-18
Beattie, 245 .... B-15
Beattie B-3
Beaumont, 200 .... I-15
Beaver, 40 .... E-10
Beeler, 45 .... F-6
Bellaire, 6769 .... H-13

Bellaire B-9
Belle Plaine, 1681 .... I-13
Belleville, 1991 .... B-12
Belmont, 35 .... I-11
Beloit, 3835 .... C-11
Belpre, B H-8
Belvidere, 25 .... I-8
Bendena, 117 .... B-18
Benedict, 73 .... I-16
Bennington, 672 .... D-12
Bentley, 530 .... H-12
Benton, 880 .... H-13
Bern, 166 .... B-16
Berryton, 400 .... E-17
Berwick B-10
Beulah, 60 .... I-19
Beverly, 162 .... D-11
Big Bow, 95 .... I-2
Big Sprs., 75 .... D-17
Bird City, 447 .... B-3
Bison, 255 .... F-8
Blaine, 80 .... D-16
Blair, 40 .... D-16
Blakeman B-4
Bloom, 75 .... I-6
Bloomington, 60 .... C-9
Blue Mound, 275 .... G-18
Blue Rapids, 1019 .... B-14
Bluff City, 65 .... I-11
Bogue, 143 .... C-7
Boicourt, 30 .... G-19
Bolton, 40 .... I-16
Bonita *N-1
Bonner Spgs., 7314 .... D-18
BOURBON CO.,
15173 .... H-18
Boyle, 36 .... I-7
Brainerd, 70 .... H-13
Brazilton, 80 .... H-19
Bremen, 80 .... B-14
Brenham I-8
Brewster, 305 .... C-3
Bridgeport, 75 .... E-12
Bronson, 323 .... H-18
Brookville, 262 .... E-11
BROWN CO.,
9984 .... B-17
Brownell, 29 .... F-7
Bucklin, 794 .... H-7
Bucyrus, 193 .... E-19
Buffalo, 232 .... H-17
Buhler, 1327 .... G-12
Bunker Hill, 95 .... E-9
Burden, 535 .... I-14
Burdett, 247 .... G-7
Burdick, 75 .... F-14
Burlingame, 934 .... E-16
Burlington, 2674 .... G-16
Burns, 228 .... G-14
Burr Oak, 174 .... B-10
Burrton, 901 .... G-12
Bush City G-18
Bushong, 34 .... F-15
Bushton, 279 .... F-10
BUTLER CO.,
65880 .... H-14
Byers, 35 .... H-9
Cadmus F-18
Cairo, 20 .... I-10
Caldwell, 1068 .... I-12
Calista G-12
Calvert, 25 .... B-7
Cambridge, 82 .... I-14
Canada, 75 .... F-13
Caney, 2203 .... J-16
Canton, 748 .... F-12
Capaldo I-19
Carbondale, 1437 .... E-16
Carlton, 42 .... F-13
Carlyle, 100 .... H-17
Carneiro, 25 .... E-11
Cassoday, 129 .... G-14
Castleton, 25 .... H-11
Catharine, 104 .... E-8
Cawker City, 469 .... C-10
Cedar, 14 .... C-9
Cedar Bluffs, 35 .... A-5
Cedar Pt., 28 .... G-14
Cedar Vale, 579 .... I-15
Centerville, 100 .... H-18
Centralia, 512 .... B-15
Centropolis, 170 .... F-17
Chanute, 9119 .... H-17
Chapman, 1393 .... E-13
Charleston, 25 .... H-5
Chase, 477 .... F-10
CHASE CO., 2790 .... G-14
Chautauqua, 111 .... J-15
CHAUTAUQUA CO.,
3669 .... J-15
Cheney, 2094 .... H-12
Cherokee, 714 .... I-19
CHEROKEE CO.,
21603 .... J-18
Cherryvale, 2367 .... J-17
Chetopa, 1125 .... J-18
CHEYENNE CO.,
2726 .... B-2
Cimarron, 2184 .... H-5
Circleville, 200 .... C-16
Claflin, 645 .... F-10
CLARK CO., 2215 .... J-6
Claudell B-9
Clay Ctr., 4334 .... D-13
CLAY CO., 8535 .... D-13
Clayton, 59 .... B-6
Clearwater, 2481 .... I-12
Clements, 100 .... G-14
Clifton, 554 .... C-13
Climax, 77 .... H-15
Clinton, 40 .... E-17
Clonmel B-18
CLOUD CO., 9533 .... C-11
Clyde, 716 .... C-12
Coats, 83 .... H-10
Codell, 75 .... D-8
COFFEY CO.,
8601 .... G-16
Coffeyville, 10295 .... J-17
Colby, 5387 .... C-4
Coldwater, 828 .... I-8
Collyer, 109 .... D-6
Colony, 408 .... G-17
Columbus, 3312 .... J-19
Colwich, 1327 .... H-12
COMANCHE CO.,
1891 .... J-8
Concordia, 5395 .... C-12
Conway, 75 .... G-11
Conway Sprs., 1272 .... I-12
Coolidge, 95 .... G-1
Copeland, 310 .... H-5
Corbin, 100 .... I-11

Corning, 157 .... B-16
Corwin, 25 .... I-10
Cottonwood Falls,
903 .... G-15
Council Grv., 2182 .... E-15
Countryside, 295 .... *J-2
Courtland, 285 .... B-11
COWLEY CO.,
36311 .... J-14
Coyville, 46 .... H-16
CRAWFORD CO.,
39134 .... I-18
Crestline, 110 .... J-19
Croweburg, 75 .... I-19
Cuba, 156 .... B-12
Cullison, 101 .... I-9
Culver, 121 .... E-12
Cummings, 70 .... C-17
Cunningham, 454 .... I-10
Dalton, 61 .... B-17
Damar, 132 .... D-7
Danville, 38 .... I-11
De Graff G-13
De Soto, 5720 .... D-18
Dearing, 431 .... I-17
Decatur, 100 .... C-6
DECATUR CO.,
2961 .... B-5
Deerfield, 700 .... H-3
Delavan, 26 .... F-14
Delia, 169 .... D-16
Delphos, 359 .... D-12
Denison, 187 .... C-17
Denmark D-11
Dennis, 150 .... I-17
Densmore, 35 .... C-7
Denton, 148 .... B-17
Derby, 22158 .... I-13
Detroit, 174 .... E-13
Devon, 30 .... H-19
Dexter, 278 .... I-14
Diamond Sprs. F-14
DICKINSON CO.,
19754 .... E-13
Dighton, 1038 .... F-5
Dodge City, 27340 .... H-6
Doniphan, 48 .... B-18
DONIPHAN CO.,
7945 .... B-17
Dorrance, 185 .... E-10
Douglass, 1700 .... I-13
Dover, 140 .... E-16
Downs, 900 .... C-10
Dresden, 41 .... C-5
Dunlap, 30 .... F-15
Duquoin I-18
Durham, 112 .... F-13
Dwight, 272 .... E-14
Eastborough, 773 .... M-9
Easton, 253 .... C-18
Edgerton, 1671 .... E-18
Edmond, 49 .... C-7
Edna, 442 .... J-17
Edson, 40 .... C-4
EDWARDS CO.,
3037 .... H-8
Edwardsville, 4340 .... *I-1
Effingham, 546 .... C-17
El Dorado, 13021 .... H-14
Elbing, 229 .... G-13
Elgin, 89 .... K-15
Elk City, 325 .... I-16
ELK CO., 2882 .... I-15
Elk Falls, 107 .... I-15
Elkhart, 2205 .... K-1
Ellinwood, 2131 .... F-10
Ellis, 2062 .... E-7
ELLIS CO., 28452 .... D-8
Ellsworth, 3120 .... E-11
ELLSWORTH CO.,
6497 .... E-11
Elmdale, 55 .... F-14
Elmo, 40 .... E-13
Elmont, 100 .... D-16
Elsmore, 77 .... H-18
Elwood, 1224 .... B-18
Elyria, 75 .... F-12
Emmett, 191 .... C-16
Emporia, 24916 .... F-15
Englevale, 25 .... I-18
Englewood, 77 .... J-6
Ensign, 187 .... H-6
Enterprise, 855 .... E-13
Erie, 1150 .... H-17
Esbon, 99 .... B-9
Eskridge, 534 .... E-16
Eudora, 6136 .... E-18
Eureka, 2633 .... H-15
Everest, 284 .... B-17
Fairmount, 100 .... B-18
Fairview, 260 .... B-16
Fairway, 3882 .... *J-3
Fall River, 162 .... I-16
Falun, 87 .... F-12
Farlington, 75 .... H-18
Farlinville G-18
Faulkner, 30 .... I-18
Fellsburg H-7
Finney G-5
FINNEY CO.,
36776 .... G-5
Floral, 40 .... I-14
Florence, 465 .... G-14
Fontana, 224 .... F-19
Ford, 216 .... H-7
FORD CO., 33848 .... I-6
Formoso, 93 .... B-10
Fostoria D-14
Fowler, 590 .... I-6
Frankfort, 726 .... B-15
Franklin, 375 .... I-19
FRANKLIN CO.,
25992 .... F-17
Frederick, 18 .... F-10
Fredonia, 2482 .... I-16
Freeport, 5 .... *J-3
Friend, 30 .... G-6
Frontenac, 3437 .... I-19
Fulton, 163 .... G-18
Furley, 100 .... H-13
Galatia, 39 .... F-9
Galena, 3085 .... J-19
Galesburg, 136 .... H-17
Galva, 870 .... F-12
Garden City, 26658 .... H-4
Garden Plain, 841 .... H-12
Gardner, 11923 .... E-18
Garfield, 190 .... G-8

Garland, 100 .... H-19
Garnett, 3415 .... G-18
Gas, 564 .... H-17
Gaylord, 114 .... C-9
GEARY CO.,
34362 .... E-14
Gem, 88 .... C-4
Geneseo, 267 .... F-11
Geuda Sprs., 185 .... J-13
Girard, 2789 .... I-19
Glade, 96 .... B-8
Glasco, 498 .... C-11
Glen Elder, 445 .... C-10
Glendale, 35 .... E-11
Goddard, 4344 .... I-12
Goessel, 539 .... G-13
Goff, 126 .... B-16
Goodland, 4489 .... C-2
Goodrich, 40 .... G-18
Gorham, 334 .... E-9
Gove, 80 .... E-5
GOVE CO., 2695 .... E-5
Graham, 30 .... F-16
GRAHAM CO.,
2597 .... D-6
Grainfield, 277 .... D-5
Grandview Plaza,
1560 .... D-14
GRANT CO., 7829 .... I-3
Grantville, 180 .... D-17
Gray Hawk K-14
Great Bend, 15995 .... F-9
Greeley, 302 .... F-18
Green, 128 .... C-13
Greenleaf, 331 .... B-13
Greensburg, 777 .... I-8
Greenwich, 80 .... H-13
Greenwich Hts.,
960 .... H-13
GREENWOOD CO.,
6689 .... H-15
Grenola, 216 .... I-15
Gretna B-8
Gridley, 341 .... G-16
Grigston F-4
Grinnell, 259 .... D-5
Gross, 50 .... I-18
Grove D-16
Groveland G-12
Gypsum, 405 .... E-12
Hackney, 25 .... J-13
Haddam, 104 .... B-13
Half Mound C-17
Hallowell, 200 .... J-18
Halls Summit F-17
Halstead, 2085 .... H-12
Hamilton, 268 .... H-15
Hanover, 206 .... B-14
Harding G-6
Hardtner, 172 .... J-9
Harlan, 25 .... C-9
Harper, 1473 .... I-11
HARPER CO.,
6034 .... J-11
Harris, 51 .... F-18
Hartford, 371 .... G-16
HARVEY CO.,
34684 .... G-13
Harveyville, 236 .... E-16
Haskell, 4256 .... J-4
Havana, 100 .... J-16
Haven, 1237 .... H-12
Havensville, 133 .... C-16
Haviland, 701 .... I-8
Hays, 20510 .... E-8
Haysville, 10826 .... I-13
Hazelton, 93 .... J-10
Healy, 234 .... F-5
Hedville, 50 .... E-12
Heizer, 125 .... F-9
Hepler, 132 .... H-18
Herington, 2526 .... F-14
Herkimer, 50 .... B-14
Herndon, 129 .... B-4
Hesston, 3709 .... G-13
Hewins, 40 .... I-15
Hiattville, 60 .... H-18
Hiawatha, 3172 .... B-17
Hickok, 80 .... I-2
Highland, 1012 .... B-17
Highland Pk. M-16
Hill City, 1474 .... C-7
Hillsboro, 2993 .... F-13
Hillsdale, 229 .... E-18
Hitschmann, 20 .... F-10
HODGEMAN CO.,
1916 .... G-6
Hoisington, 2706 .... F-9
Holcomb, 2094 .... H-4
Holland F-13
Hollenberg, 21 .... B-13
Hollis C-12
Holton, 3329 .... C-16
Holyrood, 447 .... F-10
Home, 160 .... B-14
Homewood, 80 .... F-17
Hope, 368 .... F-13
Hopewell H-8
Horace, 70 .... F-2
Horton, 1776 .... B-17
Howard, 780 .... I-15
Hoxie, 1201 .... C-5
Hoyt, 669 .... C-16
Hudson, 129 .... G-10
Hugoton, 3904 .... J-3
Humboldt, 1953 .... H-17
Hunnewell, 47 .... J-13
Hunter, 57 .... D-10
Huron, 57 .... B-17
Hutchinson, 42080 .... G-11
Idana, 70 .... C-12
Independence, 9483 .... J-17
Industry D-13
Ingalls, 306 .... H-5
Inman, 1377 .... G-12
Iola, 5704 .... H-17
Ionia, 80 .... C-10
Iowa Pt., 35 .... B-17
Isabel, 90 .... I-10
Iuka, 163 .... H-9
JACKSON CO.,
13462 .... C-16
Jamestown, 286 .... C-12
Jarbalo, 100 .... D-18
Jefferson, 50 .... H-17
JEFFERSON CO.,
19126 .... D-17

Jennings, 96 .... B-6
Jetmore, 867 .... G-6
Jewell, 432 .... B-11
JEWELL CO.,
3077 .... B-11
Johnson, 1495 .... J-2
JOHNSON CO.,
544179 .... E-18
Junction City,
23353 .... D-14
Kackley, 25 .... B-11
Kalvesta, 40 .... G-6
Kanopolis, 492 .... E-11
Kanorado, 153 .... C-1
Kansas City,
145786 .... D-19
KEARNY CO., 3977 .... G-3
Keats, 170 .... D-14
Kelly, 40 .... B-16
Kendall, 250 .... H-2
Kensington, 473 .... B-9
Kimball B-18
Kincaid, 122 .... G-18
Kingman, 3177 .... I-11
KINGMAN CO.,
7858 .... I-11
Kingsdown, 200 .... I-6
Kinsley, 1457 .... H-8
Kiowa, 1026 .... K-10
KIOWA CO., 2553 .... I-8
Kipp, 59 .... E-12
Kirwin, 171 .... B-9
Kismet, 459 .... J-4
La Crosse, 1342 .... F-8
La Cygne, 1149 .... F-19
La Harpe, 578 .... H-18
Labette, 78 .... J-18
LABETTE CO.,
21607 .... J-18
Labette, 100 .... J-16
Lake City, 50 .... J-9
Lakin, 2216 .... H-3
Lamont, 45 .... G-16
Lancaster, 298 .... C-17
Lane, 225 .... F-18
LANE CO., 1750 .... F-5
Langdon, 42 .... H-10
Langley I-18
Lansing, 11265 .... D-18
Larkinburg, 30 .... C-17
Larned, 4054 .... G-8
Latham, 139 .... I-14
Latimer, 20 .... E-14
Lawrence, 87643 .... D-18
Leavenworth,
35471 .... I-16
Leavenworth, 80 .... C-18
LEAVENWORTH CO.,
76227 .... D-18
Leawood, 31867 .... J-3
Lebanon, 218 .... B-10
Lebo, 940 .... F-16
Lecompton, 625 .... D-17
Lehigh, 175 .... F-13
Lenexa, 48190 .... D-19
Lenora, 250 .... C-6
Leon, 704 .... H-14
Leona, 48 .... B-17
Leonardville, 449 .... C-14
Leoti, 1534 .... F-3
Leoville, 50 .... C-5
Levant, 61 .... C-3
Lewis, 451 .... H-8
Liberal, 20525 .... J-4
Liberty, 123 .... J-17
Liebenthal, 103 .... F-8
Lillis C-15
Lincoln, 1297 .... D-11
LINCOLN CO.,
3241 .... D-11
Lincolnville, 203 .... F-13
Lindsborg, 3458 .... F-12
Linn, 410 .... B-13
LINN CO., 9656 .... G-18
Linn Valley, 804 .... F-19
Linwood, 375 .... D-18
Little River, 557 .... F-11
Logan, 589 .... B-7
LOGAN CO., 2756 .... E-3
Lone Elm, 25 .... G-18
Lone Star E-17
Long Island, 134 .... B-7
Longford, 79 .... D-13
Longton, 348 .... I-16
Loretta, 30 .... F-8
Lorraine, 138 .... F-11
Lost Sprs., 70 .... F-13
Louisburg, 4315 .... E-19
Louisville, 188 .... D-15
Lowell J-19
Lowemont C-18
Lucas, 393 .... D-10
Ludell, 100 .... B-4
Luray, 194 .... D-9
Lyndon, 1052 .... F-17
LYON CO., 33690 .... F-15
Lyons, 3739 .... G-11
Macksville, 549 .... H-9
Madison, 701 .... G-15
Mahaska, 83 .... A-12
Maize, 3420 .... H-12
Manchester, 85 .... D-13
Manhattan, 52281 .... D-14
Mankato, 869 .... B-10
Manning F-5
Manter, 171 .... J-2
Maple City, 20 .... J-14
Maple Hill, 620 .... D-16
Mapleton, 84 .... G-19
Marienthal, 71 .... F-4
Marion, 1927 .... F-13
MARION CO.,
12660 .... G-13
Marquette, 641 .... F-11
MARSHALL CO.,
10177 .... B-14
Marysville, 3294 .... B-14
Matfield Green, 47 .... G-14
Mayetta, 341 .... C-16
Mayfield, 113 .... J-12
McCracken, 190 .... F-7
McCune, 405 .... I-18
McDonald, 160 .... B-3
McFarland, 256 .... D-15
McLouth, 880 .... D-18
McPherson, 13155 .... F-12
MCPHERSON CO.,
29180 .... F-11
Meade, 1721 .... J-5

MEADE CO., 4575 .... J-5
Medicine Lodge,
2009 .... J-10
Medora, 50 .... G-11
Melrose, 50 .... J-18
Melvern, 385 .... F-17
Menlo, 61 .... C-5
Mentor, 100 .... E-12
Mercier, 25 .... B-17
Meriden, 813 .... D-17
Merriam, 11003 .... *J-2
MIAMI CO.,
32287 .... F-18
Michigan Valley,
150 .... E-17
Midway I-11
Milan, 82 .... I-12
Milberger, 25 .... E-9
Mildred, 28 .... G-18
Milford, 530 .... D-14
Miller, 50 .... F-16
Milton, 155 .... I-12
Miltonvale, 539 .... C-12
Mingo, 40 .... D-4
Minneapolis, 2045 .... D-12
Minneola, 745 .... I-6
Minneola, 9323 .... *J-1
Mission, 9504 .... *J-3
Mission Hills, 3498 .... *J-3
Mission Woods, 178 .... *J-3
Mitchell F-11
MITCHELL CO.,
6373 .... D-11
Modoc, 35 .... F-4
Moline, 371 .... I-15
Monmouth I-18
Mont Ida, 50 .... G-17
Montana, 50 .... E-8
Montezuma, 966 .... I-5
MONTGOMERY CO.,
35471 .... I-16
Montrose B-11
Monument, 75 .... D-4
Moran, 558 .... H-18
Morehead, 50 .... I-17
Morganville, 192 .... C-13
Morland, 154 .... C-6
Morrill, 230 .... B-16
MORRIS CO.,
5923 .... F-14
Morrowville, 155 .... B-13
MORTON CO.,
3233 .... J-2
Moscow, 310 .... J-3
Mound City, 694 .... G-19
Mound Valley, 407 .... J-17
Moundridge, 1737 .... G-12
Mt. Hope, 813 .... H-12
Mulberry, 520 .... I-19
Mullinville, 255 .... I-7
Mulvane, 6111 .... I-13
Munden, 100 .... B-12
Munjor, 213 .... E-8
Murdock, 75 .... I-11
Muscotah, 176 .... C-17
Narka, 94 .... B-12
Nashville, 64 .... I-10
Natoma, 335 .... D-9
Navarre, 75 .... E-13
Neal, 65 .... H-15
Nekoma, 80 .... F-8
NEMAHA CO.,
10178 .... B-16
Neodesha, 2486 .... I-17
NEOSHO CO.,
16512 .... I-17
Neosho Falls, 141 .... G-17
Neosho Rapids, 265 .... F-16
Ness City, 1449 .... F-6
NESS CO., 3107 .... F-7
Netawaka, 143 .... C-16
Neutral J-19
New Albany, 56 .... I-16
New Almelo, 50 .... C-6
New Cambria, 126 .... E-12
New Lancaster, 25 .... F-19
New Salem, 80 .... H-14
New Strawn, 394 .... G-16
Newman, 40 .... D-7
Newton, 19132 .... G-13
Nickerson, 1070 .... G-11
Niles, 40 .... E-12
Niotaze, 82 .... J-16
Norcatur, 151 .... B-6
N. Newton, 1759 .... G-13
N. Topeka C-16
Northbranch, 29 .... B-10
NORTON CO.,
5671 .... B-6
Nortonville, 637 .... C-17
Norway, 40 .... C-12
Norwich, 491 .... I-11
Oak Hill, 24 .... D-13
Oak Valley, 25 .... I-16
Oakland L-14
Oaklawn, 3000 .... N-9
Oakley, 2045 .... D-4
Oberlin, 1788 .... B-5
Ochelbee, 100 .... E-19
Odin, 101 .... F-10
Offerle, 199 .... H-7
Ogallah, 40 .... E-7
Ogden, 2087 .... D-14
Oketo, 60 .... B-14
Olathe, 125872 .... E-19
Olivet, 67 .... F-16
Olmitz, 114 .... F-9
Olpe, 546 .... G-15
Olsburg, 215 .... C-15
Onaga, 702 .... C-15
Oneida, 75 .... B-16
Opolis, 130 .... I-19
Osage City, 2943 .... F-16
OSAGE CO.,
16295 .... E-16
Osawatomie, 4447 .... F-18
Osborne, 1431 .... C-9
OSBORNE CO.,
3858 .... C-9
Oskaloosa, 1113 .... D-17
Oswego, 1829 .... J-18
Otis, 282 .... F-9
Ottawa, 12649 .... F-18
OTTAWA CO.,
6091 .... D-12
Overbrook, 1058 .... E-17
Overland Pk.,
173372 .... J-3
Oxford, 1049 .... J-13
Ozawkie, 645 .... D-17
Page City, 40 .... D-4
Palco, 272 .... D-7
Palmer, 121 .... C-12
Paola, 5602 .... F-18
Paradise, 49 .... D-9
Park, 126 .... D-6
Park City, 7297 .... H-13
Parker, 277 .... F-18
Parkerfield, 426 .... J-14
Parkerville, 59 .... F-14
Parsons, 10500 .... I-18

Partridge, 248 .... H-11
Pauline N-15
PAWNEE CO., 6973 .... G-7
Pawnee Rock, 252 .... G-9
Paxico, 221 .... D-15
Peabody, 1210 .... G-13
Peck, 110 .... I-13
Penalosa, 17 .... H-10
Penokee, 150 .... C-6
Peoria, 40 .... F-18
Perry, 929 .... D-17
Perth, 50 .... J-13
Peru, 139 .... J-16
Petrolia, 85 .... H-17
Pfeifer, 80 .... E-8
Philipsburg, 2581 .... B-8
Pickrell Cor., 40 .... H-14
Piedmont, 250 .... I-15
Pierceville, 100 .... H-5
Pilsen, 200 .... F-13
Piqua, 107 .... H-17
Plains, 1146 .... I-5
Plainville, 1903 .... D-8
Plevna, 98 .... H-10
Plymouth, 50 .... F-15
Pomona, 830 .... F-17
Portis, 103 .... C-9
POTTAWATOMIE CO.,
21604 .... C-15
Potter, 100 .... C-18
Powhattan, 77 .... B-17
Prairie View, 134 .... B-7
Prairie Vil., 21447 .... J-3
Pratt, 6835 .... I-9
PRATT CO., 9656 .... I-9
Prescott, 264 .... G-19
Preston, 158 .... H-10
Pretty Prairie, 680 .... H-11
Princeton, 277 .... F-18
Prospect, 500 .... H-14
Protection, 514 .... J-7
Quenemo, 388 .... F-17
Quincy H-16
Quinter, 918 .... D-6
Radium, 25 .... G-8
Radley, 200 .... I-19
Rago, 30 .... I-11
Ramona, 187 .... F-13
Randall, 65 .... C-11
Randolph, 163 .... C-14
Ransom, 294 .... F-6
Rantoul, 184 .... F-18
RAWLINS CO.,
2519 .... B-4
Raymond, 79 .... G-10
Reading, 231 .... F-16
Redfield, 146 .... H-19
Redwing, 20 .... F-9
Reece, 140 .... H-15
RENO CO.,
64511 .... H-11
Republic, 116 .... B-11
REPUBLIC CO.,
4980 .... B-12
Reserve, 84 .... A-17
Rexford, 232 .... C-5
Rice I-12
RICE CO., 10083 .... F-10
Richfield, 43 .... J-2
Richmond, 464 .... F-18
Riley, 939 .... D-14
RILEY CO., 71115 .... C-14
Riverdale, 60 .... I-13
Riverton, 929 .... J-19
Robinson, 234 .... B-17
Rock, 80 .... I-13
Rock Creek, 50 .... D-17
Rocky Ford D-14
Roeland Pk., 6731 .... *J-3
Rolla, 442 .... J-2
Rose, 120 .... I-17
Rosalia, 171 .... H-14
Rose Hill, 3931 .... I-13
Roseland, 77 .... J-19
Rossville, 1151 .... D-16
Roxbury, 104 .... F-12
Rozel, 156 .... G-8
Rush Ctr., 170 .... F-8
RUSH CO., 3307 .... F-8
Russell, 4505 .... E-9
RUSSELL CO.,
6970 .... D-9
Russell Sprs., 24 .... E-3
Sabetha, 2571 .... B-16
St. Benedict, 70 .... B-15
St. Clere C-15
St. Francis, 1329 .... B-2
St. George, 639 .... D-15
St. John, 1295 .... H-9
St. Joseph, 55 .... C-12
St. Leo, 25 .... H-11
St. Mark, 100 .... G-13
St. Marys, 2627 .... D-16
St. Paul, 629 .... I-18
St. Peter, 30 .... D-6
SALINE CO.,
55606 .... E-11
Sanford I-10
Satanta, 1133 .... I-4
Savonburg, 109 .... H-18
Sawyer, 124 .... I-9
Saxman, 25 .... F-10
Scammon, 482 .... I-19
Scandia, 372 .... B-11
Schoenchen, 207 .... E-8
Schulte, 50 .... C-12
Scipio F-18
SCOTT CO., 4936 .... F-4
Scott City, 3816 .... E-4
Scottsville, 20 .... C-11
Scranton, 710 .... E-16
Sedan, 1124 .... J-16
Sedgwick, 1695 .... H-12
SEDGWICK CO.,
498365 .... I-12
Selden, 219 .... C-5
Seldkirk, 35 .... F-3
Selma G-18
Seneca, 1991 .... B-16
Severance, 96 .... B-17
Severy, 250 .... H-16
Seward, 64 .... G-10
SEWARD CO.,
22952 .... J-4
Shallow Water, 40 .... F-4
Sharon, 173 .... I-10
Sharon Sprs., 748 .... E-2

Sharpe G-17
Shaw I-13
Shawnee, 62209 .... D-19
SHAWNEE CO.,
177934 .... E-16
SHERIDAN CO.,
2556 .... D-5
Sherman, 50 .... I-13
SHERMAN CO.,
6010 .... C-2
Sherwin, 40 .... J-19
Shields, 30 .... F-5
Silver Lake, 1439 .... D-16
Silverdale, 50 .... J-14
Simpson, 86 .... C-11
Sitka J-7
Skiddy E-14
Smith Ctr., 1665 .... B-9
SMITH CO., 3853 .... B-9
Smolan, 215 .... E-12
Soldier, 136 .... C-16
Solomon, 1095 .... E-13
Somerset, 40 .... F-19
S. Haven, 363 .... J-12
S. Hutchinson,
2457 .... G-11
S. Mound, 20 .... H-18
Sparks, 50 .... B-18
Spearville, 773 .... H-7
Speed, 37 .... B-8
Spivey, 78 .... I-11
Spring Hill, 5437 .... E-19
Springdale, 30 .... D-18
Stafford, 1042 .... H-10
STAFFORD CO.,
4437 .... G-9
Stanley *M-2
Stark, 103 .... H-18
STANTON CO.,
2235 .... H-1
Sterling, 2328 .... G-11
Stilwell, 250 .... *J-4
STEVENS CO., 5724 .... J-3
Stippville, 30 .... J-19
Stockton, 1329 .... C-8
Strauss I-18
Strong City, 485 .... F-15
Studley, 50 .... C-7
Stull, 45 .... D-17
Stuttgart, 75 .... B-8
Sublette, 1453 .... I-4
SUMNER CO.,
24132 .... J-12
Sun City, 53 .... I-9
Susank, 34 .... F-9
Sycamore, 200 .... I-17
Sylvan Grv., 279 .... D-10
Sylvia, 218 .... H-10
Syracuse, 1812 .... G-2
Talmage, 99 .... D-13
Talmo, 50 .... B-12
Tampa, 112 .... F-13
Tasco C-6
Tecumseh, 650 .... M-17
Terra Hts. N-15
Tescott, 319 .... D-11
Thayer, 497 .... I-17
THOMAS CO.,
7900 .... C-3
Thrall G-17
Timken, 70 .... F-8
Tipton, 210 .... C-10
Tonganoxie, 4996 .... D-18
Topeka, 127473 .... D-16
Toronto, 281 .... H-16
Towanda, 1450 .... H-13
Trading Post G-19
Traer, 25 .... B-5
Trego Ctr. E-6
Tribune, 741 .... F-2
Trousdale H-8
Troy, 1010 .... B-18
Turon, 387 .... H-10
Tyro, 200 .... J-17
Udall, 746 .... I-13
Ulysses, 6161 .... I-3
Uniontown, 272 .... H-18
Upland, 25 .... B-13
Urbana, 30 .... I-17
Utica, 158 .... F-6
Valeda, 70 .... J-17
Valley Ctr., 6822 .... H-13
Valley Falls, 1192 .... C-17
Varner H-11
Vassar, 537 .... F-17
Venango, 100 .... F-11
Verdi F-16
Vermillion, 102 .... B-15
Vernon H-17
Victoria, 1214 .... E-8
Vilas I-16
Vine Creek D-7
Vining, 45 .... C-13
Vinland, 30 .... E-18
Viola, 130 .... I-12
Virgil, 71 .... H-16
Vliets, 35 .... B-15
Voda D-6
Wabaunsee, 710 .... D-15
WABAUNSEE CO.,
7053 .... E-15
Wagstaff, 20 .... F-18
Wakarusa, 260 .... E-16
Wakeeney, 1831 .... D-7
Wakefield, 980 .... D-13
Waldo, 30 .... D-10
Waldron, 11 .... K-11
Walker, 60 .... E-8
Wallace, 57 .... E-2
WALLACE CO.,
1485 .... D-2
Walnut, 220 .... H-18
Walton, 235 .... G-13
Wamego, 4372 .... D-15
Washington, 1131 .... B-13
WASHINGTON CO.,
5799 .... B-13
Waterloo, 30 .... H-13
Waterville, 680 .... B-14
Wathena, 1364 .... B-18
Waukena G-5
Waverly, 592 .... F-17
Wayne, 30 .... C-11
Wayside, 65 .... J-16
Weaver, 200 .... F-13
Beaver Dam, 3409 .... K-5
Weir, 686 .... I-19
Welda, 150 .... G-17
Wellington, 8172 .... I-12
Wells, 40 .... D-12
Wellsford, 25 .... I-8
Wellsville, 1857 .... F-18
Weskan, 161 .... E-2
W. Mineral, 185 .... I-19
W. Westphalia, 40 .... F-13
Westmoreland, 778 .... C-15
Westphalia, 163 .... G-17
Westwood, 1506 .... *J-3

Westwood Hills,
359 .... *J-3
Bellefonte, 888 .... *B-14
Bellemeade, 865 .... B-9
Bellevue, 343 .... C-19
Bellewview, 5955 .... A-17
Belmont, 100 .... J-10
Belton, 250 .... L-4
Bengal K-9
Benham, 500 .... L-18
Bennettstown, 35 .... M-2
Benton, 4349 .... K-4
Berea, 13561 .... J-13
Berkley, 125 .... F-2
Berlin, 45 .... E-13
Berry, 264 .... F-13
Bethany, 65 .... I-10
Bethel, 200 .... K-4
Bethelridge, 30 .... K-12
Bethlehem, 260 .... G-11
Betsy Layne, 688 .... I-18
Beulah, 50 .... K-6
Beulah Hts., 50 .... M-13
Beverly, 30 .... L-15
Bewleyville, 100 .... I-7
Big Clifty, 300 .... I-7
Big Creek, 300 .... L-15
Big Eddy, 150 .... K-12
Big Laurel, 100 .... L-17
Big Spr., 90 .... I-7
Bighill, 200 .... J-13
Bimble, 200 .... M-15
Birdsville J-3
Black Gnat, 50 .... K-9
Black Snake, 200 .... M-16
Blackey, 120 .... L-17
Blackford, 100 .... J-3
Blaine, 47 .... H-18
Blandville, 90 .... J-2
Bledsoe, 56 .... L-16
Bloomfield, 838 .... I-10
Blue Licks Spr. G-14
Blue Ridge Mnr., 767 .... B-9
Blue River, 30 .... I-18
Bluehole L-15
Board Tree, 50 .... J-20
Boaz, 20 .... K-4
Bohon, 30 .... I-11
Boldman, 130 .... I-18
Bon, 90 .... K-14
Bondville M-1
Bonnieville, 255 .... K-8
Boone J-12
Boone, 100 .... L-16
Boonesborough I-13
Booneville, 81 .... L-15
Boons Camp, 125 .... I-18
Boradus K-7

BELL CO., 28691 .... M-15
Bosco, 200 .... J-3
Boston, 266 .... I-9
Boston, 80 .... K-7
Bostona, 40 .... J-9
Boundary, 100 .... L-12
Bow, 25 .... M-10
Bowen, 35 .... I-15
Bowling Green,
58067 .... K-7
BOURBON CO.,
19985 .... H-13
Bracht E-18
BRACKEN CO.,
8488 .... F-13
Bradfordsville, 294 .... I-10
Brainard H-12
Brandenburg, 2643 .... H-7
BREATHITT CO.,
13878 .... J-16
Breckinridge L-2
BRECKINRIDGE CO.,
20059 .... I-7
Breeding, 60 .... K-9
Bremen, 197 .... K-6
Brewers, 125 .... K-4
Briarwood, 435 .... B-9
Bridgeport, 200 .... H-11
Brodhead, 1211 .... K-13
Bromley, 763 .... B-9
Bronston, 400 .... L-12
Brooks, 2401 .... H-9
Brooksville, 642 .... F-14
Broughtentown, 40 .... J-11
Browder, 300 .... K-6
Brownsboro Farm,
648 .... A-9
Brownsboro Vil., 319 .... B-8
Brownsville, 836 .... K-7
Bruin, 60 .... H-17
Brush Grv. I-10
Bryantsville, 80 .... I-12
Buckhorn, 162 .... K-16
Buckner, 5837 .... G-9
Buechel, 7272 .... C-8
Buffalo, 498 .... J-9
Buford, 75 .... I-13
Bulan, 600 .... K-17
Bullitt H-9
BULLITT CO.,
74319 .... H-9
Burgin, 965 .... I-12
Burkesville, 1521 .... M-10
Burkhart, 20 .... K-16
Burlington, 15926 .... D-12
Burna, 250 .... K-3
Burnaugh, 175 .... G-18
Burning Spr., 100 .... L-11
Burnside, 611 .... L-12
Burns, 3148 .... A-17
Burtonville, 60 .... G-15
Bush, 15 .... L-14
Butler, 623 .... E-13

DAVIESS CO.,
96656 .... J-4
Davis G-12
Dawson Spr., 2764 .... L-2
Day L-18
Daysville, 75 .... M-4
Dayton, 5338 .... A-20
Deane, 80 .... I-18
Deatsville, 80 .... I-9
Decoy, 30 .... J-17
Dekle, 50 .... G-11
Dekoven, 125 .... K-2
Delphia, 100 .... L-17
Demossville, 60 .... E-13
Dennistown, 75 .... I-13
Denton, 30 .... G-17
Depoy, 70 .... K-6
Dexter, 277 .... K-4
Diablock, 453 .... K-17
Diamond, 150 .... K-17
Dice, 20 .... K-16
Dixie, 100 .... L-12
Dixon, 786 .... L-2
Dog Walk I-11
Dorton, 250 .... K-18
Douglass Hills, 5484 .... B-9
Dover, 252 .... E-14
Draffenville, 300 .... K-4
Drakesboro, 515 .... K-4
Dreyfus, 150 .... J-13
Drift, 300 .... J-18
Dry Ridge, 2191 .... F-12
Dublin, 50 .... G-3
Duckers H-11
Dukedom, 50 .... K-4
Dundee, 50 .... J-5
Dunmore, 200 .... L-4
Dunnville, 225 .... K-11
Dwale, 329 .... I-18
Dwarf, 100 .... K-17
Dycusburg, 26 .... K-1
Dyer, 125 .... J-17
Earlington, 1413 .... K-3
E. Bernstadt, 716 .... K-14
E. Union G-18
Eastview, 60 .... I-7
Eddyville, 2554 .... L-1
Edgewood, 8575 .... C-18
EDMONSON CO.,
12161 .... K-6
Edmonton, 1595 .... L-9
Egypt, 30 .... K-4
Eighty Eight, 75 .... M-8
Ekron, 135 .... I-7
Elba, 30 .... J-3
Eli, 100 .... L-11
Elizabethtown, 28531 .... I-8
Elizaville, 181 .... G-14
Elk Creek, 30 .... H-10
Elk Horn, 50 .... J-10

FORKS OF ELKHORN
Fordsville, 524 .... J-5
Forest Grv., 125 .... H-13
Forest Hills, 444 .... C-9
Forest Hills, 300 .... J-19
Forks of Elkhorn,
.... A-13
Ft. Mitchell, 8207 .... D-12
Ft. Thomas, 16325 .... D-12
Ft. Wright, 5723 .... B-19
Foster, 40 .... E-13
Fount L-15
Fountain Run, 217 .... M-8
Four Oaks, 140 .... K-17
Fourmile, 450 .... M-15
Foxport, 50 .... F-15
Frakes, 125 .... N-14
Frances, 50 .... K-1
Franfort, 25527 .... G-11
Franklin, 8408 .... M-6
FRANKLIN CO.,
49285 .... G-11
Franklin Cross Roads,
.... G-11
Fredericktown, 150 .... I-10
Fredonia, 401 .... K-1
Freedom M-10
Frenchburg, 486 .... H-15
Fruit Hill L-3
Fulgham, 60 .... K-3
Fulton, 2445 .... K-3
FULTON CO., 6813 .... G-2
Future City, 200 .... K-3
Gage, 40 .... L-3
GALLATIN CO.,
8589 .... E-11
Gamaliel, 376 .... N-8
Gap in Knob, 180 .... I-9
Garden Vil., 100 .... I-19
Gardnersville, 50 .... E-12
Garfield, 150 .... I-7
Garner, 150 .... K-17
GARRARD CO.,
16912 .... J-12
Garrett, 500 .... J-18
Garret, 150 .... I-7
Garrison, 866 .... F-16
Gasper L-5
Gatliff, 60 .... M-14
Gays Creek, 80 .... K-16
Geneva, 150 .... J-2
Georgetown,
29098 .... G-12
Germantown, 154 .... F-14
Ghent, 323 .... E-11
Gilbertsville, 458 .... K-4
Gilley, 50 .... I-18
Girdler, 250 .... L-14
Glasgow, 14028 .... L-8
Gleanings J-5
Glen Dean, 50 .... J-6
Glencoe, 360 .... E-11
Glendale, 350 .... I-8
Glens Fork, 100 .... L-10
Glensboro, 100 .... H-11
Goldbug J-13

Kentucky

Aaron, 70 .... M-10
Aberdeen, 200 .... K-5
Acton, 125 .... K-10
Adairville, 852 .... N-5
Adamson K-18
Adolphus, 150 .... N-7
Airport Gdns., 700 .... K-17
Akersville N-7
Albany, 2033 .... M-11
Alexandria, 8477 .... D-13
Allegre, 100 .... M-4
Allen City, 193 .... I-18
Allen, 199556 .... M-7
Allensville, 157 .... M-4
Almo, 100 .... K-4
Alpha, 25 .... M-11
Alpine, 50 .... L-11
Alton, 300 .... H-11
Alton Sta., 450 .... H-11
Altro, 35 .... K-16
Alvaton, 80 .... M-7
Amandaville, 40 .... J-3
Amos, 50 .... L-17
Anchorage, 2348 .... B-10
Anco, 360 .... J-17
ANDERSON CO.,
21421 .... H-11
Anna L-6
Annville, 1095 .... K-14
Anthoston, 250 .... K-3
Anton, 200 .... K-3
Appalachia, 200 .... N-17
Argillite, 50 .... G-17
Argo J-20
Arjay, 400 .... M-15
Arlington, 590 .... K-3
Artemus, 590 .... M-15
Ary, 60 .... K-17
Ashbyburg, 40 .... K-5
Ashcamp, 150 .... I-20
Asher, 150 .... L-16
Ashland, 21684 .... F-18
Athertonville, 28 .... I-9
Athol, 75 .... K-15
Auburn, 1340 .... M-5
Audubon Pk., 1473 .... C-7
Augusta, 1190 .... F-14
Aurora, 200 .... K-4
Austin, 150 .... M-8
Auxier, 669 .... I-18
Avawam, 250 .... K-16
Axtel, 60 .... I-10
Bagdad, 220 .... H-11
Baizetown, 25 .... K-5
Bakerton, 30 .... M-10
BALLARD CO.,
8249 .... J-2
Ballardsville, 200 .... B-9
Balltown, 80 .... I-9
Bancroft, 472 .... B-9
Bandana, 203 .... J-3
Bandy M-16
Banner, 100 .... I-18
Barbourmeade, 1186 .... A-9
Barbourville, 3165 .... M-14
Bardstown, 11700 .... I-10
Bardstown Jct. H-9
Bardwell, 723 .... K-3
Barlow, 675 .... J-2
BARREN CO.,
42173 .... M-8
Barrier, 75 .... M-12
Baskett, 200 .... K-3
Bath, 125 .... J-3
BATH CO., 11591 .... G-15
Battletown, 150 .... H-7
Baxter, 800 .... M-16
Bays, 25 .... K-15
Bear Branch, 80 .... K-15
Beauty, 600 .... I-20
Beaver, 200 .... I-18
Beaverlick, 75 .... E-12
Beda L-9
Bedford, 599 .... G-10
Bee Spr., 50 .... K-6
Beech Creek, 25 .... K-5
Beech Grv., 30 .... K-4
Beechmont, 689 .... L-6
Beechwood Vil.,
1324 .... B-8
Belcher, 125 .... I-20
Belfry, 600 .... I-19

Canada, 400 .... J-19
Cane Valley, 150 .... L-10
Caney, 100 .... L-16
Caneyville, 608 .... K-6
Canmer, 140 .... K-8
Cannel City, 250 .... I-16
Cannon, 150 .... M-14
Cannonsburg, 856 .... G-18
Canton, 75 .... M-3
Carlisle, 2010 .... G-14
Carlisle, 2010 .... G-14
CARLISLE CO.,
5104 .... F-2
Carrie, 80 .... K-17
CARROLL CO.,
10811 .... F-11
Carrollton, 3938 .... F-10
Carrsville, 50 .... K-1
Carter, 50 .... F-17
CARTER CO.,
27720 .... G-17
Cartwright, 40 .... J-18
CASEY CO.,
15955 .... K-11
Casey Creek, 50 .... K-10
Caseyville, 40 .... J-2
Catlettsburg, 1856 .... G-18
Causey K-15
Cave City, 2240 .... L-8
Cawood, 731 .... M-16
Cayce, 125 .... G-2
Cecil, 125 .... K-3
Cecilia, 572 .... I-8
Centertown, 423 .... K-4
Centerville, 120 .... G-13
Central City, 5978 .... K-4
Cerulean, 314 .... L-2
Chalybeate, 50 .... L-7
Chapel Hill, 50 .... M-7
Chaplin, 418 .... I-10
Chappell, 50 .... L-16
Charleston, 200 .... K-2
Charters F-16
Chavies, 170 .... K-16
Cherokee B-8
Cherry Grv. G-13
Cherrywood Vil., 327 .... B-8
Chestnut Grv., 60 .... G-10
Chloe, 150 .... J-19
Choateville, 200 .... H-11
Christeanburg I-11
CHRISTIAN CO.,
73955 .... L-3
Cinda, 50 .... L-16
Clarkson, 875 .... J-7
Clay, 1181 .... L-1
Clay City, 1077 .... I-14
Claylick, 50 .... K-5
Claymour M-4
Claypool M-7
Clayton, 80 .... I-18
Clearfield, 1300 .... H-16
Cleaton, 500 .... K-4
Clementsville, 75 .... K-11
Clermont, 250 .... I-9
Clifford H-18
Clifton, 200 .... H-11
Cliffty, 275 .... L-4
Clinton, 1388 .... G-2
CLINTON CO.,
10272 .... N-11
Clio M-11
Cloverport, 1152 .... I-6
Coal Run Vil., 1706 .... I-19
Cobb, 30 .... L-2
Coburn K-10
Cold Spr., 5912 .... C-20
Coldiron M-16
Coldstream, 1100 .... A-10
Coldwater, 120 .... K-4
Coleman J-20
Colesburg, 90 .... I-8
College Hill J-13
Colonial Ter. B-9
Columbia, 4452 .... L-10
Columbus, 170 .... F-2
Colville G-11
Combs, 900 .... K-17
Comer J-13
Compton J-16
Confederate I-10
Connersville, 35 .... L-18
Constance A-18
Conway, 50 .... J-13
Cool Spr., 50 .... K-4
Cooper L-11
Coopersville, 80 .... M-12
Coral Ridge C-8
Corbin, 7304 .... L-14
Corinth, 232 .... F-12
Corinth H-10
Cornettsville, 90 .... L-17
Cornishville, 90 .... I-11
Corydon, 720 .... J-3
Cottle I-16
Covington, 40640 .... D-12
Cowan, 150 .... G-14
Coxs Creek, 50 .... I-9
Crab Orchard, 841 .... J-12
Cranks, 120 .... N-16
Crayne, 113 .... L-1
Craynor, 85 .... J-18
Crescent Pk. C-20
Crescent Spr. C-19
Crestwood, 475 .... C-20
Crider, 60 .... L-1
Crittenden, 3815 .... E-12
CRITTENDEN CO.,
9315 .... K-1
Crockett, 40 .... H-18
Crofton, 749 .... L-3
Cromona, 400 .... K-18
Cromwell, 240 .... K-5
Cropper, 150 .... G-10
Crossland, 50 .... N-4
Crown Spr., 60 .... I-3
Crutchfield, 85 .... G-2
Crystal, 200 .... I-18
Cub Run, 125 .... K-7
Cubage M-15
Cuba, 100 .... K-4
Culver, 30 .... K-9
CUMBERLAND CO.,
6856 .... M-9
Cundiff K-9
Cunningham, 400 .... J-3
Curdsville, 50 .... J-4
Custer, 125 .... I-7
Cutshin, 50 .... L-15
Cynthiana, 6402 .... G-13
Daisy, 200 .... L-17
Danville, 16218 .... J-12
Darfork K-17
David, 300 .... I-18

FLOYD CO., 39451 .... I-18
Gillmore, 20 .... G-17
Gilpin L-17
Gilreath, 50 .... J-20
Goldbug J-13
Gold City M-6
Golden Pond L-3
Goochland M-13
Goose Rock, 200 .... L-15
Gordon, 100 .... L-17
Goshen, 909 .... A-8
Gracey, 138 .... M-2
Gradyville, 75 .... L-10
Graham, 700 .... K-4
Grahamville, 200 .... J-3
Grahn, 550 .... G-17
Grange City, 75 .... G-15
Grangertown, 100 .... I-13
GRANT CO.,
4662 .... F-12
Grants Lick, 100 .... D-13
Grassy Creek I-16
Grassy Pt., 78 .... J-11
Gravel Switch, 75 .... J-10
GRAVES CO.,
37121 .... F-4
Gray, 750 .... L-14
Gray Hawk, 100 .... K-14
Graymoor-Devondale,
2870 .... B-9
Grays Branch, 125 .... F-17
Grays Knob, 300 .... M-16
Grayson, 4217 .... G-17
GRAYSON CO.,
25746 .... J-7
Grayson Spr. J-7
Green Spr., 75 .... I-18
GREEN CO., 11258 .... K-9
Greensburg, 2163 .... K-9
Greenup, 1188 .... F-18
GREENUP CO.,
36910 .... F-17
Greenville, 4312 .... K-4
Greenwood, 95 .... M-12
Grethel, 100 .... I-18
Griders, 50 .... M-8
Groom M-9
Grove Ctr., 70 .... J-3
Guffie J-12
Gulnare J-18
Gum Sulphur K-13
Gunlock J-12
Guston, 50 .... I-7
Guthrie, 1419 .... N-4
Habit, 100 .... J-5
Hadley, 25 .... L-7
Hagerhill, 450 .... I-18
Haldeman, 250 .... G-16
Halfway, 35 .... M-7
Halls Gap, 90 .... J-11
Hamlin, 50 .... K-4
Hampton, 175 .... K-1
Hammonville, 163 .... K-8
Hampton, 100 .... K-1
HANCOCK CO.,
8565 .... J-5
Hanson, 742 .... K-3
Hardin, 615 .... K-4
Hardinsburg, 2343 .... I-6
HARDIN CO.,
105543 .... I-8
Hardinsburg, 2343 .... I-6
Hardy, 200 .... I-20
Hardyville, 163 .... K-8
Hardy, 65 .... I-19
Hargett J-14
Harlan, 1745 .... M-16
HARLAN CO.,
29278 .... M-16
Harned, 140 .... I-7
Harold, 400 .... I-18

Maine

Page locator
Map keys A–J — Atlas pages 92–93

Abbot Vil., 150 D-5
Acton, 40 I-1
Addison, 250 E-9
Albion, 230 F-5
Alexander, 50 D-9
Alfred, 600 I-2
Allagash, 100 B-12
Allens Mills, 200 E-3
Alna, 130 G-4
Amherst, 130 E-7
Andover, 600 E-2
ANDROSCOGGIN CO., 107702 G-3
Anson, 752 E-4
AROOSTOOK CO., 71870 B-8
Ashland, 709 B-13
Athens, 280 D-4
Atlantic, 60 G-7
Auburn, 23055 G-3
Augusta, 19136 F-4
Aurora, 60 E-7
Bailey Island, 650 H-3
Bancroft, 30 B-8
Bangor, 33039 E-6
Bar Hbr., 2552 F-8
Bar Mills, 280 I-2
Baring, 130 D-10
Bass Hbr., 500 G-7
Bath, 8514 H-4
Bay Pt. H-4
Beals, 400 F-9
Beans Cor. E-3
Belfast, 6668 F-6
Belgrade, 200 F-4
Belgrade Lakes, 300 F-4
Belmont Cor., 30 F-5
Benedicta, 60 A-7
Benton, 120 E-5
Bernard, 200 J-11
Berwick, 2187 J-1
Bethel, 1200 F-2
Biddeford, 21277 I-2
Bingham, 758 D-4
Blaine, 301 C-14
Blaisdell Cors., 200 I-1
Blanchard C-4
Blue Hill, 943 F-7
Blue Hill Falls, 100 F-7
Bolsters Mills, 90 G-2
Boothbay, 450 H-4
Boothbay Hbr., 1086 H-4
Bowdoinham, 722 G-4
Bowerbank, 70 C-5
Bradford, 80 D-6
Bremen, 100 G-5
Brewer, 9482 E-6
Bridgewater, 330 C-14
Bridgton, 2071 G-2
Brighton, 40 D-4
Bristol, 300 H-5
Brooklin, 230 G-7
Brooks, 400 F-6
Brooksville, 120 F-7
Brookton, 170 B-9
Brownville, 350 C-6
Brownville Jct., 800 C-6
Brunswick, 15175 H-4
Bryant Pond, 500 F-2
Buckfield, 400 F-3
Bucks Hbr., 120 E-10
Bucksport, 2885 F-6
Burlington, 140 C-7
Burnham, 200 E-5
Byron, 80 E-2
Calais, 3123 C-10
Cambridge, 130 D-5
Camden, 3570 G-6
Canaan, 400 E-4
Canton, 400 F-3
Cape Elizabeth, 8850 I-3
Cape Neddick, 2568 J-2
Cape Porpoise, 500 I-2
Caratunk, 70 C-4
Cardville, 150 D-7
Caribou, 8189 B-14
Carmel, 550 E-6
Carrabassett, 230 D-3
Carthage E-2
Casco, 587 G-2
Castine, 1029 F-6
Center Lovell, 200 G-1
Charleston, 280 D-6
Chebeague Island, 340 H-3
Cherryfield, 350 E-8
Chester, 100 C-7
Chesterville, 110 F-3
Chesuncook A-5
China, 450 F-5
Chisholm, 1380 F-3
Clark Island, 120 G-5
Clayton Lake, 20 B-12
Clifton, 150 E-7
Clinton, 1419 E-5
Coburn Gore, 10 C-2
Columbia Falls, 250 E-9
Coopers Mills, 250 G-5
Corea, 300 F-8
Corinna, 1100 D-5
Cornish, 600 H-2
Cornville E-4
Costigan, 60 D-7
Cranberry Isles, 90 J-12
Crescent Lake, 200 G-2
Crouseville, 180 B-14
Cumberland Ctr., 2499 H-3
CUMBERLAND CO., 281674 H-2
Cushing, 50 G-5
Cutler, 200 E-10
Damariscotta, 1142 G-5
Danforth, 500 B-8
Deblois, 30 E-8
Dedham, 130 E-7
Deer Isle, 400 G-7
Denmark, 130 G-2
Dennysville, 150 D-10
Derby C-6
Detroit, 180 E-5
Dexter, 2158 D-5
Dickey A-12
Dixfield, 1076 F-2
Dixmont, 80 E-5
Dixmont Ctr. E-6
Dover-Foxcroft, 2528 D-5
Dresden Mills, 140 G-4
Dry Mills, 350 H-3
Dyer Brook, 60 A-8
Eagle Lake, 625 B-13
E. Andover, 150 E-2
E. Blue Hill, 150 F-7
E. Brownfield, 80 H-1
E. Corinth, 400 D-6
E. Dixfield, 120 E-3
E. Eddington, 250 E-7
E. Exeter D-6
E. Hampden, 1200 J-6
E. Hiram, 250 H-2
E. Holden, 180 E-7
E. Lamoine, 50 F-7
E. Livermore, 60 F-3
E. Machias, 300 E-10
E. Millinocket, 1567 B-7
E. Newport, 120 E-5
E. Peru, 100 F-3
E. Sebago, 320 H-2
E. Sumner, 100 F-3
E. Vassalboro, 300 F-4
E. Waterboro, 250 I-2
E. Wilton, 350 E-3
E. Winn C-7
Eastbrook, 130 E-8
Easton, 300 B-14
Eastport, 1331 D-10
Eaton, 40 B-9
Eden, 75 G-12
Edgecomb, 110 H-4
Eggemoggin F-6
Eliot, 90 J-2
Ellsworth, 7741 F-7
Emery Mills, 200 I-1
Enfield, 350 C-7
Estcourt Sta., 30 A-12
Etna, 140 E-6
Eustis, 80 C-2
Exeter Cors., 80 D-5
Fairbanks, 180 E-3
Fairfield, 2638 E-4
Falmouth, 1855 H-3
Falmouth Foreside, 1511 H-10
Farmingdale, 1970 G-4
Farmington, 4288 E-3
Farmington Falls, 300 E-3
Fayette, 100 F-3
Forest City, 50 B-9
Ft. Fairfield, 1825 B-14
Ft. Kent, 2488 A-13
Frankfort, 180 E-6
Franklin, 300 E-8
FRANKLIN CO., 30768 D-2
Freedom, 150 F-5
Freeport, 1485 H-3
Frenchboro, 61 G-7
Frenchville, 480 A-13
Friendship, 600 G-5
Frye, 60 E-2
Fryeburg, 1631 G-1
Fryeburg Ctr. G-1
Gardiner, 5800 G-4
Garland, 150 D-5
Georgetown, 150 H-4
Gilead, 50 F-1
Glenburn Ctr., 60 D-6
Goodwins Mills, 50 I-2
Gorham, 6882 H-2
Gouldsboro, 200 F-8
Grand Isle, 380 A-13
Grand Lake Stream, 140 D-9
Gray, 884 H-3
Great Pond, 50 D-7
Greeleys C-5
Green Lake E-7
Greenbush, 150 D-7
Greene, 500 G-3
Greenfield, 40 D-7
Greenville, 1257 C-4
Greenville Jct., 450 C-4
Greenwood F-2
Grindstone, 50 B-7
Grove, 40 D-9
Guerette, 50 A-13
Guilford, 903 D-5
Hall Quarry, 100 H-12
Hallowell, 2381 F-4
Hampden, 4343 E-6
Hampden Highlands, 800 E-6
Hancock, 400 F-8
HANCOCK CO., 54418 D-8
Hancock Pt., 40 F-8
Hanover, 180 F-2
Harborside, 100 F-6
Harmony, 280 D-5
Harrington, 300 E-9
Harrison, 600 G-2
Hartford, 60 F-3
Hartland, 813 E-5
Haynesville, 70 A-8
Hebron, 300 G-2
Hinckley, 120 E-4
Hiram, 350 H-2
Hodgdon, 350 A-8
Holden, 130 E-7
Hollis Ctr., 250 I-2
Hope, 100 G-5
Houlton, 4856 C-14
Howland, 1096 C-7
Hudson, 150 D-6
Hulls Cove, 250 F-8
Indian River, 40 E-9
Island Falls, 600 A-7
Isle au Haut, 70 G-7
Islesboro, 140 F-6
Islesford, 80 I-13
Jackman, 800 B-3
Jackson, 100 E-6
Jacksonville, 150 E-10
Jay, 600 F-3
Jefferson, 280 G-5
Jonesboro, 220 E-9
Jonesport, 1100 F-9
Keegan, 200 A-14
Kenduskeag, 350 D-6
Kennebago Lake Camps D-2
KENNEBEC CO., 122151 F-4
Kennebunk, 5214 I-2
Kennebunkport, 1238 I-2
Kents Hill, 200 F-3
Kingfield, 850 D-3
Kingman, 140 B-8
Kittery, 4562 J-2
Kittery Pt., 1012 J-2
Knights, 20 C-6
Knowles Cor. C-13
KNOX CO., 39736 G-5
Kokadjo, 10 B-5
Lagrange, 120 D-6
L. Moxie C-4
Lakewood, 80 E-4
Lambert Lake, 130 B-9
Lebanon, 90 I-1
Lee, 250 C-7
Leeds, 80 F-3
Levant, 250 E-6
Lewiston, 36592 G-3
Liberty, 180 F-5
Limerick, 400 H-2
Limestone, 1075 B-14
Limington, 220 H-2
Lincoln, 2884 C-7
LINCOLN CO., 34457 G-4
Lincolnville, 300 F-6
Linneus, 100 A-8
Lisbon, 1400 G-3
Lisbon Falls, 4100 G-3
Litchfield Cors., 200 G-3
Little Deer Isle, 150 F-6
Littleton, 200 C-14
Livermore, 200 F-3
Livermore Falls, 1594 F-3
Locke Mills, 200 F-2
Lookout I-14
Lovell, 230 G-1
Lubec, 349 E-10
Ludlow, 40 C-14
Lynchville G-2
Machias, 1274 E-9
Machiasport, 250 E-10
Macwahoc, 80 B-7
Madawaska, 2967 A-13
Madison, 2630 E-4
Madrid E-2
Manchester, 650 F-4
Manset, 200 I-12
Mapleton, 683 B-14
Maplewood, 30 H-1
Mars Hill, 980 C-14
Martin G-5
Martinsville, 100 H-5
Matinicus, 50 H-6
Mattawamkeag, 650 B-7
Mechanic Falls, 2237 G-3
Meddybemps, 70 D-10
Medway, 900 B-7
Mexico, 1743 F-2
Milbridge, 600 F-8
Milford, 2233 D-7
Millinocket, 4466 B-6
Milo, 1847 C-6
Minturn, 90 G-7
Molunkus, 40 B-7
Monarda B-7
Monhegan, 70 H-5
Monmouth, 600 G-3
Monroe, 140 E-6
Monson, 500 C-5
Monticello, 400 C-14
Moose River, 200 B-3
Moosehead, 20 B-4
Morrill, 150 F-5
Moscow, 400 D-4
Mt. Vernon, 200 F-3
Naples, 428 G-2
New Hbr., 500 H-5
New Portland, 200 D-3
New Sharon, 300 E-3
New Sweden, 60 B-14
New Vineyard, 220 E-3
Newagen, 130 H-4
Newburgh Vil., 120 E-6
Newcastle, 667 G-5
Newfield, 225 H-1
Newport, 1776 E-5
Newry, 150 F-2
Nobleboro, 150 G-5
Norridgewock, 1438 E-4
N. Amity A-8
N. Anson, 750 E-4
N. Berwick, 1615 J-2
N. Bradford, 50 D-6
N. Bridgton, 500 G-2
N. E. Carry A-4
N. Fryeburg, 70 G-1
N. Haven, 280 G-6
N. Jay, 200 F-3
N. Lovell G-1
N. Monmouth, 200 F-3
N. New Portland, 225 D-3
N. Newcastle G-4
N. Palermo F-5
N. Parsonsfield, 50 H-1
N. Penobscot F-7
N. Searsmont F-5
N. Sebago, 280 H-2
N. Sedgwick F-7
N. Shapleigh, 130 I-1
N. Turner, 350 F-3
N. Vassalboro, 900 F-4
N. Waldoboro, 180 G-5
N. Waterboro, 200 I-2
N. Waterford, 300 G-2
N. Whitefield, 60 G-4
N. Windham, 4904 H-2
Northeast Harbor, 650 F-7
Northport, 90 F-6
Norway, 2748 G-2
Oakland, 2602 F-4
Oceanville, 70 G-7
Ogunquit, 892 J-2
Olamon, 220 D-7
Old Orchard Bch., 8624 I-3
Old Town, 7840 D-7
Oquossoc, 150 D-2
Orient, 30 A-8
Orland, 300 F-6
Orono, 9474 E-7
Orrington, 400 E-6
Otter Creek, 250 I-13
Owls Head, 350 G-6
Oxford, 1263 G-2
OXFORD CO., 57833 F-2
Palermo, 120 F-5
Palmyra, 160 E-5
Parkman, 80 D-5
Passadumkeag, 150 D-7
Patten, 1000 A-7
Peaks Island J-10
Pembroke, 280 D-10
Penobscot, 100 F-6
PENOBSCOT CO., 153923 A-7
Perham, 150 B-13
Perry, 90 D-10
Phillips, 750 E-3
Phippsburg, 150 H-4
PISCATAQUIS CO., 17535 A-5
Pittsfield, 3150 E-5
Pittston, 150 G-4
Pittston Farm A-4
Pleasant Hill, 900 H-9
Pleasant Pond, 20 C-4
Plymouth, 200 E-5
Poland, 350 G-3
Popham Bch., 40 H-4
Port Clyde, 600 H-5
Portage, 350 B-13
Porter, 200 H-1
Portland, 66194 H-3
Pownal Ctr., 50 H-3
Presque Isle, 9692 B-14
Prides Corner H-8
Princeton, 750 C-9
Prospect, 100 F-6
Prospect Hbr., 400 F-8
Prouts Neck, 50 I-3
Purgatory, 300 G-4
Randolph, 1772 G-4
Rangeley, 700 D-2
Raymond, 600 H-2
Readfield, 400 F-4
Richmond, 1760 G-4
Ripley, 110 D-5
Robbinston, 200 D-10
Rockland, 7297 G-6
Rockport, 1200 G-6
Rockwood, 300 B-4
Rome, 200 E-4
Roque Bluffs, 100 E-9
Round Pond, 400 H-5
Roxbury, 180 E-2
Rumford, 4218 F-2
Sabattus, 1300 G-3
Saco, 18482 I-2
SAGADAHOC CO., 35293 G-4
St. Agatha, 500 A-13
St. Albans, 250 D-5
St. Francis, 300 A-13
St. George, 280 G-5
St. John, 130 A-13
Salem, 50 D-3
Salsbury Cove, 250 G-12
Sanford, 9761 I-2
Sangerville, 650 D-5
Scarborough, 4403 I-3
Seal Cove, 100 F-7
Seal Hbr., 250 I-13
Searsmont, 180 F-5
Searsport, 992 F-6
Seawall, 50 J-12
Sebago Lake, 600 H-2
Sebasco Estates, 200 H-4
Sebec, 100 C-6
Sebec Lake, 5 C-5
Seboeis, 30 C-6
Seboomook A-4
Sedgwick, 150 F-7
Shapleigh, 180 I-1
Sherman Mills, 450 A-7
Sherman Sta., 325 A-7
Shin Pond C-13
Shirley Mills, 150 C-4
Sidney F-4
Skowhegan, 6297 E-4
Small Pt. Bch. H-4
Smithfield, 230 E-4
Smyrna Mills, 250 C-14
Solon, 450 D-4
SOMERSET CO., 52228 B-3
Somesville, 250 H-12
S. Addison, 100 F-9
S. Arm, 20 E-2
S. Berwick, 3000 J-1
S. Brewer J-6
S. Bristol, 500 H-4
S. China, 500 F-4
S. Eliot, 3550 J-2
S. Gouldsboro, 175 G-14
S. Harpswell, 230 H-3
S. Lagrange, 60 D-6
S. Lebanon, 230 J-1
S. Liberty F-5
S. Lincoln, 180 C-7
S. Lubec, 120 E-10
S. Orrington, 300 E-6
S. Paris, 2267 G-2
S. Portland, 25002 I-3
S. Sanford, 4536 I-2
S. Surry F-7
S. Waterford, 180 G-2
S. Windham, 1374 H-2
S. Woodstock, 70 F-2
Southwest Harbor, 720 F-7
Springfield, 120 C-8
Springvale, 3292 I-2
Spruce Head, 220 G-5
Stacyville, 40 A-7
Standish, 469 H-2
Starboard, 50 E-10
Starks, 140 E-4
Steep Falls, 1139 H-2
Stetson, 150 D-5
Steuben, 150 F-8
Stockton Sprs., 330 F-6
Stonington, 800 G-7
Stow G-1
Stratton, 400 D-2
Strong, 700 E-3
Sullivan, 180 F-8
Sunshine, 60 G-7
Surry, 230 F-7
Swanville, 150 F-6
Temple, 230 E-3
Tenants Hbr., 400 G-5
The Forks, 10 C-4
Thomaston, 1875 G-5
Thorndike, 140 F-5
Topsfield, 130 C-9
Topsham, 5931 H-4
Town Hill, 60 G-12
Tremont, 80 J-11
Trenton, 170 F-7
Troy, 60 E-5
Turner, 500 G-3
Union, 600 G-5
Unity, 469 E-5
Upper Gloucester, 300 G-3
Upton, 50 E-1
Van Buren, 1937 A-14
Vanceboro, 190 B-9
Vassalboro, 200 F-4
Veazie, 1630 E-6
Vienna, 70 F-4
Vinalhaven, 800 G-6
Waite, 40 C-9
WALDO CO., 38786 F-5
Waldoboro, 1233 G-5
Waltham, 80 E-7
Warren, 400 G-5
Washburn, 997 B-14
Washington, 240 F-5
WASHINGTON CO., 32856 E-9
Waterboro, 750 I-2
Waterford Flat, 120 G-2
Waterville, 15722 F-4
Wayne, 250 F-3
Weld, 200 E-2
Wellington, 50 D-4
Wells, 1200 J-2
Wells Bch., 500 J-2
Wesley, 50 D-9
W. Baldwin, 150 H-2
W. Bethel, 180 F-1
W. Bowdoin, 10 G-3
W. Buxton, 300 H-2
W. Enfield, 600 C-7
W. Forks, 30 C-3
W. Jonesport F-9
W. Levant D-6
W. Mills, 100 E-3
W. Minot, 130 G-3
W. Newfield, 100 I-1
W. Paris, 550 F-2
W. Peru, 120 F-2
W. Poland, 330 G-2
W. Rockport, 250 G-5
W. Scarborough, 900 I-3
W. Sumner, 30 F-2
W. Tremont, 80 G-7
W. Trenton G-11
Westbrook, 17494 H-3
Weston, 90 B-8
Whitefield, 100 G-4
Whiting, 110 E-10
Whitneyville, 150 E-9
Willimantic, 40 C-5
Wilsons Mills, 30 D-1
Wilton, 2198 E-3
Windsor, 120 F-4
Winn, 200 C-7
Winslow, 7794 F-4
Winter Hbr., 426 F-8
Winterport, 1340 E-6
Winthrop, 2650 F-4
Woodland, 952 D-9
Woolwich, 600 H-4
Wytopitlock, 150 B-8
Yarmouth, 5869 H-3
York Bch., 900 J-2
YORK CO., 197131 I-1
York Hbr., 3033 J-2
York Vil., 1000 J-2

Maryland

Page locator
Map keys — Atlas pages
1–10 — 94–95
11–20 — 96–97
* City keyed to pp. 224–225

Abell, 160 I-13
Aberdeen, 14959 B-15
Abingdon, 2000 C-15
Accident, 325 B-2
Accokeek, 10573 G-12
Adamstown, 2372 C-10
Adelina, 150 H-13
Adelphi, 15086 *D-7
Airey, 30 H-16
Albeth Hts., 140 J-1
Alesia, 230 A-12
ALLEGANY CO., 75087 B-5
Allen, 210 I-18
Allens Fresh, 100 H-12
Alpha, 100 C-12
Altamont C-2
American Corner F-17
Ammendale *C-9
Andersontown, 30 F-17
Andrews, 130 I-16
Annapolis, 38394 E-14
Annapolis Jct., 800 N-3
ANNE ARUNDEL CO., 537656 F-13
Antietam, 89 C-8
Appleton Acres, 200 A-17
Aquasco, 981 H-13
Arbutus, 20483 K-4
Ardmore *F-9
Argonne Hills *B-10
Arnold, 23106 E-14
Arundel Gdns., 1250 L-6
Arundel on the Bay, 1100 F-14
Arundel Vil., 2700 L-6
Ashton, 1500 D-12
Aspen Hill, 48759 *C-6
Athol, 50 H-17
Avenue, 450 I-13
Avilton A-3
Baden, 2128 G-13
Baldwin, 420 B-14
Ballard *I-9
Baltimore, 620961 C-13
BALTIMORE CO., 805029 B-13
Baltimore Corner E-17
Baltimore Highlands, 7019 K-5
Barclay, 120 D-17
Barnaby Vil., 5300 *H-7
Barnesville, 172 D-10
Barrelville, 73 A-4
Barstow, 200 H-13
Barton, 457 B-3
Bartonsville, 1451 C-10
Bay City E-15
Bay Ridge, 2200 C-20
Bay View, 300 B-16
Baynesville G-7
Bayside Bch., 950 D-14
Beachville, 300 J-14
Beallsville, 400 D-10
Beantown G-12
Beaver Creek, 251 B-9
Beaver Dam, 50 K-18
Bel Air, 10120 B-15
Bel Alton, 1000 H-12
Belhaven, 500 N-9
Bellevue, 330 G-15
Belltown F-2
Beltsville, 16772 E-12
Bembe Bch. B-20
Benedict, 261 H-13
Benevola B-9
Bennsville, 11923 G-12
Benson B-14
Bentley Sprs., 130 A-13
Berlin, 4485 I-20
Berwyn Hts., 3123 *D-8
Bestgate B-19
Bethany Manor, 500 J-1
Bethesda, 60858 E-11
Bethlehem, 150 G-16
Betterton, 345 C-16
Beverly Bch., 170 F-14
Big Pines, 500 *B-3
Big Pool, 82 B-7
Big Spring, 84 B-8
Birdsville, 250 F-14
Bishop, 40 H-20
Bishops Head, 200 I-16
Bishopville, 531 H-20
Bittinger, 70 B-2
Bivalve, 201 I-17
Black Horse, 130 B-14
Bladensburg, 9148 *F-8
Bloomington, 305 B-3
Bloomsbury K-4
Bonnie Brae, 1250 C-12
Boonsboro, 3336 B-9
Boonsboro E-17
Boring, 300 B-13
Bowens, 50 H-13
Bowie, 54727 E-13
Bowleys Quarters, 6755 C-14
Bowling Green, 1077 B-4
Boxiron, 110 J-19
Boyds, 900 D-10
Bozman, 440 F-15
Bradshaw, 500 C-14
Brandywine, 6719 G-12
Breezewood Farms, 50 I-1
Breezy Pt., 230 G-14
Brentwood, 3046 *F-8
Bridgeport, 860 M-17
Bridgetown, 80 E-17
Brighton, 110 D-12
Brightwood Acres N-17
Brinkleigh Mnr., 2500 J-2
Brinklow, 300 D-12
Bristol, 30 F-13
Broad Run C-9
Brookeville, 134 D-11
Brooklandville, 1700 F-5
Brooklyn Pk., 14373 K-6
Brookmead, 260 *B-2
Brookmont, 3468 *E-5
Brookview, 60 H-17
Brookwood, 2200 *J-10
Broomes Island, 405 H-14
Browns Woods Villa, 400 A-20
Brownsville, 100 E-16
Brownsville, 89 C-9
Bruceville, 60 G-16
Brunswick, 5870 C-9
Bryans Road, 7244 G-11
Bryantown, 655 H-12
Bryantown E-15
Buckeystown, 1019 C-10
Bucktown, 30 H-16
Budds Creek I-13
Burkittsville, 151 C-9
Burrisville, 100 E-16
Burrsville, 130 F-17
Burtonsville, 8323 E-12
Bush B-15
Bushwood, 400 I-13
Butler, 350 B-13
Butlertown, 505 D-16
Byrdtown, 110 K-17
Cabin John, 2280 *E-4
California, 11857 I-14
Callaway, 470 I-14
Calvert, 150 A-16
Calvert Bch., 808 H-14
CALVERT CO., 88737 H-13
Calverton, 17724 *C-8
Cambridge, 12326 H-16
Camp Sprs., 19096 F-12
Canton J-7
Cape Isle of Wight, 750 I-20
Cape St. Claire, 8747 E-14
Capitol Hts., 4337 *G-8
Cardiff, 300 A-15
Carmichael, 30 E-16
Carney, 29941 G-8
CAROLINE CO., 33066 F-17
CARROLL CO., 167134 B-12
Carroll Highlands, 2000 C-12
Carrollton B-12
Carsins Run, 100 B-15
Cascade, 1000 A-10
Castleton, 200 A-15
Catonsville, 41567 J-4
Catonsville Manor, 2600 J-4
Cavetown, 1473 B-9
Cayots B-17
Cearfoss, 178 A-8
CECIL CO., 101108 B-17
Cecilton, 663 C-17
Cedar Bch., 500 J-10
Cedar Grv., 500 D-11
Cedar Hts., 1150 *F-8
Cedar Lawn, 400 M-16
Cedarhurst Acres, 300 D-19
Cedarville, 717 G-13
Centreville, 4285 E-16
Ceresville, 70 L-20
Champ, 100 J-17
Chance, 353 J-16
Chaney G-13
Chaneyville, 90 G-13
Chaptico, 850 I-13
CHARLES CO., 146551 H-12
Charlestown, 1183 B-16
Charlotte Hall, 1420 H-13
Chase, 920 C-14
Chateau Valley, 1900 K-1
Chattolanee G-3
Cheltenham, 950 G-13
Cherry Hill, 500 A-17
Chesaco Pk., 450 I-8
Chesapeake Bch., 5753 G-14
Chesapeake City, 673 B-17
Chesapeake Haven, 250 C-16
Chesapeake Hts., 550 I-18
Chester, 4167 E-15
Chestertown, 5252 D-16
Chesterville, 100 D-16
Chestnut Hill Estates J-2
Chestnut Ridge, 230 E-4
Cheverly, 6173 *F-8
Chevy Chase, 9545 *E-5
Chevy Chase View, 920 *D-5
Chewsville, 238 B-9
Chicamuxen, 100 H-11
Childs, 370 A-17
Chillum, 33513 *E-7
Choptank, 129 G-16
Christs Rock, 120 H-16
Church Creek, 125 H-16
Church Hill, 745 D-16
Churchton F-14
Churchville, 600 B-15
Claggettsville, 400 C-11
Claiborne, 170 F-15
Clarksburg, 13766 D-11
Clarksville, 830 D-12
Clarysville, 73 A-4
Clear Spr., 358 A-8
Clements, 270 I-13
Cliffs City, 60 D-16
Clinton, 35970 F-12
Clopper, 1000 *A-3
Clover Hill, 3260 L-19
Cloverly, 15126 *B-7
Cobb Island, 1166 I-12
Cockeysville, 20776 B-13
Cohasset *E-4
Cokesbury, 110 J-18
Coleman, 130 C-16
Colesville, 14647 E-12
College Pk., 30413 *D-8
Colmar Mnr., 1404 *F-8
Colonial Pk. N-17
Colora, 120 A-16
Coltons Pt., 500 J-13
Columbia, 99615 L-1
Columbia Pk., 1000 *F-9
Compton, 250 I-13
Comus D-10
Conowingo, 150 A-15
Contee *C-9
Cooksville, 500 C-12
Coral Hills, 9895 *G-8
Cordova, 562 F-16
Cornersville, 100 G-15
Corriganville, 455 A-4
Cottage City, 1305 *F-8
Cove Pt., 1200 I-14
Coxs Corner I-17
Craigtown, 200 B-16
Cranberry, 200 B-12
Crapo, 130 I-16
Creagerstown, 150 B-10
Crellin, 264 C-1
Cresaptown, 4592 B-4
Crestwood, 200 I-18
Crisfield, 2726 K-17
Crocheron, 120 I-16
Crofton, 27348 E-13
Croom, 2631 G-13
Cropley *E-3
Crosby, 50 D-15
Crownsville, 1757 E-13
Crumpton, 550 D-16
Crystal Bch., 250 C-16
Cub Hill G-8
Cumberland, 20859 A-4
Damascus, 15257 D-11
Dameron, 350 J-15
Dames Quarter, 167 J-17
Daniel, 100 C-12
Danville, 271 B-3
Dares Bch., 500 H-14
Dargan, 165 C-9
Darlington, 409 B-15
Darnestown, 6802 E-10
Davidsonville, 780 F-13
Dawson, 103 B-3
Dawsonville, 120 D-10
Dayton, 800 D-12
Deal Island, 471 J-16
Deale, 4945 F-14
Deer Harbour, 250 F-19
Deer Pk., 399 C-2
Defense Hts., 2250 *E-9
Delight F-2
Delmar, 3003 H-18
Denton, 4418 F-17
Dentsville, 50 H-12
Derwood, 2381 *B-4
Detour, 520 B-11
Dickerson, 1000 D-10
District Hts., 5837 *G-8
Dominion, 470 E-15
Doncaster, 200 H-11
DORCHESTER CO., 32618 H-16
Dorrs Cor., 170 E-13
Dorsey, 1350 M-3
Doubs, 160 C-10
Dowell, 300 I-14
Downsville, 355 B-8
Drayden, 110 J-14
Drum Pt., 2731 I-14
Drury, 300 F-13
Drybranch A-14
Dublin, 500 A-15
Dumbarton G-4
Dundalk, 63597 D-14
Dunkirk, 2520 G-13
Dynard, 50 I-13
Eagle Hbr., 63 H-13
Earleville, 500 C-16
E. New Market, 400 G-17
Easton, 15945 F-16
Eastpines, 1250 *E-8
Eastpoint J-8
Eastview, 330 M-18
Eden, 823 I-18
Edesville, 169 D-15
Edgemere, 8669 D-14
Edgewater, 9023 C-18
Edgewood, 25562 C-15
Edmonston, 1445 *E-8
Ednor *A-7
Eldersburg, 30531 C-12
Eldorado, 59 G-17
Elioak, 290 K-1
Elk Mills, 700 A-17
Elk Neck, 130 B-16
Elkridge, 15593 D-13
Elkton, 15443 B-17
Ellerslie, 572 A-4
Ellerton B-9
Ellicott City, 65834 D-13
Elliott, 52 I-16
Ellwood, 130 G-17
Elmwood, 1650 H-8
Emmitsburg, 2814 A-10
Emmorton, 1400 B-15
Emory Grv., 5300 *A-4
Epping Forest A-19
Essex, 39262 C-14
Etchison, 200 D-11
Evergreen Pk., 70 D-14
Evitts Creek E-4
Ewell, 250 K-16
Ewingville, 120 D-16
Fair Haven, 500 G-14
Fair Hill, 100 A-17
Fairbank G-15
Fairland, 23681 E-12
Fairlee, 490 D-15
Fairmount, 457 J-17
Fairmount Hts., 1494 *F-8
Fairplay, 580 B-8
Fairview, 680 M-8
Fallston, 8958 B-14
Farmington, 180 A-16
Faulkner, 450 H-12
Feagaville, 220 C-10
Federalsburg, 2739 G-17
Fells Pt. J-6
Ferndale, 16746 L-5
Fiddlersburg, 180 M-17
Finksburg, 1000 B-12
Finzel, 547 A-3
Fishing Creek, 163 I-15
Flintstone, 177 A-5
Flohrville, 800 C-12
Florence, 100 C-11
Font Hill, 890 K-3
Font Hill Mnr., 2500 J-1
Forest Hts., 2447 *H-7
Forest Hill, 900 B-14
Forestville, 12353 F-12
Fork, 500 C-14
Ft. Foote Vil., 5000 *I-6
Ft. Howard, 890 D-14
Fountain Green, 1400 B-15
Fountain Head, 1350 A-9
Fountaindale C-10
Fowblesburg, 250 B-12
Foxhall *C-6
Frederick, 65239 C-10
FREDERICK CO., 233385 B-10
Freeland, 600 A-13
Friendly, 9250 *J-7
Friendly Farms *J-7
Friendship, 447 G-14
Friendsville, 491 A-1
Frizzelburg, 280 B-11
Frostburg, 9002 A-3
Fruitland, 4866 E-19
Fullerton, 2400 H-8
Fulton, 2049 *A-8
Funkstown, 904 B-9
Furnace Branch M-6
Gaither, 300 C-12
Gaithersburg, 59933 D-11
Galena, 612 C-17
Galestown, 138 H-17
Galesville, 684 F-14
Gamber, 250 C-12
Gambrills, 2800 E-13
Gapland, 109 C-9
Garland, 1800 L-6
GARRETT CO., 30097 B-2
Garrett Pk., 992 *D-5
Garrison, 8823 G-3
George Island J-19
Georgetown, 143 C-17
Germantown, 86395 D-11
Gibson Island, 400 E-14
Gingerville Manor Estates B-18
Girdletree, 149 J-19
Glassmanor, 17295 *H-7
Glen Arm, 730 F-8
Glen Burnie, 67639 D-13
Glen Echo, 255 *E-4
Glen Hills, 1400 *C-3
Glen Mar Pk. *E-5
Glenarden, 6000 F-12
Glencoe, 220 B-13
Glenelg, 1000 D-12
Glenmar K-2
Glenmont, 13529 *C-6
Glenn Dale, 13466 *E-10
Glenwood, 200 D-12
Glyndon, 900 B-13
Golden Bch., 3796 H-13
Golden Hill, 40 I-15
Goldsboro, 246 E-17
Golts, 150 C-17
Good Hope *B-7
Goodwill, 50 J-18
Gorman, 106 C-1
Gortner, 230 C-1
Goshen, 530 D-11
Governors Run, 30 H-14
Graceham, 120 B-10
Granite, 950 I-1
Grantsville, 766 A-2
Grasonville, 3425 E-15
Gratitude D-15
Great Mills, 700 I-14
Green Haven D-14
Green Hill, 70 I-17
Green Valley, 3000 C-10
Greenbelt, 23068 E-12
Greenberry Hills, 1400 N-16
Greensboro, 1931 E-17
Greentree N-6
Guilford, 1000 D-12
Hack Pt., 500 C-17
Hagerstown, 39662 B-9
Halethorpe, 2000 K-4
Halfway, 10701 B-8
Hampden I-6
Hampstead, 6323 B-12
Hampton, 5052 F-6
Hancock, 1545 A-7
Hanesville, 30 D-16
Hanover, 210 L-4
Harewood Pk., 1100 C-15
HARFORD CO., 244826 B-14
Harmans, 400 M-4
Harmony, 150 F-17
Harney, 240 A-11
Harrisonville, 270 G-2
Harundale M-6
Harwood, 450 F-13
Harwood Pk. D-13
Havre de Grace, 12952 B-16
Hearn Bailey Farm, 500 D-19
Hebbville, 2500 H-3
Hebron, 1084 H-18
Helen, 70 I-13
Henderson, 146 E-17
Herald Hbr., 2603 E-14
Hereford, 700 B-13
Hernwood Hts., 960 H-2
Hickory, 610 B-15
Hidden Pt., 70 A-20
High Pt., 3700 M-8
High Ridge, 2500 N-1
Highfield, 210 A-10
Highland, 1034 D-12
Highland Bch., 96 F-14
Hill Top, 50 H-11
Hillcrest Hts., 16469 *H-7
Hillcrest Hts., 380 M-1
Hillsboro, 161 F-16
Hillsmere Shores, 2977 C-20
Hobbs, 60 F-17
Holbrook, 200 G-1
Hollywood, 1000 I-14
Homewood D-3
Honga, 100 I-15
Hoopersville, 250 I-15
Hopewell K-17
HOWARD CO., 287085 D-12
Hoyes B-1
Hudson, 250 G-15
Hughesville, 2197 H-13
Hunting Pk., 290 E-19
Huntingtown, 3311 G-13
Hurlock, 2092 G-17
Hutton, 86 C-1
Huyett, 100 A-8
Hyattstown, 120 D-10
Hyattsville, 17557 *E-8
Hydes, 250 B-14
Ijamsville, 400 C-10
Ilchester, 23476 K-3
Indian Head, 3844 G-11
Indian Sprs., 64 B-7
Ingleside, 350 E-17
Ironshire I-20
Ironsides, 180 H-11
Island Creek, 100 H-14
Island View Bch., 80 J-10
Issue, 430 I-12
Jacksonville, 600 B-14
Jacobsville N-8
Jarrettsville, 2916 B-14
Jefferson, 2111 C-9
Jefferson Hts., 800 M-17
Jessup, 7137 D-13
Johnsville, 1200 C-12
Johnsville, 550 B-11
Jonestown, 250 G-17
Joppatowne, 12616 C-15
Keedysville, 1152 B-9
Kemp Mill Estates, 3050 *D-6
Kemptown C-11
Kennedyville, 199 C-16
Kensington, 2213 *D-5
KENT CO., 20197 D-16
Kent Vil., 2700 *F-9
Kentmore Pk., 250 C-16
Kenwood, 2500 I-8
Kettering, 12790 F-13
Keymar, 520 B-11
Keysers Ridge, 30 A-2
Kings Pk., 3000 H-2
Kingston, 50 J-17
Kingstown, 1733 D-16
Kingsville, 4318 C-14
Kitzmiller, 321 C-2
Knollwood, 1250 *D-7
Knoxville, 340 C-9
La Plata, 8753 H-12
La Vale, 3551 D-3
Ladiesburg, 230 B-11
L. Shore, 19477 E-14
Lakesville, 30 I-16
Lakeview, 750 N-1
Landover, 640 *F-8
Landover Hills, 1687 *E-9
Langley Pk., 18755 *E-7
Lanham, 10157 *E-9
Lansdowne, 8409 K-5
Lappans, 30 B-9
Largo, 10709 *F-10
Laurel, 25115 E-12
Lawsonia K-17
Layhill, 5169 *B-6
Laytonsville, 353 D-11
Le Gore, 110 B-10
Leitersburg, 573 A-9
Leonardtown, 2930 I-13
Level, 400 B-15
Lewisdale, 3100 *E-7
Lewistown, 270 B-10
Lexington Pk., 11626 I-14
Liberty Grv., 90 A-16
Liberty Manor, 920 H-3
Libertytown, 950 B-11
Libertytown I-19
Lime Kiln C-10
Lineboro, 350 A-12
Linhigh, 2100 H-8
Linkwood, 240 H-16
Linthicum, 10324 L-5
Linwood, 130 B-11
Lipins Cor., 80 N-7
Lisbon, 1150 C-11
Little Orleans, 42 B-6
Lloyds, 30 G-15
Loch Lynn Hts., 552 C-1
Loch Raven Vil. G-7
Lochearn, 25333 H-4
Locust Grv., 30 C-16
Lonaconing, 1214 B-3
Londontown, 4000 F-14
Long Bch., 1821 H-14
Long Green, 500 B-14
Longwoods, 50 F-16
Loretta Hts. B-19
Lothian, 300 F-13
Louisville, 200 C-12
Love Pt., 290 E-15
Loveville, 640 I-13
Lower Marlboro, 170 G-13
Luke, 65 B-3
Lusby, 1835 H-14
Lutherville, 6504 F-6
Luxmanor, 2500 *C-5
Lynch, 200 C-16
Lynne Acres, 6700 H-3
Lyons Creek, 50 G-13
Maddox, 230 I-13
Madison, 204 H-15
Madonna, 200 B-14
Magnolia C-15
Malcolm, 50 G-13
Manchester, 4808 A-12
Manokin, 350 D-19
Manokin, 250 J-17
Manor B-14
Manor View E-8
Maple Plains, 390 D-20
Maplewood, 1100 I-1
Marbury H-11
Mardela Sprs., 347 H-17
Margate, 1500 M-6
Marion, 1050 K-17
Marley, 1500 M-6
Marlton, 9031 F-13
Marriottsville, 110 H-1
Marshall Hall, 230 G-11
Marston, 50 B-11
Martinsburg D-10
Marydel, 141 D-17
Maryland City, 16093 *B-10
Maryland Line, 400 A-13
Mason Sprs., 30 H-11
Massey, 150 C-17
Matthews, 30 F-16
Maugansville, 3071 A-8
Mayo, 8298 F-14
Mays Chapel, 11420 F-6
McAlpine, 4400 K-2
McCoole, 511 C-3
McDaniel, 170 F-15
McHenry, 1000 B-1
Meadowcliff F-8
Meadowood, 1100 *C-7
Mechanicsville, 1508 H-13
Melitota, 70 D-15
Melrose, 200 A-12
Middle River, 25191 I-9
Middleburg, 70 B-11
Middletown, 4136 C-9
Middletown, 100 A-13
Midland, 446 B-3
Midlothian, 320 B-3
Milford, 690 H-3
Millers, 180 A-12
Millersville, 950 E-13
Millington, 642 D-17
Monie, 110 J-17
Monkton, 800 B-13
Monrovia, 416 C-11
Montevideo, 230 M-3
MONTGOMERY CO., 971777 D-11
Montgomery Vil., 32032 D-11
Montpelier, 3600 *C-9
Montrose *C-5
Morgantown, 200 I-12
Morganza, 150 I-13
Morningside, 2015 *H-9
Moscow, 240 B-3
Motters A-10
Mt. Aetna, 561 B-9
Mt. Airy, 9288 C-11
Mt. Harmony G-13
Mt. Hebron, 2000 I-2
Mt. Lena, 515 B-9
Mt. Pleasant, 330 C-10
Mt. Pleasant Bch., 2100 M-8
Mt. Rainier, 8080 *F-7
Mt. Savage, 873 A-4
Mt. Vernon, 779 I-17
Mt. Victoria, 150 I-12
Mt. Zion, 80 E-17
Mountain Lake Pk., 2092 C-1
Muirkirk, 650 *C-9
Myersville, 1626 B-9
Nanjemoy, 240 H-11
Nanticoke, 225 I-17
Neavitt, 300 G-15
New Carrollton, 12135 E-12
New Germany, 30 B-2
New London, 170 C-11
New Market, 656 C-11
New Midway, 380 B-10
New Windsor, 1396 B-11
Newark, 336 I-19
Newburg, 720 I-12
Newcomb, 250 G-15
Newport, 80 H-12
Newtown, 330 H-12
Newtown, 80 C-15
Nikep, 116 B-3
Norbeck *B-5
Normans, 100 E-15
Norrisville, 250 A-14
N. Beach, 1978 G-14
North East, 3572 B-16
North Point J-9
North Point Vil. J-9
N. Potomac, 24410 E-11
Norwood, 250 *B-6
Notch Cliff F-8
Oak Court B-18
Oak Pk., 30 C-1
Oak Ridge, 580 N-16
Oak View, 3400 *D-7
Oakland, 2500 *G-8
Oakland, 1925 C-1
Oakland F-1
Oaklawn, 1600 *I-8
Oakley, 50 I-13
Oakmont *D-5
Oakville I-13
Oakwood A-15
Ocean City, 7102 I-20
Ocean Pines, 11710 I-20
Odenton, 37132 E-13
Oella J-3
Old Farm, 3450 *C-4
Oldtown, 86 B-5
Olivet, 500 I-14
Olney, 33844 D-11
Oraville, 50 H-13
Orchard Bch., 2200 M-8
Orchard Hills, 1250 L-16
Oriole, 100 J-17
Overlea, 12275 H-8
Owings, 2149 G-14
Owings Mills, 30622 C-13
Oxford, 651 G-15
Oxon Hill-Glassmanor, 35355 *I-7
Palmer Pk. *F-9
Paradise Bch., 350 M-9
Paramount, 1450 L-17
Park Hall, 700 J-14
Parkside, 4650 *D-5
Parkton, 500 B-13
Parkville, 30734 C-14
Parole, 15922 B-19
Parsonsburg, 339 I-19
Patapsco, 200 B-12
Pen Mar, 210 A-10
Pendennis Mount, 350 A-20
Perry Hall, 28474 C-14
Perryman, 2342 B-15
Perryville, 4361 B-16
Pfeiffer Cors. L-2
Phoenix, 600 B-13
Pikesville, 30764 H-4
Pine Knoll Ter., 350 C-20
Pine Orchard Meadows, 690 J-1
Pinefield, 8800 G-12
Pinehurst on the Bay, 570 N-10
Pinesburg, 449 B-8
Piney Glen Farms, 470 *C-3
Piney Grv. A-6
Piney Pt., 864 J-14
Pinto, 300 B-4
Pioneer City N-4
Piscataway G-12
Pisgah, 300 H-11
Pittsville, 1417 I-19
Pleasant Hill, 250 A-17
Pleasant Hills, 3379 B-14
Plum Pt., 200 G-14
Pocomoke City, 4184 J-18
Pt. Lookout, 70 K-15
Pt. of Rocks, 1466 D-9
Pt. Pleasant, 1000 M-6
Pomfret, 517 H-12
Pomona, 60 D-16
Pomonkey, 500 G-11
Poolesville, 4883 D-10
Popes Creek, 80 I-12
Poplar Grv., 550 B-15
Poplar Hill G-13
Poplar Sprs., 220 C-11
Port Deposit, 653 B-16
Port Herman, 270 B-17
Port Republic, 200 H-14
Port Tobacco, 13 H-12
Pot Spr. F-6
Potomac, 44965 E-11
Potomac Hts., 1117 G-11
Powellville, 189 I-19
Preston, 719 G-17
Price, 180 E-16
Prince Frederick, 2538 H-14
PRINCE GEORGES CO., 863420 G-12
Princess Anne, 3290 J-18
Principio Furnace, 130 B-16
Providence, 1400 F-7
Public, 230 J-19
Pumphrey, 5317 L-6
Putnam, 300 B-14
Putty Hill H-8
Pylesville, 693 A-14
Quaker Neck, 30 D-16
Quantico, 133 I-17
Queen Anne, 222 F-16
QUEEN ANNES CO., 47798 E-16
Queenstown, 664 E-15
Quince Orchard, 5500 E-11
Randallstown, 32430 C-13
Randolph Hills, 6150 *C-5
Rawlings, 693 B-4
Rayville, 100 B-13
Redhouse, 30 C-1
Redland, 17242 *A-4
Rehobeth, 50 K-18
Reids Grv., 50 H-17
Reisterstown, 25968 C-12
Relay K-4
Reliance, 30 G-17
Rhodes Pt., 150 K-16
Rhodesdale, 50 H-17
Ricmar, 350 D-20
Riderwood G-5
Ridge, 450 J-15
Ridge Lake, 1000 J-1
Ridgely, 1639 E-17
Ridgeway, 500 N-5
Ringgold, 166 A-9
Ripley, 110 H-11
Rippling Ridge, 2100 L-6
Rising Sun, 2781 A-16
Rison, 450 H-11
Riva, 4076 E-14
Riverdale Pk., 6956 *E-8
Riviera Bch., 12677 M-8
Roberts, 50 D-16
Roblee Acres *H-10
Rock Creek Forest *D-6
Rock Hall, 1310 D-15
Rock Hill Bch., 1350 M-8
Rock Pt., 107 I-12
Rockdale, 6700 H-3
Rockville, 61209 E-11
Rocky Ridge, 900 B-10
Rodgers Forge G-6
Rohrersville, 175 C-9
Romancoke, 470 F-15
Rosaryville Estates, 1250 G-13
Rose Haven, 550 G-14
Rosedale, 19257 I-8
Rosemont, 294 C-9
Rossville, 15147 H-9
Royal Oak, 550 G-15
Royal Oak, 50 I-17
Rumbley, 200 J-17
Ruthsburg, 30 E-16
Ruxton G-5
Sabillasville, 354 A-10
St. Augustine B-17
St. Charles G-12
St. Clement Shores, 400 I-13
St. George Island, 257 J-14
St. Inigoes, 500 J-14
St. James, 2953 B-8
St. Leonard, 742 H-14
St. Margarets, 350 A-20
St. Martin I-20
St. Marys City, 3300 J-14
ST. MARYS CO., 105151 I-13
St. Michaels, 1029 F-15
Salem, 60 H-17
Salisbury, 30343 I-18
Sanders Pk., 450 M-8
Sandgates, 450 H-13
Sandy Bottom D-15
Sandy Hook, 188 C-9
Sandy Spr., 1200 *A-6
Sandyville, 650 B-12
Sang Run, 180 B-1
Sassafras, 70 C-17
Savage, 7054 N-2
Scaggsville, 270 M-1
Scientists Cliffs, 750 H-14
Scotland, 350 J-15
Seabrook, 17287 *E-9
Seat Pleasant, 4542 F-12
Secretary, 535 G-16
Security, 270 M-17
Selbysport, 50 A-1
Seneca E-10
Severn, 44231 D-13
Severn Grv. A-19
Severna Pk., 37634 E-14
Shad Pt., 390 E-19
Shady Side, 5803 F-14
Shallmar, 150 C-2
Shane A-14
Sharpsburg, 705 C-8
Sharptown, 651 H-17
Shawsville, 80 B-14
Shelltown, 100 K-18
Sherwood, 250 F-15
Sherwood Forest, 630 E-14
Shiloh, 130 I-12
Shipley L-5
Shookstown, 550 M-18
Showell, 400 H-20
Silesia, 240 *J-7
Silver Hill, 5950 *H-8
Silver Run, 180 A-12
Silver Sands, 350 M-7
Silver Spr., 71452 E-12
Skidmore, 450 E-14
Smithsburg, 2975 A-9
Smithville, 100 H-15
Smithville, 50 F-17
Snow Hill, 2103 J-19
Solomons, 2368 I-14
Somerset, 1216 *E-5
SOMERSET CO., 26470 J-17
S. River Pk., 550 F-14
Sparks, 670 B-13
Sparrows Pt. L-9
Spence J-19
Spencerville, 1594 *B-7
Spring Gap, 55 B-4
Springbrook, 1100 *C-7
Springdale, 3850 B-13
Starkey Cor. D-16
Starr, 30 E-16
Stemmers Run I-9
Stepney, 350 B-15
Stevenson, 750 G-4
Stevensville, 6803 E-15
Still Pond, 400 C-16
Stockton, 92 J-19
Stonecrest Hill, 1250 K-2
Street, 900 A-14
Suburban Acres, 390 E-19
Sudlersville, 497 D-17
Suitland, 25825 F-12
Summit Pk., 2900 G-5
Sunderland, 600 G-14
Sunnybrook, 980 B-14
Sunshine, 100 D-11
Swan Pt., 280 D-14
Swanton, 58 B-2
Sweet Air Mnr., 450 B-14
Sykesville, 4436 C-12
Takoma Pk., 16715 *E-7
TALBOT CO., 37782 F-16
Tall Timbers, 462 J-14
Taneytown, 6728 A-11
Tanyard G-16
Taylors Island, 173 H-15
Taylorsville, 150 C-11
Taylorville, 30 I-20
Temple Hills, 7852 *H-8
Templeville, 138 D-17
The Lakes, 9000 C-13
Thomas H-15
Thurmont, 6170 B-10
Tilghman, 784 G-15
Tilghmanton, 465 B-8
Timber Ridge C-11
Timberview L-3
Timonium, 9925 F-6
Tobytown, 210 *C-2
Toddville, 250 I-16
Tolchester Bch., 329 D-15
Tompkinsville, 150 I-12
Towson, 55197 C-13
Tracys, 440 F-14
Trappe, 1077 G-16
Travilah, 12159 *C-2
Tunis Mills, 70 F-15
Tuscarora, 150 D-10
Tuxedo *F-8
Tyaskin, 236 I-17
Tylerton, 150 K-16
Union Br., 975 B-11
Union Mills, 150 A-12
Uniontown, 350 B-11
Unionville, 230 J-18
Unionville, 220 B-11
Unionville, 80 F-16
Unity, 80 D-11
University Pk., 2548 *E-8
Upper Crossroads, 300 B-14
Upper Fairmount, 450 J-17
Upper Falls, 450 C-14
Upper Hill, 190 J-17
Upper Marlboro, 631 F-13
Upperco, 700 B-12
Urbana, 9175 C-10
Vale Summit, 139 B-3
Valley Lee, 500 J-14
Valley Mede, 4700 J-2
Van Bibber, 1000 C-15
Van Lear Manor, 1050 N-15
Venice on the Bay, 300 M-9
Venton, 150 J-17
Vienna, 271 H-17
Viers Mill Vil. *C-5
Villa Nova, 940 H-4
Waldorf, 67752 G-12
Walkersville, 5800 B-10
Wallville H-14
Walston, 50 D-20
Wards Chapel, 270 G-2
Warfieldsburg B-12
Warwick, 850 C-17
WASHINGTON CO., 147430 A-7
Washington Grv., 555 *A-4
Waterloo M-3
Waterview, 40 I-17
Webster Vil., 380 B-15
Welcome, 600 H-11
Wellington Estates, 280 M-1
Wenona, 390 J-16
W. Denton, 52 F-17
W. Edmondale, 3450 J-4
W. Friendship, 1200 C-12
W. Ocean City, 4375 I-20
W. River F-14
Westernport, 1888 B-3
Westgate *E-5
Westminster, 18590 B-12
Westover, 800 J-18
Westwood G-13
Wetipquin, 80 I-17
Weverton, 140 C-9
Whaleyville, 149 I-19
Wheaton, 48284 E-12
White Hall, 700 B-13
White Marsh, 9513 C-14
White Oak, 17403 *C-7
White Plains G-12
White Pt. Bch., 450 J-13
Whiteford, 750 A-15
Whitehaven, 43 I-17
Whitehouse B-13
Whiteleysburg E-17
Whiton, 60 I-19
WICOMICO CO., 98733 H-18
Widgeon I-17
Wild Rose Shores, 300 C-19
Wild Wood Bch., 200 K-10
Willards, 958 I-19
Williamsburg, 100 G-17
Williamsport, 2137 B-8
Williston, 155 F-17
Willow Bch. Colony, 230 G-14
Wilson, 50 A-8
Wilton Farm Acres, 1900 I-2
Winchester on the Severn, 700 A-19
Windham Mnr., 290 E-19
Winfield, 200 C-11
Wingate, 230 I-16
Wiseburg B-13
Wittman, 600 F-15
Wolfsville, 150 B-9
Wood Pt. M-16
Woodbine, 500 C-11
Woodensburg, 150 B-12
Woodfield D-11
Woodland, 113 B-3
Woodlawn, 37879 C-13
Woodlawn, 150 B-16
Woodlawn Hts., 2400 L-5
Woodmont *D-5
Woodmoor, 8400 H-4
Woodmore, 3936 *F-10
Woodsboro, 1141 B-10
Woodstock, 850 I-1
Woodville C-11
Woolford, 290 H-15
WORCESTER CO., 51454 I-19
Worthington, 2350 K-2
Worthington, 90 E-3
Worton, 249 D-16
Wye Mills, 400 E-16
Yellow Sprs., 450 B-10

Massachusetts

Page locator
Map keys — Atlas pages
1–10 — 98–99
11–20 — 100–101
* City keyed to p. 185

Abington, 15985 G-15
Acoaxet, 220 L-14
Acton, 2300 D-12
Acushnet, 3073 J-15
Adams, 5515 C-3
Adamsville C-5
Agawam, 28144 G-5
Aldenville L-12
Alford, 160 F-1
Allerton L-10
Amesbury, 12327 A-15
Amherst, 19065 E-6
Andover, 8762 C-14
Arlington, 42844 E-14
Ashburnham, 1500 C-9
Ashby, 700 C-10
Ashfield, 1050 D-4
Ashland, 12100 F-12
Ashley Falls, 850 G-1
Ashley Hts., 110 I-15
Assinippi, 1400 G-15
Assonet, 1300 I-14
Athol, 8265 C-8
Attleboro, 43593 H-13
Auburn, 15000 F-10
Avon, 4300 G-14
Ayer, 2868 D-11
Back Bay K-7
Baldwinville, 2028 C-8
Ballardvale, 1400 C-13
Bancroft E-3
Barnstable, 45193 J-18
BARNSTABLE CO., 215888 J-17
Barre, 1009 E-8
Barre Plains, 400 E-8
Barrowsville, 250 H-13
Bass River J-19
Bayview, 200 K-15
Beach Pt., 50 G-19
Beacon Hill I-2
Becket, 600 E-3
Becket Ctr., 80 F-3
Bedford, 13300 D-13
Bedford Sprs. H-4
Beechwood, 500 F-15
Belchertown, 2899 F-7
Bellingham, 4854 G-12
Belmont, 24729 E-13
Berkley, 200 I-14
Berkshire, 200 D-2
BERKSHIRE CO., 131219 E-2
Berlin, 700 E-11
Bernardston, 900 C-6
Beverly, 39502 D-15
Billerica, 6850 D-13
Blackstone, 5000 H-11
Blandford, 393 F-4
Bliss Cor., 5466 F-20
Bolton, 550 E-11
Bondsville, 1850 F-7
Boston, 617594 E-14
Bourne, 1418 J-17
Bournedale, 150 I-17
Boxborough, 500 D-11
Boxford, 2339 C-14
Boylston Ctr., 950 E-11
Bradstreet, 200 E-6
Braintree, 33698 F-14
Braleys, 350 J-15
Brant Rock, 1800 G-16
Brewster, 2000 J-20
Bridgewater, 7841 H-15
Briggsville B-3
Brighton K-6
Brightwood M-11
Brimfield, 800 G-8
BRISTOL CO., 548285 J-14
Brockton, 93810 G-14
Brookfield, 833 F-8
Brookline, 58732 E-14
Bryantville, 1800 G-15
Buckland, 200 C-4
Burlington, 24498 D-13
Buzzards Bay, 3859 J-17
Byfield, 1300 B-15
Cambridge, 105162 E-14

*, †, ‡, §, ◊ See explanation under state title in this index.
County and parish names are listed in capital letters & boldface type.
Independent cities (not included in a county) are listed in italics.

*, †, ‡, §, ◊   See explanation under state title in this index.
County and parish names are listed in CAPITAL LETTERS & boldface type.
Independent cities (not included in a county) are listed in italics.

Wilsonville, 93.....M-9
Winnebago, 774.....G-18
Winnetoon, 68.....F-14
Winside, 427.....G-16
Winslow, 103.....I-18
Wisner, 1170.....G-17
Wolbach, 283.....I-13
Wood Lake, 63.....F-9
Wood River, 1325.....K-13
Woodland Pk., 1866.....G-16
Worms, 30.....J-14
Wymore, 1457.....M-17
Wynot, 166.....E-16
York, 7766.....K-15
YORK CO., 13665.....K-15
Yutan, 1174.....J-18

Nevada

Page locator
Map keys Atlas pages
A–N 130–131
* City keyed to p. 30
† City keyed to pp. 132–133

Alamo, 1080.....J-8
Amargosa Valley, 380.....K-6
Ash Sprs., 50.....J-8
Austin, 192.....F-5
Baker, 68.....G-10
Battle Mtn., 3635.....D-6
Beatty, 1010.....K-6
Belmont, 25.....H-6
Beowawe, 280.....D-6
Black Sprs., 230.....†G-1
Blue Diamond, 290.....L-8
Boulder City, 15023.....L-9
Bunkerville, 1303.....K-10
Caliente, 1130.....J-9
Cal-Nev-Ari, 244.....M-9
Carlin, 2368.....D-7
Carp.....J-9
Carson City, 55274.....F-2
Carvers.....G-5
Caselton, 40.....I-9
Cherry Creek, 30.....E-8
CHURCHILL CO., 24877.....F-4
CLARK CO., 1951269.....K-8
Coaldale, 20.....I-4
Cold Sprs., 20.....F-4
Cosgrave, 50.....C-4
Cottonwood Cove, 180.....M-9
Crescent Valley, 392.....D-6
Crystal Bay, 305.....*F-9
Currant.....G-8
Currie.....D-9
Dayton, 8964.....F-2
Deeth, 100.....C-8
Denio, 47.....A-3
Dixie Valley, 20.....E-4
DOUGLAS CO., 46997.....G-2
Duckwater, 25.....G-7
Dunphy, 25.....D-6
Dyer, 259.....I-4
Elgin.....J-9
Elk Pt., 250.....*G-9
Elko, 18297.....C-7
ELKO CO., 48818.....C-7
Ely, 4255.....F-9
Empire, 217.....D-2
ESMERALDA CO., 783.....I-5
Eureka, 610.....F-7
EUREKA CO., 1987.....E-6
Fallon, 8606.....F-3
Fernley, 19368.....F-2
Gabbs, 269.....G-4
Gardnerville, 5656.....G-2
Genoa, 939.....*G-10
Gerlach, 206.....D-2
Glenbrook, 215.....G-1
Glendale, 50.....K-9
Golconda, 214.....C-5
Gold Pt., 20.....J-5
Golden Valley, 1556.....F-2
Goldfield, 268.....I-5
Goodsprings, 229.....M-8
Hadley.....G-5
Halleck, 40.....C-8
Hawthorne, 3269.....H-3
Hazen, 50.....F-3
Henderson, 257729.....L-8
Hidden Valley, 1000.....†I-3
Hiko, 119.....J-8
HUMBOLDT CO., 16528.....B-4
Imlay, 171.....D-4
Incline Vil., 8777.....F-1
Indian Sprs., 991.....K-7
Ione, 20.....G-5
Jackpot, 1195.....A-9
Jacks Valley, 250.....*G-10
Jarbidge, 80.....B-8
Jean, 200.....M-8
Jiggs, 30.....D-7
Kingsbury, 2152.....*G-10
Kingston, 113.....F-5
Lakeridge, 371.....*G-9
Lamoille, 105.....D-8
LANDER CO., 5775.....E-5
Las Vegas, 583756.....L-8
Laughlin, 7323.....N-9
Lee, 100.....D-7
Lemmon Valley, 5040.....F-1
Lida.....J-5
LINCOLN CO., 5345.....I-9
Logandale.....K-9
Lovelock, 1894.....E-3
Lund, 282.....G-8
Luning, 60.....H-4
LYON CO., 51980.....G-2
Majors Pl.....G-9
Manhattan, 70.....H-5
Mason, 400.....G-2
McDermitt, 172.....A-5
McGill, 1148.....F-9
Mercury, 50.....K-7
Mesquite, 15276.....K-10
Midas, 70.....C-6
Mill City.....D-4
Mina, 155.....H-4
Minden, 3001.....G-2
MINERAL CO., 4772.....H-3
Moapa, 1025.....K-9
Montello, 84.....C-9
Mountain City, 100.....B-7
Nelson, 37.....M-9
New Washoe City.....*E-10
Nixon, 374.....E-2
N. Las Vegas, 216961.....L-8
NYE CO., 43946.....H-6
Oasis, 29.....C-9
Oreana, 100.....D-4
Orovada, 155.....B-4
Overton.....K-9
Owyhee, 953.....A-7
Pahrump, 36441.....L-7
Panaca, 963.....I-9
Paradise, 223167.....M-2
Paradise Valley, 109.....B-5
PERSHING CO., 6753.....D-3
Pioche, 1002.....I-9
Preston, 78.....G-8
Primm, 50.....M-8
Rachel, 54.....I-7
Reno, 225221.....F-2
Round Hill, 400.....*G-9
Ruby Valley, 100.....D-8
Ruth, 440.....F-8
Sandy Valley, 2051.....M-8
Schurz, 658.....G-3
Scotty's Jct., 10.....J-5
Searchlight, 539.....M-9
Silver City, 150.....F-2
Silver Peak, 107.....I-5
Silver Sprs., 5296.....F-2
Skyland, 376.....*G-9
Smith, 160.....G-3
S. Hills, 1100.....†J-2
Sparks, 90264.....F-2
Spring Creek, 12361.....D-7
Spring Valley, 178395.....M-1
Stagecoach, 1874.....F-2
Stateline, 842.....G-1
Steamboat, 300.....F-2
Stillwater, 200.....F-3
STOREY CO., 4010.....F-2
Sun Valley, 19299.....F-2
Sunnyside, 30.....H-8
Sunrise Mnr., 189372.....L-3
Sutcliffe, 253.....E-2
Tonopah, 2478.....H-5
Topaz Lake, 157.....G-2
Tuscarora, 100.....B-7
Unionville, 35.....D-4
Ursine, 91.....I-10
Valmy, 37.....C-5
Verdi, 1415.....F-1
Virginia City, 855.....F-2
Vya.....B-2
Wabuska, 100.....F-2
Wadsworth, 834.....F-2
Walker Lake, 275.....G-3
Warm Sprs.....H-6
Washoe City, 500.....F-2
WASHOE CO., 421407.....D-2
Weed Hts., 240.....G-2
Wellington, 300.....G-2
Wells, 1292.....C-8
W. Wendover, 4410.....D-10
WHITE PINE CO., 10030.....F-8
Whitney, 38585.....M-3
Winchester, 27978.....K-3
Winnemucca, 7396.....C-4
Yerington, 3048.....G-2
Zephyr Cove, 565.....G-1

New Hampshire

Page locator
Map keys Atlas pages
A–N 132–133

Acworth, 230.....K-5
Albany.....H-9
Alexandria, 150.....I-6
Alstead, 500.....L-4
Alstead Ctr., 70.....L-4
Alton, 501.....I-8
Alton Bay, 900.....I-8
Amherst, 613.....M-7
Andover, 500.....I-6
Antrim, 1397.....L-6
Ashland, 1244.....I-7
Ashuelot, 370.....M-4
Atkinson, 900.....M-9
Auburn, 450.....L-8
Barnstead, 380.....K-8
Barrington, 350.....K-9
Bartlett, 373.....G-8
Bath, 250.....G-6
Bedford, 1800.....M-7
Beebe River, 60.....H-7
BELKNAP CO., 60088.....J-8
Belmont, 1301.....J-7
Bennington, 381.....L-6
Benton, 80.....G-6
Berlin, 10051.....E-8
Bethlehem, 972.....F-7
Boscawen, 400.....K-7
Bow Mills, 700.....F-2
Bowkerville, 70.....M-5
Bradford, 356.....K-6
Brentwood, 400.....L-9
Bretton Woods, 30.....F-8
Bridgewater, 130.....I-7
Bristol, 1688.....I-7
Brookfield, 40.....J-9
Brookline, 700.....N-7
Campton, 700.....H-7
Canaan, 524.....I-5
Canaan Ctr., 250.....I-5
Canaan Street, 300.....I-5
Candia, 400.....L-8
Candia Four Corners, 150.....L-8
Canobie Lake, 700.....M-8
Canterbury, 300.....K-7
Carroll.....F-7
CARROLL CO., 47818.....I-8
Cascade, 180.....E-8
Cedar Pond, 60.....E-8
Center Barnstead, 350.....K-8
Center Conway, 400.....H-9
Center Effingham, 150.....I-9
Center Harbor, 650.....I-7
Center Ossipee, 561.....I-9
Center Sandwich, 123.....H-8
Center Strafford, 250.....K-9
Center Tuftonboro, 450.....I-8
Charlestown, 1152.....K-4
Chase Vil., 150.....L-6
Chesham, 120.....M-5
CHESHIRE CO., 77117.....L-5
Chester, 600.....M-8
Chesterfield, 450.....M-4
Chichester, 230.....K-8
Chocorua, 400.....H-8
Christian Hollow, 70.....L-4
Claremont, 13355.....J-4
Clinton Vil., 400.....L-6
Cold River, 70.....L-4
Colebrook, 1394.....C-7
Concord, 42695.....K-7
Contoocook, 1444.....K-7
Conway, 1823.....H-9
COOS CO., 33055.....D-8
Cornish Ctr., 150.....J-4
Cornish Flat, 350.....J-5
Cornish Mills, 100.....J-4
Croydon, 130.....J-5
Croydon Flat, 100.....J-5
Cushman, 90.....F-7
Dalton, 100.....E-7
Danbury, 350.....J-6
Danville, 700.....M-9
Davisville.....K-7
Deerfield, 250.....L-8
Deerfield Parade, 200.....L-8
Deering, 100.....L-6
Derry, 22015.....M-8
Dixville Notch, 20.....C-8
Dorchester, 60.....I-6
Dover, 29987.....K-10
Drewsville, 150.....L-4
Dublin, 650.....M-5
Dunbarton Ctr., 230.....L-7
Durham, 10345.....L-9
E. Alstead, 200.....L-5
E. Andover, 350.....J-6
E. Candia, 120.....L-8
E. Concord.....K-7
E. Conway, 130.....G-9
E. Derry, 850.....M-8
E. Grafton.....I-6
E. Hampstead, 1400.....M-9
E. Haverhill, 110.....G-6
E. Hebron, 150.....I-6
E. Lempster, 300.....K-5
E. Rindge, 250.....M-6
E. Sullivan, 170.....L-5
E. Sutton.....K-6
E. Swanzey, 350.....M-5
E. Unity, 130.....K-5
E. Wakefield, 90.....I-9
E. Washington, 60.....K-6
Eaton Ctr., 100.....H-9
Effingham, 80.....I-9
Effingham Falls, 100.....H-9
Elkins, 120.....J-6
Elmwood, 80.....L-6
Enfield, 1540.....I-5
Enfield Ctr., 250.....I-5
Epping, 1681.....L-9
Epsom, 250.....K-8
Errol, 170.....D-9
Etna, 350.....I-5
Exeter, 9242.....L-9
Fabyan.....F-8
Farmington, 3885.....J-9
Fitzwilliam, 650.....M-5
Fitzwilliam Depot, 500.....M-5
Francestown, 250.....L-6
Franconia, 600.....F-6
Franklin, 8477.....J-7
Freedom, 400.....H-9
Fremont, 900.....L-9
Georges Mills, 400.....J-5
Gilford, 600.....J-8
Gilmanton, 700.....J-8
Gilmanton Ironworks, 600.....J-8
Gilsum, 400.....L-5
Glen, 250.....G-8
Glencliff, 90.....H-6
Glendale, 400.....I-8
Goffstown, 3196.....L-7
Gorham, 1600.....F-8
Goshen, 350.....K-5
Gossville, 350.....K-8
Grafton, 330.....J-6
Grafton Ctr., 50.....J-6
GRAFTON CO., 89118.....I-6
Grantham, 300.....J-5
Greenfield, 900.....M-6
Greenland, 1400.....L-10
Greenville, 1108.....M-6
Groton, 140.....I-6
Groveton, 1118.....E-7
Guild, 325.....J-5
Hampstead, 900.....M-8
Hampton, 9656.....M-10
Hampton Bch., 2275.....M-10
Hampton Falls, 550.....M-10
Hancock, 204.....L-6
Hanover, 8636.....I-5
Hanover Ctr., 60.....I-5
Happy Corner.....B-8
Harrisville, 500.....M-5
Haverhill, 400.....G-5
Hebron, 150.....I-6
Henniker, 1747.....K-6
High Br., 100.....K-6
Hill, 280.....J-7
Hillsborough, 1976.....L-6
Hillsborough Ctr., 150.....L-6
HILLSBOROUGH CO., 400721.....L-6
Hillsborough Lower Vil., 250.....L-6
Hillsborough Upper Vil., 340.....L-6
Hinsdale, 1548.....M-4
Holderness, 400.....I-7
Hollis, 600.....N-7
Hooksett, 4147.....L-8
Hopkinton, 400.....K-7
Hudson, 7336.....M-8
Hudson Ctr.....M-8
Intervale, 300.....G-9
Jackson, 350.....G-8
Jaffrey, 2757.....M-6
Jaffrey Ctr., 400.....M-5
Jefferson, 230.....E-7
Kearsarge, 100.....G-9
Keene, 23409.....M-5
Kelleys Corner.....K-8
Kellyville, 200.....K-5
Kensington, 240.....M-9
Kidderville.....C-8
Kingston, 700.....M-9
Laconia, 15951.....J-7
Lancaster, 1725.....E-7
Landaff Ctr., 30.....G-6
Langdon, 200.....L-4
Lebanon, 13151.....I-5
Lee, 150.....L-9
Lempster, 170.....K-5
Lincoln, 993.....G-7
Lisbon, 980.....F-6
Little Boars Head, 120.....L-10
Littleton, 4412.....F-6
Lochmere, 200.....J-7
Londonderry, 11037.....M-8
Loudon, 559.....K-7
Lower Gilmanton.....J-8
Lyme, 450.....H-5
Lyme Ctr., 120.....H-5
Lyndeborough, 100.....M-6
Madbury, 150.....K-9
Madison, 250.....H-9
Manchester, 109565.....L-7
Marlborough, 1094.....M-5
Marlow, 450.....L-5
Marshall Cor., 80.....L-9
Martin.....A-5
Mason, 200.....M-6
Melvin Vil., 241.....I-8
Meredith, 1718.....I-7
Meredith Ctr., 220.....I-7
Meriden, 500.....J-5
Merrimack, 2400.....M-7
MERRIMACK CO., 146445.....K-6
Middleton Cors., 150.....J-9
Milan, 230.....E-8
Milford, 8835.....M-7
Milton, 575.....J-9
Milton Mills, 299.....J-9
Mirror Lake, 300.....I-8
Monroe, 280.....F-6
Mont Vernon, 600.....M-7
Moultonborough, 350.....I-8
Mt. Sunapee, 250.....K-5
Munsonville, 230.....L-5
Nashua, 86494.....M-7
Nelson, 130.....L-5
New Boston, 850.....L-7
New Castle, 840.....L-10
New Durham, 350.....J-9
New Hampton, 351.....I-7
New Ipswich, 800.....M-6
New London, 1415.....J-6
Newbury, 200.....K-5
Newfields, 301.....L-9
Newmarket, 5297.....L-9
Newport, 4769.....K-5
Newton, 650.....M-9
Noone, 80.....M-6
N. Branch, 150.....L-6
N. Charlestown, 150.....K-4
N. Chatham, 80.....F-9
N. Chichester, 250.....K-8
N. Conway, 2349.....G-9
N. Hampton, 500.....L-10
N. Haverhill, 450.....G-6
N. Newport, 200.....K-5
N. Pelham, 400.....M-8
N. Salem, 300.....M-8
N. Sanbornton, 300.....J-7
N. Sandwich, 100.....H-8
N. Stratford, 400.....D-7
N. Sutton, 270.....K-6
North Village, 160.....M-6
N. Walpole, 828.....L-4
N. Woodstock, 528.....G-7
Northfield, 1500.....J-7
Northumberland, 100.....E-7
Northwood, 650.....K-9
Northwood Ctr., 270.....K-8
Northwood Ridge, 250.....K-8
Nottingham, 280.....L-9
Orange, 120.....I-6
Orford, 400.....H-5
Orfordville, 120.....H-5
Ossipee, 250.....I-9
Pages Cor., 90.....J-8
Parker Hill.....F-6
Passaconaway, 40.....H-8
Pelham, 1200.....N-8
Pembroke, 400.....L-8
Percy, 60.....D-8
Peterborough, 3103.....M-6
Piermont, 200.....H-5
Pike, 220.....G-6
Pinardville, 4780.....B-4
Pittsburg, 400.....B-8
Pittsfield, 1576.....K-8
Plainfield, 205.....J-4
Plaistow, 2200.....M-9
Plymouth, 4456.....I-7
Portsmouth, 20779.....L-10
Potter Pl., 60.....J-6
Randolph, 200.....F-8
Raymond, 2855.....L-8
Redstone, 150.....G-9
Richmond, 130.....M-5
Rindge, 400.....M-6
Riverdale, 50.....L-7
Rochester, 29752.....K-9
ROCKINGHAM CO., 295223.....L-8
Rollinsford, 1500.....K-10
Rumney, 430.....H-6
Rumney Depot, 320.....H-6
Rye, 850.....L-10
Rye Bch., 450.....L-10
Salem, 12000.....M-8
Salisbury, 330.....J-7
Salisbury Hts., 100.....J-7
Sanbornton, 320.....J-7
Sanbornville, 1056.....J-9
Sandown, 600.....M-8
Sandwich, 60.....H-8
Scotland, 70.....M-4
Seabrook, 900.....M-10
Sharon, 80.....M-6
Shelburne.....F-9
Short Falls, 90.....K-8
Silver Lake, 300.....H-9
Snowville, 50.....H-9
Somersworth, 11766.....K-10
S. Acworth, 200.....K-5
S. Barnstead, 70.....K-8
S. Charlestown.....K-4
S. Chatham, 90.....G-9
S. Danville, 250.....M-9
S. Deerfield.....L-8
S. Effingham, 120.....I-9
S. Hooksett, 5418.....L-8
S. Lyndeboro, 250.....M-6
S. Merrimack, 200.....M-7
S. Newbury, 150.....K-6
S. Stoddard.....L-5
S. Sutton, 170.....K-6
S. Tamworth, 200.....H-8
S. Weare, 250.....L-7
S. Wolfeboro, 400.....J-8
Spofford, 500.....M-4
Springfield, 80.....J-5
Squantum, 120.....M-6
Stark, 130.....E-8
Stewartstown, 180.....C-7
Stewartstown Hollow, 30.....C-8
Stinson Lake, 60.....H-6
Stoddard, 300.....L-5
Strafford, 300.....K-8
STRAFFORD CO., 123143.....K-9
Stratford, 150.....D-7
Stratham, 800.....L-9
Sugar Hill, 200.....F-6
SULLIVAN CO., 43742.....K-4
Sunapee, 1000.....J-5
Suncook, 5379.....L-8
Surry, 150.....L-4
Sutton, 200.....K-6
Swanzey, 900.....M-5
Swiftwater, 120.....G-6
Tamworth, 600.....H-8
Temple, 400.....M-6
The Glen.....G-8
Thornton, 100.....H-7
Tilton, 1300.....J-7
Troy, 1221.....M-5
Tuftonboro, 70.....I-8
Twin Mtn., 300.....F-7
Union, 204.....J-9
Unity, 150.....K-5
Wakefield, 140.....J-9
Walpole, 605.....L-4
Warner, 444.....K-6
Warren, 550.....H-6
Washington, 150.....K-5
Water Vil., 50.....I-8
Waterloo, 60.....K-6
Waterville Valley, 120.....H-7
Wawbeek, 20.....I-8
Weare, 300.....L-7
Webster, 120.....K-7
Wendell, 120.....K-5
Wentworth, 280.....H-6
W. Alton.....J-8
W. Campton, 140.....H-7
W. Canaan, 120.....I-5
W. Center Hbr., 70.....I-7
W. Chesterfield, 550.....M-4
W. Epping, 350.....L-9
W. Hampstead, 200.....M-8
W. Henniker, 300.....K-6
W. Hopkinton, 30.....K-6
W. Milan, 100.....E-8
W. Nottingham, 170.....K-9
W. Ossipee, 150.....H-8
W. Peterborough, 500.....M-6
W. Plymouth.....I-6
W. Rindge, 330.....M-5
W. Rumney, 150.....H-6
W. Rye, 300.....L-10
W. Springfield, 90.....J-5
W. Stewartstown, 386.....C-7
W. Swanzey, 1308.....M-4
W. Thornton, 160.....H-7
W. Wilton, 200.....M-6
Westmoreland, 300.....L-4
Westport, 500.....M-4
Westville, 400.....M-9
Whitefield, 1142.....F-7
Whittier, 50.....H-8
Wilmot, 120.....J-6
Wilmot Flat, 350.....J-6
Wilton, 1163.....M-7
Winchester, 1733.....M-4
Windham, 300.....M-8
Winnisquam, 650.....J-7
Wolfeboro, 2838.....I-8
Wolfeboro Ctr.....I-9
Wolfeboro Falls, 600.....I-8
Wonalancet, 60.....H-8
Woodman, 80.....J-9
Woodstock, 280.....H-7
Woodsville, 1126.....G-5

New Jersey

Page locator
Map keys Atlas pages
A–J 134–135
K–T 136–137
* City keyed to p. 50
† City keyed to pp. 146–147
‡ City keyed to p. 148
§ City keyed to p. 182

Absecon, 8411.....P-10
Adamston.....K-12
Adelphia, 150.....I-12
Aldene.....†J-4
Aldine, 50.....O-5
Allamuchy, 78.....D-8
Allendale, 6505.....C-12
Allenhurst, 496.....J-13
Allentown, 1828.....I-10
Allerton, 100.....G-8
Alloway, 3467.....O-5
Almonesson, 800.....M-6
Alpha, 2369.....F-6
Alpine, 1849.....‡B-11
Amwell, 100.....H-8
Anderson, 342.....F-7
Andover, 606.....D-9
Annandale, 1695.....G-8
Asbury, 273.....F-7
Asbury Pk., 16116.....J-13
Atco, 3500.....N-8
Atlantic City, 39558.....Q-10
ATLANTIC CO., 274549.....P-9
Atlantic Highlands, 4385.....H-13
Auburn, 150.....N-5
Audubon, 8819.....M-7
Audubon Pk., 1023.....§F-5
Augusta, 100.....C-9
Avalon, 1334.....S-9
Avenel, 17011.....†L-4
Avon-by-the-Sea, 1901.....J-13
Awosting, 500.....C-11
Bakersville, 200.....Q-9
Baleville, 90.....C-8
Bamber Lake, 250.....M-11
Baptistown, 200.....H-7
Bargaintown, 1600.....Q-10
Barnegat, 2817.....N-12
Barnegat Bch., 300.....N-12
Barnegat Light, 574.....N-12
Barnegat Pines, 400.....M-12
Barrington, 6983.....M-7
Bartley.....E-9
Basking Ridge, 4000.....F-10
Batsto, 10.....O-9
Bay Head, 968.....K-13
Bay Shore.....L-12
Bayonne, 63024.....F-13
Bayville, 900.....L-12
Beach Haven, 1170.....O-12
Beach Haven Crest, 100.....O-12
Beach Haven Hts., 300.....O-11
Beach Haven Ter., 400.....O-12
Beach Haven West, 3896.....N-12
Beachwood, 11045.....L-12
Beattystown, 4642.....E-8
Beaver Lake, 250.....C-10
Bedminster, 3000.....F-9
Beesleys Pt., 850.....Q-9
Belcoville, 850.....P-9
Belford, 1768.....H-12
Belle Mead, 216.....H-9
Belleplain, 597.....Q-8
Belleville, 35928.....E-12
Bellmawr, 11262.....§G-6
Belmar, 5794.....J-13
Belvidere, 2681.....E-7
BERGEN CO., 905116.....D-13
Bergenfield, 26764.....D-13
Berkeley Hts., 13407.....F-10
Berlin, 7588.....M-7
Bernardsville, 7707.....F-10
Beverly, 2577.....K-7
Bivalve, 50.....R-7
Blackwood, 4545.....M-7
Blairstown, 515.....D-7
Blawenburg, 280.....H-9
Bloomfield, 47683.....C-2
Bloomingdale, 7656.....D-11
Bloomsbury, 870.....G-6
Blue Anchor.....N-8
Bogota, 8187.....A-5
Bonhamtown.....†M-2
Boonton, 8347.....E-11
Bordentown, 3924.....K-9
Bound Brook, 10402.....G-10
Bradevelt, 150.....I-12
Bradley Bch., 4298.....J-13
Brainards, 202.....F-6
Branchville, 841.....C-8
Brant Bch., 300.....O-12
Brass Castle, 1555.....F-7
Breton Woods.....K-12
Bricksboro, 40.....Q-7
Bridgeboro.....L-7
Bridgeport, 700.....M-5
Bridgeton, 25349.....P-6
Bridgeville, 106.....E-7
Bridgewater, 7000.....G-9
Brielle, 4774.....K-13
Brigantine, 9450.....P-11
Brighton Bch., 150.....O-12
Broadway, 244.....F-7
Brooklawn, 1955.....§G-5
Brookside, 1800.....E-10
Brookville.....M-11
Brotmanville, 150.....O-6
Browns Mills, 11223.....L-10
Browntown, 2400.....I-11
Buckshutem, 100.....Q-7
Budd Lake, 8968.....E-9
Buddtown, 70.....L-9
Buena, 4603.....P-7
Bunnvale, 400.....F-8
Burleigh, 725.....S-8
Burlington, 9920.....K-8
BURLINGTON CO., 448734.....L-9
Butler, 7539.....D-11
Buttzville, 146.....E-7
Caldwell, 7822.....E-11
Califon, 1076.....F-8
Camden, 77344.....L-6
CAMDEN CO., 513657.....N-8
Candlewood, 4000.....K-12
Canton, 350.....P-4
Cape May, 3607.....T-7
CAPE MAY CO., 97265.....R-8
Cape May Court House, 5338.....S-8
Cape May Pt., 291.....T-7
Cardiff, 400.....P-9
Carlls Cor., 900.....P-6
Carlstadt, 6127.....B-4
Carlton Hill.....B-4
Carmel, 150.....P-6
Carneys Pt., 7382.....N-4
Carpenterville, 90.....G-6
Carteret, 22844.....G-12
Cecil.....O-7
Cedar Brook, 800.....N-8
Cedar Crest Manor, 150.....N-4
Cedar Grv., 12300.....B-1
Cedar Knolls.....E-10
Cedar Run, 400.....N-11
Cedarville, 776.....Q-6
Center Sq., 150.....N-5
Centerton, 150.....O-6
Centerton, 30.....§D-9
Centerville, 150.....G-8
Centre Grv.....G-6
Chadwick, 250.....L-13
Chambers Corners.....L-9
Changewater, 250.....F-7
Chatham, 8962.....F-11
Chatsworth, 500.....M-10
Cheesequake, 300.....H-11
Cherry Hill, 2100.....L-7
Cherryville, 50.....G-8
Chesilhurst, 1634.....N-8
Chester, 1649.....F-9
Chesterfield, 200.....K-9
Chrome.....†L-5
Cinnaminson.....L-7
Clark, 14597.....†J-3
Clarksboro, 1700.....M-6
Clarksburg, 400.....J-10
Clarkstown, 200.....P-9
Clayton, 8179.....N-6
Clementon, 5000.....M-7
Clermont, 100.....R-8
Cliffside Pk., 23594.....C-6
Cliffwood, 1500.....H-12
Cliffwood Bch., 3194.....H-12
Clifton, 84136.....E-12
Clinton, 2719.....G-8
Closter, 8373.....*A-11
Clover Leaf Lakes, 900.....P-9
Cloverhill, 150.....H-9
Cohansey, 50.....P-5
Cokesbury, 150.....F-8
Cold Spr., 600.....T-7
Colesville, 120.....B-9
Collings Lakes, 1706.....O-8
Collingswood, 13926.....L-7
Collingwood Park, 200.....J-12
Cologne, 1100.....P-9
Colonia, 17795.....G-11
Colonial Manor, 2000.....§G-4
Colts Neck, 800.....I-12
Columbia, 229.....D-6
Columbus, 700.....K-9
Convent Sta., 1800.....F-10
Cookstown, 300.....K-10
Corbin City, 492.....Q-8
Cornish.....E-7
Country Lake Estates, 3943.....L-10
Cranberry Lake, 1000.....D-9
Cranbury, 2181.....I-10
Cranford, 22578.....G-11
Cream Ridge, 150.....K-10
Cresskill, 8573.....‡B-11
Crestwood Vil., 7907.....L-11
Cross Keys, 600.....N-7
Crosswicks, 800.....K-9
Croton, 60.....H-7
Culvers Lake, 1100.....C-8
Cumberland, 100.....Q-7
CUMBERLAND CO., 156898.....Q-6
Daretown, 125.....O-5
Dayton, 7063.....I-10
Deal, 750.....J-13
Deans, 600.....I-10
Deepwater, 500.....N-4
Deerfield, 350.....O-6
Del Haven, 1200.....S-7
Delanco.....K-7
Delaware, 150.....E-7
Delmont, 650.....R-7
Delran, 13200.....L-7
Demarest, 4881.....‡B-11
Dennisville, 600.....R-8
Denville, 13800.....E-10
Devonshire, 250.....O-9
Dias Creek.....S-8
Dividing Creek, 500.....Q-6
Dorchester, 600.....Q-7
Dorothy, 900.....P-8
Dover, 18157.....E-10
Dumont, 17479.....†B-10
Dunellen, 7227.....G-10
Dutch Neck, 175.....I-9
E. Hanover.....E-11
E. Keansburg, 3000.....H-12
E. Millstone, 579.....H-10
E. Newark, 2406.....D-3
E. Orange, 64270.....D-2
E. Rutherford, 8913.....B-4
E. Vineland, 300.....P-7
E. Windsor, 4000.....J-10
Eatontown, 12709.....I-13
Edgewater, 11513.....B-6
Edgewater Pk., 2000.....K-8
Edinburg.....J-9
Edison, 97597.....H-11
Egg Hbr. City, 4243.....O-9
Eldora, 120.....R-8
Eldridge Pk., 3000.....R-13
Elizabeth, 124969.....F-12
Elm, 200.....N-8
Elmer, 1395.....O-6
Elmwood Pk., 19403.....A-3
Elwood, 1437.....O-9
Emerson, 7401.....†A-9
Englewood, 27147.....E-13
Englewood Cliffs, 5281.....A-7
Englishtown, 1847.....I-11
Erma, 2134.....T-8
ESSEX CO., 783969.....F-11
Estell Manor, 1735.....Q-8
Eta, 30.....I-10
Everittstown, 90.....G-7
Evesboro, 100.....L-7
Ewan, 250.....N-6
Ewansville, 300.....L-9
Ewing, 35707.....J-8
Ewingville.....R-12
Fair Haven, 6121.....I-13
Fair Lawn, 32457.....†B-7
Fairton, 1264.....Q-6
Fairview, 13835.....C-6
Fairview.....M-6
Fanwood, 7318.....G-11
Far Hills, 919.....F-9
Farmingdale, 1329.....J-12
Farmington, 450.....H-1
Fenwick.....O-5
Ferrell, 80.....N-6
Fieldsboro, 540.....K-9
Finderne, 5600.....G-10
Finesville, 175.....G-6
Five Points.....Q-8
Flagtown, 600.....H-9
Flanders, 1200.....E-9
Flatbrookville, 5.....C-7
Flemington, 4581.....H-8
Florence, 5500.....K-8
Florham Pk., 11696.....E-11
Folsom, 1885.....O-8
Fords, 15187.....H-11
Forest Grv.....K-3
Forked River, 5244.....M-12
Ft. Lee, 35345.....E-13
Fortescue, 500.....R-6
Foul Rift, 40.....E-6
Franklin, 5045.....C-10
Franklin Pk., 13295.....H-10
Franklinville, 1500.....O-7
Freehold, 12052.....J-11
Freewood Acres, 1900.....J-12
Frenchtown, 1373.....H-7
Fries Mill, 200.....N-7
Gandys Bch., 60.....Q-6
Garfield, 30487.....A-4
Garwood, 4226.....†J-3
Georgetown, 60.....K-9
Germania.....P-9
Gibbsboro, 2274.....M-7
Gibbstown, 3739.....M-5
Gilford Pk.....L-12
Gillette, 900.....F-10
Glassboro, 18579.....N-6
Glen Gardner, 1704.....F-7
Glen Ridge, 7527.....C-2
Glen Rock, 11601.....†B-7
Glendola, 2400.....J-13
Glenwood, 200.....B-10
Gloucester City, 11456.....M-6
GLOUCESTER CO., 288288.....O-7
Golf Mnr., 200.....*D-9
Golf View, 500.....§D-9
Goshen, 600.....R-8
Gouldtown, 700.....P-6
Grassy Sound, 80.....S-3
Great Meadows, 303.....E-7
Great Notch.....A-2
Green Bank, 150.....O-10
Green Brook, 2400.....G-10
Green Creek, 900.....S-8
Green Pond, 900.....D-10
Green Vil., 400.....F-10
Greendell, 200.....D-8
Greenwich, 700.....P-5
Grenloch, 450.....M-7
Griggstown, 819.....H-9
Groveville, 2945.....J-9
Guttenberg, 11176.....C-5
Hackensack, 43010.....E-13
Hackettstown, 9724.....E-8
Haddonfield, 11593.....M-7
Hainesburg, 91.....D-7
Hainesport, 1200.....L-8
Haineville, 100.....B-8
Haledon, 8318.....†B-6
Haleyville, 120.....Q-7
Halsey, 60.....C-9
Hamburg, 3277.....C-10
Hamden.....G-8
Hamilton Sq., 12784.....J-9
Hammonton, 14791.....O-8
Hampton, 1401.....F-7
Hancocks Br., 254.....P-4
Harbourton.....I-8
Harding Lakes, 1000.....P-8
Harlingen, 297.....H-9
Harmersville.....P-4
Harmony, 441.....F-6
Harrington Pk., 4664.....†A-10
Harrison, 27472.....D-3
Harrisonville, 500.....N-5
Hartford, 300.....L-8
Harvey Cedars, 337.....N-12
Hasbrouck Hts., 11842.....B-4
Haven Bch., 200.....O-12
Haworth, 3382.....†B-10
Hawthorne, 18791.....†B-7
Hazen, 30.....E-7
Hazlet, 12000.....H-12
Hedding, 150.....K-9
Heislerville, 500.....R-7
Helmetta, 2178.....I-10
Hewitt, 200.....C-11
Hibernia, 200.....D-10
High Br., 3648.....F-8
Highland Lake, 4933.....B-10
Highland Pk., 13982.....H-10
Highlands, 5005.....I-13
Hightstown, 5494.....J-10
Hillsdale, 10219.....D-13
Hillside, 21747.....E-1
Hoboken, 50005.....F-13
Holgate.....O-11
Holiday City, 800.....L-12
Holly Pk., 700.....M-12
Holmdel, 900.....I-12
Holmeson.....J-11
Hopatcong, 15147.....D-9
Hope, 195.....E-7
Hopelawn, 800.....†M-4
Hopewell, 1922.....I-8
Hornerstown, 150.....K-10
HUDSON CO., 634266.....F-12
HUNTERDON CO., 128349.....G-7
Hurdtown.....D-9
Hurffville, 350.....N-6
Hutchinson, 135.....F-6
Hyson, 2000.....K-11
Imlaystown, 250.....J-10
Indian Mills, 150.....M-9
Interlaken, 820.....J-13
Iona.....O-7
Ironia, 800.....E-9
Irvington, 60695.....E-1
Iselin, 18695.....†L-3
Island Hts., 1673.....L-12
Jacksonburg, 200.....D-7
Jacksons Mills.....K-11
Jacksonville, 125.....K-8
Jacobstown, 150.....K-10
Jamesburg, 5915.....I-10
Jefferson, 125.....N-6
Jenkins, 60.....N-10
Jersey City, 247597.....E-4
Jerseyville, 50.....J-12
Jobstown, 100.....K-9
Johnsonburg, 101.....D-8
Juliustown, 429.....L-9
Keansburg, 10105.....H-12
Kearny, 40684.....D-3
Kendall Pk., 9339.....H-10
Kenilworth, 7914.....†I-4
Kenvil, 3009.....E-9
Keyport, 7240.....H-12
Kingsland.....C-3
Kingston, 700.....H-9
Kinnelon, 10248.....D-11
Kresson, 200.....M-7
Lafayette, 350.....C-9
L. Como, 1759.....J-13
L. Hiawatha.....E-11
L. Hopatcong, 3000.....D-9
L. Lenape, 700.....D-9
L. Pine, 500.....M-8
L. Riviera.....K-12
L. Swannanoa, 1600.....D-10
L. Tamarack, 800.....C-10
L. Telemark, 1255.....D-10
Lakehurst, 2654.....L-11
Lakeside, 400.....B-11
Lakewood, 53805.....K-12
Lambertville, 3906.....I-7
Lamington, 150.....F-9
Lanoka Hbr., 2500.....M-12
Larison's Cor., 15.....H-8
Laurel Lake, 2989.....Q-7
Laureldale, 300.....P-9
Laurelton.....K-12
Laurence Hbr., 6536.....H-12
Lavallette, 1875.....L-13
Lawrenceville, 3887.....I-9
Layton, 250.....B-8
Lebanon, 1358.....G-8
Ledgewood, 1200.....E-9
Leeds Pt., 400.....P-10
Leektown.....O-10
Leesburg, 750.....R-7
Leisuretowne, 3582.....M-9
Leonardo, 2757.....H-13
Leonia, 8937.....B-6
Liberty Corner, 800.....F-10
Lincoln Pk., 10521.....D-11
Lincroft, 6135.....I-12
Linden, 40499.....G-12
Lindenwold, 17613.....M-7
Linvale, 30.....I-8
Linwood, 7092.....Q-10
Little Falls, 11793.....A-1
Little Ferry, 10626.....B-5
Little Silver, 5950.....I-13
Little York, 150.....G-7
Livingston, 27391.....E-11
Loch Arbour, 194.....J-13
Lodi, 24136.....E-13
Long Branch, 30719.....I-13
Long Valley, 1879.....F-8
Longport, 895.....Q-10
Loveladies, 200.....N-12
Lower Bank, 200.....O-10
Lower Squankum.....J-12
Lumberton, 900.....L-8
Lyndhurst, 19383.....C-3
Macopin, 100.....C-11
Madison, 15845.....F-10
Mahwah, 12000.....C-12
Malaga, 2100.....O-7
Manahawkin, 2303.....N-12
Manalapan, 90.....I-11
Manasquan, 5897.....K-13
Mansfield, 40.....K-9
Mansfield Sq.....K-9
Mantoloking, 296.....K-13
Mantua, 2400.....M-6
Manunkachunk, 150.....E-7
Manville, 10344.....G-9
Maple Shade, 18700.....L-7
Maplewood, 23868.....†H-4
Marcella.....D-10
Margate City, 6354.....Q-10
Marksboro, 82.....D-8
Marlboro, 1100.....I-12
Marlton, 10133.....M-7
Marmora, 1700.....R-9
Marshalls Corner.....I-8
Martinsville, 11980.....G-10
Masonville, 400.....L-8
Matawan, 8810.....H-12
Mauricetown, 550.....Q-7
Mayetta, 250.....N-11
Mays, 2135.....P-9
Maywood, 9555.....A-4
McAfee, 1400.....B-10
McKee City, 1200.....P-9
Meadford Farms, 100.....M-9
Meadowbrook Vil., 150.....K-11
Medford, 2400.....L-8
Medford Lakes, 4146.....M-8
Mendham, 4981.....F-9
Menlo Pk. Ter.....†M-3
MERCER CO., 366513.....I-8
Mercerville, 13230.....J-9
Meriden, 80.....D-10
Metedeconk.....K-12
Metuchen, 13574.....G-11
Mickleton, 1200.....M-6
Middle Valley, 150.....F-8
Middlebush, 2326.....H-10
Middlesex, 13635.....G-10
MIDDLESEX CO., 809858.....I-10
Middletown, 24000.....I-12
Middleville, 100.....C-8
Milford, 1233.....G-6
Mill Brook, 1700.....E-10
Millbrook, 5.....C-7
Millburn, 19765.....F-11
Millhurst, 100.....I-11
Millington, 2500.....F-10
Millstone, 418.....H-9
Milltown, 6893.....H-10
Millville, 28400.....P-7
Milmay, 350.....P-8
Milton, 400.....D-10
Mine Hill, 2800.....E-9
Mizpah, 1000.....P-8
Monmouth Bch., 3279.....I-13
MONMOUTH CO., 630380.....J-11
Monmouth Jct., 2887.....H-10
Monroe, 75.....C-9
Monroeville, 200.....O-6
Montague, 40.....A-8
Montclair, 38658.....E-12
Montvale, 7844.....C-13
Montville, 2600.....D-11
Moonachie, 2708.....B-5
Moorestown, 19000.....L-7
Morganville, 5040.....I-12
MORRIS CO., 492276.....E-9
Morris Plains, 5532.....E-10
Morristown, 18411.....E-10
Mt. Airy, 60.....H-8
Mt. Arlington, 5050.....D-9
Mt. Ephraim, 4676.....§G-6
Mt. Freedom, 1900.....E-10
Mt. Hermon, 141.....D-7
Mt. Holly.....L-8
Mt. Hope, 375.....D-10
Mt. Laurel, 300.....L-8
Mt. Pleasant, 120.....G-7
Mt. Royal, 900.....M-6
Mountain Lakes, 4160.....E-10
Mountain View.....D-11
Mountainville, 75.....F-8
Mullica Hill, 3982.....N-6
Mystic Island, 8493.....O-11
National Pk., 3036.....§G-4
Naughright, 100.....F-9
Navesink, 2020.....I-13
Neptune, 19000.....J-13
Neptune City, 4869.....J-13
Nesco.....O-9
Neshanic, 150.....H-9
Neshanic Sta., 500.....H-9
Netcong, 3232.....E-9
New Brooklyn, 4000.....N-7
New Brunswick, 55181.....H-10
New Egypt, 2512.....K-10
New Gretna, 600.....O-10
New Hampton, 200.....F-7
New Lisbon, 350.....L-9
New Market, 20000.....†L-1
New Milford, 16341.....†B-10
New Providence, 12171.....F-10
New Sharon.....J-10
New Vernon, 600.....F-10
New Vil., 421.....F-6
Newark, 277140.....F-12
Newfield, 1553.....O-7
Newfoundland, 400.....C-10
Newport, 700.....Q-6
Newton, 7997.....C-8
Newtonville, 200.....O-8
Norma, 400.....P-6
Normandy Bch.....L-13
N. Arlington, 15392.....C-3
N. Beach, 200.....N-12
N. Beach Haven, 2235.....O-12
N. Bergen.....C-5
N. Branch, 1300.....G-9
N. Caldwell, 6183.....B-1
N. Cape May, 3226.....T-7
N. Church, 100.....C-9
N. Haledon, 8417.....†B-6
N. Plainfield, 21936.....G-10
N. Wildwood, 4041.....T-8
Northfield, 8624.....Q-10
Northvale, 4640.....D-13
Norton, 60.....G-7
Nortonville, 100.....M-4
Nutley, 27362.....E-12
Oak Ridge, 900.....C-10
Oak Ridge Estates, 1600.....L-12
Oakhurst, 3995.....J-13
Oakland, 12754.....D-11
Oaklyn, 4038.....§F-6
Oakwood Bch., 200.....O-4
Ocean Bch., 1800.....L-13
Ocean City, 11701.....Q-10
OCEAN CO., 576567.....M-11
Ocean Gate, 2011.....L-12
Ocean Grv., 3342.....J-13
Ocean View, 200.....R-9
Oceanport, 5832.....I-13
Oceanville, 300.....P-10
Ogdensburg, 2410.....C-9
Old Br., 23753.....H-11
Old Tappan, 5750.....D-13
Oldwick, 200.....F-9
Olivet, 1408.....O-6
Oradell, 7978.....†B-9
Orange, 32868.....D-1
Ortley Bch., 1500.....L-13
Osbornsville.....K-12
Othello.....P-5
Oxford, 1090.....E-7
Oyster Creek.....P-11
Palermo, 1200.....R-9
Palisades Pk., 19622.....B-6
Palmyra, 7398.....L-7
Paradise Lakes, 150.....O-5
Paramus, 26342.....D-13
Parkertown, 800.....O-11
Parkway Pines, 1100.....K-12
Parsippany.....E-10
Passaic, 69781.....E-12
PASSAIC CO., 501226.....C-11
Paterson, 146199.....D-12
Pattenburg, 150.....G-7
Paulina, 100.....D-7
Paulsboro, 6097.....M-6
Peapack & Gladstone, 2582.....F-9
Pebble Bch., 2000.....N-12
Pedricktown, 524.....N-4
Pemberton, 1409.....L-9
Pennington, 2585.....I-8
Penns Grv., 5147.....N-4
Pennsville, 11888.....N-4
Penton, 70.....O-4
Penwell, 50.....F-8
Pequannock.....D-11
Perrineville, 400.....J-10
Perth Amboy, 50814.....H-11
Petersburg, 900.....R-9
Phillipsburg, 14950.....F-6
Pierces Pt., 40.....S-8
Pine Bch., 2127.....L-12
Pine Hill, 10233.....M-7
Pine Lake Pk., 8707.....L-12
Pinewald, 1700.....M-12
Piscataway, 56044.....H-10
Pitman, 9011.....N-6
Pittstown, 600.....G-7
Plainfield, 49808.....G-10
Plainsboro, 2000.....I-9
Pleasant Grv.....F-8
Pleasant Mills.....O-9
Pleasant Plains.....L-12
Pleasant Run.....G-8
Pleasant Valley, 200.....F-7
Pleasantville, 20249.....Q-10
Pluckemin, 300.....G-9
Plumbsock.....B-9
Pt. Pleasant, 18392.....K-13
Pt. Pleasant Bch., 4665.....K-13
Pointers, 200.....O-4
Polkville.....D-7
Pomona, 7124.....P-10
Pompton Lakes, 11097.....D-11
Pompton Plains.....D-11
Port Colden, 122.....F-7
Port Elizabeth, 650.....Q-7
Port Monmouth, 3818.....H-12
Port Murray, 129.....F-7
Port Norris, 1377.....R-7
Port Reading, 3728.....†L-5
Port Republic, 1115.....O-10
Potterstown, 100.....G-8
Pottersville, 600.....F-9
Princeton, 12307.....I-9
Princeton Jct., 2465.....I-9
Prospect Pk., 5865.....†B-6
Pumptown, 2000.....†L-2
Quakertown, 200.....G-7
Quinton, 588.....O-4
Rahway, 27346.....†K-4
Ralston, 150.....F-9
Ramblewood, 5907.....L-7
Ramsey, 14473.....C-12
Ramtown, 6242.....K-12
Rancocas, 500.....L-8
Rancocas Hts., 750.....§D-10
Rancocas Woods, 1400.....§D-10
Raritan, 6881.....G-9
Raven Rock.....H-7
Readington, 500.....G-9
Reaville, 250.....H-8
Red Bank, 12206.....I-13
Red Bank, 1100.....§G-4
Red Lion.....M-9
Reeds Bch., 70.....S-8
Repaupo, 100.....M-5
Richland, 600.....P-8
Richwood, 3459.....N-6
Ridgefield, 11032.....B-5
Ridgefield Pk., 12729.....B-5
Ridgeway.....K-11
Ridgewood, 24958.....†A-7
Riegel Ridge, 250.....G-6
Riegelsville, 150.....G-6
Ringoes, 600.....H-8
Ringwood, 12228.....C-11
Rio Grande, 2670.....S-8
River Edge, 11340.....†B-9
River Vale, 9449.....†A-10
Riverdale, 3559.....‡C-12
Riverside.....K-7
Riverton, 2779.....L-7
Roadstown, 200.....P-5
Robbinsville, 3041.....J-9
Robertsville, 11297.....I-11
Rochelle Pk., 5528.....A-4
Rockaway, 6438.....E-10
Rocky Hill, 682.....I-9
Roebling, 3715.....K-8
Roosevelt, 882.....J-10
Roosevelt City, 35.....L-11
Roselle, 21085.....F-1
Roselle Pk., 13297.....†J-4
Rosemont, 185.....H-7
Rosenhayn, 1098.....P-6
Ross Corner, 13.....C-9
Roxburg, 120.....F-6
Rudeville.....C-10
Rumson, 7122.....I-13
Runnemede, 8468.....M-7
Rutherford, 18061.....B-3
Saddle Brook, 13155.....A-4
Salem, 5146.....O-4
SALEM CO., 66083.....O-5
Sand Brook.....H-7
Saxton Falls, 100.....E-8
Sayerwood South, 10000.....I-11
Sayreville, 42704.....H-11
Schooleys Mtn., 200.....E-8
Scobeyville, 15.....I-12
Scotch Plains, 22732.....G-11
Scullville, 40.....Q-9
Sea Breeze, 50.....Q-5
Sea Bright, 1412.....I-13
Sea Girt, 1828.....K-13
Sea Isle City, 2114.....R-9
Seabrook, 1340.....P-6
Seabrook Farms, 1484.....P-6
Seaside Hts., 2887.....L-13
Seaside Pk., 1579.....L-13
Seaville, 300.....R-9
Secaucus, 16264.....C-4
Sergeantsville, 400.....H-7
Sewaren, 2756.....†M-4
Sewell, 2000.....N-6
Sharptown, 120.....N-5
Shiloh, 516.....P-5
Ship Bottom, 1156.....O-12
Shirley.....O-6
Shore Acres.....L-12
Short Hills.....F-11
Shrewsbury, 3809.....I-13
Sicklerville, 1800.....N-7
Sidney, 250.....G-8
Silverton, 4800.....L-12
Singac, 3618.....A-1
Skillman, 242.....H-9
Slackwoods, 6000.....J-9
Smithburg.....J-11
Smithville, 7242.....P-10
Somerdale, 5151.....M-7
Somers Pt., 10795.....Q-9
SOMERSET CO., 323444.....H-9
Somerville, 12098.....G-9
S. Amboy, 8631.....H-11
S. Bound Brook, 4563.....G-10
S. Branch, 150.....G-9
S. Dennis, 350.....R-8
S. Egg Hbr., 600.....O-9
S. Hackensack, 2106.....A-5
S. Orange, 16964.....D-1
S. Plainfield, 23385.....G-11
S. River, 16008.....H-11
S. Seaside Pk., 400.....L-13
S. Seaville, 500.....R-8
S. Toms River, 3684.....L-12
Sparta, 1900.....D-9
Spotswood, 8257.....I-11
Spray Bch., 200.....O-12
Spring Lake, 2993.....J-13
Spring Lake Hts., 4713.....J-13
Spring Mills, 125.....G-6
Springdale, 400.....D-8
Springfield, 14429.....F-11
Springside, 1600.....K-8
Springtown, 100.....G-6
Springville, 200.....L-8
Staffordville, 150.....N-11
Stanhope, 3610.....E-9
Stanton, 100.....G-8
Stanton Sta.....G-8
Stanwick Glen, 300.....§D-8
Star Cross, 150.....O-7
Stephensburg, 100.....E-8
Stevens, 300.....K-8
Stewartsville, 349.....F-6
Stillwater, 200.....C-8
Stirling, 1800.....F-10
Stockholm, 200.....C-10
Stockton, 538.....H-7
Stone Hbr., 866.....S-8
Strathmere, 158.....R-9
Succasunna, 9152.....E-9
Summit, 21457.....F-11
Surf City, 1205.....N-12
Sussex, 2130.....B-9
SUSSEX CO., 149265.....B-9
Swainton.....S-8
Swartswood, 250.....C-8
Swedesboro, 2584.....N-5
Sweetwater, 150.....O-9
Sykesville, 60.....K-9
Tabernacle, 150.....M-9
Tansboro, 300.....N-7
Taunton Lake, 250.....M-8
Taylortown, 150.....D-11
Teaneck, 39260.....A-5
Tenafly, 14488.....‡C-11
Tennent, 100.....I-11
Teterboro, 67.....B-5
Thorofare, 1700.....M-6
Three Bridges, 500.....H-8
Tinton Falls, 17892.....I-12
Titusville, 900.....I-8
Toms River, 88791.....L-12
Totowa, 10804.....E-12
Town Bank, 1500.....T-7
Townley.....F-1
Townsbury, 50.....E-7
Tranquility, 100.....D-8
Trenton, 84913.....J-8
Troy Hills.....E-11
Tuckahoe, 800.....Q-8
Tuckerton, 3347.....O-11
Turnersville, 3742.....N-7
Twin Rivers, 7443.....I-10
Union, 54405.....F-11
Union Bch., 6245.....H-12
Union City, 66455.....D-5
UNION CO., 536499.....G-11
Uniontown, 120.....F-6
Upper Saddle River, 8208.....C-12
Vail, 30.....D-7
Vanhiseville, 80.....K-11
Ventnor City, 10650.....Q-10
Verga, 800.....§G-4
Vernon, 250.....B-10
Verona, 13533.....B-1
Victory Gdns., 1520.....E-10
Vienna, 981.....E-8
Villas, 9483.....S-7
Vincentown, 900.....L-9
Vineland, 60724.....P-7
Wading River, 30.....O-10
Wallington, 11335.....B-4
Wallpack Ctr., 20.....C-8
Walnut Valley, 80.....D-7
Wanamassa, 4532.....J-13
Wanaque, 11116.....D-11
Waretown, 1569.....M-12
WARREN CO., 108692.....E-8
Warren Glen, 300.....G-6
Warren Grv.....N-11
Warrenville, 1000.....G-10
Washington, 6461.....F-7
Washington Crossing, 500.....I-8
Watchung, 5801.....G-10
Waterford Works, 1000.....N-8
Wayne, 54069.....D-11
Weehawken.....D-5
Weekstown, 140.....O-9
Wenonah, 2278.....M-6
W. Atlantic City, 900.....Q-10
W. Cape May, 1024.....T-7
W. Collingswood Hts., 1000.....§F-5
W. Creek, 800.....O-11
W. Freehold, 13613.....J-11
W. Keansburg, 1500.....H-12
W. Long Branch, 8097.....I-13
W. Milford, 26410.....C-11
W. New York, 49708.....E-13
W. Orange, 44943.....F-12
W. Paterson, 10987.....A-2
W. Portal, 100.....F-7
W. Tuckerton, 700.....O-11
W. Wildwood, 603.....T-8
Westfield, 30316.....†J-3
Westville, 4500.....§G-5
Westville Grv., 1500.....§G-5
Westwood, 10908.....†A-9
Weymouth, 200.....P-8
Wharton, 6522.....E-10
Whippany.....E-10
White Horse, 9494.....T-13
White House Sta., 2089.....G-8
Whitehouse, 800.....G-9
Whitesbog.....L-10
Whitesboro, 1100.....S-8
Whitesville, 120.....K-11
Whiting, 950.....L-11
Whitman Sq., 3500.....N-7
Wickatunk, 300.....I-12
Wildwood, 5325.....T-8
Wildwood Crest, 3270.....T-8
Williamstown, 15567.....N-7
Willingboro.....K-8
Willow Grv.....K-3
Windsor, 250.....J-9
Winslow, 800.....N-8
Woodbine, 2472.....R-8
Woodbridge, 19265.....G-11
Woodbury, 10174.....M-6
Woodbury Hts., 3055.....M-6
Woodglen, 150.....F-8
Wood-Lynne, 2978.....§F-5
Woodport, 200.....D-9
Wood-Ridge, 7626.....B-4
Woodruff, 70.....P-6
Woods Tavern, 200.....H-9
Woodstown, 3505.....N-5
Wrightstown, 802.....K-9
Wyckoff, 16508.....D-12
Yardville, 7186.....J-9
Yellow Frame.....D-8
Yorktown, 50.....O-5
Zarephath, 37.....G-10

New Mexico

Page locator
Map keys Atlas pages
A–N 138–139

Abbott.....C-8
Abiquiu, 231.....C-5
Acoma, 400.....E-3
Acomita, 800.....E-3
Adobe Acres, 2500.....N-8
Agua Fria, 2800.....M-4
Alameda.....E-4
Alamillo, 102.....F-4
Alamogordo, 30403.....I-6
Albert, 30.....C-9
Albuquerque, 545852.....E-4
Alcalde, 285.....C-5
Algodones, 814.....D-5
Alma, 100.....H-1
Alto, 800.....H-6
Amalia, 200.....A-6
Ambrosia Lake.....D-3
Amistad, 30.....C-10
Anaconda, 200.....E-3
Ancho.....G-6
Angel Fire, 1216.....B-7
Animas, 237.....J-1
Antelope Wells.....L-2
Anthony, 9360.....J-5
Anton Chico, 188.....E-7
Arabela.....H-7
Aragon, 94.....G-2
Arch.....G-10
Arenas Valley, 1522.....I-2
Armijo.....E-4
Arrey, 232.....I-3
Arroyo Hondo, 474.....B-6
Arroyo Seco, 1785.....B-6
Artesia, 11301.....I-8
Atoka, 1077.....I-8
Atrisco.....M-7
Aztec, 6763.....B-3
Bayard, 2328.....I-2
Beaverhead, 30.....H-2
Beclabito, 317.....B-1
Belen, 7269.....F-4
Bell Ranch, 20.....D-8
Bellview.....E-10
Bennett.....J-10
Bent, 119.....H-6
Berino, 1441.....J-4
Bernalillo, 8320.....D-5
BERNALILLO CO., 662564.....E-4
Black Lake.....C-7
Black River Vil.....J-8
Black Rock, 1323.....E-1
Blanco, 388.....B-3
Bloomfield, 8112.....B-3
Bluewater, 628.....E-3
Boles, 450.....I-5
Bosque Farms, 3904.....E-4
Brazos, 44.....B-5
Broadview, 30.....E-10
Buckhorn, 200.....I-1
Bueyeros, 30.....C-9
Butterfield Pk., 500.....I-4
Caballo, 112.....I-3
Canjilon, 256.....B-5
Canon, 327.....D-4
Capitan, 1489.....H-6
Caprock, 30.....H-9
Capulin, 66.....B-8
Carlsbad, 26138.....J-8
Carrizozo, 996.....G-6
CATRON CO., 3725.....G-2
Causey, 104.....G-10
Cebolla, 100.....B-5
Cedar Crest, 958.....E-5
Cedar Hill, 847.....A-3
Cedarvale, 20.....F-6
Cerro, 250.....B-6
Chacon, 250.....C-6
Chama, 1022.....B-5
Chamberino, 919.....J-4
Chamisal, 310.....C-6
Chaparral, 14631.....J-5
CHAVES CO., 65645.....G-9
Chilili, 137.....E-5
Chimayo, 3177.....C-6
Chloride, 50.....H-3
Church Rock, 1128.....D-2
CIBOLA CO., 27213.....E-2
Cimarron, 1021.....B-7
Claunch, 3025.....G-5
Clayton, 2980.....B-10
Cliff, 293.....I-1
Clines Corners, 90.....E-6
Cloudcroft, 674.....I-6
Clovis, 37775.....F-10
Cochiti, 528.....D-5
COLFAX CO., 13750.....B-7
Colonias, 30.....E-7
Columbus, 1664.....K-3
Conchas Dam, 186.....D-8
Continental Divide, 250.....D-2
Cordova, 414.....C-6
Corona, 172.....F-6
Corrales, 8329.....E-5
Costilla, 205.....A-6
Cotton City, 388.....J-1
Counselor, 40.....C-3
Coyote, 128.....C-5
Coyote Canyon, 200.....D-2
Crossroads, 50.....H-10
Crownpoint, 2278.....D-2
Cruzville, 72.....G-1
Crystal, 311.....C-1
Cuba, 731.....C-4
Cubero, 289.....E-3
Cuchillo, 70.....H-3
Cuervo, 90.....E-8
CURRY CO., 48376.....F-9
Dalton Pass, 100.....D-2
Datil, 54.....G-3
DE BACA CO., 2022.....F-8
Deming, 14855.....J-3
Derry, 120.....I-4
Des Moines, 143.....B-9
Dexter, 1266.....H-8
Dilia, 80.....E-7
Dixon, 926.....C-6
Doña Ana, 1211.....J-4
DOÑA ANA CO., 209233.....J-4
Dora, 133.....G-10
Dulce, 2743.....B-4
Duran, 35.....F-6
Dusty, 30.....G-3
Eagle Nest, 290.....B-7
EDDY CO., 53829.....J-8
Edgewood, 3735.....E-5
El Morro, 100.....E-2
El Porvenir, 100.....D-6
El Pueblo, 50.....D-6
El Rito, 808.....C-5
El Vado.....B-4
Elephant Butte, 1431.....H-4
Elida, 197.....G-9
Elk.....I-7
Encino, 82.....F-6
Engle.....H-4
Ensenada, 107.....B-5
Escabosa, 150.....E-5
Espanola, 10224.....C-5
Estancia, 1655.....E-5
Eunice, 2922.....J-10
Fairacres, 824.....M-1
Farley.....C-8
Farmington, 45877.....B-2
Fence Lake, 42.....F-1
Field.....F-9
Five Points, 4200.....M-8
Flora Vista, 2191.....B-2
Floyd, 133.....F-9
Flying H, 50.....I-7
Folsom, 56.....B-8
Forrest, 60.....F-9
Ft. Stanton, 100.....H-6
Ft. Sumner, 1031.....F-8
Ft. Wingate, 950.....D-2
Fruitland.....B-2
Galisteo, 253.....D-6
Gallina, 286.....C-4
Gallup, 21678.....D-1
Gamerco, 400.....D-1
Garfield, 137.....I-4
Garson.....C-6
Gila, 314.....I-2
Gila Hot Sprs., 40.....H-2
Gladstone, 50.....C-8
Glenrio, 30.....E-10
Glenwood, 143.....H-1
Glorieta, 430.....D-6
Golden, 37.....E-5

*, †, ‡, §, ◊ See explanation under state title in this index.
County and parish names are listed in capital letters & boldface type.
Independent cities (not included in a county) are listed in italics.

*, †, ‡, §, ◊   See explanation under state title in this index.
County and parish names are listed in CAPITAL LETTERS & boldface type.
Independent cities (not included in a county) are listed in italics.

E. Monroe, 120......SE-7
E. Norwalk, 80......NG-11
E. Palestine, 4721......NL-20
E. Richland, 300......NN-18
E. Rochester, 231......NJ-18
E. Sparta, 819......NJ-16
E. Springfield, 350......NL-19
E. Townsend, 80......NG-11
E. Trumbull, 80......NE-18
E. Union, 30......SE-6
Eastlake, 18577......NE-16
Easton, 200......NI-15
Eastview......SL-9
Eaton, 8407......SC-2
Eaton Estates, 1222......NG-13
Eber, 300......SD-7
Eckmansville......SH-6
Eden Pk., 430......SE-7
Edenton, 300......SF-4
Edgerton, 2012......NF-1
Edgewater Pk., 700......SB-10
Edgewood, 4432......NC-19
Edinburg, 250......NH-17
Edison, 437......NK-10
Edon, 834......NE-1
Elba, 70......SD-16
Eldorado, 509......NG-4
Elery, 25......NG-4
Elgin, 57......NJ-2
Elida, 1905......NJ-4
Elizabethtown, 350......SF-1
Elkton, 80......NJ-19
Ellerton......SE-4
Elliot Crossroads......SD-14
Ellisonville, 50......SJ-1
Ellsberry, 60......SL-4
Ellsworth, 280......NH-18
Elm Grv., 25......SG-8
Elmore, 1410......NH-8
Elmwood Pl., 2188......SL-3
Elroy, 35......NM-1
Elyria, 54533......NF-13
Empire, 299......NK-20
Englewood, 13465......SB-3
Enon, 2415......SB-5
Enterprise, 170......SD-12
Epworth......NI-11
Epworth Hts., 150......SK-6
Era, 130......SC-8
ERIE CO., 77079......NF-11
Eris, 25......NN-5
Erlin, 80......NF-9
Espyville, 80......NK-8
Essex, 90......NI-1
Etna, 1215......SB-11
Euclid, 48920......NE-15
Eureka, 100......SL-13
Evansport, 300......NF-3
Evansville, 200......NC-12
Evendale, 2767......SK-4
Everett, 25......NG-15
Ewing, 30......SL-12
Ewington, 65......SG-12
Excello, 50......SC-8
Fairborn, 32352......SB-5
Fairfax, 1699......SL-4
Fairfax, 40......SD-2
Fairfield, 42510......SE-2
Fairfield, 50......NL-8
FAIRFIELD CO., 146156......SB-11
Fairhaven, 200......SC-1
Fairhope, 1720......NJ-17
Fairlawn, 7437......NH-15
Fairpoint, 500......NN-18
Fairport Hbr., 3109......ND-17
Fairview, 83......SB-16
Fairview, 50......SF-6
Fairview Lanes, 1000......NF-10
Fairview Pk., 16826......NF-14
Falsburg, 200......NM-12
Farmdale, 200......NF-20
Farmer, 120......NF-2
Farmers, 45......SE-6
Farmerstown, 330......NL-15
Farmersville, 1009......SC-3
Fawcett......NF-17
Fayette, 1283......NE-3
FAYETTE CO., 29030......SD-8
Fayetteville, 330......SF-5
Feesburg, 500......SF-4
Felicity, 818......SH-4
Fernald, 25......SJ-1
Fernell Hts., 330......SM-6
Fincastle, 85......SG-6
Findlay, 41202......NH-6
Finneytown, 12741......SK-3
Firestone Pk.......NL-15
Fitchville, 350......NH-11
Five Points, 1824......SD-4
Five Points, 30......SD-4
Fivemile......SG-5
Flat Rock, 233......NG-9
Fleming, 40......SE-16
Fletcher, 473......NN-4
Florence, 200......NG-12
Florence, 150......NN-9
Florence, 50......SC-16
Florida, 232......NG-4
Flushing, 879......NN-18
Fly, 80......NC-18
Footville......NE-18
Foraker, 130......NJ-7
Forest, 1461......NJ-7
Forest Hill......NB-8
Forest Hills, 200......NA-15
Forest Pk., 18720......SF-2
Forestville, 10532......SL-3
Ft. Jefferson, 80......NA-2
Ft. Jennings, 485......NI-3
Ft. Loramie, 1478......NL-3
Ft. McKinley, 3989......SL-7
Ft. Recovery, 1430......NL-1
Ft. Seneca, 234......NG-8
Ft. Shawnee, 3726......NJ-4
Foster......SE-3
Fosterville......NB-7
Fostoria, 13441......NH-7
Fowler, 250......NG-19
Fowlers Mill, 320......NE-17
Fox, 25......SD-9
Frankfort, 1064......SE-9
Franklin, 11771......SD-3
FRANKLIN CO., 1163414......NN-10
Franklin Furnace, 1660......SI-10
Franklin Sq., 240......NN-19
Frazeysburg, 1316......NN-13
Frederick, 150......NB-4
Fredericksburg, 423......NJ-14
Fredericksdale, 50......SC-16
Fredericktown, 2493......NN-11

Fredericktown, 200......NJ-20
Freeburg, 90......NN-17
Freedom, 90......NG-17
Freeport, 369......NM-17
Fremont, 16734......NG-8
Frenchtown, 60......NM-2
Fresno, 140......NL-15
Friendship, 351......SJ-10
Fruit Hill, 3755......SM-3
Fruitdale, 50......SE-7
Fryburg, 150......NK-4
Frytown, 45......SC-3
Fulda, 40......SC-16
Fulton, 258......NL-10
FULTON CO., 42698......NE-3
Fultonham, 176......SB-13
Funk, 110......NI-13
Gahanna, 33248......SA-10
Galena, 653......NN-9
Galion, 10512......NJ-10
Gallia......SH-11
GALLIA CO., 30934......SH-12
Gallipolis, 3641......SH-13
Galloway, 250......NN-9
Gano, 200......SF-3
Garden Acres, 250......NB-17
Garden City, 300......SL-10
Garfield, 110......NI-18
Garfield Hts., 28849......NF-15
GEAUGA CO., 93389......NE-17
Geneva, 6215......ND-18
Geneva-on-the-Lake, 1288......ND-18
Genoa, 2336......NF-7
Georges Run, 400......NM-20
Georgesville, 160......SB-8
Georgetown, 4331......SH-5
Georgetown, 150......NM-18
Gephart......SI-10
Gerald, 50......NJ-8
Germano, 200......NL-18
Germantown, 5547......SD-3
Germantown, 35......SD-17
Getaway, 100......SJ-12
Gettysburg, 513......NN-2
Gettysburg, 80......NG-4
Ghent, 1600......NH-15
Gibisonville, 130......SF-11
Gilboa, 184......NH-5
Gillivan......SB-8
Gilmore, 85......NM-16
Ginghamsburg, 250......SB-4
Girard, 9958......NH-19
Givens, 75......SG-10
Gladstone, 30......SC-6
Glandorf, 1001......NH-4
Glasgow, 40......NJ-19
Glasgow, 150......NN-19
Glen Este, 350......SM-6
Glen Karn, 40......SA-1
Glen Roy, 100......SG-12
Glencoe, 310......NN-19
Glendale, 2155......SJ-3
Glenford, 150......SB-12
Glenmont, 272......NK-13
Glenmoor, 1987......NJ-20
Glenmore, 50......NK-19
Glouster, 1791......SD-13
Gnadenhutten, 1288......NL-16
Goes, 100......SC-5
Golf Manor, 3611......SL-4
Gomer, 350......NI-4
Good Hope, 234......SE-8
Goodyear Hts.......NH-15
Gordon, 212......SB-2
Gore, 240......SE-14
Goshen, 730......SF-4
Goshen, 200......NL-16
Gould Pk.......SG-20
Grafton, 6636......NG-13
Grand Rapids, 965......NF-5
Grand River, 399......ND-17
Grandview, 699......NB-18
Grandview Hts., 6536......SB-9
Grandview Hts., 170......NN-4
Grange Hall, 200......SB-8
Granger, 90......NH-15
Grant, 60......NJ-6
Grantville, 5646......NN-17
Granville, 5409......NM-12
Grape Grv., 35......SC-6
Gratiot, 221......SB-13
Gratis, 881......SC-2
Graysville, 76......SC-18
Graytown, 180......NG-8
Green Camp, 374......NK-8
Green Sprs., 1368......NG-9
Greenbush......SD-2
Greenbush......SC-10
Greencastle......SC-10
Greendale, 80......SD-13
GREENE CO., 161573......SC-6
Greenfield, 4639......SE-7
Greenford, 700......NJ-19
Greenhills, 3615......SJ-3
Greenland......SE-9
Greensburg, 600......NI-16
Greentown, 3804......NJ-16
Greenview......SA-13
Greenville, 13227......NN-2
Greenwich, 1476......NH-11
Greenwood, 40......SG-8
Greer, 50......NK-12
Grelton, 110......NG-4
Groesbeck, 6788......SK-2
Grove City, 35575......SB-9
Groveport, 5363......SJ-20
Grover Hill, 400......NH-3
Guerne, 250......NH-11
Guernsey, 50......NM-16
GUERNSEY CO., 40087......NM-16
Guilford, 320......NJ-18
Gurneyville......NN-7
Gustavus......NF-19
Gutman, 35......NK-4
Guysville, 250......SF-14
Gypsum, 200......NF-9
Hackney, 40......NB-17
Hallock, 100......NE-2
Hallsville, 230......SD-10
Hambden, 180......NE-17
Hamburg......SH-4
Hamden, 879......SF-11

Hamersville, 546......SH-5
Hamilton, 62477......SE-2
HAMILTON CO., 802374......SF-1
Hamilton Meadows, 2100......SB-9
Hamler, 576......NG-4
Hamlet, 160......SG-4
Hammansburg, 100......NG-6
Hammondsville, 400......NK-19
HANCOCK CO., 74782......NI-5
Hanging Rock, 221......SJ-10
Hanley Vil.......NL-12
Hannibal, 411......NC-19
Hanover, 921......NN-12
Hanover......NL-18
Hanoverton, 408......NJ-18
Harbor View, 123......ND-7
Hardin, 80......NM-3
HARDIN CO., 32058......NJ-6
Harlem, 150......NN-10
Harlem Sprs., 80......NK-18
Harmon, 250......NJ-15
Harmony, 250......SB-6
Harper, 70......NL-6
Harpersfield......ND-18
Harpster, 200......NJ-8
Harriett, 30......NG-3
Harriettsville, 60......SD-17
Harrington, 320......SC-8
Harrisburg, 500......NI-17
Harrison, 9897......SF-1
HARRISON CO., 15864......NM-17
Harrisville, 150......SJ-13
Harrisville, 298......NN-18
Harrod, 417......NJ-5
Hartford, 350......NG-20
Hartland......NH-11
Hartsgrove, 300......NE-18
Hartsville......SC-17
Hartville, 2944......NI-16
Harveysburg, 546......SD-5
Haselton......ND-4
Haskins, 1188......NF-6
Hatton, 50......NJ-5
Havana, 100......NH-16
Havensport, 60......SC-11
Haverhill, 120......SJ-10
Haviland, 215......NH-2
Haydenville, 381......SD-12
Hayesville, 448......NJ-12
Heath, 10310......SA-12
Hebbardsville, 50......SF-13
Hebron, 2336......SB-12
Hecla, 200......NJ-17
Helena, 224......NG-8
Hemlock, 155......SD-13
Hemlock Grv., 70......SG-14
Hendrysburg, 150......NN-17
Henry, 50......NM-10
HENRY CO., 28215......NG-4
Hepburn, 100......NJ-6
Hessville, 214......NF-8
Hicksville, 3581......NG-1
Higginsport, 251......SI-5
Highland, 254......SE-8
HIGHLAND CO., 43589......SF-6
Highland Hts., 8345......SK-20
Highland Hills, 1130......SM-19
Highland Pk., 700......NJ-15
Highlandtown......NK-19
Highpoint, 1503......NJ-5
Hill Grv., 100......NM-1
Hilliard, 28435......NA-8
Hills & Dales, 221......NB-9
Hillsboro, 6605......SF-6
Hinckley, 500......NG-14
Hiram, 1406......NG-17
Hiram Rapids, 250......NF-17
Hiramsburg......SD-16
Hitchcock......SH-11
Hoagland, 50......NE-2
Holgate, 1109......NG-4
Holiday City, 50......NF-2
Holland, 1784......NB-1
Hollansburg, 227......SA-1
Holloway, 338......NM-17
Holmesville, 372......NK-14
Homer, 250......NM-11
Homerville, 80......NH-13
Homeworth, 481......NJ-18
Honeytown, 40......NK-14
Hooker......NE-2
Hooven, 534......SF-1
Hopedale, 950......NM-18
Hopetown, 50......SE-9
Hopewell, 250......SB-13
Hopkinsville......SF-12
Hoskinsville, 50......SC-15
Houcktown, 180......NI-6
Houston, 220......NM-3
Howard, 242......NL-12
Howenstein, 160......NJ-17
Howland Ctr.......NG-19
Hoytville, 303......NG-5
Hubbard, 7874......NH-20
Huber Hts., 38101......SB-4
Huber Pk., 4604......SF-19
Hudson, 22262......NG-16
Hulington, 100......SB-4
Hunter......SB-18
Hunting Valley, 705......NF-16
Huntington, 226......NL-8
Huntsburg, 300......NE-17
Huntsville, 431......NK-5
Huron, 7149......NF-11
HURON CO., 59626......NH-11
Hustead, 100......SB-5
Hyatts, 50......NN-9
Iberia, 452......NK-10
Idaho, 50......SG-4
Iler......SL-10
Ilesboro......NL-18
Independence, 7133......NF-15
Independence, 100......NJ-16
Ingomar......NL-18
Irondale, 387......NK-19
Ironspot, 50......SB-13
Ironton, 11129......NK-17
Irwin......SK-7
Irwin, 50......SA-7
Island View, 300......NK-5

Isle St. George, 50......ND-10
Isleta......NM-15
Ithaca, 136......SB-2
Jackson, 6397......SG-11
Jackson Ctr., 1462......NL-4
JACKSON CO., 33225......SH-11
Jacksonburg, 63......SD-2
Jacksontown, 350......SB-12
Jacksonville, 481......SD-13
Jacksonville, 75......SN-17
Jacobsburg, 200......SB-19
Jamestown, 1993......SC-6
Jasper, 250......SG-9
Jasper Mills, 40......SD-7
Jaysville, 30......NM-2
Jefferson, 3120......ND-19
Jeffersonville, 1203......SC-7
Jelloway, 90......NK-12
Jenera, 221......NI-5
Jericho, 200......SE-3
Jerome, 200......NN-8
Jeromesville, 562......NJ-13
Jersey City, 427......NG-6
Jersey, 250......NN-10
Jerusalem, 161......SB-18
Jewell, 250......NF-3
Jewett, 692......NL-18
Johnston, 250......NF-19
Johnstown, 4632......NN-10
Jonestown, 80......NJ-2
Joy......SE-14
Junction, 100......NG-2
Junction City, 819......SC-12
Justus, 100......NJ-16
Kalida, 1542......NI-4
Kanauga, 125......SH-13
Kansas, 179......NG-8
Keene, 100......NM-15
Kelleys Island, 312......NE-10
Kellogsville, 200......NC-19
Kemp, 70......SI-6
Kendall Hts., 850......NI-8
Kennard, 40......NM-6
Kennonsburg, 50......SB-17
Kensington, 320......NJ-18
Kent, 28904......NH-16
Kenton, 8262......NJ-6
Kenwood, 6981......SK-4
Kerr, 90......SH-13
Kessler, 150......SB-3
Kettering, 56163......SC-4
Kettlersville, 179......NL-3
Key......NJ-19
Kidron, 944......NJ-15
Kieferville, 40......NI-3
Kilbourne, 139......NM-9
Kileville, 25......NN-8
Kilgore, 100......NL-18
Killbuck, 817......NL-13
Kimball, 110......NM-9
Kimberly, 40......SE-13
Kimbolton, 144......NN-15
Kingman......NB-8
Kings Creek, 300......NN-6
Kings Mills, 1319......SE-3
Kingston, 1032......SE-10
Kingsville, 650......NC-19
Kingsway......NF-8
Kinnikinnick, 65......SE-9
Kinsman, 600......NF-20
Kiousville......SB-8
Kipling, 150......SA-16
Kipton, 243......NG-12
Kirby, 118......NJ-7
Kirkersville, 525......SB-11
Kirkpatrick, 80......NJ-9
Kirkwood, 60......NM-1
Kitts Hill, 200......NK-17
Klondike, 250......NK-19
Knockemstiff......SF-9
Knockoff......NL-18
KNOX CO., 60921......NM-12
Knoxville, 180......NK-19
Kossuth, 80......NK-3
Kunkle, 246......NE-2
Kyger, 60......SH-13
La Croft, 1144......NK-20
La Grange, 70......NG-13
La Rue, 747......NK-7
Lacarne, 200......NF-9
Lafayette, 445......NI-5
Lafayette, 250......SB-7
Lafayette, 250......NL-17
Lafferty, 304......NN-18
Lagrange, 2103......NG-13
Laings, 30......SC-18
L. Cable, 250......NB-9
Lake, 350......NK-3
Lakeland......NC-18
Lakemore, 3068......NI-16
Lakeside, 694......NE-10
Lakeside, 200......NN-19
Lakeview, 1072......NL-5
Lakeville, 130......NK-14
Lakewood, 52131......NF-14
Lancaster, 38780......SC-11
Landeck, 100......NI-3
Langsville, 80......SF-13
Lansing, 634......NN-19
LaPorte, 400......NG-13
Latham, 250......SF-8
Latty, 193......NH-2
Laura, 474......SA-3
Laurel Ridge, 2350......NI-16
Laurelville, 527......SE-10
Lawrence, 200......NK-3
LAWRENCE CO., 62450......SI-11
Lawrenceville, 300......NA-8
Lawshe, 60......SH-7
Layhigh, 60......SE-1
Layland, 50......NK-14
Lebanon, 18555......SD-4
Leavittsburg......NG-18
Leavittsville, 100......NK-18
Lebanon, 20033......SE-4
Leechburg, 40......NJ-13
Lees Creek, 160......SE-6
Leesburg, 1314......SE-7
Leesville, 200......NJ-10
Leesville, 158......NL-17
Leetonia, 1959......NJ-19
Leipsic, 2093......NH-5
Leistville, 60......SD-10
Lemert, 30......NJ-9
Lemoyne, 300......NF-7
Lena, 100......NN-5
Leno Ctr., 60......NL-9
Leo......SF-11

Leonardsburg......NL-9
Letart Falls, 180......SH-14
Levanna, 80......SI-5
Lewis Ctr., 350......NM-9
Lewisburg, 1820......SB-2
Lewiston, 222......NL-5
Lewisville, 176......SC-17
Lexington, 4822......NJ-11
Liberty, 240......SC-11
Liberty Ctr., 1180......NF-4
LICKING CO., 166492......NN-11
Lightsville, 30......NM-1
Lilly Chapel, 200......SB-8
Lima, 38771......NJ-4
Limaville, 151......NI-17
Lime City, 120......NF-7
Limecrest, 400......SB-6
Limestone, 50......SH-4
Limestone City, 40......NB-13
Lincoln Hts., 3286......SK-3
Lincoln Vil., 9032......SA-9
Lindale, 200......SL-5
Lindsey, 446......NF-8
Linndale, 179......SM-16
Linnville, 90......SA-12
Linnville, 60......SB-12
Linton, 80......NK-18
Linworth......NB-8
Lisbon, 2821......NJ-19
Litchfield, 400......NH-13
Lithopolis, 1106......SC-10
Little Hocking, 263......SF-15
Little Sandusky, 50......NJ-8
Little Walnut, 80......SC-10
Little Washington......NJ-11
Little York, 400......SK-7
Lloydsville, 150......NN-18
Lock......NM-11
Lockbourne, 237......SC-9
Lockington, 141......NM-3
Lockland, 3449......SK-3
Lockville, 90......SC-11
Lockwood, 30......NF-18
Locust Grv., 220......SG-8
Locust Ridge......SG-5
Lodi, 2746......NH-13
Logan, 7152......SD-12
LOGAN CO., 45858......NL-5
Logan Elm Vil., 1118......SD-9
Logansville, 55......NL-5
Londonderry, 40......NH-9
London, 9904......SB-7
Londonderry, 400......SF-10
Londonderry, 40......NN-17
Long Bottom, 70......SG-14
Lorain, 64097......NF-13
LORAIN CO., 301356......NG-12
Lordstown, 3417......NH-18
Lore City, 325......SA-16
Lottridge......SF-14
Louden......SG-7
Loudonville, 2641......NK-13
Louisville, 9186......NI-17
Loveland, 12081......SL-4
Loveland Pk., 1523......SL-6
Lowell, 549......SD-16
Lowellville, 1155......NH-20
Lower Salem, 86......SC-17
Lucas, 615......NJ-12
Lucasville, 9186......SH-10
Lucasville, 2757......SH-9
Luckey, 1012......NF-7
Ludlow Falls, 208......SA-3
Lumberton, 50......SD-5
Luray, 110......SB-11
Lykens, 70......NK-9
Lynchburg, 1499......SF-6
Lyndhurst, 14001......NE-16
Lyndon, 200......SE-8
Lynx, 220......SH-7
Lyons, 562......NE-4
Lytle, 200......SD-5
Macedon, 70......NL-5
Macedonia......SH-18
Mack, 11585......SL-1
Macksburg, 186......SD-16
Macon, 140......SH-4
Madeira, 8726......SL-4
Madison, 3184......ND-18
MADISON CO., 43435......NN-7
Madison Mills, 60......SC-8
Madison-on-the-Lake, 950......ND-18
Magnetic Sprs., 268......NL-8
Magnolia, 978......NK-17
Maineville, 975......SE-4
Malaga, 200......SC-17
Malinta, 265......NG-4
Mallet Creek, 300......NH-14
Malta, 671......SC-14
Malvern, 1189......NJ-17
Manchester, 4000......NI-15
Manchester, 2023......SI-6
Mandale, 50......NM-3
Mansfield, 47821......NJ-11
Mantua, 1043......NG-17
Mantua Sta., 50......NG-17
Maple Hts., 23138......SM-18
Maple Valley......NB-5
Mapleton, 90......NJ-18
Maplewood, 230......NL-4
Marathon, 800......SF-4
Marble Cliff, 573......NB-8
Marblehead, 903......NE-10
Marcy......SD-10
Marengo, 342......NL-10
Maria Stein, 300......NL-2
Mariemont, 3403......SL-4
Marietta, 14085......SE-16
Marion, 36837......NK-8
MARION CO., 66501......NK-7
Mark Ctr., 200......NF-2
Marlboro, 50......NI-17
Marseilles, 113......NJ-7
Marshall, 110......SF-7
Marshallville, 756......NJ-15
Martel......NK-9
Martin, 100......NF-7
Martins Ferry, 6915......NN-19
Martinsburg, 237......NM-12
Martinsville, 463......SE-5
Marysville, 22094......NM-7
Mason, 30712......SE-3
Massieville, 400......SE-9
Massillon, 32149......NJ-16
Masury, 2064......NG-20
Matamoras, 939......NA-19
Maud, 500......SE-3

Maumee, 14286......NC-1
Maximo, 200......NJ-17
Maxville, 100......SD-12
May Hill, 50......SG-7
Mayfield, 3460......SK-20
Mayfield Hts., 19155......NE-16
Mayflower Vil.......NC-7
Maynard, 400......NN-19
Maysville, 100......NJ-14
Maysville, 50......NL-5
McArthur, 1701......SF-12
McCartyville, 160......NL-3
McClimansville, 60......SC-8
McClure, 725......NG-5
McComb, 1648......NH-5
McConnelsville, 1784......SC-14
McCuneville, 90......SD-13
McCutchenville, 400......NI-8
McDermott, 434......SH-9
McDonald, 3263......NH-19
McDonaldsville......NI-16
McGill, 20......NM-16
McGonigle, 150......SE-2
McGuffey, 501......NJ-5
McKinley Hts.......NL-15
McLuney, 75......SC-13
McZena, 40......NJ-13
Mecca, 60......NF-19
Mechanicsburg, 1644......NN-6
Mechanicstown, 30......NK-18
Medina, 26678......NH-14
Medway, 2000......SB-5
Meeker, 150......NK-8
Meigs, 40......SC-13
MEIGS CO., 23770......SG-13
Melbern, 200......NF-2
Melmore, 153......NH-8
Melrose, 275......NH-3
Melvin, 90......SE-6
Memphis......SE-6
Mendon, 662......NJ-2
Mentor, 47159......NE-16
Mentor-on-the-Lake, 7443......ND-16
Mercer, 50......NL-12
Mercerville, 100......SH-13
Mermill......NG-6
Mesopotamia, 30......NF-18
Metamora, 627......ND-5
Metzger, 200......SE-9
Mexico, 60......NK-8
Meyers Lake, 569......NC-9
MIAMI CO., 102506......NN-3
Miami Shores......SN-1
Miami Vila.......SB-4
Miamisburg, 20181......SD-3
Miamitown, 1259......SF-1
Miamiville, 242......SK-5
Middle Bass, 100......ND-10
Middle Pt., 576......NI-2
Middleboro......SE-3
Middlebourne, 80......NM-16
Middlebranch, 220......NI-16
Middleburg, 220......NM-6
Middleburg Hts., 15946......SM-16
Middlebury, 30......NI-1
Middlefield, 2694......NF-17
Middleport, 2530......SG-14
Middleton, 80......NI-19
Middleton, 48694......SD-3
Middletown, 90......NN-16
Midland, 315......SE-5
Midvale, 754......NL-16
Midway, 322......SC-7
Mifflin, 137......NJ-12
Milan, 1367......NG-11
Milford, 6709......SL-5
Milford Ctr., 792......NM-7
Millbrook, 60......NJ-13
Millbury, 1200......NE-7
Milledgeville, 112......SD-7
Miller City, 137......NH-4
Millersburg, 3025......NK-14
Millersport, 1044......SB-11
Millersville, 90......NN-6
Millersville, 150......NI-8
Millfield, 341......SE-13
Millport, 70......NJ-18
Millville, 708......SE-2
Millwood, 200......NL-12
Milton Ctr., 144......NG-5
Miltonsburg, 43......SB-18
Miltonville, 90......SD-2
Mineral, 150......SF-12
Mineral City, 727......NL-16
Mineral Ridge, 3892......NH-19
Minerva, 3720......NJ-17
Minerva Pk., 1272......NN-9
Minford, 693......SH-10
Mingo, 100......NN-6
Mingo Jct., 3454......NL-20
Minster, 2805......NL-3
Mitiwanga, 50......NF-11
Modest......SB-14
Mogadore, 3853......NH-16
Mohicanville, 100......NJ-13
Moline, 470......NC-2
Monclova, 90......NC-1
Monfort Hts., 11948......SL-2
Monnett, 60......NK-9
Monroe, 12442......SD-3
Monroe Ctr., 100......ND-18
MONROE CO., 14642......SC-18
Monroeville, 1400......NG-10
Monroeville, 30......NM-14
Monterey, 100......SE-6
Montezuma, 165......NL-2
Montgomery, 10251......SK-5
MONTGOMERY CO., 535153......SC-3
Monticello, 40......NL-13
Montpelier, 4072......NE-2
Montra, 140......NL-4
Montra Jct.......NB-8
Montville, 100......NE-7
Montville, 300......NF-17
Montville, 100......NL-5
Moorefield, 100......NM-18
Mooresville, 70......SG-4
Moraine, 6307......SC-4
Moreland, 100......NJ-14
Moreland Hills, 3320......SM-20
Morgan, 2064......NK-15
MORGAN CO., 15054......SC-15

Morganville, 25......SD-14
Morgantown, 50......SG-8
Morning Sun, 200......SD-1
Moral, 399......NJ-8
Morning, 303......NI-18
Morristown, 70......SE-6
Morrow, 1188......SE-4
MORROW CO., 34827......NK-9
New Waterford, 1238......NJ-20
New Weston, 136......NL-1
New Westville, 90......SB-1
New Winchester, 30......NJ-9
Newark, 47573......NN-12
Newburgh Hts., 1200......NM-13
Newbury, 4795......NG-16
Newcastle, 100......NM-13
Newcomerstown, 3822......NM-15
Newell Run......SE-16
Newhope, 500......SH-5
Newman, 300......NJ-5
Newport, 1003......SE-17
Newport, 200......NM-16
Newport, 198......NM-3
Newton, 50......SB-7
Newton Falls, 300......NG-18
Newtonsville, 392......SF-4
Newtown, 2672......SM-4
Ney, 354......NF-2
Nicholsville, 200......SH-4
Nickel Plate......NH-19
Niles, 19266......NG-19
Nipgen, 100......SF-9
NOBLE CO., 14645......SC-16
N. Auburn, 40......NH-6
N. Baltimore, 3432......NH-6
N. Bend, 857......SL-1
N. Benton, 200......NI-18
N. Bloomfield, 500......NF-18
N. Bristol, 160......NF-18
N. Canton, 17488......NI-16
N. College Hill, 9397......SJ-2
N. Creek, 80......NK-3
N. Fairfield, 560......NH-11
N. Fork Vil., 1700......SC-9
N. Georgetown, 150......NJ-18
N. Hampton, 478......SA-5
N. Industry, 2700......NJ-16
N. Jackson, 900......NH-18
N. Kingsville, 2923......NC-19
N. Lawrence, 268......NJ-15
N. Lewisburg, 1490......NN-6
N. Liberty, 80......NL-12
N. Lima, 900......NI-19
N. Madison, 8547......ND-18
N. Monroeville, 40......NG-10
N. Olmsted, 32718......NF-14
N. Perry, 893......ND-17
N. Randall, 1027......SM-19
N. Ridgeville, 29465......NF-13
N. Robinson, 205......NJ-10
N. Royalton, 30444......NG-15
N. Salem, 100......NN-12
N. Star, 236......NM-1
N. Warren......NA-12
N. Woodbury, 90......NI-15
New Antioch, 220......SE-6
New Athens, 320......NM-18
New Baltimore, 661......SF-2
New Baltimore, 250......NH-15
New Bavaria, 99......NG-4
New Bedford, 200......NL-15
New Bloomington, 515......NK-8
New Boston, 2272......SI-9
New Bremen, 2978......NL-3
New Burlington, 5069......SD-5
New California, 1411......NN-8
New Carlisle, 5785......SB-5
New Concord, 2491......SA-15
New Cumberland, 150......NK-17
New Dover, 130......NM-8
New England, 60......NL-13
New Franklin, 230......NI-17
New Gdn., 100......NJ-18
New Germany......SL-9
New Hagerstown, 40......NL-17
New Hampshire, 174......NK-5
New Harmony, 100......NL-5
New Harrison, 50......NN-2
New Haven, 50......NI-19
New Haven, 399......NH-10
New Holland, 801......SD-8
New Hope, 150......SC-1
New Jasper, 100......SC-6
New Knoxville, 879......NL-3
New Lebanon, 3995......SC-3
New Lexington, 100......SC-12
New Lexington, 4731......SC-12
New London, 2461......NH-11
New Madison, 892......SB-1
New Marshfield, 326......SN-14
New Martinsburg, 150......SD-8
New Matamoras, 896......SD-18
New Miami, 2249......SE-2
New Middletown, 1621......NI-20
New Milford......SH-16
New Moorefield, 300......SA-5
New Moscow, 35......NM-14
New Paris, 1629......SB-1
New Petersburg, 150......SD-10
New Philadelphia, 17288......NL-16
New Pittsburg, 388......NJ-13
New Plymouth, 120......SE-11
New Richland, 100......NL-5
New Richmond, 2582......SM-4
New Riegel, 248......NH-8
New Rochester, 75......NF-7
New Rumley, 140......NL-18
New Somerset, 150......NK-19

New Springfield, 600......NI-20
New Stark, 70......NJ-6
New Straitsville, 722......SD-13
New Vienna, 1224......SE-6
New Washington, 967......NI-10
New Waterford......
New Weston......
New Winchester......
Newark......
Newburgh Hts., 2167......NF-15
Newcomerstown......
Newark......
Newport, 1238......
Niles......
Nippert, 100......SC-14
NOBLE CO.......

N. Aberdeen......
Outville, 110......SA-11
Overlook......SL-8
Overpeck, 300......SC-2
Overton, 140......NC-13
Owensville, 794......SG-4
Oxford, 21371......SD-1
Padua, 70......NM-2
Page Manor......SL-8
Pageton, 40......NL-10
Painesville, 19563......ND-17
Painesville on the Lake, 850......NC-17
Painter Creek, 150......NN-2
Paintersville, 70......SD-5
Palestine, 200......NM-1
Palmyra, 240......NH-18
Pancoastburg, 87......SD-8
Pandora, 1153......NI-5
Pansy......NE-5
Paris, 220......NI-17
Park Ridge Acres, 300......NB-15
Parkertown, 25......NL-10
Parkman, 600......NF-18
Parma, 81601......NF-15
Parma Hts., 20718......NF-14
Parral, 218......NL-16
Parrott......SD-7
Parrott, 40......SC-7
Pataskala, 14962......SA-11
Patmos......SG-8
Patriot, 140......SI-12
Pattersonville, 139......NJ-17
Pattersonville, 30......NJ-18
Paulding, 3605......NH-1
PAULDING CO., 19614......NH-1
Pavonia, 160......NJ-11
Payne, 1194......NH-1
Peebles, 1782......SH-7
Pekin, 250......SD-4
Pekin, 100......NJ-14
Pemberton, 350......NM-4
Pemberville, 1371......NF-7
Penfield, 100......NH-13
Peninsula, 565......NG-15
Pennsville, 156......SD-14
Peoli, 30......NM-16
Peoria, 230......NM-7
Pepper Pike, 5979......NF-16
Perry, 1663......ND-17
Perrysburg, 20623......NE-6
Perrysville, 735......NK-12
Perrysville, 60......NC-17
Petersburg, 500......NI-19
Pettisville, 498......NE-3
Pfeiffer Sta., 30......NK-7
Phalanx......NG-18
Pharisburg, 50......NM-8
Phillipsburg, 557......SB-3
Philo, 733......SB-14
Philothea, 100......NL-1
Phoneton, 220......SB-4
Pickerington, 18291......SB-10
Pickrelltown, 60......NM-6
Piedmont, 200......NM-17
Pierce......SM-4
Pierpont, 420......ND-20
Pigeon Run, 250......NJ-15
Piketon, 2172......SG-10
Pikeville, 40......SH-7
Pine Grv., 50......SH-12
Piney Fork, 350......NM-19
Piqua, 20522......NN-3
Pisgah, 1000......SE-3
Pitchin, 150......SB-6
Pitsburg, 388......NN-3
Plain City, 4225......NN-8
Plainfield, 157......NM-15
Plants, 150......SH-14
Pleasant Bend, 80......NG-4
Pleasant City, 447......SB-16
Pleasant Corners, 80......NL-9
Pleasant Grove, 300......NC-9
Pleasant Hill, 1200......NN-3
Pleasant Home, 200......NI-14
Pleasant Plain, 154......SF-4
Pleasant Ridge......SL-4
Pleasant Run, 4654......SJ-2
Pleasant Run Farm, 279......SK-2
Pleasant Valley, 500......SE-9
Pleasant View......SC-9
Plum......SD-10
Olive Branch, 200......SG-4
Olive Green, 65......NM-10
Olivesburg, 80......NI-11
Olivet, 80......SA-18
Olmsted Falls, 9024......SN-14
Omega, 150......SF-11
Oneida, 100......NM-17
Ontario, 6225......NJ-11
Opperman, 30......NF-3
Ora, 100......SF-13
Orange, 3323......SM-20
Orange, 35......NM-15
Orangeville, 197......NG-20
Orbiston, 40......SD-13
Orchard Island, 300......NL-5
Oregon, 20291......NC-7
Oregonia, 300......SE-4
Orient, 270......SC-9
Orleton, 40......SC-12
Orrville, 8380......NJ-14
Orwell, 1660......NE-18
Osborn......SB-5
Osgood, 300......NM-2
Ostrander, 643......NM-8
Otsego......SB-13
Otterbein Home, 200......SE-4
Otterville......SD-15
Otto, 200......SG-12
Ottoville, 1006......NI-3
Ottawa, 4460......NH-4
OTTAWA CO., 41428......NE-7
Ottawa Hills, 4517......NB-1
Otterbein Home......
Otterville......
Otway, 87......SH-8

Powellsville, 50......SI-10
Powhatan Pt., 1592......NB-19
Pratts Fork, 150......SF-14
Prattsville, 30......SD-4
Preble......
PREBLE CO., 42270......SC-1
Pricetown, 60......SE-6
Princeton, 120......SE-3
Proctorville, 574......SK-12
Prospect, 1112......NL-8
Pulaski, 132......NF-2
Pulaskiville, 50......NL-10
Put-in-Bay, 138......NE-10
Putnam......
PUTNAM CO., 34499......NI-4
Pyro, 150......SI-11
Queen Acres, 650......SE-7
Quincy, 706......NL-5
Raccoon Island, 50......SI-13
Racine, 675......SG-14
Radcliff, 50......SF-12
Radnor, 201......NL-8
Ragersville, 150......NL-15
Rainsboro, 280......SF-7
Raleigh, 417......NM-19
Randolph, 750......NH-17
Range, 40......SC-7
Ranten, 159......SH-8
Ravenna, 11724......NH-17
Rawson, 570......NI-5
Ray, 100......SF-11
Raymond, 257......NM-7
Reading, 10385......SK-3
Red Lion, 200......SD-3
Redfield, 50......SC-13
Redhaw, 50......SH-6
Redoak......SH-5
Redtown......SE-13
Reedsburg, 150......NJ-13
Reedsville, 160......SG-15
Reedtown, 50......NH-10
Reedurban, 4400......NI-16
Reese, 40......SI-19
Reesville, 250......SD-6
Rehoboth, 100......SC-13
Reily, 200......SE-1
Reinersville, 160......SC-15
Remington, 328......SL-5
Reminderville, 3404......NG-16
Remsen Cors., 75......NG-13
Renick, 36......SD-13
Reno, 1293......SE-17
Renrock, 20......SC-15
Republic, 549......NH-9
Resaca, 40......SC-16
Residence Pk.......SL-7
Reynoldsburg, 36......SA-10
Rice......NI-4
Riceland, 200......NJ-14
Rich Hill, 75......NM-16
Richfield, 3648......NG-15
Richfield Ctr., 110......NE-5
RICHLAND CO., 124475......NI-11
Richmond, 481......NL-19
Richmond Ctr.......
Richmond Dale, 200......SF-10
Richmond Hts., 10546......NE-16
Richville, 3324......NJ-16
Richwood, 2229......NL-8
Ridgeland, 50......SD-11
Ridgeton, 20......NJ-9
Ridgeville, 200......SD-4
Ridgeville Corners, 435......NF-3
Ridgeway, 338......NK-6
Ridgewood Hts.......SM-7
Rimer, 50......NH-3
Ringgold, 250......SD-10
Ringgold, 25......SC-15
Rinard Mills, 50......SD-18
Rio Grande, 830......SH-12
Ripley, 1750......SI-5
Risingsun, 606......NG-7
Rittman, 6491......NI-14
River Cors., 80......NF-18
Riverlea, 545......SF-18
Riverside, 25201......SC-4
Rix Mills, 80......SB-15
Roachester, 300......SE-4
Roads, 160......SG-11
Roaming Shores, 1508......NE-18
Robertsville, 331......NJ-17
Robins, 90......SE-10
Robtown......SG-12
Rochester, 182......NG-12
Rock Camp, 80......SK-17
Rock Creek, 529......NE-18
Rock Way, 160......SE-7
Rockbridge, 182......SD-11
Rockford, 1120......NJ-2
Rockport, 90......NI-4
Rocky Fork......SF-6
Rocky Ridge, 417......NE-8
Rocky River, 20213......NF-14
Rodney, 200......NK-2
Rogers, 237......NJ-19
Roland, 2555......NM-20
Rome, 1450......SK-12
Rome, 60......NE-19
Romohr Acres, 300......SL-5
Rootstown, 300......NH-17
Rose Farm, 200......SC-13
Rosedale, 180......NN-7
Roseland, 2150......NN-10
Rosemont, 60......SM-6
Rosemount, 2112......SH-10
Roseville, 1812......SC-13
Rosewood, 257......NM-5
Ross, 3417......SC-2
ROSS CO., 78064......SE-9
Rossburg, 231......NN-1
Rossford, 6293......NC-6
Roswell, 219......NL-16
Roundhead, 300......NK-5
Rowsburg, 50......NI-13
Roxabell, 20......SE-9
Royal......
Royalton, 260......NM-13
Rubyville......SI-10
Rudolph, 458......NG-6

S. Salem, 204......SE-8
S. Solon, 355......SC-6
S. Vienna, 384......SB-6
S. Webster, 866......SI-10
S. West Hubbard, 100......NC-14
S. Woodbury, 30......NI-8
Southington, 400......NG-18
Sparta, 161......NL-10
Spencer, 753......NG-13
Spencerville, 2223......NJ-3
Spring Hill, 100......NJ-15
Spring Mtn., 30......NL-13
Spring Valley, 479......SD-5
Springboro, 17409......SD-4
Springdale, 11223......SJ-3
Springfield, 60608......SB-6
Springhills, 150......NN-5
St. Bernard, 4368......SL-3
Springville, 40......NJ-13
Squirrel Town......
St. Clairsville......
Stafford, 81......SC-17
Standley......
Stanleyville, 40......SE-13
Stanwood, 30......NK-18
Staunton, 120......NN-4
Staunton, 80......SD-13
Steam Cors., 30......NJ-10
Steamburg, 123......SB-17
Steinersville, 200......SB-19
Stelvideo, 90......NN-2
Sterling, 457......NI-14
Steuben, 60......NH-10
Steubenville, 18659......NL-20
Stewart, 247......SE-14
Stewartsville, 200......NN-19
Stewartville, 30......SF-11
Stillwater, 150......NM-17
Stockdale, 130......SH-10
Stockdale, 135......NK-16
Stockport, 503......SD-15
Stone Creek, 177......NL-15
Stonelick, 100......SG-4
Stony Ridge, 411......NF-7
Stout, 94......SI-8
Stoutsville, 560......SD-10
Stovertown, 35......SB-14
Stow, 34837......NH-16
Strasburg, 2608......NK-16
Stratford, 80......NM-4
Stratton, 294......NK-20
Streetsboro, 16028......NG-16
Scio, 763......NL-18
Strongsville, 44750......NG-14
Struthers, 10713......NH-20
Stryker, 1335......NF-3
Sugar Bush Knolls, 177......NH-16
Sugar Grv., 426......SD-11
Sugar Grv., 150......SD-6
Sugar Grv., 110......SL-9
Sugar Grv. Hill, 200......NC-14
Sugar Ridge, 130......NG-6
Sugar Tree Ridge, 110......SG-6
Sugarcreek, 2287......NL-15
Sullivan, 450......NH-12
Sulphur Sprs., 194......NI-9
Sulphurgrove......SK-7
Summerfield, 254......SC-17
Summerford, 250......SB-7
Summerside, 5083......SL-3
Summerside Estates, 1700......SL-3
Summersville, 80......NL-17
Summit, 700......NC-13
SUMMIT CO., 541781......NH-15
Summithill, 200......SD-8
Summitville, 135......NJ-18
Sumner......NI-16
Sun Valley......SJ-20
Sunbury, 4389......NM-10
Sunbury, 110......SD-5
Sunnyland, 250......NL-16
Surrey Hill, 700......NJ-16
Swanders, 80......NM-3
Swanton, 3690......NE-5
Swartz Creek......
Sybene, 200......SK-12
Sycamore, 861......NI-8
Sycamore Valley, 25......SC-17
Sylvania, 18965......NC-6
Syracuse, 826......SG-14
Tacoma, 100......SA-18
Tallmadge, 17537......NH-16
Tallow......SD-8
Tarlton, 282......SD-10
Tawawa, 100......NM-4
Taylors Creek, 660......SK-1
Taylorsburg......SC-3
Taylorsville......SB-3
Tedrow, 173......NE-4
Temperanceville, 80......NN-18
Terrace Pk., 2251......SL-5
Terre Haute, 100......SD-7
Terry Acres, 165......SL-10
Texas, 180......NF-5
Thackery, 120......NN-6
The Bend, 100......NG-2
The Plains, 3000......SE-13
The Vil. of Indian Hill, 5785......SK-5
Thomastown......NI-9
Thompson, 370......NE-17
Thornville, 991......SB-12
Thurman, 100......SH-12
Thurston, 604......SB-11
Tiffin, 17963......NH-8
Tiltonsville, 1372......NM-19
Timberlake, 675......NE-16
Tipp City, 9689......SB-4
Tippecanoe, 121......NM-17
Tiro, 280......NI-10
Tiverton, 80......NL-13
Tobias......
Tobasco, 200......SM-4
Toboso, 200......SA-12
Toledo, 287208......NB-7
Tontogany, 367......NF-6
Topeka, 75......SC-10
Torch, 300......SE-12
Toronto, 5091......NL-20
Townwood......SD-7
Trail......NL-15
Tranquility, 100......SH-6
Tremont City, 375......SA-5
Trenton, 11869......SD-2
Trimble, 390......SD-13
Trinway, 365......NN-13
Trotwood, 24431......SC-3
Trowbridge, 50......NG-8
Troy, 25058......NN-3
Trumbull, 200......ND-18
TRUMBULL CO., 210312......NG-18
Tucson......SE-10
Tuppers Plains, 465......SF-14
Turpin Hills, 5099......SM-4
Tuscarawas, 1056......NL-16
TUSCARAWAS CO., 92582......NM-16
Twenty Mile Stand, 300......SE-3
Twightwee......SJ-6
Twin Lakes, 300......NG-16
Twin Valley, 300......SD-8
Twinsburg, 18795......NG-16
Tymochtee, 30......NI-8
Tyndall, 150......NM-4
Uhrichsville, 5413......NL-16
Union, 6419......SC-3
UNION CO., 52300......NL-7
Union Furnace, 430......SE-12
Union Sta.......SE-11
Unionport, 150......NL-19
Uniontown, 3309......NI-16
Uniontown, 230......NN-18
Unionvale, 90......NM-18
Unionville Ctr., 233......NN-7
Uniopolis, 250......NK-4
Unity, 100......NI-20
Unity, 30......NI-7
University Hts., 13539......NF-15
University View, 500......SH-13
Upper Arlington, 33771......SA-9
Upper Sandusky, 6596......NJ-8
Urbana, 11793......NN-5
Urbancrest, 960......SB-9
Utica, 2132......NM-11
Utopia, 70......SI-4
Valley City, 400......NG-14
Valley Hi, 212......NN-4
Valley View, 2034......SN-18
Valley View, 620......SN-17
Valleywood......SM-9
Van Buren, 328......NH-6
Van Wert, 10846......NI-2
VAN WERT CO., 28744......NJ-2
Vanatta, 130......NN-11
Vandalia, 15246......SB-4
Vanlue, 359......NI-7
Vaughnsville, 262......NI-4
Venedocia, 124......NJ-3
Venice Hts., 1300......NA-12
Vera Cruz......SF-5
Vermilion, 10594......NF-12
Vernon, 100......NF-20
Vernon, 20......NK-3
Verona, 494......SB-2
Versailles, 2687......NN-2
Veto, 110......SE-15
Vickery, 121......NF-9
Vienna, 600......NG-19
Vigo, 220......SF-13
Viking Vil., 1230......SM-5
Villa, 120......NA-8
Villa Nova, 800......SL-4
Vincent, 300......SE-15
Vinton, 222......SG-12
VINTON CO., 13435......SF-11
Wabash, 70......NL-4
Waco, 380......NJ-16
Wade......SE-18
Wadsworth, 21567......NI-14
Wagram, 125......NN-16
Wahlsburg, 30......NK-5
Wainwright, 250......NL-16
Waite Hill, 471......NE-16
Wakatomika, 140......NM-13
Wakefield, 140......SH-9
Wakeman, 1047......NG-12
Walbridge, 3019......NC-3
Waldo, 350......NL-8
Walhonding, 90......NL-13
Walhonding, 90......NL-13
Walnut Creek, 878......NK-15
Walton Hills, 2281......SN-19
Wamsley, 90......SH-13
Wapakoneta, 9867......NK-4
Warner, 130......SD-16
Warner, 200......SD-16
Warren, 41557......NG-19
WARREN CO., 212693......SE-4
Warrensville Hts., 13542......NF-15
Warsaw, 682......NL-13
WASHINGTON CO., 61778......SD-6
Washington Court House, 14192......SD-7
Washingtonville, 801......NJ-19
Waterford, 450......SD-15
Waterloo, 90......NH-11
Waterloo, 170......SH-18
Waterville, 5523......NF-6
Watkins......NN-10
Wauseon, 7332......NE-4
Waverly, 4408......SG-10
Wayland, 50......NG-17
Wayne, 887......NG-7
Wayne, 60......NF-20
WAYNE CO., 114520......NI-14
Wayne Lakes Pk., 718......SA-2
Waynesburg, 923......NJ-17
Waynesfield, 847......NK-5
Waynesville, 2834......SD-5
Webb Summit......SD-12
Webster......SE-10
Webster......SK-3
Weeksville......SG-10
Weimer......NL-20
Welcome......NL-16
Wellington, 4802......NH-12
Wellston, 5663......SF-11

*, †, ‡, §, ◊   See explanation under state title in this index.
County and parish names are listed in CAPITAL LETTERS & boldface type.
Independent cities (not included in a county) are listed in italics.

Wellsville, 3541 NK-19
Welshfield, 150 NF-17
Wengerlawn, 85 SB-3
W. Akron NC-5
W. Alexandria, 1340 SC-2
W. Andover, 100 NE-19
W. Bedford, 60 NM-13
W. Carlisle, 30 NM-13
W. Carrollton City, 13818 SC-3
W. Charleston, 100 SB-4
W. Chester, 800 SE-3
W. Chester, 100 NM-16
W. Clarksfield, 100 NG-11
W. Elkton, 197 SD-2
W. Farmington, 499 NF-18
W. Florence, 40 SC-1
W. Hill, 2273 NG-20
W. Independence, 40 NH-7
W. Jefferson, 4222 SB-8
W. Jefferson, 120 NE-2
W. Lafayette, 2321 NM-15
W. Lancaster, 75 SD-6
W. Lebanon, 120 NJ-15
W. Leipsic, 206 NH-4
W. Liberty, 1805 NM-5
W. Liberty, 50 NI-10
W. Liberty, 40 NL-9
W. Lodi, 80 NH-9
W. Manchester, 474 SB-2
W. Mansfield, 682 NL-6
W. Mecca, 120 NF-19
W. Middletown, 550 SD-3
W. Millgrove, 174 NG-7
W. Milton, 4630 SB-3
W. Newton NK-5
West Point, 220 NJ-19
W. Portsmouth, 3149 SI-9
W. Rushville, 134 SC-12
W. Salem, 1464 NI-13
W. Sonora, 100 SB-2
W. Union, 3241 SI-7
W. Unity, 1671 NE-3
W. Williamsfield, 110 NE-20
Westboro, 270 SF-5
Westerville, 36120 NN-9
Westfield, 110 NL-9
Westfield Ctr., 1115 NH-14
Westhope, 80 NG-5
Westlake, 32729 NF-14
Westminster, 100 NJ-4
Weston, 1590 NG-5
Westview, 530 NG-14
Westville, 250 NI-18
Westville, 200 NN-5
Wetsel NI-2
Weymouth, 180 NG-14
Wharton, 358 NI-7
Wheelersburg, 6437 SI-10
Whipple, 130 SD-16
Whisler, 120 SD-10
White Cottage, 300 SB-13
White Oak, 19167 SF-2
White Sulphur NM-8
Whitehall, 18062 SB-10
Whitehouse, 4149 NF-5
Whiteoak, 40 SC-8
White's, 375 NF-9
Wick, 90 NE-19
Wickliffe, 12750 NE-16
Wiggonsville, 80 SH-4
Wilberforce, 2271 SC-5
Wildbrook Acres, 1500 SK-3
Wilgus, 30 SJ-12
Wilkesville, 149 SG-12
Willard, 6236 NH-10
Willetsville, 50 SF-6
Williams Ctr., 300 NF-2
WILLIAMS CO., 37642 NE-2
Williamsburg, 2490 SG-4
Williamsdale, 581 SE-2
Williamsfield, 400 NE-20
Williamsport, 1023 SD-9
Williamsport, 70 NK-10
Williamstown, 100 NJ-6
Williston, 487 NE-7
Willoughby, 22268 NE-16
Willoughby Hills, 9485 NE-16
Willow Wood, 20 SJ-12
Willowdale Lake, 600 NA-8
Willowdell, 75 NM-2
Willowick, 14171 NE-16
Willowville, 500 SG-3
Willshire, 397 NJ-1
Wilmington, 12520 SE-5
Wilmot, 304 NK-15
Wilson, 125 SB-18
Winchester, 1051 SH-6
Winchester, 50 SG-11
Windham, 2209 NG-18
Windsor, 400 NE-18
Windsor, 120 NJ-11
Windsor SF-4
Winesburg, 352 NK-15
Winfield, 200 NK-15
Wingett Run, 40 SD-17
Winona, 250 NI-18
Winterset, 150 NN-16
Wintersville, 3924 NL-19
Withamsville, 7021 SG-3
Wolf Run, 120 NL-18
WOOD CO., 125488 NG-6
Woodbourne, 6050 SN-8
Woodington, 100 NM-1
Woodlawn, 3294 SK-3
Woodmere, 884 SL-20
Woodsdale, 200 SE-2
Woodsfield, 2384 SC-18
Woodstock, 305 NM-7
Woodville, 2135 NF-7
Woodville SF-5
Woodworth, 700 NI-19
Wooster, 26119 NJ-14
Wooster Hts., 850 NJ-11
Worstville, 25 NH-1
Worthington, 13575 NN-9
Wren, 194 NJ-1
Wrightsville SB-8
Wyandot, 50 NJ-8
WYANDOT CO., 22615 NJ-7
Wyoming, 8428 SK-3
Xenia, 25719 SC-5
Yankee Lake, 79 NG-20
Yankeetown, 250 SH-5
Yatesville, 20 SC-7
Yellow Sprs., 3487 SC-5
Yellowbud, 120 SD-9
York, 90 NM-19
York Ctr., 100 NL-7
Yorkshire, 96 NM-2
Yorkville, 1079 NM-19
Youngs, 110 SH-8
Youngstown, 66982 NH-19
Youngsville, 50 SH-7
Zahns Corners SG-9
Zaleski, 278 SF-12
Zanesfield, 197 NL-6
Zanesville, 25487 SB-14
Zimmerman SM-10
Zoar, 169 NK-16
Zoarville, 230 NK-16
Zone, 30 NE-3

Oklahoma

Page locator

Map keys	Atlas pages
1–10	166–167
11–20	168–169

Achille, 492 K-16
Ada, 16810 H-15
Adair, 790 D-18
ADAIR CO., 22683 E-19
Adams, 200 C-5
Adamson, 150 H-18
Addington, 114 J-12
Afton, 1049 C-19
Agawam, 50 H-12
Agra, 339 E-14
Ahloso, 90 H-15
Akins, 493 F-20
Albany, 143 K-16
Albert, 120 G-11
Albion, 106 H-19
Alderson, 304 H-17
Alex, 550 H-12
Alfalfa, 100 G-11
ALFALFA CO., 5642 C-11
Aline, 207 C-11
Allen, 932 H-16
Alluwe, 90 C-18
Alma, 80 I-13
Altus, 19813 I-9
Alva, 4945 C-10
Amber, 419 G-12
Ames, 239 D-11
Amorita, 37 B-11
Anadarko, 6762 G-11
Antioch, 80 H-13
Antlers, 2453 J-17
Apache, 1444 H-11
Apple, 40 J-18
Arapaho, 796 F-10
Arcadia, 247 F-13
Ardmore, 24283 J-14
Arkoma, 1989 G-20
Arlington, 25 F-15
Armstrong, 105 J-16
Arnett, 524 D-8
Arpelar, 272 H-17
Asher, 393 H-14
Ashland, 66 H-16
Atoka, 3107 I-16
ATOKA CO., 14182 J-16
Atwood, 74 H-16
Avant, 320 C-16
Avard, 30 C-10
Avery, 60 E-15
Aydelotte F-14
Baker, 50 B-5
Bald Hill F-17
Balko, 100 C-6
Ballard, 120 D-20
Barnsdall, 1243 C-16
Baron, 140 E-20
Bartlesville, 35750 C-16
Battiest, 250 I-19
Baum J-14
Bearden, 133 G-16
Beaver, 1515 B-6
BEAVER CO., 5636 C-7
BECKHAM CO., 22119 G-8
Bee, 140 J-15
Beggs, 1321 F-16
Bengal, 100 H-19
Bennington, 334 J-17
Bentley, 100 J-16
Bernice, 562 C-19
Bessie, 181 G-10
Bethany, 19051 F-13
Bethel, 260 I-19
Bethel Acres, 2895 G-14
Big Cabin, 265 C-18
Billings, 509 C-13
Binger, 672 G-11
Bison, 65 D-12
Bixby, 20884 E-17
Blackburn, 108 D-15
Blackwell, 7092 C-14
BLAINE CO., 11943 E-11
Blair, 818 H-9
Blanchard, 7670 G-13
Blanco, 200 H-17
Blocker, 200 G-18
Blue, 195 J-16
Bluejacket, 339 B-19
Boatman, 100 D-18
Boise City, 1266 C-2
Bokchito, 632 J-16
Bokoshe, 512 G-19
Boley, 1184 F-15
Boone, 25 H-11
Boswell, 709 J-17
Bowden G-1
Bowlegs, 405 G-15
Bowring, 100 B-16
Boynton, 248 F-17
Braden G-20
Bradley, 130 H-13
Braggs, 259 F-18
Braman, 217 B-13
Bray, 1209 I-12
Breckinridge, 245 D-13
Briartown, 150 G-18
Bridge Creek, 336 G-13
Bridgeport, 116 F-11
Bristow, 4222 E-16
Britton J-4
Broken Arrow, 98850 E-17
Broken Bow, 4120 J-20
Bromide, 165 I-15
Brooksville, 63 G-14
Brushy, 900 F-19
BRYAN CO., 42416 K-16
Bryans Cor., 100 C-5
Buffalo, 1299 B-8
Bunch, 80 F-19
Burbank, 141 C-15
Burlington, 152 B-11
Burneyville, 60 K-14
Burns Flat, 2057 G-9
Bushyhead, 1314 C-18
Butler, 287 F-9
Butner, 100 G-15
Byars, 255 H-14
Byng, 1175 H-15
Byron, 35 B-11
Cache, 2796 I-10
Caddo, 997 J-16
CADDO CO., 29600 H-11
Calera, 2164 K-16
Calhoun, 50 G-19
Calumet, 507 F-12
Calvin, 294 H-16
Camargo, 178 E-9
Cameron, 302 G-20
Camp Houston C-9
Canadian, 220 G-17
CANADIAN CO., 115541 F-12
Caney, 205 J-16
Caney Ridge, 130 E-19
Canton, 625 E-11
Canute, 541 F-9
Capron, 23 B-11
Carmen, 355 C-11
Carnegie, 1723 G-11
Carney, 647 E-14
Carrier, 85 C-12
Carter, 256 G-8
CARTER CO., 47557 J-13
Cartwright, 609 K-15
Cashion, 802 E-13
Castle, 106 F-16
Catoosa, 7151 D-17
Cedar Crest, 312 D-18
Cedar Valley, 288 E-13
Cement, 501 H-12
Center, 120 H-15
Centerview F-15
Centrahoma, 97 I-16
Central High, 1199 I-12
Centralia, 35 C-18
Ceres C-14
Chandler, 3100 F-14
Chattanooga, 461 I-10
Checotah, 3335 F-18
Chelsea, 1964 C-18
Cherokee, 1498 C-11
CHEROKEE CO., 46987 E-19
Cherry Tree, 883 E-20
Chester, 117 D-10
Chewey, 135 D-19
Cheyenne, 801 F-8
Chickasha, 16036 H-12
Childers, 40 C-17
Chilocco, 30 B-14
Choctaw, 11146 F-14
CHOCTAW CO., 15205 J-17
Chouteau, 2097 D-18
Christie, 218 E-19
Cimarron City, 150 E-13
CIMARRON CO., 2475 B-2
Claremore, 18581 D-17
Clarita, 150 I-16
Clayton, 821 I-18
Clearview, 48 G-16
Clebit I-19
Cleo Sprs., 338 D-11
Cleora, 1463 C-19
Cleveland, 3251 D-15
CLEVELAND CO., 255755 G-13
Clinton, 9033 F-10
Cloud Chief, 50 G-10
Cloudy, 50 J-18
COAL CO., 5925 I-16
Coalgate, 1967 I-16
Cobb J-16
Cogar, 25 G-12
Colbert, 1140 K-15
Colcord, 815 D-19
Cole, 555 G-13
Coleman, 180 J-16
Collinsville, 5606 D-17
Colony, 136 G-10
Comanche, 1663 I-12
COMANCHE CO., 124098 I-11
Commerce, 2473 B-19
Connerville, 250 I-15
Cookietown J-11
Cookson, 900 F-19
Cooperton, 16 H-10
Copan, 733 B-17
Copeland, 1629 C-19
Cordell, 2915 G-10
Corn, 503 G-10
Cornish, 163 J-13
Corum, 30 I-12
COTTON CO., 6193 J-11
Cottonwood, 160 I-16
Council Hill, 158 F-17
Countyline, 300 I-13
Covington, 527 D-13
Cowden G-10
Coweta, 9943 E-17
Cowlington, 155 G-19
Cox City, 100 H-13
Coyle, 325 E-14
CRAIG CO., 15029 C-18
Crawford, 50 E-8
CREEK CO., 69967 E-15
Crescent, 1411 E-13
Criner, 50 H-13
Cromwell, 286 G-15
Crowder, 430 G-17
Cushing, 7826 E-15
Custer City, 375 F-10
CUSTER CO., 27469 F-9
Cyril, 1059 H-11
Dacoma, 107 C-11
Daisy, 50 I-17
Dale, 181 G-14
Davenport, 814 F-15
Davidson, 315 J-9
Davis, 2683 I-14
Deer Creek, 130 C-13
Del City, 21332 F-13
Delaware, 417 C-17
DELAWARE CO., 41487 C-19
Delhi, 60 G-8
Depew, 476 E-15
Devol, 151 J-11
Dewar, 888 F-17
Dewey, 3432 C-17
DEWEY CO., 4810 E-9
Dibble, 878 H-13
Dickson, 1207 J-14
Dill City, 562 G-9
Disney, 311 C-19
Dixon, 250 G-15
Dotyville, 101 B-19
Dougherty, 215 I-14
Douglas, 32 D-13
Dover, 464 E-12
Dow, 100 H-17
Driftwood, 25 B-11
Drummond, 455 D-12
Drumright, 2907 E-15
Duke, 424 I-8
Duncan, 23431 I-12
Dunjee Pk. K-7
Durant, 15856 J-16
Durham, 120 E-7
Dustin, 395 G-16
Eagle City, 50 E-11
Eagletown, 528 J-20
Eakly, 338 G-11
Earlsboro, 628 G-15
Eastborough, 1000 F-6
Edmond, 81405 F-13
El Reno, 16749 F-12
Eldon, 368 E-19
Eldorado, 446 I-8
Elgin, 2156 H-11
Elk City, 11693 F-9
ELLIS CO., 4151 D-8
Elmer, 96 I-9
Elmore City, 697 I-13
Elmwood, 25 C-6
Empire City, 955 I-12
Enid, 49379 D-12
Enos K-15
Enterprise, 200 G-18
Enville K-14
Eram F-17
Erick, 1052 G-8
Erin Sprs., 87 H-13
Etowah, 92 G-14
Eufaula, 2813 G-18
Fair Oaks, 103 D-17
Fairfax, 1380 C-15
Fairland, 1057 C-19
Fairmont, 134 D-13
Fairview, 2579 D-11
Falconhead, 300 K-14
Fallis, 27 F-14
Fame G-17
Fanshawe, 419 H-19
Fargo, 364 D-8
Farris, 150 J-17
Faxon, 136 I-11
Fay, 150 E-10
Felker, 100 J-19
Felt, 93 C-1
Fillmore, 45 J-15
Finley, 150 I-18
Fittstown, 500 I-15
Fitzhugh, 230 I-15
Fletcher, 1177 H-11
Folsom, 50 J-16
Foraker, 19 B-15
Forest Pk., 998 K-5
Forgan, 547 B-6
Ft. Cobb, 634 G-11
Ft. Coffee, 424 G-20
Ft. Gibson, 4154 E-18
Ft. Supply, 330 C-8
Ft. Towson, 519 J-18
Foss, 151 F-9
Foster, 161 I-13
Fox, 300 I-13
Foyil, 344 D-18
Francis, 315 H-15
Frederick, 3940 I-10
Freedom, 289 C-9
Friendship, 24 H-9
Gage, 442 D-8
Gans, 312 F-20
Garber, 822 D-13
GARFIELD CO., 60580 C-12
Garvin, 256 J-19
GARVIN CO., 27576 I-13
Gate, 93 B-7
Geary, 1280 F-11
Gene Autry, 158 J-14
Geronimo, 1268 I-11
Gerty, 118 H-16
Glencoe, 601 D-14
Glenpool, 10808 E-16
Glover, 150 J-19
Golden, 200 J-19
Goldsby, 1801 G-13
Goltry, 249 C-12
Goodland, 50 J-18
Goodwell, 1293 C-4
Gore, 977 F-19
Gotebo, 226 G-10
Gould, 141 I-8
Gowen, 250 H-18
Gracemont, 318 G-11
GRADY CO., 52431 H-12
Graham, 250 J-13
Grainola, 31 B-15
Grandfield, 1038 J-10
Granite, 2065 H-9
Grant, 289 K-18
GRANT CO., 4527 B-12
Gray Horse, 60 C-15
Grayson, 159 F-17
Green Pastures J-7
Greenfield, 93 F-11
GREER CO., 6239 H-8
Grimes F-8
Grove, 6623 C-19
Guthrie, 10191 E-13
Guymon, 11442 C-4
Haileyville, 813 H-18
Hallett, 125 D-15
Hammon, 568 F-9
Hanna, 138 G-17
Hanson, 150 F-20
Hardesty, 212 C-5
Harjo G-15
Harmon, 25 D-8
HARMON CO., 2922 H-7
HARPER CO., 3685 C-8
Harrah, 5095 F-14
Harris, 150 K-20
Hartshorne, 2125 H-18
Haskell, 2007 E-17
HASKELL CO., 12769 G-18
Hastings, 143 J-12
Haworth, 297 K-20
Hayward, 30 D-13
Haywood, 300 H-17
Headrick, 94 I-9
Healdton, 2788 J-13
Heavener, 3414 H-20
Helena, 1403 C-11
Hendrix, 79 K-16
Hennepin, 250 I-13
Hennessey, 2131 E-12
Henryetta, 5927 F-17
Hess, 50 I-9
Hester H-9
Hickory, 71 I-15
Hillsdale, 121 C-12
Hinton, 3196 F-11
Hitchcock, 121 E-11
Hitchita, 88 F-17
Hobart, 3756 H-9
Hodgen, 260 H-20
Hoffman, 127 F-17
Holdenville, 5771 G-16
Hollis, 2060 I-7
Hollister, 50 J-10
Homer, 100 H-15
Homestead, 70 D-11
Hominy, 3565 D-16
Honobia, 150 I-19
Hooker, 1918 B-5
Hopeton, 40 C-10
Horntown, 97 G-16
Hough, 100 B-4
Howe, 802 H-20
HUGHES CO., 14003 G-16
Hugo, 5310 J-18
Hulbert, 590 E-18
Humphreys, 150 I-9
Hunter, 165 C-13
Hydro, 969 F-11
Idabel, 7010 K-19
Indiahoma, 344 I-10
Indianola, 162 G-17
Ingalls, 60 E-14
Ingersoll, 20 C-11
Inola, 1788 D-18
Isabella, 136 D-11
JACKSON CO., 26446 I-8
Jacktown, 30 F-14
Jay, 2448 D-19
Jefferson, 12 C-12
JEFFERSON CO., 6472 J-12
Jenks, 16924 E-17
Jennings, 363 D-15
Jesse I-15
Jet, 213 C-11
Johnson, 247 F-15
JOHNSTON CO., 10957 J-15
Jones, 2692 F-14
Joy I-14
Kansas, 802 D-19
Katie, 348 I-13
Kaw City, 375 C-15
KAY CO., 46562 B-14
Keefton, 100 F-18
Kellyville, 1150 E-16
Kemp, 133 K-16
Kendrick, 139 E-15
Kenefic, 196 J-16
Kent J-17
Kenton, 17 B-1
Kenwood, 1224 D-19
Keota, 564 G-19
Ketchum, 442 C-19
Keyes, 324 B-2
Keys, 565 E-19
Kiefer, 1685 E-16
Kildare, 100 C-14
Kingfisher, 4633 E-12
KINGFISHER CO., 15034 E-12
Kingston, 1601 J-15
Kinta, 297 G-18
Kiowa, 731 H-17
KIOWA CO., 9446 H-10
Knowles, 11 B-7
Konawa, 1298 H-15
Krebs, 2053 H-17
Kremlin, 255 C-12
Lacey E-12
Lahoma, 611 D-12
L. Aluma, 88 J-5
L. Valley G-10
Lamar, 158 G-16
Lambert, 6 C-11
Lamont, 417 C-13
Lane, 414 J-17
Langley, 819 C-19
Langston, 1724 E-14
LATIMER CO., 11154 H-18
Laverne, 1344 C-8
Lawrence Creek, 149 E-16
Lawton, 96867 I-11
LE FLORE CO., 50384 I-19
Leach, 237 D-19
Lebanon, 303 K-14
Leedey, 435 E-9
Leflore, 190 H-19
Lehigh, 356 I-16
Lenapah, 293 B-17
Lenna, 40 G-17
Lenora E-9
Leon, 91 K-13
Leonard, 550 E-17
Lequire, 250 G-19
Lewisville G-18
Lexington, 2152 H-13
Liberty, 220 E-17
Liberty, 220 F-20
Lillard Pk. L-3
Lima, 53 G-15
LINCOLN CO., 34273 E-14
Lindsay, 2840 H-13
Little City, 150 J-15
Loco, 122 J-13
Locust Grv., 1423 D-18
LOGAN CO., 41848 E-13
Lone Grv., 5054 J-14
Lone Wolf, 438 H-9
Longdale, 262 D-11
Longtown, 2739 G-18
Lookeba, 166 G-11
LOVE CO., 9423 J-13
Loveland, 13 J-10
Lovell, 60 E-13
Loyal, 79 E-12
Lucien, 88 D-13
Lula, 30 H-16
Luther, 1221 F-14
Lutie H-18
Macomb, 32 G-14
Madill, 3770 J-15
MAJOR CO., 7527 D-10
Manchester, 103 B-12
Mangum, 3010 H-8
Manitou, 181 I-10
Mannford, 3076 D-16
Mannsville, 863 J-15
Maramec, 91 D-15
Marble City, 263 F-19
Marietta, 2626 K-14
Marland, 225 C-14
Marlow, 4662 I-12
Marshall, 272 D-13
MARSHALL CO., 15840 J-14
Martha, 162 H-9
Martin F-18
Mason, 100 F-16
Matoy J-16
Maud, 1048 G-15
May, 39 C-8
MAYES CO., 41259 D-18
Mayfield, 10 G-8
Maysville, 1232 H-13
Mazie, 91 D-18
McAlester, 18383 H-17
McBride, 80 K-15
MCCLAIN CO., 34506 H-13
McCurtain, 516 G-19
MCCURTAIN CO., 33151 I-19
MCINTOSH CO., 20252 G-17
McLain F-18
McLoud, 4044 F-14
Mead, 122 J-15
Medford, 996 C-13
Medicine Pk., 382 H-11
Meeker, 1144 F-14
Meno, 235 D-12
Meridian, 38 E-14
Miami, 13570 B-19
Midwest City, 54371 F-13
Milburn, 317 J-15
Milfay, 170 F-15
Mill Creek, 319 I-15
Miller J-17
Millerton, 320 J-19
Minco, 1632 G-12
Moffett, 128 F-20
Monroe, 200 H-20
Moore, 55081 G-13
Mooreland, 1190 D-9
Morris, 1479 F-17
Morrison, 733 D-14
Mounds, 1168 E-16
Mt. Herman, 150 I-19
Mountain Pk., 409 I-10
Mountain View, 795 G-10
Moyers, 100 J-17
Muldrow, 3466 F-20
Mulhall, 225 E-13
MURRAY CO., 13488 I-14
Muse, 200 H-19
Muskogee, 39223 E-18
MUSKOGEE CO., 70990 F-17
Mustang, 17395 G-13
Mutual, 61 D-9
Narcissa, 99 B-19
Nardin, 52 C-13
Nash, 204 C-12
Nashoba, 150 I-18
Nelagoney, 120 C-16
New Woodville, 132 K-15
Newcastle, 7685 G-13
Newkirk, 2317 B-14
Newport, 50 J-14
Nichols Hills, 3710 J-4
Nicoma Pk., 2393 K-7
Nida, 30 J-15
Ninnekah, 1002 H-12
Noble, 6481 G-13
NOBLE CO., 11561 C-14
Non, 40 H-16
Norge, 145 H-12
Norman, 110925 G-13
N. Enid, 860 D-12
Notchietown, 373 F-19
Nowata, 3731 C-17
NOWATA CO., 10536 B-17
Oakhurst, 2185 E-16
Oakland, 1057 J-15
Oaks, 288 D-19
Oakwood, 65 E-10
Ochelata, 424 C-16
Octavia, 50 I-20
Oglesby, 100 C-17
Oil Ctr. H-15
Oilton, 1013 E-15
Okarche, 1215 F-12
Okay, 620 E-18
Okeene, 1204 E-11
Okemah, 3223 F-16
Okesa, 120 C-16
OKFUSKEE CO., 12191 F-15
Oklahoma City, 579999 F-13
OKLAHOMA CO., 718633 F-13
Okmulgee, 12321 F-17
OKMULGEE CO., 40069 E-17
Oktaha, 390 F-18
Oleta, 50 J-18
Olive, 200 E-15
Olney, 130 I-16
Olustee, 607 I-9
Onapa F-18
Oologah, 1146 D-17
Optima, 356 C-4
Ord K-18
Orienta, 25 D-11
Orlando, 148 D-13
Orr, 30 J-13
Osage, 156 D-16
OSAGE CO., 47472 C-15
Oscar, 20 K-12
OTTAWA CO., 31848 B-19
Overbrook, 100 J-14
Owasso, 28915 D-17
Paden, 461 F-15
Page, 25 H-20
Panama, 1413 G-20
Panola, 300 H-18
Paoli, 610 H-14
Paradise Hill, 85 F-19
Park Hill, 3909 E-19
Parkland, 50 E-15
Pauls Valley, 6187 H-14
Pawhuska, 3584 C-16
Pawnee, 2196 D-15
PAWNEE CO., 16577 D-14
PAYNE CO., 77350 E-14
Pearson, 25 G-14
Peckham, 75 B-14
Peggs, 813 E-19
Pensacola, 125 C-18
Perkins, 2831 E-14
Pernell, 200 I-13
Perry, 5126 D-14
Pershing, 50 C-16
Phillips, 135 I-16
Pickens, 170 I-19
Piedmont, 5720 F-12
Pink, 2058 G-14
Pittsburg, 207 H-17
PITTSBURG CO., 45837 I-17
Plunkettville, 80 I-20
Pocasset, 156 G-12
Pocola, 4056 G-20
Ponca City, 25387 C-14
Pond Creek, 856 C-12
Pontotoc, 200 I-15
PONTOTOC CO., 37492 I-15
Pooleville, 100 I-13
Porter, 566 E-18
Porum, 727 G-18
Poteau, 8520 G-20
POTTAWATOMIE CO., 69442 G-14
Prague, 2386 F-15
Preston, 500 F-17
Proctor, 231 E-19
Prue, 465 D-16
Pryor, 9539 D-18
Pumpkin Ctr. I-11
Purcell, 5884 H-13
Purdy, 45 H-13
PUSHMATAHA CO., 11572 I-18
Putnam, 29 E-10
Pyramid Cors., 45 B-18
Quapaw, 906 B-19
Quinlan D-10
Quinton, 1051 G-18
Ralston, 330 C-15
Ramona, 535 C-17
Randlett, 438 J-11
Ratliff City, 120 I-13
Rattan, 310 J-18
Ravia, 528 J-15
Reagan, 50 I-15
Red Bird, 137 E-17
Red Oak, 549 H-19
Red Rock, 283 D-14
Reed, 40 H-8
Renfrow, 12 B-13
Rentiesville, 128 F-18
Retrop G-9
Reydon, 210 F-7
Richards Spur H-11
Richland, 400 F-12
Ringling, 1037 J-13
Ringold, 100 J-19
Ringwood, 497 D-11
Ripley, 403 E-14
Rock Island, 646 G-20
Rocky, 162 G-9
Rocky Pt., 370 E-18
Roff, 725 I-15
ROGER MILLS CO., 3647 F-8
ROGERS CO., 86905 D-17
Roland, 3169 F-20
Roll, 25 E-8
Roosevelt, 248 H-10
Rose, 285 D-19
Rosedale, 68 H-14
Rosston, 31 C-8
Rubottom, 70 K-13
Rufe, 200 J-19
Rush Sprs., 1231 H-12
Russell, 25 H-8
Russett J-15
Ryan, 816 J-12
St. Louis, 158 G-15
Salina, 1396 D-18
Sallisaw, 8880 F-19
Salt Fork C-13
Sand Sprs., 18906 D-16
Sapulpa, 20544 E-16
Sasakwa, 150 H-15
Savanna, 686 H-17
Sawyer, 321 J-18
Sayre, 4375 G-8
Schulter, 509 F-17
Scipio, 50 G-17
Scraper, 191 D-19
Scullin I-15
Seiling, 860 D-10
Selman, 25 C-9
Seminole, 7488 G-15
SEMINOLE CO., 25482 H-15
Sentinel, 901 G-9
Sequoyah, 698 D-17
SEQUOYAH CO., 42391 F-20
Seward, 50 E-13
Shady Pt., 1026 G-20
Shamrock, 101 E-15
Sharon, 135 D-9
Shattuck, 1356 D-8
Shawnee, 29857 G-14
Shay K-15
Sherwood, 80 I-19
Shidler, 441 C-15
Sickles, 110 G-11
Silo, 331 J-15
Silver City E-15
Skedee, 51 D-15
Skiatook, 7397 D-16
Slapout, 20 C-7
Slaughterville, 4137 G-13
Slick, 131 E-16
Smith Vil., 66 L-5
Smithville, 113 I-20
Snow, 130 I-18
Snyder, 1394 I-10
Soper, 261 J-17
S. Coffeyville, 785 B-17
Southard, 80 E-11
Sparks, 169 F-15
Spaulding, 178 H-16
Spavinaw, 437 D-19
Spencer, 3912 J-6
Spencerville, 200 J-18
Sperry, 1206 D-16
Spiro, 2164 G-20
Springer, 700 J-14
Stafford, 25 F-9
STEPHENS CO., 45048 I-12
Sterling, 793 H-11
Stidham, 18 G-17
Stigler, 2685 G-19
Stillwater, 45688 E-14
Stilwell, 3949 E-20
Stonewall, 470 I-15
Straight B-4
Stratford, 1525 H-14
Stringtown, 410 I-16
Strong City, 47 F-8
Stroud, 2690 F-15
Stuart, 180 H-16
Sugden, 43 J-12
Sulphur, 4929 I-14
Summerfield, 150 H-19
Summit, 139 F-18
Surrey Hills I-1
Sweetwater, 87 F-7
Swink, 66 J-18
Tabler H-12
Taft, 250 E-18
Tahlequah, 15753 E-19
Taiwah, 189 D-17
Talala, 273 C-17
Talihina, 1114 H-19
Taloga, 299 E-10
Tamaha, 176 F-19
Tangier D-8
Tatums, 151 I-13
Tecumseh, 6457 G-14
Temple, 1002 J-11
Terlton, 106 D-15
Terral, 382 K-12
Texanna, 2261 G-18
TEXAS CO., 20640 B-4
Texhoma, 926 C-3
Texola, 36 G-7
Thackerville, 445 K-14
The Village, 8929 J-4
Thomas, 1181 F-10
TILLMAN CO., 7992 I-10
Timber Brook, 1000 E-17
Tipton, 847 I-9
Tishomingo, 3034 J-15
Tom, 150 K-20
Tonkawa, 3216 C-13
Tribbey, 391 G-14
Troy, 40 J-15
Tryon, 491 E-14
Tullahassee, 106 E-18
Tulsa, 391906 D-17
TULSA CO., 603403 D-17
Tupelo, 329 I-16
Turley, 2756 D-17
Turpin, 467 B-5
Tushka, 312 J-16
Tuskahoma, 151 I-18
Tussy, 80 I-13
Tuttle, 6019 G-12
Twin Oaks, 198 D-19
Tyler J-14
Tyrone, 762 B-5
Union City, 1645 G-12
Utica, 50 K-16
Valley Brook, 765 L-5
Valliant, 754 J-19
Vamoosa, 80 H-15
Vanoss, 100 H-15
Velma, 620 I-13
Vera, 241 D-17
Verden, 530 G-12
Verdigris, 3993 D-17
Vernon, 60 G-17
Vian, 1466 F-19
Vici, 699 D-9
Victory, 25 I-9
Vinita, 5743 C-18
Vinson, 50 H-8
Vivian G-17
Wade, 70 K-16
Wagoner, 8323 E-18
WAGONER CO., 73085 E-18
Wainwright, 165 F-17
Wakita, 344 B-12
Walters, 2551 I-11
Wanette, 350 H-14
Wann, 125 B-17
Wapanucka, 438 I-16
Wardville I-16
Warner, 1641 F-18
Warr Acres, 10043 J-3
Warren, 80 H-9
Warwick, 148 F-14
Washington, 618 G-13
WASHINGTON CO., 50976 C-17
Washita, 130 G-11
WASHITA CO., 11629 G-9
Watonga, 5111 E-11
Watova, 150 C-17
Watson, 300 I-20
Watts, 324 D-20
Waukomis, 1286 D-12
Waurika, 2064 J-12
Wayne, 688 H-14
Waynoka, 927 C-10
Weatherford, 10833 F-10
Webb City, 62 C-15
Webbers Falls, 616 F-18
Welch, 619 B-18
Weleetka, 998 G-16
Welling, 771 E-19
Wellston, 788 F-14
Welty, 120 F-16
W. Siloam Sprs., 846 D-20
Westport, 298 D-16
Westville, 1639 E-20
Wetumka, 1282 G-16
Wewoka, 3430 G-15
Wheatland M-2
Whippoorwill, 100 B-16
White Eagle, 100 C-14
White Oak, 263 C-18
Whitefield, 391 G-18
Whitesboro, 250 H-19
Wilburton, 2843 H-18
Williams, 120 G-20
Willow, 149 G-8
Wilson, 1724 J-13
Winchester, 516 E-16
Wister, 1102 H-19
Wolco, 30 C-16
Wolf, 100 G-15
Woodford, 50 J-14
Woodlawn Pk., 153 K-2
WOODS CO., 8878 C-10
Woodward, 12051 D-9
WOODWARD CO., 20081 C-9
Wright City, 762 J-19
Wyandotte, 333 B-19
Wynnewood, 2212 I-14
Wynona, 437 C-16
Yale, 1227 D-15
Yanush, 60 H-18
Yeager, 75 G-16
Yuba, 60 K-16
Yukon, 22709 F-12
Zoe H-20

Oregon

Page locator

Map keys	Atlas pages
1–10	170–171
11–20	172–173

Adair Vil., 840 F-4
Adams, 350 C-13
Adel, 80 M-11
Adrian, 177 H-16
Agness, 120 L-2
Airlie, 100 F-3
Albany, 50158 F-4
Alfalfa H-8
Alicel D-14
Alkali Lake Sta. K-10
Allegany, 120 I-2
Alma, 30 H-3
Aloha, 49425 C-4
Alpine, 171 G-3
Alsea, 164 G-3
Alston, 270 B-4
Amity, 1614 D-4
Antelope, 46 E-9
Applegate, 100 M-3
Arago, 110 J-1
Arch Cape, 200 B-2
Arlington, 586 C-10
Arock, 60 K-16
Ashland, 20078 M-4
Ashwood, 30 F-9
Astoria, 9477 A-2
Athena, 1126 B-13
Aumsville, 3584 E-4
Aurora, 918 D-5
Austin F-13
Azalea, 430 K-3
Baker City, 9828 E-15
BAKER CO., 16134 E-15
Ballston, 80 E-3
Bandon, 3066 J-1
Banks, 1777 C-4
Barview, 1844 J-1
Barview, 170 C-2
Bates, 100 F-13
Bay City, 1286 C-2
Bayshore, 350 F-2
Beatty, 280 L-8
Beaver, 122 D-2
Beaver Marsh, 110 J-6
Beaverton, 89803 C-4
Beech Creek F-12
Bellfountain, 75 G-3
Bend, 76639 H-7
BENTON CO., 85579 G-3
Biggs Jct., 22 C-8
Bingham Sprs., 30 C-14
Birkenfeld, 60 B-3
Blachly, 100 G-3
Blodgett, 58 F-3
Blue River, 400 G-5
Bly, 700 L-8
Boardman, 3220 B-11
Bonanza, 415 M-7
Bonneville, 30 C-6
Boring, 730 D-5
Boyd C-8
Breitenbush, 40 E-6
Brickerville, 90 G-2
Bridgeport, 50 F-15
Brightwood, 240 D-6
Broadbent, 350 K-1
Brogan, 90 G-15
Brookings, 6336 M-1
Brothers, 150 H-9
Brownlee, 60 E-17
Brownsmead A-3
Brownsville, 1668 G-4
Buchanan, 30 I-13
Bunker Hill, 1444 J-1
Burlington, 100 J-17
Burns, 2806 I-12
Burns Jct. K-15
Burnt Woods F-3
Butte Falls, 423 L-5
Buxton, 100 C-4
Camas Valley, 380 J-2
Camp Sherman, 233 F-7
Canby, 15829 D-5
Cannon Bch., 1690 B-2
Canyon City, 703 G-12
Canyonville, 1884 K-3
Cape Meares, 99 C-2
Capitol Hill L-18
Carlton, 2007 D-4
Carson, 30 E-16
Carver, 480 M-20
Cascade Locks, 1144 C-6
Cascade Summit, 100 I-6
Cascadia, 147 G-5
Cave Jct., 1883 M-2
Cayuse, 68 C-13
Cecil C-10
Cedar Hills, 8300 L-17
Cedar Mill, 14546 L-17
Celilo, 80 C-8
Central Pt., 17169 L-4
Charleston, 700 J-1
Chemult, 270 J-6
Chenoweth, 1855 C-8
Cherry Grv., 300 D-4
Cheshire, 350 G-3
Chiloquin, 734 L-6
Christmas Valley, 300 J-9
Clackamas, 5177 M-19
CLACKAMAS CO., 375992 E-5
Clatskanie, 1737 B-4
CLATSOP CO., 37039 B-3
Cloverdale, 250 D-2
Coburg, 1035 G-4
Colton, 600 D-5
Columbia City, 1946 B-4
COLUMBIA CO., 49351 B-4
Condon, 682 D-10
Coos Bay, 15967 J-1
COOS CO., 63043 J-2
Coquille, 3866 J-1
Cornelius, 11869 C-4
Corvallis, 54462 F-3
Cottage Grv., 9686 H-4
Cove, 552 D-15
Crabtree, 391 F-4
Crane, 129 I-13
Crawfordsville, 332 G-4
Crescent, 770 I-7
Crescent Lake, 150 I-6
Creswell, 5031 H-4
CROOK CO., 20978 H-10
Crow, 100 H-3
Culp Creek, 220 I-4
Culver, 1357 F-8
CURRY CO., 22364 L-1
Curtin, 270 I-3
Dairy, 70 M-7
Dale, 80 E-12
Dallas, 14583 E-3
Damascus, 10539 M-20
Days Creek, 272 K-3
Dayton, 2534 D-4
Dayville, 149 F-11
Deadwood, 200 G-2
Dee, 200 C-7
Deer Island, 294 B-4
Dellwood, 50 I-2
Depoe Bay, 1398 E-2
DESCHUTES CO., 157733 H-8
Detroit, 202 F-6
Dexter, 300 H-4
Diamond, 70 K-13
Diamond Lake, 110 J-6
Diamond Lake Jct., 40 J-6
Dillard, 478 J-3
Dilley, 200 C-4
Donald, 979 D-4
Dorena, 350 H-4
DOUGLAS CO., 107667 J-4
Drain, 1151 I-3
Drew K-4
Drewsey, 100 H-14
Dufur, 604 D-8
Dundee, 3162 D-4
Dunes City, 1303 H-2
Durham, 1351 M-18
Durkee, 160 F-15
Eagle Creek, 430 D-5
Eagle Pt., 8469 L-4
Echo, 699 C-12
Eddyville, 240 F-2
Elgin, 1711 C-14
Elk City, 50 F-2
Elk Lake H-6
Elkhorn E-5
Elkton, 195 I-3
Elmira, 600 H-3
Elsie, 50 B-3
Enterprise, 1940 C-16
Eola, 45 F-18
Errol Hts. L-19
Estacada, 2695 D-5
Eugene, 156185 H-4
Fairview, 8920 C-5
Fairview, 100 J-2
Falcon Hts., 800 M-7
Fall Creek, 110 H-4
Falls City, 947 E-3
Fields, 30 M-13
Finn Rock, 80 G-5
Five Corners M-9
Flora B-16
Florence, 8466 H-2
Forest Grv., 21083 C-4
Ft. Klamath, 250 L-6
Ft. Rock, 50 J-8
Fossil, 473 E-10
Four Cors., 15947 F-20
Fox, 50 F-12
Frenchglen, 30 K-13
Fruitdale, 1177 L-3
Gales Creek, 100 C-4
Galice L-3
Garden Home L-18
Gardiner, 248 H-2
Garibaldi, 779 C-2
Gaston, 637 C-4
Gates, 471 F-5
Gateway, 40 F-8
Gaylord, 40 K-2
Gearhart, 1462 B-2
Gervais, 2464 E-4
Gibbon C-14
Gilbert L-20
Gilchrist, 500 I-7
GILLIAM CO., 1871 D-10
Gladstone, 11497 M-19
Glasgow, 763 I-1
Glenada, 270 H-2
Glendale, 874 K-3
Gleneden Bch., 900 E-2
Glengary, 300 J-3
Glenwood, 80 C-3
Glenwood B-8
Glide, 1795 J-4
Goble, 200 B-4
Gold Bch., 2253 L-1
Gold Hill, 1220 L-4
Goshen, 170 H-4
Government Camp, 193 D-7
Grand Ronde, 1661 E-3
Granite, 38 E-13
GRANT CO., 7445 E-13
Grants Pass, 34533 L-3
Grass Valley, 164 D-9
Green, 7515 J-3
Green Acres, 230 J-1
Greenberry, 50 F-3
Greenleaf, 100 G-3
Gresham, 105594 C-5
Haines, 416 E-14
Halfway, 288 E-16
Halsey, 904 G-4
Hampton I-10
Happy Valley, 13903 M-20
Harbor, 2391 M-1
Hardman, 30 D-11
Harlan, 130 F-3
HARNEY CO., 7422 J-12
Harper, 109 H-15
Harrisburg, 3567 G-4
Hauser, 700 I-1
Hayesville, 19936 E-20
Hebo, 232 D-2
Heceta Bch., 340 H-2
Helix, 184 B-13
Heppner, 1291 D-11
Hereford, 60 F-14
Hermiston, 16745 B-12
Hilgard D-14
Hillsboro, 91611 C-4
Hines, 1563 I-12
Homestead E-17
Hood River, 7167 C-7
HOOD RIVER CO., 22346 C-7
Horton, 50 G-3
Hoskins, 90 F-3
Hot Sprs., 50 M-8
Hubbard, 3173 D-4
Huntington, 440 G-16
Idanha, 134 F-6
Idleyld Pk., 320 J-4
Illinois Valley, 250 M-2
Imbler, 306 C-14
Imnaha, 90 C-17
Independence, 8590 E-4
Ione, 329 C-11
Ironside, 50 G-15
Irrigon, 1826 B-11
Irving, 450 G-4
Island City, 989 D-14
JACKSON CO., 203206 L-4
Jacksonville, 2785 M-4
Jamieson, 90 G-16
Jasper, 90 H-4
Jeffers Gdn., 368 A-2
Jefferson, 3098 F-4
JEFFERSON CO., 21720 F-8
Jewell, 50 B-3
John Day, 1744 G-12
Johnson City, 566 M-19
Jordan Valley, 181 K-17
Joseph, 1081 D-16
JOSEPHINE CO., 82713 L-3
Junction City, 5392 G-4
Juntura, 57 H-14
Kamela, 30 D-13
Keizer, 36478 E-4
Keno, 1100 M-6
Kent, 40 D-9
Kenton K-18
Kerby, 595 M-2
Kernville, 50 E-2
Kimberly, 50 F-11
King City, 3111 M-17
Kings Valley, 65 F-3
KLAMATH CO., 66380 L-7
Klamath Falls, 20840 M-6
Knappa, 400 A-3
La Grande, 13082 D-14
La Pine, 1653 I-7
Lacomb, 546 F-5
Lafayette, 3742 D-4
LAKE CO., 7895 K-9
L. Oswego, 36619 D-5
Lakeside, 1699 I-1
Lakeview, 2294 M-10
LANE CO., 351715 H-4
Langell Valley, 400 M-8
Langlois, 177 K-1
Lawen, 60 I-13
Leaburg, 250 G-5
Lebanon, 15518 F-4
Lee's Camp, 60 C-3
Lewisburg, 250 F-3
Lexington, 238 D-11
Lincoln Bch., 2045 E-2
Lincoln City, 7930 E-2
LINCOLN CO., 46034 F-2
LINN CO., 116672 F-5
Logsden, 300 F-2
London I-4
Lonerock, 21 E-10
Long Creek, 197 F-12
Lorane, 220 H-3
Lorella M-8
Lostine, 213 C-15
Lowell, 1045 H-4
Lyons, 1161 E-5
Madras, 6046 F-8
MALHEUR CO., 31313 J-15
Malin, 805 N-7
Manning, 110 C-4
Manzanita, 598 C-2
Mapleton, 900 H-2
Marcola, 560 G-4
Marion, 313 F-4
MARION CO., 315335 E-6
Marion Forks, 100 F-6
Marquam, 60 E-5
Maupin, 418 D-8
Mayger, 120 A-4
Mayville, 30 E-10
Maywood Pk., 752 K-19
McCoy, 50 E-4
McDermitt, 200 M-15
McKee Br., 50 M-4
McKenzie Br., 400 G-6
McMinnville, 32187 D-4
McNulty, 800 B-4
Meacham, 50 C-13
Medford, 74907 M-4
Medical Sprs., 30 E-15
Mehama, 292 E-5
Melrose, 735 J-3
Merlin, 1615 L-3
Merrill, 844 N-7
Metolius, 710 F-8
Metzger, 3765 M-18
Midland, 300 M-6
Mill City, 1855 F-5
Millington, 100 J-1
Milo, 320 K-4
Milton-Freewater, 7050 B-13
Milwaukie, 20291 M-19
Minam C-15
Mission, 1037 C-13
Mist, 60 B-4
Mitchell, 130 F-10
Modoc Pt., 30 L-6
Mohler, 60 C-2
Molalla, 8108 D-5
Monmouth, 9534 E-3
Monroe, 617 G-3
Monument, 128 E-11
Moro, 324 C-9
MORROW CO., 11173 C-11
Mosier, 433 C-7
Mt. Angel, 3286 E-4
Mt. Hood, 286 C-7
Mt. Vernon, 527 G-12
Mulino, 2103 D-5
MULTNOMAH CO., 735334 C-6
Murphy, 420 M-3
Myrtle Creek, 3439 K-3
Myrtle Pt., 2514 J-1
Nedonna, 450 C-2
Nehalem, 271 C-2
Neotsu, 350 E-2
Nesika Bch., 463 L-1
Neskowin, 134 D-2
Netarts, 748 C-2
New Br., 30 E-16
New Hope, 1515 L-3
New Pine Creek, 120 N-10
New Princeton, 150 J-13
Newberg, 22068 D-4
Newport, 9989 F-2
Nonpareil, 70 I-4
N. Bend, 9695 I-1
N. Plains, 1947 C-4
N. Powder, 439 E-15
Norway, 150 J-1
Noti, 200 H-3
Nyssa, 3267 H-17
Oak Grv., 16629 M-19
Oakland, 927 I-3
Oakridge, 3205 H-5
O'Brien, 504 M-2
Oceanside, 361 C-2
Odell, 2255 C-7
Odessa, 40 L-8
Olene, 30 M-7
Olex C-10
Olney, 210 B-3
Ontario, 11366 H-17
Ophir, 220 L-1
Oregon City, 31859 D-5
Otis, 230 E-2
Otter Rock, 200 E-2
Outlook, 100 M-20
Owyhee H-16
Pacific City, 1035 D-2
Paisley, 243 L-9
Parkdale, 311 C-7
Parkrose K-20
Paulina, 40 G-10
Pedee, 100 F-3
Pendleton, 16612 C-13
Peoria, 94 F-4
Perry, 90 D-14
Philomath, 4584 F-3
Phoenix, 4538 M-4
Pilot Rock, 1502 C-13
Pine Grv., 148 E-7
Pinehurst, 40 M-5
Pistol River, 84 M-1
Pittsburg, 40 B-4
Pleasant Hill, 110 H-4
Plush, 57 L-10
POLK CO., 75403 E-3
Port Orford, 1133 K-1
Portland, 583776 C-5
Post, 40 G-9
Powell Butte, 770 G-8
Powers, 689 K-2
Prairie City, 909 F-13
Prescott, 55 B-4
Prineville, 9253 G-8
Prospect, 455 K-5
Rainier, 1895 B-4
Raleigh Hills, 5896 L-18
Redmond, 26215 G-8
Reedsport, 4154 I-2
Remote, 30 K-2
Rhododendron, 800 D-6
Richland, 156 E-16
Rickreall, 77 E-4
Riddle, 1185 K-3
Rieth, 70 C-12
Riley, 50 I-11
Ritter, 50 E-12
Rivergrove, 289 M-18
Riverside, 10 I-14
Riverton, 100 J-1
Rockaway Bch., 1312 C-2
Rockville, 30 J-16
Rockwood L-20
Rocky Pt., 110 L-6
Rogue River, 2131 L-3
Rome K-15
Rose Lodge, 1894 E-2
Roseburg, 21181 J-3
Ruch, 840 M-4
Rufus, 249 C-9
Ruggs D-11
Russellville L-20
Saginaw, 100 H-4
St. Helens, 12883 B-4
St. Paul, 421 D-4
Salem, 154637 E-4
Sandy, 9570 D-6
Santa Clara A-7
Scappoose, 6592 C-4
Scio, 838 F-4
Scotts Mills, 357 E-5
Scottsburg, 210 I-2
Seal Rock, 600 F-2
Seaside, 6457 B-2
Selma, 695 M-2
Seneca, 199 G-12
Shady Cove, 2904 L-4
Shaniko, 36 E-9
Shaw, 80 E-4
Shedd, 204 F-4
Sheridan, 6127 D-3
SHERMAN CO., 1765 D-9
Sherwood, 18194 D-4
Siletz, 1212 F-2
Siltcoos, 30 H-2
Silver Lake, 149 J-8
Silverton, 9222 E-4
Simnasho E-7
Sisters, 2038 G-7
Sitkum J-2
Sixes, 220 K-1
Sodaville, 308 F-4
Sprague River, 350 L-7
Spray, 160 E-11
Springfield, 59403 H-4
Stanfield, 2043 C-12
Stayton, 7644 E-4
Steamboat, 60 J-4
Sublimity, 2681 E-4
Summer Lake, 70 K-9
Summerville, 135 C-14
Sumner, 50 J-1
Sumpter, 204 F-14
Sunny Valley, 180 L-3
Sunnyside, 6791 M-20
Sunriver, 1393 H-7
Sunset Bch., 320 B-2
Sutherlin, 7810 I-3
Suver, 50 F-4
Svensen, 550 A-3
Sweet Home, 8925 G-5
Swisshome, 300 H-2
Sylvan L-18
Takilma, 378 M-3
Talent, 6066 M-4
Tangent, 1164 F-4
Telocaset D-15
Tenmile, 260 J-3
Terrebonne, 1257 G-8
The Dalles, 13620 C-8
Thornhollow C-13
Three Lynx, 70 D-6
Tidewater, 300 F-2
Tiernan H-2
Tierra Del Mar, 220 D-2
Tigard, 48035 D-4
Tillamook, 4935 C-2
TILLAMOOK CO., 25250 C-3
Tiller, 210 K-4
Timber, 260 C-3
Toketee Falls, 300 J-5
Toledo, 3465 F-2
Tollgate B-14
Trail, 702 L-4
Triangle Lake, 70 G-3
Tri-City, 3931 K-3
Troutdale, 15962 C-5
Troy, 30 B-15
Tualatin, 26054 D-4
Tumalo, 488 G-7
Turner, 1854 E-4
Twin Rocks, 510 C-2
Tygh Valley, 206 D-8
Ukiah, 186 D-12
Umapine, 315 B-13
Umatilla, 6906 B-12
UMATILLA CO., 75889 D-13
Umpqua, 240 J-3
Union, 2121 D-15
UNION CO., 25748 D-14
Union Creek, 30 K-5
Unionvale D-4
Unity, 71 F-14
Vale, 1874 H-16
Valley Falls L-10
Vaughn, 60 H-3
Veneta, 4561 H-3
Vernonia, 2151 B-4
Vida, 450 G-5
Wagontire J-11
Waldport, 2033 F-2
Wallowa, 808 C-15
WALLOWA CO., 7008 C-16
Walterville, 250 H-4
Walton, 200 H-3
Wamic, 85 D-8
Wapato D-4
Wapinitia E-8
Warm Sprs., 2945 F-8
Warren, 1787 B-4
Warrenton, 4989 A-2
Wasco, 410 C-9
WASCO CO., 25213 E-8
WASHINGTON CO., 529710 C-3
Waterloo, 229 F-4
Wedderburn, 330 L-1
W. Linn, 25109 N-19
W. Portland M-18
W. Salem F-19
W. Slope, 6554 L-18
Westfall, 80 H-15
Westfir, 253 H-5
Weston, 667 B-13
Westport, 321 A-3
Wheeler, 414 C-2
WHEELER CO., 1441 F-10
White City, 7975 L-4
Whiteson, 100 D-4
Wilbur, 200 J-3
Wilderville, 380 L-3
Willamina, 2025 E-3
Williams, 1072 M-3
Willowcreek G-16
Willowdale E-8
Wilsonville, 19509 D-4
Winchester, 2700 J-3
Winchester Bay, 382 I-1
Winston, 5379 J-3
Wolf Creek, 550 K-3
Woodburn, 24080 D-4
Woods, 80 D-2
Woodson, 60 B-3
Worden, 30 M-6
Wren, 110 F-3
Yachats, 690 G-2
Yamhill, 1024 D-4
YAMHILL CO., 99193 D-3
Yoncalla, 1047 I-3
Zigzag, 300 D-6

Pennsylvania

Page locator

Map keys	Atlas pages
WA1–WJ14	174–175
WK1–WT14	176–177
EA1–EJ14	178–179
EK1–ET14	180–181

* City keyed to p. 50
† City keyed to p. 137
‡ City keyed to pp. 182–183

Aaronsburg, 613 EK-2
Abbottstown, 1011 EQ-4
Abington, 10000 ‡A-5
Academia, 30 EM-2
Academy Cors., 60 EE-2
Ackermanville, 610 EK-12
Acme, 180 WO-6
Acmetonia, 1500 ‡I-8
Acosta, 400 WO-8
Adah, 450 WP-4
ADAMS CO., 101407 EP-2
Adamsburg, 172 WN-5
Adamstown, 1789 EN-8
Adamsville, 67 WG-2
Addison, 207 WQ-7
Adrian, 200 WK-6
Afton Vil., 700 EC-4
Aiken WE-10
Airville, 100 EQ-6
Akeley WD-8
Akron, 3876 EO-7
Alba, 157 EF-4
Albany, 20 EL-9
Albert, 60 EI-8
Albion, 1516 WE-2
Albrightsville, 202 EJ-10
Alburtis, 2361 EM-10
Aldan, 4152 ‡F-2
Alden, 200 EI-8
Aldenville, 170 EF-11
Aleppo, 60 WQ-2
Alexandria, 346 WM-12
Alfarata, 149 EL-2
Alford, 25 EE-9
Alinda EN-2
Aliquippa, 9438 WL-3
Allandale, 1000 ET-3
ALLEGHENY CO., 1223348 WM-4
Allemans, 60 WL-11
Allen, 375 EO-3
Allenport, 648 WN-13
Allens Mills WI-9
Allensville, 503 WM-13
Allentown, 118032 EL-10
Allenwood, 321 EI-4
Allison, 625 WP-4
Allison Pk., 21552 WL-4
Allport, 264 WJ-12
Almedia, 1078 EJ-6

*, †, ‡, §, ◊ See explanation under state title in this index.
County and parish names are listed in capital letters & boldface type.
Independent cities (not included in a county) are listed in italics.

Almont, 75 ... EN-11
Alsace Mnr., 478 ... ER-14
Altenwald, 40 ... EQ-1
Altoona, 46320 ... WM-11
Alum Bank, 198 ... WO-10
Alverda, 400 ... WL-9
Alverton, 350 ... WO-5
Ambler, 6417 ... EO-12
Ambridge, 7050 ... WL-3
Amity, 400 ... WO-3
Amityville, 250 ... EN-9
Amsbry, 65 ... WM-10
Analomink, 200 ... EJ-12
Ancient Oaks, 6661 ... EM-10
Andalusia, 3500 ... ‡B-8
Andersonburg, 50 ... EN-2
Andreas, 200 ... EK-9
Andrews Settlement, 40 ... WE-13
Angelica, 100 ... EN-8
Angels ... EH-11
Anita, 600 ... WJ-8
Annandale, 275 ... WI-4
Annisville, 35 ... WI-5
Annville, 4767 ... EN-6
Ansonia, 50 ... EF-2
Ansonville, 100 ... WK-10
Antes Fort, 400 ... EI-3
Antrim, 400 ... EF-2
Apollo, 1647 ... WL-6
Appenzell, 150 ... EJ-11
Applebachsville, 120 ... EM-11
Applewold, 310 ... WK-6
Ararat ... EE-10
Arbuckle, 50 ... WD-4
Arcadia, 220 ... WK-9
Arch Rock, 100 ... EL-2
Archbald, 6984 ... EG-10
Ardara, 300 ... ‡L-10
Ardenheim, 25 ... WM-13
Ardmore, 12455 ... ‡D-2
Ardsley, 4500 ... ‡A-4
Arendtsville, 952 ... EP-2
Argentine, 60 ... WI-5
Aristes, 311 ... EK-7
Armagh, 122 ... WM-8
Armbrust, 230 ... WN-6
ARMSTRONG CO., 68941 ... WL-6
Arnold, 5157 ... WL-5
Arnot, 332 ... EF-3
Arona, 370 ... WN-5
Asaph, 100 ... EF-2
Asbury ... WB-9
Ashfield, 300 ... EK-9
Ashland, 2817 ... EK-7
Ashland, 60 ... WK-11
Ashley, 2790 ... EI-9
Ashtola, 150 ... WO-9
Ashville, 227 ... WM-10
Aspers, 350 ... EP-3
Aspinwall, 2801 ... ‡J-7
Atco, 200 ... EF-12
Atglen, 1406 ... EP-8
Athens, 3367 ... EE-6
Atlantic, 77 ... WG-2
Atlantic ... WK-11
Atlas, 809 ... EK-6
Atlasburg, 401 ... WN-2
Atwood, 107 ... WK-7
Auburn, 741 ... EL-8
Auburn Ctr., 50 ... EF-8
Auburn Four Corners, 60 ... EF-8
Audubon, 8433 ... EO-11
Aultman, 225 ... WM-7
Austin, 562 ... WF-12
Austinburg, 60 ... ED-2
Austinville, 150 ... EE-4
Avalon, 4705 ... WM-3
Avella, 804 ... WN-2
Avis, 1484 ... EI-2
Avoca, 2661 ... EB-10
Avon, 1667 ... EN-6
Avondale, 1265 ... EQ-9
Avonia, 1205 ... WD-3
Avonmore, 1011 ... WM-6
Axemann, 150 ... WK-14
Bachmanville, 200 ... EN-6
Baden, 4135 ... WL-3
Baggaley, 600 ... WN-6
Bainbridge, 1355 ... EO-5
Bair, 400 ... EP-5
Bairdford, 698 ... WL-4
Bakers Summit, 110 ... WN-11
Bakerstown Sta., 400 ... WL-4
Bakersville, 200 ... WP-7
Bakerton, 900 ... WL-9
Bala-Cynwyd, 8000 ... ‡D-3
Bald Eagle, 250 ... WL-12
Baldwin, 19767 ... WN-4
Ballietsville, 250 ... EA-1
Balls Mills, 60 ... EH-4
Bally, 1090 ... EM-10
Bandanna, 225 ... EQ-4
Banetown, 100 ... WO-3
Bangor, 5273 ... EK-12
Bannerville, 110 ... EL-2
Barbours, 120 ... EH-5
Bard, 50 ... WP-10
Bareville, 1250 ... EO-8
Barkeyville, 207 ... WI-4
Barnes, 200 ... WF-8
Barnesville, 300 ... EK-8
Barnsley, 100 ... EQ-8
Barree, 70 ... WL-12
Barto, 180 ... EN-10
Bath, 2693 ... EL-11
Baumstown, 422 ... EN-9
Bausman, 300 ... ET-8
Bavington, 50 ... WM-2
Baxter ... WI-8
Beach Haven, 500 ... EJ-7
Beach Lake, 320 ... EG-12
Beallsville, 466 ... WO-4
Bear Creek Vil., 257 ... EI-9
Bear Lake, 164 ... WD-6
Beartown, 200 ... EQ-2
Beartown ... EO-8
Beaumont, 200 ... EH-8
Beaver, 4531 ... WL-2
Beaver Brook, 400 ... EJ-8
Beaver Ctr., 40 ... WE-2
BEAVER CO., 170539 ... WK-2
Beaver Dam, 130 ... WE-5
Beaver Falls, 8987 ... WK-2
Beaver Lake ... EH-6
Beaver Meadows, 869 ... EJ-9
Beaver Sprs., 674 ... EL-3
Beaverdale, 1035 ... WN-9
Beavertown, 965 ... EL-3
Beavertown, 90 ... EO-4
Beavertown, 40 ... WN-11
Beccaria, 175 ... WK-11
Bechtelsville, 942 ... EN-10
Beckersville, 200 ... EO-9
Bedford, 2841 ... WP-10
BEDFORD CO., 49762 ... WO-10
Bedminster, 500 ... EM-12
Beech Creek, 701 ... EJ-1
Beechwood ... WG-11
Beersville, 250 ... EK-10
Belair, 1310 ... ER-8
Belden ... WO-10
Belfast, 1257 ... EK-11
Belknap, 40 ... WK-7
Bell Acres, 1388 ... WL-3
Bellaire ... EO-6
Belle Vernon, 1093 ... WO-4
Bellefonte, 6187 ... WK-14
Bellegrove, 300 ... EN-6
Belleville, 1827 ... WL-14
Bellevue, 8370 ... WM-3
Bells, 75 ... WK-10
Belltown, 60 ... EL-2
Bellwood, 1828 ... WL-11
Belmont, 2784 ... WT-2
Belmont Hills, 1500 ... ‡C-2
Belsano, 400 ... WM-9
Ben Avon, 1781 ... ‡I-4
Ben Avon Hts., 371 ... ‡I-5
Bendersville, 641 ... EP-3
Bendertown, 50 ... EI-7
Benezette, 200 ... WH-11
Benfer, 100 ... EK-3
Bensalem, 3000 ... ‡A-8
Benson, 191 ... WO-8
Bentley Creek, 160 ... EE-5
Bentleyville, 2581 ... WO-4
Benton, 824 ... EI-6
Benvenue, 25 ... EN-4
Berkley, 200 ... EM-8
Berkleys Mill, 60 ... WQ-8
BERKS CO., 411442 ... EM-8
Berlin, 2104 ... WP-8
Berlinsville, 200 ... EK-10
Bermudian, 40 ... EP-4
Berne, 130 ... EM-8
Bernville, 955 ... EM-8
Berrysburg, 368 ... EL-5
Berwick, 10477 ... EJ-7
Berwyn, 3631 ... EP-11
Bessemer, 1111 ... WJ-2
Bethany, 246 ... EF-11
Bethel, 499 ... EM-7
Bethel Pk., 32313 ... WN-4
Bethesda, 45 ... EQ-7
Bethlehem, 74982 ... EL-11
Bethlehem, 25 ... WK-9
Betula ... WF-11
Beyer, 100 ... WK-7
Big Beaver, 1970 ... WK-2
Big Cove Tannery, 200 ... WQ-12
Big Pond, 100 ... EE-5
Big Run, 624 ... WJ-9
Bigler, 398 ... WJ-11
Biglerville, 1200 ... EP-3
Bigmount, 100 ... EP-4
Bingen, 350 ... EC-5
Bingham, 40 ... WE-10
Bingham Ctr. ... WE-14
Birchardville, 40 ... EE-8
Bird in Hand, 402 ... EP-7
Birdsboro, 5163 ... EN-9
Birmingham, 90 ... WL-12
Bishop, 800 ... WN-3
Bittersville, 150 ... EP-6
Black Gap ... EP-1
Black Lick, 1462 ... WM-7
Black Walnut, 150 ... EF-8
Blacktown, 50 ... WI-3
Blackwell, 80 ... EG-2
Blain, 263 ... EN-1
Blain City, 250 ... WK-10
Blaine Hill, 1100 ... WN-4
Blainsport, 110 ... EN-8
BLAIR CO., 127089 ... WN-11
Blairs Mills, 100 ... WN-14
Blairsville, 3412 ... WM-7
Blairtown, 60 ... WP-3
Blakely, 6564 ... EG-10
Blakeslee, 300 ... EI-10
Blanchard, 740 ... EJ-1
Blandburg, 402 ... WL-11
Blandon, 7152 ... EM-9
Blawnox, 1432 ... ‡J-8
Blooming Glen, 650 ... EN-12
Blooming Grv., 200 ... EH-12
Blooming Grv., 100 ... EQ-4
Blooming Valley, 337 ... WF-4
Bloomingdale, 2100 ... ES-9
Bloomington, 80 ... WJ-10
Bloomsburg, 14855 ... EJ-6
Bloserville, 200 ... EO-2
Blossburg, 1538 ... EF-3
Blough, 80 ... WO-8
Blue Ball, 1031 ... EO-8
Blue Bell, 6067 ... EO-11
Blue Knob ... WN-10
Blue Ridge Summit, 891 ... ER-2
Blythedale, 250 ... WN-5
Boalsburg, 3722 ... WK-13
Boardman, 35 ... WK-11
Bobtown, 757 ... WQ-4
Bocktown ... ‡I-1
Bodines, 50 ... EG-4
Boiling Sprs., 3225 ... EO-3
Bolivar, 465 ... WN-7
Bolivar Run, 350 ... WD-10
Boltz, 160 ... WM-8
Bon Air, 600 ... WS-2
Bonneauville, 1800 ... EQ-3
Booneville, 75 ... EJ-2
Booths Cor., 200 ... EQ-10
Boothwyn, 4933 ... *B-10
Bordnersville ... EM-6
Bossardsville ... EJ-11
Boston, 545 ... ‡M-8
Boswell, 1277 ... WO-8
Bovard, 700 ... WN-6
Bovard, 40 ... WJ-4
Bowmanstown, 937 ... EK-10
Bowmansville, 2077 ... EO-8
Boyds Mills, 85 ... EF-12
Boydstown, 50 ... WJ-4
Boyertown, 4055 ... EN-10
Boynton, 200 ... WQ-8
Brackenridge, 3260 ... WL-5
Brackney, 200 ... ED-8
Braddock, 2159 ... ‡L-8
Braddock Hills, 1880 ... ‡K-8
Braden Plan, 250 ... WP-3
Bradenville, 545 ... WN-7
Bradford, 8770 ... WD-10
BRADFORD CO., 62622 ... EE-5
Bradford Woods, 1171 ... WL-3
Bradleytown, 50 ... WG-4
Bradys Bend, 150 ... WJ-5
Branch Dale, 388 ... EL-7
Branchton, 80 ... WJ-4
Branchville ... WD-3
Brandamore, 300 ... EP-9
Brandonville, 197 ... EK-7
Brandtsville ... EO-3
Brandy Camp, 200 ... WH-10
Brandywine Manor, 200 ... EO-9
Brave, 201 ... WQ-2
Breezewood, 300 ... WP-11
Breinigsville, 4138 ... EM-10
Brent, 90 ... WI-3
Brentwood, 9643 ... ‡L-6
Breslau, 500 ... EA-7
Bressler, 1437 ... ET-4
Briar Creek, 660 ... EJ-7
Brickerville, 1309 ... EO-7
Bridesburg ... ‡D-6
Bridgeburg ... WK-6
Bridgeport, 4554 ... ‡A-1
Bridgeport, 40 ... EN-2
Bridgeton ... EQ-6
Bridgeville, 5148 ... WN-3
Bridgewater, 704 ... WL-2
Bridgewater, 250 ... ‡B-9
Brisbin, 411 ... WK-11
Bristol, 9726 ... EO-13
Bristoria, 40 ... WP-2
Britton Run ... WE-5
Broad Top City, 452 ... WO-12
Brockport, 300 ... WI-9
Brockton, 500 ... EL-8
Brockway, 2072 ... WI-9
Brodbecks ... EQ-5
Brodhead, 100 ... EA-5
Brodheadsville, 1800 ... EJ-11
Brogue, 200 ... EQ-6
Brookdale, 60 ... ED-9
Brookhaven, 8006 ... EQ-11
Brookland, 15 ... WE-13
Brooklyn, 250 ... EF-9
Brookside, 2200 ... WC-4
Brookside ... EH-3
Brookston, 90 ... WF-8
Brookville, 3924 ... WI-8
Broomall, 10789 ... EP-11
Brotherton, 60 ... WP-8
Broughton, 3000 ... ‡M-6
Browndale, 525 ... EF-10
Brownfield, 400 ... WQ-5
Brownstown, 2816 ... EO-7
Brownstown, 744 ... WN-8
Brownstown, 30 ... WM-6
Brownsville, 2331 ... WP-4
Browntown, 1418 ... EB-9
Browntown, 90 ... EF-7
Bruin, 524 ... WJ-5
Brunnerville, 250 ... EO-7
Brush Valley, 300 ... WM-8
Brushtown, 340 ... EQ-4
Brushtown ... EO-2
Bryan, 30 ... WK-7
Bryn Athyn, 1375 ... EO-12
Bryn Mawr, 3779 ... ‡C-1
Buck, 120 ... EQ-7
Buck Hill Falls, 950 ... EI-11
Buck Mtn., 70 ... EJ-9
Buck Run, 176 ... EL-7
Buck Run, 150 ... EP-9
Buck Valley ... WQ-11
Buckhorn, 318 ... EJ-6
Buckhorn, 130 ... WM-10
Buckingham, 2000 ... EN-12
BUCKS CO., 625249 ... EM-11
Bucktown, 60 ... EO-10
Buena Vista, 600 ... WN-5
Buena Vista, 60 ... WJ-5
Buffalo, 120 ... WN-2
Buffalo Mills, 100 ... WP-10
Buffalo Run, 75 ... WK-13
Buffalo Valley, 120 ... WK-5
Bulger, 407 ... WM-2
Bullion, 40 ... WI-4
Bullis Mills ... WD-11
Bully Hill, 150 ... WH-5
Bungalow Pk., 200 ... EC-2
Bunker Hill, 170 ... EN-6
Bunkertown, 60 ... EL-3
Bunola, 300 ... WN-4
Burgettstown, 1388 ... WM-2
Burlington, 156 ... EF-5
Burnham, 2054 ... EL-1
Burning Well ... WF-10
Burnside, 234 ... WK-9
Burnt Cabins, 125 ... WO-13
Burtville ... WF-12
Bushkill, 1200 ... EI-12
Bustleton ... ‡B-7
Butler, 13757 ... WK-4
BUTLER CO., 183862 ... WJ-4
Buttonwood, 620 ... EB-6
Buttonwood ... EG-3
Butztown, 1500 ... EA-5
Byrnedale, 427 ... WH-10
Byromtown ... WG-8
Cabot, 400 ... WK-5
Cadogan, 400 ... WK-6
Cairnbrook, 520 ... WO-9
Caledonia, 200 ... WH-11
California, 6795 ... WO-4
Callensburg, 207 ... WI-6
Callery, 394 ... WK-4
Caln, 1519 ... EP-9
Calvin, 90 ... WN-12
Cambra, 70 ... EI-7
CAMBRIA CO., 143679 ... WL-10
Cambridge, 140 ... EO-8
Cambridge Sprs., 2595 ... WE-4
Cameron, 50 ... WG-12
CAMERON CO., 5085 ... WG-11
Camp Hill, 7888 ... EN-4
Campbelltown, 3616 ... EN-6
Camptown, 180 ... EF-7
Canadensis, 1200 ... EI-11
Canan, 140 ... WB-12
Candor, 60 ... WM-2
Cannelton, 100 ... WK-2
Canoe Camp, 150 ... EF-3
Canoe Creek, 250 ... WM-11
Canonsburg, 8992 ... WN-3
Canton, 1976 ... EF-4
CARBON CO., 65249 ... EJ-9
Carbondale, 8891 ... EG-10
Carlisle, 18682 ... EO-3
Carlisle Sprs. ... EN-3
Carlton, 80 ... WG-4
Carmichaels, 483 ... WP-4
Carnegie, 7972 ... ‡K-4
Carnot, 4500 ... ‡I-2
Carroll ... EJ-3
Carroll Valley, 3876 ... EQ-2
Carrolltown, 853 ... WL-9
Carter Camp, 20 ... WF-14
Carversville, 400 ... EN-12
Carverton, 500 ... EA-9
Casanova, 90 ... WJ-12
Cashtown, 459 ... EQ-2
Cassandra, 147 ... WM-10
Casselman, 94 ... WP-7
Cassville, 143 ... WN-12
Castanea, 1125 ... EI-2
Castle Gdn., 45 ... WH-12
Castle Shannon, 8316 ... ‡L-5
Catasauqua, 6436 ... EL-11
Catawissa, 1552 ... EJ-6
Cavettsville, 120 ... ‡L-9
Cecil, 900 ... WN-3
Cedar Hts., 800 ... ‡B-2
Cedar Ledge, 25 ... EF-4
Cedar Run, 100 ... EG-2
Cedar Sprs., 90 ... EJ-2
Cedarbrook, 2800 ... ‡B-4
Cementon, 1538 ... EL-10
Center Mills, 80 ... EP-3
Center Moreland ... EH-8
Center Road ... WF-2
Center Valley, 900 ... EM-11
Centerport, 387 ... EM-8
Centerville, 3263 ... WO-4
Centerville, 1700 ... ES-7
Centerville, 218 ... WF-5
Centerville, 125 ... WQ-10
Central, 100 ... EH-6
Central City, 1124 ... WO-9
Central Highlands, 700 ... ‡N-8
Centralia, 10 ... EK-7
CENTRE CO., 153990 ... EK-1
Centre Hall, 1265 ... WK-14
Cessna, 60 ... WO-10
Cetronia ... EC-2
Chadds Ford, 1200 ... EQ-10
Chalfant, 800 ... ‡K-8
Chalfont, 4009 ... EN-12
Chalkhill, 141 ... WQ-5
Challenge ... WH-10
Chambers Hill, 1500 ... ES-4
Chambersburg, 20268 ... EP-1
Chambersville, 100 ... WL-7
Champion, 300 ... WO-6
Chandlers Valley, 250 ... WE-7
Chaneysville, 80 ... WQ-10
Chapman, 199 ... EK-11
Chapmanville, 90 ... WG-5
Charleroi, 4120 ... WO-4
Charleston, 100 ... WI-2
Charlesville ... WP-10
Chase, 978 ... EA-7
Chatham, 300 ... EQ-9
Chatwood, 1000 ... EP-10
Chelsea, 160 ... EQ-11
Cheltenham ... ‡B-5
Cherry Flats, 250 ... EF-3
Cherry Grv. ... WF-8
Cherry Hill, 300 ... EK-11
Cherry Hill, 60 ... WE-2
Cherry Hill, 35 ... EQ-7
Cherry Tree, 364 ... WL-9
Cherry Valley, 200 ... WN-2
Cherry Valley, 66 ... WI-5
Cherrytown, 120 ... WN-11
Cherrytree ... WG-5
Cherryville, 1580 ... EK-10
Chest Sprs., 149 ... WL-10
Chester, 33972 ... EQ-11
CHESTER CO., 498886 ... EP-9
Chester Hts., 2531 ... EP-11
Chester Hill, 883 ... WK-12
Chester Sprs., 450 ... EO-10
Chestnut Grv., 100 ... WJ-10
Chestnut Level, 200 ... EQ-7
Chestnut Ridge, 100 ... ES-7
Cheswick, 1746 ... ‡I-9
Chevy Chase Hts., 1502 ... WL-8
Chewton, 488 ... WK-2
Cheyney, 150 ... EP-10
Chicora, 1043 ... WJ-5
Childs, 450 ... EG-10
Chillisquaque, 400 ... EJ-4
Chinchilla, 2098 ... EA-13
Choconut, 50 ... ED-8
Christiana, 1168 ... EP-8
Christmans, 100 ... EJ-10
Christy Mnr., 75 ... WK-6
Chrome ... EQ-8
Churchill, 3011 ... ‡K-8
Churchtown, 470 ... EO-8
Churchville, 60 ... WO-10
Circleville, 450 ... ‡M-10
Cito, 20 ... WQ-13
Clairton, 6796 ... WN-4
Clappertown, 110 ... WN-11
Clarence, 626 ... WJ-13
Clarendon, 450 ... WF-8
Claridge, 1200 ... WN-5
Clarington, 125 ... WH-8
Clarion, 5276 ... WI-6
CLARION CO., 39988 ... WJ-6
Clark, 640 ... WH-2
Clarks Green, 1476 ... EA-13
Clarks Mills, 120 ... WH-3
Clarks Summit, 5116 ... EG-9
Clarksburg, 180 ... WM-6
Clarkstown, 200 ... EI-5
Clarksville, 230 ... WP-3
Claussville, 40 ... EL-10
Clay, 1559 ... EO-7
Claylick ... WQ-13
Claysburg, 1625 ... WN-10
Claysville, 829 ... WO-2
Clear Ridge, 30 ... WO-13
Clear Run, 350 ... WI-9
Clear Spr., 40 ... EP-3
Clearfield, 6215 ... WJ-11
Clearfield, 200 ... EK-11
CLEARFIELD CO., 81642 ... WI-11
Clearview Estates, 2500 ... ET-2
Clearville, 200 ... WP-11
Cleona, 2080 ... EN-6
Clermont, 100 ... WF-10
Cleversburg, 100 ... EP-2
Clifford, 500 ... EF-10
Clifton, 300 ... EI-10
Clifton Hts., 6652 ... ‡F-2
Climax, 40 ... WJ-6
Clinton, 434 ... WM-2
Clinton, 75 ... WL-6
CLINTON CO., 39238 ... EI-1
Clintondale, 100 ... EJ-1
Clintonville, 508 ... WI-4
Cloe, 250 ... WJ-8
Clover Creek, 170 ... WN-11
Clyde, 50 ... WM-8
Clymer, 1357 ... WL-8
Coal Ctr., 139 ... WO-4
Coal City, 25 ... WH-5
Coal Glen, 25 ... WI-9
Coal Hill, 120 ... WH-6
Coal Run, 310 ... WM-7
Coaldale, 2281 ... EK-9
Coaldale, 161 ... WO-12
Coalmont, 106 ... WO-12
Coalport, 523 ... WL-10
Coaltown, 1200 ... WJ-2
Coatesville, 13100 ... EP-9
Cobham ... WF-7
Coburn, 236 ... EK-2
Cocalico ... EN-7
Cochranton, 1136 ... WG-4
Cochranville, 668 ... EP-9
Cocolamus, 50 ... EL-3
Cogan Sta., 600 ... EH-3
Cokeburg, 630 ... WO-3
Colebrookdale, 130 ... EN-10
Colegrove ... WF-11
Colesburg ... WE-13
Colesville, 150 ... EC-4
Coleville, 250 ... WK-13
College Hts., 550 ... ES-13
College Pk., 160 ... EJ-4
Collegeville, 5089 ... EO-11
Collingdale, 8786 ... ‡F-2
Collinsville, 150 ... EQ-6
Collomsville, 200 ... EI-3
Colmar, 800 ... EN-12
Colonial Mnr., 550 ... ET-8
Colonial Pk., 13229 ... EN-5
Colony Pk., 1076 ... ET-11
Columbia, 10400 ... EP-6
COLUMBIA CO., 67295 ... EI-6
Columbia Cross Roads, 220 ... EE-5
Columbus, 824 ... WE-6
Colver, 959 ... WM-9
Colwyn, 2546 ... ‡F-3
Commodore, 331 ... WL-8
Compass, 140 ... EP-8
Concord, 135 ... WN-14
Conestoga, 1258 ... EP-7
Coneville ... WE-12
Conewago Hts., 900 ... EO-5
Confluence, 780 ... WQ-6
Conneaut Lake, 653 ... WF-3
Conneaut Lake Pk., 200 ... WF-2
Conneautville, 774 ... WE-2
Connellsville, 7637 ... WP-5
Connoquenessing, 528 ... WK-4
Conrad ... WG-13
Conshohocken, 7833 ... EO-11
Conway, 2176 ... WL-3
Conyngham, 1914 ... EJ-8
Cookport, 75 ... WL-9
Cooksburg, 20 ... WH-7
Coolspring, 180 ... WJ-8
Coon Hunter, 40 ... EK-3
Coopersburg, 2386 ... EM-11
Cooperstown, 460 ... WG-4
Cooperstown, 200 ... WL-4
Coplay, 3192 ... EL-10
Coral, 325 ... WM-7
Coraopolis, 5677 ... WM-3
Coraopolis Hts., 1400 ... ‡J-2
Cork Lane, 700 ... EB-10
Cornwall, 4112 ... EN-6
Cornwells Hts., 1391 ... ‡B-8
Corry, 6605 ... WE-5
Corsica, 357 ... WI-7
Cortez, 350 ... EG-10
Coryville, 70 ... WE-11
Costello, 50 ... WG-12
Coudersport, 2546 ... WF-12
Coulter, 300 ... ‡N-9
Countryside, 2500 ... ES-2
Coupon, 275 ... WM-10
Courtdale, 732 ... EA-8
Cove Gap, 60 ... WQ-13
Coventryville, 350 ... EO-10
Covington, 650 ... EF-3
Covode, 75 ... WK-8
Cowan ... EJ-4
Cowanesque, 150 ... EE-2
Cowansville, 140 ... WK-6
Coyleville ... WK-5
Crabtree, 277 ... WN-6
Crafton, 5951 ... WM-3
Craigsville, 150 ... WK-5
Craley, 300 ... EP-6
Cramer, 100 ... WM-8
Cranberry, 300 ... WH-5
Cranesville, 638 ... WE-2
Crates ... WI-7
CRAWFORD CO., 88765 ... WF-4
Creekside, 309 ... WL-7
Creighton, 1500 ... WL-5
Crenshaw, 468 ... WI-9
Cresco, 500 ... EI-11
Cresson, 1711 ... WM-10
Cressona, 1651 ... EL-7
Crestmont, 90 ... EI-2
Crestmont Vil., 700 ... ‡H-1
Creswell ... EP-6
Croft, 60 ... WJ-11
Crooked Creek, 50 ... EE-3
Crosby, 225 ... WF-11
Cross Creek, 137 ... WN-2
Cross Fork, 60 ... WG-13
Cross Keys, 200 ... WM-11
Cross Keys, 70 ... WN-14
Cross Roads, 512 ... EQ-6
Crossingville, 60 ... WE-3
Crosswicks, 540 ... ‡B-5
Crown, 183 ... WH-7
Croydon, 9950 ... ‡B-9
Crucible, 725 ... WP-4
Crystal Spr., 100 ... WP-11
Cuba Mills, 90 ... EL-2
Culmerville, 600 ... WL-4
CUMBERLAND CO., 235406 ... EO-3
Cumbola, 443 ... EL-8
Curllsville, 110 ... WI-6
Curry Run, 45 ... WK-10
Curryville, 200 ... WN-11
Curtisville, 1064 ... WL-4
Curwensville, 2542 ... WJ-10
Custards, 30 ... WG-3
Custer City, 300 ... WE-10
Cyclone, 450 ... WE-10
Daggett, 50 ... EE-4
Dagus Mines, 400 ... WH-10
Daguscahonda, 120 ... WH-10
Daisytown, 326 ... WS-2
Dale, 1234 ... WN-8
Dale Summit, 180 ... WS-7
Daleville, 420 ... EH-10
Dallas, 2804 ... EH-8
Dallastown, 4049 ... EP-5
Dalmatia, 488 ... EL-4
Dalton, 1234 ... EG-9
Damascus, 365 ... EF-12
Danboro, 500 ... EN-12
Danielsville, 750 ... EK-10
Danville, 4699 ... EJ-5
Darby, 10687 ... EP-12
Darlington, 254 ... WK-2
Darlington Cors. ... EP-10
Dauberville, 848 ... EM-8
Dauphin, 791 ... EN-4
DAUPHIN CO., 268100 ... EN-4
Davidsburg, 25 ... EP-4
Davidsville, 1130 ... WO-8
Davistown, 60 ... WQ-3
Dawson, 367 ... WO-5
Dawson Ridge, 1200 ... WL-2
Day, 40 ... WI-7
Dayton, 553 ... WK-7
Dayton, 100 ... EM-5
Dean, 90 ... WL-10
Deanville, 65 ... WJ-6
Deckers Pt., 50 ... WK-8
Deemston, 722 ... WP-3
Deep Valley, 75 ... WQ-1
Deer Lake, 687 ... EL-8
Defiance, 239 ... WO-12
Degolia ... WE-10
Delano, 342 ... EK-8
DELAWARE CO., 558979 ... EP-11
Delaware Grv., 25 ... WH-3
Delaware Water Gap, 746 ... EJ-12
Delmont, 2686 ... WM-6
Delroy, 200 ... EP-6
Delta, 728 ... EQ-7
Dempseytown, 200 ... WG-5
Denholm, 75 ... EL-2
Dents Run ... WH-11
Denver, 3861 ... EO-8
Deodate, 80 ... EO-5
Derrick City, 1000 ... WD-10
Derry, 2688 ... WN-7
Desire, 90 ... WJ-9
Devault, 100 ... EO-10
Devon, 1515 ... EP-11
Dewart, 1471 ... EI-4
Diamond, 50 ... WF-5
Diamondville, 100 ... WL-8
Dice ... EK-4
Dickerson Run, 400 ... WP-5
Dickinson, 100 ... EO-2
Dickson City, 6070 ... EG-10
Dicksonburg ... WF-2
Dillsburg, 2563 ... EO-4
Dilltown, 250 ... WM-8
Dime ... WL-6
Dimock, 300 ... EF-8
Dingmans Ferry, 1000 ... EI-13
Distant, 750 ... WJ-7
Dixonville, 600 ... WL-8
Doe Run, 100 ... EP-9
Dolington, 250 ... EN-13
Donaldson, 328 ... EL-6
Donegal, 120 ... WO-6
Donnally Mills, 80 ... EM-3
Donora, 4781 ... WO-4
Dora, 50 ... WJ-7
Dormont, 8593 ... WM-4
Dorneyville, 4406 ... EC-2
Dornsife, 100 ... EL-5
Dorrance, 50 ... EI-8
Dorseyville, 650 ... WL-4
Dott, 40 ... WQ-12
Doubling Gap ... EN-2
Douglassville, 448 ... EN-9
Dover, 2007 ... EP-4
Downingtown, 7891 ... EP-10
Doylesburg, 150 ... WO-14
Doylestown, 8380 ... EN-12
Drakes Mills, 40 ... WE-4
Draketown, 60 ... WQ-6
Dravosburg, 1792 ... ‡M-7
Drehersville, 40 ... EL-8
Drexel Hill, 28043 ... EP-11
Drifting, 150 ... WJ-12
Drifton, 800 ... EJ-9
Driftwood, 67 ... WH-12
Drumore, 115 ... EQ-7
Drums, 600 ... EJ-8
Drury Run, 100 ... WH-14
Dry Run, 200 ... WO-14
Dry Tavern, 697 ... WP-4
Dryville, 398 ... EM-9
Dublin, 2158 ... EN-12
DuBois, 7794 ... WI-9
Duboistown, 1205 ... EI-4
Dudley, 184 ... WO-12
Duke Ctr., 850 ... WE-11
Dunbar, 1042 ... WP-5
Duncannon, 1522 ... EN-4
Duncansville, 1233 ... WM-11
Dundaff, 175 ... EF-10
Dundore, 30 ... EL-4
Dunkard, 150 ... WQ-4
Dunlevy, 381 ... WO-4
Dunlo, 342 ... WN-9
Dunmore, 14057 ... EH-10
Dunnstown, 1360 ... EI-2
Dupont, 2711 ... EC-10
Duquesne, 5565 ... ‡L-8
Durham, 200 ... EL-12
Duryea, 4917 ... EB-10
Dushore, 608 ... EG-6
Dutch Hill, 110 ... WJ-5
Dysart, 120 ... WL-10
Eagle, 130 ... EO-10
Eagle Rock, 60 ... WG-6
Eagles Mere, 120 ... EH-6
Earlston, 1122 ... WP-11
Earlville, 500 ... EN-9
E. Altoona, 200 ... WM-11
E. Athens, 400 ... EE-6
E. Bangor, 1172 ... EK-12
E. Benton, 175 ... EG-10
E. Berlin, 1521 ... EP-4
E. Berwick, 2007 ... EJ-7
E. Brady, 942 ... WJ-5
E. Brook, 300 ... WJ-3
E. Butler, 732 ... WK-4
E. Canton, 25 ... EF-5
E. Conemaugh, 1220 ... WN-9
E. Earl, 1144 ... EO-8
E. Finley ... WP-2
E. Freedom, 972 ... WN-11
E. Greenville, 2951 ... EM-10
E. Hickory, 150 ... WG-6
E. Kane, 135 ... WF-9
E. Lansdowne, 2668 ... ‡E-2
E. Lemon, 400 ... EG-9
E. McKeesport, 2126 ... ‡L-9
E. Millsboro, 400 ... WP-4
E. New Castle, 250 ... WJ-2
E. Petersburg, 4506 ... EO-7
E. Pittsburgh, 1822 ... ‡L-8
E. Prospect, 905 ... EP-6
E. Rochester, 567 ... WL-3
E. Salem, 186 ... EL-3
E. Sharpsburg, 110 ... WN-11
E. Side, 317 ... EJ-9
E. Smethport, 500 ... WE-11
E. Smithfield, 500 ... EE-5
E. Springfield, 400 ... WD-2
E. Stroudsburg, 9840 ... EJ-12
E. Texas, 450 ... EC-2
E. Titusville, 60 ... WF-5
E. Towanda, 400 ... EF-6
E. Troy, 140 ... EF-5
E. Vandergrift, 674 ... WL-6
E. Washington, 2234 ... WO-3
E. Waterford, 190 ... EN-1
E. York, 8777 ... WS-14
Eastland Hills, 550 ... ES-9
Easton, 26800 ... EL-12
Eastvale, 225 ... WK-2
Eastville, 80 ... EJ-3
Eatonville, 200 ... EG-8
Eau Claire, 316 ... WI-5
Ebenezer, 200 ... EN-6
Ebensburg, 3351 ... WM-9
Echo, 150 ... WR-3
Echo, 30 ... WK-7
Echo Lake, 80 ... EJ-12
Eckley, 30 ... EJ-9
Eckville ... EL-8
Economy, 8970 ... WL-3
Eddington, 1906 ... ‡B-8
Eddington Gdns., 800 ... ‡A-8
Eddystone, 2410 ... ‡G-1
Eden, 700 ... EO-7
Edenborn, 294 ... WP-4
Edenburg, 681 ... EM-8
Edendale, 100 ... WK-11
Edenville, 150 ... WP-13
Edgegrove, 500 ... EQ-4
Edgemont, 900 ... ES-3
Edgewood, 3118 ... ‡K-7
Edgewood, 2384 ... EK-6
Edgeworth, 1680 ... WM-3
Edie, 83 ... WO-8
Edinboro, 6438 ... WE-3
Edinburg, 200 ... WJ-2
Edmon, 120 ... WM-6
Edwardsville, 4816 ... EA-7
Effort, 2269 ... EJ-11
Egypt, 2391 ... EA-2
Ehrenfeld, 228 ... WN-9
Eighty Four, 657 ... WO-3
Elam, 200 ... EQ-10
Elberta, 180 ... WM-11
Elbon ... WH-10
Eldersville, 200 ... WN-2
Elderton, 356 ... WL-7
Eldred, 825 ... WE-11
Elgin, 218 ... WE-5
Elimsport, 65 ... EI-4
Elizabeth, 1493 ... WN-4
Elizabethtown, 11545 ... EO-6
Elizabethville, 1510 ... EM-5
Elk City, 80 ... WI-6
ELK CO., 31946 ... WG-10
Elk Grv., 45 ... EH-6
Elk Lake, 100 ... EF-8
Elkins Pk., 4700 ... ‡B-5
Elkland, 1821 ... ED-2
Ellenton, 25 ... EG-5
Ellerslie, 550 ... ‡A-9
Elliott Mills ... WJ-3
Elliottsburg, 220 ... EN-2
Ellisburg, 55 ... WE-13
Ellport, 1180 ... WK-3
Ellsworth, 1027 ... WO-4
Ellwood City, 7921 ... WK-2
Elm, 150 ... EO-7
Elmer ... EE-1
Elmhurst, 830 ... EH-10
Elrama, 307 ... WN-4
Elstonville, 60 ... EO-6
Elton, 600 ... WN-9
Elverson, 1225 ... EO-9
Elysburg, 2194 ... EK-6
Embreeville, 90 ... EP-9
Emeigh, 400 ... WL-9
Emerald, 240 ... EL-10
Emerickville, 150 ... WI-8
Emigsville, 2672 ... EP-5
Emlenton, 625 ... WI-5
Emmaus, 11211 ... EM-10
Emmaville, 40 ... WP-11
Emporium, 2073 ... WG-12
Emsworth, 2449 ... WM-3
Endeavor, 200 ... WG-7
Enders, 65 ... EM-4
Energy, 50 ... WJ-3
English Ctr., 60 ... EH-2
Enhaut, 1007 ... ET-4
Enid ... WO-12
Enlow, 1013 ... ‡K-2
Ennisville ... WL-13
Enola, 6111 ... EN-4
Enon Valley, 306 ... WK-2
Enterprise, 50 ... WF-6
Entriken, 125 ... WN-12
Ephrata, 13394 ... EO-7
Equinunk, 130 ... EE-11
Ercildoun, 100 ... EP-9
Erdenheim ... ‡B-3
Erdman, 200 ... EL-5
Erie, 101786 ... WC-4
ERIE CO., 280566 ... WD-4
Erlen, 800 ... ‡B-4
Ernest, 462 ... WL-7
Erwinna, 140 ... EM-12
Eshcol ... EM-2
Espy, 1642 ... EJ-6
Espyville, 300 ... WF-2
Essington ... ‡G-2
Estella, 50 ... EG-5
Estherton, 1200 ... ER-3
Etna, 3451 ... ‡J-6
Euclid, 90 ... WJ-4
Evans City, 1833 ... WK-3
Evans Falls, 270 ... EG-8
Evansburg, 2129 ... EO-11
Evendale, 165 ... EL-3
Everett, 1834 ... WP-11
Evergreen, 70 ... EF-6
Everson, 793 ... WO-5
Ewingsville, 400 ... ‡L-4
Exchange, 100 ... EI-5
Exeter, 5652 ... EH-9
Export, 917 ... WM-5
Exton, 4842 ... EP-10
Eyers Grv., 105 ... EJ-6
Factoryville, 1158 ... EG-9
Fair Acres, 500 ... ET-3
Fairbank, 600 ... WP-4
Fairbrook, 225 ... WL-13
Fairchance, 1975 ... WQ-5
Fairdale, 2059 ... WP-4
Fairdale, 40 ... EE-8
Fairfield, 1100 ... WC-4
Fairfield, 507 ... EQ-2
Fairhope, 50 ... WQ-9
Fairless Hills, 8466 ... EO-13
Fairmont City, 300 ... WJ-7
Fairmount Sprs., 40 ... EI-7
Fairoaks, 800 ... ‡H-2
Fairplay ... EQ-2
Fairview, 2348 ... WD-3
Fairview, 250 ... WJ-8
Fairview, 198 ... WJ-5
Fairview, 50 ... WH-3
Fairview Hts., 600 ... ‡I-8
Fairville, 150 ... *A-7
Fall Brook, 200 ... EF-4
Fallentimber, 150 ... WL-10
Falling Spr., 200 ... EP-1
Falls, 230 ... EG-9
Falls Creek, 1037 ... WI-9
Fallsington, 1300 ... †T-12
Fallston, 266 ... WK-2
Falmouth, 420 ... EO-5
Fannettsburg, 950 ... WO-13
Farmers Valley, 120 ... WE-11
Farmersville, 991 ... EO-7
Farmersville, 50 ... EA-6
Farmington, 800 ... EB-4
Farmington, 767 ... WQ-6
Farragut, 60 ... EH-4
Farrandsville, 120 ... EI-2
Farrell, 5111 ... WI-2
Farwell, 350 ... WH-14
Fassett, 175 ... ED-5
Fawn Grv., 452 ... EQ-6
Fayette City, 596 ... WO-4
FAYETTE CO., 136606 ... WP-5
Fayetteville, 3128 ... EP-1
Fayetteville, 300 ... ‡K-2
Fellsburg, 1180 ... WO-4
Felton, 506 ... EQ-6
Feltonville ... ‡C-5
Fenelton, 110 ... WK-5
Fern Brook, 550 ... EH-8
Fern Glen, 350 ... EJ-7
Ferndale, 1636 ... WN-8
Ferndale, 400 ... EM-12
Fernridge ... EJ-10
Fernville, 556 ... EJ-6
Fernway, 12414 ... WL-3
Fertigs, 65 ... WH-6
Finleyville, 461 ... WN-4
Fisher, 130 ... WH-7
Fishertown, 400 ... WO-10
Fisherville, 60 ... EM-4
Five Forks, 50 ... EQ-1
Five Points, 600 ... WL-3
Five Points, 100 ... ES-14
Five Points, 20 ... WL-7
Five Points ... WM-6
Fivepointville, 1156 ... EO-8
Flat Rock, 140 ... WQ-6
Fleetville, 350 ... EG-9
Fleetwood, 4085 ... EM-9
Flemington, 1330 ... EI-2
Flicksville, 100 ... EK-12
Flinton, 250 ... WL-10
Florence, 250 ... WM-2
Flourtown, 4538 ... ‡A-3
Fogelsville, 950 ... EL-10
Folcroft, 6606 ... ‡F-2
Folsom, 8323 ... ‡F-1
Fombell, 100 ... WK-3
Fontana, 150 ... EN-6
Foot of Ten, 672 ... WC-12
Forbes Road, 650 ... WN-6
Force, 253 ... WI-10
Ford City, 2991 ... WK-6
Ford Cliff, 371 ... WK-6
Fordyce, 20 ... WQ-3
Forest City, 1911 ... EF-10
FOREST CO., 7716 ... WG-7
Forest Grv., 2600 ... ‡J-4
Forest Hills, 6518 ... ‡K-8
Forest Lake, 100 ... EE-8
Forest Pk., 300 ... EI-9
Forestville, 100 ... WI-4
Forks ... EI-7
Forkston, 70 ... EG-8
Forksville, 145 ... EG-5
Ft. Hill, 35 ... WQ-7
Ft. Hunter, 150 ... EN-4
Ft. Littleton, 100 ... WP-13
Ft. Loudon, 886 ... WP-13
Ft. Washington, 5446 ... EO-12
Forty Fort, 4214 ... EH-9
Foster Brook, 1251 ... WD-10
Fostoria, 40 ... WL-11
Foundryville, 256 ... EJ-7
Fountain, 250 ... EL-6
Fountain Dale, 150 ... EQ-2
Fountain Hill, 4597 ... EL-11
Fountain Sprs., 278 ... EK-7
Foustown, 200 ... WR-12
Fox Chapel, 5388 ... ‡I-7
Fox Chase ... ‡B-6
Fox Hill, 125 ... EC-8
Foxburg, 183 ... WI-5
Frackville, 3805 ... EK-7
Franconia, 430 ... EN-11
Frankford ... ‡C-6
Frankfort Sprs., 130 ... WM-2
Franklin, 6545 ... WH-5
Franklin, 323 ... WN-9
Franklin Ctr., 30 ... WD-3
FRANKLIN CO., 149618 ... WP-13
Franklin Forks, 110 ... EE-9
Franklin Pk., 13470 ... WL-3
Franklindale, 100 ... EF-6
Franklintown, 489 ... EO-4
Franklinville, 75 ... WL-12
Frankstown, 200 ... WM-11
Frazer, 2000 ... EP-10
Frederick, 120 ... EN-10
Fredericksburg, 1357 ... EM-6
Fredericksburg, 733 ... WF-3
Fredonia, 502 ... WH-3
Freeburg, 575 ... EK-4
Freedom, 1569 ... WL-3
Freeland, 3531 ... EJ-9
Freemansburg, 2636 ... EB-5
Freeport, 1813 ... WL-5
Frenchtown, 60 ... WF-4
Frenchville, 200 ... WI-12
Freysville, 400 ... EP-6
Friedens, 1523 ... WP-8
Friedensburg, 858 ... EL-7
Friedensville, 800 ... EC-4
Friendsville, 111 ... EE-8
Frisco, 850 ... WK-3
Fritztown, 200 ... EN-8
Frogtown, 70 ... WJ-5
Frogtown, 40 ... WI-7
Frostburg, 120 ... WJ-8
Fryburg, 375 ... WH-6
Frystown, 380 ... EM-7
Fullerton, 14925 ... EL-10
FULTON CO., 14845 ... WP-12
Furlong, 700 ... EN-12
Gabby Hts., 1200 ... WO-2
Gaines, 120 ... EF-1
Galeton, 1149 ... EF-1
Galilee, 180 ... EF-12
Gallatin, 250 ... WO-4
Gallitzin, 1668 ... WM-10
Ganister, 85 ... WM-12
Gap, 1931 ... EP-8
Gapsville ... WP-11
Garards Fort, 100 ... WQ-3
Garden City ... ‡G-1
Garden View, 2503 ... EI-4
Gardenville, 250 ... EN-12
Gardners, 150 ... EP-3
Garland, 300 ... WE-6
Garrett, 456 ... WQ-8
Garrett Hill ... ‡C-1
Garrison, 50 ... WQ-2
Gastonville, 2818 ... WN-4
Gastown, 150 ... WL-7
Gatchellville, 60 ... EQ-6
Gatesburg, 100 ... WL-13
Gauff Hill, 350 ... EB-4
Gayly, 300 ... ‡K-3
Geeseytown, 100 ... WM-11
Geiger, 90 ... WP-8
Geigertown, 500 ... EO-9
Geistown, 2467 ... WN-9
Gelatt, 50 ... EE-10
Genesee, 300 ... WD-13
Geneva, 109 ... WG-3
Georgetown, 1640 ... EB-7
Georgetown, 1022 ... EP-8
Georgetown, 200 ... EL-11
Georgetown, 174 ... WL-2
Georgeville, 30 ... WK-8
Germania, 130 ... EF-1
Germansville, 250 ... EL-9
Germantown ... ‡C-4
Geryville ... EM-11
Gettysburg, 7620 ... EQ-3
Ghennes Hts., 900 ... WO-4
Gibbon Glade, 65 ... WQ-5
Gibraltar, 680 ... EN-9
Gibson, 200 ... EE-10
Gibsonia, 2733 ... WL-4
Gifford, 500 ... WE-10
Gilbert, 700 ... EK-11
Gilberton, 769 ... EK-7
Gilbertsville, 4832 ... EN-10
Gilfoyle, 20 ... WG-7
Gillett, 300 ... EE-5
Ginter, 120 ... WK-11
Ginther, 75 ... EK-8
Gipsy, 125 ... WK-9
Girard, 3104 ... WD-3
Girardville, 1519 ... EK-7
Girty, 30 ... WL-6
Glade City, 130 ... WQ-8
Gladwyne, 4000 ... ‡C-2
Glasgow, 250 ... WL-11
Glasgow, 60 ... WL-1
Glassport, 4483 ... WN-4
Gleason ... EF-4
Gleasonton ... WH-14
Glen Campbell, 245 ... WK-9
Glen Forney, 120 ... EQ-2
Glen Hazel ... WG-10
Glen Hope, 142 ... WK-10
Glen Iron, 150 ... EK-3
Glen Lyon, 1873 ... EI-8
Glen Mawr, 100 ... EH-5
Glen Moore, 1000 ... ES-9
Glen Osborne, 547 ... ‡I-3
Glen Richey, 270 ... WJ-10
Glen Rock, 2025 ... EQ-5
Glen Roy ... EQ-8
Glen Savage, 15 ... WP-9
Glen Summit, 250 ... EI-9
Glenburn, 953 ... EG-9
Glencoe, 15 ... WQ-9
Glendale, 75 ... EC-10
Glendon, 440 ... EL-11
Glenfield, 205 ... ‡I-4
Glenmar Gdns., 200 ... WD-4
Glenmoore, 900 ... EO-9
Glenolden, 7153 ... ‡F-2
Glenshaw, 8981 ... ‡I-6
Glenside, 8384 ... ‡A-4
Glenville, 100 ... EQ-5
Glenwillard, 1100 ... ‡H-2
Glenwood, 3000 ... ES-3
Glenwood, 50 ... EF-9
Globe Mills, 45 ... EK-4
Goheenville, 50 ... WK-7
Gold, 50 ... WE-13
Goldsboro, 952 ... EO-5
Good Intent, 25 ... WO-2
Good Spr., 90 ... EL-6
Goods Cor., 500 ... WR-2
Goodtown, 20 ... WP-8
Goodville, 482 ... EO-8
Goodyear, 100 ... EP-3
Gordon, 763 ... EL-7
Gordonville, 508 ... EP-8
Goshenville, 150 ... EP-10
Gouldsboro, 890 ... EI-11
Gowen City, 220 ... EL-6
Graceton, 257 ... WM-7
Graceville, 50 ... WP-11
Gradyville, 500 ... EP-11
Grampian, 356 ... WJ-10
Grand Valley, 175 ... WF-6
Grandview Hts., 2050 ... ES-9
Grantham, 500 ... EO-4
Grantville, 230 ... EN-5
Granville, 440 ... EM-1
Granville Ctr., 110 ... EF-5
Granville Summit, 85 ... EF-5
Grassflat, 511 ... WJ-12
Grassmere Pk., 50 ... EH-6
Graterford, 900 ... EO-11
Gratz, 765 ... EL-5
Gray, 275 ... WO-8
Graysville, 160 ... WP-2
Grazierville, 665 ... WL-11
Greason, 150 ... EO-2
Great Bend, 734 ... ED-9
Greble, 100 ... EM-7
Greece City, 40 ... WJ-5
Greeley, 1000 ... EH-12
Green Lane, 508 ... EN-11
Green Pt., 75 ... EM-6
Green Tree, 4432 ... ‡K-5
Green Vil., 400 ... EP-1
Greenawalds, 1200 ... EB-2
Greenburr, 130 ... EJ-2
Greencastle, 3996 ... WQ-14
Greendale ... WF-9
GREENE CO., 38686 ... WQ-3
Greenes, 894 ... EE-6
Greenfield, 40 ... WI-2
Greenfields, 1170 ... ES-12
Greenmount, 70 ... EQ-3
Greenock, 2195 ... ‡M-9
Greensboro, 260 ... WQ-4
Greensburg, 14892 ... WN-6
Greentown, 1000 ... EH-11
Greenville, 5919 ... WH-2
Greenwood, 2458 ... WM-11
Greenwood, 30 ... EI-6
Gresham, 75 ... WF-5
Grill, 1468 ... ET-12
Grindstone, 498 ... WP-4
Gringo, 600 ... ‡H-1
Grovania ... EJ-6
Grove City, 8322 ... WI-3
Grover, 200 ... EG-4
Groveton, 500 ... ‡J-3
Guffey, 100 ... ‡N-9
Guitonville, 50 ... WG-7
Gulph Mills, 450 ... ‡B-1
Guys Mills, 124 ... WF-4
Gwynedd, 600 ... EO-11
Hadley, 180 ... WH-3
Hahntown, 400 ... ‡M-10
Halifax, 841 ... EM-4
Hallam, 2673 ... EP-6
Hallstead, 1303 ... ED-9
Hallton, 30 ... WH-8
Hamburg, 4289 ... EM-8
Hametown, 80 ... EQ-5
Hamilton, 125 ... WJ-8
Hamilton Pk., 3500 ... ES-8
Hamlin, 1100 ... EH-11
Hamlin, 85 ... EM-6
Hammett ... WD-4
Hamorton, 100 ... *A-7
Hampton, 632 ... EP-4
Haneyville ... EH-2
Hannahstown, 80 ... WK-5
Hannastown, 350 ... WN-6
Hannaville, 176 ... WG-4
Hanover, 15289 ... EQ-4
Hanover, 800 ... EA-4
Hanover Hills, 160 ... ES-5
Hanoverdale ... EN-5
Harborcreek, 1500 ... WC-4
Harding, 400 ... EA-10
Harford, 250 ... EF-9
Harlansburg, 300 ... WJ-3
Harleigh, 1104 ... EJ-8
Harleysville, 9286 ... EN-11
Harmar Hts., 1050 ... ‡H-8
Harmarville, 1100 ... ‡I-8
Harmonsburg, 401 ... WF-3
Harmonville, 1500 ... ‡B-2
Harmony, 890 ... WK-3
Harnedsville, 90 ... WQ-7
Harper Tavern, 50 ... EN-6
Harrisburg, 49528 ... EN-4
Harrison City, 134 ... WN-5
Harrison Valley, 250 ... EE-1
Harrisonville, 50 ... WP-12
Harrisville, 897 ... WI-4
Harshaville ... WM-2
Hartleton, 283 ... EK-3
Hartstown, 201 ... WG-2
Hartsville, 700 ... EN-12
Harveys Lake, 2791 ... EH-8
Harveyville, 50 ... EI-7
Harwick, 899 ... ‡H-9
Harwood, 420 ... EJ-8
Hastings, 1278 ... WL-9
Hatboro, 7360 ... EO-12
Hatfield, 3290 ... EN-11
Haverford, 6000 ... ‡D-2
Havertown, 30000 ... ‡D-1
Hawk Run, 534 ... WK-12
Hawley, 1211 ... EG-12
Hawstone, 60 ... EM-2
Hawthorn, 494 ... WJ-7
Haydentown, 120 ... WQ-5
Haysville, 70 ... ‡I-3
Hayti, 950 ... EP-9
Hazel Hurst, 300 ... WF-10
Hazen, 125 ... WI-8
Hazleton, 25340 ... EJ-8
Heart Lake, 130 ... EE-9
Heathville, 15 ... WI-7
Hebe, 70 ... EL-5
Hebron Ctr. ... WE-13
Heckscherville, 220 ... EL-7
Hecktown, 1200 ... EL-11
Hecla, 100 ... EL-8
Hegins, 812 ... EL-6
Heidelberg, 1244 ... WM-3
Heidlersburg, 707 ... EP-3
Heilwood, 711 ... WL-9
Helfenstein, 100 ... EL-6
Helixville ... WO-9
Hellertown, 5898 ... EL-11
Helvetia, 90 ... WJ-9
Hemlock ... WE-8
Hendersonville ... WH-4
Henrietta, 100 ... WN-11
Henrys Bend, 60 ... WG-6
Henryville, 300 ... EI-11
Hepburnia, 140 ... WJ-10
Hereford, 930 ... EM-10
Herman, 400 ... WK-5
Herminie, 789 ... WN-5
Hermitage, 16220 ... WI-2
Herndon, 324 ... EL-4
Herrick Ctr., 125 ... EF-10
Herrickville, 75 ... EE-7
Hershey, 14257 ... EN-5
Heshbon, 50 ... WM-8
Hessdale, 100 ... EP-7
Hesston, 175 ... WM-12
Hetlerville ... EJ-7
Hibbs, 200 ... WP-4
Hickernell, 50 ... WE-3
Hickory, 740 ... WN-2
Hickory Cors., 60 ... EL-4
Hickory Grv., 30 ... ED-9
Highland Pk., 1900 ... ET-2
Highland Pk., 1380 ... EL-1
Highspire, 2399 ... EO-5
Hilldale, 1246 ... EB-9
Hiller, 1155 ... WP-4
Hilliards, 120 ... WI-5
Hillsdale, 250 ... WK-9
Hillsgrove, 200 ... EH-5
Hillside, 200 ... WN-7
Hillsville, 600 ... WJ-2
Hilltown, 800 ... EN-12
Hilltown, 60 ... EE-12
Hilltown ... EQ-2
Hinkletown, 175 ... EO-8
Hoadleys, 110 ... EG-11
Hobbie, 350 ... EJ-8
Hoernerstown, 50 ... ES-5
Hogestown, 300 ... EN-4
Hokendauqua, 3378 ... EA-3
Holbrook, 40 ... WQ-2
Holland, 5300 ... EO-13
Hollidaysburg, 5791 ... WM-11
Hollisterville ... EH-11
Hollsopple, 500 ... WO-8
Hollywood, 800 ... ‡B-5
Holmes, 2800 ... ‡F-2
Holmesburg ... ‡C-7
Holtwood, 200 ... EQ-7
Home, 400 ... WL-8
Home Camp ... WI-10
Homer City, 1707 ... WM-7
Homestead, 3165 ... ‡K-7
Hometown, 1349 ... EK-8
Homeville, 50 ... EQ-8
Homewood, 109 ... WK-2
Honeoye, 20 ... WD-12
Honesdale, 4480 ... EG-11
Honey Brook, 1713 ... EO-9
Honey Grv., 200 ... EN-1
Hooker, 100 ... WJ-5
Hookstown, 147 ... WL-2
Hooversville, 645 ... WO-8
Hop Bottom, 337 ... EF-9
Hopeland, 738 ... EO-7
Hopewell, 230 ... WO-11
Hopwood, 2090 ... WP-5
Horsham, 14842 ... EO-12
Hosensack ... EM-10
Host, 25 ... EM-7
Hostetter, 740 ... WN-6
Houserville, 1814 ... WK-13
Houston, 1296 ... WN-3
Houtzdale, 797 ... WK-11
Howard, 720 ... EJ-1
Hoytville, 40 ... EG-2
Hublersburg, 104 ... EJ-1
Hudson, 1443 ... EB-8
Hudsondale, 100 ... EK-9
Huey, 125 ... WJ-6
Huffs Church, 150 ... EM-10
Hughestown, 1392 ... EB-10
Hughesville, 2128 ... EI-5
Humboldt, 120 ... EJ-8
Hummels Wharf, 1353 ... EK-4
Hummelstown, 4538 ... EN-5
Hunker, 291 ... WO-5
Hunlock Creek, 300 ... EI-8
Hunters Run, 60 ... EO-3
Hunterstown, 547 ... EQ-3
Huntersville, 50 ... EH-5
Huntingdon, 7093 ... WM-12
HUNTINGDON CO., 45913 ... WN-12
Huntingdon Valley, 10000 ... ‡A-6
Huntington Mills, 175 ... EI-7
Huntsdale, 300 ... EO-2
Huntsville, 100 ... EH-8
Husband ... WP-8
Hustontown, 450 ... WP-12
Hyde, 1399 ... WJ-11
Hyde Pk., 2528 ... ES-13
Hydetown, 526 ... WF-5
Hyndman, 910 ... WQ-9
Hyner, 150 ... EH-1
Ickesburg, 280 ... EM-2
Idamar, 30 ... WL-8
Idaville, 177 ... EP-3
Imler, 150 ... WO-10
Imperial, 2541 ... WM-3
Independence, 110 ... WN-1
Independence, 100 ... ‡H-1
Independence, 70 ... EL-4
Indian Crossing, 20 ... WD-11
Indian Head, 175 ... WP-6
Indian Head ... WE-4
Indian Lake, 394 ... WP-9
Indian Orchard, 300 ... EG-11
Indiana, 13975 ... WL-7
INDIANA CO., 88880 ... WK-8
Indianola, 900 ... WL-4
Industry, 1835 ... WL-2
Ingram, 3330 ... ‡K-5
Inkerman, 1819 ... EB-9
Intercourse, 1274 ... EP-8
Iola, 144 ... EI-6
Iona, 800 ... EN-7
Irishtown, 430 ... EQ-4
Iron Sprs., 200 ... EQ-2
Ironton, 300 ... EA-1
Irvine, 200 ... WE-7
Irvona, 647 ... WK-10
Irwin, 3973 ... WN-5
Isabella, 275 ... WP-4
Iselin, 275 ... WM-6
Ithan ... ‡C-1
Ivyland, 1041 ... EO-12
Ivywood, 40 ... WL-4
Jackson, 90 ... EE-10
Jackson Ctr., 224 ... WH-3
Jackson Summit ... EE-4
Jacksonville, 637 ... WM-7
Jacksonville, 100 ... EL-11
Jacksonville, 95 ... EJ-1
Jacksonwald, 3393 ... ET-14
Jacktown, 200 ... ‡M-10
Jacobs Creek, 275 ... WO-5
Jacobus, 1841 ... EQ-5
James City, 287 ... WF-9
Jamestown, 617 ... WG-2
Jamestown, 400 ... WN-10
Jamison, 850 ... EN-12
Jamison City, 134 ... EH-7
Janesville, 600 ... WK-11
Jeannette, 9654 ... WN-5
Jeddo, 98 ... EJ-9
Jefferson, 733 ... EQ-4
Jefferson, 270 ... WP-3
Jefferson Ctr., 80 ... WK-4
JEFFERSON CO., 45200 ... WH-8
Jefferson Hills, 10619 ... WN-4
Jenkintown, 4422 ... EO-12
Jenners, 250 ... WO-8
Jennerstown, 695 ... WO-8
Jennersville, 45 ... EQ-9
Jenningsville, 100 ... EG-7
Jericho, 20 ... WH-12
Jermyn, 2169 ... EG-10
Jerome, 1017 ... WO-8
Jersey Mills, 55 ... EH-2
Jersey Shore, 4361 ... EI-3
Jerseytown, 184 ... EJ-6
Jessup, 4676 ... EG-10
Jim Thorpe, 4781 ... EK-9
Joanna, 80 ... EO-9
Jobs Corners ... EE-4
Joffre, 536 ... WM-2
Johnsonburg, 2483 ... WG-10
Johnstown, 20978 ... WN-8
Joliett, 275 ... EL-6
Jollytown, 25 ... WQ-2
Jonas, 60 ... EJ-10
Jones Mills, 300 ... WO-7
Jonestown, 1905 ... EM-6
Jonestown, 64 ... EI-7
Josephine, 300 ... WM-7
Julian, 152 ... WK-13
Juneau, 30 ... WK-8
Junedale, 200 ... EK-8
JUNIATA CO., 24636 ... EM-2
Juniata Gap, 1100 ... WA-12
Juniata Ter., 542 ... EM-1
Justus ... EB-14
Kane, 3730 ... WF-9
Kanesholm ... WF-9
Kaneville ... WG-5
Kantner, 80 ... WO-8
Kantz, 35 ... EK-4
Kaolin, 150 ... EQ-9
Karns City, 209 ... WJ-5
Karthaus, 250 ... WI-12
Kasiesville, 30 ... WQ-13
Kauffman, 150 ... WQ-14
Kaylor, 200 ... WJ-5
Kearney ... WO-12
Kearsarge ... WB-10
Keating ... WI-13
Keating Summit, 100 ... WF-12
Kecksburg, 140 ... WO-6
Keelersville, 100 ... EM-11
Keeneyville, 100 ... EE-2
Keewaydin ... WI-12
Keisterville, 300 ... WP-5
Kelayres, 533 ... EK-8
Kellersburg, 100 ... WJ-6
Kellettville, 100 ... WG-7
Kelly, 70 ... WL-6
Kelly Crossroads, 70 ... EJ-4
Kelton, 140 ... EQ-9
Kemblesville, 125 ... EQ-9
Kempton, 169 ... EL-9
Kendall ... WM-2
Kenhorst, 2877 ... ET-12
Kenilworth, 1907 ... EO-10
Kenmar, 4124 ... EI-4
Kennard, 20 ... WG-2
Kennerdell, 247 ... WH-5
Kennett Sq., 6072 ... EQ-10
Kensington ... ‡D-5
Kenwick Vil., 200 ... ER-9
Kenwood, 25 ... WL-8
Kerr, 250 ... WJ-11
Kerrmoor, 25 ... WK-10
Kerrtown, 305 ... WF-3
Kersey, 937 ... WH-10
Khedive, 40 ... WP-3
Killinger, 75 ... EM-4
Kimberton, 450 ... EO-10
Kimmelton, 80 ... WO-8
King ... WN-10
King of Prussia, 19936 ... EO-11
Kings Manor, 650 ... ‡B-1
Kingsdale, 200 ... ER-3
Kingsley, 200 ... EF-9
Kingston, 13182 ... EI-9
Kingwood, 120 ... WP-7
Kintnersville, 100 ... EM-12
Kinzers, 450 ... EP-8
Kirby, 35 ... WQ-3
Kirkwood, 396 ... EQ-8
Kirwan Hts., 500 ... ‡L-4
Kissimmee, 100 ... EK-3
Kistler, 320 ... WN-13
Kistler, 40 ... EN-2
Kittanning, 4044 ... WK-6
Klecknersville, 300 ... EK-11
Kleinfeltersville, 250 ... EN-7
Klinesville, 100 ... EM-9
Klinesville, 60 ... EP-6
Klingerstown, 127 ... EL-5
Knapp ... EF-2
Knauers ... EN-8
Knobsville, 100 ... WP-13
Knox, 1146 ... WI-6
Knox Dale, 300 ... WJ-8
Knoxville, 629 ... EE-2
Koonsville, 200 ... EI-7
Koppel, 762 ... WK-2
Korn Krest, 850 ... EB-6
Kossuth, 150 ... WH-6
Kralltown, 75 ... EP-4
Kratzerville, 383 ... EK-4
Kreamer, 822 ... EK-4
Kreidersville, 270 ... EL-10
Kremis, 20 ... WH-2
Kresgeville, 400 ... EK-10
Krings, 150 ... WT-2
Krumsville, 140 ... EL-9
Kuhnsville, 500 ... EB-1
Kuhntown, 30 ... WQ-2
Kulpmont, 2924 ... EK-6
Kulpsville, 8194 ... EN-11
Kunkle, 150 ... EH-8
Kunkletown, 200 ... EK-11
Kushequa, 60 ... WF-10
Kutztown, 5012 ... EM-9
Kylertown, 340 ... WJ-12
Kyleville, 25 ... EQ-7
La Anna ... EI-11
La Belle, 350 ... WP-4
La Gonda, 70 ... WO-2
La Plume, 400 ... EG-9
Laboratory, 850 ... WO-3
Labott, 50 ... EP-4
Laceyville, 379 ... EF-7
LACKAWANNA CO., 214437 ... EH-10
Lackawaxen, 600 ... EG-12
Laddsburg, 60 ... EG-6
Lafayette, 40 ... WE-10
Lafayette Hill, 6700 ... ‡B-3
Laflin, 1487 ... EB-9
Lahaska, 200 ... EN-12
Lairdsville, 120 ... EI-5
L. Ariel, 1250 ... EG-11
L. Carey, 400 ... EG-8
Lake City, 3031 ... WD-2
L. Como, 280 ... EE-11
L. Harmony, 850 ... EJ-10
L. Winola, 748 ... EG-9
L. Wynonah, 2640 ... EL-7
Lakemont, 1868 ... WM-11
Lakeside, 200 ... EE-10
Lakeview Hts., 600 ... ES-4
Lakeville, 500 ... EG-11
Lakewood, 300 ... EE-11
Lamar, 562 ... EJ-1
Lamartine, 200 ... WI-5
Lambertsville, 70 ... WO-8
Lamott, 800 ... ‡B-5
Lampeter, 1669 ... ET-10
Lanark, 400 ... EC-4
Lancaster, 59322 ... EP-7
LANCASTER CO., 519445 ... EP-8
Landenberg, 100 ... EQ-9
Lander, 150 ... WD-7
Landingville, 159 ... EL-8
Landis Valley, 800 ... ER-9
Landisburg, 218 ... EN-2
Landisville, 1893 ... EO-6
Lanes Mills, 30 ... WI-9
Lanesboro, 506 ... ED-10
Langdondale, 100 ... WO-11
Langeloth, 717 ... WN-2
Lansdale, 16269 ... EN-11
Lansdowne, 10620 ... ‡E-2
Lanse, 450 ... WJ-12
Lansford, 3941 ... EK-9
Lantz Cors., 40 ... WF-10
Laporte, 316 ... EH-6
Larabee ... WE-11
Larimer, 750 ... ‡M-10
Larksville, 4480 ... EI-8
Latimore, 60 ... EP-3
Latrobe, 8338 ... WN-6
Latta Grv. ... WN-13
Lattimer, 600 ... EJ-8
Laughlintown, 950 ... WO-7
Laurel, 25 ... EQ-6
Laurel Lake, 300 ... EE-8
Laurel Mtn., 167 ... WO-7
Laurel Run, 500 ... EI-9
Laureldale, 3911 ... EN-9
Laurelton, 221 ... EK-3
Laurelville, 150 ... WO-6
Laurys Sta., 1243 ... EL-10
Lavansville, 150 ... WP-7
Lavelle, 742 ... EK-6
Laverock, 1100 ... ‡B-4
Lawn, 300 ... EO-6
Lawndale ... ‡C-6
Lawnton, 3813 ... ES-4
Lawrence, 540 ... WN-3
LAWRENCE CO., 91108 ... WI-2
Lawrence Pk., 3982 ... WC-4
Lawrenceville, 581 ... ED-3
Lawsonham, 50 ... WJ-6
Lawsville Ctr., 75 ... EE-9
Lawton, 85 ... EF-8
Le Raysville, 290 ... EE-7
Leaders Hts., 1200 ... WT-13
Leamersville, 80 ... WN-11
Lebanon, 25477 ... EN-6
LEBANON CO., 133568 ... EM-6
Leck Kill, 200 ... EL-5
Leckrone, 250 ... WQ-4
Lecontes Mills, 125 ... WJ-11
Lee Pk., 3600 ... EI-8
Leechburg, 2156 ... WL-5
Leeper, 200 ... WH-7
Lees Cross Roads, 200 ... EP-2
Leesburg, 100 ... WI-3
Leesport, 1918 ... EM-8
Leetsdale, 1218 ... WL-3
Lehigh, 100 ... EH-10
LEHIGH CO., 349497 ... EL-10
Lehighton, 5500 ... EK-9
Lehman, 250 ... EH-8
Leinbachs, 150 ... ES-11
Leisenring, 600 ... WP-5
Leith, 900 ... WP-5
Leithsville, 300 ... EM-11
Lemasters, 250 ... WQ-13
Lemon ... EF-8
Lemont, 2270 ... WK-13
Lemont Furnace, 827 ... WP-5
Lemoyne, 4553 ... ET-3

*, †, ‡, §, ◊ See explanation under state title in this index.
County and parish names are listed in capital letters & boldface type.
Independent cities (not included in a county) are listed in italics.

Lenape, 200 ....EP-10
Lenhartsville, 165 ......EM-9
Lenoxville, 130 ....EF-10
Leola, 7214 ....EO-7
Leroy, 90 ....EF-5
Lester *G-2
Level Green, 4020 ....WN-5
Levittown, 52983 ....EO-13
Lewis Run, 617 ....WE-10
Lewisberry, 362 ....EJ-4
Lewisburg, 5792 ....EJ-4
Lewistown, 8338 ....EL-1
Lewisville, 225 ....EJ-3
Liberty, 2551 ....*M-8
Liberty, 249 ....EJ-4
Liberty Cors., 100 ......EF-2
Library, 6000 ....‡N-5
Lickingville, 60 ....WH-7
Lightner, 1400 ....WR-13
Lightstreet, 1093 ....EJ-4
Ligonier, 1573 ....WM-4
Lilly, 968 ....WM-10
Lima, 2735 ....EP-11
Lime Ridge, 890 ....EJ-7
Limehill EF-7
Limeport, 250 ....EM-11
Limerick, 860 ....EN-10
Limestone, 150 ....WI-7
Limestoneville, 70 ......EJ-5
Lincoln, 1072 ....‡M-8
Lincoln Hts., 300 ....WN-5
Lincoln Hill, 150 ....WG-9
Lincoln Pk., 1615 ....ET-11
Lincolnville, 96 ....WE-5
Lincolnway, 950 ....WS-12
Linconia, 950 ....‡A-8
Linden, 270 ....EI-3
Linden, 100 ....EM-3
Lincville, 1040 ....WF-2
Linfield, 650 ....EO-10
Linglestown, 6334 ....EN-5
Linntown, 1489 ....EJ-4
Linwood, 3281 ....*B-10
Lionville, 6189 ....EO-10
Lippincott, 400 ....WP-3
Lisburn, 400 ....EO-4
Listie, 700 ....WM-8
Listonburg WQ-7
Litchfield, 80 ....EE-6
Lititz, 9369 ....EO-7
Lithia Sprs., 90 ....EK-5
Little Cooley, 50 ....WF-4
Little Cors., 45 ....WF-3
Little Gap, 300 ....EK-8
Little Hope, 60 ....WD-7
Little Marsh, 80 ....EE-2
Little Meadows,
  273 ....ED-7
Littlestown, 4434 ....EQ-3
Liverpool, 955 ....EM-1
Llewellyn, 800 ....EL-7
Llewellyn Cors. EC-8
Loag, 200 ....EO-10
Lobachsville EM-9
Lock Haven, 9772 ....EI-1
Locke Mills EL-1
Locust WM-7
Locust Gap, 450 ....EK-6
Locust Run, 100 ....EK-7
Locustdale, 177 ....EK-7
Loganton, 468 ....EJ-2
Loganville, 1240 ....EQ-5
London, WI-3
Lone Pine, 50 ....WO-3
Long Pond, 900 ....EJ-10
Longfellow, 215 ....EM-1
Longstown, 100 ....WS-14
Longswamp, 300 ....EM-10
Loop, 60 ....WM-7
Lopez, 180 ....EG-7
Lorain, 759 ....WS-2
Lorane, 4236 ....EN-9
Lords Valley, 70 ....EH-12
Loretto, 1302 ....WM-10
Lost Creek, 100 ....EK-7
Lottsville, 100 ....WL-8
Lovejoy, 50 ....WL-8
Lovelton, 100 ....EG-7
Lover WN-3
Lower Allen, 6694 ....ET-3
Lower Burrell,
  11761 ....*H-10
Lowville, 130 ....WO-9
Loyalsockville, 400 .....WH-4
Loyalton, 450 ....WM-6
Loysburg, 330 ....WO-11
Loysville, 200 ....EL-2
Lucerne Mines,
  937 ....WM-7
Lucinda, 300 ....WH-7
Luciusboro, 100 ....WM-8
Ludlow, 500 ....WL-8
Lumber City, 76 ....WJ-10
Lumberville, 200 ....EM-12
Lundys Lane, 180 ....WE-2
Lurgan, 50 ....EO-1
Luthersburg, 325 ....WJ-9
Luxor, 70 ....EH-9
Luzerne, 2845 ....EH-9
LUZERNE CO.,
320918 ....EH-8
Lycippus, 90 ....WN-6
LYCOMING CO.,
116111 ....EH-3
Lykens, 1779 ....EM-5
Lyleville, 135 ....WL-10
Lynch WM-11
Lyndell, 400 ....EP-9
Lynnport, 100 ....EL-9
Lyndora, 1300 ....WK-4
Lynn, 120 ....EP-2
Lynnport, 100 ....EL-8
Lynnwood, 1300 ....EB-7
Lyons, 478 ....EM-9
Macdonaldton,
  130 ....WP-8
Mackeyville, 250 ....EI-2
Macungie, 3074 ....EM-10
Maddensville WO-13
Madera, 1000 ....WK-11
Madison, 397 ....WN-6
Madisonburg, 168 ....EI-1
Madisonville, 150 ....EH-10
Madley WP-10
Mahaffey, 350 ....WK-10
Mahanoy City, 4162 ......EK-8
Maiden Creek, 200 ....EM-9
Mainland, 2000 ....EN-11
Mainsville, 150 ....EO-1
Maitland, 357 ....EL-2

Malta EL-4
Malvern, 2998 ....EP-10
Mammoth, 525 ....WN-6
Mamont WM-6
Manatawny, 200 ....EN-9
Manchester, 2763 ....EL-5
Mandata, 60 ....EL-5
Manheim, 4858 ....EO-8
Manns Choice,
  300 ....WP-10
Mannsville, 25 ....EM-3
Manor, 3290 ....WN-6
Manor Ridge, 1000 ....ES-8
Manorville, 410 ....WK-6
Mansfield, 3625 ....EE-3
Mantz, 300 ....EL-6
Maple Bch., 100 ....‡B-10
Maple Glen, 135 ....WU-6
Mapledale, 200 ....WM-8
Mapleton, 441 ....WN-13
Maplewood, 130 ....WO-4
Maplewood,
  200 ....EE-3
Maplewood, 405 ....EL-8
Maplewood Pk.,
  1700 ....‡F-1
Marble, 130 ....WH-6
Marchand, 90 ....WK-8
Marcus Hook,
  2397 ....EP-12
Margo Gdns., 300 ....‡A-10
Marianna, 494 ....WP-3
MIFFLIN CO.,
46682 ....EK-2
Marietta, 2588 ....EP-6
Marion, 953 ....WQ-14
Marion Ctr., 451 ....WK-8
Marion Hts., 451 ....EK-6
Markes, 100 ....WQ-13
Marklesburg, 204 ....WN-12
Markleton, 40 ....WQ-7
Markleysburg, 284 ....WQ-6
Markton WO-4
Marlin, 661 ....EL-7
Mars, 1699 ....EO-4
Marsh Hill EG-4
Marshallton, 1441 ....EK-6
Marshallton, 600 ....EP-10
Marshburg, 50 ....WE-9
Millardsville, 100 ......EK-6
Marshlands, 50 ....EF-1
Marstown, 150 ....EM-6
Martha Furnace,
  25 ....WK-13
Marticville, 400 ....WP-7
Martin, 110 ....WQ-4
Martindale, 180 ....EO-8
Martindale, 140 ....WN-10
Martins Creek,
  631 ....EK-12
Martinsburg,
  1958 ....WN-11
Martinsville, 100 ....EP-6
Marwood, 60 ....WK-5
Marysville, 2534 ....EM-4
Masontown, 3450 ....WQ-4
Mastersonville, 185 .....EO-6
Masthope, 685 ....EG-12
Matamoras, 2469 ....EH-14
Mather, 737 ....WP-3
Mattawanna, 276 ....WM-14
Mausdale, 75 ....EJ-5
Maxatawny, 250 ....EM-10
Mayburg WG-8
Mayfield, 1807 ....EG-10
Mayport, 80 ....WI-7
Maysville, 60 ....WM-9
Mayville, 150 ....WF-3
Maytown, 3824 ....EO-6
Maytown, ...WO-5
Maze EL-3
Mazeppa, 225 ....EJ-4
McAdoo, 2300 ....EK-8
McAlevys Fort, 70 ......WL-13
McAlisterville, 971 .....EL-3
McCartney, 70 ....WM-5
McClure, 941 ....EL-2
McConnellsburg,
  1220 ....WO-14
McConnellstown,
  1194 ....WN-12
McCoysville EM-1
McCracken, 60 ....WO-3
McCrea WM-9
McElhattan, 598 ....EI-2
McEwensville, 279 ....EJ-5
McGees Mills, 100 ....WK-9
McGovern, 2742 ....WN-3
McGrann, 700 ....WK-6
McIntyre, 20 ....WM-7
McKean, 388 ....WD-3
MCKEAN CO.,
43450 ....WF-10
McKeansburg, 163 ....EL-8
McKee, 200 ....WO-3
McKee Half Falls,
  130 ....EL-4
McKees Rocks,
  6104 ....WM-3
McKeesport,
  19731 ....WN-3
McKinney EO-1
McKnightstown,
  226 ....EQ-2
McLane, 70 ....WG-2
McMichael, 50 ....EJ-11
McMurray, 4647 ....WN-3
McSherrystown,
  3038 ....EQ-2
McVeytown, 342 ....WM-14
Meadow Lands,
  822 ....WN-3
Meadowbrook,
  1000 ....‡A-5
Meadville, 13388 ....WF-3
Mechanics Grv.,
  120 ....EQ-8
Mechanicsburg,
  8981 ....WO-13
Mechanicsville,
  7828 ....EO-9
Mechanicsville,
  500 ....EN-11
Mechanicsville, 120 .....EA-2
Mechanicsville, 35 ......WP-10
Mecks Corner, ...WO-11
Media, 5327 ....EP-11
Mehoopany, 350 ....EG-8
Meiserville, 100 ....EL-4
Melcroft, 250 ....WN-6
Melrose Pk., 6500 ......‡B-9
Mendenhall, 600 ....EQ-10

Menges Mills, 200 ......EQ-4
Menno, 80 ....WM-14
Mentcle, 100 ....WL-9
Mercer, 2002 ....WI-3
MERCER CO.,
116638 ....WH-2
Mercersburg,
  1561 ....WQ-13
Meridian, 3881 ....WK-4
Merion Sta., 700 ....*D-3
Mertztown, 664 ....EM-10
Meshoppen, 563 ....EG-8
Metal, 100 ....WP-13
Mexico, 472 ....EL-3
Meyersdale, 2184 ....WQ-8
Middle Creek, ...EK-3
Middle Lancaster,
  100 ....WK-5
Middle Spr., 80 ....EO-1
Middleburg, 1309 ....EK-4
Middleburg, 90 ....EJ-9
Middlebury Ctr.,
  200 ....EE-3
Middleport, 405 ....EL-8
Middlesex, 250 ....EO-3
Middletown, 8901 ....EO-5
Middletown, 7378 ....EL-5
Midland, 2635 ....WL-2
Midvale EL-4
Midway, 913 ....WN-4
Mt. Wolf, 1393 ....EP-5
Mt. Zion, 350 ....EM-6
Mt. Zion, 100 ....ES-1
Mt. Zion, 200 ....EA-10
Mountain Top,
  10982 ....EI-9
Mountainhome,
  1182 ....EI-11
Mountville, 2802 ....EP-6
Mourersville, 40 ....EO-1
Muddy Creek Forks,
  650 ....EQ-6
Muhlenberg, 200 ....EI-7
Muhlenberg Pk.,
  120 ....EA-12
Muir, 451 ....EL-6
Mummasburg, 200 ....EQ-2
Muncy, 2477 ....EI-5
Muncy Valley, 270 ......EH-6
Mundert, 30 ....WH-8
Munhalls Corner,
  205 ....WN-3
Munson, 275 ....WJ-12
Murdocksville, ...WN-2
Murrell EO-7
Murrysville,
  20079 ....WM-5
Muse, 2504 ....WN-3
Myerstown, 3062 ....EN-7
Myers Hts., 3762 ....EL-11
Myerstown, 5414 ....EK-10
Myoma, 100 ....EK-8
Myrtle WD-12
Nanticoke, 10465 ....EI-8
Nant Mead Vil., ...
Nanty Glo, 2734 ....WM-9
Narberth, 4282 ....EP-12
Nassau Vil., 1500 .....‡G-1
Natrona, 2800 ....WL-5
Natrona Hts., 2800 .....WL-5
Nauvoo, 40 ....EG-3
Nazareth, 5746 ....EL-11
Neckscott WO-3
Nectarine WI-4
Needmore, 170 ....WQ-12
Neelyton, 80 ....WO-13
Neffs, 650 ....EL-10
Neiltown, 3 ....EO-7
Neilton, 300 ....EO-3
Nemacolin, 937 ....WP-4
Nescopeck, 1583 ....EJ-7
Nesquehoning,
  3349 ....EK-9
New Albany, 356 ....EG-6
New Alexandria,
  560 ....WM-6
New Baltimore,
  180 ....WP-9
New Beaver, 1502 ......WK-2
New Bedford, 825 ......WI-2
New Berlin, 873 ....EK-4
New Berlinville, ...EN-10
New Bethlehem,
  989 ....WJ-7
New Bloomfield,
  1247 ....EM-3
New Boston, 230 ....EK-7
New Br.ville, 320 .....EO-7
New Brighton,
  6025 ....WK-3
New Britain, 3152 .....EN-12
New Buena Vista,
  80 ....WP-11
New Buffalo, 129 ......EM-4
New Castle, 23273 .....WJ-2
New Centerville,
  3835 ....WP-9
New Columbia,
  133 ....WJ-7
New Columbus,
  1013 ....EJ-4
New Columbus, 227 .....EL-7
New Cumberland,
  7277 ....EO-4
New Danville, 500 .....EP-8
New Derry, 800 ....WN-7
New Eagle, 2184 ....WN-4
New Enterprise,
  300 ....WO-11
New Era, 35 ....EP-7
New Florence, 689 .....WN-8
New Franklin, 150 .....EO-1
New Freedom,
  4464 ....EQ-5
New Freeport, 150 .....WQ-2
New Galilee, 379 ......WK-2
New Gdn., 300 ....*B-6
New Geneva, 150 ....WQ-4
New Germantown,
  200 ....EM-1
New Grenada, 90 ....WO-12
New Hamburg, 70 ....WI-3
New Holland, 5378 .....EO-8
New Hope, 2528 ....EN-13
New Jerusalem,
  649 ....EM-9
New Kensington,
  13116 ....WL-5
New Kingstown,
  495 ....EO-3
New Lebanon, 188 ......WH-4

Ohiopyle, 59 ....WQ-6
Ohioville, 3533 ....WK-1
Ohl, 75 ....WJ-7
Oil City, 10557 ....WG-5
Oklahoma, 809 ....WL-6
Oklahoma, 782 ....WK-10
Old Boston, 200 ....EK-7
Old Concord, 30 ....WR-2
Old Forge, 8313 ....EH-9
Old Port, 90 ....EM-2
Oley, 1282 ....EN-9
Oliphant Furnace,
  250 ....WQ-5
Oliveburg, 150 ....WJ-8
Oliver, 2535 ....WP-5
Olney, ...‡C-5
Olyphant, 5151 ....LG-10
Oneida, 200 ....EK-8
Oneida, 100 ....EK-8
Ono, 300 ....EN-6
Opp, ...WM-1
Orange, 300 ....EN-9
Orangeville, 508 ......EI-6
Orbisonia, 428 ....WN-13
Orchard Bch., 125 .....WC-5
Orchard Hills, 1952 ...WL-6
Ore Hill, 95 ....WN-11
Ore Valley, 200 ....WT-14
Orefield, 250 ....WO-10
Oreland, 5678 ....‡A-4
Oriental, 100 ....EL-4
Oriole, 100 ....EL-3
Ormrod, 300 ....EA-12
Ormsby, 100 ....WE-10
Orrstown, 262 ....EP-1
Orrtanna, 173 ....EQ-2
Orson, 125 ....EE-10
Orviston, 95 ....WH-14
Orwell, 100 ....EE-7
Orwigsburg, 3099 ......EL-8
Orwin, 314 ....EM-6
Osceola, 400 ....ED-2
Osceola Mills,
  1141 ....WK-13
Osgood, 40 ....WO-2
Osterburg, 250 ....WO-10
Oswayo, 139 ....WC-12
Ottsville, 250 ....EM-12
Oval, 361 ....EI-3
Overbrook *D-3
Overlook, 200 ....EK-2
Overlook Hts., ...WS-5
Overton, 85 ....EG-6
Overview, 50 ....ER-2
Oxford, 5077 ....EQ-8
Packerton, 20 ....EK-9
Paint, 1023 ....WN-9
Painterville, ...EL-2
Painterstown, 120 .....‡L-11
Palm, 370 ....EM-10
Palmer Hts., 3762 .....EL-11
Palmerton, 5414 ....EK-10
Palmyra, 7320 ....EN-6
Palo Alto, 1032 ....EL-7
Pancic, 80 ....WJ-8
Paoli, 5575 ....EP-11
Paradise, 1129 ....EP-8
Paradise, 250 ....EN-6
Paradise Valley, 1 ....EI-11
Pardoe, 50 ....WI-3
Park Carbon, 1889 .....EL-7
Park Clinton, 326 .....EL-8
Park Griffith, 1350 ...EB-9
Park Hall, 1952 ....WQ-11
Park Royal, 925 ....EM-3
Port Trevorton, 769 ...EL-4
Park Vue, 3798 ....WN-4
Parker, 840 ....WI-5
Parker Ford, 800 ......EO-10
Parkesburg, 3593 ......EP-9
Parkhill, 300 ....WL-11
Parkside, 2328 ....EQ-11
Parksorn, 175 ....WS-2
Parryville, 525 ....EK-10
North East, 4294 ......WC-5
North Fork, 30 ....WM-8
N. Hills, 3000 ....‡A-3
N. Irwin, 846 ....WN-5
N. Liberty, 100 ....WH-2
N. Mountain, 150 ......EH-6
N. Oakland WK-4
N. Orwell, 100 ....EE-7
N. Point, 75 ....WM-8
N. Rome, 65 ....EE-6
N. Springfield, 300 ...WD-2
N. Towanda, 400 ....EF-6
N. Versailles, 10027 ..WN-5
N. Wales, 3229 ....EO-11
N. Warren, 1934 ....WE-8
N. Washington, ...
  500 ....WM-5
N. Washington, 200 ....WK-5
N. York, 1914 ....EO-5
Northampton,
  9926 ....EL-10
NORTHAMPTON CO.,
297735 ....EK-11
North Cambria,
  3804 ....WL-9
Northumberland,
  3804 ....EK-5
NORTHUMBERLAND CO.,
94528 ....EK-5
Northview, 700 ....WJ-4
Northwood, 296 ....WL-12
Northwd, 948 ....WO-6
Norwood, 5890 ....‡F-2
Nottingham, 3000 ......‡A-8
Nottingham, 200 ....WL-9
Norwmtn, 150 ....WM-4
Noxen, 633 ....EH-8
Numidia, 244 ....EK-6
Nu.Mine, 300 ....WK-7
Nuremberg, 434 ....EJ-7
Nyesville, 75 ....WL-9
Oak Forest, 60 ....WL-9
Oak Grv., 200 ....WN-7
Oak Hall, ...EK-1
Oak Pk., 700 ....EN-11
Oakdale, 1459 ....WM-3
Oakland, 1600 ....WS-2
Oakland, 1569 ....WJ-3
Oakland, 616 ....ED-10
Oakland Mills, 110 ....EL-2
Oakleigh, 1000 ....ES-4
Oakmont, 6303 ....WM-4
Oaks, 850 ....EO-11
Oberlin, 588 ....ES-4
Ogdensburg, 75 ....WJ-9
Ogletown, 150 ....WO-9

Phillips, 225 ....WP-5
Phillipston, 45 ....WJ-6
Phillipsville WP-4
Phoenixville, ...EN-9
  16440 ....EO-10
Picture Rocks, 678 ....EI-5
Pigeon, 20 ....WG-8
PIKE CO., 57369 .....EH-12
Pilgrim Gdns., 1650 ...*E-1
Pillow, 298 ....EL-5
Pine, 80 ....EI-2
Pine Flats, 30 ....WL-8
Pine Glen, 190 ....WJ-12
Pine Grv., 2186 ....EM-6
Pine Grv. Furnace EP-3
Pine Grv. Mills, ...
  1502 ....WL-13
Pine Summit, 15 ....EJ-8
Pinecroft, 100 ....WM-11
Piney Fork, 400 ......*N-6
Pinola, 20 ....EL-7
Pipersville, 600 .....EM-12
Pitcairn, 3294 ....*K-9
Pitman, 300 ....EL-6
Pittsburgh, ...
  305704 ....WM-4
Pittsfield, 500 ......WE-7
Pittston, 7739 ....EI-9
Pittsville, 35 ....WP-4
Plainfield, 399 ......EO-2
Plains, 4335 ....EI-8
Plainsville, 350 .....EI-8
Platea, 430 ....WD-3
Pleasant Gap,
  2879 ....WK-14
Pleasant Grv., 150 ...WJ-4
Pleasant Hall, 150 ...EP-1
Pleasant Hills, 8268 ..*M-6
Pleasant Mount,
  125 ....EF-11
Pleasant Union, ...WQ-9
Pleasant Unity,
  600 ....WN-6
Pleasant Valley,
  200 ....EM-11
Pleasantville,
  1000 ....WR-13
Pleasureville, ...EO-5
Ples, 732 ....WN-7
Plum, 27126 ....WM-5
Plumer, 150 ....WF-5
Plumsteadville, ...EM-12
Plumville, 307 ....WK-7
Plymouth, 5951 ....EI-8
Plymouth Meeting,
  6177 ....*A-2
Pocahontas, 250 ......WP-8
Pocono Lake, 750 ......EI-10
Pocono Mnr., 200 ......EI-11
Pocono Pines, 1409 ...EI-11
Pocono Summit,
  1500 ....EI-11
Point, ...WO-10
Pt. Marion, 1159 .....WQ-4
Pt. Pleasant, 800 ....EM-12
Pointer View Pk., ...
  3380 ....ES-12
Poland, 75 ....WH-4
Polk, 816 ....WH-4
Pomeroy, 401 ....EP-9
Pond Bank, 200 ....EQ-1
Pond Eddy, 50 ....EG-13
Pond Hill, 200 ....EI-8
Port Allegany,
  2157 ....WE-11
Port Carbon, 1889 ....EL-7
Port Clinton, 326 ....EL-8
Port Griffith, 1350 ..EB-9
Port Matilda, 606 ....WK-12
Port Royal, 925 ......EM-3
Port Trevorton, 769 ..EL-4
Port Vue, 3798 ....WN-4
Portage, 2638 ....WN-10
Porter, 25 ....WJ-7
Porters Sideling,
  100 ....EQ-4
Portersville, 235 ....WJ-3
Portland, 519 ....EJ-12
Portland Mills, 40 ...WH-9
Portville, 6706 ......EQ-4
Potter Brook, 200 ....EC-1
Pottersdale, 100 .....WJ-12
Potterville, 75 ......EE-7
Potts Grv., 140 ......EJ-5
Pottstown, 22377 .....EN-10
Pottsville, 14324 ....EL-7
Powell, 150 ....EF-6
Powells Valley, 600 ..EM-4
Prescott, 100 ....EN-6
President, 100 ....WH-6
Preston, 240 ....EE-10
Preston Pk., 100 .....EE-11
Pricetown, 180 ....EN-9
Primos, 900 ....*F-2
Primrose, 400 ....EK-7
Princeton, 150 ....WJ-3
Pringle, 979 ....EA-8
Prittstown, ...WP-9
Proctor, 50 ....EG-4
Progress, 9765 ....ES-3
Prompton, 250 ....EG-11
Prospect, 1169 ....WJ-4
Prospect Pk., 6454 ...EP-11
Prospect, 327 ....WQ-12
Prospectville, 500 ...EO-12
Prosperity, 175 ......WO-2
Pulaski, 300 ....WI-2
Punxsutawney,
  5962 ....WJ-8
Purcell, 25 ....WL-10
Purchase Line, 40 ....WL-8
Putneyville, 140 .....WJ-7
Puzzletown, ...WN-10
Quakake, 300 ....EK-8
Quaker Hills, ...ET-8
Quaker Lake, 70 ......ED-8
Quakertown,
  8979 ....EM-11
Quarryville, 2576 ....EP-7
Queen Col, 57369 .....EH-10
Queens Run, 50 ....EI-2
Quentin, 594 ....EN-6
Quicktown, 100 ....WN-6
Quiggleville, 50 .....EI-4
Quincy, 400 ....EQ-1
Radnor, ...*C-1
Railroad, 278 ....EQ-5
Rainsburg, 140 ....WP-10
Ralston, 330 ....EG-4
Ramey, 451 ....WK-11
Ramsey, 45 ....WI-7
Ransom, 250 ....EH-9
Rankin, 2112 ....*K-7
Rathmel, 150 ....WJ-8
Raubsville, 1088 .....EL-12
Ravine, 420 ....EM-6
Rawlinsville, 150 ....EQ-7

Raymilton, ...WH-4
Raymond, ...WE-13
Rea, 50 ....WN-2
Reading, 88082 ....EN-9
Reagantown, 70 ....WO-5
Reamstown, 3361 ......EO-8
Rebersburg, 494 ......EJ-1
Rebuck, 150 ....EL-5
Rector, 400 ....WO-7
Red Br., 200 ....EP-1
Red Cross, 70 ....EL-8
Red Hill, 2383 ....EN-10
Red Hill, 100 ....WA-12
Red Lion, 6373 ....EP-5
Red Rock, 30 ....EH-7
Redcliffe, 20 ....EP-3
Reeders, 350 ....EJ-11
Reeds Gap, 30 ....EM-1
Reedsville, 641 ......EL-1
Reels Cors., 25 ......WO-9
Reese, 80 ....WM-11
Reesedale, 50 ....WJ-6
Refton, 298 ....EP-7
Rehrersburg, 319 .....EM-7
Reidsburg, 40 ....WI-6
Reiffton, 4178 ....ET-13
Reinerton, 424 ....EL-6
Reinholds, 1803 .....EN-8
Reistville, 100 ......EN-7
Renfrew, 350 ....WK-4
Renovo, 1272 ....WH-14
Republic, 1096 ....WP-4
Revere, 400 ....EM-12
Revloc, 570 ....WM-9
Rew, 199 ....WE-10
Rexford, 100 ....EF-2
Rexis, 45 ....WM-9
Reynoldsville, 2759 ..WJ-9
Rheems, 1598 ....EO-6
Rices, 463 ....WM-8
Riceville, 68 ....WE-5
Rich Hill, 50 ....EM-11
Richardsville, 40 ....WI-8
Richboro, 6563 ....EO-12
Richfield, 549 ....EL-3
Richland, 1519 ....EN-7
Richlandtown,
  1327 ....EM-11
Richmond, 100 ....EK-12
Richmond Furnace,
  50 ....WP-13
Richvale, 35 ....WP-3
Riddlesburg, 300 .....WO-11
Ridgebury, 800 ....EE-4
Ridgeview, 800 ....ER-5
Ridgway, 4078 ....WH-9
Ridley Farms, 1500 ...*F-1
Ridley Pk., 7002 .....‡F-2
Riegelsville, 868 ....EL-12
Rimer, 40 ....WJ-6
Rimersburg, 951 ......WJ-6
Rinely, ...WO-12
Ringgold, 225 ....WJ-7
Ringtown, 818 ....EK-7
River View Pk., ...
  3380 ....ES-12
Riverside, 1896 ......EK-5
Riverside, 381 ....WT-2
Rixford, 400 ....WE-10
Roaring Branch,
  100 ....EF-4
Roaring Creek, 156 ...EK-6
Roaring Spr.,
  2585 ....WN-11
Robertsdale, 240 .....WO-12
Robesonia, 2061 ......EN-8
Robinson, 614 ....WM-7
Rochester, 3657 ......WL-3
Rochester Mills,
  2802 ....WK-8
Rock, 60 ....WM-8
Rock Glen, 300 ....EJ-7
Rockhill, 371 ....WO-13
Rockingham, 40 ....WO-3
Rockland, 30 ....WH-5
Rockledge, 2543 .....EO-12
Rockport, 85 ....EJ-9
Rockspring, ...WL-13
Rockton, 200 ....WJ-10
Rockville, 170 ....EN-4
Rockville, 85 ....EN-4
Rockwood, 890 ....WP-7
Roderfield, 300 .....EM-6
Rodgersville, 249 ....WP-2
Rogertown, 140 ....WE-8
Rohrerstown, 1200 ....EP-6
Rohrsburg, 145 ....EI-6
Rome, 441 ....EF-7
Ronco, 256 ....WP-4
Roscoe, 812 ....WO-4
Rose Pt., 90 ....WJ-3
Rose Valley, 913 .....EP-11
Rosebud, 450 ....WK-10
Rosecrans, ...EI-2
Roseglen, 110 ....EN-3
Rosemont, ...*C-1
Roses, 140 ....WO-8
Roseto, 1567 ....EK-11
Roseville, 189 ....EE-4
Roseville, 100 ....WJ-6
Roslyn, 10047 ....EO-12
Rossiter, 646 ....WK-8
Rossland, 60 ....WP-4
Rosslyn Farms, 427 ...*K-4
Rossmoyne, 1100 ......ET-2
Rote, 507 ....EI-2
Rothsville, 3044 .....EO-7
Roulette, 210 ....WD-12
Round Top, 125 ....EQ-3
Rouseville, 523 ......WG-5
Roweville, 180 ....EM-9
Rowes Run, 564 ....WP-4
Rowland, 200 ....EG-12
Roxbury, 275 ....EO-1
Roxbury, 50 ....EM-6
Royal, 100 ....EF-10
Royalton, 907 ....EO-5
Royer, 45 ....WN-11
Royersford, 4752 .....EO-10
Ruff Creek, 40 ....WP-3
Ruffs Dale, 800 .....WN-5
Rummel, 600 ....WN-9
Rummerfield, 35 ......EF-6
Runville, 250 ....WJ-13
Rupert, 150 ....EJ-6
Ruppsville, 400 .....EA-11
Rural Ridge, 1000 ...*I-8
Rural Valley, 876 ....WK-7
Rushland, 30 ....EN-12
Rushville, 45 ....EF-7
Russell, 1408 ....WD-8
Russell City, 40 ....WG-8
Russell Hill, 125 ...EH-8
Russellton, 1440 ....WL-5
Rutherford, 4303 ....ES-4

Rutledge, 784 ....‡F-1
Shelocta, 130 ....WL-7
Shenandoah, 5071 .....EK-7
Shenandoah Hts.,
  1233 ....EK-1
Shenango, 80 ....WI-2
Shepherd Hills,
  2030 ....EC-1
Shepherdstown, ...
  200 ....EO-4
Sherman, 239 ....EK-8
Sherman Dale, ...
  120 ....EN-3
Shermansville, 50 ....WF-2
Sherrett, 125 ....WK-6
Sheshequin, 550 ......EE-6
Shickshinny, 838 .....EI-7
Shillington, 5273 ....EN-8
Shiloh, 11218 ....EP-5
Shimerville, 130 .....EM-10
Shimpstown, 80 ......WQ-13
Shindle, 70 ....EL-2
Shinglehouse,
  1127 ....WD-12
Shinglestown, ...
  150 ....WK-13
Shintown, 75 ....WH-13
St. Lawrence, 1809 ...EN-9
St. Lawrence, 40 .....WL-10
St. Marys, 13070 .....WH-10
St. Michael, 408 .....WN-9
St. Paul, 75 ....WQ-2
St. Peters, 400 ......EO-9
St. Petersburg, 400 ..WI-5
St. Thomas, 900 ......WP-13
Salem, 150 ....EE-5
Salem, 30 ....WG-2
Salemville, 10 ....WO-11
Saltillo, 346 ....WO-12
St. Boniface, 120 ....WM-11
St. Clair, 3004 ......EL-7
St. Clairsville, 78 ..WO-10
St. George, 50 ....EM-7
St. Johns, 300 ....EJ-8
St. Joseph, 150 ......EL-8
St. Lawrence, 1809 ...EN-9
St. Petersburg, 400 ..WI-5
Saltsburg, 873 ......WM-6
Salunga, 2695 ....EO-6
Saluvia, ...WP-12
Sanatoga, 8378 .....EN-10
Sand Bch., 300 ......EN-5
Sand Hill, 2496 .....EN-6
Sand Lake, 150 ......EE-8
Silver Spr., 300 ....EN-3
Sandts Eddy, ...EK-12
Sandy, 1429 ....WJ-9
Sandy Creek, ...WP-2
Sandy Hollow, 55 ....WO-4
Sandy Lake, 659 .....WH-3
Sandy Ridge, 407 ....WK-12
Sandy Run, 60 ....EF-8
Sandy Valley, 40 ....WO-3
Sankertown, 675 .....WM-10
Santiago, 400 ......EL-13
Santon, 400 ....WN-9
Sassamansville, ...
  350 ....EN-10
Satterfield, ...EN-10
Saulsburg, ...WL-13
Saville, 20 ....EK-12
Saxton, 736 ....WO-11
Saybrook, ...EN-6
Saylorsburg, 1126 ...EK-11
Sayre, 5587 ....EE-6
Scalp Level, 778 ....WN-9
Scandia, 25 ....WE-8
Scenery Hill, 600 ...WO-4
Schaefferstown,
  941 ....EN-7
Schellsburg, 338 ....WP-10
Schenley, 55 ....WL-6
Schnecksville,
  2935 ....EL-10
Schoeneck, 1056 .....EN-7
Schoenersville, 400 ..EA-12
Schubert, 249 ....EM-8
Schuster Hts., 75 ...WL-5
Schwenksville,
  1370 ....EO-11
School Lane Hills, ...ES-8
Schuylkill Haven,
  5437 ....EL-7
Schuylkill Haven, ...
Sciota, 300 ....EJ-11
Scotch Hill, ...EN-4
Scotdale, 6578 ......WO-5
Scotia, ...WK-13
Scotland, 1395 ......EP-1
Scotrun, 650 ....EJ-11
Scottdale, 4384 .....WO-5
Scottsville, 2400 ...WN-3
Scranton, 76089 .....EH-10
Scullton, 100 ....WP-8
Seanor, 130 ....WN-9
Searights, 350 ......WP-4
S. Bethlehem, 481 ...WJ-7
S. Bradford, 150 ....EF-6
S. Canaan, 250 ......EG-11
S. Coatesville, 1303 .EP-9
S. Connellsville, ...WP-5
S. Fork, 928 ....WN-9
S. Gibson, 175 ......EF-8
S. Greensburg,
  2117 ....WN-6
S. Heights, 475 .....WL-3
S. Lakemont, ...WN-11
S. Montrose, 400 ....EE-8
S. Mountain, 600 ....EQ-1
S. New Castle, 709 ..WJ-2
S. Philipsburg, ...WK-12
S. Renovo, 439 ......WH-14
S. Sterling, 150 ....EH-11
S. Tamaqua, 200 .....EK-8
S. Temple, 1424 .....ER-13
S. Uniontown, ...WP-4
S. Waverly, 1027 ....EC-6
S. Williamsport,
  6379 ....EI-4
Southampton,
  11500 ....EO-12
Southmont, 2284 .....WN-9
Southview, 276 ......WN-3
Southwest, 600 ......WO-6
Southwest Greensburg,
  2155 ....WN-6
Sparta, 30 ....WQ-12
Spartansburg, 305 ...WE-5
Speers, 1154 ....WO-4
Spinnerstown, ...EM-11
Spraggs, 30 ....WQ-2
Sprankle Mills, 60 ..WJ-8
Spring Brook, 450 ...EH-10
Spring City, 3323 ...EO-10
Spring Creek, 100 ...WD-7
Spring Glen, 200 ...EL-5
Spring Grv., 2167 ...EQ-4
Spring Hill, 839 ...WN-10

Taylor, 6263 ....EH-9
Taylorstown, 217 .....WO-3
Taylorville, 20 ......WF-4
Telford, 4872 ....EN-11
Temple, 1877 ....EM-9
Ten Mile, 60 ....WP-3
Terre Hill, 1295 .....EO-8
Terrytown, 100 ....EF-7
Thomas, 325 ....WN-5
Thomas Mills, 50 .....WP-9
Thomasville, 450 .....EP-4
Thompson, 299 ....EE-10
Thompsontown, ...
  697 ....EL-3
Thornburg, 500 ......‡K-4
Thornton, 100 ....EP-11
Thornville, 400 .....EE-8
Three Sprs., 444 ....WO-13
Tidal, 75 ....WJ-6
Tideoute, 688 ....WF-6
Tidi Jct., 616 ......WO-5
Timberly Hts., 400 ..WJ-4
Timblin, 157 ....WJ-7
Tioga, 666 ....EE-3
Tinicum, 100 ....EM-12
Tioga Jct., 100 .....EE-3
Tiona, 400 ....WF-8
Tipton, 1083 ....WL-11
Tire Hill, 900 ......WN-9
Titusville, 5601 ....WF-5
Tobyhanna, 1200 .....EI-11
Todd, 952 ....WN-12
Tobyhanna, 1200 .....EI-11
Toftrees, 2053 ......WS-5
Tolna, 40 ....EQ-5
Tomhicken, 160 ......EJ-8
Tompkinsville, 200 ..EG-10
Torranceville,
  135 ....WQ-2
Topton, 2069 ....EM-9
Toughkenamon,
  1492 ....EQ-9
Towanda, 2919 ....EF-6
Townville, 512 ......WF-4
Towne City, 1346 ....EL-6
Townville, 300 ......EK-4
Trafford, 3174 ......WN-5
Trainer, 1828 ......*B-10
Transfer, 500 ......WH-2
  350 ....WL-12
Trappe, 3509 ....EO-11
Treichlers, 600 ....EL-10
Tremont, 1752 ......EL-6
Trent, ...WP-7
Tresckow, 880 ......EK-8
Trevorton, 1834 ....EK-5
Trevose, 5744 ....EO-13
Trexler, ...EM-9
Trexlertown, 1988 ..EM-10
Trout Run, 350 ......EH-4
Troutville, 243 ....WJ-9
Troxelville, 221 ....EK-3
Troy, 1354 ....EE-5
Troy Ctr., ...EE-5
Trucksville, 2152 ...EA-8
Trumbauersville, ...
  1878 ....EM-11
Tuckerton, 300 .....EN-9
Tullytown, 1872 ....*T-12
Tunkhannock, 1836 ..EG-8
Tunnelhill, 303 .....WM-10
Tunnelton, 110 .....WM-6
Turbotville, 705 ...EJ-5
Turkey City, 100 ...WH-6
Turtle Creek, 5349 ..WM-4
Turtlepoint, 90 ....WD-11
Tuscarora, 980 .....EK-8
Twin Lakes, 125 ....EH-13
Twin Rocks, 600 ....WM-9
Two Taverns, 50 ....EQ-3
Tyler Hill, 80 .....EF-12
Tyler Hill, 450 ....EF-12
Tylersburg, 200 ....WH-7
Tylersport, 300 ....EN-11
Tylersville, 225 ...EI-2
Tyrone, 5477 ....WL-11
Uledi, 250 ....WP-5
Ulster, 300 ....EE-6
Ulysses, 621 ....WE-14
UNION CO.,
44947 ....EJ-3
Union Dale, 267 .....EF-10
Union Deposit, 400 ..EN-6
Uniontown, 10372 ....WP-5
Unionville, 962 .....WL-13
Unionville, 110 .....ES-8
Unionville, 291 .....WK-13
Unityville, 60 .....EI-5
Universal, ...*J-9
Upper Black Eddy,
  992 ....EM-12
Upper Darby, ...*F-2
Upper Exeter, 707 ...EA-9
Upper St. Clair,
  19200 ....WN-3
Upper Strasburg,
  223 ....WP-13
Urban, 45 ....EL-5
Urey, ...WO-8
Ursina, 225 ....WP-7
Utica, 189 ....WG-5
Valencia, 551 ......WL-4
Valier, 600 ....WJ-8
Valley Forge, 1500 ..EO-11
Valley View, 1683 ...EL-6
Valley View, 400 ...ES-4
Van, 60 ....WL-7
Van Ormer, 150 .....WM-10
Van Voorhis, 560 ...WO-4
Vandergrift, 5205 ...WL-6
Vandling, 751 ......EF-10
Vankirk, ...WO-3
  1294 ....WL-5

Varden, 150 ....EG-11
Venango, 239 ....WE-3
VENANGO CO.,
54984 ....WG-5
Venetia, 250 ....WN-3
Venus, 150 ....WH-5
Vera Cruz, 250 .....EM-10
Verona, 2411 ....WM-4
Versailles, 1515 ...WN-4
Vestaburg, 975 .....WO-4
Vicksburg, 261 .....EJ-4
Victory Hts., 150 ..EF-2
Villa Maria, 150 ...WI-2
Villanova ....‡C-1
Vinco, 1305 ....WN-9
Vinemont, 100 ......EN-8
Vintage, 200 ....EP-8
Vintondale, 414 ....WM-8
Vira, 150 ....EL-1
Virginville, 309 ...EM-9
Volant, 168 ....WJ-3
Vosburg, ...WG-8
Vowinckel, 139 .....WH-7
Wagner, 128 ....EL-2
Wagnerville, 150 ...EA-6
Wagontown, 500 .....EP-9
Wakefield, 609 .....EQ-7
Walbert, 200 ....EA-11
Wall, 580 ....‡L-7
Wallaceton, 313 ....WJ-11
Wallace *F-1
Wallingford ....‡F-1
Walls Cors., 30 ....EG-9
Walnut, 45 ....EM-10
Walnut, 115 ....EM-2
Walnut Bottom,
  300 ....EO-2
Walnutport, 200 ....EK-10
Walnuttown, 484 ....EM-9
Walston, 275 ......WJ-8
Waltersburg, 275 ...WP-5
Walton, 300 ....WJ-8
Wampum, 717 ....WK-2
Wanamakers, 55 .....EL-9
Wanamie, 612 ....EI-8
Wapwallopen, 150 ...EJ-8
Warfordsburg,
  135 ....WQ-13
Warminster ....
  31400 ....EO-12
Warren, 9710 ......WE-8
Warren Ctr., 200 ...EE-7
WARREN CO.,
41815 ....WE-7
Warrendale, 560 ....WL-3
Warrensville, 300 ..EH-4
Warrington, 300 ....EN-12
Warrior Run, 584 ...EI-8
Warriors Mark,
  350 ....WL-12
Warwick, 200 ....EO-9
Washington, ...
  13663 ....WO-3
Washington Boro,
  729 ....EP-6
WASHINGTON CO.,
207820 ....WN-2
Washington Crossing,
  850 ....EN-13
Wassergass, 200 ....EL-11
Water Street, 15 ...WM-12
Waterford, 1517 ....WD-4
Waterford, 300 .....WO-12
Waterloo, 50 ....WN-14
Waterman, 140 ......WM-8
Waterside, 50 ......WO-11
Waterville, 150 ....EH-3
Watrous, 150 ....EF-3
Watsontown, 2351 ...EJ-4
Wattsburg, 438 .....WD-5
Wattsville, 403 ...WO-5
Waverly, 604 ....EH-9
Waymart, 1341 ......EG-11
Wayne Hts., 2545 ...EQ-1
WAYNE CO.,
52822 ....EF-11
Waynesboro, ...
Waynesburg, ...
  10568 ....WP-2
Weatherly, 2525 ....EJ-9
Webster, 255 ....WO-4
Webster Mills, 250 ..WQ-12
Weedville, 542 .....WH-10
Weigelstown, ...
  12875 ....EO-4
Weikert, 215 ....EK-2
Weishample, 100 ....EL-8
Weissport, 412 .....EK-9
Weldbank, 100 ......WL-6
Welcome, 4300 ......‡A-4
Wells Tannery, ...
  100 ....WO-12
Wellersville, 3341 ..WP-4
W. Alexander, 800 ..WO-1
W. Auburn, 100 .....EF-8
W. Bangor, 300 .....EK-11
W. Bingham, 50 .....WE-13
W. Bristol, 5000 ...EN-13
W. Brownsville, ...
  1929 ....WO-4
W. Cameron, 165 ...EL-5
W. Catasauqua,
  700 ....EA-12
W. Chester, 18461 ..EP-10
W. Clifford, 50 ....EF-9
W. Conshohocken,
  1320 ....‡B-1
W. Decatur, 533 ...WJ-11
W. Elizabeth, 518 ..WN-4
W. Enola, 800 .....ES-2
W. Fairfield, 60 ...WN-7
W. Fairview, 1282 ..ES-2
W. Finley, 150 ....WO-2
W. Franklin, 40 ...WO-5
W. Freedom, 240 ...WI-5
W. Grove, 2854 ...EO-9
W. Hazleton, 4594 ..EJ-8
W. Hickory, 300 ...WG-7
W. Kittanning,
  1175 ....WK-6
W. Lancaster, 800 ..EP-6
W. Lawn, 1715 .....EN-11
W. Lebanon, 150 ...WM-7
W. Leechburg, ...
  1294 ....WL-5

*, †, ‡, §, ◊   See explanation under state title in this index.
County and parish names are listed in CAPITAL LETTERS & boldface type.
Independent cities (not included in a county) are listed in italics.

*, †, ‡, §, ◊   See explanation under state title in this index.
County and parish names are listed in CAPITAL LETTERS & boldface type.
Independent cities (not included in a county) are listed in *italics*.

WINKLER CO.,
7110 .... WK-8
Winnie, 3254 ....EK-12
Winnsboro, 3434 .....EE-10
Winona, 576 ....ZZ-14
Winter Haven, 25 .... WR-14
Winters, 2562 ....WK-14
WISE CO., 59127 ...ED-5
Wixon Valley, 254 .....EI-8
Woden, 250 ....EE-14
Wolfe City, 1412 ......ED-8
Wolfforth, 3670 ......WH-10
WOOD CO., 41964..EE-9
Woodbury, 40 ....EG-6
Woodcreek, 1457 ......EK-5
Woodlake, 120 ....EI-10
Woodlake, 800 ....EF-11
Woodland, 60 ....EC-10
Woodland, 250 ....EE-11
Woodrow, 120 ....WH-10
Woods, 100 ....EG-12
Woodsboro, 1512 ......EO-6
Woodson, 264 ....EE-3
Woodville, 2586 .....EI-12
Woodway, 8452 ....EH-6
Wortham, 1073 ....EG-8
Wrightsboro, 50 ....EM-6
Wylie, 41427 ....EE-7
Yancey, 200 ....EN-3
Yantis, 388 ....EE-9
Yarrelton, 30 ....EH-6
Yellowpine, 60 ....EH-13
Yoakum, 5815 ....EM-6
YOAKUM CO.,
7879 .... WH-8
Yorktown, 2092 ....EM-6
YOUNG CO.,
18550 .... ED-3
Youngsport, 30 ....EI-5
Zapata, 5089 ....ER-3
ZAPATA CO.,
14018 .... ER-2
ZAVALA CO.,
11677 .... WR-14
Zavalla, 713 ....EH-11
Zephyr, 300 ....EH-3

Utah

Page locator
Map keys ... Atlas pages
1–10 ... 206–207
11–20 ... 208–209

Adamsville, 50 ....K-6
Alta, 383 ....E-9
Altamont, 225 ....E-12
Alton, 119 ....M-7
Altonah, 40 ....E-12
American Fork,
26263 ....E-9
Aneth, 501 ....M-14
Annabella, 795 ....H-8
Antimony, 122 ....K-8
Apple Valley, 701 .....N-6
Aurora, 1016 ....H-8
Avon, 367 ....B-9
Axtell, 70 ....H-9
Ballard, 801 ....E-12
Bear Valley City, 853...B-8
Beaver, 3112 ....J-6
BEAVER CO., 6629...J-6
Beryl, 120 ....L-5
Beryl Jct., 197 ....L-5
Bicknell, 327 ....J-9
Big Water, 475 ....N-9
Birdseye, 92 ....G-9
Blanding, 3375 ....L-13
Bluebell, 293 ....E-12
Bluff, 258 ....M-13
Bluffdale, 7598 ....E-6
Bonanza, 1 ....F-14
Boulder Town, 226 .....L-9
Bountiful, 42552 ......D-8
BOX ELDER CO.,
49975 ....B-5
Brian Head, 83 ....L-6
Bridgeland, 87 ....E-12
Brigham City, 17899 ...B-8
Bryce Canyon City,
198 ....M-8
Bullfrog, 200 ....M-11
Burrville, 40 ....J-8
CACHE CO.,
112656 ....B-9
Caineville, 15 ....J-9
Callao F-5
Cannonville, 167 ......M-8
CARBON CO.,
21403 ....G-11
Carbonville, 1567 ....G-10
Castle Dale, 1630 ....H-10
Castle Valley, 319 ...H-11
Cedar City, 28857 .....L-6
Cedar Fort, 368 ....E-8
Centerfield, 1367 .....H-8
Centerville, 15335 ....D-8
Central, 613 ....M-5
Central Valley, 528 ...H-8
Charleston, 415 ....E-9
Circleville, 547 ......K-8
Cisco I-14
Clarkston, 666 ....A-8
Clawson, 163 ....H-10
Clear Creek, 4 ....G-10
Clearfield, 30112 .....C-8
Cleveland, 464 ....H-10
Clinton, 20426 ....C-8
Coalville, 1363 ....D-9
Copperton, 826 ....E-8
Corinne, 685 ....B-8
Cornish, 288 ....A-8
Cottonwood C-9
Cottonwood Hts.,
33433 ....E-8
Cove Fort J-7
Croydon, 50 ....C-9
DAGGETT CO.,
1059 ....D-12
Daniel, 938 ....E-9
DAVIS CO., 306479..D-7
Delta, 3436 ....H-7
Deseret, 353 ....H-7
Devils Slide C-9
Draper, 42274 ....E-8
Dry Fork, 30 ....E-13
Duchesne, 1690 ......F-11
DUCHESNE CO.,
18607 ....E-11
Duck Creek Vil., 400 ..M-7
Dugway, 795 ....F-6
Dutch John, 140 .....D-13
Eagle Mtn., 21415 .....E-8

---

*, †, ‡, §, ◊   See explanation under state title in this index.
County and parish names are listed in capital letters & boldface type.
Independent cities (not included in a county) are listed in italics.

* , †, ‡, §, ◊   See explanation under state title in this index.
County and parish names are listed in CAPITAL LETTERS & boldface type.
Independent cities (not included in a county) are listed in italics.